NEPAL IN TRANSITION

Since emerging in 2006 from a 10-year Maoist insurgency, the "People's War," Nepal has struggled with the difficult transition from war to peace, from autocracy to democracy, and from an exclusionary and centralized state to a more inclusive and federal one. The present volume, drawing on both international and Nepali scholars and leading practitioners, analyzes the context, dynamics, and key players shaping Nepal's ongoing peace process. Although the peace process is largely domestically driven, it has been accompanied by wide-ranging international involvement, including initiatives in peacemaking by nongovernmental organizations, the United Nations (UN), and India; significant investments by international donors; and the deployment of a Security Council–mandated UN field mission. This book shines a light on the limits, opportunities, and challenges of international efforts to assist Nepal in its quest for peace and stability and offers valuable lessons for similar endeavors elsewhere.

Sebastian von Einsiedel works in the policy planning unit of the UN's Department of Political Affairs. From 2007 to 2008, he served as a political affairs officer with the UN Mission in Nepal, providing analysis on a range of peace-process–related issues. He also served as Senior Program Officer of the International Peace Academy (now Institute) and as Special Assistant to its president. He was a member of the research team of the UN Secretary-General's High-Level Panel on Threats, Challenges and Change and worked for two years in the Secretary-General's strategic planning unit. Einsiedel has published a number of journal articles and book chapters on multilateral security issues.

David M. Malone was appointed as President of the International Development Research Center (IDRC) in July 2008 for a term of five years. Before that, he served as Canada's High Commissioner to India and nonresident Ambassador to Bhutan and Nepal. He currently serves as Adjunct Professor at the New York University School of Law and is a Senior Fellow of Massey College in the University of Toronto. He has published extensively on peace and security issues, and his books include *Does the Elephant Dance? Contemporary Indian Foreign Policy* (2011), *The Law and Practice of the United Nations* (2008), *The UN Security Council: From the Cold War to the 21st Century* (2004), and *The International Struggle over Iraq: Politics in the UN Security Council, 1980–2005* (2006).

Suman Pradhan is a former Nepali journalist who has written extensively on the struggle to institutionalize democracy in Nepal, as well as c...... .... have been published in leading Nepal-based newspa...... ...... Kathmandu Post newspaper from 2000 to 2003 wher ...... dent for the Inter Press Service. He also was a Nepa ...... Group from 2003 to 2005. Since late 2006, he has wo ...... in Nepal, Afghanistan, Pakistan, and New York.

Nepal in Transition

FROM PEOPLE'S WAR TO FRAGILE PEACE

Edited by

SEBASTIAN VON EINSIEDEL

DAVID M. MALONE

SUMAN PRADHAN

NYU | CENTER ON
—— | INTERNATIONAL
CIC | COOPERATION

CAMBRIDGE
UNIVERSITY PRESS

CAMBRIDGE UNIVERSITY PRESS
Cambridge, New York, Melbourne, Madrid, Cape Town,
Singapore, São Paulo, Delhi, Mexico City

Cambridge University Press
32 Avenue of the Americas, New York, NY 10013-2473, USA

www.cambridge.org
Information on this title: www.cambridge.org/9781107668980

© Cambridge University Press 2012

First published 2012

Printed in the United States of America

A catalog record for this publication is available from the British Library.

Library of Congress Cataloging in Publication data

Nepal in transition : from people's war to fragile peace / [edited by] Sebastian von Einsiedel, David M. Malone, Suman Pradhan.
  p. cm.
Includes bibliographical references and index.
ISBN 978-1-107-00567-9 (hardback) – ISBN 978-1-107-66898-0 (pbk.)
1. Peace-building – Nepal – International cooperation. 2. Nation-building – Nepal – International cooperation. 3. United Nations – Nepal. 4. Nepal – Politics and government – 1990–
I. Einsiedel, Sebastian von, 1972– II. Malone, David, 1954– III. Pradhan, Suman, 1965–
JZ5584.N35N487 2012
954.96–dc23   2011040846

ISBN 978-1-107-00567-9 Hardback
ISBN 978-1-107-66898-0 Paperback

Contents

Contributors

EDITORS

Sebastian von Einsiedel works in the policy-planning unit of the United Nations (UN) Department of Political Affairs. From 2007 to 2008, he served as a political affairs officer with the UN Mission in Nepal, providing analysis on a range of issues related to the peace process. He was a member of the research team of the UN Secretary-General's High-Level Panel on Threats, Challenges and Change and worked for two years in the Secretary-General's strategic planning unit. Mr. von Einsiedel also worked with the International Peace Academy (now Institute) in New York, the German Bundestag in Berlin, and the NATO Parliamentary Assembly in Brussels. He has published a number of journal articles and book chapters on multilateral security issues.

David M. Malone was appointed as President of International Development Research Center (IDRC) on July 1, 2008, for a term of five years. Prior to that, Mr. Malone served as Canada's High Commissioner to India and nonresident Ambassador to Bhutan and Nepal. Other positions he has held include: Assistant Deputy Minister (Global Issues) in Canada's Department of Foreign Affairs and International Trade; President, International Peace Academy (now Institute), New York; and Canadian Ambassador to the UN in New York.

Mr. Malone has published extensively on peace and security issues, in book form and in journals. He has taught at Columbia University and the University of Toronto. He currently serves as Adjunct Professor at the New York University School of Law and is a Senior Fellow of Massey College in the University of Toronto. His books include *The Law and Practice of the United Nations* (Oxford University Press, 2008); *The UN Security Council: From the Cold War to the 21st Century* (LRP, 2004); *The International Struggle over Iraq: Politics in the UN Security Council, 1980–2005* (Oxford University Press, 2006); and *Does the Elephant Dance? Contemporary Indian Foreign Policy* (Oxford University Press, 2011).

Suman Pradhan is a former Nepali journalist who wrote extensively on the struggle to institutionalize democracy in Nepal, as well as on the Maoist conflict. His articles have been published in leading Nepal-based newspapers, such as *The Kathmandu Post, Nepali Times,* and *Himal Southasian,* as well as abroad in publications including *The Times of India, Asian Age,* and numerous others through Inter Press Service, for which he served as Nepal correspondent. He has also written for research publications such as *South Asia Intelligence Review* and served as a Nepal Analyst for the International Crisis Group in 2003–5. He was the News Editor of *The Kathmandu Post* newspaper in 2000–3. He was also a coeditor of "Asia Media Report 2006: The Crisis Within," published by Inter Press Service as a review of the media trends and issues in the region. He was a Knight Journalism Fellow at Stanford University in 2005–6. Since late 2006, he has been working for the UN as a political officer in Nepal, Afghanistan, Pakistan, and New York.

AUTHORS

Aditya Adhikari is a political writer based in Kathmandu who writes a column for *The Kathmandu Post.* He was previously Opinion Editor at the paper. He has written about the Maoists' aims and strategies, the place of the Nepal Army in the new political order, the role of the UN in the peace process, and the recent upsurge of ethnic assertion for regional publications. In addition to *The Kathmandu Post,* he has written for publications such as *Himal Southasian,* the academic journal *Studies in Nepali History and Society,* and the bulletin of the Indian Institute of Defence Studies and Analyses. Mr. Adhikari also worked as the Political Analyst at the Carter Center International Election Observation in Nepal where, among other things, he wrote briefings for former U.S. President Jimmy Carter and was a codrafter of the Carter Center's final report on the elections in Nepal.

Rhoderick Chalmers is the former South Asia Deputy Project Director for the International Crisis Group (ICG), where he was primarily responsible for its reporting on Nepal's Maoist insurgency. In addition to examining the roots of the conflict and means of resolving it, he coordinated research on specific areas, including political parties and constitutional reform, cross-border security issues, ethnic movements, and Maoist politics. Before joining the ICG, Mr. Chalmers was a Visiting Fellow at the Centre for Nepal and Asian Studies at Tribhuvan University, Kathmandu, Nepal. He has written extensively on various issues relating to Nepal in numerous articles and book chapters. In addition, Mr. Chalmers authored *"We Nepalis": The Formation of a Nepali Public Sphere in India, 1900–1940,* and *The Politics of Language in Nepal* (both forthcoming).

Rajeev Ranjan Chaturvedy is Senior Assistant Director–International Affairs at the Federation of Indian Chambers of Commerce and Industry (FICCI) in New Delhi.

He completed one year of research and writing on Indian foreign policy and Chinese strategic access during his tenure as a Professional Development Award recipient in 2009 at the Canadian International Development Research Centre in Ottawa. Before going to Ottawa, Mr. Chaturvedy was engaged in a major research project at the Indian Council for Research on International Economic Relations (ICRIER), which was aimed at outlining the future of India's external policy from the point of view of India's national interest. He has worked on energy, nuclear, and proliferation issues with the Indian Pugwash Society and was part of the "Nuclear Cluster" at the Institute for Defence Studies and Analyses. Mr. Chaturvedy has published extensively on India's foreign and security policy, India-China strategic access, energy security, nuclear issues, and hydro-diplomacy in various journals, magazines, and websites. He also writes regularly on Indian foreign policy and India's South Asian neighbors in leading Indian newspapers, including *The Hindu* and the *Business Standard.*

Jörg Frieden is Executive Director for Switzerland at the World Bank. He has extensive experience in the development field, acquired serving in the Swiss Agency for Development and Cooperation (SDC). He worked for many years in conflict-affected countries, including as Head of the Demobilization Unit at the United Nations Peacekeeping Mission in Mozambique. Mr. Frieden spent five years in Nepal as Country Director at the Swiss Cooperation Office and as Advisor to the UN Mission. In addition to authoring numerous policy papers, Mr. Frieden has contributed to the guest column of the *Nepali Times.*

Prashant Jha is a journalist based in Kathmandu, Nepal. He is the Nepal correspondent of *The Hindu* newspaper. He is also a writer for *The Kathmandu Post,* where he contributes a weekly column, regular news analysis pieces, and on-the-ground reports. Mr. Jha has written extensively on the peace process, the evolution of the Maoists, politics in the Tarai, and geo-politics, especially India-Nepal relations. Mr. Jha is also a contributing editor with *Himal Southasian* magazine, where he has reported on the changing dynamics of Indian foreign policy, the Naxalite insurgency, the aftermath of the Gujarat riots, and elections in Nepal. Between 2007 and 2011, he was a columnist for the *Nepali Times.* He also worked as an analyst for the International Crisis Group and has written for several international and regional publications, including *Jane's Intelligence Review*, opendemocracy.net, *The Times of India, Seminar, Frontline* magazine, and *Tehelka* weekly. He has contributed to several research projects and regularly speaks on Nepal to diverse audiences. Mr. Jha is currently working on a book on Nepal's political transition.

Mahendra Lawoti is a professor of political science at Western Michigan University, an Associate Fellow of the Asia Society, and a columnist for *The Kathmandu Post.* His research has covered democratization, political institutions, ethnic politics, governance, social movements, conflicts, and state building. In addition to numerous articles and book chapters, Dr. Lawoti has published various books, including

Towards a Democratic Nepal: Inclusive Political Institutions for a Multicultural Society (2005); *Contentious Politics and Democratization in Nepal* (2007); *Federal State-Building in Nepal: Challenges in Framing the Nepali Constitution* (2009); *The Maoist Insurgency in Nepal: Revolution in the Twenty-First Century* (2010); *Ethnicity, Inequality and Politics in Nepal* (2010); and *Nationalism and Ethnic Conflict* (2011).

Ian Martin served in Nepal from 2005 to early 2009, latterly as the Special Representative of the United Nations Secretary-General and Head of the UN Mission (UNMIN). He came to Nepal as the Representative of the UN High Commissioner for Human Rights and then served as the Personal Representative of the Secretary-General in support of the peace process. Mr. Martin has also held senior posts in Timor-Leste, Ethiopia and Eritrea, Bosnia and Herzogovina, Rwanda, and Haiti. Prior to working for the UN, Mr. Martin was Secretary General of Amnesty International from 1986 to 1992. His writings include *Self-Determination in East Timor: The United Nations, the Ballot, and International Intervention* (2001).

S. D. Muni is Visiting Research Professor at the Institute of South Asian Studies, Singapore. He was nominated to India's first National Security Council Advisory Board. Previously, he served as India's Ambassador to Laos and later as Special Envoy to Cambodia and Laos. In addition, Mr. Muni was a member of the official delegation during the visits of India's Foreign Minister and Prime Minister to Nepal, Sri Lanka, Mauritius, and Vietnam. Mr. Muni taught at Jawaharlal Nehru University (1974–2006) and other Indian universities and held several academic assignments abroad. A regular commentator in national and international print and electronic media and author of more than a dozen books and nearly a hundred research papers, Mr. Muni is internationally acknowledged as an authority on South Asian and Nepalese political and security affairs. His recent publications include *The Maoist Insurgency* (New Delhi, 2003), *Responding to Terrorism in South Asia* (New Delhi, 2005), *Asian Strategic Review* (New Delhi, 2008), *India's Foreign Policy: The Democratic Dimension* (New Delhi, 2009), and *Resurgent China: South Asian Perspectives* (New Delhi, 2011).

Devendra Raj Panday is a well-known civil society leader and human rights defender based in Kathmandu, Nepal. He is the Founding Vice Chairman of the Human Rights Organisation of Nepal, a founding member of South Asians for Human Rights, the Rural Self Reliance Development Centre, the Nepal South Asia Centre, and Transparency International, Nepal, of which he also is the former president. In Transparency International he was also elected twice to its International Board of Directors in Berlin. Previously, Mr. Panday held the posts of Finance Minister of Nepal in the interim government of 1990 and, before that, Secretary of the Ministry of Finance. In addition to being a lead researcher and contributor to the first UN Human Development Report of Nepal in 1998, Mr. Panday has written and edited many books on development and democracy, including *Nepal's Failed*

Development: Reflections on the Mission and the Maladies (1999/2009) and *Looking at Development and Donors: Essays from Nepal* (2011).

Bhojraj Pokharel served as the Chief Election Commissioner of Nepal from October 2006 to June 2009. Mr. Pokharel had a distinguished career working for the government of Nepal, where he was appointed permanent secretary for various ministries, including the Ministry of Health, Home Affairs, Supplies, and Information and Communication. He also served as the chairperson of numerous public and private companies, such as Nepal Telecommunication Corporation, Nepal Oil Corporation, and Standard Chartered Bank Nepal. In addition, Mr. Pokharel led various high-level commissions and task forces formed by the government and worked extensively with external development partners in Nepal. He was one of the members of the UN Secretary-General's Panel on the Referendum in South Sudan. Mr. Pokharel has authored the report *HIV/AIDS Situation Analysis of Nepal, 2000*, and contributed to various other election and governance-related publications. His new book on the Nepalese peace process (*Bringing a Bullet to the Ballot*) and personal reflections on managing a post-conflict election in Nepal are expected to be published in 2012.

Frederick Rawski is an international lawyer and the Nepal Country Representative for the International Commission of Jurists. He previously worked as Coordinator for Accountability and Rule of Law issues with the Office of the United Nations High Commissioner for Human Rights in Nepal. In the past, he has done human rights work for the United Nations Transitional Administration in East Timor, the United Nations International Criminal Tribunal for Rwanda, human rights non-governmental organizations (NGOs), and as a private attorney. He has published widely on a range of international legal and political issues, including transitional justice mechanisms, UN peacekeeping, the Security Council, indigenous rights, armed groups, and the World Bank.

Sujeev Shakya is a business executive based in Kathmandu, Nepal and through his firm, beed, he works with various corporations, bilaterals, multilaterals, and INGOs. Mr. Shakya is Chair of the Nepal Economic Forum. From 2001 to 2011, Mr. Shakya wrote a fortnightly column on economic issues in *The Nepali Times*. Most recently, Mr. Shakya authored the book *Unleashing Nepal: Past, Present and Future of the Economy* (Penguin, 2009).

Mandira Sharma is a lawyer and the Executive Director of Advocacy Forum-Nepal, a human rights NGO campaigning for international human rights standards to be incorporated into Nepalese law. Ms. Sharma's organization played a key role in defending the rights of Nepali people caught in the Nepali civil war. A leading human rights advocate, Ms. Sharma has been awarded the Human Rights Watch award, one of the most prestigious honors in the field of human rights. Ms. Sharma has written extensively on human rights issues and is a contributing author to *Himalayan People's War: Nepal's Maoist Rebellion* (2004).

Catinca Slavu is an independent consultant with 13 years of experience in electoral assistance, political processes, and coordination in transitional, conflict, and post-conflict contexts in the Balkans, the Caucasus, the Middle East, and South Asia. In Nepal, Ms. Slavu advised the Personal Representative of the Secretary-General on the development of a UN strategy for support to the Constituent Assembly election. She also advised the Nepal Election Commission on matters related to the system of representation, donor coordination, and general electoral administration. Later, she became involved in establishing the framework for the UN Mission's role as coordinator of the UN support to the peace process. In addition to numerous papers and reports, Ms. Slavu is a contributing author to the *International IDEA External Voting Handbook* (2007), and the Afghanistan Analysts Network's *Lessons Learned? Documenting Projects Past in Afghanistan 2001–2009* (2011).

Deepak Thapa is the Director of Social Science Baha, a center founded to foster and facilitate the development of social science studies in Nepal. Previously, Mr. Thapa worked as a journalist for, among others, the *Himal Southasian* and *The Nepali Times*. Mr. Thapa is an acknowledged expert on the Maoist movement and has written widely on the subject. Among other works, he edited *Understanding the Maoist Movement of Nepal* (2003) and coauthored *A Kingdom under Siege: Nepal's Maoist Insurgency 1996–2004* (2005).

Teresa Whitfield is a Senior Advisor and Fellow at the Center on International Cooperation (CIC) and Senior Adviser to the Geneva-based Centre for Humanitarian Dialogue, responsible for liaison with the UN. Her research interests are the dynamics of internal conflict, peacemaking, mediation, and UN peace operations. She has published widely on these subjects and in March 2010 was awarded a grant by the United States Institute of Peace to research and write a book examining efforts to end the Basque conflict in Spain. Prior to joining CIC in May 2008, Ms. Whitfield spent three years as Director of the Conflict Prevention and Peace Forum, a program of the Social Science Research Council that facilitates access by UN officials to outside sources of expertise on countries in conflict or crisis. From 1995 to 2000, Ms. Whitfield worked as an official within the UN's Department of Political Affairs, latterly in the Office of the Under-Secretary-General of Political Affairs. She was a Visiting Fellow at CIC from 2003 to 2005. Ms. Whitfield is a member of the Board of Trustees of the Conciliation Resources, which is based in London, and serves on the Advisory Board of the Conflict Prevention and Peace Forum.

Acknowledgments

The editors are deeply indebted to a number of key individuals and institutions without whose help this volume would not have been possible.

The editors are particularly grateful to New York University's Center on International Cooperation (CIC) for agreeing to host this project, several of whose members became actively involved. Special thanks are due to Alischa Kugel for keeping the editors and authors on track, providing thoughtful comments on various chapters, and being the force behind the scenes that kept the project moving forward. Richard Gowan oversaw the project at CIC and provided helpful editorial advice. Throughout this project and beyond, Bruce D. Jones, CIC's director, has been an invaluable friend and supporter of the editors.

This volume would not have seen the light of day without the support of Canada's International Development Research Centre (IDRC), long engaged in funding policy-relevant research in Nepal. We are particularly grateful to Bruce Currie-Alder for being a champion of this book.

Thanks to CIC and IDRC, the editors and the authors of this book's chapters were able to meet in New York in 2009, along with a number of other interested individuals to discuss our collective approach, having read and commented on each other's early contributions. The spirited, friendly, and highly involved discussion that unfolded on this occasion has done much to shape this volume's outlook. Since then, the editors have worked hard to challenge the authors to move well beyond their first drafts, in terms of both breadth and depth. We are very grateful to them all for the very significant commitment of time and effort they have made to the volume – and for their patience in enduring and responding to multiple comments in several rounds of drafts and redrafts.

David M. Malone would like to thank the Canadian Cooperation Office in Kathmandu, particularly its leader, Prabin Manandhar, as well as Canada's representative in Kathmandu, 2005–2010, Ed Doe, for so frequently and generously hosting him in Nepal and guiding his education thereon.

Finally, we would like to thank John Berger and Cambridge University Press for publishing this book. In particular, we are deeply grateful to John for his patience and strong support throughout the gestation of its chapters.

1

Introduction

Sebastian von Einsiedel, David M. Malone, and Suman Pradhan

WHY THIS BOOK?

Asia today has wind in its sails. In one significant shift in international relations emerging from the global economic and financial crisis of 2008–10, the balance of influence is tilting toward Asia, and away from the West, based on the momentum (if not yet the weight) of Asia's economic performance and the geostrategic potential with which this rapidly increasing wealth endows the continent.

Conventional wisdom suggests that the West frittered away its moment of advantage at the conclusion of the Cold War. Meanwhile, Asia tended to its vulnerabilities, which remained, overwhelmingly, economic ones. The focus on economic growth throughout much of Asia has paid off.

When we think of Asian prosperity, we tend to think of the three main regional powers – China, India, and Japan – or of the Asian Tigers: South Korea, Taiwan, and several of the countries of Southeast Asia. We tend to forget about the poverty that continues to afflict so much of Asia, and we think of Nepal hardly at all.

In the minds of Westerners, Nepal evokes the Himalayas, the impressive and elegant Gurkha troops that India and the United Kingdom continue to employ, the hippie trail of the 1970s that led by many roads to Kathmandu, and its rich cultural heritage, so spectacularly on display in the Kathmandu Valley and beyond. Yet, even though Nepal is bigger than it looks on a map, where it appears as a sliver backing onto the Himalayas between the vast territories of India and Tibet, and although its population approaches 30 million, it remains out of focus for distant peoples. In the words of Nepal's founding father, Prithvi Narayan Shah, it is a "yam caught between two boulders" – China and India, the two fastest growing large economies in the world and two of the fastest rising global powers.

The views expressed in this chapter are solely those of the authors and do not represent the official views of the United Nations or the International Development Research Centre.

Few beyond South Asia are aware that for the past six decades Nepal has been caught in an internal struggle for peace, development, and justice. This struggle has involved failed attempts at democratization in the 1950s and 1990s interspersed with 30 years of monarchical dictatorship, which were followed by a Maoist insurgency, an imploding monarchy, and, in recent years, tentative and inconclusive efforts to craft a constitutional solution to the country's political, social, economic, and other woes. This volume aims to contribute to a wider understanding and public awareness of the upheavals that have marked Nepal's trajectory over the past decade, focusing in particular on the country's critical transition from 2005–11 and the international role in those developments.

After 10 years of civil war and the gradual reinstitution of absolute monarchy, the Nepali people in April 2006 took to the streets and forced the king to hand power back to the political parties. Peace negotiations between the leaders of the newly reempowered political parties and the Maoists, which had already led to an important framework agreement in part facilitated by India in 2005, gained new momentum, culminating first in a ceasefire agreement in May 2006 and then in the signing of the Comprehensive Peace Agreement (CPA) in December 2006. In April 2008, after a rocky period and significant delays, elections to a Constituent Assembly took place, bringing to power a Maoist-led coalition under Prime Minister Pushpa Kamal Dahal, known as Prachanda, the former leader of the insurgency. This government resigned in May 2009 after a tussle over control of the Nepalese Army. Since then political life has been unstable, and policy making has been largely paralyzed. Yet, political violence continues to be mostly contained, and the "peace process" is still formally under way, regaining momentum in August 2011 after a long period of stasis when the Maoists returned to power under a coalition government led by the Maoist ideologue turned pragmatist Dr. Baburam Bhattarai.

Why should Nepal's transition be of wider interest? First, Nepal is situated between Asia's two giants, China and India, whose relationship teeters between tension and cooperation, with India very sensitive to any advances by China or Chinese influence in what it perceives as its own backyard. In many ways, Nepal represents a microcosm of the wider geopolitical struggles playing out in the region. Second, the recent political developments there, involving first a Maoist insurgency and then a political process in which the Maoists rather improbably joined in electoral politics, may hold valuable lessons for other countries beset by insurgency, even India itself. Third, although the peace process and the wider transition were largely domestically driven, various international efforts supported Nepal's quest for peace. These efforts included initiatives in peacemaking by NGOs, the UN Secretary-General, and India that throughout the process wielded considerable political influence; significant investments by international donors; and the deployment of two UN field missions: one led by the Office of the High Commissioner on Human Rights (OHCHR) to monitor the human rights situation and the other, the UN Mission in Nepal

(UNMIN), mandated by the Security Council to assist in the implementation of key aspects of the CPA.

Although the jury is still out on the degree to which the transition period lastingly altered the dynamics of Nepali politics and sustainably placed the country on a path of peace and stability, this volume seeks to offer both a "midterm assessment" and a country case study of internationally supported peacemaking and peacebuilding efforts. Placing Nepal's transition in a larger context of its history and international relations and approaching the subject matter from multiple perspectives – from academia and practitioners, Nepali and international – this volume seeks to critically review this period and the international role, in the hope of identifying lessons for other countries undergoing similar transitions.

WHY THESE CONTRIBUTORS?

As the book's editors, we came together because of our interest in, indeed our commitment to, a better future for Nepal and gaining a greater understanding of what that will require. We hail from different backgrounds. One of us, a long-time journalist and analyst turned international public servant, is from Nepal. One of us, a German, served the United Nations political mission in Nepal in 2007–8. And one of us, a Canadian, served as his country's non-resident envoy to Nepal, traveling there from Delhi every now and then during the years 2006–8, after having visited Nepal a couple of decades earlier and been thoroughly seduced by its beauty and its compelling people.

Rather than limit the reader to our own views, we wanted to draw on a wide range of individuals with valuable ideas and genuine expertise on aspects of Nepal's history, economy, politics, and interaction with the rest of the world. Even more, we wanted the book to draw heavily on Nepali voices and engage them in a dialogue with international scholars and practitioners. A volume drawing so heavily on Nepali authors proved possible because Nepal harbors a large number of insightful activists, commentators, and academics with in-depth knowledge of the recent crisis. They include former finance minister and civil society leader *Devendra Raj Panday* (writing about the country's development failure); leading Nepali human rights activist *Mandira Sharma* (writing alongside former OHCHR staffer *Frederick Rawski* on international human rights monitoring); and *Bhojraj Pokharel*, the former head of Nepal's Election Commission who played such a critical role in organizing the Constituent Assembly elections. Two of Nepal's most prolific political scientists, *Deepak Thapa* and *Mahendra Lawoti*, are part of this volume, examining the making of the Maoist insurgency and Nepal's ethnic politics, respectively. Providing a unique view from Nepal's private sector on impediments and opportunities for economic growth is business executive *Sujeev Shakya*. We are particularly proud to be able to introduce to a wider international readership, two startlingly vivid younger writers at work in Nepal, *Aditya Adhikari* and *Prashant Jha*, writing about the transformation of the Maoist party and the role of key international actors in the peace process, respectively.

Most of the international contributors to this volume are practitioners who played an active role in international efforts to support the peace process. *Ian Martin*, who served consecutively as the head of OHCHR's Nepal Office and UNMIN, reflects in this volume on his experience and the role of the UN. *S. D. Muni*, one of India's most insightful foreign policy scholars, who was personally involved in the early phase of the Nepali peace process, sheds light on Indian interests in and perspectives on Nepal and on the specific role of India in brokering the entry of the Maoists into the country's mainstream politics. *Jörg Frieden*, who led the Swiss Development Cooperation's Nepal Program for many years, critically reviews the donor community's struggles to adapt to Nepal's transition. Other non-Nepali authors include *Rhoderick Chalmers* (on state power and the security sector), the former head of the International Crisis Group's Nepal Office, which was long a lone voice within the international nongovernmental community in informing and advocating on Nepal, and *Teresa Whitfield* (on peacemaking), who as the former head of the New York-based Conflict Prevention and Peace Forum (CPPF) promoted analysis and provided support for a greater involvement of the international community in resolving the crisis.

HISTORY OF NEPAL

Before the king of the small western principality of Gorkha, Prithvi Narayan Shah, launched his campaign to unify the country in the latter half of the 18th century, the geographical area occupied by today's Nepal was dotted with small principalities. Kathmandu Valley itself was divided into three kingdoms – Kathmandu, Lalitpur, and Bhaktapur – ruled by different but related Malla dynasties. Out west, there existed what is collectively known as the 22 Baise and 24 Chaubise rajyas (states) ruled by various clans. The eastern hills were dominated by the Kirat rulers, and the southern plains were divided into several kingdoms, both large and small.

In 1769, King Prithvi Narayan Shah, commanding an army comprised primarily of Magars and Gurungs but mainly led by members of the ruling Hindu warrior caste (Chhettris), embarked on a campaign to unify this conglomerate of mini-states under his leadership. What could not be won with friendship and diplomacy was won over by the khukuri, the traditional Nepali curved knife. In the decades that followed, the Gorkhalis not only unified Nepal but also expanded the territory over significant swathes of modern-day India's east, north, and northwest. They also succeeded, through several campaigns, in extracting favorable trade concessions from the rulers of Tibet. When the latter refused to provide those concessions, the Gorkhalis coerced them through punitive military expeditions into paying tributes to the Nepali king.

This rapid expansion of the Nepali state came to an abrupt halt in 1816 with the Gorkhali army's defeat at the hands of the British East India Company and the signing of the Treaty of Sugauli, forcing the Shah regime to cede all the territory won by the Gorkhali army in India to the British colonial power. After Sugauli, Nepal would never add another inch to its territory through military means, and its borders as defined by the treaty, would remain fixed. The only exception was when the British gave back some western districts as a token of appreciation for Nepal's support in suppressing the Indian Sepoy Mutiny of 1857.

The country's frenzied territorial expansion in the first five decades of its existence significantly shaped its character. Before unification, tribal, ethnic, linguistic, and social caste groups in Nepal's constituent parts pursued their affairs largely autonomously within their own small borders. The Nepali state's expansion forced these myriad groups to live together under the authority of the new Gorkha rulers. By the time Nepal's unification was completed, Nepali society had become multicultural, multiethnic, and multilingual. The failure to recognize and accommodate through active nurturing this new reality would continue to trouble Nepal in the ensuing centuries.

From its earliest days, Nepal was a top-down society governed by a strict hierarchical structure. Before 1846, all power and authority were vested in the Shah ruler and his family. Power flowed from them to the Bhardars – the ministers, aides, and officials who assisted the king and the royal family. Because almost all of the royal court hailed from the higher Hindu castes, spoke Nepali, and wore a particular style of dress, these emblems of the rulers gradually became the norm. The institution of the monarchy therefore drew its sustenance and support from a sense of nationalism embodied by a single religion (Hinduism), a single language (Nepali), and a single dress (Daura Suruwal). It was as if the immense diversity within Nepal's borders – its very multiethnic, multilingual, multireligious, multicultural fabric – did not matter in the eyes of the monarchical state.

Nepal's history took a new turn in 1846 when Jung Bahadur Rana, a military official serving at the court, seized power in a bloody coup and instituted the Rana autocracy that lasted for 104 years. The Ranas, who ruled as prime ministers through a hereditary system, kept the monarchy in place, but left it powerless. They further institutionalized alienation and exclusion by introducing the Muluki Ain (Civil Code) that codified Hinduism's caste structure and incorporated all groups – whether Hindu or non-Hindu – residing within Nepal's borders within its hierarchy. The result was official discrimination practiced on a massive scale, marginalizing large parts of the population.

The first half of the 20th century witnessed growing popular dissatisfaction with the Rana regime, especially among the educated classes. Spurred by the success of the struggle for independence in India, Nepal's opposition in Indian exile called for an uprising against Rana rule. Leading the anti-regime activism was the newly founded Nepali Congress Party (NC), which was secretly in alliance with the politically impotent Shah King Tribhuwan. Faced with growing turmoil, the Ranas were forced to give back power in 1951. Nehruvian India, itself newly independent from British rule, brought its vast influence to bear in helping fashion the Rana-king-Nepali Congress political compromise of 1951, which officially ended Rana rule and ushered in democracy for the first time in Nepal. The period from 1951 to 1960 saw a flowering of political parties of all ideological hues. This was also the time when the communists, who had founded their first party in exile in India in 1949, burst on the Nepali scene only to find themselves banned in 1952 for anti-government activism (the ban was lifted in 1956 in return for a secret pledge by communist party leaders not to oppose the monarchy).[1] More importantly, however, it was also the time when the monarchy firmly clawed power back not only from the still entrenched Rana clan but also from the nascent and idealistic political parties. A signal of what lay ahead was King Tribhuwan's inordinate delay in implementing his commitment to call a Constituent Assembly election to draft a constitution for the country. He also routinely changed governments, handpicking prime ministers at will to govern a newly awakening country. His death in 1955 and the ascension of his son Mahendra to the throne altered the course of Nepali politics profoundly, as would become clear within just a few years.

After much political turmoil and a succession of short-lived governments, King Mahendra finally called Nepal's first general election in 1959. The NC won resoundingly, led by Bisheswhar Prasad Koirala (brother of the late Girija Prasad Koirala, the four-time prime minister in the 1990s and 2000s who would play such a crucial role in Nepal's recent transition). However, his subsequent government was overthrown by King Mahendra with the help of the army in December 1960. Mahendra banned political parties, and two years later, he instituted the party-less Panchayat system, which bred corruption, nepotism, and all the ills that often accompany highly authoritarian forms of government. An armed cross-border insurgency in 1961/1962 led by exiled NC and communist leaders was brutally crushed by the army.

The Panchayat regime sought to strengthen its legitimacy and popular support by actively fostering a Nepali national identity based on Hindu culture as practiced in the hilly highlands, thereby deepening exclusion of the marginalized groups. The ascension of King Birendra after Mahendra's death in 1972 did little to soften the Panchayat's hard edge. However, in 1979, with the spark provided by Zulfikar Ali Bhutto's execution in Pakistan, Nepali students, always more attuned to politics than the common people, rose up in revolt. Many Nepalis today consider the 1979 student movement the precursor to the 1990 People's Movement. Faced with escalating student violence, King Birendra seemingly loosened the reins of power and, in a major political gamble, called for a referendum on whether Nepalis wanted a reformed Panchayat system or multiparty parliamentary democracy as demanded

---

[1] John Whelpton, *A History of Nepal* (Cambridge: Cambridge University Press, 2005), p. 91.

by the students and their affiliated political parties. Massive vote rigging led to the Panchayat's victory in the 1980 referendum, but it only provided a limited new lease on life to the regime.

With the advent of perestroika in the Soviet Union under Gorbachev, other closed societies, including some outside the Warsaw Pact, such as Nepal, Bangladesh, and Pakistan, became caught up in the new democratic winds blowing in the late 1980s. The fall of the Berlin Wall in 1989 inspired many Nepali youths to actively urge the still-banned political parties to press for more direct action to reestablish democracy. Thus, the First People's Movement (*Jana Andolan I*) was born in February 1990 under the unprecedented joint leadership of the NC and seven communist parties, which came together as the United Left Front (ULF). As the movement progressed, it drew large swathes of Nepali society, including marginalized groups, professional classes, and trade unions, into a broad alliance with the pro-democracy political parties, challenging the Panchayat's grip.

The protestors drew support not just from within but also from across the southern borders. Many of India's political parties, particularly those on the left, socialists, and even elements of the National Congress (Indira) as well as Indian civil society, pledged support to the movement. At this time Nepal was still under an economic and transit blockade by India, imposed in 1989 in the context of a dispute over Nepal's arms purchases from China. By April of that year, just when it appeared that the rising popular tide of the people was about to sweep away the monarchy, King Birendra, despite strong reservations within the palace and opposition from the Royal Nepalese Army, offered to start talks with the opposition parties. The NC and ULF seized the moment to demand dissolution of the Panchayat regime and institution of a true constitutional monarchy with multiparty parliamentary democracy. A new constitution was promulgated in November 1990, which largely reflected the demands of the democratic forces but, in a compromise with the palace and the generals, confirmed Nepal as a Hindu state and the king as the supreme commander of the army. Multiparty elections were held in 1991. Significantly, the transitional NC-ULF government, led by the NC's Krishna Prasad Bhattarai, managed to negotiate a new transit treaty with India, leading to a lifting of the blockade.

Thus, in the post-1990 years Nepal embarked on its second journey along the path of multiparty democracy. However, in a repetition of the ills that befell Nepal's first democratic experiment in the 1950s, the country experienced a series of short-lived governments that provided little stability and failed to advance the people's aspirations for inclusion, economic development, and good governance.[2] It was in this context that the Maoists launched their People's War in 1996, the causes of which are analyzed in the next section.

---

[2] For further detail on this period, see Michael Hutt (ed.), *Nepal in the Nineties: Versions of the Past, Visions of the Future* (New Delhi: Oxford University Press, 1994).

CAUSES OF CONFLICT

To analyze the conditions and developments contributing to the outbreak of violent conflict in Nepal, it is helpful, following Michael Brown, to distinguish between long-term structural factors that make countries more conflict prone, and short- or mid-term proximate causes that serve as catalytic factors helping to trigger violent conflict.[3]

Structural Causes

Two of the most important structural causes of violent conflict in Nepal are endemic poverty and group inequality, both of which show a strong association with the outbreak of civil war in cross country studies.[4] Indeed, with a per capita GDP of around USD 200 in the early 1990s, Nepal, statistically, faced a civil war risk almost twice as high than a country with a GDP of USD 2,000.[5] In 1996, the year the conflict started, 42% of the population were living under the national poverty line.[6] That same year, Nepal ranked in the bottom 12% of the Human Development Index (a composite index measuring life expectancy, literacy, education, standard of living, and GDP per capita), in the unhappy company of a number of conflict-ridden countries in sub-Saharan Africa.[7]

A closer look at Nepal's development indicators over time shows a more nuanced picture. Indeed, in the half-century from 1951 to 2001, Nepal enjoyed significant development gains, with the literacy rate growing from 2% to 43%, infant mortality decreasing from 300 to 61 per 1,000 live births, and life expectancy increasing from

---

[3] Michael Brown, "The Causes of Internal Conflict," in Michael Brown et al. (eds.), *Nationalism and Ethnic Conflict: An International Security Reader* (Cambridge: MIT Press, 2000), pp. 3–25.

[4] Paul Collier et al., *Breaking the Conflict Trap: Civil War and Development Policy*, A World Bank Policy Research Report (Oxford: Oxford University Press, 2003); Fearon, James D. and David D. Laitin, "Ethnicity, Insurgency, and Civil War," *American Political Science Review* 97 (2003): 75–90; Collier, Paul and Anke Hoeffler, "Greed and Grievance in Civil War," *Oxford Economic Papers* 56 (2003): 563–95. Although empirical research on the motivation of those joining the conflict has yet to be undertaken in the Nepali context, such research in other contexts suggests that grievance-based models are incomplete because poverty is also a factor in people's decisions to join both insurgency and counterinsurgency rebellion and counter-rebellion. In addition, involuntary participation is a fundamental, poverty-related aspect of revolutionary mobilization and political violence. See Macartan Humphreys and Jeremy Weinstein: "Who Fights? The Determinants of Participation in Civil War," at http://www.columbia.edu/~mh2245/papers1/who_fights.pdf.

[5] For Nepal's historical GDP per capita figures, see http://www.indexmundi.com/nepal/gdp_per_capita_%28ppp%29.html. For the civil war risk associated with certain GDP per capita levels, see Macartan Humphreys and Ashutosh Varshney: *Violent Conflict and the Millennium Development Goals: Diagnosis and Recommendations*, CGSD Working Paper No. 19, August 2004, p. 9.

[6] World Bank, *Nepal: Resilience amidst Conflict An Assessment of Poverty in Nepal, 1995–96 and 2003–04*, Report No. 34834-NP, June 26, 2006.

[7] UNDP, 1996 Human Development Index.

35 to 59.[8] Surprisingly, over the past 40 years, Nepal has been among the top ten countries in the world in the rate of improvement in the Human Development Index (although, as of 2010, the country remained in the bottom 20%).[9] Paradoxically, not even the decade-long People's War stopped Nepal's steady progress in improving average national income, health, and education indicators.[10] Although the $11 billion in international development aid that Nepal received between 1980 and 2008 surely helped,[11] Nepal made these gains in spite of receiving only 70% of the average per capita disbursement to low-income countries over the same period.[12] (Reflecting international support for the peace process, net development aid received per capita has been increasing since 2005, following 15 years of steady decline.)[13]

Yet, human development indicators based on average national figures can be deceptive. They tell only part of the story and leave out what is the most distinct feature of Nepali society that has made Nepal ripe for conflict: deep social inequalities and injustices. For one, urban areas benefited from much of the development improvements, with poverty in Nepal increasingly becoming a rural phenomenon. In 1995–6, the rural poverty rate at 43.27% was almost exactly twice as high as the urban one (by 2004, the urban–rural poverty ratio had further widened to 3.6 to 1).[14] This urban–rural divide is partly the result of the difficulties of bringing development to the more remote parts of the country and partly a reflection of the Kathmandu-based rulers' neglect of the rest of the country throughout Nepal's history.

Interestingly, in terms of income inequality as measured by the Gini coefficient, Nepal in 1996 compared rather favorably on a global level. Of 110 countries for which data were available, Nepal ranked 55, with most countries in Latin America and sub-Saharan Africa, 10 countries in Asia, and the United States all having greater

[8] Sarah Kernot, "Nepal" A Development Challenge," *Journal of South Asian Studies*, 23 (August 2006): 297.

[9] The top ten improvers were identified by comparing performances of countries against those with similar HDI starting points in 1970; see UNDP, *The Real Wealth of Nations: Human Development Report 2010 Summary* (New York: UNDP, 2010), p. 4.

[10] The Nepali case thus seems to confirm other studies that have identified the paradox of improving health and declining mortality indicators in wartime. For instance, from 1970 to 2008, the child mortality rate has declined in 90% of country-years in war (i.e., the sum of years in which countries have been at war). Reasons for this paradox can be found in the largely localized nature of today's low-intensity conflicts, the lasting effect of the decades-long international campaign to promote public health in developing countries, and the increase in the level and scope of international humanitarian assistance. See Human Security Centre, Human Security Report 2009/2010.

[11] See http://data.worldbank.org/indicator/DT.ODA.ALLD.CD/countries/NP?display=graph.

[12] Between 1980 and 2008, Nepal received an average of $17.6 per Nepali per year compared to $25 per capita received by the average low-income country. Calculations made by authors based on World Bank data; see http://data.worldbank.org/indicator/DT.ODA.ODAT.PC.ZS/countries/NP-XM?display=graph.

[13] Ibid.

[14] Government of Nepal, Central Bureau of Statistics, *Poverty Trends in Nepal (1995–96 and 2003–04)*, Kathmandu, September 2005, at www.cbs.gov.np/Others/Poverty%20Assessment.pdf.

levels of income inequality. (Income inequality has since worsened in Nepal, and the country now ranks, alongside China, as the country with the highest Gini coefficient in Asia.)[15] However, Nepal has some of the world's highest levels of "horizontal" inequality, that is, inequality not among individuals but between groups or regions. No data or rankings are available for the mid-1990s, but the Failed States Index, which ranks states according to a number of indicators associated with state failure, in 2007 placed Nepal in the bottom 10 countries in terms of uneven development and 176 out of 177 in terms of group grievance, with only Zimbabwe ranking worse.[16]

These rankings are all the more relevant because quantitative studies, although failing to detect a correlation between income inequality and increased conflict risk, have identified major group or regional inequalities in economic, social, or political spheres as an important underlying cause of conflict in multiethnic societies. In these cases mass grievances can facilitate recruitment for violence, in particular where political and social inequalities overlap.[17] In Nepal, recent studies found a strong relationship between regional deprivation and the origin and intensity of the Maoist rebellion across districts, with caste polarization having had an additional impact on conflict intensity.[18] Poverty and malnutrition are concentrated particularly in the Maoist stronghold areas such as the hills of the far west and mid-west (see Fig. 1.1).[19] In Chapter 2, Deepak Thapa explains how the Maoists exploited this sense of deprivation in their recruitment and mass mobilization campaign in the run-up to the People's War.

Horizontal inequality is even more pronounced among groups than among regions. Indeed, the pervasive exclusion of large parts of the population based on caste, ethnicity, religion, gender, or regional provenance features prominently in almost every chapter of this volume. Inequality and exclusion in Nepal have to be

---

[15] For global income inequality data for the mid-1990s, see UNDP, 2001 *Human Development Report: Making New Technologies Work for Human Development* (New York: UNDP, 2001), pp. 182–5; for developments in Nepal's income inequality ranking since then, see Asian Development Bank, *Inequality in Asia: Key Indicators 2007 Special Chapter Highlights* (Manila, ADB, 2007), p. 3.

[16] See Fund for Peace, 2007 Failed States Index, at http://www.fundforpeace.org/web/index.php?option= com_content&task=view&id=229&Itemid=366.

[17] For an overview of recent cross-country and intra-country studies establishing a link between horizontal inequality and conflict, see Frances Stewart, *Horizontal Inequality and Conflict: Understanding Group Violence in Multiethnic Societies* (Palgrave: Houndsmills, 1998), p. 287. For a more critical review of the relevant literature, see James D. Fearon, "Governance and Civil War Onset," Background paper for 2011 World Development Report, August 31, 2010, at http://wdr2011.worldbank .org/governance-and-civil-war-onset.

[18] John Bray, Leiv Lunde, and Mansoob Murshed, "Nepal: Economic Drivers of the Maoist Insurgency," in Karen Ballentine and Jake Sherman (eds.), *The Political Economy of Armed Conflict: Beyond Greed and Grievance* (Boulder, CO: Lynne Rienner Publishers, 2003), pp. 107–32; S. M. Murshed and S. Gates, "Spatial-Horizontal Inequality and the Maoist Insurgency in Nepal," *Review of Development Economics* 9 (2004): 121–34; Quy-Toan Do and Lakshmi Iyer, *Geography, Poverty and Conflict in Nepal*, Harvard Business School Working Paper 07–065, 2009 at http://www.hbs.edu/research/pdf/ 07–065.pdf.

[19] See http://www.un.org.np/node/10125.

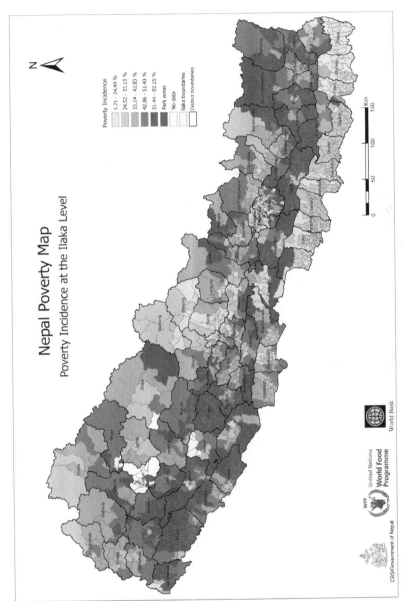

FIGURE 1.1. Nepal Poverty Map. *Source:* UN Office for the Coordination of Humanitarian Affairs.

understood in the context of Nepal's being among the most ethnically diverse – and socially stratified – countries in the world, with 36% of its population belonging to one of the more than 100 different indigenous nationalities with their own language and traditional culture. In several Terai districts, more than 90 different ethnic and caste groups are present.[20] Reflecting the ethnic diversity, some 93 different languages are currently spoken in Nepal, with well over 30 different languages spoken within many Terai districts.[21]

Anthropologist David Gellner has noted that "[it] is unimaginable to meet people in Nepal who do not know what their caste is."[22] Yet, a neat classification of Nepalis into different clearly delineated groups is difficult for several reasons. For one, the terms "caste" and "ethnic group" are overlapping categories in the Nepali context (the Nepali word "jat" can mean tribe, caste, ethnic group, or nation).[23] As Arjun Guneratne explains, "Ethnic groups can be absorbed into [the caste system] as new castes.... [And] an ethnic group can itself be internally organized into castes."[24] Moreover, identities in Nepal are rarely congruent in ethnic, caste, religious, linguistic, cultural, or geographic terms, and any group may be further subdivided along religious, language, caste, or cultural lines.[25]

The exclusionary nature of the state predates unification, when many small principalities, although not all, were ruled by Hindu rulers and thus practiced the caste system. Caste-based exclusion was reinforced when Nepal's founding fathers imposed the caste system as the unifying framework to facilitate political control over the newly conquered territories' diverse subjects. Close to a century later, in the 1854 civil code (Muluki Ain), the autocratic Rana regime, aiming at greater cultural homogenization of the kingdom, force-fit all of Nepal's linguistically, religiously, and culturally diverse populations into a strict hierarchy of castes. Translating cultural differences into hierarchical caste categories, the Muluki Ain placed the high-caste Hindu hill elite on top of the hierarchy, the "enslaveable" ethnic groups and "untouchable" castes at the bottom, and the so-called "non-enslaveable alcohol-consuming classes," which comprised the bulk of the ethnic groups, in between, even though as non-Hindu groups they had been outside the caste system until then.[26]

---

[20] Gauri Nath Rima, based on 2001 population census. Map 19.

[21] Gauri Nath Rima, based on 2001 population census. Map 21.

[22] David Gellner, "Caste, Ethnicity and Inequality in Nepal," *Economic and Political Weekly*, May 19, 2007, p. 1823.

[23] Arjun Guneratne, *Many Tongues, One Nation*, (Ithaca, NY: Cornell University Press, 2002), p. 1.

[24] Ibid., p. 37.

[25] For instance, Newaris, an indigenous group predominant in the Kathmandu valley and bound together by a common language, are further subdivided along religious lines (with a Hindu majority and a Buddhist minority) and caste lines (with around 20 castes and subcastes). Indeed, some authors consider different Newar castes so culturally different as to represent different ethnicities. See Guneratne, *Many Tongues, One Nation*, pp. 37f.

[26] Rajendra Pradhan, "Ethnicity, Caste, and a Pluralist Society," in Kanak Mani Dixit and Shastri Ramachandaran (eds.), *State of Nepal* (Kathmandu: Himal Books, 205), p. 9.

Although it was formally replaced by a new civil code in the 1960s, the social stratification prescribed by the Muluki Ain reverberates to this very day. As Thapa writes in Chapter 2, "there seems to be a clear link between group status in the 1854 Muluki Ain and positions of influence in Nepal today because caste status continued to affect social mobility and individual accomplishment."

Nepal has often been contrasted to other parts of South Asia as a zone of interethnic harmony. Yet, as Mahendra Lawoti points out in Chapter 5, the exclusionary nature of the state has, throughout the 19th and 20th century, repeatedly led to violent uprisings and militant opposition movements among ethnic groups, a ferment of discontent that the Maoists effectively tapped in the 1990s.

In rural areas the most glaring manifestation of social injustice and group inequality, given Nepal's continuously heavy reliance on agriculture,[27] can be found in control over land and the labor necessary to cultivate it. It is the relationship between landlords and the peasant population that gave rise to the Maoist claim, not without justification, that Nepal remained a feudal society. Indeed, the practice by which the state assigned its revenue collection rights on land to employees or favored individuals – common until the 1960s – created a class of landlords drawn almost exclusively from the Hindu hill elite. As John Whelpton, the author of Nepal's so far only comprehensive English-language history, writes in 2005, "In many cases, throughout Nepal, the wealthiest individuals are very often still those whose ancestors obtained revenue collection rights during the 18th and 20th century."[28] That Dalits, the "untouchable" caste who make up 13% of the population, only own 1% of arable land illustrates this point.[29]

Arjun Guneratne, an anthropologist who has done extensive field research in the Terai, links the low-intensity ethnic tension and conflict that have existed for many years in many parts of Nepal to the control of land by one ethnic group (with ethnicity and class being congruent).[30] He concludes, "[T]he high intensity violence of the Maoist insurgency in Nepal . . . is in part a reaction to the everyday violence of 'normal' life and the grinding inequality of Nepal's agrarian sector."[31] This everyday violence is particularly glaring with respect to bonded labor practices, which remain common in Nepal to this day. Although the Kamaiya system, in which the bonded laborer works to pay off a loan, was nominally abolished by law in 2002, coercion through indebtedness and undervalued labor remain a fact of life for thousands of Nepali families, in particular in rural areas. Indeed, in Nepal, the Kamaiya system

---

[27] Although the reliance on agriculture, which in 1951 made up more than 90% of the economy, has declined over the years because of the expansion of tourism, the service sector, and manufacturing, it still accounts for 40% of Nepal's GDP. See World Bank, "Nepal: Priorities for Agriculture and Rural Development," at http://go.worldbank.org/D9M3ORHVL0.

[28] Whelpton, *A History of Nepal*, p. 51.

[29] Ramesh Chandra, *Liberation and Social Articulation of Dalits* (New Delhi: Isha Books, 2004), p. 152.

[30] Guneratne, *Many Tongues, One Nation*, pp. 92ff.

[31] Ibid., p. 92.

"is changing into . . . a practice of share-cropping under which produce is divided between landlords and tenants, and tenants are required to till additional land for the landlords without any wages."[32] Meanwhile, other bonded labor practices, such as the Haliya system in the western hill districts of Nepal, in which women often work for moneylender landlords while their husbands work seasonally in India, continue to thrive.[33]

As Jörg Frieden and Devendra Raj Panday point out in Chapter 4.1 and 4, respectively, the international donor community working in Nepal woke up distressingly late to the realities of social exclusion and only began to address them in their programming in the early 2000s. One reason for this blindness to ethnic and caste politics among donors was the Panchayat regime's lasting success in propagating the image of a common national identity based on a dominant Hindu hill culture.[34] Another reason was the fact that for many years many of the diplomats, aid workers, and international NGO members stationed in Nepal remained ghettoized in Kathmandu and rarely ventured out into the rural areas to witness these realities firsthand.

Proximate Causes

Underlying causes are helpful in explaining *why* a country faces a higher conflict risk in general. To find some hints to *when* and in which context organized violence is likely to break out, one needs to turn to shorter term proximate causes. Chief among these are the dysfunctional features of the fledgling democracy and its inability to bring about meaningful change for much of the population, particularly with respect to poverty and exclusion. This led to disappointed expectations and widely felt disillusionment with the political parties and the political system, fueling popular support for the Maoists, a movement with a charismatic leader, revolutionary agenda, and readiness to resort to the use of force.[35]

The 1990 constitution, although acknowledging for the first time Nepal's multiethnic and multilingual character, continued to define the country as a "Hindu kingdom" and affirmed the status of Nepali as the national language, underpinning the continued cultural exclusion of ethnic groups. A winner-takes-all electoral system prevented meaningful representation of marginalized groups in parliament, as Catinca Slavu explains in Chapter 9. As Lawoti illustrates in Chapter 5, in

---

[32] Krishna Prasad Upadhyaya, "Poverty, Discrimination and Slavery: The Reality of Bonded Labour in India, Nepal and Pakistan," Anti-Slavery International, 2008, pp. 7f.

[33] Ibid., p. 24.

[34] Gellner, "Caste, Ethnicity and Inequality in Nepal, p. 1824.

[35] Joanna Pfaff-Czarnecka, "High Expectations, Deep Disappointment: Politics, State and Society in Nepal after 1990," in Michael Hutt (ed.), *Himalayan People's War: Nepal's Maoist Revolution* (Bloomington: Indiana University Press, 2004), pp. 166–91.

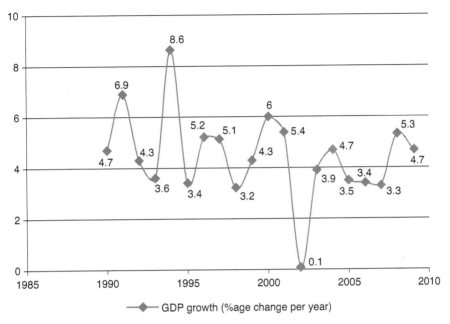

FIGURE 1.2. Percentage Change in GDP Growth Rates per Year, 1990–2010. *Source:* Asian Development Bank.

the bureaucracy, minority representation actually declined throughout the 1990s. Lagging progress in addressing exclusion contrasted sharply with the awakening of ethnic identities that took place in the context of the opening of democratic space, leading one prominent anthropologist to describe the period since 1990 as "a time of ethnicity building."[36]

In terms of development, the democratic transition brought some progress in some indicators. In the decade from 1990 to 2000, infant mortality fell from 10% to 7%, literacy rose from 39% to 58%, the road network more than doubled to 15,308 kilometers, and the number of telephone lines quadrupled to more than 255,000 (translating into a meager 10 lines per 1,000 inhabitants, most of them in urban areas).[37] Yet, as Devendra Raj Panday writes in Chapter 4, "the democratic transition in 1990 brought little change . . . [and] failed to leave a positive impact on the GDP growth rate, which continued to linger around an average of 5% for the first half of the 1990s – roughly the same rate Nepal saw during the last five years of the Panchayat regime (see Fig. 1.2)."[38]

36 Gellner, "Caste, Ethnicity and Inequality in Nepal," p. 1823.
37 Whelpton, *A History of Nepal*, p. 200.
38 See http://www.adb.org/Documents/Books/Key_Indicators/2009/pdf/nep.pdf.

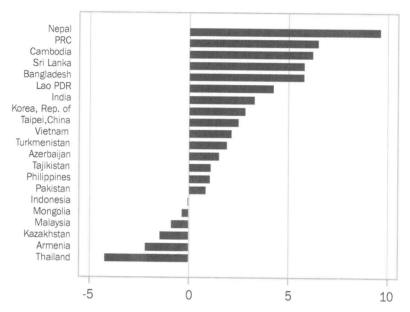

FIGURE 1.3. Changes in Gini Coefficient for Expenditure/Income Distributions, 1990s–2000s (percentage points). *Source:* Asian Development Bank.[39]

    While the growth rate remained stagnant, Nepal's income inequality increased at the highest rate in Asia throughout the 1990s, making Nepal the country with the highest income inequality on that continent (see Fig. 1.3). According to the Asian Development Bank, had Nepal been able to achieve its recent growth at the more equitable Gini Index level of 1995, extreme poverty in Nepal would have been cut by half within eight years.[40]
    The state's weak capacity only partly explains its failure to deliver essential services to its population. Indeed, as Pfaff-Czernanka has written, growing discontent with these service delivery shortfalls in the early 1990s occurred against the background not of the absence of state institutions but of the significant centralization and expansion of the state during the Panchayat years; this context gave rise to growing expectations that the state would play a redistributive role and provide services to the people. This expectation contrasted sharply with the de facto "gatekeeper" function played by centrally appointed state officials at the local level who, by diverting resources, "created scarcities and delays in provision [of goods and services] . . . to which the population holds legitimate right but has no means of claiming."[41] These state officials, as Pfaff-Czernanka points out, were often part, alongside politicians

[39] Asian Development Bank, *Inequality in Asia: Key Indicators 2007 Special Chapter Highlights,* p. 6.
[40] Ibid., p. 8.
[41] Pfaff-Czarnecka, "High Expectations, Deep Disappointment," p. 175.

and entrepreneurs, of "distributional coalitions," which channeled resources away from their rightful recipients and into their own pockets. (It should be noted that low government salaries, even by Nepali standards, facilitated the emergence of such corrupt practices.)[42]

Thus it was the abuse rather than the absence of the capacity for state service provision that exacerbated discontent, which only grew worse with the lack of recourse mechanisms and any form of accountability. As Panday explains in Chapter 4, development actors, by channeling significant amounts of aid money into the system, fed these corrupt dynamics. According to one study from the year 2000, only 15% of Nepalis benefited from foreign aid, many of them businessmen and powerful bureaucrats.[43]

The structure of Nepali parties and their role in the political system did not help. The two main parties alternating in power throughout the 1990s were the Nepali Congress (NC) and the Communist Party of Nepal (Unified Marxist-Leninist [UML]), either alone or in coalitions, and often, particularly in the case of the latter, as a prop for the royalist Rashtriya Prajatantra Party (RPP). The NC, formed in the 1940s modeled after India's Congress party, is the country's leading conservative party and a long-time supporter of the constitutional monarchy,[44] with its support base drawn largely from the establishment, the middle class, the business community, and sections of the security forces. Meanwhile, the UML, founded in 1991 and emerging as the largest party in the parliamentary election in 1994, was communist in name only and over time adopted a social democratic agenda.

Inexperienced in democratic and parliamentary processes and programmatically unprepared, the mainstream parties were also autocratically structured, with all major decisions (during the 1990s as well as later during the peace process) made by a small circle of largely male, Hindu high-caste party leaders. Their room for maneuver – already circumscribed by the 1990 constitution, which forced them to share power with the king – was further limited from within by internal divisions and constant struggles for party leadership. As a result, governments during the 1990s, in particular after the 1994 election, were increasingly instable – with the period of 1991–2002 seeing no less than 12 governments – a disarray that the Maoists (as well as the palace) readily exploited.

Only faintly resembling in form and function their counterparts in many Western democracies, the traditional parties in Nepal tended to be organized around individuals rather than programs. Party politics was a Kathmandu-centered "game of government making and unmaking" that led the parties to "grossly ignore the

---

[42] The monthly salary of a joint secretary at one of the government ministeries is Rs 11,000, around USD 150.

[43] Dhruba Kumar, "What Ails Democracy in Nepal?", in Dhruba Kumar (ed.), *Domestic Conflict and Crisis of Governability in Nepal* (Kathmandu: Center for Nepal and Asian Studies, 2000), p. 24.

[44] The NC dropped the term "constitutional monarchy" from its statute in September 2005.

need for party-building at the grassroots-level."[45] Meanwhile, the local presence of mainstream parties was often in the form of "strongmen," many of them landowners, who were key beneficiaries of the earlier mentioned "distributional coalitions" and who used their privileged access to state resources to maintain these coalitions and keep key members of their constituencies happy. Moreover, in rural areas, parties drew on established youth gangs, which had been used by the Panchayat regime to suppress the opposition, to intimidate rival parties and voters during election time.[46]

The poorly performing democracy significantly contributed to the radicalization of the left in the early 1990s and the emergence of the Maoist Party, which can trace its lineage back to the 1940s and the foundation of the Communist Party of Nepal in 1949. From their early days, the Nepali communists combined class struggle ideology with anti-imperialist rhetoric directed at newly independent India (and at the Nepali Congress party, which they considered a "stooge" of the Indian government).[47] Central to their demands was the end of "the feudal system" in Nepal and the replacement of the monarchy by a republic formed by an elected Constituent Assembly (demands that the Maoists took up four decades later to justify their insurgency). In well-rehearsed communist tradition, the following decades saw ideological divisions and leadership struggles (as well as international developments such as the Sino-Russian split) that led to a series of schisms, splits, and partial reunifications of the Communist Party. One breakaway (and Maoist precursor) faction that emerged in the 1980s, the CPN (Mashal), toyed with the idea of launching an armed struggle in the hope of triggering a mass uprising, but the idea was abandoned.[48]

Shortly after the 1990 People's Movement, several hard-line communist factions merged to form the (underground) Communist Party of Nepal (Unity Center) with a Maoist platform.[49] The new party chose as its general secretary Pushpa Kamal Dahal, better known by his nom-de-guerre Prachanda, a Brahmin former high school teacher turned full-time communist who, up to the peace process in 2006, had spent all of his political career underground. Although the party's above-ground electoral vehicle, the United People's Front, emerged in the 1991 elections as the third largest force, key party leaders believed that their goals could not be achieved within the parliamentary process. That same year a party conference endorsed Prachanda's policy of achieving a "People's Republic" through a "People's War."

Over the next three years, the United People's Front showed little interest in legislative work and focused instead on extraparliamentary opposition tactics, such as

---

[45] Krishna Hachhethu, "The Nepali State and the Maoist Insurgency," in Michael Hutt (ed.), *Himalayan People's War: Nepal's Maoist Revolution* (Bloomington: Indiana University Press, 2004), p. 61.

[46] International Crisis Group, *Nepal's Political Rites de Passage*, ICG Report 194, September 29, 2010, p. 19.

[47] Deepak Thapa, "Radicalism and the Emergence of the Maoists," in Michael Hutt (ed.), *Himalayan People's War: Nepal's Maoist Revolution* (Bloomington: Indiana University Press, 2004), p. 23.

[48] Ibid., p. 35.

[49] Ibid., p. 36.

street protests, strikes, and blockades. In 1994, the Unity Center split over the question whether the time was ripe for an armed uprising. The following year, Prachanda's pro-war faction of the Unity Center renamed itself the Communist Party of Nepal (Maoist) and engaged in an extensive recruitment and propaganda campaign in the Maoist mid-western stronghold districts, Rukum and Rolpa, harnessing the disaffection of ethnic groups in the region. Excessive and indiscriminate use of force by the Nepal Police in response to Maoist mobilization fed local resentment of the state.[50]

THE PEOPLE'S WAR

On February 13, 1996, the Maoist insurgency started with attacks on police posts in six districts in western, mid-western, and eastern Nepal. Initially, the conflict remained confined both geographically (in a number of mid-western hill districts) and in terms of fatalities (which, four years into the insurgency, numbered less than 500 annually), allowing the Kathmandu-based elite to treat it as a minor irritant.

However, over the next four years, the Maoist insurgency, relying on hit-and-run guerrilla tactics, slowly spread further to districts in central and western Nepal. With no outside support, Maoists had to be self-sufficient in their war-making capabilities, capturing weapons by overrunning police posts in isolated areas and financing themselves through bank robberies, extortion of local businesses (including private schools), and taxation of land in areas under their control. (Only an estimated 40% of its force permanently carried weapons, many of them homemade.)[51] As Rhoderick Chalmers notes, "[Maoist] violence was almost never random and their efforts to move among the people and win their support were in most respects genuine – though undercut by the casual brutality with which they sometimes sought to create shortcuts."[52]

For the first five years of the conflict, on the government's side, the war was exclusively fought by Nepal's police forces, first by the poorly trained and equipped Nepal Police, which from 1999 onward was supplemented by the newly formed counterinsurgency Armed Police Force (APF). An important shift in conflict dynamics occurred in June 2001 when King Birendra and much of the royal family were killed in a drug-infused (and conflict-unrelated) rampage by Crown Prince Dipendra (who then committed suicide). Whereas King Birendra had been reluctant to deploy the army against its own people – its role during the Panchayat years in suppressing internal political dissent notwithstanding – the newly enthroned king, Birendra's brother Gyanendra, decided to deploy the Royal Nepalese Army (RNA) in November 2001, six months after the royal massacre.

[50] Whelpton, *A History of Nepal*, pp. 202–5.
[51] Ashok Mehta, *The Royal Nepal Army: Meeting the Maoist Challenge* (New Delhi: Rupa, 2005).
[52] Rhoderick Chalmers, "Nepal: From Conflict to Consolidating a Fragile Peace," in Thania Paffenholz (ed.), *Civil Society and Peacebuilding: A Critical Assessment* (Boulder, CO: Lynne Rienner Publishers, 2010), p. 262.

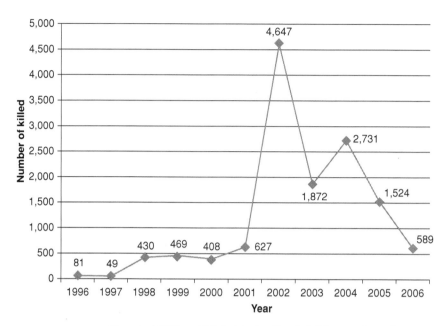

FIGURE 1.4. Reported Killings Related to the People's War, 1996–2006.

Although it was similarly incapable of suppressing the Maoist insurgency, the RNA deployment did lead to a massive escalation of the conflict and a skyrocketing number of battle deaths (more than 4,500 in the conflict's peak year in 2002; see Fig. 1.4). That same year, the Maoists improved their war-making capabilities by forming the People's Liberation Army (PLA). Estimates of its strength at the height of the conflict generally range from 8,000 to 12,000 combatants. The intensification of the conflict in 2001 also precipitated an increasing number of human rights violations, leading to mounting international concern.

The insurgency dramatically curtailed the reach of the already weak Nepali state. By the end of the People's War, the Maoists had denied the state control over around 80% of its territory (which does not necessarily mean it was under Maoist control). During the 10-year conflict, the PLA destroyed about 90% of the buildings of the roughly 4,000 village development committees (VDCs), the Nepali equivalent to municipalities, and displaced 68% of VDC secretaries, forcing them to withdraw to district capitals.[53] Of 1,979 police units in the country, 1,271 were forced to withdraw, and in areas under their control, the Maoists established parallel state structures, in particular the "People's Courts" and "People's Governments."

[53] Data collected by UN Office of Coordination of Humanitarian Affairs (OCHA) in May–July 2006; see http://www.un.org.np/sites/default/files/maps/tid_188/2006-8-11-VDCSec_in_2006_final.pdf.

In the aftermath of the People's War and the peace accords, the government struggled to reestablish its administrative presence, particularly in response to increasing unrest in the Terai (discussed in more detail later). Indeed, the UN estimated that, as of 2008, only 45% of VDC secretaries were "present" at their duty station.[54] This continued to hamper the state's already minimal ability to deliver development and security at the local level. Mirroring the contraction of the state's presence, the party structures of the main parties, mainly the NC and the UML, were also significantly weakened, ensuring a lasting dominance of the Maoists in many rural areas.

The history of the People's War is also a history of the erosion of the nascent – and in many ways only nominal – democratic state. The Maoist displacement of local state and elected representatives cut off the limbs of Nepal's young democracy. Meanwhile, King Gyanendra complemented the Maoists' work by beheading democracy through his twin coups in October 2002 and February 2005, which forced a return to absolute monarchy.

Gyanendra's attack on democracy was encouraged by the RNA, whose senior officer corps, staunchly royal in orientation, promised him – unrealistically, as it turned out – to swiftly put down the Maoist insurgency once freed from the shackles of democratic oversight. One leading general declared at the time that "[n]ow we can go single-mindedly after the Maoist without having to worry about the street."[55] With its increasing involvement in the People's War, the RNA roughly doubled in size to 90,000 soldiers in the course of the conflict, and military expenditures increased more than threefold between 2000 and 2006 to almost $180 million annually (and have only increased since, placing a huge burden on Nepal's budget and diverting funds away from the development effort; see Fig. 1.5).[56]

Yet, the state's arms build up did not translate into military success. Why did the combined force of roughly 110,000 Royal Nepalese Army and Armed Police Force[57] eventually fail to contain, let alone to put down, a 10,000-strong, largely self-sufficient insurgency that had no international sources of support? First, the counterinsurgency force was comparatively small by historical standards, in particular in Nepal's mountainous and hilly terrain that favors guerrilla warfare.[58] Second,

---

[54] Survey conducted between February and May 2008 by UN Office of Coordination of Humanitarian Affairs (OCHA); see http://www.un.org.np/node/9851.

[55] Mehta, *The Royal Nepal Army*.

[56] Asian Development Bank, "Nepal's Economic Indicators: 1990–2009," at http://www.adb.org/Documents/Books/Key_Indicators/2010/pdf/nep.pdf.

[57] Originally 15,100 strong when it was established in 1999, the APF had grown to 25,000 by 2008.

[58] Counterinsurgency experts suggest a counterinsurgent-to-insurgent ratio of between 10:1 and 20:1 depending on the circumstances. The Nepalese Army and APF only enjoyed an 11:1 advantage against an enemy familiar with the terrain and enjoying a great degree of sympathy among the population. In terms of counterinsurgent-to-population ratio, the Nepalese Army had a ratio of 3 counterinsurgents per 1,000 residents. By comparison, British forces in Northern Ireland and Malaya peaked at about 20 per 1,000 residents; international forces in Bosnia and Kosovo at 20 and 25, respectively; French

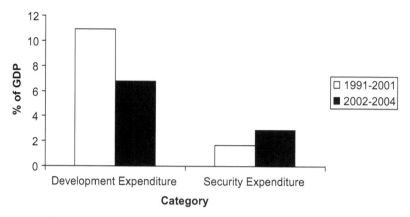

FIGURE 1.5. Government Expenditure (FY1991–FY2004). *Source:* Asian Development Bank.[59]

the RNA, which had largely been a ceremonial force (apart from deployments in UN peacekeeping missions), showed little desire for combat, engaging instead in static warfare primarily aimed at defending district capitals. Third, the Maoist social agenda resonated widely, whereas the army and police's excessively brutal security response alienated many, making it difficult for the state to win over the hearts and minds of the general population.

As the war progressed and the casualty figures increased, international involvement and concern grew. China, embarrassed by what it saw as a Maoist copyright infringement of its own brand, supported the palace throughout the conflict. In the aftermath of the 9/11 attacks, the United States was receptive to the Nepali government's assertion that by fighting the Maoists it was engaged alongside Washington in the global war on terror, and so it offered increasing political support and military aid. The United States also placed the Maoists on one of its terrorist designation lists (where they remain at the time of this writing),[60] leading the Maoists to increasingly adopt strong anti-American rhetoric.

While China's and the United States' involvement to date in Nepal have been limited, India's shadow has loomed large. Of the six countries bordering India, Nepal

forces in Algeria at just below 60; and Russian forces in Chechnya at 150 soldiers per 1,000 residents. See Steven M. Goode, "A Historical Basis for Force Requirements in Counterinsurgency," *Parameters* (Winter 2009/10); Andrew Krepinevich: *The Army and Vietnam* (Baltimore: Johns Hopkins University Press, 1986), p. 157; Bernard B. Fall, *Street without Joy* (Mechanicsburg, PA: Stackpole Books, 1964), pp. 17–172; Bernard B. Fall, *Last Reflections on a War: Bernard B. Fall's Last Comments on Vietnam* (Mechanicsburg, PA: Stackpole Books, 2000), p. 235.

59 Sungsup Ra and Bipul Singh, *Measuring the Economic Cost of Conflict*, Asian Development Bank Working Paper Series No. 2, Nepal Resident Mission, June 2005, p. 9.

60 Placement on the Terrorist Exclusion List only affects and restricts travel associated with terrorist organizations and thus carries less punitive measures than placement on the better known and more selective list, "Foreign Terrorism Organizations." See http://www.state.gov/s/ct/list/.

is the one most closely woven into the fabric of Indian life. The two countries have an open border and significant movements of population, and they have overlapping ethnicities; deep and broad political, social, and economic links; and extensive defense ties. India has hosted much of the Nepali elite for university education and serves as the principal market for Nepali goods. Even the political parties of Nepal to some extent parallel those of India. In addition, over the years, India has provided a good deal of assistance to Nepal.

New Delhi also wields unparalleled influence over the political process in Nepal which has given rise to resentment in Nepal and a tendency to see the hegemon's hand in all local developments. To a degree, Nepal's sovereignty concerns are understandable. In 1950, Jawaharlal Nehru mused publicly about incorporating Nepal into India, only then to settle on the 1950 Treaty of Peace and Friendship under which Nepal ceded considerable sovereignty, particularly over defense and security issues. India's annexation of Sikkim in 1975 and the Indian trade embargo in 1989 reinforced the widely held Nepali view of India as an overbearing neighbor. Nepalis, a proud people who often point out that they were never colonized by outsiders, tend to be deeply aggravated by what they consider to be excessive meddling by New Delhi.

Yet, as Rajeev Chaturvedy and David Malone explain in Chapter 11, India also has greater and more varied interests in Nepal than any other country, ranging from concerns about third-party (in particular Chinese and Pakistani) activities in its "backyard," links between the Maoists and India's own Maoist-inspired Naxalite insurgency to trade interests and hydropower. Interpretations of India's policy are further complicated by the fact that, as S.D. Muni explains in Chapter 12, India's approach to Nepal at any given point in time is shaped by the balance of forces among multiple stakeholders in Delhi's Nepal policy; these stakeholders include India's Ministry of External Affairs, the bureaucracy, the Indian army, the business community, members of the former princely rulers, Indian political parties, Hindu interest groups, and, finally, the Indian states bordering Nepal. It is partly because of this interplay of often incompatible interests that India's Nepal policy may seem confusing on occasion, with the defense establishment's strong support of the Nepalese Army (NA) contrasting with the Maoists' seemingly unimpeded use of Indian territory in Bihar, West Bengal, and Uttar Pradesh as safe havens. (Against this background, parts of the NA, after the peace accord, cultivated the legend that it would have won the war had it not been for the "safe haven" Maoists enjoyed across the border.)

However, the attitude of the world community took a dramatic turn after Gyanendra's seizure of power in February 2005 and the de facto reintroduction of absolute monarchy. His actions served as a wake-up call to the international community that then turned against a king who had gambled away the remaining vestiges of his legitimacy, at home and abroad. Led by India, it shifted its strategy from supporting the king in his military campaign against the Maoists to considering the Maoists as part of a negotiated solution.

PEACE PROCESS

In Chapter 6, Teresa Whitfield describes a series of failed efforts at mediation and peace negotiations, starting in 2000. Only after more than nine years of conflict and the loss of around 15,000 lives did the conditions for successful peace negotiations emerge. The first condition was that the two conflict parties had reached a "mutually hurting stalemate." In particular the humiliating defeats the Maoists and the RNA suffered in 2005 in the battles of Khara and Pili, respectively, convinced the leadership in both camps that victory on the battlefield was elusive and that the time was right to engage in serious peace negotiations.[61]

The second condition for successful peace negotiations was the growing unpopularity, at home and abroad, of King Gyanendra, who – already facing lingering suspicions among many Nepalis of having a hand in the royal massacre in 2001 – had driven a dagger through the heart of Nepali democracy with the twin coups of 2002 and 2005 while failing to translate his unconstrained power into military success.

The 2005 coup united the mainstream parliamentary parties against the king in a Seven Party Alliance (SPA), which then sought peace negotiations with the Maoists. A major step was achieved in November 2005, when both sides signed an Indian-facilitated 12-Point Understanding,[62] whose fascinating diplomatic history is detailed in S. D. Muni's Chapter 12. The 12-Point Understanding set the stage for the April 2006 People's Movement (*Jana Andolan II*), which forced the king to reinstate the elected parliament that he had dismissed in 2002 and to renounce all executive power. It then led to a Ceasefire Code of Conduct,[63] which formally started the peace process between the SPA and the Maoists, culminating in November 2006 in the Comprehensive Peace Agreement (CPA) and an Agreement on Monitoring of the Management of Arms and Armies.

The CPA provided an ambitious roadmap for the peace process. In return for being accorded a central role in open politics, the Maoists agreed to withdraw the PLA to 28 newly erected cantonment sites, dismantle parallel state structures, and return confiscated land. PLA members were also promised subsequent partial integration into the country's security forces, including a "democratically restructured Army." Other key elements of the CPA and the arms agreement, which were to be sequentially implemented in a short time frame, were the adoption of an interim constitution; the institution of an interim parliament and an interim government,

---

[61] For an expose of "mutually hurting stalemate theory" see I. William Zartman, *Ripe for Resolution* (New York: Oxford University Press, 1989). For the impact of the battles of Khara and Pili, see Sam Cowan, "Inside the People's Liberation Army: A Military Perspective," *European Bulletin of Himalayan Research* 37 (Winter 2010).

[62] Text: http://www.unmin.org.np/downloads/keydocs/12-point%20understanding-22%20Nov%202005 .pdf.

[63] Code of Conduct between the Government of Nepal and the CPN (Maoist), published on May 26, 2006. The exact time of signature is not known.

both with Maoist participation; the holding of elections to a Constituent Assembly in June 2007, which would decide on the future of the monarchy and give birth to a new Nepal; and the "restructuring of the State in an inclusive, democratic and progressive way by ending its present centralized and unitary structure"[64] designed to address the concerns of the marginalized groups.

Building on three years of quiet dialogue with the conflict parties carried out since 2003 in the context of the UN Secretary-General's "good offices function," as well as the work of the OHCHR Mission, which had operated effectively in Nepal since 2005, the Maoists and the SPA jointly requested the deployment of a UN peace mission to support the peace process and help Nepal create an atmosphere for free and fair elections to a Constituent Assembly without foreseeing an explicitly political role for that mission. In January 2007, the UN Security Council established the UN Mission to Nepal (UNMIN) as a "focused mission of limited duration," which, for the following four years became an important player in international efforts to help Nepal make the transition from war to peace. In Chapter 8, Ian Martin describes the difficulty the UN had in playing a meaningful role within the constraints of a narrow mandate and operating under the watchful eye of a suspicious regional power, India.

THE TERAI AND IDENTITY POLITICS

The period after the ceasefire also saw the emergence of fervent identity politics that deeply affected transition dynamics and, if not managed properly, holds the potential for a new round of violent conflict. The most intense manifestation of identity politics was the outbreak, in January 2007, of the Madhesi movement (or Andolan), an at times violent uprising of the Madhesi people in the Terai; this movement has placed a stark spotlight on a region that is playing an increasingly significant role in Nepali politics.

The Terai is the southern flatlands bordering India, inhabited in its eastern and central regions mostly by Madhesis, who share a common culture and languages with people across the border in India, and in its western portion by Tharus, an indigenous group with a separate identity from Madhesis. Several small kingdoms existed in the east and central Terai before the wars of unification brought them into the fold of the expanding Nepali state in the mid-18th century. Before the 1960s, few hill dwellers (Pahadis) descended to the plains, primarily because of the heat, humidity, and the prevalence of malaria there. Those who did were government officers sent to tax and administer the local population, as well as traders and entrepreneurs who saw opportunities in Nepal's new territories. The eradication of malaria in the 1960s brought large-scale migration from the hills, which was encouraged by the Panchayat governments as a demographic counter to a Madhesi population

---

[64] Comprehensive Peace Agreement, para. 3.5.

that had been steadily growing over the previous century due to migration from neighboring Indian districts. The influx of populations from both the north and the south, combined with the rapid clearing of forests for agriculture, gradually turned the Terai into Nepal's bread-basket. To this day, agriculture remains the main activity of the overwhelming majority of Terai inhabitants, although industry has also been slowly expanding since the 1960s.

Although Madhesis make up roughly a fifth of Nepal's population,[65] they look back on a long history of discrimination, when they were routinely denied meaningful representation in state institutions like the army, police, and bureaucracy and were restricted from being eligible for citizenship. In the Panchayat years, the monarchy actively promoted a vision of nationalism centered around Pahadi (hill-origin) ideals, reinforcing a notion that the Madhesis were essentially foreign. In the context of anti-Indianism, nurtured since the 1950s by communists and the monarchy alike, Madhesis were often depicted as New Delhi's fifth column.

Among the more recent attempts to organize Madhesis into a political force was the Nepal Sadbhavana Council, formed in 1985 by Gajendra Narayan Singh and later renamed the Nepal Sadbhavana Party (NSP). The NSP never posed a serious challenge to the mainstream parties, which successfully co-opted Madhesis within their respective Madhesi wings. Throughout the 1990s, the political influence of Madhesis was by and large limited to serving as a vote bank for Pahadi (hill-origin) politicians, such as the late Girija Prasad Koirala, who made the Terai their political base.

In the course of the People's War, Maoists actively encouraged identity politics and mobilized Madhesis in the Terai. However, only very few Madhesis rose through the ranks of the Maoist hierarchy, the leadership of which was primarily made up of Pahadis who showed little inclination to represent Madhesi interests in the ensuing peace process. Indeed, it was the fear of being once again left out when Nepal's social contract would be renegotiated in a newly elected Constituent Assembly that triggered the outbreak of the Madhesi *Andolan* in January 2007 with sometimes violent street protests and occasional mob violence, often targeting Maoist cadres, who had been sent from the hills to the Terai to organize the Madhesis into a coherent political force. The Madhesi *Andolan* dramatically weakened Maoist influence in much of the Madhesi heartland and led to a political realignment, with the emergence of new political groups and parties that posed a serious challenge both to the Maoists and the traditional parties.

Worryingly, the Madhesi *Andolan* also gave rise to a number of armed groups in the Terai that have contributed to a widespread sense of insecurity. By some counts, in 2008, more than 100 such armed groups operated in the eastern and central Terai, although most were small criminal outfits involved in extortion and abductions.

---

[65] This figure excludes the Terai indigenous nationalities such as Tharus (8.96%) as well as Nepal's Muslims, who mainly reside in the Terai (4.29%).

A few of these groups however, such as the Jantantrik Terai Mukti Morcha (JTMM), founded in 2004 by former Maoist functionary Jay Krishna Goit, managed to generate a degree of pan-Madhesi appeal, with demands for independence for the Terai. Yet the JTMM was weakened by several splits, and neither the JTMM nor any of the other groups possesses the popular support or organizational capability to mount a serious challenge to the state, at least for the time being.

The Pahadi reaction to Madhesi activism, particularly from the armed groups, has been one of open fear and concern. Thousands of Pahadi families who had resided in the Terai for decades have sold off their property and fled to the hills. Those who remain rue the loss of their once paramount influence in the Terai. Still others have vowed to fight back by joining or supporting Pahadi self-defense groups such as the Chure Bhawar Ekta Samaj, whose militant rhetoric has yet to be matched by action. Clearly, Nepal as a whole and its major constituent parts, particularly the Terai, are passing through a delicate phase. Nepal's new ethnic politics places an ever greater premium on the careful management of Nepal's transition and the development of a model of government that will satisfy the aspirations of Nepal's major ethnic groups.

THE CHAPTERS IN BRIEF

In **Chapter 2**, *Deepak Thapa*, a Nepali commentator, analyzes the root and proximate causes that gave rise to the Maoist insurgency and draws on social movement literature to provide an understanding of the rapid expansion and popular support for the Maoist movement. Although the Maoists' People's War seems anachronistic in a post–Cold War context, Thapa argues that it was Nepal's social political background that allowed the Maoists to emerge. He explores three theorems based in social movement literature to explain the social processes that facilitated the success of the Maoists. The first argues that relative deprivation of large parts of the population plays a major role in providing a conducive environment for an insurgency. Yet Thapa argues that the second factor, political opportunity, was a more important factor in facilitating the Maoists' success. When the 1990 democratic period did not deliver the expected radical social transformation and instead gave way to political instability, many Nepalis lost their faith in democracy and in the parties that lay at its core. The Maoists meanwhile used the political space provided to operate openly and gather public support for their cause. Equally important, the Maoists were able to effectively mobilize their constituencies through the skillful use of rhetoric that cut across class, ethnic, and gender divides, enticing people to join their People's War. Thapa concludes that the People's War was waiting to happen – and only needed the right circumstances and most importantly the right protagonists to set it in motion.

In **Chapter 3**, *Rhoderick Chalmers*, the former head of the International Crisis Group's Nepal office, provides historical context to one of the most contentious points of the peace agreement: the future of the two armed forces that fought against each other during the People's War: the Maoist People's Liberation Army (PLA) and the Royal Nepalese Army (RNA). In doing so, Chalmers provides insights into the ideologies, interests, and institutional cultures of the two actors. The peace negotiations that began in 2006 and included both armies were based not on a military victory of one side over the other but rather on a military stalemate, with both the NA and the PLA having important sources of leverage. Advances in security sector reform have been hampered by mistrust among the parties and prevailing differences on how to proceed: the Maoists want to negotiate a final deal on future military structures that would include integration of some of its force into the NA before demobilizing the PLA, while the NA firmly resists reform efforts and refuses to integrate Maoist combatants into its forces. The peace agreement meanwhile does not provide guidance on these issues, and international assistance to the negotiating process has not had an impact. The author concludes that, instead of agreeing to compromise, both forces have hardened their position and increased their political influence over the process because they recognize that control over military force, as well as the ability to shape it, remains the backbone of political power in Nepal.

In **Chapter 4**, renowned civil society leader and former Nepali Finance Minister *Devendra Raj Panday* analyzes Nepal's development trajectory since the 1950s, looking at Nepal's institutional, political, and cultural dynamics; the role of the international donor community; and the role of India. He argues that the main causes of Nepal's failed development are engrained in the country's societal and political culture, particularly in the exclusionary nature of the state. Donors, some of which have been providing aid to Nepal for decades, have largely failed to address the necessary structural changes that would enable more equitable and sustainable development. Instead, foreign aid has sustained traditional power structures, leading even positive aid achievements to ultimately become sources of conflict and making the entire development process conflict-prone. The donor communities' failure to address the causes of failed development in Nepal is partly a result of the international aid system's tendency to follow a one-size-fits-all approach to development with little regard to local conditions. However, Panday concludes that the recent political developments in Nepal provide hope for the future. He urges development actors to design strategies that are tailored to the realities on the ground and to let national actors take the lead in these processes so they can become accountable for results.

Complementing Panday's chapter with a donor's perspective, *Jörg Frieden*, in **Chapter 4.1** provides an account of the struggles of the development community to adapt to conflict realities in Nepal, drawing on his years-long experience as the head of the Nepal office of the Swiss Agency for Development and Cooperation during this critical period. He argues that, since the beginning of the conflict in 1996, aid agencies have struggled to understand three critical dimensions of the conflict: its political nature, the development regime's intimate association with an ever more illegitimate state, and the Maoists' role as a political movement and their effective control of most of Nepal's territory. A decisive change in donor practice only came about after the king's 2005 takeover, which forced development actors to distance themselves from his regime. The author argues that, although not all efforts to adjust to the conflict environment had positive outcomes, the continuous engagement of donors had some moderating effects on conflict dynamics and contributed to the ongoing political transition. At the same time, the prevailing impasse in the political process also underlines the limitations of international influence. Still, Frieden urges development actors to shed the deeply ingrained notions of development cooperation as a technical and apolitical process and to address issues around democracy, peace, and development simultaneously.

In another perspective on Nepal's development woes, Nepali business executive *Sujeev Shakya*, in **Chapter 4.2** examines the impediments to and opportunities for economic growth in Nepal. Looking back at Nepal's history since becoming a modern state, Shakya describes patronage and a predatory elite as well as dependence on India as long-standing obstacles to economic growth. However, the author also sees important potential for Nepal's development, highlighting the country's comparative advantages in various sectors, such as in hydropower generation, its vast biodiversity, and tourism that could stimulate domestically driven growth if they were fully exploited. To tap into this potential, Shakya urges decision makers in Nepal to introduce stringent reforms that promote transparency and good governance, strengthen the education sector, and shore up investments into infrastructure development. To stamp out exclusionary practices of the past, policy makers also have to ensure that the reforms benefit all regions and groups in society.

In **Chapter 5**, the U.S.-based Nepali academic *Mahendra Lawoti* provides an overview of Nepal's diverse ethnic makeup and analyzes both the extent to which ethnic politics has influenced the peace process and how political developments before and during the peace agreement have shaped ethnic politics. For most of its history the Nepal state has been dominated by one group, the high-caste Pahadi Hindu elite, that discriminated against other ethnic, caste, and religious groups both culturally and economically and excluded them from formal politics. Although for the past two centuries the polity succeeded in suppressing resistance to the discriminatory practices through tight control and oppression, democratization of the political system in the 1990s enabled marginalized ethnic groups to organize and challenge the elite's hegemony. Indeed, Nepal's history since 1990 has been marked by a progressive ethnic awakening. Yet, Lawoti cautions that the transition has so far failed to address deeply engrained exclusion, leading various ethnic groups to seek extrasystemic methods for achieving their goals, which could – and have in the past – turn violent, thereby jeopardizing the achievements of the peace process.

In **Chapter 6**, conflict resolution expert *Teresa Whitfield* assesses the role and effectiveness of international actors, including the UN, bilateral actors, and NGOs, in assisting in peacemaking efforts between the conflict parties and in bringing about the peace agreement. The impact of these actors on peacemaking processes is hard to assess, although long-term engagement by some actors can be credited with creating a conducive environment to pursue a political solution to the conflict. The author argues that the Nepali experience demonstrates the benefits of sustained dialogue and the necessity to create space for the dialogue to take place. She also stresses that actors who were committed to long-term engagement had more viable results than those who dealt with the conflict in the shorter term, because the latter were less familiar with the full complexity of the conflict's dynamics. Finally, the author argues that India, instead of resisting international involvement, could have made better use of the various international actors to deflect repeated criticisms that it played an overly dominant role in Nepal's peace process.

Chapter 7 is a collaboration between *Frederick Rawski,* a long-time staff member of the Office of the High Commissioner of Human Rights' mission in Nepal, and *Mandira Sharma,* a leading Nepali human rights advocate. In it, they analyze successes and failures of human rights monitoring before and after the conflict. Although increased international attention and scrutiny, particularly through the 2005 establishment of the OHCHR Nepal Office, of abuses committed by both the Royal Nepalese Army and the Maoists had moderating effects on the conflict, soon after the peace agreement was put into effect, human rights monitoring lost its leverage. This was primarily due to the failure to tackle impunity in the postconflict setting. However, the authors point out that rights defenders also struggled to effectively address the social, structural, and institutional causes of the conflict. They conclude that human rights monitoring can play an important role at key moments, but when it comes to addressing long-term systemic problems, international interventions, because of their inherent short-term engagements, have serious limitations. The authors further caution that international and past Nepali experiences suggest that the transitional justice mechanisms that Nepal is currently putting in place rarely result in accountability mechanisms or have a lasting impact on impunity. They therefore urge international and national actors to focus on systematically reforming rule of law institutions.

In **Chapter 8,** *Ian Martin,* who led the United Nations Mission in Nepal (UNMIN) from 2006–9, details how the mission came into being, describes its work, and discusses its strengths and weaknesses in the context of its mandate. The engagement of the UN in Nepal was unique in many ways, and its various mandated tasks, including one of its core functions – monitoring the commitments of the peace agreements regarding the forces of the Nepalese Army and the Maoists and their weapons – were designed during close negotiations with UN representatives and peace process parties to suit Nepal's specific needs. The author argues that success in implementing provisions relating to the future of the two armies was ultimately hampered by flaws in the agreements, which failed to spell out details on procedure and sequencing. In addition, the various governments throughout the transitional period did not follow through on their commitments, impeding the process further. UNMIN's mandate meanwhile restricted its ability to enforce compliance with the agreements. Nevertheless, the author concludes that the UN presence was able to provide encouragement and support to the political actors and hope for the Nepali people that peace would endure, both of which prevented a renewed confrontation and a return to conflict.

In **Chapter 9**, electoral expert *Catinca Slavu* places the Constituent Assembly (CA) elections in the context of Nepal's electoral experience in the 1990s and explores the struggles to ensure they would lead to the establishment of a representative body that could credibly address the very root cause of the violent conflict: the exclusionary nature of Nepal's state. The author argues that one of the key factors that contributed to the success of the election was the establishment of a new electoral system that introduced proportional representation with inclusion quotas alongside the traditional first-past-the-post system. Combined with the Maoists' selection of candidates from minority groups for the first-past-the-post race, the electoral system helped make the Constituent Assembly the most inclusive state institution in Nepal's history. Notwithstanding this important achievement, the author warns that in the absence of a roadmap for peace and for building a genuinely democratic state, the positive outcome of the elections can only be sustained if the political parties work together in advancing the democratic transformation agenda and the peacebuilding process.

In the complementary contribution, *Bhojraj Pokharel*, in **Chapter 9.1** provides a unique insiders' perspective on the Constituent Assembly (CA) elections by drawing on his past experience as Nepal's Chief Election Commissioner from 2006–9. Seen as the first step to restore peace and stability in Nepal, the CA elections carried enormous significance in the postpeace agreement period. The Election Commission began its work in the context of strong political commitment but a weak electoral infrastructure. Challenges included widespread insecurity, an administrative vacuum, particularly in rural areas, as well as the lack of a legislative framework that would detail, among other elements, the model of the electoral system, eligibility requirements for voters, and the eventual size of the CA. These shortcomings in combination with evolving political developments led to repeated postponements of the elections. The author concludes that the Election Commission's commitment to maintaining flexibility to accommodate the highly volatile political situation as well as the support of the international community, particularly the UN, were decisive factors in the success of the elections. However, the Nepali people, civil society organizations, the media, and the political parties, all of which sustained their enthusiasm and commitment to the elections, played the most crucial part in bringing the elections to their successful conclusion. The author further urges the political actors to seize the chance that the elections provided to break away from Nepal's past problems to achieve real and lasting change.

In **Chapter 10**, Nepali journalist *Aditya Adhikari* details the Maoists' transformation in thought, strategy, and structure as they made the transition from an insurgent group to a party engaging in competitive politics, emerging as the strongest political force in Nepal. Although two actors, India and the UN Mission in Nepal, were instrumental in bringing the rebels into the democratic fold, the Maoists' message of change and their far-reaching reform agenda soon awarded them overwhelming popular support. Yet the Maoists also used other, sometimes illicit, means to extend their reach into society and to shore up support. Once in government, the party's strict discipline and tightly controlled organizational structure largely prevented frictions among the leadership from causing dissent and enabled the party to withstand attempts at manipulation by other political forces, at least for the first few years of the peace process. The author argues that the quick pace and rigor with which the Maoists set out to reform corrupt and dysfunctional state structures combined with their political power threatened the traditional political institutions and contributed to an increasing anti-Maoist stance among the other parties. The resulting conflict between the Maoists and the traditional parties has led to a deep polarization of Nepali politics that largely paralyzed the state. The author concludes that it has become clear that it will be difficult for the Maoists to control Nepal's political space. However, they have no option but to engage in the multiparty state system, making compromises and enduring negotiations to pursue their goals.

In **Chapter 11**, *Rajeev Chaturvedy*, an Indian academic, and *David M. Malone*, a former Canadian High Commissioner to India and Ambassador to Nepal, discuss Nepal's international significance and particularly Kathmandu's relations with India and China, its influential neighbors. The authors identify Nepal's geography as a major factor determining its international relations and argue that if Nepal is to achieve domestic stability, peace, and development and pursue an independent foreign and domestic policy agenda, it will have to better exploit its position between the two fastest growing economies in the world. Recent developments in the country have not altered Nepal's foreign policy options. Although China is exerting growing influence in South and Southeast Asia and expanding its sway over Nepal, Beijing's interests are largely limited to holding in check the activities of the Tibetan diaspora. India will thus continue to exert its pervasive influence in Nepali economic, cultural, and political matters, although Delhi's approach is no longer as heavy-handed as it was in the past. The authors stress that cooperation with India on Nepal's immense water reserves is particularly promising and could benefit both countries, if more trust developed between them.

In **Chapter 12**, *S. D. Muni*, a leading Indian academic, diplomat, and authority on South Asian security affairs, discusses India's role in facilitating the negotiations that led to the peace agreement, an episode in which the author was personally involved as a key actor. Muni provides insights on New Delhi's changing attitudes toward the monarchy and the Maoists in the run-up to and the early phase of the peace process. Although India's approach to Nepal is largely defined by New Delhi's security concerns, the multiple stakeholders shaping its policy have diverse and often incompatible positions. Differences in approaches and opinions started to emerge particularly after Nepal's political developments forced India to abandon its support for the constitutional monarchy in favor of bringing the Maoists into the democratic fold. However, once the former rebels emerged as the strongest political party in the Constituent Assembly, New Delhi began a campaign to marginalize and weaken them in the long run. The author argues that this tactic endangers the peace process and jeopardizes its objective of establishing a new constitution. He further warns that as long as the Maoists are denied a meaningful role in a power-sharing arrangement, Nepal's peace and stability will hang in a precarious balance.

In **Chapter 13**, Nepali journalist *Prashant Jha* provides a Nepali perspective on the role and influence of outside actors, specifically India, the UN Mission in Nepal, China, and the United States, during the transition period. India undoubtedly played the most prominent and influential role in creating space for a political solution to the conflict and in helping implement key aspects of the peace agreement. However, all external actors shaped the process, although not all international interventions have been conducted in concert or had positive outcomes. The author observes that because international actors, with their respective interests in mind, have varying approaches and often conflicting prescriptions, domestic problems become more difficult to solve and political polarization begins to sharpen. The author thus concludes that constructive international engagement depends on the consensus among national actors: as long as domestic actors work together constructively, the activities of international actors can be channeled positively. However, when political fragmentation emerges, international actors, bringing their own interests into play, can deliberately or inadvertently enhance political instability.

The Context

2

The Making of the Maoist Insurgency

Deepak Thapa

In a remote corner of the western Nepal district of Rolpa, in a gently sloping river valley lies the village of Jelbang. Nothing distinguishes this village from the hundreds of others that dot the Nepali mountainside. It does not straddle any of the main trails that crisscross the mountain heartland of Nepal, and unless one purposely intends to visit this village, it is very unlikely to be part of anyone's travel itinerary.

Despite its obscurity, Jelbang stands out in one aspect: although not generally known, this small village (or, more precisely, Jelbang VDC[1]) probably suffered the highest number of deaths during the Maoist conflict of the approximately 4,000 VDCs in Nepal. Sixty-eight people from Jelbang lost their lives, of whom 30 died in the first three years of the fighting, all within the village boundaries.[2]

It is difficult to say what role Jelbang played in the larger Maoist conflict and what and how it might have contributed to its perpetuation. However, there is no doubt that it was villages like Jelbang and the internecine bloodshed that tore at the communities' social fabric that sustained the Maoist conflict in those initial years and contributed to creating a mystique around both the Maoists and districts like Rolpa and Rukum in the national consciousness.

One can certainly identify several socioeconomic factors that could suggest that Jelbang was ripe for a communist insurgency, but then not all the villagers became Maoists. It has been argued that, in Jelbang's case, police high-handedness, along with preexisting factionalism within the village, was the reason why the place suffered so many casualties in such a brief period.[3] However, experiences from other villages that saw heightened Maoist activity are often at complete variance with what

---

[1] VDC, or the village development committee, is the smallest administrative unit in Nepal.
[2] Thapa et al., 2009. Not all of the 68 died in the village because, with the widening of the conflict zone, people from Jelbang were being killed elsewhere as well.
[3] Thapa et al., 2009.

happened in Jelbang.[4] In other words, a number of factors propelled people into the Maoist conflict, and any explanation proffered will only be partial at best. It is with this caveat in mind that this chapter approaches its subject matter.

This chapter sets out the background to the Maoists' "People's War" that began with simultaneous attacks on three police posts and a local office of a government-owned bank on February 13, 1996, in western Nepal. It briefly recounts the history of Nepal from the state's formation to the present time as it relates to the exclusionary policies of the state that were partly responsible for the unprecedented and unexpected strength of the Maoist insurgency. It then draws on literature on social movements to provide a framework for understanding the Maoist movement's rapid expansion.

STATE FORMATION

Until the mid-18th century, the area that today is Nepal comprised a number of kingdoms and principalities – some rich and powerful, others less so, but all small. The state of Nepal was created out of these disparate small principalities by the ruler of one of the more impoverished ones, Gorkha, located in central Nepal.

In 1744, Prithvi Narayan Shah, the youthful king of Gorkha, set out on a campaign to conquer lands far and wide. Within seven decades, through his own efforts and those of his successors as well as some capable military commanders, the tiny kingdom of Gorkha reached proportions that qualified it to be called a little empire. It covered an area that was nearly twice the size of present-day Nepal, and its rapid expansion was viewed with disquiet by the English East India Company, which was consolidating its own presence in South Asia.

As expected, in 1814, a war broke out between the two expanding powers in which the Gorkha empire was defeated and reduced to a size coinciding more or less with today's borders of Nepal. The war with the British was followed by intense court rivalries and intrigues that lasted for three decades until, in 1846, a young general, Jang Bahadur Rana, took over as an all-powerful prime minister by literally eliminating all opposition in the court in a bloodbath known as the Kot Massacre. He reduced the Shah king to a ceremonial figurehead and ensured that the office of prime minister would stay within his family, thus laying the foundation for 104 years of hereditary rule by the Rana family. With all state power vested in them, the Rana prime ministers ruled Nepal as their personal fiefdom, using the country's treasury for whatever purpose they thought fit, which usually meant aggrandizement of themselves and their family. Rule by the Ranas lasted until 1951 when, after the decolonization of South Asia and the departure of the British, the Ranas' patrons in the region, their oligarchic rule came to an end.

---

[4] See, for instance, Shneiderman and Turin (2005).

Yet Jang Bahadur's takeover in 1846 brought a measure of stability to Nepali politics after a century of uncertainty engendered first by the furious pace of territorial conquests and then by perennial intrigues and rivalries around the royal palace. It was this calm after the long period of uncertainty that allowed the Ranas to accelerate the process of social stratification that had already begun in the initial years of the Gorkha conquests. As Pradhan puts it, the political process that gave birth to Nepal as a state had "created a unified kingdom, but not a unified society."[5] He concludes that the unification of Nepal resulted in

> the subjugation of the original inhabitants, mostly Tibeto-Burman-speaking Mongoloids, by the high order Hindu migrants from the Indian plains. . . . In the economic sphere, the very nature of the Gorkha conquests gave birth to a privileged landholding gentry or a feudal class of jagir and birta owners[6] drawn from the same "two superior classes of the Hindoos."[7] They occupied all the positions of trust, enjoyed civil and military power and maintained themselves on exactions from the humble peasantry.[8]

The Ranas instituted laws and rules for the benefit of high-caste Bahuns and Chhetris, while gradually marginalizing those outside the ruling elite.[9] The Limbus, an indigenous group concentrated in eastern Nepal, had to compromise on their traditional rights to land; the Tamangs, a predominant ethnic group in the central hill region, were forced to serve the growing class of rulers in Kathmandu; and the Terai, the lowlands alongside the border with India, was treated as a colony.[10] Even the Magars and Gurungs, the two "Tibeto-Burman-speaking Mongoloid" groups that formed part of the vanguard of the Gorkhali expansion, found themselves sidelined soon after the conquests were over.[11]

The Ranas were instrumental in institutionalizing Hinduism and Nepali as the official religion and language of the state, with the result that the languages, religions, and cultures of nonprivileged groups were gradually sidelined. One of their most pernicious acts was Jang Bahadur's codification of the Hindu caste system through the 1854 Muluki Ain (Civil Code), which "integrate[d] three historically

---

[5] Pradhan, 1991, p. 222.

[6] *Jagir* and *birta* were two forms of landownership granted by the state for services rendered.

[7] Namely, Bahuns and Chhetris, including the ruling subgroup of Thakuris.

[8] Pradhan, 1991, pp. 225–6.

[9] Ibid., chapter 7.

[10] Whelpton, 2005.

[11] Mahesh Chandra Regmi's survey of around 49 men who became *kaji*, or the highest ranking nonroyal courtier, in the years 1768–1814 showed that at least 10 were Magars and Gurungs. However, after Rana Bahadur Shah's assassination in 1806, representation by these two groups came almost to an end. Regmi 1995, pp. 43–6. Abhiman Singh Rana, a Magar general killed in the Kot Massacre of 1846 that catapulted Jung Bahadur Rana to power, was the last major figure in the state nobility from either of these two groups.

and regionally autonomous caste hierarchies, i.e. that of the Parbatiya,[12] the Newar and of the Terai people, as well as a number of ethnic groups into an all-embracing 'national' hierarchy of castes."[13]

In effect, the Muluki Ain subsumed the entire population of Nepal into a rigid social pecking order based on caste and ethnicity. This legacy of the Ranas' century in power continues to have an impact on the country and helps explain why a seemingly anachronistic Maoist insurgency emerged in Nepal in the waning years of the 20th century.

THE PANCHAYAT YEARS

A short and chaotic experiment with popular rule started in 1951 with the ouster of the Ranas and ended with the takeover by King Mahendra in 1960. The king justified his power grab by claiming that parliamentary democracy was not suited for the country. Instead he claimed he would institute a "democratic system" that was rooted in the country's panchayats (traditional village councils). As it turned out, democracy was the least of his concerns, for, as Rose notes, "the most notable characteristic of the immediate period after the coup was the haphazard manner with which new institutions were grafted on what was essentially an absolute monarchy."[14]

For the next 30 years, Nepal lived through an authoritarian regime that curtailed all overt political activity outside of what was called the party-less Panchayat system. This system delayed democratic consolidation and political development by decades. A perhaps more insidious effect of this environment of intolerance was the stifling of various social movements that had emerged in the 1950s to establish the rights of those who had been consigned to the margins of the state, namely the Dalits (formerly, the "untouchables" of the Hindu caste system), the Janajatis (the groups that mainly spoke Tibeto-Burman languages, as mentioned earlier), and the Madhesis (whose origin is traced to the Terai plains of southern Nepal).[15]

The new Panchayat constitution further consolidated the privileges of the Kathmandu-based elite by enshrining Nepali as the official language and declaring Nepal to be a Hindu kingdom. This was followed by crafting policies that favored the sociocultural values of the ruling upper castes, leading to the systematic marginalization of Dalits, Janajatis, Madhesis, and religious minorities and their worldviews. In doing so, the Panchayat system crafted a sense of Nepali nationhood based on a set of features with which more than two-thirds of the population could not identify. Conformity was demanded by the state, and dissent was penalized severely. After

---

[12] The "upper castes," mainly the Bahun and Chhetri in Nepal.
[13] Hoefer, 2004, p. 8.
[14] Rose, 1963, p. 17.
[15] These are the same three groups that were to make themselves heard with considerable force in the second half of the 2000s.

the Panchayat system finally came to an end in 1990, democracy was reestablished, opening up political space for a diversity of voices to claim rights as equal citizens.

During the 30 years of authoritarian rule, marginalized groups had no choice but to acquiesce in the policies of the state but at the same time they had also been quietly organizing under various guises and become more conscious of their marginalized situation.[16] After the Panchayat system came to an end, they demanded that their voices be recognized and that they have a say in how the character of the state evolved. First to mobilize were the Madhesis and the Janajatis, both of whom could build on many years of awareness-raising during the Panchayat system and earlier, albeit under the guise of community-based work.

Hangen's brief recounting of Janajati mobilization describes how various social groups began organizing in the pre-1990 period.[17] Starting in the Rana period through the brief democratic interlude and the later Panchayat period, Janajati groups established organizations such as the Tharu Welfare Society and Thakali Society Reform Organization. Most of these entities were founded to promote "social cohesion and cultural preservation within single ethnic groups,"[18] but there were some attempts to form organizations that brought together more than one group under a single umbrella. Although the very act of coming together indicated a political purpose, the political environment was hardly conducive to such actions. After 1990, a number of parties and organizations claiming to speak for Janajatis emerged, but none had any electoral success. However, Janajati activism was at its loudest in the early 1990s, or so it seemed at that time given its very novelty. For instance, the little-known Magarat Mukti Morcha (Magarat Liberation Front) warned that it would opt for "separation" if the government did not heed its demand to create a separate state for Magars, the largest of the Janajati groups.[19] The language used perhaps made the Morcha sound more radical than it actually was, but at that time an ethnic conflict looked probable. Of course, that perception was fostered by the country's recent emergence from an era in which the polity had tried to suppress all expressions of difference: Nepalis were not used to such views being aired in public.

In contrast, the Madhesis had the advantage of having in place a political machine rooted in a longer history of political organizing. Since the 1950s Madhesi demands, first articulated by the Nepal Terai Congress, focused mainly on recognition of Hindi as a second national language and the Terai as an autonomous region. Championing Madhesi rights was the Nepal Sadbhavana Party led by Gajendra Narayan Singh, formerly of the Nepali Congress.[20] Although Singh had formed the Nepal

---

[16] See chapter 2, Hangen, 2009.

[17] Ibid.

[18] Ibid.

[19] Lecomte-Tilouine, 2005, p. 118.

[20] Singh was following in the footsteps of Vedananda Jha who split off from the Nepali Congress to form the Nepal Terai Congress, and this trend accelerated after 2006 as many Madhesi leaders quit the Nepali Congress to form or join more militantly Madhesi parties. The setback faced by the Nepali

Sadbhavana Parishad (Nepal Goodwill Council) in 1985, it was only after the restoration of democracy in 1990 that it could come out openly as a political force (as the Nepal Sadbhavana Party). For more than a decade thereafter, despite achieving only limited electoral success, it was the party that championed the Madhesi cause, even though the Nepali Congress had many more leaders of Madhesi origin in its ranks, including at the highest levels.[21]

The success of the third group, Dalits, was hobbled by the fact that despite its members' early attempts to lead social reform movements, their lowly social status translated into lower levels of readiness for effective mobilization. Yet the democratic space of post-1990 Nepal awarded them a level of freedom to make a push for their rights, even though none of the many governments that came to power throughout the decade bothered to respond meaningfully. For both Janajatis and Dalits, their interactions with their respective international "sister organizations" – the international indigenous movement and India's Dalit movement – also played a role in raising consciousness about their own situation.

This, then, was the general sociopolitical situation when the Communist Party of Nepal (Maoist), or CPN-M, launched the People's War in February 1996. The CPN-M itself had arrived at this juncture after a long journey that began with the founding of the Communist Party of Nepal – the mother of all communist parties in Nepal – in 1949, followed by brutal suppression and co-optation during the Panchayat regime, as well as a series of seemingly never ending splits and mergers. As part of the short-lived United People's Front, the political front of the CPN (Unity Center) was formed in 1991, and the Maoists even won seats in the first parliament elected after 1990. An ideological split within the CPN (Unity Center) in 1994 resulted in the more radical faction renaming itself the CPN-M and disavowing parliamentary politics in favor of an armed revolt in a bid to capture state power by force.

Why and how the CPN-M succeeded to such a large extent in such a short time can be partly explained using a framework derived from work on social movements. This approach relates the dynamics unleashed by the Maoist movement to the broader theoretical literature to gain an understanding of the social processes at play in Nepal.

RELATIVE DEPRIVATION

In his classic work on challenges facing a modernizing state, Huntington writes, "Urbanization, literacy, education, mass media, all expose the traditional man to new forms of life, new standards of enjoyment, new possibilities of satisfaction.

Congress in the 2008 Constituent Assembly elections was due mainly to the Terai slipping from its grip.

[21] For a brief history of Madhesi mobilization, see International Crisis Group, 2007.

These experiences break the cognitive and attitudinal barriers of the traditional culture and promote new levels of aspirations and wants."[22]

Huntington's analysis uses the idea of "relative deprivation" to explain why people seek change in the status quo. Gurr defines relative deprivation as "actors' perception of discrepancy between their value expectations and their value capabilities."[23] Phrased differently, it is the perceived gap between what ought to be and what is. As Norman Maier puts it, responses triggered by frustration can take the form of "regression, fixation and resignation as well as aggression."[24] Rebellion is one of the forms in which aggression is expressed. A sense of deprivation has been acute throughout Nepal's history, and even a cursory look at the nature of the Nepali state shows that the ruling class has been nothing but a rapacious bunch of self-serving individuals all the way down to the modern era, and most jarringly in the post-1990 democratic era.

Olson provides a useful basis for understanding the relationship between the state and the ruler with his conception of the formation of the state using the metaphor of roving and stationary bandits. The shift from anarchy to stability results from the transformation of a roving bandit into a stationary one. Whereas roving bandits indulge in intermittent but thorough plunder of the population, with the stationary bandit there is "rational monopolisation of theft" in the form of taxes that the people pay willingly. Thus, "the rational, self-interested leader of a band of roving bandits is led . . . to settle down, wear a crown, and replace anarchy with government."[25]

Following Olson, Riaz and Basu argue that "the Nepali state has never gone through this dramatic, yet necessary, transformation. Although geographically speaking over time the Nepali State had become 'stationary,' it essentially remained the 'roving bandit.' It is roving in the sense that the Nepali state has failed to demonstrate that it has [any] stake in long-term development of the country."[26] It is noteworthy that the authors use the term "state" to describe the ruling elite, a justifiable equation because the ruling elite did personify the state until recently.

The level of deprivation felt by the majority of the Nepali population contrasted sharply with the advantages enjoyed by others. An absolute monarchy in the garb of the Panchayat system was King Mahendra's gift to Nepal, as the 1962 constitution firmly identified the state with the monarch's sociocultural and religious values. State sanction of the caste system ended with the promulgation of the new Muluki Ain of 1963, but the hierarchical social structure was still deeply rooted in Nepali society, not only in people-to-people relations but also in differential access to the state. Traditional elite groups continued to monopolize power. As Rana pointed out

---

[22] Huntington, 1968, p. 53.
[23] Gurr, 1970, p. 24.
[24] Cited in Gurr, 1970, p. 34.
[25] Olson, 1993.
[26] Riaz and Basu. 2007.

TABLE 2.1. *Caste category of Muluki Ain, 1854*

Hierarchy status	Category	Social group
A	Wearers of the holy cord	Bahun[27]/Chhetri, Newar Brahman, Tarai Brahman, Newar Hindu
B	Nonenslavable alcohol drinkers	Magar & Gurung, Sunuwar, Newar (assorted Janajati groups)
C	Enslavable alcohol drinkers	Bhote, Chepang/Kumal/Hayu, Tharu, Gharti (assorted Janajati groups)
D	Impure but touchable	Low-caste Newar, Muslim, Christian
E	Impure and untouchable	*Parbate* artisan castes, Newar scavenger castes (Dalits)

Source: Gurung, 2005.

nearly four decades ago, "Analysis of the occupancy of all governmental positions at the level of under-secretary or above shows that Newars, Brahmans, Chettris, the three dominant castes of Nepal, held 93 per cent of these posts in 1969. . . . Thus some 77 per cent of the total population of Nepal are represented at the seats of power by a mere 7 per cent, while 23 per cent hold 93 per cent of the administrative posts."[28]

Since then various writers have analyzed the representation of marginalized groups in the state structure and unanimously concluded that not much has changed, and the situation might even have worsened toward the close of the 20th century. In fact, there seems to be a clear link between group status in the 1854 Muluki Ain and positions of influence in Nepal today because caste status continued to affect social mobility and individual accomplishment.

Table 2.1 shows the ranking of some of the major groups in the Muluki Ain, and Table 2.2 shows how they fared in public life in 1999. The population categories in the two tables do not match neatly, and the tables are meant to be indicative only. Madhesis as a separate group are not even mentioned in the Muluki Ain's caste hierarchy except for the Terai Brahmans.[29] Group A of Table 2.1 corresponds with Group I of Table 2.2 (except for Madhesi Brahmans, who would be placed in Group IV). The Newars of Group II from Table 2.2 are spread across Groups A and B of Table 2.1. At the bottom in both tables are the Dalits.

The clear link between group status and individual accomplishment can also be seen in the political arena, as demonstrated by Table 2.3. Just a single Dalit was

---

[27] Nepali expression for Brahmin.

[28] Pashupati Shumshere J. B. Rana cited in Wildavsky, 1972. Rana was writing at a time when the national censuses did not enumerate on the basis of caste and ethnicity, and hence they were quite different from the 1991 and 2001 censuses. The combined strength of these three groups, according to these censuses, is nearly 35%.

[29] Hoefer, 2004, p. 9.

TABLE 2.2. *Integrated caste/ethnicity index of representation in governance, 1999*

Institutions	I. Bahun/Chhetri	II. Newar	III. Hill Janajati	IV. Madhesi	V. Hill Dalit	VI. Others	Total
1. Judiciary	181	32	4	18	0	0	235
2. Constitutional bodies & commissions	14	6	2	3	0	0	25
3. Council of ministers	20	3	4	5	0	0	32
4. Civil administration	190	43	3	9	0	0	245
5. Legislature	159	20	36	46	4	0	265
6. Political party leaders	97	18	25	25	0	0	165
7. DDC chair, mayors/vice-mayors	107	30	23	31	0	0	191
8. Industry & trade leaders	7	20	0	15	0	0	42
9. Education sector leaders	75	11	2	7	1	1	97
10. Cultural organizations leaders	85	22	6	0	0	0	113
11. Science & technology	36	18	2	6	0	0	62
12. Civil society leaders	41	8	1	4	0	0	54
Total	**1,012**	**231**	**108**	**169**	**5**	**1**	**1,526**
Row %	66.3	15.2	7.1	11.1	0.3	0	100

Source: Onta, 2005. This table has been adapted by Onta from Govinda Neupane, *Nepalko Jatiya Prashna: Samajik Banot ra Sajhedariko Sambhavana*, 2000, with some rectifications made by referring to the original source.

TABLE 2.3. *Legislative representation of social groups*

	1991	1994	1999
Bahun-Chhetri	57.7	63.9	61.5
Janajati	22.4	17.6	18.5
Madhesi	20	18.5	20
Dalit	0.5	0	0

Source: Adapted from Suvash Darnal, "Naya Sambidhanma Dalit le Chhaheka Kura," *Himal Khabarpatrika*, 1–15 Asar 2066; and http://www.inseconline.org/index.php?type=opinionforums&id= 29&lang=en.

elected in the three parliaments since 1990, while the Bahun-Chhetri group retained its stranglehold over political power.

On another scale, Murshed and Gates use econometrics to demonstrate a direct correlation between marginalization and conflict and conclude that "[g]roup differences based on caste and ethnicity are central to explaining the genesis of the present conflict."[30] The 1999/2000 Human Development Index of Nepal's population groups (see Figure 2.1; Table 2.4) illustrates how status in the 1854 Muluki Ain continues to yield an effect on the group's general well-being.[31]

Caste/ethnicity alone, however, cannot explain the wide divergence in the quality of life. Regional variations are equally stark. In 1972 Rana commented, "A geographic analysis would show a similar disproportionate control by Kathmanduites or Kathmandu-based people of the major seats of power. There is no doubt at all that it is this bias which has caused the disproportionate regional distribution of resources. In the last three plans[32] development expenditure has been concentrated either around Kathmandu or in the Narayani Zone, where this power-elite has a strong landed interest."[33]

The situation of unequal development has not improved much since. In fact, the rural–urban divide is even more striking, as is evident from Table 2.4. Note the figures from the Central Region, which is where Kathmandu is located. Thus, when the Maoists arrived on the scene, there was already a groundswell of grievances they could readily exploit with their all-embracing rhetoric that promised a sea change in social relations and an end to all forms of discrimination.[34]

---

[30] Murshed and Gates, 2005.
[31] Leading the group is the Madhesi Brahman/Kshatriya group, which stands in sharp contrast to other Madhesi groups. However, it should be noted that the former make up only 1.9% of the population, whereas the latter account for 12.9% according to the 2001 census.
[32] That is, the five-year national development plans drawn up by the government.
[33] Pashupati Shumshere J. B. Rana cited in Wildavsky, 1972.
[34] See the famous 40-Point Demands handed to the Maoists just days before the fighting began. Annex III, Thapa and Sijapati, 2005, p. 211.

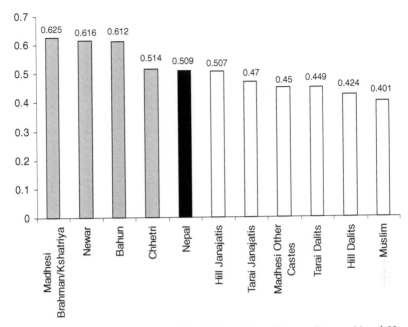

FIGURE 2.1. Human Development Index by Population Group. *Source:* Nepal Human Development Report, 2009, p. 44.

POLITICAL OPPORTUNITY

Although relative deprivation and social strain provide a conducive environment for setting off insurgencies, there is not always a direct causal link between the two. Instead, as McAdam puts it, "social insurgency is shaped by broad social processes

TABLE 2.4. *Human development indicators for Nepal, 1999–2000*

	PPP GDP per capita	Gap	HDI	Gap
Nepal	**1,237**		0.466	
Rural	1,094	88%	0.446	96%
Urban	2,133	172%	0.616	132%
Region				
Eastern	1,073	87%	0.484	104%
Central	1,713	138%	0.493	106%
Western	1,022	83%	0.479	103%
Mid-western	861	70%	0.402	86%
Far western	899	73%	0.385	83%

Gap is the percentage difference from the corresponding figure for Nepal.
Source: Murshed and Gates, 2005.

that usually operate over a longer period of time. As a consequence, the processes shaping insurgency are expected to be of a more cumulative, less dramatic nature."[35] Tilly et al. also give due credit to what is called "breakdown theory"[36] and to relative deprivation because they "are by no means irrelevant to collective violence. It is just that their effects do not work as . . . [classical] theories say they should. Instead of a short-run generation of strain, followed by protest, we find a long-run transformation of the structures of power and of collective violence."[37]

Such a transformation can come about through various means such as war, industrialization, and urbanization; that is, some sort of shift in the politico-economic structure that encourages excluded groups to engage in political activism, either peaceful or otherwise, against the status quo. In the early 1990s, Nepal was undergoing just such a shift. The marginalized began raising their voice seeking recognition from the state, but in the end there was no change in the status quo. Those who felt discrimination from the state on the basis of their ethnicity, language, or religion had hoped that that the new constitution would recognize the country's diversity. In the end, the only recognition of the country's diversity was the definition of the nation as "multiethnic" and "multilingual" and acceptance of the various languages spoken in the country as the "national languages of Nepal." Other demands, such as for Nepal to become a secular state, were simply ignored.

The radical social transformation that was expected to be the promise of democracy after 30 years of authoritarianism lay unfulfilled. Instead politics in its basest form took over. Among its initial manifestations was the internal discord within the Nepali Congress that led to the fall of the first post-1990 elected government within three years of taking office.[38] Still, the first Nepali Congress government was to prove to be the longest of any in post-1990 Nepal (see the appendix for a list of the 17 governments from 1990–2004). The see-saw battle for political supremacy between the Nepali Congress and the Communist Party of Nepal (UML) led to the political instability that has plagued Nepal ever since. Public faith in democracy itself eroded while governance lay in shambles, with the major political parties engaging in an all-out scramble for power. Such was the political environment in which the CPN-M launched its People's War.

---

[35] McAdam, 1999, p. 41.
[36] According to Useem, "Breakdown theory is the classic sociological explanation of contentious forms of collective action such as riots, rebellion, and civil violence. The crux of the theory is that these sorts of events occur when the mechanisms of social control lose their restraining power." Useem, 1998.
[37] Tilly et al. cited in McAdam, 1999, p. 41.
[38] To its credit, it should be noted that intra-party wrangling was not a feature limited to the Nepali Congress. The four largest parties in the parliament elected in 1991, representing 95% of the seats – Nepali Congress, Communist Party of Nepal (UML), United People's Front, and Nepal Sadbhavana Party – were wracked by infighting that resulted in each undergoing at least one split in the years to come. The other major player of the 1990s, the Rastriya Prajatantra Party, contested as Rastriya Prajatantra Party (Chand) and Rastriya Prajatantra Party (Thapa) in 1991 and later merged and split a number of times.

Literature on internal conflict shows that countries in transition are more prone to internal conflict than either autocracies or stable democracies.[39] Nepal was no exception. The democratic space provided by the 1990 political change gave the CPN-M the opportunity to operate openly and mobilize public support for its cause, while highlighting the failure of successive governments to deliver.[40] Although an armed uprising against the state had been the dream of the myriad communist forces operating in Nepal for decades, including the group of which the Maoists were formerly part, any insurgent group would have faced swift and costly repression before 1990. The experience of the first Mao-inspired rebellion in Nepal, the Jhapa uprising of 1971 that was crushed almost immediately, had brutally demonstrated the resolve of the Panchayat-ruled state.

Although the political opportunity available after 1990 may have served as the key to mobilization, it is also true that the insurgent groups had to decide to take advantage of the opening. Rebel groups are always aware of the cost of failure. After 1990 the largest communist force, the CPN (UML), had given up its own version of Maoism and had embraced multiparty democracy. Radical left politics had become the preserve of smaller forces such as the CPN (Unity Center) and, after its split in 1994, also of the CPN-M. It was the latter that discerned a shift in its favor, and recognizing the disarray in the central authority and having gradually built up a broad popular base, albeit in isolated pockets of the country, it made its move. The scale of the Maoists' subsequent expansion could not have been foreseen at the time, but it certainly established the CPN-M as a formidable force within a short period. In the words of a political analyst, the Maoists "took the high-risk, quick-rewards road."[41]

The Maoists were not without their detractors, especially within the broader communist movement. In fact, the former mentor of many of the top Maoist leaders, Mohan Bikram Singh, termed the People's War nothing more than "ultra-left adventurism" (which, incidentally, was the same characterization he had heaped on the 1971 Jhapa uprising as well).[42] The Maoists were also criticized for taking up arms in a period of political freedom. As Mishra points out, in post-1990 Nepal, "the newly legitimised freedom of political association and political organisation and freedom of speech and expression could have been instrumentally utilised in order to advance and fortify a popular political movement and to seek a basically political resolution to the political, economic and cultural contradictions."[43]

---

[39] Gurr et al, 2000, p. 20.

[40] See chapter 3 in Thapa and Sijapati, 2005, for a discussion on Maoist preparations for the People's War.

[41] Shridhar Khatri quoted in "Mao the Designer Revolution" by Binod Bhattarai, *Nepali Times*, #7, Aug. 30, 2000–Sep. 5, 2000.

[42] Singh, 2002, p. 154.

[43] Mishra, 2007, p. 97.

Another reason why internal conflicts arise in countries in transition is because the state is not in a position either to work out a peaceful settlement or, alternatively, use all-out force to subdue challenges to its authority.[44] The Nepali state talked of negotiations from the very beginning, but it also held the belief that the Maoist insurgency was a simple law-and-order issue that could be tackled by the police.[45] In the end, neither negotiation nor police intervention succeeded because all attempts were half-hearted, as the attention of successive governments was primarily focused on their own longevity.[46]

RESOURCE MOBILIZATION

In contrast to the grievance model, discussed earlier in the context of relative deprivation, is the resource mobilization theory of social movements. Here, resources do not refer to finances alone but to other sources of strength such as human and social capital. The main point of departure from the grievance model is "that there is always enough discontent in any society to supply the grassroots support for a movement if the movement is effectively organized."[47] That is, "[g]rievances are either structurally given or, increasingly in the contemporary setting, manufactured by the mobilizing efforts of movement entrepreneurs."[48] This is not to understate the importance of grievances: when they matter and how they matter will shape an uprising. Yet, the role of movement entrepreneurs is paramount, because it is they who mobilize the masses using frames of reference that highlight the grievances.

The resource mobilization thesis also recognizes that social movements often receive support, both moral and material, from external actors. In the case of intrastate conflicts, backing often comes from foreign countries. Long before it became known with certainty that the Maoist leadership was operating out of India,[49] there existed a strong body of opinion within Nepal that the Maoists were founded and funded by New Delhi,[50] even though there is every indication that the Maoist insurgency was homegrown. Widespread suspicions of Indian machinations can be partly explained by the long history of India being a source of insurrections against the Nepali state; more recently, India played a role in the 1950–1 armed revolt

---

[44] Gurr et al., 2000, p. 20.

[45] The prime minister, Sher Bahadur Deuba, indicated his willingness to negotiate with the Maoists, while the home minister, Khum Bahadur Khadka, advocated the use of force against them. *Janabhavana*, February 26, 1996, cited in Nepal Rastriya Buddhijibi Sangathan, *Nepalma Janayuddha*, Nepal Rastriya Buddhijibi Sangathan, Kathmandu, 2054 BS (CE 1997), p. 134.

[46] See Upadhya, 2002,for a concise discussion of politics of Nepal in the 1990s and early 2000s.

[47] McCarthy and Zald, 1977, p. 1216.

[48] Jenkins, 1983, p. 530.

[49] Note, for instance, the convening of Nepal's top communist leaders, including the then-General Secretary of CPN (UML), Madhav Kumar Nepal, for a meeting with the CPN-M chair, Prachanda, in Siliguri of the Indian state of West Bengal, in August 2001, during the first ceasefire.

[50] See, for instance, Shah, 2005.

against the Rana regime and, arguably, also the People's Movement of April 2006. The gradual moderation of the Maoists' anti-India rhetoric over the years also gave rise to further suspicion of India's involvement.[51] Perhaps a much more balanced summation is offered by Mishra: "Both the CPN-M and the GOI [Government of India] are seeking to use each other in specific and separate ways in order to attain their respective objectives."[52]

The issue of Indian support to the Maoists is likely to be debated into the future, but even if it were to be proven true, it hardly detracts from the fact that the Maoists were able to effectively mobilize the people by blaming the leaders of the 1990s democracy era for failing to even attempt – let alone succeed – to change the exploitative land relationships under which the rural peasantry suffered in the villages or to address the exclusion of the many social groups by the state. Under democracy the lives of most people remained no different from what they had been for decades. What had changed, however, was a growing consciousness of the outside world among a peasantry that had become more educated and more mobile and could also compare and contrast the difference between their lives and those of others. A committed group of grassroots organizers in the villages were able to channel this frustration into the People's War.[53]

The use of brute and indiscriminate force by the police against a hapless population, as in Jelbang, exacerbated the conflict by pushing more people into the Maoist fold. The public held these security actions responsible for rapid expansion of the insurgency. In a country-wide survey in early 2001, a plurality of respondents (30 percent) from the mid- and far-western regions of Nepal, which was where the fighting had been concentrated up to that time, believed that police high-handedness was responsible for the growing success of the Maoists. (It is noteworthy that poverty/unemployment/corruption was believed to be the number one reason nationally in the same poll.[54]) A chilling example of the mood of ordinary folks at the receiving end of police brutality is given in Gautam and coauthors, who quote a girl in her teens whose brother had been killed by the police: "Yes, my brother has been killed. But we have another 1,000 brothers of the same kind. We will all come together and take revenge. We will not spare those responsible for our grief."[55]

The particular manner in which the Maoists presented their struggle proved to be highly effective in drawing people to their cause. Their rhetoric skillfully presented their fight as being everything for everyone, encompassing aggrieved groups and cutting across class and ethnic boundaries.

---

[51] Of the nine demands grouped under "Concerning nationality" in the 40-Point Demand of 1996, eight had a direct bearing on Nepal's relationship with India.

[52] Mishra, 2007, p. 129.

[53] See de Sales, 2003, for her description of Kham Magar youth in the Maoist heartland.

[54] Himal Association, 2001.

[55] Gautam et al., 2003, p. 110.

The following two extracts are from the much-cited 1998 document, *Politico-Economic Rationale of People's War in Nepal*, by one of the top Maoist leaders, Baburam Bhattarai, It begins as follows:

An armed People's War has been initiated in Nepal on February 13, 1996, under the leadership of the Communist Party of Nepal (Maoist) with the proclaimed aim of establishing a new democratic socio-economic system and state by overthrowing the present socio-economic system and state. This should be understood against the background that Nepal has slid to the status of the second poorest country in the world in terms of physical and cultural developments; 71% of its population fall below the absolute poverty level; 46.5% of national income is in the hands of 10% of the richest people; more than 60% of its total population are illiterate, more than 90% of its total population live in rural areas and 81% of the labour force is engaged in the backward agricultural occupation; 10% are fully unemployed and 60% are under-employed or in disguised employment. Similarly the growth rate of food grain production, the most important national production, has shown decline in the last 30 years; foreign debt constitutes more than 60% of gross domestic product and its intensity is increasing as years pass. . . . In this context it is necessary to find out the root cause . . . of this condition and provide a scientific solution . . . by analyzing the problem with a historical materialist method, or the concept of Marxist-Leninist-Maoist political economy; and today in Nepal the Maoist People's War is trying just that.[56]

Here, Bhattarai's emphasis is economic in highlighting the glaring inequality in Nepali society, and he asserts that only a violent overthrow of the existing state can bring any change to the situation. As Mishra notes, the Maoists locate "the causes, among others, in the structure and process of underdevelopment which creates (or exacerbates) poverty in the first place."[57] That provides their rationale for a People's War to bring about structural transformation in the politics and economy of the country.

Later in the same document, Bhattarai deals mainly with ethnic issues, drawing from the writings of communist luminaries like Lenin, Stalin, and, of course, Mao on the "nationality question":

The oppressed regions within the country are primarily the regions inhabited by the indigenous people since time immemorial. These indigenous people [who] dominated regions that were independent tribal states prior to the formation of the centralized state in the later half of the eighteenth century, have been reduced to the present most backward and oppressed condition due to the internal feudal exploitation and the external semi-colonial oppression. They have been left behind

[56] Bhattarai, 1998. Sections within sentences that seemed superfluous have been excised for the sake of clarity. I have also slightly edited the original language to correct grammatical errors.
[57] Mishra, 2007, p. 101.

the historical development process because of a blockade of their path of independent development and [the] imposition of socio-cultural along with economic oppression upon them with the backing of the state by those forces who had come from outside. Thus it is quite natural that the question of regional oppression of Mongol-dominated [i.e., Tibeto-Burman-speaking] eastern, central and the western Hilly regions or the Austro-Dravid dominated Inner Terai[58] and Terai regions are manifested in the form of national oppression.... Besides this, the problem of the Khas dominated far western Karnali region... [is a] regional question instead of a nationality question and it will have to be tackled accordingly. Thus, according to the concrete situation it is necessary to solve the problem of oppressed regions and nationalities by granting regional and national autonomy.[59]

The domination by one particular group at the expense of all the others was a recurring theme in the Maoist repertoire. Even in their earlier incarnation as part of the CPN (Unity Center), they had raised the question of regional disparity to bring about an end to "discrimination towards people living in the Terai and remote areas" while also calling for an end to "discrimination against oppressed people and the Dalits" and "equal opportunity in the media, including radio and TV, for all languages."[60] They repeated similar demands later when they handed the famous charter, the 40-Point Demand, to the government on the eve of their armed movement. These demands included the following:

- Regional discrimination of the Terai by the hill-based elite should be eliminated. Backward areas should be given regional autonomy. Rural and urban areas should be treated equally.
- All racial exploitation and suppression should be stopped. Where ethnic communities are in the majority, they should be allowed to form their own autonomous governments.
- Discrimination against downtrodden and backward people[61] should be stopped. The system of untouchability should be eliminated.
- All languages and dialects should be given equal opportunities to prosper. The right to education in the mother tongue up to higher levels should be guaranteed.[62]

---

58 Bhattarai seems to have conflated the few Janajati Austro-Asiatic- and Dravidian-language speakers with the many other Janajati groups of Terai origin who lived in those areas.

59 Bhattarai, 1998. The last point is included in the 40-Point Demand. No 20 states: "Where ethnic communities are in the majority, they should be allowed to form their own autonomous governments."

60 The 14-point charter of demands presented to Prime Minister Girija Prasad Koirala by Nirmal Lama of the Communist Party of Nepal (Unity Center) on March 5, 1992.

61 "Backward" is the literal translation of the Nepali term *pichhadiyeko*, which was commonly used to denote marginalized groups.

62 The 40-Point Demand presented to Prime Minister Sher Bahadur Deuba by Dr. Baburam Bhattarai of the United People's Front Nepal on February 4, 1996. Thapa and Sijapati, 2005.

This was the message used by the Maoists in their attempt to reach out to their main constituencies – the impoverished and socially excluded. It stands in sharp contrast to the left's general antipathy to any assertion of ethnic identity at the expense of class identity. As it turned out, their strategy paid off very well in terms of finding willing recruits to their cause. Prachanda himself admitted as much when he said in an interview, "Peoples of the oppressed nationalities – the Mongolian peoples, the Terai peoples and the far western peoples – have been very sympathetic to the People's War. They feel it is the only alternative for them. And this is also a big victory for the People's War and a big defeat for the reactionary ruling class."[63]

The creation of various "liberation fronts," representing the different "nationalities" of the country, was another strategy used to great effect as the Maoists expanded eastward and southward from their stronghold in the mid-western hills. After building up a strong base among a substantial section of the population while withstanding the assault by the police – the only force the government was able to deploy against them – the Maoists took the natural next step of taking on the army itself. When they did do so in November 2001, succeeding in capturing a big haul of arms and ammunition with the army close on their heels, the stage was set for a confrontation on a much larger scale. Five times more people died in the second half of the decade-long People's War than in the first.[64] In contrast to the initial period in which the deaths were overwhelmingly concentrated in their first "base areas" of the mid- and far-west regions, after 2001 the fighting and the killings were spread out across the country, reflecting the military and recruitment success of the Maoists.

CONCLUSION

The Maoist insurgency was certainly the most serious internal challenge the Nepali state has ever faced in its nearly two and a half centuries of existence. The insurgency was instrumental, although not solely responsible, in bringing monumental changes to Nepal's social and political spheres. It was driven primarily by the quest for a more just and equitable society, but its rapid growth over a short period of time would not have been possible had it not been for a number of factors at play at the same time. The first was the squandering of the promise of the immediate post-1990 period manifested by its gradual transformation into the politics of power without regard for the well-being of the people. Second, the continued neglect of the aspirations of the excluded gave the Maoists a convenient pretext to launch an armed struggle for the liberation of these groups. Without the constitutionally guaranteed freedom to organize politically, the Maoists would not have been able to build up their strength so quickly in preparation for armed action.

---

[63] Onesto, 2000.

[64] "No. of Victims Killed by State and Maoist in Connection with the 'People's War,'" at http://insec. org.np/pics/1247467500.pdf.

A war to establish a communist state was considered an anomaly in a world that had just witnessed the unraveling of the communist regimes of the Warsaw Pact states under the weight of their own contradictions. Yet for the reasons outlined earlier, there was never a time in Nepal's past in which anything on a comparable scale could have been undertaken. The People's War was perhaps waiting to happen. All it required was a provocateur to light the flame, and it was the CPN-M that fulfilled that role.

APPENDIX

17 Governments in 20 Years

Prime Minister	Party of Prime Minister	Tenure
1 Krishna Prasad Bhattarai	Nepali Congress	April 1990–May 1991
2 Girija Prasad Koirala	Nepali Congress	May 1991–Nov 1994
3 Man Mohan Adhikari	CPN (UML)	Nov 1994–Sep 1995
4 Sher Bahadur Deuba*	Nepali Congress	Sep 1995–March 1997
5 Lokendra Bahadur Chand*	Rashtriya Prajatantra Party (Chand)	March–Oct 1997
6 Surya Bahadur Thapa*	Rashtriya Prajatantra Party (Thapa)	Oct 1997–April 1998
7 Girija Prasad Koirala*	Nepali Congress	April 1998–May 1999
8 Krishna Prasad Bhattarai	Nepali Congress	May 1999–March 2000
9 Girija Prasad Koirala	Nepali Congress	March 2000–July 2001
10 Sher Bahadur Deuba	Nepali Congress	July 2001–Oct 2002
11 Lokendra Bahadur Chand#	Rashtriya Prajatantra Party (Chand)	Oct 2002–June 2003
12 Surya Bahadur Thapa	Rashtriya Prajatantra Party (Thapa)	June 2003–June 2004
13 Sher Bahadur Deuba*	Nepali Congress (Democratic)	June 2004–Feb 2005
14 King Gyanendra Bir Bikram Shah Dev#	NA	Feb 2005–April 2006
15 Girija Prasad Koirala*	Nepali Congress	April 2006–Aug 2008
16 Pushpa Kamal Dahal Prachanda*	CPN-M	Aug 2008–May 2009
17 Madhav Kumar Nepal*	CPN (UML)	May 2009–

* Coalition government.
# Nonparty government.

REFERENCES

Bhattarai, Baburam. 1998. *Politico-Economic Rationale of People's War in Nepal.* Kathmandu: Utprerak Publications.
de Sales, Anne. 2003. "The Kham Magar Country, Nepal: Between Ethnic Claims and Maoism," in Deepak Thapa (ed.), *Understanding the Maoist Movement of Nepal.* Kathmandu: Martin Chautari. Pp. 59–88.

Gautam, Shobha, Amrit Baskota, and Rita Manchanda. 2003. "Where There Are No Men: Women in the Maoist Insurgency in Nepal," in Deepak Thapa (ed.), *Understanding the Maoist Movement of Nepal*. Kathmandu: Martin Chautari. Pp. 93–124.

Gurr, Ted. 1970. *Why Men Rebel*. Princeton, NJ: Princeton University Press.

Gurr, Ted Robert, Monty G. Marshall, and Deepa Khosla. 2000. *Peace and Conflict 2001: A Global Survey of Armed Conflicts, Self-Determination Movements, and Democracy*. College Park, MD: Center for International Development and Conflict Management.

Gurung, Harka. 2005. "Social Exclusion and Maoist Insurgency," Paper presented at the National Dialogue Conference on ILO Convention 169 on Indigenous and Tribal Peoples, Kathmandu, January 19–20.

Hangen, Susan I. 2009. *The Rise of Ethnic Politics in Nepal: Democracy in the Margins*. London: Routledge.

Himal Association. 2001. *Political Opinion Survey Nepal 2001*. Kathmandu: Himal Association.

Hoefer, Andras. 2004 [1979]. *The Caste Hierarchy and the State in Nepal: A Study of the Muluki Ain of 1854*. Kathmandu: Himal Books.

Huntington, Samuel P. 1968. *Political Order in Changing Societies*. New Haven, CT: Yale University Press.

International Crisis Group. 2007. *Nepal's Troubled Region*, Asia Report No. 136, July 9.

Jenkins, J. Craig. 1983. "Resource Mobilization Theory and the Study of Social Movements," *Annual Review of Sociology*, 9: 527–53.

Lecomte-Tilouine, Marie. 2005. "Ethnic Demands within Maoism: Questions of Magar Territorial Autonomy, Nationality and Class," in Michael Hutt (ed.), *Himalayan People's War: Nepal's Maoist Rebellion*. London: Hurst and Co. Pp. 112–35.

McAdam, Doug. 1999. *Political Process and the Development of Black Insurgency 1930–1970*. Chicago and London: The University of Chicago Press.

McCarthy, John D. and Mayer N. Zald. 1977. "Resource Mobilization and Social Movements: A Partial Theory," *American Journal of Sociology*, 82(6): 1212–41.

Mishra, Chaitanya. 2007. *Essays on the Sociology of Nepal*. Kathmandu: Fineprint.

Murshed, S. Mansoob and Scott Gates. 2005. "Spatial–Horizontal Inequality and the Maoist Insurgency in Nepal," *Review of Development Economics*, 9(1): 121–34.

Olson, Mancur. 1993. "Dictatorship, Democracy, and Development," *American Political. Science Review*, 87(3): 567–76.

Onesto, Li. 2000. "Red Flag Flying on the Roof of the World: Inside the Revolution in Nepal: Interview with Comrade," *Revolutionary Worker*, #1043, www.rwor.org/a/v21/1040–049/1043/interv.htm.

Onta, Pratyoush. 2005. "Public Discourse and Action to Address Adivasi Janajati Exclusion," in 'Gender and Social Exclusion Assessment' report prepared by The World Bank and DFID, Kathmandu.

Pradhan, Kumar. 2009 [1991]. *The Gorkha Conquests: The Process and Consequences of the Unification of Nepal, with Particular Reference to Eastern Nepal*. Kathmandu: Himal Books.

Regmi, Mahesh C. 1995. *Kings and Political Leaders of the Gorkhali Empire 1768–1814*. Hyderabad: Orient Longman.

Riaz, Ali and Subho Basu. 2007. "The State–Society Relationship and Political Conflicts in Nepal (1768–2005)," *Journal of Asian and African Studies*, 42(2): 123–42.

Rose, Leo E. 1963. 'Nepal's Experiment with "Traditional Democracy,"' *Pacific Affairs*, 36:1.

Shah, Saubhagya. 2005. "A Himalayan Red Herring?: Maoist Revolution in the Shadow of the Legacy Raj," in Michael Hutt (ed.), *Himalayan People's War: Nepal's Maoist Rebellion*. London: Hurst and Co. Pp. 192–224.

Shneiderman, Sarah and Mark Turin. 2005. "The Path to Jan Sarkar in Dolakha District," in Michael Hutt (ed.), *Himalayan People's War: Nepal's Maoist Rebellion*, pp. 79–111. London: Hurst and Co.

Singh, Mohan Bikram. 2002. *RIM ra Maobadiharuko Kathit Janayuddha* [RIM and the Maoists' so-called People's War]. Kathmandu: Jana Sikshya Griha. (in Nepali)

Thapa, Deepak and Bandita Sijapati. 2005. *A Kingdom under Siege: Nepal's Maoist Insurgency, 1996–2004*. Kathmandu: Zed Books.

Thapa, Deepak, Kiyoko Ogura, and Judith Pettigrew. 2009. "The Social Fabric of the Jelbang Killings, Nepal," *Dialectical Anthropology*, 33.

Tilly, Charles, Louise Tilly, and Richard Tilly. 1975. *The Rebellious Century, 1830-1930*. Cambridge, Mass: Harvard University Press. (cited in McAdam 1999)

Upadhya, Sanjay. 2002. "A Dozen Years of Democracy: Games That Parties Play," Kanak Mani Dixit and Shastri Ramachandaran (eds.), *State of Nepal*. Kathmandu: Himal Books. Pp. 39–61.

Useem, Bert. 1998. "Breakdown Theories of Collective Action," *Annual Review of Sociology*, 24.

Whelpton, John. 2005. "Thoughts on the Maoist Problem," *Peace and Democracy in South Asia*, 1:2.

Wildavsky, Aaron. 1972. "Why Planning Fails in Nepal," *Administrative Science Quarterly*, 17:4.

3

State Power and the Security Sector: Ideologies and Interests

Rhoderick Chalmers

INTRODUCTION

Nepal's peace process will not be complete until the future of the two major forces that fought the war is resolved. The November 2006 Comprehensive Peace Agreement (CPA) called for parallel processes of integrating and rehabilitating Maoist combatants and bringing the Nepalese Army (NA) under democratic control, as well as adjusting its size and making its composition more inclusive. These processes were not mapped out in detail, nor has there been significant progress on either. Members of the Maoist People's Liberation Army (PLA) have remained in cantonments since the end of 2006, and discussions over their future have made little headway. The NA dropped its "Royal" designation but has maintained its full conflict-era strength and, despite the introduction of a 2006 Army Act bringing it nominally under cabinet control, retains both day-to-day autonomy and a significant political role.

The measures that need to be taken to resolve this impasse do not neatly fit standard international models. The peace deal emerged from a military stalemate, in which neither force had been defeated. This has reduced incentives to accept compromise and understandably led the Maoists to reject forcefully the imposition of typical disarmament, demobilization, and rehabilitation models. The NA and its political backers have similarly rejected the need for systematic security sector reform, arguing that the transition away from palace control is complete and that the NA's exclusive legitimacy should not be tarnished by equating it with former rebel fighters. Therefore reforming the security sector presents much more than a technical challenge.

The Maoists and their opponents do agree on one point: that the army is the central pillar of state power. For the Maoists, this renders any political settlement that leaves the NA untouched irrelevant and unacceptable: without restructuring the army it will be impossible to deliver radical social and political change on other fronts. For the NA and the many Nepalis who fear the Maoists and their radical agenda of state transformation, the army is the last bastion protecting Nepal from possible Maoist totalitarianism, disintegration, or a breakdown in social unity and national sovereignty.

This chapter examines the ideologies, interests, and institutional cultures that lie at the heart of the deadlock. It does not offer a detailed examination of technical issues (many of which have been well examined elsewhere), nor does it present a roadmap for security sector reform. Instead, it covers four areas: the historical relationship between army and state in Nepal, the outlook of the (Royal) Nepalese Army and the ways in which it developed in the course of the conflict, the structure of the PLA and the ways in which its expansion and political role at the end of the conflict and start of the peace process shaped its political stance and power, and a brief summary of the political challenges involved in bringing about a stable, mutually acceptable resolution of core disputes.

ARMY AND STATE

At the center of the Nepalese Army's doctrine lies a strong belief that it is the embodiment of Nepali nationalism and its strongest defender. As the only historian within the army's ranks put it, "the Royal Nepalese Army and Nepal are bound together as the flowers and thread of a garland."[1] For eminent nationalist historian Yogi Naraharinath, "of the seven limbs of the state, the army acts as the arm and hand."[2] As long as it was firmly under the control of the palace, the NA did not need to have a sophisticated political understanding of the country's internal dynamics nor, given the slim likelihood of external aggression, did it have to develop a clearly defined national security strategy. Its primary threat scenario was an Indian invasion, in the event of which it would try to delay the inevitable defeat while international political support was rallied – and, failing that, would resort to precisely the type of guerrilla warfare that the Maoists came to embrace. Its established training did little to prepare it for its new role:

> Military planning and training, at least theoretically, was largely focused towards defending the country from potential foreign invasion. In the absence of a comprehensive national security doctrine, large portions of the course of study in the Royal Nepalese Army Command and Staff College established on 30 December 1990 is [sic] essentially an adaptation and synthesis of materials taught in several foreign military academies, especially of India, Pakistan and the UK. Considerable time was devoted to studying histories of large unit actions that had limited relevance to Nepalese realities.[3]

[1] Prem Singh Basnyat, *Shahi nepali sena*, p. 1.
[2] Preface to Bista.
[3] Nepali and Subba, 2005.

As an institution the army had enjoyed a relatively comfortable existence: the palace's patronage reinforced the crown-centered nationalistic rationale for its existence while insulating it from the challenge of making tough strategic decisions. The counterinsurgency role into which it was suddenly thrown five years into the People's War was a rude awakening. The Maoists' initial success at overrunning army bases could be attributed to catching the army off guard, but it did raise serious questions about the NA's readiness to fight. Nor could the army claim to be surprised as the police were when the conflict erupted in February 1996 – they had more than five years to learn about Maoist tactics and evaluate their strengths and weaknesses. Taking serious casualties was both a blow to morale and a harsh introduction to a tougher adversary than any the army had faced in decades. Insofar as it existed, military doctrine had rested on the assumption that Nepal's people shared the reverence toward the army that it felt was its due. Yet the conflict tested this assumption and immediately found it wanting. A successful counterinsurgency would depend on close cooperation from ordinary people, but soldiers were widely seen as, at best, aloof and detached from their fellow countrymen.

The RNA instilled in its officers one clear duty: "The safety, honour and welfare of your king and country come first always and every time."[4] The order of priority is no accident: since the 1950s resurgence of the Shah dynasty, the monarchy has been central to the army's culture, structure, and sense of mission. Service to the country has been seen as an extension of loyalty to the crown and the army's own sense of identity. Army officers continue to be proud of their role in Nepal's history and national development. As its official history proclaims, "Throughout history, the RNA has remained an apolitical institution, forever committed to selfless service of the Nation."[5] Yet the army sees itself as having defined the nation, rather than the other way round. In its own words, "the history of Nepal, in one sense, is largely a history of the RNA."[6] It is through this prism that one must understand the army's insistence that it is an apolitical servant of the nation.

The army argues that it has always followed the orders of civilian governments, as its website notes: "Even after the unification campaigns, the institution of the RNA has consistently remained . . . firmly apolitical and always supportive of legitimate civilian authority. This is a rare distinction in the history of nations."[7] However, in practice this was far from the truth. The 1990 transition from absolute monarchy to multiparty democracy offered the first real opportunity to bring the army under meaningful democratic control by building bridges between military and civilian leaders. Yet the effort was doomed from the start. The constitution of 1990 was deliberately ambiguous. Although it foresaw the establishment of a National Defense

---

[4] RNA Honor Code, available at http://www.rna.mil.np/organisation/index.php?hdng=Missions&pg=1/.
[5] Royal Nepalese Army, "RNA History" (Kathmandu, undated), p. 28, available at http://www.rna.mil. np/organisation/images/history.pdf.
[6] Ibid.
[7] See http://www.rna.mil.np/hr/index.php?hdng=introduction&pg=1.

Council chaired by the defense minister to provide oversight over the army, it confirmed the king as the supreme commander of the armed forces, which continued to be subservient to none other than the monarchy. All army appointments and promotions had to be approved by the king, not the government. The government's job simply was to ensure that the army had enough resources. The newly elected civilian government refrained from challenging the arrangement by making proactive efforts to exert civilian oversight out of fear that any radical change would invite a backlash by the army. As the years went by, both the monarchy and the army became increasingly assertive, making reforms to the civil–military relationship increasingly difficult. The Ministry of Defense served little purpose other than to push paper prepared and finalized in military headquarters.

The cumulative effect of these failures to manage the security sector's transition to democratic control was largely to the political benefit of the Maoists – although the army's ability to stand its ground and defend strategic locations in the later phase of the conflict was also a crucial factor in persuading the Maoists that total victory was not an option. Ironically, the army's assiduous support for the palace's two power grabs in October 2002 and February 2005 ended up as a decisive factor in the loss of the monarchy's remaining political power. The army encouraged King Gyanendra to overreach, partly through its dedicated advocacy of an active monarchy but more significantly through its falsely confident assurances that, once unrestrained by meddling muddle-headed politicians, it could deliver a decisive blow to the Maoists.

Political–Military Tensions

The army's poor opinion of the democratic political leadership was rooted in its own self-image as the most dedicated and professional servant of the nation. In contrast, it saw the political parties as weak, divided, self-interested, and incapable of defending national interests. Army officers insisted that after 1990 they were ready to offer more wholehearted support of democracy but that the political parties were the main obstacle. As one officer wrote, "The political party governments instead of democratizing the army, considered the army anti-democratic."[8] A political scientist observes, "The politicians never made the effort to bring the [army] officers into their advisory circles, and the RNA was rarely discussed in the parliament. The politicians were wary of the army because the senior-most generals made no secret of their distrust for the political parties, nor their anxiousness to remain within the royal umbrella."[9] The RNA accused the parties of marginalizing it, preferring to lavish budgets and attention on the police rather than to build working relationships with

[8] Prem Singh Basnyat, 2004, p. 138.
[9] Kumar, 2006.

the army. "Suddenly the police were all driving around in brand-new Prados while we were left with our old Gypsies," complained one officer.[10]

As the conflict unfolded, the army developed more specific grievances against what it viewed as mismanagement by successive governments. It blamed political leaders for the failure to develop a coherent civil–military counterinsurgency campaign and felt that it had to shoulder the brunt of the task without adequate political support or planning. In terms of political strategies to deal with the Maoists, the army saw even royalist governments as weak, too willing to compromise, and reluctant to take the army's advice. For example, it viewed the 2003 ceasefire as a cunning Maoist ploy to escape from successful military pressure; the RNA was frustrated that governments failed to allow it to deliver the killer blow that it believed it was capable of – and also that the ceasefire gave space to the rebels to regroup and prepare for intensified conflict.

Aggrieved by loudly voiced national and international criticism of its poor human rights record, the army also felt that the government failed to protect it from unfair abuse and to take its own share of responsibility. When critics pointed to human rights violations committed by the army, officers were quick to remind them that patterns of abusive behavior were established by the police under Nepali Congress Prime Ministers Koirala and Deuba, rather than by the army or the palace.[11] Indeed, some of the army's most intensive offensives against the Maoists were sanctioned by party-led governments happy to endorse its brutal techniques when they appeared to be to their benefit.

Moreover, the army complained – with some justification – that many civil society and human rights groups were quick to exaggerate its failings while going easy on the Maoists and forgetting the context in which the fighting was taking place. Army officers felt that the people did not take into account the losses suffered by the RNA. In its four-year involvement in the war, the RNA suffered more than 900 casualties and many serious injuries. For those fighting on the frontlines, conditions were often grim. Soldiers and mid-ranking officers had little home leave while they coped with long postings in remote areas and poor resources; their families were often threatened and harassed by Maoists. They felt isolated and deprived of solid public support. In addition, the top brass reacted strongly to complaints that the army was dominated by high-caste Shahs and Rana clans, arguing that many members of ethnic groups (Janajatis) were in senior positions and that the RNA was more representative than any of the major political parties. Although this assertion may have been true, major population groups, such as the Madhesis, Tharus, and Dalits,

---

[10] The police had diverted vehicles intended for delegation use – even Deputy Inspector General-level officers were unable to use them.

[11] For instance Operation Romeo, launched in 1995 even prior to the People's War in response to Maoist mobilization and Operation Sierra Kilo II, a brutal police operation carried out by Nepal Police for over a year starting in 1998 and 1999.

were almost completely absent from the army's upper echelons and continue to be so today.

Commanders were not shy about broadcasting the army's distaste for political leaders and those it saw as being unfairly critical. Shortly after its November 2001 mobilization to fight the Maoists, then-Chief of Army Staff (COAS) Prajwalla Shamsher Rana publicly berated the political parties: "Who is responsible for the present state of the country? Was it malgovernance or was it the army? How just is it to burden the army with this difficult situation created for political reasons?"[12] Despite such attacks on the democratic system – or at least its representatives – the army's protestations that it was a strictly apolitical body dedicated to serving the nation as a whole hold some truth. The army has historically been a central pillar of Nepal as a sovereign nation-state, being a central force in the unification of the country under the Shah kings in the early decades of Nepal's existence; it was transformed into a tool of the Rana clans that ruled the country for more than a hundred years until 1951. It only lost the capacity for independent political intervention in national affairs when King Mahendra (r. 1955–72) brought it firmly under the control of the royal palace in the early 1960s. For the most part since then, it has remained free from party-political manipulation.

Still, the army's track record on supporting democracy was poor. It has always been a powerful political player concerned for its own interests, the interests of its leadership, and also the interests of the monarchy and of the state. It served as King Gyanendra's primary support in his twin power grabs of October 2002 and February 2005 – each of which was heralded in advance by coded warnings in the press penned under a pseudonym by palace protégé Rookmangad Katawal, who would become COAS in 2006–9. In this it was following tradition: it had also been the instrument for bringing about Mahendra's royal coup against Nepal's first elected government in 1960, and its main fighting experience in the decades before the Maoist insurgency had been garnered in brutally effective operations against Nepali Congress guerrillas who took up arms after the royal takeover. The army had taken a strong political stance even in the negotiations leading to the framing of the 1990 constitution, attempting to intimidate interim Prime Minister Krishna Prasad Bhattarai into preserving royal sovereignty and allowing the army to retain substantive autonomy.[13]

---

[12] Gen Prajwalla Shamsher Rana, Speech at the RNA Command and Staff College, March 27, 2002.

[13] K. P. Bhattarai, interviewed in Hoftun et al., p. 301 (date of interview given as October 10, 1990, but must be 1991 as they describe it as "a year later" than the events he is talking about): "One day the commander-in-chief rang at eight o'clock and said he was coming at nine. He walked in uniform and gave me a file. It said that the king's prerogatives and powers and sovereignty should all remain with him. So I said that this in not my business, it is the business of the Constitution Commission. I put it before the commission and they rejected it. Then I duly informed the commander-in-chief. Then one day I had a telephone call in the office. Some generals and the commander-in-chief wanted to see me personally. All of the came – 22 generals in uniform led by the commander-in-chief. They saluted and sat down. I gave them a cup of tea each. They gave me a file which was the same thing again."

The autonomy of the RNA from democratic control was evident during the first phase of the insurgency when the army refused to take part in operations against the Maoists. In July 2001, the RNA categorically refused to obey the Congress government's order to engage the Maoists at Holery village in the western hill district of Rolpa, claiming it could only act on royal command.[14] During the April 2003 peace talks, the RNA reportedly refused to accede to Maoist demands aimed at restricting their movement to a five-kilometer radius of their barracks, despite the agreement of Prime Minister Lokendra Bahadur Chand and the alleged sanction of the king.[15] The loss of the RNA's confidence in the Chand government following this concession is widely believed to have led to its replacement by the government of Surya Bahadur Thapa in May 2003.

Morale and Internal Relations

Since its formation, the Nepalese Army has recruited from a limited range of caste and ethnic groups. There has been a traditional divide between the officer corps – traditionally drawn from a small number of noble families that surrounded the Gorkha court that unified Nepal and later the Rana clans that ruled until 1951 – and the bulk of ordinary soldiers. Prithvi Narayan Shah described Nepal as "a country earned by the shield of the Pandeys and the sword of the Basnets,"[16] two of the leading families that still dominate many senior positions. The rank and file were drawn mainly from the Chhetri, Magar, and Gurung communities.

Nevertheless, in its early days, the Gorkha army was very much of the people. Almost all able-bodied men took turns serving as soldiers, and military service was part of the everyday social fabric. The shift to a postunification national standing army rapidly distanced the army from the people. The previously respectable position of being a *dhakre* (a former soldier on temporary furlough) became an insult; the narrow ethnic base of recruitment that Prithvi Narayan had specified might have suited the Gorkha court, but produced a force that looked far from representative as the nation expanded to encompass many more groups.

Rana rule entrenched the army as an integral part of the ruling elite. Male members of the ruling Rana family were appointed to senior army positions at birth, and command positions were assigned according to the roll of succession to the office of prime minister. The army also retained its important political and cultural role as a Hinduizing force, promoting (and to some extent imposing) the emerging national culture, religion, and language. Historically, their central position in the military helped bring Magars and Gurungs into an acceptable place in the Hindu hierarchy.

---

[14] Roka, 2003.

[15] Ibid.

[16] Presumably *Divyopadesh* – one of the epigraphs to Somdhvaj Bista's book (which was published by Narayan Jang Shah and Narendra Man Singh Basnyat).

However, especially since 1990, the army's continued embrace of an increasingly questioned vision of unitary national culture became problematic. While the nation was starting to come to terms with a more diverse self-image, the army continued to promote Hinduism symbolically and practically, partly because of its cultural dependence on the monarchy. Unlike the British Gurkhas and Indian Gorkhas, the Nepalese Army's main symbol is not the renowned khukuri knife but Shiva's trident; the army's celebration of Hindu rituals such as the Taleju Dasain sacrifices formed part of a long tradition of public legitimization of divine kingship. Even after Nepal became a republic, the army insisted that there should be a referendum on the question of making Nepal a secular state – a step taken by the reinstated parliament immediately after the April 2006 People's Movement.

The fact that the officer class has continued to be recruited partially on the basis of family heritage has undermined both professionalism and vertical integration between the ranks. Hierarchy within the military has been strict and slower to change than in society at large. Thousands of lower caste soldiers were traditionally recruited purely to work as servants in army messes and officers' private homes, a practice that has continued to this day. It was only in 1999 that Dalit soldiers were first allowed to eat alongside their higher caste colleagues in army canteens.

Although there are now many more senior officers drawn from ethnic communities – especially Limbus, Magars, and Gurungs – they are largely isolated from real decision-making power, even if they have advanced to the highest ranks.[17] A retired officer who maintains close links with the army recently complained that the inner core of influential officers still form a "Praetorian guard" that makes key decisions privately.[18] The most powerful army officer used to be the Principal Military Secretary (PMS) to the king, rather than the Chief of Army Staff, and King Mahendra's tight grip on the military depended on the palace-based staff officers remaining detached from the rest of the army. The PMS retained final authority over promotions and postings forwarded by the army and Ministry of Defense.[19] After this structure was changed when the 2006 Army Act removed the army from palace control, a Janajati, General Chhatraman Singh Gurung, was appointed for the first time as COAS in 2009. Nevertheless, the bulk of influential senior officers are acculturated to the former system, and systematic change is likely to be slow.

Engaging with Society

The army's difficulty in coping with even constructive criticism is a product of its combination of arrogance and naivety. Unlike seasoned royalist politicians, who had learned to cope with the rough and tumble of heated public debate, army officers

---

17 Interviews with retired *janajati* senior officers.
18 Interview, Kathmandu, September 2006.
19 Nepali and Subba, 2005.

have found it extremely difficult to adapt to a more exposed position in national life. To this extent they are indeed apolitical – unaccustomed to having to argue their case in the face of opposition, they have appeared thick-skinned and heavy-handed in rebutting any allegations of mistakes or misbehavior. Despite an intensive effort to develop better public relations skills they have been slow to adopt the basic political skills of persuasion. When upset by misleading reports from local journalists they have tended to respond with exaggerated force – a counterproductive strategy.[20] As for any broader debate on national security issues – be it with journalists, academics, civil society organizations, or even serving governments – the stock response has been that this is a sacrosanct topic that can only be opened to outsiders on a need-to-know basis. Even the mildest suggestions prompt heated accusations of "vilification"[21] rather than being treated as an entry point to healthy dialogue.

The NA's resistance to engaging in more open debate with the rest of society has been most damaging to the army itself. Its largely self-imposed isolation from the people of the nation it serves and unwillingness to listen to criticism, however well intentioned, have translated directly into operational weakness, especially in the areas central to a successful counterinsurgency campaign.

For an army that views itself as the central embodiment of nationhood, it is remarkable how little the nation has been permitted to know of it. In stark contrast to the dozens of books celebrating the glorious record of Nepali soldiers in the service of the British and Indian armies, only four books have been written about the Nepalese Army. The only one still in print is the highly critical account written by retired Indian general Ashok Mehta and published in Delhi;[22] the three works by Nepali soldiers have been deliberately hidden from view, despite the fact that they were all approved by the army and contain no sensitive information. The most authoritative book, a serious academic history edited by professional historians,[23] was commissioned and published by the army itself – but was only for sale in the army headquarters canteen because of concerns that it should not be shared with the public.[24]

Prem Singh Basnyat, the sole military officer to write publicly on civil–military relations, argues that the army should only share its thoughts with civilians on a

---

[20] See, for example, "RNA summons Dailekh-based reporter," *Kathmandu Post*, July 28, 2005: "Royal Nepal Army Wednesday summoned Dailekh-based reporter Harihar Singh Rathour regarding his published news reports on July 20. Rathour's story was published in The Kathmandu Post that said the RNA soldiers were using local children as spies. The Army called Rathour at its barrack in Dailekh Bazaar, the district headquarters, and handed him a letter asking him to be present before the barracks on Thursday with evidences on which the story was based. Although Rathour was asked to be present before the barrack alone, many local journalists had joined him."

[21] Cf. C. K. Lal.

[22] Ashok Mehta, *The Royal Nepal Army: Meeting The Maoist Challenge*. Mehta himself comments on the lack of published material relating to the army. His own book, despite being a short monograph with a particular focus on the Maoist insurgency and Indian policy considerations, is now the most substantial work on the army in print.

[23] Sharma, Vaidya, and Manandhar, *Military History of Nepal*.

[24] Interviews, serving and retired army officers, Kathmandu, September 2006.

need-to-know basis.[25] He suggests that the Panchayat period was a missed opportunity for enhancing civil–military relations: the Ministry of Defense should have taken the initiative to introduce a school curriculum "right from primary to higher level" on "what is security, why is security important, why are security organs required, what sort of relationship should be there between security organ and civil society, between defence and democracy."[26] The army's ventures into publicity through the state media, with weekly television and twice-weekly radio programs, have adopted this lecturing tone.[27]

Basnyat argues that the army should have enhanced capacity to teach all citizens what is their role in building good relations (which is necessary because "society itself preferred to be aloof from the army"[28] and therefore needs to correct its ways), but not once does he suggest that the military might benefit from listening to the rest of society. Blame for all weaknesses in the system can simply be laid at the door of those who fail to appreciate the military's qualities: "Is it not cowardice on the part of our so-called great leaders and scholars in the eyes of the foreigners to criticize an army who is loyal to its master? . . . [B]ackbiting of defense by democracy and lack of democratization in the defense is the result of complete lack of security awareness in the political leadership."[29] Unfortunately, Basnyat's serving and retired colleagues in the military share his perspective that education or discussion about civil–military relationships is a purely one-way process.

Of course, this sensitivity to criticism and fear of open debate about the role of security forces are not limited to Nepal. As military historian Richard H. Kohn observes, "Military establishments which are unused to having their judgment or authority questioned by anyone, much less the cacophony of groups and individuals (many of whom most flagrantly do not subscribe to the values and behaviors traditional to military groups) typical of democratic governance, will experience an . . . uncomfortable challenge."[30] Perhaps revealingly, the only other published study of civil–military relations in Nepal – a 2005 article by Prakash Nepali and Phanindra Subba that offers a more subtle exposition of the army's stance – does not touch on the topic of communication between the military and society at large beyond noting the "lack of empathy for the military among key segments of the Nepali political establishment, media and the academic circle."[31]

There are indications that the army, partly under pressure from its international backers, particularly the Americans and British, has started to accept the need to

---

[25] Basnyat, *New Paradigm*, p. 142.

[26] Ibid., p. 141.

[27] One report claimed that the army had also sought permission to operate 10 mobile FM radio stations across the country "to counter Maoist propaganda." "RNA to run 10 mobile FM stations," *Kathmandu Post*, March 1, 2006.

[28] Basnyat, *New Paradigm*, p. 142.

[29] Ibid., p. 140.

[30] Richard Kohn, "An Essay on Civilian Control of the Military."

[31] Nepali and Subba.

revise its attitude to engaging with the public. In an interview with the author, one
senior army officer explained:

> The army is an element of national power so some consideration for security is
> natural. We don't hide away intentionally – we were keeping a very low profile.
> We didn't want to politicize ourselves or intrude and partly because of that lack of
> political ambition we didn't open up: we're not a high-profile army. Our intention
> wasn't secretive but this was our nature. When we joined the army we never
> imagined we'd have a Department of Public Relations, that we'd be talking to
> someone like you . . . we are willing now to engage with people – and we know it's
> in our own interests.[32]

That the army has generated few strategic analysts of any substance is not surprising
given the complete lack of public debate on the role and work of the security forces –
thinkers within the army have been deprived of the stimulus of engaging with experts
from different backgrounds. Even as widespread (and sympathetic) concern about
the Maoist insurgency and the need for a coordinated military response grew, it was
not until December 2004 that a Nepali officer, retired general Sadip Bahadur Shah,
became the first to address an international seminar on strategic issues.[33]

THE ROYAL NEPALESE ARMY IN ACTION

When the army was drawn into the conflict, it found itself confronting challenges that
it had never had to deal with before. The insurgency was far more widespread and
intractable than most senior officers had imagined; they had accurately observed
that the Maoists were, in conventional terms, a pathetic military force, but had
failed to understand that the insurgents' strengths lay in an unconventional strategy
and a far less visible political mobilization. Furthermore, the army was suddenly
exposed to political decision making and public scrutiny from which it had earlier
been sheltered. Questions about its basic loyalties assumed a new significance,
whereas its poor relations with democratic governments that remained suspicious
of its intentions became a crippling block to developing a viable political–military
strategy. From the moment of its mobilization, war and politics were inescapably
entwined.

"All indications from the first week of army action are that after Dang, where the
RNA was caught napping, the Maoist rank-and-file is now taking a heavy beating,"
reported the *Nepali Times*, a mainstream English language weekly newspaper, when
the army was finally forced into the conflict after the Maoist attack on its barracks
in Ghorahi in the southern Dang district in November 2001. "As repeated often,
the killing of Nepalis by Nepalis cannot be a victory for anyone. But that is exactly

---

[32] Interview, Kathmandu, September 2006.
[33] Mehta, *The Royal Nepal Army*.

what the Maoists were doing these past years, and now the tables may turn. The Royal Nepal Army, which has held its fire for so long, now has the difficult job of bringing this campaign to a swift, effective and conclusive end with the least amount of Nepali blood shed."[34]

For more than five years, the army had held its fire as the Maoists gained ground across the country. While the rebels picked off poorly defended police posts, well-armed soldiers sat tight in their barracks, their officers insisting this was not their fight. The military remained on the sidelines of the conflict for several reasons. King Birendra was reportedly reluctant to escalate the fighting and see the RNA deployed against its own people – and he and his military advisors believed the situation could still be brought under control fairly easily. The king was also hoping to negotiate with the Maoists and indeed had designated his brother Dhirendra to establish contact with their leadership. In addition, political leaders were still distrustful of the RNA, and its open refusal to obey the elected governments forced them to rely more on the civil police – and later a new Armed Police Force. Finally, it was in the army's self-interest to stand aside: the failures of the inept anti-Maoist campaign attached to the police and politicians, while the army quietly ran its own hearts and minds campaign, building roads and setting up temporary health camps in rural areas providing basic health services free of cost to local villagers, even where this meant tacitly coexisting with the Maoists.[35]

The army's masterly inaction – coupled with its strident public critiques of the government's botched strategy – had inspired many observers to assume that it was indeed capable of delivering a "swift, effective, and conclusive end" to the insurgency. The prospect of a rapid resolution tempered concerns about the state of emergency that the army had demanded as a condition for its mobilization. Most analysts focused on the Maoists' apparently suicidal decision to invite full-scale confrontation with a force that was so clearly superior by every conventional measure.

However, translating superiority in numbers and equipment into a viable offensive strategy was not straightforward. It was often said that Nepal's army was purely a ceremonial force that, despite the odd skirmish, had not fought a serious war since the Gorkha army's conquests were brought to an end with defeat at the hands of the British East India Company in 1816. Many Nepalis themselves often dismissed the army as a *"salami, malami, gulami* outfit" – good only for salutes, funeral processions, and servitude (to the palace). Yet this characterization was not accurate: the army's role as a backbone of national security during the Panchayat years was more than just ceremonial, and it had strengths that were not just on paper.

Therefore even before its mobilization against the Maoists, the army was more than a token force. Since its modernization began in the 1960s, the army had

---

[34] Dixit, 2001.
[35] For example, Rukum, where army road builders would share the same paths with armed Maoist units without qualms.

received significant training and equipment not only from India, its main benefactor, but also from the United Kingdom, China, and the United States; after the 9/11 attacks, the United States expanded its aid, providing modern weaponry, as well as tactical training and equipping of a special forces battalion. Thus, by the time it was eventually pressed into military action against the Maoists in November 2001, the army, in theory, was adequately trained and equipped – but just not for this sort of counterinsurgency.

Although somewhat neglected by post-1990 democratic governments, at a strength of 55,000 the NA was larger than the civil police and more than half the size of the entire civil service; its officers had been trained in prestigious international military academies, and it had many years of experience as part of UN peacekeeping missions around the world. More significantly, its most senior officers had direct experience fighting Nepali Congress guerrillas in the hills and suppressing the proto-Maoist Jhapa insurgency in the early 1970s – tasks that they managed with proficiency and relative ease. To their minds, they could not be dismissed as a ceremonial force: given solid political cover (as they had enjoyed under palace rule until 1990) they could impose their will and restore order.

However, the struggle to devise a new doctrine suited to a messy internal counterinsurgency illustrated the tensions – and seriously conflicting strategic outlooks – that were to undermine the army's campaign. The instinct of senior officers was to go in hard and take the fight, perhaps dirtily but effectively, to the Maoists: this was how it had mopped up resistance in the 1970s, and it was how the Gorkha army had won its victories and its place at the heart of the nation. Some of the army's core values had been adapted to frame this belligerent approach in modern terms. In 2005 the RNA adopted a Soldier's Code of Conduct closely modeled on the U.S. Army Soldier's Creed. New recruits learned by rote that "I am a Warrior . . . I shall always remain ready to enter the field of battle and destroy my Country's enemies."

Yet there was also a growing awareness that dealing with the Maoists would require a more subtle approach than simply "destroying" them as enemies of the country. Of the U.S. Army Soldier's Creed, a senior British officer who served alongside U.S. counterparts in Iraq observed, "Note that it enjoins the soldier to have just the one type of interaction with his enemy – 'to engage and *destroy* him': not *defeat*, which could permit a number of other politically attuned options, but *destroy*. . . . it is very decidedly a war-fighting creed, which has no doubt served well to promote the much sought conventional warfighting ethos, but cannot be helping soldiers to understand that on many occasions in unconventional situations they have to be soldiers, not warriors."[36] The same caveat applied to the RNA's emphasis on destruction of the enemy in a counterinsurgency environment, a point that was not lost on its top brass. COAS Pyar Jung Thapa publicly instructed his personnel that "the people involved in the Maobadi [Nepali term for Maoist] terrorist activities are our own people who

[36] Aylwin-Foster, 2005, p. 14.

have been misled and have taken the wrong path . . . .(our) mission is not to totally eliminate them but to disarm them."[37]

If rank-and-file soldiers were confused, it is not surprising: their training and rules of engagement were an awkward and inconsistent effort to bridge seriously contrasting approaches. This inconsistency was partly a failure of top-level strategy but also a nearly inescapable consequence of the political confusion that had bedeviled attempts to forge a coherent civil–military approach. For junior officers who had to translate these conflicting demands into action in the field, the frustration was evident. "Now we're being asked to do what is effectively policing – being told not to open fire, to ask insurgents nicely to hand over their weapons. How's that meant to work?", asked a mid-ranking officer with wide experience of counterinsurgency operations across the country. "We're not equipped to do this. We're trained for full-on fighting, not community policing. We wouldn't hold them off for long but we're probably still better prepared to fight the Indian army than our own Maoists."[38]

THE MAOIST FORCES

Ideology and the Use of Violence

The major question for the Maoists was not whether resorting to violence was politically legitimate – all strands of the Nepali communist movement accepted, in theory, that armed struggle could be a valid revolutionary tool – but whether it was an appropriate and viable strategy. For the precursors of the Communist Party of Nepal (Maoist) (CPN-M), the first trial of armed tactics, which came to be known as the "Sector Kanda," was less than encouraging. On April 1, 1986 cadres of the CPN (Mashal), a communist (and Maoist precursor) faction then led by Mohan Baidya, attacked several police posts in Kathmandu. The assault was far from decisive and led to the police uncovering Mashal networks and activists and, eventually, to Baidya's resignation as chairman; he was replaced by Prachanda, who then went by the party name "Biswas."[39] By 1990, the democracy movement had led to the restoration of multiparty politics and the promulgation of a new constitution. Although the 1991 election delivered a decisive Nepali Congress majority, the mainstream left, principally the Unified Marxist-Leninist (UML) party, became solidly committed to parliamentary practice.

The Maoists, however, remained determined to explore opportunities for armed revolt. In this they drew inspiration from India's Naxalites (Indian Maoists from the Naxalbari district of West Bengal State) even as their parliamentary wing – the United People's Front led by Baburam Bhattarai – maintained a tenuous role in

---

[37] Ibid.
[38] Interview with RNA soldier, Kathmandu, November 2005.
[39] Roy, 2008, pp. 28–9.

mainstream politics. According to a biographer, Prachanda was personally engaged in preparation for armed conflict:

> Although Prachanda got his initial training in guerrilla warfare from the ex-Gorkha soldiers of the Indian Army, he was in India to study from close quarters the movements in Bihar and Jharkhand. Prachanda says, "I was in contact with the Maoist Communist Centre and went to Palamau district of Bihar for training." He also visited several districts in the southern Indian state of Andhra Pradesh, a hotbed of Indian Maoist activity, to comprehend the practical problems of launching an armed struggle. It's these trainings that turned Prachanda into a genius at planning military operations and an expert in the use of arms.[40]

It does not appear that Prachanda put his own skills to use directly. However, by the time the CPN(M) had decided to press ahead with armed tactics, cadres of its youth wing were ready to transform themselves into guerrillas.

The major step of translating the People's War from theory into practice was deeply controversial. Many other leftists labeled it "adventurism"; even sympathetic Naxalites believed Nepal's Maoists had misjudged their country's political development and overestimated their chances of success. Nevertheless, the outline of their armed strategy was clear and remained intact, with tactical modifications and practical development, from its inception until the final ceasefire. The primary principle was that the party should control the gun. Even as authority was devolved to local units to decide on military targets or assassinations, it was party committees rather than military commanders who were in charge. Discipline and political control of the burgeoning combat units were maintained through a dual leadership system, with a political commissar placed alongside each military commander – and with the commissar ranking higher within the party. Major decisions had to be made jointly, and all combatants were under orders to follow the central plans laid down by the party.[41]

PLA Formation and Culture

The Maoists did not launch their armed campaign with anything approaching an organized military wing. At the time of their first attacks, on February 13, 1996, they possessed only two rifles – and one of them was not working.[42] As they expanded their attacks on poorly defended rural police stations and government buildings, they established "fighting units" (*ladaku dal*), "security units" (*suraksha dal*), and "volunteer units" (*svayamsevak dal*). It was the government's Operation Kilo Sierra 2 of May 1998–April 1999, a sometimes brutal sweep by armed police task forces,

---

[40] Ibid., p. 94.
[41] Ibid.
[42] Ibid.

which spurred rebel recruitment by antagonizing local communities and prompted the expansion of the Maoists' armed wing.[43]

The development of a more organized military was tied to the strategy of building secure "base areas" that could be protected against state assault and used to launch further attacks and broaden the scope of Maoist operations. This strategy, agreed at their August 1998 plenum, led to success in taking on the poorly armed police but still left them far short of a force capable of conventional warfare should the army be deployed. During four months of ceasefire in 2001, the Maoists sat for talks with the government, but simultaneously devoted significant energy to building their armed wing through further recruitment and more advanced training.[44] It was during the ceasefire, in September 2001, that the People's Liberation Army (PLA) was formed, and it went into action only two months later under its new name, bringing the lull in fighting to a dramatic end with an attack on the RNA barracks in Dang. This assault marked the abandonment of negotiations and a major escalation of the conflict as it drew the army into action and prompted the declaration of a state of emergency.

As the fighting went on, the CPN-M's June 2002 plenum organized the PLA into brigades. A longer ceasefire in 2003 appeared to offer more hope for political progress, but its collapse led to much more intense conflict. During the ceasefire, the Maoists had once again spent time preparing for the possibility of renewed confrontation, but so had a growing and better equipped RNA. By August 2004 the Maoists were ready to establish three "divisions," each made up of three brigades. The strength of these formations was far lower than that of their equivalents in the RNA or other regular armies, but the step marked a psychological move forward. It also brought to more prominence the senior military commanders who would shape the PLA in the later stages of the conflict and would bridge the political–military divide during the peace process: Barshaman Pun "Ananta" (eastern division commander), Nanda Kishor Pun "Pasang" (central), and Janardan Sharma "Prabhakar" (western).

Meanwhile, the building of a formally structured military wing was accompanied by the development of a more decentralized – and less well- documented or enumerated – set of militias. At the same time as the PLA's divisional structure was announced, Prachanda set the target of establishing a 100,000-strong people's militia.[45] It would consist of companies under the command of both regional and district-level headquarters. However, these militias had fluid boundaries: poorly

---

43 Interview with Sandip, then company-level PLA commander, *Nepal Samacharpatra*, December 17, 2000.

44 Video footage from one such training camp in the north of Dhading district commanded by Pasang was obtained by the RNA and subsequently broadcast on Nepal Television. The Maoists themselves filmed training sessions extensively and have compiled at least two films of more than an hour each on the activities of the PLA, many sections of which date to the ceasefire period. These films have not been widely distributed, although segments can be viewed at http://cpnm.org/video/Web Library/Final.htm.

45 Press statement, September 1, 2004.

armed and lacking uniforms, their members – many of whom were also underage – answered to village party committees and "people's governments" as well as to higher bodies (such as district or national committees).[46] Although primarily used as local muscle or sentries in their own home areas, militia members were drafted into the large forces that commanders assembled for more major attacks, such as those on district capitals.[47]

Estimates of PLA strength (discussed in more detail later) varied widely, although by the later stages of the conflict many suggested the core force was no more than several thousand – less than the total claimed by the Maoists themselves and the RNA estimates. PLA weaponry was also limited. Many fighters had to do with homemade weapons such as socket bombs rather than guns. Most of the PLA's more professional arsenal was captured from state forces; it appears arms purchases on the black market were fairly limited.

The PLA differed from the RNA not only in these organizational aspects but also in its institutional culture and the nature of its operations. Most importantly, the party's political control was strictly institutionalized, with leadership of every fighting unit from company to division level shared between a military commander and a political commissar.[48] Political training and discussion within the PLA were encouraged, as were constructive debate over military tactics and the critical assessment of operations. Although command and control remained disciplined, the PLA placed less insistence on hierarchy, emphasizing instead a sense of comradeship. PLA combatants were almost constantly on the move. Camaraderie was established, and training continued, in the midst of conflict and under frequent risk of attack. Contact with local populations was more or less constant: although Maoist fighters inspired fear as much as admiration among many civilians, they were rarely cut off from day-to-day life. With minimal resources they depended on villagers to house and feed them, either voluntarily or under duress. Their self-reliance in terms of manufacturing many weapons and improvising other equipment, as well as covering large distances on foot under tough conditions, made them more formidable in the field than most RNA units. However, they lacked access to the more professional training available to the army. Their senior commanders, much younger than their RNA equivalents and with none of their formal qualifications, had to make up with battle-hardened experience what they lacked in terms of advanced instruction.

Entering the Peace Process

The closing stages of the conflict saw changes in the Maoist military structure and strategy, which affected its posture at the start of the peace process. After the

---

[46] Dinesh, "Janamukti senako vikas ra rajnitik karya," *Janadesh*, August 10, 2004.
[47] Kiyoko Ogura, "Meeting Pasang in Rolpa." *Nepali Times, Issue* 305, 7 July 2006; Sam Cowan, "Inside the People's Liberation Army: A Military Perspective," *European Bulletin of Himalayan Research* 37 (Winter 2010).
[48] Dinesh, "Janamukti senako vikas ra rajnitik karya."

February 2005 royal coup, internal divisions in the party leadership were bound up with disputes over the efficacy of their military approach. Senior leader Baburam Bhattarai, who had argued for a conditional alliance with mainstream parties against the monarchy, was suspended from the party. Prachanda, realizing that the coup had foreclosed the possibility of immediate dialogue and keen to emphasize his strength, ordered further large-scale attacks. The assault on a well-fortified army base in Khara in the mid-western Rukum district was a bloody failure that illustrated the limits of Maoist military power. After a mid-2005 reshuffle of local commanders, the Maoists saw more headline success in a major assault: the August 2005 overrunning of an army engineering base in Pili in the far-western Kalikot district. However, the political momentum was shifting toward an emerging deal with the other parties.

October 2005 saw a decisive plenum of the party, which cleared the way for the November 12-Point Agreement launching the peace process, and made sweeping structural changes to the party. The PLA was also the subject of attention, with four more divisions established and new commanders appointed. The three existing divisional commanders were joined by Chandra Prakash Khanal "Baldev" as PLA deputy commander under Prachanda as supreme commander. In addition to eastern and western regional commands, a "special central command" was set up to mobilize local communities in the districts around Kathmandu as well as to manage military operations. This shake-up was accompanied by a new strategy, summed up in the slogan, "Stand on the spine to strike the head," which denoted increased pressure on supply routes and peripheral military bases to enable strikes against Kathmandu and other urban areas. In January 2006, the Maoists launched repeated attacks on the mid-western regional NA headquarters in Nepalgunj and, on January 14, launched the first multiple simultaneous attacks within the Kathmandu valley.

The immediate aim of these attacks was to disrupt preparations for municipal elections called by the royal government, but they also marked the completion of a shift away from the earlier approach of slowly building rural base areas. The struggle was coming to the cities, and the Maoists wanted to make the most of their political and military opportunities. PLA operations were now being planned in light of the October 2005 plenum's acceptance of a deal to join competitive multiparty politics and to work hand-in-hand with their former political foes against the monarchy. Collaborating with the mainstream Seven Party Alliance not only made for a strong united front against the royal government but also offered the Maoists a much better chance of penetrating urban areas – a long-held aim that had met with only minimal success. While they worked with other parties to plan the peaceful protests that led to the decisive April 2006 People's Movement, the PLA made parallel military preparations. If nonviolent protests failed or if state retaliation prompted sufficient disorder for them to exploit, the PLA was ready to impose its own blockade of the capital (a tried-and-tested tactic) and also, under the aegis of the special central command, to engineer an urban insurrection.

These revolutionary plans remained on the shelf. When mass protests forced the king to relinquish power, a unilaterally declared Maoist ceasefire that was soon entered into by the new interim government led by the Seven Party Alliance restrained the PLA. The Maoist military wing found itself in very new territory. For the first time it was entering a cessation of hostilities that its leaders believed could be permanent and that would, if negotiations progressed, most likely lead to the end of the PLA itself. In early May the party leadership held a special central committee meeting in Punjab, India, to prepare its roadmap for peace talks. Alongside reiterating calls for an all-party conference (rather than a restored parliament) to form an interim government to hold Constituent Assembly elections, the 10-point plan also envisaged the "restructuring" of the PLA and state armies "as per the popular mandate expressed through the election."[49] The 12-Point Agreement had already committed both sides to keeping their militaries out of politics and under neutral supervision during the election process. Attention now shifted to longer term goals and the prospect of protracted negotiations in which the PLA itself would have little direct say.

PEACE TALKS AND POWER PLAY

From the outset the atmosphere for peace talks was conditioned by the circumstances of the ceasefire: the deal was between two sides of the triangular conflict – with the king and, by extension, the army sidelined – and it was based on a military stalemate rather than a decisive victory. Neither armed party saw itself as having been vanquished; both the Nepalese Army and the Maoist PLA remained pillars of political power and important sources of leverage behind the negotiations. Each moved to secure as much legitimacy as possible: the NA by distancing itself from the royal regime and playing up its supposed role in persuading the king to give in peacefully to the mass protests; the PLA by preparing to present itself to the outside world, most importantly the UN, as an organized and disciplined force deserving recognition and legitimization within the terms of a peace deal.

The decision to request the UN to monitor arms and armies emerged from the first direct meeting of senior government and Maoist leaders in June 2006. Yet the difficulties ahead rapidly became apparent. Members of the major mainstream parties feared that their negotiators had conceded unnecessarily favorable terms to the Maoists and pressured Prime Minister Koirala to add a significant extra condition: that the reinstated parliament could only be dissolved to make way for an interim legislature including the Maoists once their arms had been dealt with. When the government wrote to request UN involvement in July, it further specified assistance in "decommissioning" Maoist weapons, a step that went beyond the 12-Point Agreement and had not been agreed to by the Maoists. As mistrust grew, the PLA divisional commanders and commissars were summoned to join a central committee meeting that discussed plans for revolt if the peace talks failed to progress. After this meeting,

---

[49] Prachanda, press statement, May 13, 2006.

which took place in Kabhre to the east of the capital, the government deployed armed police in Kathmandu to guard against a possible PLA incursion.

Underlying the mutual suspicions was a difference in perspective that has hampered efforts to address security sector reform throughout the peace process. Government negotiators feared that the Maoists were deliberately trying to retain their military capacity to influence the environment for proposed elections and to reserve the threat of a return to war if the talks did not secure their main objectives. However, the Maoists believed that earlier agreements had endorsed their view of sequential progress, with UN monitoring being sufficient to keep their armed force out of the electoral equation and full disarmament only possible as part of the restructuring of the national army and integration of some of their combatants. The Comprehensive Peace Agreement (CPA) skirted this central divergence of opinion through its carefully vague and ambiguous language. The CPA also signally failed to address the question of the Maoist militia: the narrow government focus on disarmament shut out consideration of broader issues of demilitarization.

The Maoists were happy to proceed rapidly with the cantonment of their forces, a process that they had in effect started soon after the ceasefire. After the cessation of hostilities, the PLA lost much of its immediate utility and was expensive to maintain. Rapid steps to set up cantonments signaled goodwill but also strengthened the party negotiators' case that the government should pay to maintain their combatants. The UN had agreed to monitoring the "relevant compliance" of the parties' agreement on arms and army management.[50] However, the size of the PLA had not been specified. In contrast to private Maoist estimates that the cantonments should house around 15,000 fighters, the number of personnel initially registered by the UN in early 2007 was more than 30,000. The process of verifying genuine combatants and identifying those who were underage and should be immediately discharged was to be controversial; the question of overall numbers lay at the heart of a renewed debate in 2009 over Maoist strategy and perceived insincerity toward the peace process.

The battle lines on security sector questions were drawn early and firmly. The Maoists required a viable final deal on future military structures before demobilizing their force, whereas the NA made it clear from the start that it saw no need to reform and would strongly resist accepting any more than token Maoist entrants. The CPA did not specify in detail the modalities for pursuing the twin goals of PLA integration and rehabilitation and state army "democratization," nor did it offer clear guidance on sequencing and time frames. For the first year after the CPA, the Maoists appeared keen to press for rapid progress, repeatedly urging that integration should be completed before the Constituent Assembly election. This step was resisted by the NA and other parties, and the Maoists' apparent flexibility on

---

[50] The Agreement on Monitoring of the Management of Arms and Armies was signed on November 28 and witnessed by the UN. After some technical revisions by UN lawyers in New York, Ian Martin signed the agreement on behalf of the UN on December 8.

seeing its army demobilize gave way to a determination to keep the PLA intact until after the elections, as a safeguard against a collapse in the process or unfavorable results. Against this backdrop of continued adversarial relations, both military forces increased their influence over the political process and defended their red lines.

THE REFORM CHALLENGE: SECURITY SECTOR AND STATE

The security sector remains at the heart of the peace process's unresolved business. The NA continues to view itself as the guardian of national sovereignty and the most direct inheritor of the Prithvi Narayan Shah's legacy. It has resisted many of the changes agreed to by the major parties since the ceasefire; for example, calling for a referendum on whether Nepal should be a secular state. It harbors deep suspicions about the possible damage to national unity if federalism is implemented and is determined to retain a major role in safeguarding what it sees as the nation's core values. For the Maoists, the PLA cannot be seen merely as a collection of 19,000 individuals (roughly the number subsequently "verified" by the UN to be Maoist combatants), awaiting the offer of training or employment on humanitarian grounds. It was a central spear of their revolutionary project, and the party leadership has been at pains – in contradiction to the provisions of the CPA – to ensure it retains a sharp sense of its political mission.

The mechanisms established to resolve these questions have functioned only intermittently, and in more than three years there has been little tangible progress. The CPA specified that "the Interim Cabinet shall constitute a Special Committee to carry out monitoring, adjustment and rehabilitation of the Maoist combatants."[51] The interim constitution further provided that the "functions, duties and powers of the committee shall be as determined by the Council of Ministers."[52] This special committee managed to meet only once in the two years following the interim constitution's promulgation, in July 2007. It was eventually reconstituted on January 16, 2009, and supplemented by a technical subcommittee tasked with drawing on expert advice to prepare implementable plans in line with political decisions taken by the main committee.[53]

---

[51] CPA, Art. 4.4.

[52] Ibid., Art. 146.

[53] In the Agreement between the Political Parties to Amend the Constitution and Take Forward the Peace Process, June 25, 2008, it was further decided that the special committee should "collect information regarding the circumstances of those Maoist combatants that have been registered and verified in the cantonments." "Agreement between the political parties to amend the Constitution and take forward the peace process," June 25, 2008, Art. 2.2.1 Unofficial translation at http://www. unmin.org.np/downloads/keydocs/2008–06–25-Agreement.to.Ammend.Constitution.ENG.pdf. This agreement also provided for a technical committee of experts functioning under its auspices. Ibid., Art. 2.1. The eight-member technical committee has undergone various changes in membership, but like other bodies established by the peace process, its members are nominated by the major parties – initially two each from the four largest parties.

Neither of these bodies has been able to tackle the fundamental issues still in contention. International assistance has had only marginal impact: those offering technical input are still waiting for a political framework within which to prepare more detailed options. International actors with influence over the parties to the process have done little to press for movement. The most engaged external player, India, has worked consistently to shield the NA from reform and to argue against integrating Maoist combatants into the state army. The NA itself has exerted considerable influence over the mainstream political parties and, after the fall of the postelection Maoist-led government in May 2009, has successfully protected its core interests. Neither armed force has cooperated in any investigations into war crimes; both have actively shielded personnel accused of grave crimes.

The Maoists and their opponents are well aware that security sector reform is not merely a technical exercise. The army's historical centrality to the Nepali state remains intact, and control over military force, as well as the ability to shape it, remains a fulcrum of political power.

REFERENCES

Aylwin-Foster, Nigel. 2005. "Changing the Army for Counterinsurgency Operations," *Military Review*, November-December, pp. 2–15.

Basnyat, Prem Singh. 2004. *New Paradigm in Global Security: Civil-Military Relation in Nepal*. Kathmandu: Bhrikuti Adcademic Publications.

Basnyat, Prem Singh. 2010. "*Military History of Nepal*," at http://www.premsinghbasnyat.com.np/doc/military_history_of_nepal(Eng).pdf.

Chaulagain, Yam and Rashmi Kandel. 2008/9. *Janayudhhaka netaharu*. Kathmandu: Jayakali Prakashan.

Dixit, Kunda. 2001. "Let's Get This Over With." *Nepali Times*, November 30.

Hoftun, Martin, William Raeper, and John Whelpton. 1999. *People, Politics & Ideology: Democracy and Social Change in Nepal*. Kathmandu: Mandala Book Point.

Kaplan, Robert D. 2005. "Who Lost Nepal?" *Wall Street Journal*, December 20.

Kaplan, Robert D. 2006. "Colonel Cross of the Gurkhas." *Atlantic Monthly*, May.

Kohn, Richard H. 1997. "An Essay on Civilian Control of the Military." *American Diplomacy*, 3. at http://www.unc.edu/depts/diplomat/AD_Issues/amdipl_3/kohn.html.

Kumar, Dhruba. 2006. "The 'Royal' Nepal Army." *Himal South Asian*, March-April.

Library of Congress. 1991. "Nepal." at http://www.country-data.com/cgi-bin/query/r-9175.html.

Mehta, Ashok. 2006. *The Royal Nepal Army: Meeting The Maoist Challenge*. New Delhi: Rupa & Co.

Nepali, Prakash and Phanindra Subba. 2005. "Civil-Military Relations and the Maoist Insurgency in Nepal." *Small Wars and Insurgencies*, 16(1) at http://dakbangla.blogspot.com/2005/02/study-nepal-civil-military_110961114568825804.html.

Onesto, Li. 2005. *Dispatches from the People's War in Nepal*. London: Pluto Press and Insight Press.

Rana, Gen. Prajwalla Shamsher. 2002. Speech at the Royal Nepalese Army Command and Staff College, March 27.

Rocca, Christina. 2003. Statement before the United States Senate Committee on Foreign Relations, Washington DC, March 26, at http://foreign.senate.gov/testimony/2003/RoccaTestimony030326.pdf.

Roka, Hari. 2003. "Militarisation and Democratic Rule in Nepal." *Himal South Asian,* November.

Roy, Anirban. 2008. *Prachanda: The Unknown Revolutionary.* Kathmandu: Mandala Book Point.

Royal Nepalese Army. n.d. "RNA History," at http://www.rna.mil.np/organisation/images/history.pdf.

Sharma, S., T. Vaidya, and T. Manandhar. 1992. *Military History of Nepal.* Kathmandu: Royal Nepal Headquarters.

Singh, Mohan Bikram (ed.). 2009. *Two-Line Struggle within RIM.* Kathmandu: Yug-Jyoti Publication.

Stodston, Francesca Elizabeth. 2003. "The Role of Foreign Military Assistance in Domestic Conflict Resolution: The Case of the Maoist Insurgency in Nepal." MSc Dissertation, University of Birmingham.

Newspaper Reports

"How long would the army be outside the barracks?" Nepalnews Translation Service, November 28, 2004.

"RNA summons Dailekh-based reporter," *Kathmandu Post,* July 28, 2005.

"RNA to run 10 mobile FM stations," *Kathmandu Post,* March 1, 2006.

"PM presents insignia to new army chief: 'I will follow instructions of government,'" Rashtriya Samachar Samiti *(RSS),* September 12, 2006.

"Prachanda rejects NC, UML pre-conditions to join govt," *Himalayan Times,* May 19, 2008.

"PLA to be separate security force: Pun," *Kathmandu Post,* June 14, 2008.

"Maovadi senako yogyatabare prashna uthainu anyaypurna," *Gorkhapatra,* June 17, 2008.

"Sabai sashastra shaktilai rajyako mathat rakhine," *Gorkhapatra,* June 18, 2008.

"Expert panel to decide PLA fate," *Kathmandu Post,* March 16, 2009.

4

The Legacy of Nepal's Failed Development

Devendra Raj Panday

The economic trajectory of so-called developing countries is far from uniform. Some of these countries have been truly developing, favorably affecting, in the reckoning of economist Paul Collier, the lives of four billion people over the past six decades.[1] A dozen or so have made miraculous progress in a relatively short period and have graduated to the status of developed or near-developed countries. However, a significant number of these countries, particularly in Africa, are not developing at all – trapping one billion people in poverty, despair, and conflict. With its record of failed development, Nepal belongs to this last group. Its failed development is mainly due to social and cultural rigidities that have maintained traditional power relations and underlying social norms despite the political changes since the 1950s. The outcomes of the contests between different interests currently testing the ongoing political transition will ultimately determine whether the country can break away from the grip of the status quo.

This chapter explores the nature of Nepal's failed development, identifies causative factors, and discusses possibilities for a course reversal. First, it explains the syndrome of failed development and examines the country's development record. Then it focuses on macroeconomic outcomes and some indicators of social and human development, as well as their distribution across different sections of the population. Nepal's political and institutional features that bear on its legacy of failed development and its future course are of special concern. The role of international partners, including India, in Nepal's development and peacebuilding efforts is also discussed. The chapter concludes with some suggestions for a behavioral shift that should allow Nepal to escape the failed development paradigm.

[1] Collier 2007.

CONCEPTUAL UNDERPINNINGS

I first applied the term "failed development" to Nepal in 1999 to capture the institutional, political, socioeconomic, and sociopsychological factors explaining the country's economic underperformance.[2] The development agenda's chronic failure to deliver on its promises reinforces the moral and cognitive deficits in the development endeavor and erodes public trust. The failure also weakens critical social values and institutional norms conducive to development. In the end it produces an environment that breeds conflict. Failed development is rarely the product of the inadequacy of inputs critical to development, such as capital, technology, human resources, or even governance in a technical sense. It is more systemic, signaling the inability of the people in power to design institutions, frame development policies, and promote value systems relevant to the prevailing socioeconomic realities. However, failed development does not have to be a permanent condition anywhere.

The development literature does not provide indicators or a threshold that distinguishes countries with failed development from the others. Nor does it allow us to measure when a country graduates to the next development level. However, the failed development narrative in some form can be found in the analysis of development performance in a number of African countries[3] as well as Nepal.[4] A generally agreed notion of development is that it is a continuous process without an endpoint that would constitute success once and for all. Not all developing countries that perform poorly are cases of failed development. Many of them may succeed if they hang on to the development mission, politically and institutionally, and generate some developmental outcomes that defy political setbacks, civil conflicts, and external constraints. Many underperforming poor countries are able to maintain institutions and policies and social norms that eventually foster sustainable development and prevent violent conflict. This is not the case with Nepal.

The critical issue in Nepal is that the state and the political actors have rarely valued the country's enthralling diversity and the underlying opportunities for mobilizing the people as the subject and object of development. Even when seemingly engaged with this issue and the related distributive concerns, they tend to bark up the wrong tree, taking the country's topography rather than the people as their reference point. The political leadership has not acknowledged the important role of the value system, including work culture, incentive structures, and ethical norms, in driving successful development. In addition, the people have lost trust in the political, civic, and bureaucratic actors purportedly working for development whose social realities and interests have little resemblance to theirs.

The principal obstacles reside in the political arena. However, development shortcomings are linked with the work and interests of influential actors in other domains

---

[2] Panday 2009.
[3] See Klass 2008; Eneh 2009.
[4] See Leve 2007; Bonino and Donini 2009.

as well. The structures of accountability are weak in public, private, and civic domains so that deviant behavior has become routine and entrenched as a culture unhelpful to development. The climate of impunity and the misuse of resources are rampant, with hardly anyone being held accountable. Successive changes in the nature of the polity over the years have failed to improve conditions, but have contributed to raising the people's expectations as well as their consciousness about their social situation. This raised awareness can help facilitate democracy and development if the leaders use the opportunity to reverse the process by engaging in the social and cultural issues hitherto ignored as inconvenient. However, unrealized expectations also make the country more conflict prone, begging a resolution before they take an irreversible turn.

Yet Nepal's economy is not at a standstill, and important achievements have been made in infrastructure, from roads to telecommunications, and in the social sector, including education and health. In the six decades since Nepal embraced, at least rhetorically, development as a primary objective of the state, the country has "implemented" 11 development plans. Half of this period fell under the party-less Panchayat system of governance, which sought its legitimacy not in popular consent but in the promise that it would deliver rapid development. This system was based on a political philosophy that saw democracy as incompatible with development. In the 30 years of the Panchayat regime, when the state could concentrate on development without the distractions of democratic competition, some development work was carried out that did generate certain outputs along the way. Development aid was also pouring in and produced some results, misgivings about sustainability and aid efficiency notwithstanding.[5] In addition, as mentioned earlier the growing interaction with the outside world, made possible by advances in global information and communications systems, produced new awareness and economic opportunities for a section of the population. However, the outbreak of the Maoist insurgency in the 1990s revealed that limited and disjointed activities in isolated areas do not constitute development.

The end of the People's War and the Maoists' participation in mainstream politics generated widespread hope that the newfound peace would translate into significant development gains. The 2006 Comprehensive Peace Agreement's (CPA) mandate for state restructuring reflects the widespread understanding that a major shift in the character of the state and its policies is required for peace to be sustainable and development to proceed meaningfully for all groups of society. The establishment of an inclusive state that respects the aspirations and rights of all people, including the marginalized groups, could indeed help reverse the legacy of failed development. However, it is impossible to predict when the task of restructuring the state will be completed so that the nation can focus on development all over again. The political class has yet to realize that what is involved is nothing short of an exercise in

5 See Panday 2011.

nation-building afresh. It is about asking questions that have been neglected since the country's creation in the late 18th century, such as "Who are we?" and "What makes us Nepali?" Without agreement on these fundamental questions it is not possible to even imagine, let alone design, development that will succeed.

DEVELOPMENT PERFORMANCE

When the government launched "planned development" in the 1950s, it did so without much knowledge about the economy and in the absence of any survey or research that could have provided hard data on the nation's output, employment, and wealth and its social distribution. The early development plans attempted to address sectoral shortcomings with scattershot projects without a coherent grand strategy. There was no discussion or analysis of how these projects would affect the national economy and society, and in most cases the achievements fell drastically short of the targets. These early shortfalls were understandable given that the country had just emerged from a century of feudal and oligarchic Rana rule and was only starting to learn its first lessons in development and public administration. However, this explanation does not hold for later decades when the country's rulers and policy makers had full exposure and access to available knowledge and technology of development.

Although there has been some progress in creating a database on socioeconomic status and trends — one that is still far from being adequate or reliable in many cases – the government's planning methodology has not changed much since those early days. It continues to emphasize sectoral programs and targets with some new narratives on poverty and gender. At the same time it ignores fundamental issues concerning the relationship between investment and employment, intersectoral linkages, and, most importantly, the distribution of the costs and benefits of development across different sections of society. The inadequate attention paid to fostering professionalism in economic and social analysis seriously impedes the quality and utility of information available to policy making. It also reflects the lack of seriousness with which decision makers approach the issue of development.

Nepal started setting targets for the growth of its gross domestic product (GDP) in 1965, but this too happened in a statistical and methodological void. In addition, the targets failed to take into account the country's diversity and the corresponding socioeconomic realities. According to the available record, from 1950 to 1970, the country's GDP rarely grew at a rate higher than its population. From the 1980s onward, growth picked up a bit, aided by intermittent improvement in agricultural performance and later by increased activities in the manufacturing and service sectors. In the mid-1980s, the government also adopted expansionary public expenditure policies, which in addition to stimulating growth led to unprecedented imbalances in fiscal and external accounts. This situation invited the engagement of the International Monetary Fund (IMF) with its standby credit for the stabilization program, followed by structural adjustment programs supported by the World Bank in the late

1980s. In the 1990s, Nepal accelerated "reform" as designed in the Washington Consensus, with deregulation, privatization, and market-oriented policies in industry and trade as the main planks.

From a developmental perspective, the democratic transition in 1990 brought little change. There was no attempt to reconceptualize how development would be approached from a democratic perspective. With the exception of the rulers and the rank-and-file members of the parties who enjoyed patronage, the advent of democracy – or economic liberalization – had little positive impact on the lives of average Nepalis. It also failed to affect the rate of economic growth, which continued to linger around an annual average of 5% for the first half of the 1990s. Although seemingly a respectable performance, this is roughly the same rate Nepal saw during the last five years of the Panchayat regime.[6] Supported by increased private sector activities in industry and services, the growth rate reached 7.9% in 1993–4 only to fall to 2.9% the next year. Since then and for the next 15 years, the average GDP growth rate declined to below 4% annually, with significant fluctuations from one year to another. Yet this is not necessarily a bad performance given the onset and escalation of the Maoist insurgency and the political instability reflected in the frequent changes in government starting in 1993–4.

However, economic growth rates tell only part of the story. Even low growth rates can cumulatively have a transformative impact if the gains are broad based and equitably distributed. This was not the case in Nepal. There was no significant shift in the structure of output and employment beyond the growth of the service sector (mainly banking and real estate), which did not add much to the productive capacity of the economy. This growth bypassed large sections of the population, especially in the rural areas. As a result, income inequality increased, and it is now the highest among Asian countries – on a par with China without any of its positive accomplishments. The exclusion of the majority of the population – in particular marginalized ethnic groups, women, and inhabitants of remote geographic regions – from the political process did not feature as a factor in policy making until recently. Ironically, the socioeconomic situation – the stubborn poverty, in particular – led to the introduction of yet another set of reforms inspired by the IMF. The 2002 "Poverty Reduction Strategy Paper" (PRSP), which became the country's de facto 10th development plan, tried to address the issues of inclusion and inequities as a belated response to the Maoist insurgency. However, technocratic intervention without a change in the culture and structure of power failed to produce the intended results.

The underperformance of the rudimentary and monsoon-dependent agricultural sector, in which the majority of the people earn their livelihoods, is a major factor contributing to failed development. Despite reported improvements in access to irrigation, quality of seeds and fertilizers, infrastructure, and marketing, agricultural

---

[6] The data in this section are from Panday 2009 and Panday 2011 unless otherwise indicated.

yields have increased only marginally, if at all. Because of inefficiencies, waste, and widespread corruption, the accomplishments tend to exist on paper only. Until the 1970s, Nepal's agriculture, despite its backwardness, compared favorably with that of its neighbors in South Asia. Today, it ranks rock-bottom in the region in crop yield per hectare and agricultural value added per worker. Despite being a water-rich country, Nepal's net irrigated area, too, is very low by South Asian standards, and irrigation facilities operate at a suboptimal level, urgently needing repairs. Eighty-three percent of "irrigated land" is not irrigated year-round, reducing the number of annual harvests. Even in years of good and timely rainfall, the yield rate of major crops like paddy and wheat is way below the South Asian average.[7] A number of enterprising farmers working with small-scale cash crops and dairy products have done well, but they cannot compensate for the generally laggard crop and livestock sector and the near absence of meaningful agricultural development activities in the government or the organized private sector that could produce lasting and cumulative outcomes.

The agricultural sector was hit hardest by the military conflict as a result of the displacement and migration of farm labor. Compounding the problem was that the conflict most severely affected the districts in the far-western and mid-western hills. These areas already had to cope with the country's highest rate of poverty, malnutrition, and food insecurity, making them breeding grounds for the insurgency. Very little is now being done to compensate these districts in the "postconflict" era. The country's rulers remain trapped, politically and mentally, in the abyss of failed development amidst rising frustrations among the people. There is no sign that the unaddressed issues of land relation, including dual ownership, absentee landlordism, and land fragmentation, which adversely affect both productivity and distributive justice, will be addressed any time soon. Nor is there much interest in focusing attention and investment outside Kathmandu and similarly privileged cities, a situation that may change once a federal system is instituted.

There is no notable industrial base supporting the economy, despite the prominent role of private sector activities. Until the 1980s, the value added in the manufacturing sector hovered around 4% of GDP, most of it generated in small and cottage industries. In the late 1980s and the first five years of the 1990s, the manufacturing sector grew significantly at an average annual rate of 14%. This growth was propelled by the expansion of export-oriented carpet and garment industries and the emergence of some small-scale consumer goods industries. The second half of the 1990s saw a still respectable yearly average growth rate of 5.7%. The employment generated by the labor-intensive industries was of particular significance in the context of a conflict that thrived on the frustrations of unemployed youth. However, since then, these industries have virtually collapsed, and many small-scale enterprises have either disappeared or are not doing well. As a result, the manufacturing sector grew at a

---

[7] ADB, DFID, ILO (2009).

meager rate of less than 1.5% a year from 2004 to 2009, reducing its share of total output to 6.8% in 2008–9 from 9% a decade earlier.

The unsatisfactory performance of the private sector is all the more noteworthy because of the significant emphasis, since the early 1990s, on development of a market economy, deregulation, and free trade. Both internal and external factors explain why such efforts failed to produce positive results, why there was a chasm between theoretical expectations of the outcome of liberalization and the considerably less satisfactory reality. Among the more prominent reasons were the volatile political situation, civil disturbances, and frequent transport and labor strikes. That Nepal, despite its vast hydroelectric potential, suffers from chronic power shortages, even though the demand for energy from industries has not surged in a dramatic way, is another important part of the explanation.

Equally important, but less obvious, are two structural factors that are potentially more difficult to overcome. First, Nepal's traditional private sector has been more interested in harnessing arbitrage and other means of short-term profit-making than moving into long-term economically rewarding ventures. In Nepal's social milieu a businessperson, like other professionals, can earn money, social fame, and political power without being particularly concerned about whether the business is predatory and makes no contribution to the economy. The second factor is the political and bureaucratic culture that is dominated by patrimonial relationships antithetical to representative government and inclusive governance. The predatory interests and practices that hurt the economy and the people at large continue to flourish even with the liberalization of the economy and democratization of the polity. A business–politics nexus characterized by the collusion among business and political leaders for their mutual gain prevails over the long-term interests of the nation and is particularly lethal for responsible entrepreneurship in the private sector and democratic governance in the public domain.

Moreover, the trade policies and practices of India, Nepal's economically strong and influential neighbor, have harmed its industrial development and possible diversification of its economy. Provisions of the 1996 trade treaty between India and Nepal that were expected to spur the development of the manufacturing sector in Nepal were watered down in the treaty's 2002 extension, further increasing Nepal's massive trade deficit with India. Although some of the treaty provisions favorable to Nepal have since been restored, India continues to impose trade barriers at will. Of particular concern is New Delhi's tendency to raise tariff and nontariff barriers on specific products just when they are about to establish a durable market in India. In fairness, Nepal's private sector has rarely made use of the trade concessions, when available, for real industrial development. Often it has preferred to pursue short-term gains from spurious trade. In addition, Nepal's anachronistic policy of pegging the exchange rate of its currency to the Indian rupee prevents its overvalued currency from adjusting, which dramatically hurts Nepali exporters while it subsidizes imports from India.

Nepal's trade deficit with India stood at USD 1.9 billion in 2008–9, which is many times higher than the USD 26 million of Indian aid disbursed that year through Nepal government channels.[8] The government figures do not account for the aid money disbursed directly by the Government of India through its embassy in Kathmandu. Even if total Indian aid were much higher, the lopsided economic relationship between Nepal and India would still remain. India makes up 3.5% of its overall trade deficit from its trade surplus with Nepal,[9] a remarkable figure given the huge difference in the size of the two economies. With increasing import-based consumption and no new significant export products in sight, the trade gap is widening. Overall, Nepal's exports reached a relatively high level of 13.5% of GDP in 2000–1, declining to 7.2% in 2008–9. Although foreign aid flows well, foreign direct investment is miniscule. The country is currently facing a balance of payments deficit not seen in decades.

Interestingly, the investment rate has increased to 30% of GDP even as domestic savings stagnate. This rate, which was attained with the contribution of foreign aid and remittances, is not sustainable without unceasing external inflows. One of the most ominous trends for future development is the drastic increase in current government expenditure, which will limit the scope of domestically financed investment in the public sector. Financial profligacy, together with growing disregard by political leaders and public officials of established public policies, norms, and regulations, is driving this trend. Military expenditures remain high because of the army's reluctance to reduce its seize to preconflict levels. In the meantime, dependence on foreign aid is growing, and international donors now finance not only development expenditures but also routine government work in the name of promoting governance, constitution-making, and peace and security. Any future decline in foreign aid will pose a serious challenge to the functioning of government and its ability to finance its bureaucracy, security establishments, and development enterprise. Similarly Nepal's "vibrant" civil society is dominated by donor-driven nongovernmental organizations (NGOs) engaged in activities ranging from human rights promotion to service delivery.

A surprising development, given the low rate of growth and the disruptions of the People's War, is the apparent reduction in poverty levels from 42% to 31% between 1996 and 2004. Although this is good news, it is the result of the increase in remittances from Nepali workers abroad, not economic development. The near doubling of remittances as a percentage of GDP in the last 10 years to 23% in 2010[10]

---

[8] The trade figure (Rs 133 billion) is from Nepal Rastra Bank, and the data on aid (Rs 1.8 billion) are from the Financial Comptroller General's Office in the Government of Nepal. Both figures were converted into dollar amounts at the historical exchange rate as of September 1, 2008.

[9] Bhurtel 2009.

[10] See Economic Survey, 2010, Ministry of Finance, Government of Nepal available at http://www.mof. gov.np/publication/budget/2010/table.

has significantly enhanced the purchasing power of rural households. It has also contributed to the growth of financial services and speculative rise in land prices. However, such income has thus far mainly demonstrated its value as a survival strategy for the poor households: the only possible long-term impact of remittances on development is that the receiving households are spending part of the funds on education. The migration of unskilled labor abroad for manual work, while driving up remittances, has also had a number of negative side effects, such as the growing desertion of farm land and increasing food insecurity, which has reached unprecedented levels in many districts.

Another of the few pieces of good news is the continued improvement over the past two decades in Nepal's education and health indicators, accounting for the impressive increase in Nepal's human development score from 0.309 in 1980 to 0.553 in 2007.[11] Whereas in the 1950s only 2% of Nepal's population were literate, the rate rose to 19% in 1980 and 49% in 2009. This dramatic rise is due to increased enrollment in primary and secondary schools, which are now attended by girls and boys in almost equal numbers. Similar achievements have been made in the health sector. In 2007, Nepal had a child mortality rate of 54.7 per 1,000 children under the age of five, down from 142 per 1,000 in 1990. Life expectancy at birth is now 63 years compared to 45 years in 1980.[12]

However, the aggregate data hide wide variations across class, geographic regions, gender, and ethnicity. The class divide in education and health is reflected in the disparity of the quality of services. Most quality schools and hospitals in Nepal are privately run, benefiting the privileged urban households. The majority of the population is dependent on poorly endowed government institutions and facilities. For example, 42% of first graders in government schools do not graduate to the second grade; of them 27% repeat first grade, and 15% drop out of school altogether.[13] Public hospitals and health centers in rural Nepal are few in number and are often staffed by inadequate and unqualified health personnel.

In addition to the class divide, large sections of the population are deprived of basic services because of their caste, ethnicity, gender, and geographic location. The urban–rural divide is particularly stark, with the proportion of urban population below the poverty line at 9.6% contrasting with a rural poverty rate of 34.6%. The mid- and far-western regions have particularly high poverty rates, especially in the mountainous districts. However, human development indicators vary more by caste and ethnicity than they do by geographic region. Unsurprisingly, high-caste

---

[11]　See UNDP 2009a. The Human Development Index (HDI), published in the UN's yearly *Human Development Reports*, ranks countries by their level of "human development." The reports' data are based on three main dimensions: life expectancy at birth, adult literacy rates, and standard of living (GDP per capita). For more information visit http://hdr.undp.org/en/humandev/.

[12]　World Bank 1983, 2009.

[13]　According to the Nepali English-language daily *Republica* citing official sources (January 13, 2010).

Brahmins, Chhetris, and Newars enjoy significantly higher human development standards than low-caste groups such as Dalits, Janajatis, and Muslims.[14]

A fair amount of national and international attention is now devoted to inclusion of traditionally marginalized groups. This is a welcome development with far-reaching importance for the future of democratic development in Nepal. However, there is also the need to prevent "elite capture" given the complexities of Nepali social stratification. For example, in the Terai, the progress made in empowering and ensuring representation of Madhesis in politics and state institutions has mainly benefited the Madhesi Brahmins and other high-caste privileged groups, further widening the divide between them and the less privileged in the region like Madhesi Dalits, Janajatis, and others. This dynamic is replicated within other recently empowered marginalized groups; for instance, women's groups.[15] The challenge is to increase the actual power of the powerless without merely empowering the elite within the excluded groups as Nepal proceeds to restructure the state and redistribute political and economic resources.

A major flaw in the country's development campaign from the very beginning has been the lack of will for incorporating political, social, and cultural transformation as an integral part of the process. The dominant groups that have traditionally enjoyed economic and political power have used everything from religion to nationalism and co-opted monarchic and democratic governments to hold on to their entitlements and privileges in the name of development or otherwise. This tendency inherent in Nepal's exclusionary state is the root cause of conflict and has imposed huge human and economic costs on the nation.[16] Yet the resistance to change persists, perpetuating the danger of development limiting itself "within an underdeveloped structure."[17]

POLITICAL, CULTURAL, AND INSTITUTIONAL DYNAMICS

A new constitution followed by elections is a necessary if insufficient condition to advance the country's ongoing transition to relative normalcy in politics and development. The promulgation of a constitution that reconciles competing interests and accommodates discontented groups will be an important step toward resolving the new identity-driven conflicts. How the political parties wielding power pursue the new constitutional mandate will determine future developments.

So far, the experience in the transition period has not been encouraging, notwithstanding the sacrifices of many leaders in the past. The powerful parties and their leaders have been stretching the law, including the constitution, at will to serve their

---

[14] UNDP 2009b.
[15] International Evaluation Group 2006.
[16] Upreti 2009.
[17] Chaitanya Misra and Pitamber Sharma cited in Panday 2011.

petty interests. Instead of engaging in consensual politics as mandated by the people, they have been colluding and dividing up among themselves spoils and entitlements and, in the process, dangerously prolonging the transition. If the new constitution is to fulfill its promise it must usher in a radical change in the political culture that values the will of the people and that can also inspire the emergence of enlightened leadership.

This is a daunting challenge, not least because, if anything, we are witnessing a deterioration in the political culture, with the pursuit of politics not serving the public purpose. This situation is compounded by a tendency of various social groups and interests to resort to confrontational approaches such as violent street protests rather than engaging in political dialogue. It is a challenge that would test the best leaders, and leadership is the scarcest resource in Nepal, despite landmark political achievements in recent years. The emergence of the Maoist party as a major new actor on the political scene has raised hopes for positive change. However, the party is finding it difficult to shed part of its culture carried over from the insurgency, to make its potentially constructive presence felt in politics and development. The ideological contests within the party and the existence of a vocal wing of hard-liners who question the wisdom of pursuing Maoist goals within the liberal democratic framework and harbor nostalgic feelings for the People's War have emboldened the adversarial forces within and outside the country. The moderate Maoist leaders are struggling to adapt the party's ideology to the demands of open and competitive politics. Doing so without adopting the dysfunctional culture of Nepal's "democratic politics" poses an additional challenge. Maoist leaders are already facing allegations that they are getting corrupted by the lure of "bourgeois democracy" and the opportunities it provides for personal gains.

To understand the challenges facing the other political parties, one has to return to the period of democratic transition during the early 1990s. When the first post-Panchayat government was elected in 1991, it adopted the core elements of the development strategy pursued by the departed regime. The new leaders did not know better, having failed to do their ideological work and prepare for assuming government by developing new policies and programs while in opposition. The "seventh plan" in the Panchayat period was routinely followed by the "eighth plan" in the democratic period. Another factor favoring continuity was that the new leadership was drawn as before from Nepal's traditionally dominant castes and class; it was reluctant to question the fundamental character of the Nepali state. Continuity rather than change became the convenient if irresponsible norm when short-term interests overwhelmed long-term strategic thinking. At the most mundane level, this tendency could be observed in the way many of the new leaders adopted the dress code, cultural practices, social mannerisms, and lifestyle of the rulers of the regime they fought against. The leaders of the communist parties who joined the system were no different. Perhaps realizing that challenging the "class character" of the state and fundamentally questioning the existing power structures would generate formidable opposition with resulting political costs, many found it convenient to merge into "the system" and promote their own interests.

Like the development strategies, the 1990 constitution framed by the new leadership in collaboration with the monarchy failed to reflect Nepal's new demands and aspirations. The constitutional framework did not take into account the rights and demands of marginalized communities who were already challenging the centuries-old power relationships. It did not acknowledge that democracy and development both required a sense of ownership and participation by the people, giving them a voice in decisions affecting their dignity and welfare. It adopted the previous regime's approach to "decentralization," which took local bodies for granted without entrusting them with independent decision-making authority or meaningful access to resources. Despite these design flaws, there was no serious attempt to review the constitution. The growing grievances substantiated by the widening disparities across regional, geographic, and ethnic lines eventually sparked the Maoist insurgency.

Two decades later, the emergence of the Maoists as a political force notwithstanding, the country has by and large the same leadership as in the 1990s, including individuals with severely tainted reputations. Although the institution of an inclusive Constituent Assembly with its diverse membership is certainly an achievement, nominal inclusion is not the same thing as gaining access to power to challenge the establishment and redirect public policies that favor the status quo. As in 1990–1, Nepal today is threatened by the prospect of a transition that embraces the nominal characteristics of a democratic system without the change in the underlying power structures necessary for development. Despite its republican pretensions, the country is becoming a classic case of a democracy in form, not in substance, which in Nepal's situation is not sustainable. The continued culture of impunity translates into grave human rights abuses that go unpunished, and it allows corruption to fester, making criminal behavior socially acceptable. The bumpy transition has provided opportunities to antisocial groups to hide their criminal intent behind political agendas, including autonomy and inclusion, as in the case of the Terai region. Important political parties and their leaders at the local and the national level provide protection and support to criminal, armed groups for personal and political gains at the cost of the lives and livelihoods of ordinary people.

The behavior of the ruling classes and powerful groups in Nepal generates a widespread sense of injustice, resentment, and betrayal among the rest of the population. As a result, there is a massive erosion in law-abiding behavior among the people, as well as the loss of a sense of community and camaraderie within and across castes, ethnicities, and geographic regions. The new constitution will not generate by itself the value system that supports development and a political and civic culture that enforces mutual accountability necessary for its smooth and productive functioning. The existing leadership obviously cannot do so either. It is therefore critical that the new state with its republican character and federal structure establishes rules and mechanisms for political parties, including the Maoists, that will govern recruitment and leadership succession at all levels.

Opinions are divided among political parties, experts, and activists on the best way to go about constituting the federating states. At one end of the spectrum is the conservative view that tends to see the promotion of identity and cultural rights as potential threats to Nepal's national unity and territorial integrity. At the other end of the spectrum are those who demand autonomous states based on ethnicity and regional identity with the right to self-determination. Creating states along ethnic lines seems like a difficult-to-implement proposition given that the population of any of the constituent states is likely to be as ethnically diverse as the country as a whole. From a developmental perspective one must also look at the resource endowments and development potential of each state, in addition to its ethnic, linguistic, and regional characteristics. Questions regarding how to allocate authority over expenditure and revenue are critical. In addition, in light of the earlier mentioned danger of elite capture, the unique situation of Dalits, women, and other groups whose concerns and rights cannot be subsumed in any territorial division deserves special attention. Where and how the ethnic or regional divisions intersect with the interests of the poor and marginalized groups in each federating unit will become critical issues in this context. Political and community leaders need to be mindful that the interests of the excluded groups can only be guaranteed by overcoming the dysfunctional political culture and shedding regressive social ideas and practices of the hitherto dominant groups. Federalism even with autonomous states demarcated on the basis of ethnicity does not necessarily add to the representative character of the government if the "ethnic leaders" exhibit the class character of the historically dominant group and are unmindful of their constituency.

Other major impediments to development are the practice of patronage in public service and the politicization of the bureaucracy, which has destroyed professionalism and ethical norms in the system. The political masters systematically take advantage of insecure and ambitious public servants, who then easily succumb to unethical and illegal overtures and pressures for survival and personal gain. Top posts, including those in the most important institutions of economic and development policy making, are divided up in backroom deals among party leaders, with little attention given to necessary qualifications and experience. Each major party maintains a separate, closely affiliated trade union of civil servants, a practice that is replicated in virtually every segment of society. Any attempt to reinvigorate an ethos of professionalism and end rent-seeking behavior, which is so common across many sectors in Nepal, would have to start with implementing civil service reforms that foster its independence and integrity.

INTERNATIONAL COOPERATION

Nepal's international development partners made a valuable contribution to the democratic movement in 2005–6, in particular by assuming the role of human rights "watchdogs." Similarly, their support at the political and diplomatic level and their financial contributions have been critical to the advancement of the peace process.

When the peace process stalled, they have not even refrained from chastising such sacrosanct institutions as the Nepalese Army. Concerned about the lack of interest in investigating human rights violations by the Maoists as well as the state, the United States, for example, has made military assistance conditional on the army's cooperation in such investigations.[18] The same is expected of the Maoists if they wish to get off the U.S. terrorism designation list. The support from donors was also a prerequisite for the involvement of the United Nations in promoting human rights and supporting the peace process by deploying a human rights monitoring mission in 2005 and a political mission in 2007 (UNMIN).

Many international actors, China and India included, initially favored reforming rather than abolishing the monarchy, and it took some time before they accepted the political change as the popular will. In response to the wishes of the Nepali people, they abandoned their view that the monarchy was necessary for stability in the country. Most critically, donors also understood that the Maoists had to be accommodated and integrated in the country's state affairs, although some international partners clearly had second thoughts after the Maoists' impressive showing in the Constituent Assembly elections. The growing difference in perspectives and interests between India and some prominent donors, particularly the European Union, in this respect will influence the outcomes of the ongoing transition and peace process.

On development cooperation, the experience has not been as satisfactory. International aid has been a key feature of Nepal's development endeavor from the time the country started thinking about development in the 1950s. Aid money has financed every aspect of development – economic, social, and governance areas, including recent efforts in conflict resolution and peacebuilding. Important achievements have been made in education, health, and infrastructure as well as in community development as donor-supported NGOs have contributed to people's empowerment, social mobilization, and service delivery. In the aggregate, however, the donors share responsibility for the country's failed development.

Critical development failures can be attributed at least in part to donor fatigue or reluctance to invest in productive sectors that could generate broad-based economic growth with equity and justice. The industrial sector has never been a recipient of significant foreign aid. Agriculture, an area where progress would have had the most important impact on the livelihoods of large parts of population, remains backward despite considerable technical and financial support from donors in the past. The numerous integrated rural development projects implemented in the 1970s and 1980s fell far short of their stated objective of changing the character of the rural economy and generating income and employment opportunities for rural households. Today, key donors have nearly abandoned the agricultural sector, seeming to put their faith in both internal and external migration as a promising path to development, despite

---

[18] See "US: Aid to Nepal Army Conditional," *Kathmandu Post*, February 3, 2010.

the fact that three-quarters of the labor force is officially stated to be dependent on agriculture. Remittances have been a double-edged sword in the Nepali context – useful for the households in the short term with negative consequences for the long-term growth of the economy. In addition, internal migration from the hills to the low-lying Terai region has complicated regional and ethnic relations.

The many inequities created in the development process have been a source of conflict at various levels. Deprived of due benefits from development, the economically and socially excluded groups resent the condescending and patronizing behavior of the ruling establishment, including the agents of development. In the absence of structural change that would ensure more equitable and sustainable development, even the positive outcomes of aid ultimately have become a source of conflict. For example, starting in the 1990s, foreign-aid-funded empowerment programs for marginalized groups enabled them to formulate demands and claims for political power and economic resources. However, this work was not followed by responsive programs that could in fact address these demands, and so the location of these groups in the power structure and development landscape changed little. The ruling classes took no notice of the newly awakened consciousness of the marginalized groups, and this failure, in the end, fueled the Maoist insurgency.

A Nepali analyst noted, "In the context of a country like Nepal . . . 'development' through foreign aid essentially becomes a metaphor for maintenance and strengthening of the traditional native power structure."[19] That donors took little interest in land reform during six decades of engagement in Nepal illustrates this point. By refraining from addressing policies that they feared might "rock the boat," donors became complicit in perpetuating the status quo. The fact that many of them engaged in well-intentioned efforts to improve the aid system and make it responsive to local conditions does not change this uncomfortable truth. Several steps need to be taken to reform the system for greater aid effectiveness in the Nepali context.

First, the fundamental flaw in the aid relationship is the inability of the country's leaders to take charge of the development process, provide a vision of development that is rooted in Nepali realities, and accept responsibility for the outcome. In Nepal, nearly every new idea in the area of development and shifts in the reigning development dogma over the years have originated abroad, devised by donors and dutifully adopted by the Nepali authorities. This needs to be reversed, with the Nepali authorities held responsible for priorities, policies, and aid efficiency. The donor representatives can provide advice and share their experiences from other countries, but beyond that, they should only ask for financial accountability from the Nepali recipients.

Second, the failure to address the structural causes of failed development is rooted in the character of the international aid system, which tends to establish global policies and targets with little regard to local conditions. The vast sum of money

---

[19] Chaitanya Misra and Pitamber Sharma cited in Panday 2011.

disbursed for structural adjustment and economic reform, governance, or democracy assistance has been a boon to governments that use the fungible resources to make their ends meet without working toward the promised results. Reflecting the general lack of accountability, the ineffective use of development finance has rarely resulted in denial of further aid in the mistaken belief that any such measure would be tantamount to punishing the victims, the people. When the donors do not share responsibility for aid failures, they should be able to take tough decisions on future aid to the country or to a given sector.

Third, donors' attempts to honor the principles of participation and ownership have at times been counterproductive. Even though donors have widened their engagement with civil society, they have failed to realize that it was largely dominated by dominant elites or driven by the elites' value system. In addition, civil society organizations became increasingly dependent on foreign aid and the priorities of donors. For example, whereas prominent Nepali academics can find plenty of opportunities to work as consultants on externally devised projects, little funding is made available for independent research on issues the scholars deem important. The foreign-aid-induced incentive structure is such that excellence is often sacrificed at the altar of mediocrity. Whether civil society, the media, the legal profession, or the National Planning Commission, all these institutions are co-opted by the donor community as "partners." Such partnership regimes give birth to "incestuous" relationships and inhibit learning and self-correcting opportunities for the donors and the recipient. Most importantly, this system dilutes accountability, with the people not knowing whom to hold responsible for their condition.

Fourth, despite recent initiatives to improve aid effectiveness such as the Paris Declaration and Accra Agenda for Action, aid administrators in Nepal as elsewhere continue to look at disbursement targets as their main yardsticks for success. The incentive structure associated with this fixation resonates well with Nepal's patronage culture and weak democracy in which those in power are eager to gain access to opportunities to distribute spoils. For aid administrators, quick disbursing avenues are preferable to risky ventures with long gestation. The main issue is the opportunity cost of the resources foregone and their possible alternative use in the poor country. For example, roughly USD 172 million worth of development assistance was spent in constitution-making by 2008–9.[20] This amount exceeds the combined appropriations for agriculture and irrigation in the country's budget that year.

India is Nepal's most important trading partner and donor, and its somewhat enigmatic role in Nepal's development deserves special attention. Despite its status as an emerging superpower, India's "threat perception" vis-à-vis its neighbors makes it hard for it to maintain good and mutually beneficial relations even with Nepal. The uneasy relations are based on a long-held fear that Nepal would play "the

---

[20] Bhurtel 2010.

China card" to India's disadvantage. India has not shown interest in a politically and economically strong Nepal managed by self-confident and capable leaders whose legitimacy is grounded in popular support. Reminiscent of the colonial age, it prefers to play a game of divide and rule with multiple power centers in Nepal competing for Indian support. India's strategy is facilitated by weak Nepali leadership that pays little regard to its obligations to its domestic constituency. Ultimately, however, this strategy is likely to backfire because India is losing the goodwill of the common people of Nepal in all regions and strata. Its capacity to effectively influence policies and events in the county is declining. Nepal's rulers of any political persuasion find it difficult to enlist public support for any kind of collaboration for the mutual benefit of the two countries. Meanwhile, vested interests in Nepal exploit anti-Indian sentiment against democratic development in the name of nationalism and sovereignty. One hopes that India will soon find it advisable to reassess its policies on Nepal, thereby reconciling them with the sovereignty of the Nepali people. The well-acknowledged truth is that a secure, stable, and democratic Nepal will also contribute to India's well-being and security.

LOOKING AHEAD

The developmental failures in Nepal are not caused by factors routinely seen in other underperforming developing countries. Its challenges are deeply engrained in the country's history and dominant political culture, which stubbornly resists change in policies and behavior relevant for development. The long neglected causes of failed development – the exclusionary nature of the Nepali state and its largely patrimonial character – also explain the outbreak of violent conflict in the mid-1990s. Neither the government nor its international partners were able to mobilize the nation's resources and energy to articulate a development strategy that captured the imagination of all its peoples. In the end, the contradictions in the international aid system and the weaknesses in Nepal's domestic structures conspired to undermine development and, eventually, peace in the country.

Nepal recently achieved remarkable progress on the political front, which provides hope for the country's future. Very few people could have imagined that the country could ever transform itself into a federal republic with the identity and rights of all people secured. Although the political and law-and-order situation may seem desperate at the time of this writing, it is important to remember that managing transitions and institutionalizing regime change peacefully never go smoothly. Nepal's problem is that, so far, its leaders have not risen to the occasion and shown the necessary resolve and moral authority to steer the process in the designated direction. One can only hope that the new constitution when completed will lead to the emergence of a new leadership structure that can harness its own wisdom and all available opportunities to transform the past failures into a productive future. For this to happen, the newly empowered youths, women, Dalits, and the underclass within marginalized groups must get a chance to rise to leadership positions in political parties and at all levels of government. In that event, donor contributions to social mobilization and empowerment of the marginalized groups since 1990 will have proven their value. Whether and how the Maoists will manage their culture and conduct, internally and externally, to reconcile with the imperatives of liberal democracy without succumbing to its vices will be critical in this process.

In the newly emerged federal republic of Nepal, aid donors can look at the recipient afresh and, in designing development strategies, take the reality on the ground as a guide instead of the internationally framed development doctrine devised for universal use. The national actors must take the lead in this process and become accountable for the results. The donors can approach their responsibilities imaginatively, adjusting their systems as required – and taking Nepal as a special or a test case, if necessary. From personal experience I know that Nepal's political and bureaucratic leaders show greater initiative and leadership qualities when they represent the country as "recipients" rather than as partners or "owners," which is currently the case in an effort to make the aid system more legitimate. In the current system the leaders enter into covenants with their international partners rather than their domestic constituents and obtain resources for which they do not have to answer to the people. In addition, they do not feel challenged because the donors make their life easy by "balancing the budget" for them and providing privileges and entitlements of various kinds.

For the immediate future, it would be preferable to see governance framed as a conditionality rather than a program that finances all kinds of largely unproductive expenditures for the benefit of nonperforming political leaders and their cohorts in civil society. In the event of "governance failure," donors could stop or curtail future disbursement instead of optimistically but unrealistically trying to reform governance themselves and treating it as a development sector for aid financing. Foreign aid will then become what it actually is – the temporary source of financing development – not a mechanism for rewarding unaccountable governments and rent-seeking members of the ruling elite.

Nepal's professional classes including the bureaucracy and the critical actors in civil society also need to transform their work culture and dependence on foreign aid. To contribute their full potential as watchdogs and to independently critique Nepal's development and governance processes, Nepal's professionals need home-grown and value-based incentive systems, not the benevolence of donors. They can autonomously, if also collectively, initiate measures for reforming the system they are a part of by inculcating in it the values and professional competencies essential to development. Nepal can reverse the curse of failed development if it can experience a resurgence of self-esteem, professional ethos, and national pride across society and in particular, in the life and work of the professional classes.

REFERENCES

ADB, DFID, and ILO. 2009. *Nepal: Critical Development Constraints*. Manila: Asian Development Bank.

Bhurtel, Bhim Prasad. 2009. "Red Carpet Welcome," *Kathmandu Post*, September 11.

Bhurtel, Bhim Prasad. 2010. "Praying for a 'Happy Accident.'" *Republica*, January 25. Bonino, Francesca and Antoni Donini. 2009. *Aid and Violence: Politics and Conflict in Nepal*. Medford, MA: Feinstein International Center, Tufts University.

Collier, Paul. 2007. *The Bottom Billion*. New York: Oxford University Press.

Eneh, Cyprian Onyenekewa. 2009. "Failed Development Vision, Political Leadership and Nigeria's Underdevelopment – A Critique," in Simon Sigue (ed.), *Repositioning African Business and Development for the 21st Century*. Proceedings of the 10th Annual Conference of International Academy of African Business and Development, at iadb.org/2009.

Independent Evaluation Group. 2006. *Unequal Citizens: Gender, Caste and Ethnic Exclusion in Nepal*. Washington, DC: World Bank.

Klass, Brian. 2008. "From Miracle to Nightmare: An Institutional Analysis of Development Failures in Cote d'Ivoire/" *Africa Today*, 55(1): 109–26.

Leve, Lauren. 2007. "Failed Development and Rural Revolution in Nepal: Rethinking Subaltern Consciousness." *Anthropological Quarterly* 80(1): 127–72.

Panday, Devendra Raj. 2009. *Nepal's Failed Development: Reflections on the Mission and the Maladies*. Kathmandu: Nepal South Asia Centre.

Panday, Devendra Raj. 2011. *Looking at Development and Donors: Essays from Nepal*. Kathmandu: Martin Chautari.

UN Development Program. 2009a. *Human Development Report*. New York: UNDP.

UN Development Program. 2009b. *Nepal Human Development Report*. Kathmandu: UNDP.

Upreti, Bishnu Raj. 2009. *Nepal: From War to Peace*. New Delhi: Adroit Publishers.

World Bank. 1983. *World Development Report*. Washington, DC: World Bank.

World Bank. 2009. *World Development Report*. Washington, DC: World Bank.

4.1

A Donor's Perspective on Aid and Conflict

Jörg Frieden

For more than 10 years, from 1996 to 2006, Nepal's armed conflict imposed constraints and offered opportunities to international development actors. Since the signing of the Comprehensive Peace Agreement (CPA) in 2006, donors have tried, with mixed results, to consolidate the peace process and to promote development at the same time.

Based on my experiences and direct observations, this chapter assesses the contributions of the Western bilateral and multilateral development agencies to the mitigation and possible resolution of the decade-long People's War.[1] It focuses on the period of intense armed conflict from 2002 to November 2006 and on the subsequent peace process. Although important, the contributions by humanitarian agencies such as the International Committee of the Red Cross (ICRC), the Office of the UN High Commissioner for Human Rights (OHCHR), and the many international nongovernmental organizations (NGOs) are not the focus of this analysis.

THE PECULIARITIES OF THE NEPALI CONFLICT

To understand the experiences of international development actors and their possible relevance to other conflict situations, it is important to take into account the specific characteristics of the People's War. In brief, the Maoist Party of Nepal (CPN-M), authentically Marxist-Leninist in its ideology and organization, took advantage of legitimate popular grievances and conducted a successful insurgency. The underlying causes of the conflict were the lack of legitimacy of a state built by feudal conquerors and the exclusion and marginalization of women, lower castes,

---

[1] Chapter 4 by Devendra Raj Panday provides an informed Nepali view and a good description of development cooperation in Nepal. Historical and updated information and analysis of international development activities in Nepal are available through the Web pages of the UN system (http://www.un.org.np) and the World Bank (http://www.worldbank.org.np).

ethnic groups, and inhabitants of certain regions. Moreover, the waste of public resources and widespread corruption in the 1990s seriously damaged the image of the democratic parties. The peace process that started in 2005 therefore has a chance to succeed only if the ongoing constitutional process corrects the deep structural imbalances and injustices that have been part of the Nepali state for two centuries.

Since the beginning of the armed insurgency in 1996, aid agencies struggled to recognize, understand, and internalize three critical dimensions of the conflict. First, they long refused to accept the political nature of the confrontation, reducing it to the more comfortable discourse on the socioeconomic causes of the Maoist insurrection. Following this interpretation, sustained equitable economic growth would have progressively eliminated the main sources of popular grievances and brought the conflict to an end. Second, aid agencies had difficulty admitting that the aid system had become intimately associated with a state that had lost legitimacy and that the lion's share of development resources had been captured by a small elite. Third, aid agencies denied that the CPN-M had progressively extended its political and military influence to large parts of Nepal's territory and that by 2002–3 government control, in the majority of districts, was limited to district headquarters and their immediate surroundings. King Gyanendra's coup d'etat in February 2005, in which he dismissed parliament and assumed direct power, weakened international support for the Kathmandu-based establishment. As detailed later, the king's actions served as a wake-up call to the international development community in Nepal and led many development actors to review and adjust the nature of their engagement in Nepal. In doing so, they ultimately made a modest contribution to ending the civil war and tentatively supported the uncertain transition launched by the Comprehensive Peace Agreement.

DONORS' STRUGGLE WITH THE POLITICAL CAUSES AND THE REALITIES OF THE ARMED CONFLICT

Trying to make sense of the armed conflict and forced to justify their continued presence in Nepal despite it, aid agencies focused for years on the socioeconomic "root causes" of the conflict. They mistakenly believed that an effective development strategy would mitigate and ultimately resolve a conflict that was fundamentally political in nature. Donors sought and found explanations for the persistence of structural poverty and the apparent ineffectiveness of their development activities mainly in the ill-conceived macroeconomic policies of the 1990s. Therefore, as late as 2002, they enthusiastically supported the IMF/World Bank-inspired reform program for Nepal.[2] The program contained a balanced mix of technocratic measures aimed at improving the quality of public expenditures, progressively liberalizing the

---

[2] Pokhara Development Forum, 2002. A complete summary of the reform agenda can be found in World Bank, *Interim Strategy Note for Nepal*, January 2007, Appendix 5.

inefficient and corrupt public sector, and promoting private investment. Only years later did donors recognize that governance problems and discrimination based on caste, ethnic identity, and gender as well as the armed conflict itself were the main reasons for aid ineffectiveness. The same underlying causes hindered an effective implementation of well-designed and necessary economic reforms. Donors also came to realize that channeling aid resources through an ineffective and often corrupt public administration or through local NGOs controlled by the establishment – especially by the moderately reformist United Marxist-Leninist Party (UML) – made them complicit with the illegitimate state machinery and the discredited elites.

The recognition of these shortcomings, as well as a renewed focus on the interrelationship between peace, democracy, and development, brought about a change in donor practices. However, the majority of donors only fully committed to a new approach after King Gyanendra seized absolute power in February 2005, disappointing expectations and unwillingly facilitating a rapprochement between the persecuted parliamentary parties and the CPN-M. Coupled with an intensification of the civil war and a rise in disappearances of political activists, the 2005 coup forced donors to distance themselves from the king and to put human rights and democracy high on their agenda. The new political landscape also led donors to conclude that the peaceful resolution of the conflict was a precondition for relaunching development in Nepal. Donors further acknowledged that development activities had to be impartial and not favor one side of the conflict. The political environment pushed aid agencies to sharpen the poverty focus of their programs and to improve their own governance through increased transparency of plans, expenditures, and results. Finally, aid agencies, for the first time, recognized the Maoists as a political movement and in some cases began to engage them in a dialogue on issues regarding access, security of staff, and local development.

The main lessons learned from donor experiences presented in the following section reflect the intellectual and political change the majority of donors went through and must be understood in the specific context of the Nepali conflict.

LESSONS LEARNED FROM PROMOTING DEVELOPMENT IN NEPAL DURING THE ARMED CONFLICT

From 2002 to 2006 the Maoist party controlled large parts of Nepal's territory, and government officials and police forces were absent from the vast majority of localities. Yet, development agencies remained present and engaged in all districts, almost without interruption. Often at risk of becoming a target of the violence, they protected their staff by sharing among them security-relevant information and analysis. Over time, these security assessments became essential not only to ensure safe operations but also to promote conflict-sensitive programming and a more effective provision of development services.

In reports to their respective headquarters, national and international development actors claimed for years that the Maoists respected and did not try to influence development activities as long as they were focused on poverty reduction and empowerment of local communities. In reality, however, donors experienced on a daily basis that deployment of development programs beyond district headquarters required the acceptance or at least the tolerance of the Maoist political cadres. Maoist requests for "donations" and other contributions were frequent, and the staff of international organizations or local NGOs often had to cede part of their salary to the "revolutionary cause." As long as they tacitly accepted these conditions and the corresponding risks, aid agencies were able to operate almost everywhere and could move freely across the frontlines during all phases of the armed confrontation. The unrestricted movement of aid agencies was also made possible because (1) the conflict parties engaged in rational behavior and the predictable and targeted use of violence, (2) the CPN-M strove for international recognition, and (3) the government was happy to tolerate development work in areas under Maoist influence because it gave the appearance of state presence where there was none.

When the armed conflict resumed after the short truce in the spring of 2003, the Nepalese Army and police force suspected the development agencies of providing, through the execution of their programs, resources and prestige to the insurgents. The police force in particular exerted pressure on development organizations and often demanded bribes to let them continue their work.

To defend the development space against the pretensions of the insurgents and the interference of the security forces, which were trying to limit the free movement and open communication of development workers, in October 2003 all bilateral Western aid agencies – with the exception of USAID[3] – and the UN agencies ratified 12 principles of engagement outlined in the so-called Basic Operating Guidelines or Bogs.[4] The Bogs committed agencies to provide inclusive assistance to the poor, while maintaining uncompromising impartiality in the armed political conflict. They expressed common standards for internal and external accountability. Finally, Bogs allowed development agencies to coordinate common responses to challenges and abuses by the parties to the conflict, upholding the principle that any attack or substantial restriction of the activities supported by one organization would trigger the suspension of all development activities in a given geographic area.

The conscious decision to continue operations during the conflict led aid agencies to review and seriously adjust the orientation and implementation of their work,

---

[3] The United States considered the CPN-M a terrorist organization. Strict legal provisions forbade U.S. citizens and government organizations like USAID from entertaining any relation with or even assisting members of the CPN-M in extreme humanitarian emergencies. USAID therefore could not accept the spirit of impartiality that informed the Basic Operating Guidelines.

[4] Bogs were endorsed by 11 bilateral agencies and subscribed to, in a modified version, by the UN system and the Association of International NGOs in Nepal. For more information see http://www.un.org .np/resources/index.php.

which had positive results for program effectiveness: programs and projects were modified to give more attention to poor and socially discriminated groups; agencies conducted more development work through community-based organizations that demonstrated more responsiveness to the challenges posed by the conflict than the government or newly established NGOs operating from district headquarters; and many projects helped give a voice to discriminated groups by recruiting staff from their midst or by increasingly involving women and representatives of marginalized groups in the decision-making processes, implementation, and supervision of development programs. Aid agencies also had to substantially improve their transparency and began involving beneficiaries in the monitoring of their activities through public information vehicles (public boards planted along the main roads, radio, press and even drawings and articles produced by schoolchildren) and public auditing. This effort in turn led to pressure on government-run development projects to adopt similar standards of transparency.

At least in some agencies the constant attention paid to the link between development and conflict led to the implementation of conflict-sensitive practices, starting with a specific context analysis, often conducted in the districts in order to take into account the local dimensions of the conflicts, that identified the agents and the beneficiaries of development programs. In Nepal, the classical "do no harm" approach to development activities had to be complemented by a specific analysis of the political beneficiaries of development interventions, be they the Maoists, the monarchists, or one of the democratic parties, with each trying to control and steer resources in a partisan way. To operate in a conflict-sensitive manner, donors therefore had to identify not only the agents and the beneficiaries of their interventions but also these groups' links to the conflict parties. Donors also made specific efforts to ensure that the poorest segments of the population and in particular the marginalized groups would get a fair share of the advantages generated by external interventions. In addition, donors identified channels of communication to the authorities as well as to the insurgents and used them at all levels, from Kathmandu down to the villages. Local staff underwent security training and were provided with professional identity cards, and the Basic Operating Guidelines were widely disseminated in English, Nepali, and in the major vernacular languages.

A few agencies were not content with simply "doing no harm" and aimed to influence positively the course of the conflict through development work. In their understanding, working to resolve the conflict meant a conscious interaction with the parties and in particular with Maoist cadres on development issues, with the objective of encouraging the search for solutions to the country's political and social problems through dialogue and negotiations. These agencies relentlessly repeated that respect for human rights, the impartiality of development work, and a nonviolent resolution of the armed conflict were preconditions for a political recognition of the CPN-M. This discourse allowed the insurgents to better understand the expectations of the international community and to realize the value of potential international support to the peace process. Field contacts between representatives of development agencies and Maoist cadres also fostered mutual trust between the insurgents and international actors. These interactions further provided valuable insights on the mindset and intentions of the insurgents to Western diplomats who engaged in mediation efforts leading up to the peace process.

Yet not all attempts of aid agencies to adjust to the conflict environment had positive impacts, and some had unintended negative consequences. For instance, in the later phase of the war, aid agencies reduced their capacity-building activities directed to local government authorities and increasingly sought to deliver basic services in rural areas through community-based organizations, project units, and contractors rather than public service providers. They did so in an effort to maintain impartiality in the conflict and because of the inefficiency of local authorities and their unwillingness – with the exception of health workers and village schoolteachers – to venture beyond the narrow limits of district headquarters. Although understandable under the circumstances, this practice further eroded state authority in the districts and led to a lack of coordination and duplication of local development projects, because multiple and parallel reporting lines replaced the centralized clearinghouse role of local authorities.

Some shortcomings notwithstanding, the donor community as a whole was successful in strengthening coordination and following a common agenda for conflict transformation, defense of human rights, and promotion of democratic institutions as necessary preconditions for sustainable development. Aid agencies often shared with each other their respective analysis of the conflict and its implications for development, creating the basis for independent but consistent decisions at the strategic and operational level. In this respect, the Basic Operating Guidelines represented a strong catalyst for donor operations, because they created a sense of solidarity and common purpose. Regular donor meetings to discuss the respect for and implementation of Bogs created opportunities for sharing experiences in conflict-sensitive program management and for a consistent approach to the conflict parties.

THE LIMITS OF A TECHNICAL APPROACH TO DEVELOPMENT COOPERATION

The majority of donors accepted a technical alignment with the government's development policies while refusing to endorse a state that lacked legitimacy and thus the ability to promote development by the people. Given the high quality of the government's 2002–6 Poverty Alleviation Strategy[5] and in view of the prudent

---

[5] The Poverty Alleviation Strategy (known also as "The Tenth Development Plan 2002–2007") was prepared by the government under democratic rule, but was implemented in the years of the armed conflict. The strategy defines clear priorities for public investment and public spending and demonstrates full awareness of the inequalities and discriminations that mar Nepali society. It was produced in a collective effort between committed public servants and international experts. Although the strategy became the official language of the Ministry of Finance when speaking to donors, it was never internalized in the views and actions of political leaders. For more information on the government's development plans, see the website of the National Planning Commission (http://www.npc.gov.np).

macroeconomic policies practiced by subsequent Nepali governments, multilateral and bilateral donors could plan their operations in a stable economic environment and with a sense of a shared development strategy. Some good sectoral policies reinforced this behavior. Donors maintained a strong dialogue with many technical ministries, while at the same time dissociating themselves from any attempt to solve the political crisis by military means. Instead, donors demanded full commitment to human rights and the restoration of democracy as integral parts of a successful development policy.

Differences of opinion within the international community crystallized around the desirability of providing general budgetary support to the autocratic governments that led the country in 2004 and 2005. However, the discussion remained theoretical and never reached a final conclusion, because the conditions that would have made Nepal eligible for a budgetary contribution by the World Bank International Development Agency (an "IDA Poverty Reduction Credit II") were never fulfilled. However, the arguments presented at the time deserve to be recalled because they illustrate real development dilemmas that often emerge in "fragile states."

Donors who opposed providing budgetary support to the government even in the presence of a convincing economic reform agenda put forward four arguments. First, they underscored the international isolation of the government and criticized the fact that its recurrent expenditures had been inflated by substantial increases in military spending, with the Royal Nepalese Army having doubled in size within only four years. Second, in light of the government's inability to productively spend much of its development budget because of the limited geographical reach of the state, they argued that any increase in budgetary resources was unlikely to translate into activities relevant to the majority of the population. Third, they stressed the difficulty of sustaining broad-based growth as long as the conflict persisted, thereby putting a damper on the willingness of the national and international private sector to invest in Nepal. Finally, they argued that general budgetary support was inappropriate in a situation in which traditional reform measures of a technical nature (such as necessary labor market liberalization or changes in administrative ordinances) could not be implemented without stirring new conflicts. Instead, any efforts to improve social and economic life would have to be rooted in a conflict transformation and state-building process.

The donors' dialogue with the authorities was not simple. On the one hand they were compelled to continue technical cooperation around the reasonable development strategy proposed by the government with the few capable technocrats in the Ministry of Finance and in the National Planning Commission. On the other hand, donors rejected the authoritarian style of government imposed by the king and his supporters. This tension also created a deep division in the international community, in particular between the Bretton Woods Institutions and the European bilateral agencies. Ultimately, the more political approach to development cooperation chosen by the majority of the bilateral donors found vindication in the victory of the People's Movement in April 2006. The agencies that had supported democratic values during the conflict could engage in a constructive dialogue with all political forces, including the widely popular Maoists. By contrast, those multilateral agencies, in particular the World Bank, that had opted to follow a purely technical approach in dealing with the government and had ignored its authoritarian practices found themselves out of touch with the reality of the political change, unable to exercise any influence on the main events or to promote their agenda of liberal economic reforms in the new political context.[6]

This lesson may have some general implications for donors' approaches to countries in conflict and in particular for the distribution of roles and responsibilities between (1) bilateral agencies open to engaging in a political discourse to reach development aims and (2) multilateral financial institutions that are forced by statute and by the voting power of their boards to disregard the political nature of conflicts and to pursue under all circumstances the ill-informed wisdom of economic and administrative reforms as an appropriate answer to many countries' problems. Therefore, as long as political factors determine development policies and influence the investment climate of a given country, the coordination of development aid should not be left to Bretton Woods Institutions, but should instead be facilitated by a team of elected local representatives of bilateral donors under UN leadership.

CONTRIBUTIONS TO CONFLICT TRANSFORMATION

Donors' efforts to remain engaged and relevant during the conflict had some positive, albeit modest, effects on the dynamic of the conflict, moderating some of its destructive consequences and contributing to the still ongoing political reconstruction of Nepal.

Against the background of an escalation of the conflict that started with the involvement of the Nepalese Army in 2001, donors joined Nepal's civil society organizations in requesting the deployment of a robust UN human rights mission. The credible activities of the UN Office of the High Commissioner on Human Rights (OHCHR) in Nepal, which was established in 2005, exposed the abuses committed by the parties to the conflict. The presence of OHCHR also moderated the repressive response of the authoritarian state to the People's Movement that defied the king's rule, thereby facilitating a positive and nonviolent outcome of the conflict. The activities of the OHCHR were complemented by those of the UN Resident Representative, who acted as the coordinator of the UN's development presence in Nepal and who was involved in a delicate dialogue with the state's

---

[6] The Independent Evaluation Group of the World Bank in 2008–9 assessed the relevance and effectiveness of the World Bank's country program for the year considered in this chapter. The study confirms in substance that "conflict blindness" reduced the relevance of the World Bank's contribution to development in decisive years. IEG, *Nepal Country Assistance Evaluation 2003–2008*, Washington, DC: World Bank, 2009.

security forces as well as with senior Maoist cadres. The UN's early involvement in and commitment to resolving the conflict in Nepal laid the foundations for the UN peace support mission, set up at the request of the government of Nepal by the UN Security Council in January 2007.

In addition, the provision of basic social services in all parts of the country and the employment generated by the continuous expansion of rural infrastructure in almost all districts, along with remittances transferred by migrant workers to a third of Nepali households, prevented major displacements of people and kept the social fabric of villages and rural communities largely intact. Donor programs strengthened and empowered community-based organizations such as forest and irrigation user groups, mothers' groups, as well as school, health, and roads committees. These elementary institutions partially compensated for the absence of the state in rural areas and allowed for the management of public goods in a political and security vacuum.

Strong donor engagement for the respect of human rights protected a vibrant civil rights movement and the media from total repression. The uninterrupted dialogue with the democratic political parties gave them legitimacy and voice even in periods of authoritarian rule. The civil rights movement and the media were then instrumental in launching the People's Movement and in leading the successful rhododendron revolution against the king's autocratic rule in April 2006.

Donors engaged in but did not limit their criticism to the government. They joined forces with representatives of civil society to protest the abduction of young people and their forced indoctrination by the Maoists, the frequent closure of schools caused by political strikes, and interruptions in the delivery of medicines due to general strikes and blockades. They were also directly involved in political arguments with the insurgents about government policies that had great political relevance, such as the transfer of responsibilities for running primary schools to local communities or the introduction of community-managed and financed drug programs.

The diverse engagement of aid agencies in a difficult development dialogue with Maoist cadres conveyed the message that the insurgents could be accepted as a legitimate force by at least parts of the international community, provided they laid down their arms and entered the democratic process. These messages may have encouraged the CPN-M to enter multiparty competition. Negotiations held during the acute phase of the armed conflict and the transition period also prepared the insurgents to assume executive responsibilities when they were entrusted with cabinet functions and later, after the elections for the Constituent Assembly, led the government of Nepal.

THE UNCERTAIN DONOR ROLE IN AN UNDECIDED TRANSITION

Five years after the signing of the Comprehensive Peace Agreement, the political transition in Nepal has yet to conclude and give way to a modicum of stability.

The parties to the CPA remain divided on critical questions of the peace process, such as integration of Maoist combatants into the Nepalese Army, let alone broader reform of the security sector. There has been no consensus on a common socioeconomic agenda or the transformation of the state into a federal system. The parties represented in the Constituent Assembly have been unwilling to join forces to form a stable coalition government encompassing all major political forces. Personal ambitions of party leaders and rivalries within the main parties have complicated the search for acceptable compromises and alliances. Those political parties that were temporarily excluded from executive responsibilities after the 2008 Constituent Assembly elections have not agreed to play the role of a loyal opposition, but have used all means at their disposal to disrupt economic and political activities and to force their way back into power. Strikes and agitation have frequently disrupted social and economic life, especially in the Kathmandu valley. Ethnic movements fighting for greater regional autonomy, such as the Madhesis in the Terai, have become stronger and have weakened the authority of the central state in many parts of the country without establishing credible alternatives. Representative local bodies have not been restored at the district or the village level, creating a lack of legitimate representation at a critical level of governance that has extended the institutional and political vacuum in rural areas, which is where the majority of the population lives. Under these circumstances the performance of the Nepali economy, although benefiting from prudent macroeconomic management, has been weak. The economy remains highly dependent on the remittances of Nepali migrants, tourism, and the grants and concessionary loans provided by the UN system, the development banks, and bilateral donors, including India.

The development partners in Nepal have actively engaged in the peace process since its beginning, demonstrating considerable commitment to Nepal and a much improved understanding of the particular challenges facing the country. However, against the background of a protracted impasse in the political process, the risk of resumed violence has increased. This situation underlines the limits of international influence on a complex political transition, limits that often contribute to donor fatigue.

In this period of political uncertainty, aid agencies have struggled to merge their engagement for peace and their support for development into one coherent strategy. One of the main obstacles has been the deeply ingrained view of development cooperation as a technical and apolitical process – internationally reinforced in recent years by the rhetoric of the 2005 Paris Declaration on aid effectiveness, the spirit of which is ill suited for conflict situations and peacebuilding. Further, the creation of specialized units within bilateral and multilateral agencies that deal with peace support functions has institutionalized the artificial gap between development and political functions.

The government of Nepal has contributed to this fictitious separation of the political and the development realm by launching, in the spring of 2007, a parallel

Nepal Peace Trust Fund (NPTF) and a new triennial development plan that had no explicit provisions for supporting the peace process. The NPTF was designed to finance the expenditures related to the peace process and the costs of the political transition, such as social programs for internally displaced persons, the cantonment of the Maoist combatants and their reintegration into society, the elections to the Constituent Assembly, the redeployment of police forces to the rural areas, and the reconstruction of physical infrastructure.

Because the government hoped to mobilize large amounts of foreign resources through the NPTF, it did not include NPTF expenditures in the budget of the fiscal year 2007–8. However, the fund, although initially well received, has only mobilized approximately USD 30 million in grants over three years. This disappointing result can be partially explained by the unwillingness or inability of the parties in power to include the opposition parties in the identification, selection, and approval of projects. Meanwhile the Maoists created their own obstacles to the operation of the peace fund by refusing civil servants and donor representatives access to their cantonment sites. On the technical side, many projects presented by the line ministries to the NPTF were of poor quality or were too large or too complex for a program of a transitory character aimed at supporting the peace process. Weak implementation capacity of the line ministries in the area of peacebuilding led donors to ask the United Nations to establish a parallel UN Peace Fund for Nepal. The latter has collected approximately USD 23 million in three years. These resources have been allocated to similar activities as those covered by the NPTF, but under the leadership of a specialized UN agency, thereby generating additional coordination needs. The UN Peace Fund has supported the NPTF in areas sensitive to the peace process, such as the registration of former Maoist combatants and the provision of water to the cantonment sites.

The damaging dual approach to peace and development has also been rein-forced by the government attempt to establish Local Peace Committees (LPCs) in each district, thereby sidestepping the existing local institutions, the Development Committees operating under the authority of the Ministry of Local Development. In addition to being poorly designed, only a handful of LPCs were operational two years after their launch. Rural development programs have long been disrupted by polit-ical factions that tried to divert development resources into their own pockets and used their power to promote a partisan agenda. Following this logic, political parties have often interfered in the decision-making processes of district- and village-level governance structures. It is now evident that it would have been better for the cause of peace as well as for development purposes to promote mediation activities within the established district- and local-level Development Committees instead of establishing parallel and ineffective Local Peace Committees. Nepal can hardly achieve stability and power sharing without the election of local bodies or at least – as a transitional measure – their establishment through representative political parties. The appoint-ment of District and Village Development Committee representatives through elections or by general local consensus would create the conditions for pursuing peace and development processes under the leadership of legitimate authorities.

From a development perspective, the period since the signing of the Comprehensive Peace Agreement has been characterized by an elusive quest for peace dividends. Especially in the first year of precarious peace, as preparations for elections to a Constituent Assembly were underway, the government and many international agencies alike presented Nepal as a postconflict country, entitled to substantive international support to rebuild its destroyed infrastructure and jump-start the economy. This view has proven false in many ways. First, Nepal has not yet entered the postconflict stage: the Maoist combatants still constitute an independent military force, and the constitution that may pacify the country has yet to be written and approved. Second, although Nepal's economy has suffered from frequent changes in government, a poor investment climate, and social tensions, the significant flow of remittances has ensured that savings and resources have stayed at a sustainable level. Third, the country's infrastructure has continuously expanded during the years of the armed conflict, with the insurgency targeting mainly police posts and administrative stations, leaving much of the other physical capital intact.[7] Fourth, the volume of public investments over the past few years has systematically remained below the level of funding available to the government, especially from multilateral sources like the World Bank's International Development Agency or the Asian Development Fund. In other words, implementation capacity – or better – governance of implementation has been the main constraint to the effectiveness of development activities in Nepal. This problem cannot be solved by expanding the aid volume, but only by improving the quality of management in the public sector and by involving donors more closely in the implementation of programs. In the end, the level of development expenditure has not increased significantly since the peace process began. Major improvements have been limited to the social sector, especially in health and education, where enhanced collaboration between ministries and external partners and increases in recurrent expenditures have allowed for meaningful progress.

MAIN CHALLENGES AHEAD

The experience of donors over the years in Nepal has confirmed the close linkage between governance, development, and the promotion of peace. Development actors must address these three areas simultaneously to achieve sustainable results in any. This central observation has powerful implications for the years to come.[8]

---

7 The main physical reconstruction needs result from a lack of maintenance – a structural and governance problem that the conflict has only exacerbated.

8 The need for a coherent approach in this direction underlined the renewed attempt in summer 2009 to formulate a Development Partners' Peace and Development Strategy for Nepal at the initiative

To support the transition toward a "new" Nepal, donors should remain firm in the defense of human rights, democracy, and inclusion. They should continue their dialogue with trustworthy representatives of civil society, collaborate with the media, and support intermediary organizations, while improving their own transparency and accountability vis-à-vis the government and the general population.

The management of aid resources must continue to advance dialogue and state-building from below. The Basic Operating Guidelines remain highly relevant for donors operating in Nepal, as an expression of impartial commitment to poverty alleviation and to transparency, as well as to the needs of development workers for security, respect, and independence.

The practice of inclusion is and will remain a critical component of political renewal and development in Nepal. International agencies should continue to facilitate diversity in all public and private institutions, but will have to start practicing inclusion seriously in their own recruitment and personnel policies while ensuring a similar compliance by the projects they support. Community-based organizations and NGOs should be encouraged to be more inclusive of marginalized groups, to practice power sharing, and to introduce democratic and transparent governance rules.

Above all, it is of paramount importance that poor and excluded groups benefit from basic services and public investments in a nondiscriminatory way. As donors increase the proportion of their development programs implemented through government channels, there is a major opportunity and imperative to encourage the government to adopt more conflict-sensitive development principles. If key government sectors such as education, health, and rural infrastructure are able to maximize their peacebuilding potential, they could have a real impact on rebuilding the relationship between citizens and the state and could contribute to turning the rhetoric of a "new" Nepal into reality.

The planning and the execution of development endeavors must involve emerging local bodies, especially the Village Development Committees, and respect their authority. A participatory and decentralized design of development initiatives may slow down investments and service delivery initially, but is crucial to ensure acceptance and sustainable results. Donor-supported programs should therefore always pursue poverty reduction and institution building simultaneously. These intentions should be reflected in concrete and measurable outputs and outcomes in both directions.

At the national level, donor assistance to the peace process and to development must remain well coordinated. The Nepal Peace Trust Fund created a platform for a formal dialogue between the international community and the government

of the UN Resident Coordinator. Although this strategy, which is supported by the government, is highly relevant, it reveals nevertheless that donors are still trying to identify a convincing development approach three years into the peace process.

in critical areas like the reintegration of former combatants, the elections, and the restoration of the state presence in rural areas. Overall the principal donors should continue to focus on achieving consistency and balance between the activities supported by the Nepal Peace Trust Fund, the UN responses to the peace process, and the priorities of the government development plans elaborated in consultation with the major bilateral donors and the development banks.

4.2

Unleashing Nepal's Economic Potential: A Business Perspective

Sujeev Shakya

INTRODUCTION

Nepalis generally tend to describe their country as small, poor, landlocked, and wedged between its two large neighbors, India and China. The majority of its people see these characteristics as obstacles to Nepal's development or as a threat to its territorial integrity. This self-perception, which has shaped Nepal's social consciousness as dependent on the good will of others while blinding people to its economic potential, can be traced to the time when Prithvi Narayan Shah conquered the kingdoms of the Kathmandu valley in the 1760s, creating the modern state of Nepal. During his reign, rather than ensuring economic development that would benefit the country, the king prioritized his personal gains and those of his kin, setting a pattern that has been followed by all Nepali rulers to this very day. This chapter analyzes why Nepalis have such a fatalistic outlook on their country's economic prospects and argues that this perception can be transformed by their recognition of Nepal's potential to become a vibrant economy – building on the fact that it has the world's 40th largest population and immediate land access to two economic superpowers.

POLITICAL HISTORY THROUGH THE ECONOMIC LENS

The main motivation for Prithvi Narayan Shah to conquer the Kathmandu valley was to gain control of the primary trading and financial hub along the trade route between China and India. The dominance of the Shah dynasty came to a temporary halt when in 1846 Jang Bahadur, in a coup d'etat, assumed executive power and founded the hereditary Rana rule that was to last for 104 years, reducing the monarchy to a titular role. The Ranas sought a close political relationship with the British and even resembled the British East India Company in treating Nepal as a private limited company, earning profits at the country's expense. In 1950, the

Rana dynasty came to an end when King Tribhuvan reestablished the monarchy's predominance. For the next 10 years Nepal was ruled under a democratic system that opened the country to the outside world, politically and economically. In 1952, Nepal became a member state of the Colombo Plan for Cooperative, Economic, and Social Development in Asia and the Pacific and began receiving foreign aid. In 1955 Nepal joined the United Nations. However, successive governments did little to boost the economy. Nepal's brief democratic experiment ended in 1960, when King Mahendra introduced the party-less Panchayat system under his direct rule. Under this system, the king experimented with a mix of socialism and capitalism popularly known as the Nehruvian Mixed Economy, propagated by Jawaharlal Nehru, then India's prime minister. During the 30 years of Panchayat rule (1960–90), members of the royal family controlled business enterprises, including some of the best hotels and major manufacturing companies, while also enjoying a monopoly over import licenses. The king also oversaw socialist programs including various trusts and state-owned enterprises like the Nepal Oil Corporation, the Nepal Electric Authority, and Nepal Telecom. The royal family's predominance in economic and business affairs contributed to slow economic development and growth in Nepal.

The euphoria around the restoration of democracy in 1990 was thwarted both by bitter rivalry among political parties and the attitude of the private sector, which, preferring to hoard rather than compete, pushed for the adoption of protectionist policies. These developments precipitated the stagnation of economic growth and the start of the Maoist insurgency in 1996. A half-decade later, with the insurgency still ongoing, King Gyanendra led Nepal into another phase of direct monarchial rule. However, the king, unwilling to open up the market, failed miserably in managing the economy, which was further hurt by the Maoist People's War. When the 10-year war ended in 2006, the monarchy was stripped of all executive power, and the parties agreed to renegotiate Nepal's social contract in a Constituent Assembly, triggering great hopes among the people for spurred economic development. However, instead of using the postwar period to harness the economic potential of the country, the political elites continued working for their personal benefit.

IMPEDIMENTS TO ECONOMIC GROWTH

Most economic analysis on Nepal tends to be somewhat ahistorical in that it primarily focuses on developments since 1990. During that period, international donors started commissioning economic analysis from external consultants who heavily influenced development thinking in Nepal but knew little about the country's history or political culture. However, to fully understand the impediments to the country's economic growth it is important to look back at developments since the birth of the state of Nepal. The following provides an overview of the key factors explaining Nepal's poor economic performance.

Corruption, Patronage, and a Predatory Elite

Throughout Nepal's history, the ruling elite, whether drawn from the Shah dynasty, the Rana regime, or the political parties, has always put its self-interest before the interest of the Nepali people. Holding power was understood as a means to increase personal wealth rather than assuring the distribution of economic gains among the larger population. In this embedded culture of corruption and cronyism, establishing who was given a road construction contract was always more important than identifying which area was in greatest need of a road. Similarly, a location of a new health center was selected on the basis of whose land was to be acquired, rather than which villages would benefit the most from improved health services. When Rana rulers put up the first power plant, it served merely to light their palace. Even today, electricity connections in rural areas are provided mainly to people in power. Similarly, in urban areas, affluent neighborhoods have access to uninterrupted power, while the rest of the nation suffers through 18 hours of daily power cuts.

These predatory practices of the elite are rooted in a system of patronage that originated in the Shah dynasty, which fostered a culture that revolved around *chakri* – a sycophantic custom, later institutionalized by the Ranas, of being seen around people in power at certain hours of the day to extract favors: it was the very antithesis of a meritocratic system. To this day, from appointments in the bureaucracy and the granting of business licenses to educational scholarships – all depend on relationships rather than merit. Through the extension of *jagir* – short-term land grants that are explained in more detail later – beneficiaries gained access to top positions in the government and the diplomatic service as well as teaching assignments, positions in health services, or careers in philanthropic institutions.

During the Panchayat years, the two Shah kings ensured that their family members received a cut of the profits from private and state-owned enterprises and exploited unrestricted access to high-revenue nonprofits, such as the trusts established for the Pashupati Temple, the Buddhist pilgrimage site Lumbini, and nature conservation projects. In addition, the queen and her nominees controlled the powerful Social Service National Coordination Council (SSNCC) that was created to monitor and streamline foreign aid. In the 1990s, when the Nepali Congress and United Marxist Leninist (UML) parties alternated in leading successive governments, they emulated the royal family's practice of nominating mostly incompetent political cadres to management positions of state-owned enterprises and public trusts. That Royal Nepal Airlines (Nepal Airlines), a government corporation, saw nearly a dozen chief executive officers in as many years is a reflection of this corrupt patronage system. When the Maoists temporarily came to power in 2008–9, their leadership succumbed to the temptation of profit-making that benefited the party and its cadres, continuing the system of crony capitalism. For example, the Maoists expended great effort to gain control of the Pashupati Area Development Trust, the country's most lucrative temple business earlier patronized by the queen.

In this system of patronage, academic achievement as a criterion for professional recruitment became secondary, thereby undermining educational standards. Unsurprisingly, Nepal's education system in which, until 2006, more than half the students failed the final examinations of their secondary education,[1] still performs poorly even by regional standards. Those who can afford a better education go to schools or universities in India and elsewhere. Those leaving Nepal tend to stay abroad.

Dependence

In the context of increasing geopolitical competition between India and China, culminating in a brief war in 1962, both countries, despite being themselves aid recipients, emerged as early as 1952 as donors in Nepal in their quest to win greater influence over the country. Nepal exploited this dynamic, trying to play the two powerful neighbors against each other in an effort to extract more aid. Success of high-level visits to either of the two countries was defined in terms not of agreements on investment and trade but of the amount of aid generated.

Throughout the 1990s, both India and China enjoyed considerable influence over Nepal, with the monarchy seeking their political support and the political party leaders assigning more importance to cultivating relationships with Delhi and Beijing than with their own constituencies. This situation prevailed despite the occasional tendency of Nepali political players to invoke anti-Indianism to shore up domestic political support. For example, toward the end of the 1990s some elements within Nepal, especially the different communist parties including the Maoists, succeeded in promoting Nepali nationalism with a strong anti-Indian tilt,[2] resulting in labor strikes and the closure of Indian companies by politically backed labor unions and discouraging the flow of formal Indian investment to Nepal. However, the majority of people in Nepal, particularly those living outside the Kathmandu valley near the border towns as well as in the western hills, have always seen – and continue to do so today – India as an economic and social safety net, be it for jobs, business opportunities, education, or health care. For instance, when patients cannot be treated in hospitals in the Terai, physicians tend to refer them across the border; when Nepali schools and colleges close down for long stretches, parents take their kids to schools in northern India. Nepal's strong dependence on India for financial, political, economic and social support has created a complex relationship between the two countries that will be difficult for Nepal to overcome. Meanwhile, China's interest in Nepal is primarily focused on containing anti-China activities, especially those led by the Tibetan Diaspora in Nepal.

---

[1] Department of Education, *Education for All: Secondary Education Support Program & Community School Support Program Report,* 2007 and Office of the Controller of Examinations (OCE), 2010.

[2] Anti-Indianism among the Nepali communist parties goes back to the 1950s and has its origins in the context of growing tensions between China and India.

This dependence feeds Nepalis' prevailing lack of belief in their country's potential to transform itself into an economic player in its own right and has led its leaders to aim for and its people to expect only modest development gains. Policy makers have refrained from long-term planning and instead introduced successive five-year plans that relied heavily on foreign assistance, especially from India. This reliance is best reflected in the contribution of foreign aid to Nepal's GDP, which increased from 2% in 1960 to just more than 10% by 1990. In absolute terms, Nepal saw an increase in aid from around USD 14 million during the entire decade of the 1960s to around USD 382 million between 2000 and 2002. This increase has made Nepal the most aid-dependent country in South Asia, with the highest foreign aid to GDP ratio in the region.[3]

Politics of Land Use and Rent Seeking

Nepal's successive ruling elites exploited the use and distribution of land for political purposes, thereby negating its economic potential. This exploitation was a continuation of the *jagir* system, in which land was assigned to state servants in lieu of salary or rented out to those favored by the ruling elite. These land holdings were the sole source of income for a family and as such defined one's power and weight. However, because the land was only owned temporarily, the system emphasized land exploitation over the gradual development of agricultural productivity, which as a result remained low. The per capita income for agricultural workers in Nepal today is among the lowest in South and Southeast Asia.[4] In addition, because large landholdings provided the owners with considerable political influence, the elites, instead of using their land, held onto it as a nonproductive asset. This system of landownership was an extension of Nepal's feudal system, fostering a culture in which people preferred to exploit resources rather than using them productively.

The Dominance of the Informal Sector

The Nepali economy, in particular agriculture, is dominated by the informal sector. In the nonagricultural sector, trade features more prominently than manufacturing or the service sector. Trade is largely controlled by Nepalis of Indian origin, Newar families, and some Rana families who have extensive networks in both countries.

Nepal's fragile political environment since the 1950s encouraged short-term rather than long-term investments, which, coupled with high import duties and currency exchange restrictions imposed by India until the early 1990s, contributed to the emergence of Nepal's strong informal economy. The trade in precious metals,

---

[3] *Macroeconomic Indicators of Nepal*, Research Department, Nepal Rastra Bank, July 2009.
[4] *Country Diagnostic Studies – Highlights Nepal: Critical Development Constraints*, ADB/DFID/ILO, 2009, p. 15.

especially gold, and in other goods imported from different parts of the world and then smuggled into India constituted a large part of informal economic activity in Nepal. For instance, in early 1990 gold was second only to the import of petroleum products into Nepal.[5] This trend resurfaced in 2008 with gold imports worth NPR 41.3 billion (an increase of 151% compared to previous year) following petroleum imports worth NPR. 53.2 billion.[6] Because the majority of trade consisted of exporting goods into the closed Indian economy, smuggling was not considered an immoral activity, and smugglers were not socially looked down on. The political protection that smugglers enjoyed first from the Rana rulers and then from the Shah kings and political parties meant that they could continue their activities undisturbed. However, while the individual wealth of businesspeople and their patrons grew, the state treasury remained dry.

In comparison, the private sector lacked ambition, and entrepreneurs focused on cultivating their relations with power centers, creating and doing business limited to trade, and taking advantage of arbitrage opportunities. Despite many opportunities created by the democratic transitions in 1950, 1990, and 2008 – opening of the markets by encouraging deregulation, opening opportunities for foreign joint venture investments and technology transfers, and passing reform-oriented laws – the business community shied away from making ambitious plans. Instead, business leaders focused on using their positions in various Nepali trade-related chambers and associations to influence government policies to their benefit, for instance by advocating for the imposition either of tariff barriers or export subsidies. Just as did the royal family, most Nepali entrepreneurs still consider hobnobbing with politicians a more productive investment than increasing business competencies to take on competition.

Seeking Opportunities Elsewhere

Although many see mass migration as a recent phenomenon, Nepal in fact has always had a high outflow of emigrants who have sought better economic opportunities elsewhere.[7] Although at times political compulsions were a factor in driving large waves of Nepalis abroad – for instance in the 1850s under the fledgling Rana regime or in the early 2000s at the height of the Maoist insurgency – economics has always been a driving force. The fatalist attitude of Nepalis toward their country's economic possibilities predisposes parents to encourage their children to migrate. Of nearly the half-million Nepalis who come to the job market every year, 300,000 people migrate. The large percentage of children of government servants and businesspeople migrating reflects this reality.

---

[5] *Economic Surveys*, Government of Nepal, Ministry of Finance.

[6] Oil, Gold, Vehicles top Nepal's import list. *The Kathmandu Post*, September 9, 2010.

[7] David Seddon, with Jagannath Adhikari and Ganesh Gurung, *Foreign Labor Migration and the Remittance Economy of Nepal*, Critical Asian Studies, London: Routledge, 2002.

There are four categories of migrants. First, a small number are people who have high skills like medical doctors, accountants, and nurses who migrate to the United Kingdom, Australia, and Europe. Second, there are students who go to the United States, United Kingdom, and Australia for education and never return to Nepal. To put the numbers into perspective in 2009, 11,233 Nepali students entered the United States for education,[8] making Nepal 11th in the list of countries sending students to the United States. The third category comprises semi-skilled workers – plumbers, carpenters, mechanics, etc. – who migrate to countries in the Middle East, Southeast Asia, or Korea. Finally, a significant number of unskilled workers leave, mostly for India. In 2009–10, the combined remittances from Nepalis working abroad totaled NPR 231 billion (USD 3 billion).[9] It is estimated that an additional USD 500 million enter Nepal through informal remittance channels. In 2009–10, remittances accounted for 25% of GDP.

Failed Development Reforms and Poor Infrastructure Development

In Nepali, the same word (*bikas*) is used for both aid and development. In its colloquial use, the term *bikas* also stands for commodities of nonlocal origin, thus imbuing the concept of economic development with a connotation of something imposed and foreign. Reinforcing this notion was the fact that government spending on development programs was completely dependent on foreign aid. Anything to do with development was seen as something imposed on Nepal, and debates on whether or not development was a form of imperialism were quite common. Better health care and education and an improved quality of life were perceived as something that outsiders wanted for Nepal. Successive governments viewed their development policies as something they had to put in place to please the bilateral and multilateral donors. Similarly, the economic reforms implemented in the 1990s were not driven by a homegrown desire to jump-start the Nepali economy through market-oriented and liberal economic policies, but were carried out in response to "directives" from the World Bank and IMF and later other donor agencies that wanted to reform Nepal's economy. Opening of the markets and the economy was anathema, particularly to the private sector that wanted a continuation of the protectionist policies that had benefited them so well in the past.

As with other development aspects, infrastructure development was also deemed to be something imposed on Nepal; it has relied on bilateral and multilateral funding, which partly explains why it is in such poor state. Infrastructure projects, such as highway construction, often reflected a combination of donor preferences and interests of a few influential politicians rather than strategic economic considerations. Because the government exclusively relied on donors to build and improve

---

[8] *Open Doors 2010*, Institute of International Education.
[9] Economic Survey, Government of Nepal, Ministry of Finance.

Nepal's infrastructure, its development took place at a slow pace. The government was never interested in letting the private sector take on infrastructure development under "build, operate, and transfer schemes."[10] For instance, in the energy sector, the government preferred to rely on donors for building power plants rather than allowing successful national independent power producers to take on the challenge, despite the acute shortage of power. The fact that donors continued to cooperate on questionable projects (which often fostered corruption) demonstrates that they were more interested in ticking off items on planning documents than in seeing real development in Nepal.

The Aid Playing Field

Since Nepal received its first aid package in the 1950s, the country has remained a fertile ground for experimentation in bilateral and multilateral aid activities. Foreign aid in Nepal is understood to encompass a broad range of activities, ranging from technical grants, loans, scholarships, and endowments to all forms of assistance in cash and kind provided by multilateral organizations, bilateral organizations, international nongovernmental organizations (NGOs), private foundations, and even foreign individuals. This rather nebulous understanding of foreign aid makes the term itself ambiguous and confusing. Consecutive governments viewed foreign aid as a gift or favor bestowed on Nepal in different forms. Ironically, this notion echoes the view of the governments during the Panchayat years, which considered national welfare programs an act of kindness from the crown bequeathed on the loyal subjects of the nation. Evident in both views is the creation of a hierarchical relationship that precipitates an enduring dependence.

The restoration of democracy in 1990 saw the emergence of a plethora of national NGOs, alongside the arrival of a plethora of international NGOs. Some of the national NGOs resembled political parties in that they were headed by political figures who used the organization to further their political goals. By providing perks and benefits to their members, these agencies reproduced the *jagir* system.

The presence of so many organizations involved in the development business also created a report-writing and conference-hopping culture that killed the creativity of those who were best placed to find innovative solutions to Nepal's development problems. The scores of gender-mainstreaming, social- inclusion, and community-mobilizing experts who emerged outnumbered those aid workers on the ground who would investigate reasons for shortcomings in education, help better manage small enterprises, or provide improved access to financing for the poor.

---

[10] Under this model, the government contracts infrastructure development to private sector companies for a specific lease period to cover the cost of construction. On completion the companies transfer ownership back to the government.

Currently, Nepal receives about USD 460 million annually of foreign aid as part of its budget, much of which remains unspent.[11] Bilateral and multilateral agencies continue to provide grants to Nepal that are not coordinated with the government's development plan or channeled through the government treasury. This lack of oversight means that countries are free to provide grants directly to organizations in Nepal, as India does through its embassy, which finances the building of schools, or like the Chinese government that sets up cultural centers around Nepal. The absence of aid coordination has hampered its overall effectiveness. The government's release of the guidelines, *Foreign Aid Policy, 2002*, was the first attempt to establish an aid policy for Nepal, but it has never been fully implemented. Meanwhile, from the donor perspective, extensive government corruption is seen as a strong disincentive to providing the country with direct budgetary support.

The biggest negative impact of aid has been its effect on the country's labor market, as the development sector has diverted most of the highly skilled workers away from the private sector and government toward higher paying donor-related jobs.

In combination, these factors help explain why Nepal's growth rate is so dismal 60 years after the country officially opened up its markets to and why it remains one of the poorest countries in the world in terms of per capita income.

ROAD TO CONFLICT

The Maoists long argued that, although Nepal was bestowed with many resources, the feudal lords were parasitic, exploiting these resources for their own benefit and neglecting the country's economic development. They argued that the insurgency was thus needed to replace the corrupt elite and ensure the people's participation in Nepal's future economic development.[12] Five key factors help explain the outbreak of the insurgency: the first three are socioeconomic in nature, and the last two political.

The first and most fundamental factor is pervasive exclusion. In addition to large class divides, the country has an ethnically diverse population, of which many groups are culturally, socially, and politically marginalized. The Maoists understood the frustrations of these excluded groups and enticed them to join their movement by promising not only political space but also access to economic resources and opportunities. The second factor is the absence of a middle class. In Nepal's economic structure only a handful of wealthy people enjoyed access to economic opportunities. This meant that Nepal failed to develop a significant middle class with access to economic opportunities and stakes in the country's stability. The third factor is

---

[11] See tables 2.8 and 2.9 in *Economic Survey 2009/10*, Ministry of Finance, July 2010, and *Macroeconomic Indicators of Nepal*, Research Department, Nepal Rastra Bank, July 2009, table 13.

[12] Shakya, Sujeev, *Unleashing Nepal*, London: Penguin, 2009.

Kathmandu-centric growth. For more than 240 years, Kathmandu has been Nepal's political and economic center, leading to a disconnect with the population outside the valley. As the Kathmandu-based elite dominated all economic sectors, it excluded the rest of the nation from participating in economic activities. In devising development and infrastructure projects, successive governments prioritized Kathmandu while paying little attention to development in other parts of Nepal. Budgets allocated to districts and villages were disbursed only at the end of the fiscal year, leaving the local authorities with few options but to squander it. Given its superior access to education and health services, Kathmandu valley became the prime destination for internal migration. The increasing disenchantment of the population living outside the Kathmandu valley with the elites was a primary reason for the onset of the war.

The fourth factor, political in nature and more immediate, related to the people's heightened – and eventually unrealized – expectations for improved living conditions in the wake of the restoration of multiparty democracy in 1990. In trying to build their constituencies, political parties competed with each other in offering election promises they knew they would be unable to keep. If one political party promised workers who joined their union a 100% wage increase, its rivals doubled that promise, creating unrealistic expectations among the population. When the inability of the parties to deliver on their promises became obvious, the Maoists took advantage of the widely felt sense of betrayal. Last not least, and intrinsically linked to the other factors, is malgovernance. After the restoration of democracy in 1990, political parties created structures and embarked on behavior that closely resembled those of the Rana and Shah factions during the Panchayat years of absolute monarchy. Politicians continued the system of patronage that favored their political cadres or financiers, which led to a sense of hopelessness among Nepalis. Tired of the frequent changes in coalitions, parties, and government, the people gave the benefit of the doubt to direct rule of the king for a while; however, this only escalated the conflict.

Although the economic impact of the conflict has been significant, an even greater impact has been on society. It will take time to reestablish the social fabric and trust. There is a strong undercurrent of resentment between victims and oppressors, whether they are Maoist or security forces, with feelings of anger, hatred, and revenge in people's minds and hearts. Sadly, the conflict has also shattered Nepal's reputation as a friendly and peaceful tourist destination.

UNLEASHING NEPAL'S POTENTIAL

Examining the transformation of economies that have successfully evolved from developing countries into industrialized high-income economies within 50 years, such as Malaysia, provides hope that the Nepali economy may emulate that experience. In 1950 Malaysia had a GDP 2.5 times that of Nepal, but by 2008, Malaysia's

GDP was 36 times higher. To realize its development potential, Nepal will have to undertake some fundamental changes, not only in economic terms but also in the social realm. Nepal has to realize the competitive advantage of its geopolitical location between the two emerging economic superpowers, China and India. It has to be able to harness its resources to complement the growth of these two countries and at the same time increase the income levels of its 30 million people.

Fortunately, Nepal is endowed with vast natural resources, a young and large labor force, and various world heritage sites that all provide readily available economic opportunities.

Hydropower: With its glacier-fed rivers flowing south to India, Nepal is endowed with abundant water resources that can be harnessed for irrigation and clean energy generation. The country's hydropower potential is estimated to be 42,000 MW, with neighboring India providing an energy-hungry and readily accessible export market.[13] Although Nepal ranks low in terms of actual energy consumption, this is a result of the lack of supply rather than demand. Indeed, there is a potential for vast growth in domestic energy consumption. In addition, the ready availability of electricity would attract foreign investments and spur industrial development.

Indo-Gangetic Plains: The Indo-Gangetic plains that encompass southern Nepal as well as parts of India, Pakistan, and Bangladesh are among the most fertile lands in Southern Asia, sparing Nepal the food crises and famines so common in parts of sub-Saharan Africa. Although only 16% of the total land is arable,[14] improved farming techniques would increase overall productivity levels. With 73.9% of the population engaged in the agricultural sector, which contributes 33.03% to the national GDP, the impact of increased productivity would be considerable.[15]

Biodiversity: Nepal's diverse geography, which features high-altitude mountains, plains, rain forests, and desert areas, boasts a vast biodiversity that can be harnessed for commercial purposes. For example, Nepal hosts thousands of species of plants and herbs used for medical and cosmetic purposes. A recent study on the commercial exploitation of these nontimber forest products indicates a low utilization of these resources, contributing to only USD 1.4 million in government revenues.[16] In addition, part of the trade in medical plants – for example, the trade in Yarchagumba, a plant used in the production of aphrodisiacs – is under the complete control of certain political groups that levy heavy informal taxes from collection to distribution.[17] A few companies such as Dabur, an Indian transnational, have been

---

[13] CIA, *World Fact Book*, last modified Dec. 8, 2010. Available from https://www.cia.gov/library/publications/the-world-factbook/geos/np.html, last accessed Dec. 17, 2010.
[14] Ibid.
[15] *Nepal Labor Force Survey Report*, Central Bureau of Statistics, Nepal, 2008.
[16] See, for example, *The Potential and Approach for Enhancing Private Sector Initiative in Nepal's Forestry Sector*, Nepal Economic Forum, 2010.
[17] Gold Rush in Dolpo," *Nepali Times*, 151, June 27–July, 3 2003.

able to take advantage of Nepal's biodiversity by producing an ayurvedic product that consists of ingredients that have all been derived from Nepal.

Tourism: Nepal has several world heritage sites, among them Lumbini, Buddha's birthplace, as well as 8 of the 10 highest mountains in the world and a diverse wildlife population. Close to 400,000 tourists visit every year. By 2020, India and China will each add 50 million and 100 million[18] prospective customers to the global tourist industry, and Nepal with its nearby location could become a prime destination if the appropriate infrastructure can be developed. To develop its tourist industry, Nepal needs to attract international hotel chains, operators, and service providers by providing an investor-friendly environment.

Youthful Labor Force: With a population of 30 million, Nepal is the 40th most populous country in the world, and it is also one of the youngest – half the population is under the age of 25.[19] Given the aging populations of more and more developed countries, Nepal has the potential to produce trained human resources for the world that will not only perform mundane manual labor but will also move up the value chain very quickly. Nepalis working in other countries have earned respect for their hard work and loyalty outside Nepal, even though the workforce in Nepal generates only low levels of productivity. The popularity of Nepali workers outside Nepal has been identified with the Gurkha soldiers who have been donning the uniforms of several foreign armies. This has created a "brand perception" of Nepalis as loyal and brave people in the security business. However, the biggest assets of the Nepali people remain their ubiquitous smile and charm, which have made them successful in the hospitality as well as in nursing/caregiving sectors around the world. Yet, Nepal has never been able to fully exploit the innate skills of its people in these fields and to replicate the success of service oriented businesses in Southasia and South East Asia.

Nepal has to do more to provide lucrative jobs to its half-million people who seek employment each year. One option is to increase employment opportunities in infrastructure projects. Government policies that strengthen the private sector including self-employment will help provide a solution to the prevailing unemployment and underemployment problems that Nepal faces.

Access to Dynamic Markets: Nepal has always looked at its political boundaries with India and China from a purely geopolitical perspective rather than an economic one. Yet, its position between both countries offers unique possibilities. China and India are the world's two fastest growing markets, and both of these markets are easily accessible via land routes; Nepal also shares an open border with India. Although there are already high levels of informal trade, exchange of services, and investment flow between India and Nepal, more has to be done to formalize the trade.

---

[18] Pacific Asia Travel Association reports.
[19] *World Population Prospects: The 2008 Revision*, United Nations, Department of Economic and Social Affairs, Population Division, 2009.

For example, servicing parts of the Indian market, especially its large northern and northeastern markets, is easier from the bordering towns of Nepal than from the cities in South India.

Similarly, access to the autonomous region of Tibet is easier through Nepal than through many major cities in China. Nepal could produce and supply food items like fruits and vegetables to the Tibetan region by allowing Chinese companies to establish processing and packaging plants in Nepal. Chinese companies that have established themselves as successful construction companies can then begin to build infrastructure.

The current policy prohibiting investments by Nepalis outside Nepal should be reviewed. If investments by Nepalis in India and other countries were made transparent and legal, Nepal would emerge as a beneficiary as Nepali investors rode the Indian growth wave. Although Indian businesspeople control a good portion of Nepali businesses, most of these operations, especially outside Kathmandu and in the border areas, have remained in the informal economy and so fail to generate any tax revenue.

Necessary Changes

Because of the interlinked nature of business and politics in Nepal, economic development is strongly politicized. More often than not, political bickering gets in the way of project development and unnecessarily prolongs implementation. Media and the society at large thus tend to pay more attention to the political reactions to a project than to the economic benefits it may bring. There needs to be a shift away from overpoliticizing issues toward a more hands-on economic analysis of the projects in question.

Political parties should move beyond the anachronistic debate, still going on in Nepal, over the virtues of capitalism versus socialism. Unfortunately, the development strategies of all political parties – except for some at the fringe – are rooted in socialist ideology and are largely copies of the failed Nehruvian model that India has long since shunned. Ultimately, the political ideologues are opposed to the institutionalization of an open market economy because they fear it would mean a loss of the political clout they enjoy with the current protectionist policies that benefit private sector enterprises. They also fear losing control over the country's key resources and state-owned enterprises like the airline and the electricity corporation, which provide income and job opportunities for their political cadres. Because political parties, including the Maoists, need populist handouts to ensure political survival, they are more concerned with keeping the labor unions happy than with strengthening private enterprises that could prove to be an important source of employment for Nepal.

Nepal should move in the direction of a model of welfare capitalism that combines economic freedom and free enterprise but ensures that the state provides some social safety nets to its citizen. Such a system would provide the necessary environment for the private sector to flourish, allowing wealth creation through private enterprises instead of the government or donors.

Nepal needs to make sweeping changes to successfully integrate with the global market economy. Some changes are cultural and include doing away with the national calendar in favor of the Gregorian one or substituting Nepal's fiscal year (that begins and ends in mid-July) with a more internationally compatible schedule. In addition, Nepal needs to adopt global accounting, financial, and banking practices so that domestic firms can compete with global companies.

Nepal's private sector, too, can do more to make itself competitive in the global market and to take the lead in bringing about the right impetus for economic growth of the domestic market. Because for private sector firms every individual is an existing or a future customer, they need to find innovative ways to reach consumers at the bottom of the income pyramid. If there are people who want to wash their hair with shampoo but cannot afford the shampoo bottles, then the market for the one-rupee sachets becomes a big market to tap into. If one is to sell infant food supplements in rural areas, then it will be important to make clean drinking water available, because the chances of the product failing will be due more to the quality of water than to the quality of the product. Therefore, having access to clean drinking water should be the agenda not only of the government but also of private sector players. The private sector will need to assist the government in forming policies that will facilitate a level playing field and in creating systems and processes based on transparency and good governance. In this context, the private sector should work with the government – federal and local – as well as aid agencies, community-based organizations, and other interest groups to foster the right set of policies and spearhead activities that can bring about rapid economic growth.

SUSTAINING PEACE FOR DEVELOPMENT

Nepal can do much to spur economic growth and development even before the peace process is completed. Yet, who can drive the necessary change? In the postconflict period, key political actors have lost credibility within their own constituencies as well as with the public at large. As a result, their ability to conclude the peace process has been compromised, and even if they do deliver, the sustainability of the results will be in doubt for some time, creating an unstable investment environment.

It thus becomes even more important for the private sector to take the lead in creating trust in and promoting the credibility of Nepal and in generating opportunities for itself and others. This success of this effort in turn will depend on how well Nepal can transform itself into a capitalist welfare state. Giving priority to long-term economic growth will mean relegating politics to second place, as in India today, and giving responsibility for leading and delivering the economic agenda to the private sector. The private sector will have to develop the means to deal with the exigencies of politics and of the government, but in the end, as in countries that have emerged out of long periods of economic stagnation, the results of economic recovery based on the internal development of enterprises and human resources will prove themselves to the population. In addition, the government must emerge as a strong regulator instead of a business actor in its own right and focus on harnessing resources for improved social service delivery. The increased economic activity can definitely go a long way in funding the welfare activities of the state.

5

Ethnic Politics and the Building of an Inclusive State

Mahendra Lawoti

In the course of the last two decades, ethnic politics in Nepal has received increasing attention in academia and the media. This is largely a reflection of the mobilization of marginalized ethnic, caste, regional, and religious groups after the democratic transition in 1990. The high rate of participation of ethnic and caste groups in the armed Maoist rebellion, launched in 1996, also highlighted ethnic grievances.

However, ethnic dynamics have always played a central role in Nepali politics. For most of the country's history, these dynamics were reflected in ethnic hegemony by one group – the caste hill Hindu elite (CHHE) – that discriminated against other ethnic, caste, and religious groups both culturally and economically and excluded them from formal politics. Dalits, indigenous nationalities, Madhesis, and Muslims were particularly discriminated against and repressed. Before the 1990s, tight control and effective oppression largely succeeded in suppressing public resistance, resulting in a deceptive façade of peace and ethnic harmony, which the state tirelessly propagated through school textbooks, an official narrative of Nepal's history, and the media. It was a "peace" based on hierarchy and inequality among groups and maintained through coercive force.

Since 1990, and against the background of the democratization of the political system, ethnic politics has been in a process of profound transformation from mono-ethnic to poly-ethnic politics, challenging the hegemonic ethnic domination of the CHHE in state and society. As does any challenge to the existing order, this ongoing transformation necessarily carries the potential for increased ethnic conflict and instability, thereby placing a premium on properly managing the empowerment of marginalized groups.

In this context the chapter reviews ethnic politics in Nepal to analyze possible implications for the ongoing peace process. The first section provides an overview

I would like to thank participants of the conference held in November 2009 at New York University, the editors of the volume, and Alischa Kugel for helpful feedback on an earlier draft.

of Nepal's diverse ethnic population and the challenges this diversity poses for the country. The second section describes how ethnic politics in Nepal has been changing with the increasing political assertion by and mobilization of the traditionally marginalized groups, in particular Dalits, Adibasi Janajatis (indigenous nationalities), and Madhesis. To explain this transformation, the third section discusses the role of ethnic groups in the Maoist rebellion and in the second People's Movement that forced the king to give up political power he had progressively usurped from 2002 onward. The fourth section analyzes the status of marginalized groups in various state institutions to assess the ongoing transformation in formal politics after the peace process began in 2006. The last section discusses the resistance by the conservative and status quo-ist forces to the inclusion of marginalized groups in state structures and the role of the media, which is largely controlled by the CHHE, in sustaining the status quo.

MULTIETHNIC/CASTE, MULTILINGUISTIC, AND MULTIRELIGIOUS NEPAL

Nepal is a multilinguistic, multireligious, and multiethnic/caste society. Many ethnic groups have their own languages, of which around 100 are still spoken today. Some languages even have their own scripts, whereas the languages of smaller groups are almost extinct. There are a half-dozen religious groups in Nepal led by the Hindus who, as of 2001, comprised 80.6% of the population.[1] The next largest groups are Buddhists, Muslims, Kiratis, and Christians, which make up 10.7%, 4.2%, 3.6%, and 0.5% of the population, respectively.[2] Despite the diversity in religion and language, politics is primarily underpinned by ethnicity and caste in Nepal. The four major ethnic/caste categories are the CHHE (which include the four main caste groupings: Bahun, Chhetri, Thakuri, and Sanyasi), indigenous nationalities, Madhesis, and Dalits (see Table 5.1).[3]

The CHHE, accounting for 30.89% of Nepal's total population, is the ruling hill "upper" caste group and can be considered a separate ethnic group because its constituent castes share the same language (Nepali aka Khas-kura), religion (Hinduism), lifestyle, dress code, values, and norms; these features have dominated Nepal's sociopolitical and cultural life since the state's founding in 1769. Even though all four castes that make up the CHHE have superior access to the state and

---

[1] Lawoti 2005.
[2] The hill Hindu caste system has only four castes, and the artisan caste is considered "untouchables" in the hills.
[3] The term "ethnic/caste category" refers to a broader aggregate identity designation (Dalit, Madhesi, and indigenous nationalities) in contrast to ethnic/caste group, which is used here to refer to individual entities. For example, indigenous nationalities is a category, whereas Newar is an individual indigenous group.

TABLE 5.1. *Ethnic/caste population, 2001*

Ethnic/caste group	Population	%
CHHE	7,023,220	30.89
Chhetri	4,126,743	18.15
Bahun	2,896,477	12.74
Indigenous Peoples	8,271,975	36.31
Mountain	190,107	0.82
Hill (excluding Newar)	4,793,274	21.03
Newar	1,245,232	5.48
Inner Terai	251,117	1.11
Terai	1,786,986	7.85
Unknown	5,259	0.02
Dalit	3,233,448	14.99
Hill	1,611,135	7.09
Madhesi	1,622,313	6.74
Unknown	173,401	0.76
Madhesi	3,778,136	16.59
High and other castes	2,802,187	12.30
Muslim	975,949	4.29
Other	265,721	1.16

Source: Bhattachan (2008).[4]

societal resources compared to the other three ethnic/caste groups, some variation does exist within the group in gaining access to these resources.

Indigenous nationalities (Adibasi Janajatis), which are native groups with traditional homelands, make up around 36% of the population. They face pervasive linguistic, religious, and sociocultural discrimination as well as unequal access to resources. In the late 1990s, the government came up with a list of 59 indigenous groups. Among these, the Newars are comparably privileged in terms of access to state resources, although the state has done little to support the promotion and preservation of their language. Meanwhile, Buddhist Newars (making up around 15% of that community) were considered "less equal" than their Hindu brethren.

The Madhesis, who share a language, culture, and traditions with North Indian people, are settled in the Terai. They comprise 12.30% of the population if only non-Dalit caste Hindus are counted and 32.29% when Terai indigenous nationalities (8.96%), Terai Dalits (6.74%), and Muslims[5] (4.29%) are included. They too face linguistic discrimination and unequal access to state and societal resources. Because

---

4 As mentioned earlier, some identities overlap in Nepal. The table therefore provides subgroups within different categories.
5 Hill residents often categorize Muslims as Madhesi because most of them also live in the Terai.

of their close cultural cross-border ties with India, most other groups often question the Madhesis' loyalty to Nepal. As a result, they are often not treated as equal citizens.

As the "lowest" Hindu caste, the Dalits, who constitute 14.99% of the population, are affected by the widespread practice of untouchability that considers them impure, denies them entry into "higher" caste homes, and generally segregates them from the social mainstream. The Hindi-speaking Madhesi Dalits also experience linguistic discrimination. Even though the Dalits are culturally less marginalized than indigenous nationalities and Madhesis, because they belong to the same religion – and in the case of the hill Dalits – speak the same language as the CHHE, they suffer the highest level of exclusion in terms of accessing state and societal resources.

The Dalits, indigenous nationalities, and Madhesis are not homogeneous groups, and the degree of exclusion and discrimination they experience often depends on the subgroups to which they belong. The Dalits are not only divided along hill and Terai groups but also among various subcastes. Likewise, among Madhesi Hindus, the "upper" caste groups are less excluded from socioeconomic and political power than the "lower" castes. In addition to caste divisions, Madhesis are further divided along religious lines (Hindu, Muslim, and animist), language, and ethnicity (indigenous versus others), whereas the indigenous nationalities are divided along ethnic, linguistic, and religious lines as well as in terms of geographic location: mountain, hill, inner Terai, and Terai. However, despite these differences within the various groups, individuals belonging to any of the disadvantaged groups face collective discrimination based on their ethnic/caste identity.[6]

Identities of some subgroups overlap. For instance, Terai Dalits can be considered Madhesis as well as Dalits, both based on their perception by others and in terms of self-identification. Some Terai Dalits, indigenous nationalities, and Muslims prefer to be identified as Madhesis, whereas others reject the Madhesi identity. Although some Terai-based indigenous nationalities, Dalits, and Muslims participated in the Madhesi movement that demanded rights and better representation for their people and that gained momentum in 2007, members of the same groups launched street movements in early 2009 to protest the government's categorization of all nonhill residents of Terai as Madhesis. Subgroups that fall into two disadvantaged categories face double discrimination. For instance, Madhesi Dalits face discrimination for being Dalit and for being Madhesi.

FROM MONO-ETHNIC TO POLY-ETHNIC POLITICS

Ethnic politics in Nepal is widely, but incorrectly, believed not to have been a factor before 1990 because the state and the dominant group were successful in creating the image of Nepal as a peaceful Shangri-La of ethnic harmony. A brief review of ethnic politics since the conquest of Nepal reveals that this is largely a myth.

---

[6] Bhattachan 2008, Bista 1996, Gaige 1975, Gurung 1998, Lawoti 2005.

In the mid-18th century, Prithvi Narayan Shah, a high-caste Hindu ruler of the kingdom of Gorkha in Nepal's western hills, established the state of Nepal, marking the first phase of Nepal's modern history and the CHHE's prevailing monopoly of state power. Their grip on power grew stronger with progressive consolidation of the state. The CHHE gained power by imposing hill Hindu values – placing the Bahun (hill Brahmin) and Chhetri (hill Kshetriya) at the top of the caste hierarchy, presenting the hill Hindu monarchy as the state "unifier," and promoting their language, Khaskura, as the national language (Khas-kura aka Nepali). In 1854, a civil code formalized and institutionalized the caste hierarchy, establishing a system of unequal rights and privileges in which lower castes were punished more severely for committing the same crime as someone from a higher caste.[7] More than a century later, during the Panchayat period (1960–90), the monarchy strengthened the assimilation of the various ethnic groups into the dominant CHHE culture in the name of modernization and development. The 1962 constitution formally declared Nepal as a Hindu kingdom, and hill Hindu culture, such as *daura suruwal* (the ruling class dress code), and hill nationalism were aggressively promoted.[8] The result was further marginalization of non-CHHE groups and the erosion of non-CHHE languages, religions, customs, lifestyles, and traditions.

However, the imposition of ethnic hegemony did not take place in the absence of opposition. The fledgling Hindu kingdom faced several major rebellions and resistance movements in its first 30 years.[9] Subsequently, the number and intensity of resistance movements declined as a result of the state's increasing coercive power, although occasional ethnic uprisings continued to erupt throughout the 19th century.[10] By the early 20th century, the autocratic Rana regime that ruled Nepal from 1846–1951 had become so effective in suppressing opposition that no major ethnic rebellion occurred from 1900 until 1950.[11] However, ethnic disaffection smoldered underneath the calm surface, and religious and ethnic leaders as well as activists, such as Phalgunanda (a Limbu reform movement activist in the 1930s–40s), Madhavraj Joshi (a Hindu reformist in the early 20th century), and Yogmaya (a leader of an anti-Brahminical Hindu women reform movement in the 1930s), were

---

[7] Hofer 2004.

[8] Burghart 1994, Gaige 1975, Onta 1996.

[9] The Manj Kirant rebellion in 1773–1881, the Limbus and Bhotes' assistance to China during the Nepal-China war 1792–3, and the Tamang (Murmi) rebellion in 1993; Lawoti 2007, Regmi 1995.

[10] The Khambu rebellion (1808), the Sukhdev Gurung rebellion (1858), the repression against those who participated in the Dasain boycott (1867) in Dhankuta, the Siri Thebe expulsion (1870), the Lakhan Thapa Magar rebellion (1876), and the Supati Gurung rebellion (1877) are some of the recorded resistances, but they were smaller in sizes and less threatening then the earlier rebellions. Lawoti 2007.

[11] The Limbus organized conferences (chumlung) to protect their communal landholding systems known as *Kipat*. The government backed off for some time after the mobilization and petitions submitted to the government by the Limbus, but continued encroaching on the rights granted by Prithvi Narayan after the strength of the mobilization subsided. Caplan 2000, Jones 1976.

harassed, prosecuted, or jailed.[12] Furthermore, everyday forms of passive resistance, such as disregard of laws and dictates or refusal to pay taxes, posed challenges to the state in exerting its authority.[13]

With the end of the Rana regime and the advent of democracy in 1951, grievances and dissatisfaction began to be aired publicly. The marginalized groups started to mobilize and openly challenged the CHHE domination of the state. Madhesis mobilized in the mid-1950s to protest against the imposition of Nepali as the language of instruction in schools.[14] The Nepal Terai Congress, a Madhesi party formed in the early 1950s, received 2.1% of the vote in the 1959 general election. Indigenous nationalities such as Tamangs, Tamus, Magars, Tharus, Rais, Limbus, and Thakalis established ethnic associations and organizations and came together in public rallies to voice their demands. Some activists even tried to form broader organizations across ethnic cleavages like the United People's Welfare Organization.[15] The period also witnessed the return of occasional ethnic uprisings; for instance, the Tamang rebellion against the Bahun and Chhetri moneylenders and landowners in Dhading and Nuwakot in 1959–60.[16] However, after the king took power and reimposed royal autocratic rule in 1960, these movements once again subsided, both because it became more costly to express dissent and the monarch was successful in co-opting many ethnic leaders.

After monarchical rule opened up slightly in the aftermath of the 1979 student movement and the subsequent referendum of 1980, marginalized ethnic and caste groups slowly began to organize and reassert themselves once again. Gajendra Narayan Singh quit the Nepali Congress and formed the Nepal Goodwill Council in the 1980s to represent the concerns of the Madhesis. Ethnic associations, such as the Society for the Promotion of Kirat Religion and Literature, the Nepal Bhasa Manka Khal (a joint alliance of Newari organizations aiming to promote their language), and the Forum for the Rights of All Ethnic Peoples in Nepal, reemerged as cultural promotion organizations.[17] Similarly, at the grassroots level, local communities began to work for the preservation of their languages and religion despite the continuing state repression. Limbu activists, despite facing arrest for their actions, started schools in their language, and the anthropologist Susan Hangen recorded conversions of Gurungs from Hinduism back to Buddhism in the district of Illam.[18]

This review of pre-1990 ethnic politics demonstrates that, although the CHHE were able to monopolize the state, establish ethnic and cultural hegemony, and

---

[12] Aziz 1993, Gaenszle 2009, Uprety 1992.
[13] Scott 1985, Holmberg 2000.
[14] Gaige 1975.
[15] Hangen 2000.
[16] Holmberg 2006.
[17] Hangen 2000.
[18] Ibid.

largely contain widespread resistance movements and oppositions, the marginalized ethnic groups sporadically asserted their identities. Meanwhile, many groups continued to speak their own languages and follow their own cultural practices.

Identity politics of the disadvantaged groups really took off only after 1990 when the newly constituted multiparty democracy provided space for dissent and ethnic mobilization. However, despite the 1990 constitution's declaration of the country as multiethnic, discrimination on the basis of language, religion, culture, and lifestyle persisted.[19] The state continued to promote and support not only the Hindu monarchy and religion but also Nepali as the national language, hill nationalism, the Khas dress code, and hill-Hindu norms and heritage.[20] The exclusion and injustices that continued even during the democratic period resulted in increased awareness of inequalities and greater mobilization by the marginalized groups.

Marginalized groups became more assertive and openly demanded that the state address discrimination, inequality, and exclusion. Madhesis and indigenous groups formed political parties, but only the Madhesi Nepal Goodwill Party (NGP) managed to gather enough votes in the three national elections in the 1990s to send a few members to the parliament. The indigenous nationalities formed the Nepal Federation of Indigenous Nationalities (NEFIN) consisting of more than four dozen ethnic associations. A number of linguistic associations were established in the Terai, with some demanding the elevation of Hindi as the lingua franca for the region. The Dalits, with the support of donors, mostly organized as individual NGOs, many of which later formed a national federation of Dalit NGOs. Individuals and academics also engaged in various forms of advocacy. These activities were successful in raising awareness of inequality and injustices not only within the marginalized groups but also in society at large. The state conceded some minor demands; for example, the formation of Dalit Development Committee, National Dalit Commission, and Nationalities Development Committee which was later transformed into the National Foundation for Development of Indigenous Nationalities.[21]

ETHNIC POLITICS, THE ARMED MAOIST REBELLION,
AND THE PEACE PROCESS

The increasing awareness of ethnic inequality and discrimination fueled the Maoist rebellion; the changes in government in 2002, when the king took over power from the democratically elected government; and the second People's Movement in 2006 that reestablished democratic rule. Both the rebellion and the regime changes altered the dynamics of ethnic politics, which became more salient when the competing

---

[19] See Neupane 2000, Lawoti 2005; 2008, among others, for different types and depth of exclusion.
[20] Bhattachan 2008, Lawoti 2005, Manchanda 2009.
[21] The Madhesis rarely received recognition and concession from the state or donor agencies for the duration of the 1990s.

political forces began to exploit ethnic disenchantment.[22] In the mid-1990s, the Maoists began to successfully recruit disenfranchised groups to join the rebellion, initially focusing on Dalits, indigenous nationalities, and women and later extending their efforts to the Madhesi community. The Maoists made the demands of the marginalized groups their own, calling for the right to self-determination and ethnic autonomy and even forming various ethnic fronts and declaring the formation of autonomous ethnic regions or states. In the areas under their control, they took steps to outlaw untouchability, sexism, and ethnic discrimination. As the rebel force expanded with the participation of the marginalized groups, it became an increasing threat to regime stability and ethnic hegemony. In 2002, responding to what he saw as the parliamentary parties' inability to contain the rebellion, the king, with the support of the Royal Nepalese Army, dismissed the elected government and established a royalist government under his direct control. However, the Maoists successfully obstructed local elections in 2002, parliamentary elections in 2004, and municipal elections in 2005.

In an effort to take the wind out of the rebellion's sails, between 2002 and 2006 the governments appointed by the king included a few leaders of the indigenous political parties and even featured a Madhesi deputy prime minister for the first time in Nepal's history. These governments initiated an affirmative action policy benefiting the Dalits and indigenous nationalities. However, structural exclusion and marginalization ran so deep that such half-hearted co-optation efforts that had worked to some degree during the Panchayat regime were not enough to appease ethnic groups.[23]

After their initial call to protest against the royal takeover in 2002 did not gain popular support, the parliamentary political parties realized the need to incorporate ethnic demands into their platforms. They also saw the need to promise substantive political reforms to address the grievances of the marginalized groups lest they lose the support of these groups to the rebels or the king. The political parties thus agreed to make the state inclusive, provide affirmative action policies to disadvantaged groups, and provide citizenship certificates to those without them, as demanded by the Madhesi movement.[24]

Eventually, in April 2006, with the active participation of ethnic organizations such as the NEFIN and a faction of the Madhesi Nepal Goodwill Party, the second People's Movement (*Jana Andolan II*) of the parliamentary parties, civil society

---

[22] The indigenous nationalities and Dalits commonly supported the Communist Party of Nepal (Unified Marxist-Leninist [CPN-UML], whereas the Madhesis often voted for the Nepali Congress during the 1990s. Even though these two parties were always in government during this period, they only introduced cosmetic reforms. The ethnic mobilization had not gained enough strength to pressure the parliamentary parties to amend the constitution or reform the polity substantially.

[23] Lawoti 2008.

[24] See the seven parties' statement and commitment to the People's Movement after the king's direct usurpation of power in February 2005; Khanal 2008, pp. 108–9.

organizations, and the Maoists forced the king to relinquish power, resulting in major political changes and reforms. Shortly after the *Jana Andolan*, the state was declared secular. In the aftermath of the Constituent Assembly elections in 2008, the Hindu monarchy was abolished. In addition, a provision in the interim constitution commits the Constituent Assembly to adopt federalism in the new constitution, implying that the days of the centralized unitary state are numbered. The design and adoption of the federal model will have important implications for empowerment of indigenous nationalities, Madhesis, and other disadvantaged groups like the Dalits and Muslims. However, social and economic transformation has yet to materialize, and exclusion of minority linguistic and religious groups remains pervasive.

The transition that began with the 2006 regime change has given rise to the emergence of new ethnic actors and organizations that are trying to influence the making of new rules affecting their rights and standing in state and society. The Madhesi movement that arose in early 2007 has been transformed into a powerful political force as Madhesi parties – constituting the fourth, fifth, and sixth largest parties, respectively, among a total of two dozen parties – have become king-makers in the hung Constituent Assembly. Although indigenous nationalities and Dalit parties are also represented in the Constituent Assembly for the first time in Nepal's legislative history, the number of their representatives (totaling six) is too low for them to exert much influence.

The emergence of a half-dozen or more new armed groups – Madhesi and indigenous as well as Hindu fundamentalists – in the years after the signing of the peace agreement in 2006 has made the transition period and peace process more complex and challenging. Some of these groups are seeking separatism. For example, one Limbu organization declared independence in 2007, and some Madhesi armed groups are seeking secession. Unless the claims of multiple class and identity groups are addressed to reduce inequality and exclusion, radical organizations may gain wider support among the marginalized population and the peace process may not be sustainable.

DOES THE PEACE PROCESS AND THE END OF THE HINDU MONARCHY MEAN INCLUSIVE STATE-BUILDING?

Although Nepal's post-2006 peace process has been primarily aimed at settling the Maoist-led armed conflict, its lasting success will largely depend on its ability to manage ethnic aspirations and prevent an escalation of ethnic conflict as well. The April 2006 regime change has affected ethnic politics much more than had earlier political transformations, and the rhetoric of inclusion is widespread among political leaders, civil society actors, and donor agencies. An assessment of the current status, especially through a pre- and post-2006 comparison, provides insights into the level of inclusion of marginalized groups and highlights challenging areas.

Cultural Discrimination before and after 2006

Two pillars of sociocultural exclusion, the Hindu monarchy and Hindu state, have been formally eliminated in the course of the peace process. Another pillar, exclusionary nationalism, has also been challenged, and even though its influence continues, it is no longer as dominant as before. Although these are important developments, formal changes in nomenclature can be deceptive. The act of declaring a polity as democratic or inclusive does not make it automatically democratic or inclusive.

The government's declaration of the Nepali state as secular is a significant step toward making citizens of different faiths (and nonbelievers) more equal. However, beyond this formal declaration, the government has done little to make itself secular in practice or to create a sense of equality between Hindu and non-Hindu communities. The head of state, the prime minister, and state officials still publicly lead, preside over, or attend primarily Hindu festivals, with which the Hindu king used to legitimize his rule. The Sanskrit University and the Sanskrit education system remain fully financed by the state, whereas educational institutions preserving and promoting studies of other religions or languages have not received similar support. The Lumbini Buddha University approved in 2005 is not yet fully functional, largely because of the government's lack of commitment and meager financial support. Likewise, despite the declaration of the state as secular, many laws based on Hinduism remain in the legal code, such as the 12-year prison sentence for killing a cow, which has sacred qualities in Hinduism.

A good measure of the degree of change in the government's religious policies is the comparison of public holidays across time. As of 2000, the government had not declared a single festival of the 59 indigenous nationalities a public holiday, but by 2010, indigenous festivals constituted around 10% of all public holidays,[25] in addition to a number of Christian and Muslim holidays.[26] However, although hill Hindu holidays have decreased from 69% to 56% of public holidays, their number is still high compared to the hill Hindu population proportion. Meanwhile, the number of Muslim, Madhesi Hindu, and indigenous holidays continues to be disproportionally low.

In a society in which religion and culture play an important role in the everyday lives of many people, secularity should be defined as equality among followers and non-followers of different religions. Given that the state in the past overwhelmingly supported and promoted the dominant hill variant of the Hindu religion and culture at the cost of others, the government should now initiate policies that aim to protect

---

[25] To distribute the holidays adequately, each holiday was awarded one point. If two groups shared a holiday, each group received a half-point; if the holiday was only for the concerned group, it was given a point. Tabulation based on calendars published by the Nepali government.

[26] Secular holidays have also increased from 11% in 2000–1 to 19% in 2009–10.

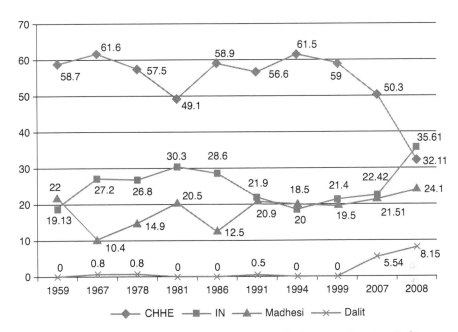

FIGURE 5.1. Representation of Various Groups in Parliament, Interim Parliament-Legislature, and Constituent Assembly, 1959–2008. *Sources:* Lawoti 2008, UNDP 2009, Darnal 2009.

cultures, traditions, and religions of minority groups to prevent the more dominant culture from encroaching and undermining them. However, the post-2006 Nepali state has done little in terms of promoting religious equality beyond declaring the state as secular.

Representation before and after 2006[27]

The Constituent Assembly: Higher Representation
The Constituent Assembly is significantly more representative than any of Nepal's previous legislatures. Not represented at all in the Lower House after elections in 1994 and 1999, Dalits attained 8% of the seats in the Constituent Assembly formed in 2008. Madhesis and indigenous nationalities, too, have achieved their highest parliamentary representation ever in the Constituent Assembly (see Fig. 5.1).[28]

---

[27] I would like to thank Medini Lawati for research assistance and Krishna Hari Pushkar for providing and verifying data on the bureaucracy.

[28] The indigenous representation is higher because of the Newar, an indigenous group from the capital that has historically fared very well politically and economically despite facing cultural (religion, language, lifestyles, etc.) discrimination.

Yet compared to their share of the overall population, Dalits and indigenous nationalities are still underrepresented,[29] whereas the CHHE are slightly overrepresented.

Although increased inclusiveness in the Constituent Assembly (and one hopes in future parliaments) is an important development, the role of marginalized groups in governance will remain constrained as long as the major political parties are led and dominated by the CHHE and do not democratize internally. Indigenous peoples and Dalits, who are mostly represented in the Constituent Assembly as individuals across a number of mainstream parties, have great difficulties making their voices heard. The less mobilized indigenous and Dalit parties elected only five and one representative, respectively, to the Constituent Assembly and are thus ineffective in pushing any agenda.

Likewise, in a continuation of practice prevalent during the 1990s, nearly all important decisions and agreements during the peace process have been hashed out in 11th-hour backroom deals by a very small group of top leaders of the major parties, most of whom are male Bahuns of advanced age. If such practice persists and key decisions affecting Nepal's future (such as the design of the federal state) are made in this manner, having proportionate and inclusive parliamentary representation will prove to be largely meaningless.

Mixed Record of Inclusion in the Cabinet

The executive, too, has become more representative in the course of Nepal's transition process.[30] Non-Dalit Madhesis are among the biggest beneficiaries of the government's greater inclusiveness, increasing their share of cabinet posts to 18%, well above their proportion of the population. This increase largely reflects the success of the Madhesi parties in positioning themself as king-makers in the coalition cabinets after the 2008 elections.

The representation of Dalits has also increased. Although not a single Dalit was appointed to the cabinet in the democratic period from 1990 to 2002, their share of ministerial posts increased to 7.5% in the post-2006 years. However, Dalit representation in the executive is still less than half of their proportion of the population. Most Dalits in the executive were either accorded the rank of junior ministers, and the few Dalit cabinet-level ministers were assigned to marginal ministries with little influence on key policy decisions.

---

[29] From around 20% representation during the 1990s, Madhesis (non-Dalit castes and Muslims) who constitute 17% of the total population, have attained 24% representation in 2008. Dalits are still nearly 50% underrepresented compared to their share of the population.

[30] The calculation of representation in the cabinet was carried out in the following way: each reshuffle of the cabinet was considered a new cabinet. A reshuffle was defined as changes in ministries along with the addition or dropping off of ministers. The additions or departures of individual ministers were not considered as a reshuffle. Groups' representations in the cabinets during different regimes were added up, and their average representation was then calculated.

By contrast, the representation of indigenous nationalities has slightly declined. The post-2006 representation of indigenous nationalities is 16%, which is lower than during the democratic years between 1990–2002 (16.7%), the royal rule of 2002–6 (16.1%), and quite significantly below the 27.1% accounted for during the Panchayat years between 1976–90.

The representation of the CHHE has also declined, but at 43% percent is still significantly higher than their 31% share of the population.[31] So far, they have maintained their ownership of the executive head of Nepal's government, a post the caste hill Hindu elite has occupied throughout Nepal's history, including during the Maoist interregnum of 2008–9.[32] And although Madhesis occupied the positions of president and vice president and a member of the indigenous nationalities was elected to the post of speaker of the legislature after the 2008 elections, these are largely ceremonial or powerless positions.

Continuation of Exclusion in the Judiciary

In the Supreme Court, the share of the CHHE has slightly declined since 2000 (76.21%), but at 64.5%, they still hold a disproportionate position, especially the Bahuns (45.1%; see Fig. 5.2).[33]

Madhesi representation in the Supreme Court increased (11.27%), but still remains below their population share. Fielding one judge each, Muslims and indigenous nationalities have a 5% share of the Supreme Court. Both groups were not represented during the royal regime and at the end of the pre-2002 democratic epoch that this dataset covers. During the periods covered, none of the judges were Dalit.

The domination of the CHHE in the Supreme Court could lead to a reversal of inclusive policies if it continues to have the right of judicial review. Indeed, in the 1990s, the majority high-caste hill Hindu judges issued a number of conservative rulings on issues affecting marginalized groups. For example, in the early 1990s when the rule that public service exams were to be conducted only in Khas-Nepali was challenged, the court ruled that this practice was constitutional. Likewise, when district governments introduced local languages as second official languages in their respective jurisdictions after the 1999 Local Government Act, the court ruled that it was unconstitutional. The Supreme Court also nullified the 1999 Citizenship Act that aimed to distribute citizen certificates to millions of

[31] Within CHHE, Chhetri (including Thakuri and Sanyansi) domination has declined considerably (20.5%) from previous years, whereas in post-2006 the Bahun still hold a significant number of positions (22.5; nearly double their proportion in the population).

[32] Marich Man Singh, a Newar, became prime minster at the end of the Panchayat regime, but the king controlled effective power during the period.

[33] The calculation for representation is similar to that of the cabinet. The count is based on the annual list of justices. If a justice is appointed for four years, his or her name will appear four times. The list was only available from 2000–1.

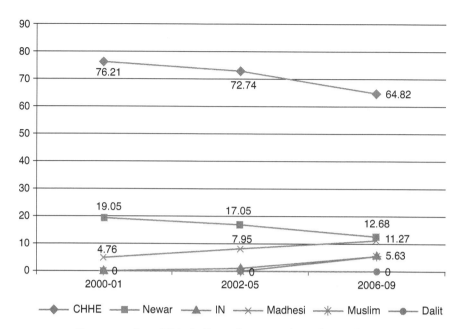

FIGURE 5.2. Representation of Ethnic/Caste Groups in the Judiciary during Democratic (2000–1), Autocratic (2002–5), and Transition Governments (2006–9). *Sources:* Calendars published by the Nepal Government.

Madhesi, Dalit, and indigenous nationalities who lacked such certificates in their families.[34]

In a federal system the frequency of judicial review would increase because of the probability that the center and regions, as well as the dominant and marginalized groups, might contest the various articles of the constitution; this could provide an opening for the Supreme Court to reinterpret socioculturally progressive articles in an conservative manner. This risk could be reduced or prevented if the right to review the constitutionality of laws is transferred from the CHHE-dominated Supreme Court to a newly created constitutional court composed of constitutional experts nominated by the regions. Doing so could ensure that different ideological, regional, and sociocultural groups have more chances of their rights being protected.[35]

Rise in Exclusion in the Bureaucracy

Data on the ethnic and caste composition at the highest level of the bureaucracy (which is referred to as the "special class" in Nepal) for four different years during

---

[34] Lawoti 2005.
[35] Lawoti 2009. Constitutional courts have been found to play an important role in new democracies by restraining the executive when it attempted to encroach on the jurisdiction of other government branches and agencies. Schwartz 1999.

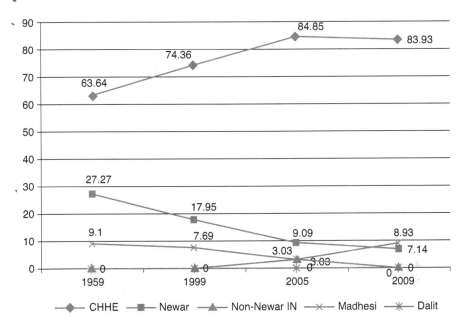

FIGURE 5.3. Ethnic/Caste Representation in the Bureaucracy (Special Class and Equivalent). *Sources:* Neupane 2000 and 2005; UNDP 2009; and self-tabulation of 2009 data.

democratic (1959 and 1999), autocratic (2005), and transitional (2009) periods show that the CHHE have actually consolidated their position in the latter two periods, reaching nearly three times their population share during the transition (see Fig. 5.3).

The representation of Madhesis in 2009 (8.93%), although slightly higher than a decade earlier (7.69%), is lower than 1959 (9.1%).[36] The Dalits, indigenous nationalities, and Muslims had zero representation at the top level of the bureaucracy in 2009, even though the groups collectively make up more than half of the population.

Despite the initiation of quotas for marginalized groups in the recruitment of civil servants since 2003, the situation at the top of the bureaucracy is unlikely to change for years to come, because it will take time for the new recruits to rise through the ranks. The data on competitive recruitment of civil service personnel show strong domination by the CHHE (especially the Bahun) throughout the 1990s. In 2001–2, CHHE recruitment through the civil service examination actually increased further to 87% from 60% in the 1980s. In the 1980s and 1990s, Dalits and Muslims never

---

[36] The Madhesis in this data and in Figure 5.3, following Neupane (2000), are composed of "upper" caste Madhesis, Dalits, Muslims, and indigenous nationalities of the Terai (32.29%). Generally, the addition of Dalits, Muslims, and indigenous groups from the Terai does not make much difference because these groups have rarely reached the highest level in the bureaucracy.

accounted for more than 1% of those recruited, that of indigenous groups never more than 3%, and that of Madhesis reached 10% only once.[37]

The overwhelming representation of the CHHE in the bureaucracy has had a negative impact on inclusion in other areas as well, because the bureaucracy often resists policies it does not like by undermining them at various levels. For instance, bureaucrats interfered with the operations of autonomous public bodies mandated to promote the welfare of Adivasi Janajatis by blocking or delaying the disbursement of government funding to these organizations.[38]

Marginalized groups have been similarly excluded in the security sector, although data on the ethnic composition of the security sector are hard to come by. According to the Nepalese Army (NA) website, its force comprises 56.54% CHHE, 30.39% indigenous nationalities, and 6.62 % Newars.[39] However, the NA does not provide an ethnic/caste breakdown of its top leadership, probably to avoid showing domination of the top echelon by the Chhetris,[40] the appointment of a member of the indigenous nationalities to the army's top position in 2009 notwithstanding.[41]

The Limits of Proportionality

Although the representation of various groups in state institutions, such as the parliament, bureaucracy, and judiciary, is an important aspect of social inclusion, it only tells part of the story. Indeed, proportional representation only goes so far in guaranteeing the rights of minorities. Even if there is perfectly proportional representation in a unitary state, numerous groups will become permanent minorities at the center. As the largest ethnic group with 31% of the population, the CHHE will continue to have more influence at the central policy level than other ethnic groups. Even the Magars, the second largest ethnic group, are more than four times smaller than CHHE at only 7% and will thus have considerable less weight in policy decisions. Meanwhile, according to the 2001 census, 29 ethnic groups have a population of less

---

[37] Lawoti 2008, Subba et al. 2002.

[38] NEFIN and indigenous activists had to fight hard to scuttle the attempts of the local government ministry's bureaucrats to control the nomination process of board members to the National Foundation for the Development of Indigenous Nationalities. In another example, in the late 1990s, the executive director of the Nationalities Development Committee complained that the funds allotted to it by the government were not released in time because the local development ministry's secretary, who belonged to the traditional hill Hindu elite, did not approve of the Committee's awareness-building program.

[39] Nepalese Army 2009; available from http://www.nepalarmy.mil.np/inclusiveness.php.

[40] Within the indigenous nationalities, the hill indigenous nationalities (population 21.86% when Newars are excluded) are slightly overrepresented, whereas the Terai indigenous nationalities (population 8.96%) are slightly underrepresented (6.5%). The Dalits have 5.87% representation, but it is comprised almost entirely by hill Dalits. The Madhesis and Muslims occupy 0.49% and 0.02% of positions, respectively.

[41] Similarly, the police force that was historically headed by members of the indigenous groups has, according to a top retired police officer, largely recruited CHHE over the last couple of decades.

than a hundred thousand, and their influence in public policies will be minimal even if they are to be proportionally represented at the center.[42] As a result, other ethnic groups than the CHHE will have to live under central level-policies, including those that guide sociocultural issues, which are likely to be heavily influenced by the CHHE.

Furthermore, the CHHE will ensure the continuation of their dominant role in society by forming majority alliances of variable geometry with other population groups (or their representatives) depending on the issue. For instance, in their pursuit of pro-Hindu policies, the CHHE often link up with Hindu Madhesis and Dalits, forming an 80% Hindu majority. On issues of hill nationalism, they appeal to fellow hill indigenous nationalities and hill Dalit "nationalists" to form an anti-Madhesi alliance, which has the weight of two-thirds of the population behind it. The CHHE often join hands with hill Dalits in devising policies to defend the privileged position of their common Khas-Nepali native language. With respect to caste, the CHHE together with Madhesis and indigenous nationalities make up the more than 80% of Nepalis who practice untouchability against Dalits. Thus, even if proportional representation based on ethnicity/caste is achieved in all governance sectors, most marginalized groups may continue to face exclusion and discrimination in various cultural spheres that affect and matter to them. Hence, in a complex society like Nepal, the country has to go beyond proportionality to attain equality and justice for its marginalized ethnic groups.

One way in which equality among groups can be provided is through group autonomy – be it territorial, nonterritorial, or through special provisions for smaller groups so that they can develop in their own sociocultural environment. Because larger groups will dominate democratic politics in ethnically divided societies,[43] group autonomy will help protect minorities from external threats emanating from large and powerful groups. Autonomy can facilitate self-governance of different groups. When groups are allowed to govern themselves based on their own norms, values, traditions, and worldviews rather than those of others, they can develop and grow.[44]

Individual equality cannot be achieved without group equality in multinational or multiethnic states. For instance, if minority groups are forced to compete in the dominant group's native language for recruitment to the public sector, the non-native-language speakers will be disadvantaged. This has been made amply clear by the low levels of recruitment of non-CHHE members into the bureaucracy whose entrance examination was conducted in the native language of the CHHE.

---

[42] Among caste groups, 1 hill Dalit caste, 9 Madhesi Dalit castes, and 19 Madhesi castes constituted less than a hundred thousand people in 2001. Likewise, five other groups – the Mali, Bengali, Kamar, Punjabi, and Jain – had an equally small population.

[43] Kymlicka 1995, Lijphart 1977.

[44] Kymlicka 1995, Lawoti 2005, Young 1990.

The debate about which kind of federal model is best suited for Nepal should consider group equality. The Nepali Congress, for instance, favors a model with only five or six federal states, but the CHHE would likely constitute the largest group in most of them, resulting in their continued dominance in governance.[45] Therefore, to break the hegemony of one ethnic group, Nepal should strive to establish a model with a higher number of federal states, which would give more number of ethnic groups a plurality status in their respective provinces. However, given that not every minority group can realistically claim its own autonomous state, minority rights and non-territorial and local autonomy within the states will have to be guaranteed so that smaller groups' rights will be protected within the autonomous provinces.[46]

RESISTANCE TO INCLUSION AND EQUALITY

Large-scale mobilization of societal forces is often necessary to achieve major political reforms. The ongoing changes in Nepal's state structure are largely a result of the pressure exerted by the Maoists and social-justice-seeking movements of the traditionally marginalized groups. For instance, the Maoist mobilization and resolution were largely responsible for ending the monarchy in 2008, whereas the Madhesi movement of 2007 forced the Constituent Assembly to amend the 2007 interim constitution to include a provision committing itself to devise a federal constitution.

Unsurprisingly, an alliance of status quo-ist and regressive forces, including the traditionally privileged groups as well as Hindu fundamentalist and royalist organizations, is resisting fundamental changes. Given that the CHHE still largely control most state and societal organs, they do not need to mobilize people to obstruct reforms. Even the supposedly "progressive" and "liberal" media are emboldening conservative ideals and groups by rallying public opinion against major reforms.

Media as a Tool of Resistance

The media, which in many societies have been a progressive agent for change, are increasingly mobilizing public opinion against inclusive reforms in Nepal. Instead of making available verifiable facts and presenting different views and perspectives to enable citizens to take informed decisions, the mainstream media have become a tool of the conservative forces that are seeking to maintain the status quo. The media's reporting on ethnic/caste movements has been largely negative and has contributed to undermining public support for the marginalized groups' social justice issues. This bias is unsurprising, given that the print media in Nepal is dominated by traditional

---

[45] Lawoti 2009.

[46] To protect the rights of individuals within groups, the aspirations of the group should be decided collectively by all members of the community, not just by the male elders, as has traditionally been the case. Kymlicka 1995. In addition, individuals also should have the right to leave if they no longer want to remain within their particular group.

elites: in 2008, of the 40 daily, weekly, and bimonthly print publications that the Nepal Press Council ranked highest in circulation and influence, not a single one had a Dalit, Muslim, or non-Newar indigenous nationalities member as editor.[47]

Traditionalist elite male intellectuals, who call themselves "democratic," "liberal," or "progressive," control major mainstream print and TV outlets and use their influence to widely disseminate conservative views and promote the status quo agenda. Indeed, a number of high-powered media personalities from that elite are among the leaders of the resistance against efforts to promote greater inclusiveness in state and society. These individuals influence public opinion through partial and selective news coverage.

Biased media commentary in the garb of fair and balanced coverage remains all too common in the "new" Nepal. One of many glaring examples of one-sided coverage is provided by Nepalnews.com, which in July 2008 ran "A Discussion on Facets of Federalism," featuring 18 interviews, news articles, and opinion pieces. Of these 18 items, 12 opposed ethnic federalism, 2 were in favor of it, and 1 was neutral. In this context, it is interesting that these and other articles tend to put the label of "ethnic federalism" on models in which marginalized groups would end up forming a majority in most federal entities, but do not attach this label to models in which traditional elites, the CHHE, would form the largest group in most entities. Of course, the large majority of the authors and interviewees came from traditional elites, with the views of Dalits, Muslims, and women not represented at all.[48] This reflects the reality that articles on minority rights issues from scholars and activists belonging to marginalized groups have either not been published or are published with significant delays or after having been heavily edited, removing "controversial" arguments along the way.

The public discourse on autonomy and federalism seems to have shifted from a largely positive stance to a largely negative one after the interim constitution, under pressure from ethnic groups, was amended to adopt federalism in 2007.[49] Opinion-makers from the traditional elites, when confronted with the very realistic prospect of a federal Nepal, have felt the need to drum up a major media campaign discrediting the very concept. Yet, despite the Nepali media's negative portrayal of federalism

---

[47] Some media organizations have hired a few reporters from marginalized groups to show an image of being "inclusive," but none have been appointed as editors.

[48] See "Facets of Federalism – a Nepalnews Discussion," available at http://www.nepalnews.com/archive/2008/jul/federal_interviews.php.

[49] See Tamang 2005 for a collection of 28 articles on state restructuring and federalism that were published before the 2006 change, in which most of the authors discussing federalism argued for "ethnic" federalism. After the interim constitution was amended to adopt federalism in 2007, antifederalists and status quo-ists have become active and have produced arguments to undermine ethnic autonomies. They have presented under various facades and pretexts models that would make the CHHE the largest group in the center as well as in most regions: such models do not provide data on "ethnic" demographic distribution, however – see *Sambidhan yatra* (Constitution Journey), a regular feature of fortnightly *Himal Khabarpatrika* for regular feature of such models.

as potentially divisive, comparative and cross-national findings have shown that all democracies with territorially concentrated ethnic and linguistic groups have federal state systems[50] and that ethnic autonomy, in many parts of the world, has contributed to mitigating ethnic conflicts.[51]

Complaints by marginalized groups about bias in major media outlets are not new. However, their frustration seems to have grown in recent years, probably because people expected the media to be a force for change during the transition. Marginalized groups are growing increasingly restive and are exploring ways to counter the media bias, for example by launching alternative media outlets that cater to their people and are primarily consumed by members of their respective groups. The CHHE most often do not read such media, partly because of their limited circulation and partly because of a lack of interest.

This segmental information dissemination, in which groups are fed different issues and often opposite perspectives, risks increasing the cleavages within society that could foment simmering ethnic conflicts. The burning of mainstream newspapers during protests by movements of the marginalized groups and violent attacks against minority religious groups by fundamentalist Hindu organizations are indicators of such deepening cleavages. With the media in Nepal turning into a force favoring the status quo instead of helping create an environment for reforms, the possibility of violent clashes between the change-seeking ethnic/caste groups, the status quo-ists, and conservative CHHE forces has increased. If violent conflicts were to occur during Nepal's transitional period, a significant part of the blame can be placed on the media for rigidifying the traditionally dominant group.

CONCLUSION

Both Nepal and the country's ethnic politics are undergoing significant transitions. The emergence of poly-ethnic politics could eliminate the prevailing mono-ethnic hegemony and create a just and equitable society. However, new democracies are at particular risk of seeing ethnic mobilization turn violent if not dealt with in the right way.[52]

In which direction ethnic politics in Nepal is heading will be ultimately determined by the level of inclusiveness both in cultural realms and in access to state resources. In cultural matters, formal discrimination has ended, but informal discrimination continues. In terms of political inclusion, the record is mixed as well. As we have seen, among the marginalized groups, the Madhesis have made the most progress, whereas other non-Newar indigenous nationalities and Muslims have not made significant gains and in some cases have even decreased in representation.

---

[50] Stepan 2001.
[51] Gurr 1993, 2000, Kohli 1997, Lijphart, 1977, Manor 1998, Saideman et al. 2002.
[52] Snyder 2000.

The Dalits continue to be the most underrepresented group in all branches of government. Meanwhile, the three traditionally dominant groups all continue to have representation higher than their population share. Although the position of Newars and Chhetri is less dominant than it used to be, the Bahun have largely maintained their control and even consolidated it in some areas.

Indeed, although the Constituent Assembly and the cabinet now show higher levels of inclusiveness, the nonpolitical branches such as the judiciary and state bureaucracy seem to be the most resistant to change. The widespread rhetoric of inclusion has yet to translate into reality in significant arenas.

Whether Nepal will evolve into a truly inclusive democratic system over time depends on at least two conditions. For one, the marginalized groups have to continue demanding progressive changes. Whatever changes, minor or substantive, have been achieved thus far have come through the mass mobilization of the marginalized groups. The more effective performance of the Madhesis in the political domain compared to the Dalits and the indigenous nationalities, for example, is to a large degree due to their higher level of mobilization. The higher representation of the Madhesis in the Constituent Assembly has given them significant leverage in that body because Madhesi votes are necessary to form coalition governments, pass bills, and approve the constitution. Because the Madhesi can exert pressure through the system, they have not engaged in major public protests since the 2008 elections.

However, the insufficient representation of marginalized indigenous nationalities and the Dalits through respective ethnic parties in the Constituent Assembly means that these groups will have to rely on extrasystemic methods for voicing their demands. Indeed, since the 2008 elections the Limbus, Tharus, and other groups have successfully organized frequent and sustained protests. The three-week-long movement in late 2008 and early 2009 led by the Tharus, which included blockades and strikes in the capital and the provinces, pressured the government to recognize their indigenous identity as separate from that of the Madhesi. However, marginalized groups may face difficulties in mobilizing people regularly for collective actions.

Experiences during the 1990s when exclusion continued under majoritarian institutions suggests that greater inclusion is not necessary a byproduct of democracy. Although the representation of Madhesis, Muslims, and Dalits at first slightly increased in the parliament during this period, it declined once the CHHE political leaders began to consolidate their hold; then non-CHHE cadres and leaders were slowly swept aside by caste- and family-oriented nepotism.

This situation could be avoided to some extent if Nepal adopts a federal system that would provide marginalized groups a degree of self-determination. However, if the CHHE continue to dominate different regions in addition to the center, then the chances of a substantive increase in inclusion in governance may be slim.

If the indigenous nationalities are not ensured effective representation in the polity, either at the center or at the regions, they may continue to revert to forms of protests, such as general strikes, shutdowns, and street movements. In due course, once their mobilization level increases the Dalit may also resort to similar techniques. Therefore, if Nepal in the post–peace-process period is to avoid prolonged street protests and the outbreak of violent conflicts, the emerging polity should develop mechanisms to effectively accommodate the various marginalized groups.

REFERENCES

Aziz, Barbara Nimri. 1993. "Shakti Yogmaya: A Tradition of Dissent in Nepal," in Charles Ramble and Martin Brauen (eds.), *Anthropology of Tibet and Himalaya*, pp. 19–29. Zurich: Ethnological Musuem of the University of Zurich.

Bhattachan, Krishna B. 2008. *Minorities and Indigenous Peoples of Nepal*. Kathmandu: National Coalition against Racial Discrimination.

Bista, Dor Bahadur. 1996. *Peoples of Nepal* (7th ed). Kathmandu: Ratna Pustak Bhandar.

Bohara, Alok. 2002. "Nepal Needs Federalism to Achieve Much Needed Political Decentralization or Devolution." *Nepalnews.com*, at http://www.nepalnews.com/archive/morepages/drbohara.htm.

Burghart, Richard. 1994. "The Political Culture of Panchayat Democracy," in Michael Hutt (ed.), *Nepal in the Nineties*, pp. 1–13. New Delhi: Oxford.

Caplan, Lionel. 2000. *Land and Social Change in East Nepal*. Kathmandu: Himal Books.

Darnal, Suvash. 2009. *Sambidhanma Dalit: Sabhasad Sambad*. Kathmandu: Jagaran Media Centre and Dalit Addhyan Kendra.

Gaenszle, Martin. 2009. "The Power of Script: Phalgunanda's Role in the Formation of Kiranti Ethnicity." Paper presented at the Annual South Asia Conference, Madison, WI.

Gaige, Frederick H. 1975. *Regionalism and National Unity in Nepal*. Delhi: Vikas.

Gurr, Ted Robert. 1993. *Minorities at Risk? A Global View of Ethnopolitical Conflicts*. Washington, DC: U.S. Institute of Peace Press.

———. 2000. *Peoples versus States: Minorities at Risk in the New Century*. Washington, DC: U.S. Institute of Peace Press.

Gurung, Harka. 1998. *Nepal: Social Demography and Expressionss*. Kathmandu: New Era.

Hangen, Susan. 2000. Making Mongols: Ethnic Politics and Emerging Identities in Nepal, Ph.D. dissertation, Anthropology, University of Wisconsin-Madison, Madison.

Hofer, Andras. 2004. *The Caste Hierarchy and the State in Nepal: A Study of the Muluki Ain of 1854*. Kathmandu: Himal Books.

Holmberg, David. 2000. "Derision, Exorcism, and the Ritual Production of Power." *American Ethnologist* 27(4): 927–49.

———. 2006. "Violence, Non-Violence, Sacrifice, Rebellion and the State." *Studies in Nepali History and Society* 11(1): 31–64.

Horowitz, Donald. 1985. *Ethnic Groups in Conflict*. Berkeley: University of California Press.

Jones, Rex L. 1976. "Sanskritization in East Nepal." *Ethnology* 15(1): 63–75.

Khanal, Krishna. 2008. *Nepal: Sankramankalin Rajniti ra Sambidhansabha Chunab* (Nepal: Transitional Politics and Constituent Assembly Election). Kathmandu: Friends for Peace.

Kohli, Atul. 1997. "Can Democracies Accommodate Ethnic Nationalism? Rise and Decline of Self-Determination Movements in India." *Journal of Asian Studies* 56(2): 325–44.

Kymlicka, Will. 1995. *Multicultural Citizenship: A Liberal Theory of Minority Rights*. Oxford: Oxford University Press.

Lawoti, Mahendra. 2005. *Towards a Democratic Nepal: Inclusive Political Institutions for a Multicultural Society*. New Delhi: Sage.

———. 2007. "Contentious Politics in Democratizing Nepal," in Mahendra Lawoti (ed.), *Contentious Politics and Democratization in Nepal*, pp. 17–47. Los Angeles: Sage.

———. 2008. "Exclusionary Democratization in Nepal, 1990–2002." *Democratization* 15(2): 363–85.

———. 2009. "The Myth of Non-Ethnic Federalism." *Kathmandu Post*, February 18, p. 8.

Lijphart, Arend. 1977. *Democracy in Plural Societies: A Comparative Exploration*. New Haven, CT: Yale University Press.

Manchanda, Rita, ed. 2009. *The No-Nonsense Guide to Minority Rights in South Asia*. New Delhi: Sage.

Manor, James. 1998. "Making Federalism Work." *Journal of Democracy* 9(3): 21–35.

Nepal Army. 2008. "State of Inclusiveness in Nepal Army." Nepalese Army website, http://www.nepalarmy.mil.np/inclusiveness.php. Accessed October 14, 2009.

Neupane, Govinda. 2000. *Nepalko Jatiya Prashna: Samajik Banot Ra Sajhedariko Sambhawana* (Nepal's National Question: Social Composition and Possibilities of Accommodation). Kathmandu: Center for Development Studies.

———. 2005, revised and expanded edition. *Nepalko Jatiya Prashna: Samajik Banot Ra Sajhedariko Sambhawana* (Nepal's National Question: Social Composition and Possibilities of Accommodation). Kathmandu: Center for Development Studies.

Onta, Praytoush. 1996. "Ambivalence Denied: The Making of Rastriya Itihas in Panchayat Era Textbooks." *Contributions to Nepalese Studies* 23(1).

Regmi, Mahesh C. 1995. *Kings and Political Leaders of the Gorkhali Empire, 1768–1814*. Hyderabad: Orient Longman.

Saideman, Stephen M., David Lanoue, Michael Campenni, and Samuel Stanton. 2002. "Democratization, Political Institutions, and Ethnic Conflict: A Pooled Time-Series Analysis, 1985–1998." *Comparative Political Studies* 35(1): 103–29.

Schwartz, Herman. 1999. "Surprising Success: The New Eastern European Constitutional Courts," in Andreas Schedler, Laryy Diamond and Marc F Plattner (eds.), *The Self-Restraining State: Power and Accountability in New Democracies*, pp. 195–214. Boulder, CO: Lynne Rienner Publishers.

Scott, James C. 1985. *Weapons of the Weak: Everyday Forms of Peasant Resistance*. New Haven, CT: Yale University Press.

Sharma, Pitamber. 2007. "Sanghiya Rajyako Adhar: Bhugol Ra Yojanaparak Dristi (Basis for Federal State: Geography and Planning Perspective)." Paper presented at the Seminar Series on Federalism, Pokhara.

Snyder, Jack L. 2000. *From Voting to Violence: Democratization and Nationalist Conflict*. New York: W.W. Norton and Company.

Stepan, Alfred. 2001. "Federalism and Democracy: Beyond the US Model" in *The Global Divergence of Democracy*, edited by Larry Diamond and Marc F. Plattner. Baltimore and London, The John Hopkins University Press: 19–34.

Subba, Chaitanya, Amrit Yonjan, Nilamber Acharya, Laxmi Limbu, Shyamlal Krishna Shrestha, Sangini Ranamagar, and Dwarika Nath Dhungel. 2002. *Adivasis/Janajatis in National Development: Major Issues, Constraints and Opportunities: Plan of Actions Proposed for the Tenth Plan, 2003–2007*. Kathmandu: IIDS.

Tamang, Sitaram, ed. 2005. *Nepalko Sandarvama Rajyako Punsanrachana*. Kathmandu, Samana Prakashan

UNDP. 2009. *Nepal Human Development Report 2009*. Kathmandu: UNDP Nepal.

Uprety, Prem R. 1992. *Political Awakening in Nepal: The Search for a New Identity*. New Delhi: Commonwealth Publishers.

Yakharai, DurgaHang. 1996. *Brahmanbad Birudha: Janajati Ra Utpiditbarga* (Janajatis and Marginalized Groups against Brahmanism). Kathmandu: Dhanrani Yakharai.

Young, Iris Marion. 1990. *Justice and the Politics of Difference*. Princeton, NJ: Princeton University Press.

Critical Transition and the Role of Outsiders

6

Nepal's Masala Peacemaking

Teresa Whitfield

Nepal's peace process was both led and driven by Nepalis, but it was also remarkably open to the involvement of a wide range of external actors. This chapter focuses on the most prominent and committed of the international peacemakers involved – among them the Swiss-based nongovernmental organization (NGO), the Centre for Humanitarian Dialogue, that worked in Nepal from 2000–6; the United Nations, whose secretary-general first offered his "good offices" in 2002 and whose presence later grew into a large Office of the UN High Commissioner for Human Rights (OHCHR, established in 2005) and a special political mission, the United Nations Mission in Nepal (UNMIN, formed in 2007); the Carter Center, whose conflict resolution program engaged with Nepal from 2004–6; and the government of Switzerland, which dispatched a special adviser for peacebuilding to Nepal in mid-2005. The chapter also analyzes the critical role played by India, which is explored more fully elsewhere in this volume.

None of these external actors came to fill a role of formal facilitation or still less mediation. For the most part, their efforts to encourage dialogue, introduce expertise gleaned from peace processes elsewhere, or provide other unspecified support were undertaken on an entrepreneurial basis, rather than in response to a clear invitation. These activities paralleled not only the presence and activity of national facilitators but also the discrete efforts of a number of individuals within Nepali civil society who encouraged dialogue between Nepal's fractious political actors. These varied actors at times appeared to crowd the peacemaking field in a confusing fashion, yet they were able to make a number of significant contributions. The result was a unique peacemaking mix – *masala peacemaking*.[1]

---

[1] I first coined this term in a paper, "Masala Peacemaking: Nepal's Peace Process and the Contribution of Outsiders," written in 2008 for the Conflict Prevention and Peace Forum and available on the website of the Center on International Cooperation at New York University, http://www.cic.nyu.edu.

After a brief review of the evolution of efforts to address Nepal's conflict by political means, the chapter analyzes the activities of external peacemakers during the three distinct phases in Nepal's progression toward the Comprehensive Peace Agreement (CPA) reached in late 2006: (1) the promotion of dialogue between Nepal's Maoists and its various royal governments between 2000 and the coup instigated by King Gyanendra on February 1, 2005; (2) the period between the coup and the People's Movement of April 2006 during which Nepalis' demands for change dislodged the king; and (3) support to the peace process as it developed through negotiations between political parties and the Maoists that culminated in the signing of the CPA. The chapter ends with an attempt to summarize the peacemaking effort as a whole. It points to the diminishing space for external peacemaking in the years since the signing of the CPA and the somewhat fragmented national efforts, periodically supplemented by the heavy hand of India, that have taken its place.

NEPAL'S CONFLICT AND THE PULL OF A POLITICAL SOLUTION

As the "People's War" launched by the Communist Party of Nepal-Maoist (CPN-M) took shape, the government addressed the insurgency as a problem of law and order. Repressive security measures introduced by a poorly trained police force, supplemented from 2001 by a new armed police force formed specifically for counterinsurgency, resulted in human rights abuses and unnecessary loss of life. Whether to mobilize the Royal Nepalese Army (RNA) against the Maoists was a controversial issue, with Maoist gains contributing to the realization that countering the insurgency lay beyond police capacity. Then, on June 1, 2001, the crown prince massacred King Birendra and 10 members of the royal family. The RNA was finally deployed later that year by Birendra's successor, his brother Gyanendra.

The political origins of the Maoist movement, the existence of a wide range of leftist parties within Nepal's political spectrum – the largest of which, the Communist Party of Nepal (United Marxist-Leninist), or UML, was second in strength only to the Nepal Congress (NC) party – and the essentially political demands of the Maoists themselves contributed to discussion of a political solution to the insurgency. Individual party leaders and other prominent figures maintained links of some sort to several members of the Maoist leadership, even during the early years of the conflict in which discussion of dialogue was taboo.

In January 2000, a commission formed to suggest ways to resolve the conflict, led by the Congress party politician Sher Bahadur Deuba, made contact with the Maoists and recommended a political settlement. An informal dialogue between the then-deputy prime minister and a member of the Maoist politburo took place in October 2000, but was soon disrupted. The Maoists intensified the conflict after the royal massacre. And when Prime Minister G. P. Koirala resigned and Deuba took his place, his government launched the first official dialogue effort. A ceasefire was announced by both sides, and three rounds of talks were held before the process collapsed in November 2001. Formal talks began again in 2003, and informally contacts across the conflict lines – between the palace, the Maoists, and individual members of political parties and civil society – continued.

In the meantime a separate conflict between the palace, with the RNA behind it, and the increasingly discredited political parties intensified. Parliament was dissolved in May 2002; on October 4, 2002, King Gyanendra dismissed the elected government and suspended elections that had been planned for the following month. A new series of peace talks began after the Maoists and the government reached a ceasefire agreement in January 2003. These talks collapsed in August 2003, three months after the appointment of yet another prime minister. The government was clearly not willing to countenance the Maoist demand for the restructuring of the Nepali state by a Constituent Assembly. In the margins of the formal talks the Maoist representatives had held unofficial talks with representatives of the Congress party and the UML, aided by like-minded individuals within other political parties and civil society. Although not successful at the time, these contacts helped build confidence and promote interaction with the Maoists that would contribute directly to the peace process's advance after 2005.

In June 2004, after weeks of street protests, Gyanendra dismissed the government again; reappointed Deuba, who was now the head of his own Nepal Congress (Democratic) party, as prime minister; and tasked him with holding elections. Deuba appointed a High Level Peace Committee (HLPC) and pressed for renewed negotiations, but his government had little credibility and was joined in the cabinet only by the UML. Meanwhile the king's increasingly authoritarian ambitions forestalled hope of a return to anything resembling a democratic political system. On February 1, 2005, Gyanendra seized power in a coup, imprisoned the leaders of the political parties and civil society, and declared a state of emergency. As he did so, he cited the need to intensify the war against the Maoists and bestowed new freedom of action on the army to enable it to do so.

The coup precipitated a profound shift in the country's political forces while also triggering the marked displeasure of Nepal's most influential neighbor and partners: India, the United States, and the United Kingdom. In the following months, as he defied international pressure to return Nepal to a democratic process, Gyanendra in effect provided the incentive for the demoralized and divided political parties to come together into the Seven Party Alliance (SPA),[2] drove that alliance into talks with the Maoists, and mobilized civil society against his regime and the monarchy as never before. The talks, which were held in New Delhi, with the tacit support of India, led to a 12-Point Understanding that was made public on November 22, 2005. A "People's Movement" gathered force in the early months of 2006 with a series of

---

[2] The members of the Seven Party Alliance were the NC, the UML, the Nepal Sadbhavana Party (Anandi Devi), the Nepal Congress (Democratic) party, Janamorcha Nepal, Nepal Workers and Peasants party, and the United Left Front.

violent strikes and protests, which in late April forced the king to abandon direct
rule and to agree to the restoration of the parliament elected in 1999.

Peace talks between the government and the Maoists resumed in May 2006, as
the parliament voted unanimously to curtail the king's political powers. The talks
took an erratic and unstructured form despite the presence of identified negotiation
teams, national observers, and, at one remove, international advisors. An inability
to delegate decision-making concentrated all decisions within the various parties'
senior leaders, with the octogenarian G. P. Koirala, who was named prime minister
for the fourth time in April, the most authoritative among them. Moving through a
series of partial agreements – including a 25-point Code of Conduct for the ceasefire
reached on May 25, an eight-point understanding agreed on June 16, and a request
for UN assistance sent to Secretary-General Kofi Annan on August 9 – the talks
culminated in the signing of the CPA in November 2006. The CPA brought a
formal end to the 10-year conflict. It provided for the entrance of the Maoists into
a transitional government and an interim constitution to be put in place, while
preparations were being made for elections to a Constituent Assembly.

ENTER THE PEACEMAKERS

Nongovernmental and other external actors who became involved in efforts to
end the conflict in Nepal saw the potential to contribute to a process that might
reduce the level of suffering of those affected by the conflict and lead toward peace
in Nepal. All the external actors proceeded from the same assumption: because
this was a political conflict over the nature of Nepal's government and social and
political inequities, rather than one rooted in secessionist or separatist demands, a
compromise between the contending parties could be found. Moreover, although
Nepal's strategic position between India and China brought its own complications,
there was a general consensus within the international community regarding what
a desirable outcome might look like: no violent takeover by the Maoists and the
emergence of a peaceful, stable, and democratic Nepal. The consensus favoring
these two outcomes, in addition to the growing realization that a military victory was
not possible, combined to encourage Nepalis and internationals alike to believe that
peace should be possible.

The presence of outside actors specifically engaged in efforts to promote dialogue and negotiation at the political level grew slowly. From 2000–3 the Centre for
Humanitarian Dialogue (HD) was the only international third party involved in a
sustained way, even as offers of help from elsewhere began to trickle in. Its involvement developed from a first visit to Kathmandu by its director and deputy director,
Martin Griffiths and Andrew Marshall, in August 2000. The two met with a small
number of well-connected journalists, representatives of civil society, and human
rights activists, including Padma Ratna Tuladhar, who promised to relay their offer

of assistance to Maoist leaders, and Sher Babadur Deuba, then the government negotiator for a dialogue process that was scarcely in existence.

The United Kingdom's Department for International Development (DFID) began thinking about building local capacity for a future peace process after the negotiations of 2001. It developed close ties to a small group of Nepalis thought likely to be involved in any future negotiations, including Tuladhar and Daman Nath Dhungana, both of whom had been facilitators of the 2001 talks. At their request, as the 2003 talks took shape, DFID organized visits to Nepal by representatives of the Community of Sant'Egidio, a lay Catholic organization that had facilitated negotiations on Mozambique, and by the former president of Finland and president of the Crisis Management Initiative, Martti Ahtisaari, to share their experiences of peacemaking. Although both these organizations would remain engaged with Nepal's efforts toward peace in the years to come, neither developed a full peacemaking involvement.

In the meantime, in his annual report to the UN General Assembly, Kofi Annan had offered to "consider the use of his good offices to help achieve a peaceful solution" to Nepal's conflict.[3] That this might be difficult to do was confirmed by a meeting with India's ambassador to inform him of Annan's intention to send a former Thai ambassador to the UN to Nepal as his envoy. At this meeting, the UN secretariat was told, as it would be on many other occasions, that Nepalis had the situation under control, competent national facilitators were available, and there was no need for third-party involvement in any effort to end the conflict. The under-secretary-general for political affairs, Kieran Prendergast, decided to send instead a mid-level official from his own department, Tamrat Samuel. Samuel arrived in Kathmandu in August 2003 as the talks were collapsing and would become a regular visitor in the coming years.

By all accounts and despite the best efforts of the national facilitators, the 2003 talks were deeply flawed. A wide gulf separated the political demands of the Maoists from the minimalist position assumed by the government; the political parties were excluded; the talks themselves were poorly managed (the government delegation in particular changed frequently, no process for the discussions was agreed to, nor were records kept of their proceedings); and communications by both parties were used to undermine the other. Conflict resolution practitioners took note of these limitations, and offers of assistance – and with them more workshops, training sessions, international experts, and trips to far-away places – began to multiply.

These offers fell on ground that was, in some respects, extremely fertile. Some of those close to the talks, including Dhungana and Tuladhar, openly appealed to international interlocutors for more help. Many politicians and members of civil

---

[3] United Nations, *Report of the Secretary-General on the Work of the Organization*, A/57/1, September 2002, para. 25. Interview, Padma Ratna Tuladhar, March 2008.

society welcomed the exposure to outside ideas offered by international experts. Others remained skeptical of the benefits to be reaped from well-intentioned people who knew more about mediation than they did about Nepal (and were largely ignorant of the national channels for communication to and between the conflict parties). Articles in the Nepali press began to appear bemoaning the "peace industry."[4]

How to relate to India was a critical question for all other external actors with an interest in Nepal's conflict. This issue was complicated by the mixed messages they heard from both Nepalis and Indians, which could be attributed to several factors. First, resentment of Indian influence was a fundamental element in the allure of non-Indian international partners for many Nepalis, even as they well knew that no solution to the conflict could be found that was not to the liking of India. Second, Indian policy toward Nepal, although since 1990 rooted in the "twin pillars" of constitutional monarchy and multiparty democracy, was shaped by a complex set of interests and priorities, with different perspectives dominant not only in different government ministries but also within distinct political parties, intelligence agencies, and the neighboring states of Bihar and Uttar Pradesh. Third, India, with its open border to Nepal, the presence of many Nepalis living in its territory, and its deep political ties to Nepal's ruling elites, engaged with Nepal on a variety of levels and with an array of political and economic levers that outsiders struggled to understand. Finally, India held well-established views on outside intervention in its neighborhood and was categorically "against third party mediation, UN or otherwise," as a senior Indian official put it. "Regardless of the irritants, no one understands each other better than India and Nepal," this official continued. "Everyone else could come and meddle . . . and if it went wrong they could dash off with their first class tickets. We could not trust anyone else to look after our concerns."[5]

Relations with Nepal's other neighbor, China, were more distant, reflecting the lower visibility of its dealings with Nepal, its long-held views on non-intervention in the affairs of others, and its underlying concern that the more than 20,000 Tibetan refugees living in Nepal not be a source of disturbance. With a critical perspective on the Maoists as an unruly force that besmirched the good name of Chairman Mao, this stance had translated into unfailing support of the government of the day. However, China began to take a much greater interest in Nepal in 2005 and after that quietly sought to increase its knowledge and engagement across the political spectrum.

PROMOTING DIALOGUE

Between 2002 and 2006 Nepal international actors flocked to provide support to Nepal's efforts to achieve a political solution to its conflict. As UN involvement

---

[4] "Foreigners Told to Keep off Nepal Affairs," *Himalayan Times*, June 7, 2003.
[5] Interview, March 2008.

continued, international NGOs engaged in peace efforts of one kind or another in Nepal included the Carter Center, the Centre for Humanitarian Dialogue, Crisis Management Initiative, Community of Sant'Egidio, Friedrich Ebert Stiftung, International Alert, International IDEA, Transcend, and the U.S. Institute for Peace. In addition, there were workshops organized in Denmark, Finland, Germany, Sweden, Switzerland, the United Kingdom, the United States, as well as in Nepal; attempts to draw comparatively on peace processes in Aceh, Cambodia, Central America, India, Northern Ireland, Peru, South Africa, and Sri Lanka; and offers of specific help in mediation from the governments of Norway and Switzerland.

Within this somewhat confusing mass of activity, the concerted efforts to promote dialogue undertaken by the HD Centre, the UN, and, from late 2004, the Carter Center stand out for the attempts they made to encourage talks among Nepali actors, as well as some of the difficulties they encountered. Over time, and particularly after the establishment of a field presence of the OHCHR, the potential for the UN to play a larger and more durable role within the peace process gradually became more evident.

HD sought to facilitate a dialogue between the government and the Maoists that would first address the humanitarian consequences of the conflict and then provide the basis for its peaceful settlement. In many respects it was a frustrating endeavor, constrained by factors both intrinsic to Nepal's political process and more directly linked to HD's own approach. Among the most significant constraints were the problems created by the frequent changes in Nepal's governments and the diminishing legitimacy with which they were able to act. HD worked hard to maintain access to the constantly changing cast of characters inside the king's government(s), but paid less attention to the politicians who had been pushed by the revolving door of Nepal's political process into increased opposition to the palace. Nor did it engage directly with Indian officials until late 2005, on the well-founded assumption that India would not welcome its involvement. Meanwhile, the lack of a consistent presence in Nepal limited its capacity to keep fully abreast of the context within which it was working and of how its initiatives might intersect with, or relate to, other developments.

On several occasions HD came close to facilitating direct meetings between the parties. Most dramatically, in early 2003 it secured agreement to hold a series of confidential talks between two representatives of the government and two senior Maoists in Geneva. However, at the last moment a security breach caused the plan to be abandoned. How such dialogue between armed actors, who were necessarily unrepresentative of the more democratic forces within Nepali society, and at the time not articulated within a broader and more inclusive strategy, might have developed is of course impossible to assess. HD's effort was quickly overtaken by that of Lt. Col Narayan Singh Pun, a former helicopter pilot and minister in the royalist Chand government. Pun carried out quiet negotiations with the Maoists that culminated in the announcement of a ceasefire on January 29, 2003, and the initiation of the second series of peace talks.

In Kathmandu a UN human rights advisor attached to UNDP met with Baburam Bhattarai, the Maoists' leading ideologue and representative in the talks, to discuss a draft human rights accord prepared by the National Human Rights Commission in May 2003. Two months later, UN official Tamrat Samuel arrived as the peace talks between the government and the Maoists were foundering. He did not manage to meet with Bhattarai, but after speaking with him on the telephone he plunged into a delicate negotiation between the Maoists and the government over how to maintain the ceasefire; this dialogue confirmed the readiness of Nepali interlocutors to engage with the UN. The Maoists quite evidently sought the legitimacy that any involvement of the UN could bring to their struggle and, from early 2004 on, appealed directly for its mediation.[6]

The ceasefire collapsed after the RNA arrested and then killed 19 suspected Maoists in Doramba on August 17, 2003. As violence surged and clashes between the police, students, and other activists became more frequent, Samuel established a pattern of regular visits to Nepal, where he met with a wide range of interlocutors. Among them was Bhekh Bahadur Thapa, who in the latter part of 2003 was Nepal's ambassador at large and in early 2004 became foreign minister. Thapa assured Samuel that he had told the Indians that Nepal had decided to use the UN "to talk about talks" with the Maoists, and Samuel became the conduit for a backchannel to the Maoists that, for a while, appeared to be working well.[7] However, the political situation was deteriorating, and the king's cabinet was coming under increasing pressure from street and other protests. In June the king dismissed the prime minister, Bhekh Thapa left the government, and so the initiative died.

In some respects the difficulties that Samuel and the UN encountered were not dissimilar to those met by the HD Centre; in other areas the UN's involvement was always going to be different from that of any other actor. Despite assistance from UNDP, the disadvantages for Samuel of working without a political presence on the ground or the ability to visit Nepal frequently were self-evident. Moreover, although it was acting with the legitimacy of the secretary-general, the UN had no clear mandate for its role in Nepal and was no less vulnerable to the political and other purposes of the parties with which it was interacting than any other entity. Yet Samuel was able to consult more broadly than the HD Centre and to meet regularly with members of Nepal's diplomatic community, including India, without jeopardizing the confidentiality of his individual discussions. He and his colleagues were also

---

[6] In March 2004 the Maoist leader Pushpa Kamal Dahal, widely known as "Prachanda," issued a statement in response to a renewed offer by Annan "to be available . . . in any manner the parties consider useful" (statement of March 22, 2004), which underlined the Maoists' recognition of "the need of mediation of the United Nations." CPN-M Press Statement, March 25, 2004, available on http://www.cpnm.org.

[7] Interviews, Tamrat Samuel and Bhekh Bahadur Thapa, March 2008.

able to send consistent messages regarding the nature of the secretary-general's good offices, which many Nepalis were surprised to learn did not necessarily involve the Security Council, and the consent-based nature of the United Nations as a whole. These messages conveyed that, if the UN were to get involved, it would be able to offer a range of resources: from limited technical involvement in issues such as human rights, arms monitoring, and electoral assistance to direct mediation and a full-scale peace operation.

Deuba became prime minister again in mid-2004 and created the HLPC and a peace secretariat to support it. However, the prospects for success were dim. Real power rested with the king, and the Maoists increasingly insisted that, on this basis, it was only Gyanendra with whom they would negotiate.

An August 2004 CPN-M central committee meeting highlighted considerable differences among the Maoist leadership on this issue, even as it reinforced the understanding that no military victory to their struggle would be possible. Bhattarai favored a more conciliatory approach to the political parties, in part because it might win the support of India and pave the way for a Constituent Assembly. However, Pushpa Kamal Dahal, better known as "Prachanda," the Maoists' chairman and commander-in-chief, preferred to reach an understanding with "patriotic forces" (including the king) to counter the threat of "Indian intervention."[8] Although in contact with Deuba and his deputy, HD had opened a highly confidential parallel track of dialogue that directly involved the palace. Intermittent discussions regarding the possibility of a meeting between the king and Prachanda continued even as tensions between the king and his government grew worse.

In the meantime, in the latter part of 2004 the Carter Center appeared on the scene as a new actor in efforts toward peace in Nepal. It had sent two missions to the country earlier in the year and had been encouraged by the palace and Deuba to invite the HLPC to meet with President Carter in Atlanta in November. In Atlanta, the HLPC, which was eager to increase pressure on the Maoists, sought help from the Carter Center in encouraging the Maoists to return to talks.[9] The Carter Center was keen to fulfill this role in the context of its growing attention to conflict resolution, but soon ran up against a number of problems: none of the king's actions favored dialogue; the Carter Center was ill prepared to initiate contacts with the Maoists that were already available to HD, the UN, and members of the peace committee itself (telephone contact with Bhattarai was eventually established in early 2005); and Carter Center staff located in the United States were poorly placed to understand the complexity of the situation with which they were becoming involved.

---

[8] International Crisis Group, *Nepal's Maoists: Purists or Pragmatists?*, Asia Report No. 132, May 18, 2007, p. 4.

[9] One indication of the fluidity of internal communication among Nepali political actors was that the UML leader Madhav Nepal, at the time chairman of the HLPC, had telephoned Prachanda to seek his advice on the Carter Center's initiative. Interview, Madhav Nepal, March 2008.

The Carter Center briefed both India and the United States on its activities and tried to be "as collaborative as humanly possible" with other external actors, especially the United Nations.[10] Although its overtures were politely received, several of its interlocutors harbored doubts about its suitability for a conflict resolution role in Nepal, given the confusing signals given by its identity as an NGO headed by a former U.S. president. In the Nepali context, obvious complications arose from the Carter Center's attempt to navigate relations with the CPN-M – which had been included on the U.S. "terrorism exclusion list" since 2003, although it was never designated a "foreign terrorist organization" – and with India. Regular contacts with Washington and with the U.S. embassy in Kathmandu, which was headed between 2001–7 by ambassadors vocal in their views that aligned the Maoist threat with global terrorism, fueled suspicions of the Carter Center's professed independence. Carter's own history with India, which included consistent support of the Non-Proliferation Treaty and opposition to any nuclear deal between the United States and India, was not an asset. In addition, Indian authorities were consistently ill disposed to look kindly on nongovernmental "freelancers" volunteering themselves a role in Nepal's complex internal conflict.

AFTER THE COUP

The robust international response to King Gyanendra's coup of February 1, 2005, was one critical element in the changes that followed. India led condemnation of the king's actions and was joined by the United States, the United Kingdom, and other EU countries. Vocal diplomatic protests were made, lethal military assistance was suspended, and ambassadors recalled. However, as the months went by with little discernible change in the king's behavior, the initial unity with which the international community had responded began to fracture.

National political developments came to the fore in a gradual realignment of the triangular dynamics of Nepal's conflict – defined by the mutual opposition of the king, the Maoists, and the mainstream political parties – into a broad front of opposition against the king. Three critical processes had a lasting impact on the shape of things to come: (1) reconciliation within the Maoists, who overcame their internal divisions with an accommodation that left Prachanda's authority in place but followed the political path outlined by Bhattarai; (2) agreement within the country's mainstream political parties to work together within the SPA; and (3) agreement between the SPA and the CPN-M in November 2005 on a joint strategy against the monarchy. In none of these processes were international actors other than India centrally involved – as Chapter 12 by S. D. Muni makes clear – even though their presence in Kathmandu was multiplying and their degree of interaction with the various political actors was increasing. Meanwhile, the quiet role

---

[10]   Interview, former Carter Center official, February 2008.

played by individual Nepalis within the political parties and from civil society, who invested time and energy in flying back and forth between Kathmandu and Delhi – encouraging progress in all three processes – represented a notable contribution to the emerging political process.

In the immediate aftermath of the coup a surprising development was agreement by the government of Nepal (and India behind it, albeit reluctantly) to the creation of an Office of the UN High Commissioner for Human Rights in Nepal. The agreement, which was endorsed within the UN's Human Rights Commission on April 20, 2005, owed a lot to the heightened attention to the dramatic curtailment of human rights since February 1 and India's frustration with the king. However, it would not have been achieved without the efforts of individual Nepalis and others who had been able to build a broad international coalition in its support. The office was headed by Ian Martin, a former secretary-general of Amnesty International with extensive experience in UN missions elsewhere. As it extended its presence across Nepal, OHCHR became not only a confidence-building measure for Nepal's beleaguered civilian population and a vital source of information on human rights abuses but also an effective means to promote communication with the conflict parties.

Martin knew Tamrat Samuel well from a period of collaboration on East Timor, and they quickly established a productive working relationship. Samuel's visits had continued in the months after February 1, but he had no illusions as to any leverage the UN might have over the king. Annan had met with Gyanendra in late April in Jakarta and had not been taken in by promises that Nepal's problems would be resolved before the king visited New York for the General Assembly meeting that September. (Because they weren't, significant international pressure ensured that he didn't.) Annan remained engaged, despite India's opposition to a more active UN role, and dispatched his most senior and trusted envoy, Lakhdar Brahimi, to Nepal in July. The king's lack of political judgment once again came to the fore. Hours after meeting with Brahimi and assuring him that things would be moving in a positive direction, he expanded his cabinet to fill it with hard-liners and former officials from the past.

Other external actors sought to accommodate themselves to the changed situation after the coup, even as the focus of political developments began to shift to the emerging dynamics between the political parties and the Maoists. A new development was the arrival in Kathmandu of two individuals – one a representative of the Swiss government, the other a South African consultant contracted by USAID – specifically tasked with the provision of support to peace efforts.

Günther Baechler's assignment as special advisor on peacebuilding derived both from Switzerland's long presence in the country as a development actor and from a determined effort by the Swiss foreign ministry to become more engaged in conflict resolution. Baechler was located in Kathmandu and thus could build relationships with a broad range of political and other actors, which positioned him well to play a useful role in support of the peace process, particularly as it evolved in 2006.

Hannes Siebert, a South African expert on conflict resolution, had first been engaged to provide support to the HLPC's peace secretariat in the fall of 2004. By mid-2005 he was working with the peace secretariat of the postcoup government of the king. Siebert struggled to overcome the tension between his roles as a USAID-funded consultant and as an independent expert whose first priority was support to the national process. He remained an advisor to the peace secretariat, at times engaging in initiatives with Baechler as part of a "task force" established to support it, but was never able to establish the independent profile that Baechler's Swiss nationality afforded him.

NEPALIS TO THE FORE

The dialogue that began in May 2005 culminated in discussions in Delhi in November that led to the 12-Point Understanding. Concluded with the tacit support of India and providing a substantive agenda for a future process, this agreement was qualitatively different from anything that had happened before. It looked forward to an elected Constituent Assembly; a Maoist commitment to multiparty democracy; and outside supervision of the armed Maoist force and RNA during the electoral process, led by the United Nations "or any other reliable international supervision," all as part of a broader effort to bring an end to "autocratic monarchy."[11]

The coup had sharply underlined the gulf separating the political parties from a position at the center of Nepal's democratic system. The palace controlled the government, but the opposition had been captured by the Maoists, both in their articulation of demands for change and in their physical presence across the country. The parties' inability to engage in dialogue with the palace and their loss of popular support rendered an attempt to seek accommodation with the Maoists the logical, if not the only, way forward. Smoothing the way were the coup's end to the Maoists' exploration of dialogue with the palace and the assuaging of divisions between Prachanda and Bhattarai. For the Maoists, dialogue with the political parties represented an opportunity to achieve both the legitimacy they craved and central elements – most importantly a Constituent Assembly – of the political agenda they had long pursued.

Indian support to the process offered both the SPA and the Maoists important guarantees. It was a product of both evolution in the thinking of the United Progressive Alliance (UPA) government that came to power in 2004 and broader shifts in policy toward Nepal precipitated by the coup. However, these changes lagged behind both the political and institutional crisis facing Nepal in the early 2000s

---

[11] Appendix, *Nepal's New Alliance: The Mainstream Parties and the Maoists*, Asia Report No. 106, November 28, 2005, pp. 29–30.

and Maoist efforts to communicate directly with Indian officials, highlighting the essentially reactive nature of Indian policy toward Nepal. The Maoists' attempt to reach out to India had begun in 2002, when Bhattarai had enlisted the help of a professor, S. D. Muni, a former Indian diplomat and noted scholar of South and Southeast Asia with deep ties to Nepal, with whom he had remained in contact since his days as a student at the Jahwaharlal Nehru University (JNU). Muni had been able to convey a message to the government of Atal Bihari Vajpayee at very high levels with some positive effect, but had found no willingness to meet the Maoists among the Indian politicians he approached.[12]

With the UPA in power and the Communist Party of India (Marxist) (CPM) a mainstay of its fragile coalition, a gradual shift in approach to the Maoists began to gain momentum. Sitarum Yechury of the CPM recalled that he had been approached by Prime Minister Manmohan Singh in about September 2004 and asked whether he would use his JNU contacts to talk to Maoists and help "bring them in to the mainstream democratic process." With Muni's assistance, he met with Maoist representatives in Delhi (Muni also facilitated a meeting between CPM leader Prakash Karat and Bhattarai in May 2005). After the coup, Yechury's involvement, and that of a Nepal Democracy Solidarity Committee he had formed with D. P. Tripathi of the Nationalist Congress Party, intensified.[13] The two – both former colleagues of Bhattarai at JNU – began working first with political party leaders already engaged in efforts to form the SPA and then, more discreetly, to encourage those leaders' engagement with the Maoists.

International actors had been aware of the mounting level of Nepali political activity in Delhi. In the latter part of November 2005 they traveled there en masse. In the case of the UN, the HD Centre, and the Carter Center, they were drawn by the opportunity presented for a first meeting with Prachanda himself (only the Carter Center did not manage a meeting with the Maoist leadership, although its representatives spoke to them on the telephone). In that of the U.S. ambassador in Nepal, James Moriarty, it was the need for "urgent consultations" with the Indian government that took him to Delhi, as he backpedaled on his earlier opposition to the Maoist–party talks.[14]

An interest by the Maoists in consultations with their most trusted international interlocutors reflected new possibilities for outsiders in the next stage of talks. These

---

[12] S. D. Muni, interview, March 2008, and e-mail, August 2008. Further details of Muni's role are provided in Chapter 12.

[13] Yechury met "five or six times" with the Maoist leadership (twice with Prachanda) in 2005–6. Interview, March 2008. See also Bharat Bhushan, "Yechury in Nepal democracy pantheon," *The Telegraph*, April 29, 2006.

[14] In mid-November, Moriarty had argued that "until and unless the Maoists lay down their weapons, the political parties cannot be in alliance with them – it would be deeply dangerous to do so." Interview, November 2005. After the agreement had been announced a U.S. spokesman "cautiously welcomed the new political understanding reached between mainstream parties and Maoists." Cited in International Crisis Group, *Nepal's New Alliance*, p. 23.

talks were conceived as proceeding in parallel to plans for a mass movement against the king in the early months of 2006. With Indian acquiescence, the 12-Point Understanding had opened the door to the possibility of a UN role in monitoring while also stating that the parties "expect reliable international mediation even during the dialogue process." The Maoists explained to both the UN and the HD Centre that they hoped for more direct involvement of third-party facilitation in any future talks, in part because of continuing sensitivities regarding India. They continued to prefer the UN, but they feared that its direct involvement would be more than India could tolerate. With India holding pronounced doubts about the Carter Center, there was agreement between the Maoists and the SPA that the HD Centre was best suited to set up the next round of talks, ideally in a third country.

As 2005 moved into 2006, discussions regarding possible international support for further talks continued. The UN maintained a deliberately low profile, in part because follow-up to an agreement that did not just exclude the government of Nepal but pointed toward its demise, was clearly a delicate matter for an intergovernmental organization. In his OHCHR capacity Martin nevertheless continued to engage the royal government and warn of the looming danger of street confrontations. Meanwhile, the HD Centre returned to Delhi and Kathmandu in late January/early February for consultations with India, the Maoists, and political parties on the possibility of arranging a new round of talks in Switzerland. The Carter Center resumed its engagement, and Baechler, on Switzerland's behalf, also increased his activity – offering at one point to host talks between the Nepali parties in the Swiss embassy in Delhi.

It gradually became evident that all these efforts were taking place at the margins of the emergence of powerful forces for political change in Nepal. The external peace-makers quite properly stood back to let the internal process run its course. An initial call by an increasingly organized civil society movement and the political parties for mass protests on January 20, 2006, was badly coordinated with the Maoists and in part preempted by widespread arrests of key civil society and other leaders. In late March the Maoists and the parties reaffirmed their commitment to work together and called for mass agitation. The movement gathered force. A succession of strikes, protests, and rallies attracted wider support than either the Maoists or the political parties had foreseen. Members of civil society, the media, the business community, professional disciplines, government bureaucrats, and the public at large took to the streets.

The end, when it came, was messy not as a consequence of the level of violence – although 19 people were killed during the course of 19 days of agitation, the number was in many respects low given the scale of the mobilization – but because of the diplomacy involved. As the need for a compromise became evident, India sent as an envoy Karan Singh, a senior Congress politician with ties to Nepal's royal family, in an effort to persuade the king to put forward an acceptable offer. He returned quickly to Delhi, but was nevertheless able to persuade Gyanendra to issue a proclamation that invited the SPA to nominate a candidate for prime minister.

Accepting the proposal would have divided the parties from the Maoists and civil society and undoubtedly would have weakened the popular movement. However, the international community (India, China, the United States, United Kingdom, and other EU states) rushed to welcome it without waiting to hear the response of the people of Nepal.

The Maoists and the agitating masses were not prepared to back down, and the parties too stood firm. After the direct intervention of its foreign secretary, Shyam Saran, India released a statement that backtracked embarrassingly on its earlier position. On April 24, the king issued a second proclamation, this time agreed in advance with the SPA leadership, as well as with India. He recognized the sovereignty inherent in the people, called for a resolution of the conflict "according to the road map of the agitating Seven Party Alliance," and announced the restoration of the parliament elected in 1999.[15]

SUPPORTING THE PEACE PROCESS

The dramatic denouement of the April 2006 popular movement underlined the extent to which Nepal's political revolution was homegrown. Yet in the following months, as Nepal's negotiations got underway, they did so amidst a plethora of offers of assistance. Governments and international NGOs alike, few of them entirely immune to the opportunities presented by the possibility of contributing to an effort that seemed to be making forward progress, sent in missions, consultants, and advisors who struggled to find a way to make a useful contribution. In September C. K. Lal, a prominent Nepali commentator, published an article – subtitled "let's oppose all foreign interference except the UN's" – that declared the "conflict tourism season" to be well underway.[16]

Accommodation to the reality of Nepali ownership was complicated by questions of role definition of the international actors already well established in the process, as well as significant problems in the negotiations. A substantive UN engagement in the peace process seemed increasingly likely, but its contours lacked definition. Even as the reinstated parliament moved quickly to endorse plans for a Constituent Assembly, the Royal Nepalese Army was stripped of its "royal" attributes – if not of any of its authority as the power behind the status quo – to become the Nepalese Army, and reciprocal ceasefires were declared.

In early May the Maoist leadership met with Andrew Marshall of the HD Centre, Günther Baechler, and Padma Ratna Tuladhar in New Delhi. The Maoists asked the HD Centre and the Swiss government to play the role of independent observers to all future negotiations with the SPA government. This role was not one that the HD Centre believed played to its comparative advantage, and so it decided to bring

---

[15] Proclamation to the Nation from His Majesty King Gyanendra, April 24, 2006.
[16] C. K. Lal, "DDR, SSR, RRR and the SPA," *Nepali Times*, September 7, 2006.

its engagement in Nepal to a conclusion soon afterward. Baechler's involvement, however, intensified. From Delhi he contacted Siebert in Kathmandu, and the two began providing support to the emerging negotiation teams of the SPA government, now led by Koirala, and the Maoists, as they worked on a draft of the ceasefire Code of Conduct that would be agreed on May 25.

In the meantime, although Indian support of some kind of UN role now seemed assured and was being actively encouraged by the United States, resistance to the UN's mediation, or even facilitation, still remained. Samuel visited Kathmandu and Delhi in mid-May with the chief military planner of the UN's department of peacekeeping operations. Their meetings confirmed that Nepali actors – in the government, the political parties, and among the Maoists – envisaged a major UN role in the peace process. During a June visit to Delhi, Koirala would put it starkly to India that either a UN role had to be accepted or India itself should assume responsibility for arms management in Nepal. Unwilling to take on this role, Indian officials eventually accepted the utility of UN involvement, not least for the international credibility that it alone could bring to the process. "I was not against a UN role for specific jobs," a senior Indian official recalled in March 2008, "so long as they did not want to take over the process."[17]

In the end a loose amalgam of support structures fell into place as the political process progressed through the Eight-Point Understanding reached on June 16 (establishing the general objective and course of the political transition) and toward the signing of the Comprehensive Peace Agreement on November 21. Baechler and Siebert provided close support to the peace secretariat (including the national observers) and the two talks' teams. They also worked in increasingly close contact with the UN, as it dispatched a "pre-assessment mission" to Nepal in late July to help forge an understanding between the government and the Maoists on the nature and scope of the UN role.

From the outset, however, the negotiations lacked the structure to guide the process in a manageable way. Despite the existence of identified negotiation teams, a peace secretariat, national observers, and international advisors, the talks reflected both the dominance of a narrow political elite and a rapid return by the mainstream political parties to exclusionary practices of the past. These features rendered decision making the province of a few individuals, most of whom had been in leadership positions throughout the 1990s. Meanwhile, the civil society movement, which had played such a prominent role in the mass mobilizations of the preceding few months, receded quickly from the scene. As one analyst commented, this withdrawal appeared to reflect "an unstated assumption that the interests of civil society were wholly represented by the political parties, combined with a shift in focus by NGOs from the protests of the April 2006 movement to ensuring their participation in

---

[17] Confidential interview conducted by the author.

donor-funded 'peacebuilding.'"[18] Within this difficult context many of the efforts of the international advisors closest to the process went unrewarded. Nepal's politicians proved surprisingly resistant to external inputs, and sound ideas – ranging from background papers from Baechler on process design and architecture, advice on the interim constitution provided by Professor Yash Ghai, whom UNDP had engaged to head a new constitutional advisory support unit, to proposals for an effective monitoring mechanism drafted by UN officials and others – found little traction.

Despite these limitations, external actors were able to make constructive contributions to a number of the different negotiations that developed in the latter half of 2006. The UN's pre-assessment mission initiated an exhausting session of negotiations between the parties on the precise terms of their request for UN support. This took place with the involvement of Baechler and Siebert and concluded only after the mission had left. Identical letters were eventually dispatched to Kofi Annan on August 9, asking for the assistance of the UN in continued human rights monitoring, monitoring of the ceasefire, management of arms and armed personnel of both sides, and in the electoral process.

Annan immediately named Ian Martin his personal representative to Nepal and authorized a small team of advisors to support him. Martin began work in early September amidst a complicated political environment. All talks appeared stalled, and the lack of trust between the parties was palpable. The government was keen for Martin to get discussions on arms management underway, but the Maoists insisted that political and arms management issues had to be discussed in parallel. Over time, an informal division of labor developed, whereby Baechler and Siebert worked with the parties on drafts of possible political agreements, sharing them regularly with Martin, while Martin himself, who was joined in October by Brig. General Jan Erik Wilhelmsen of Norway as his senior military advisor, and other advisors soon afterward, held consultations and provided input on the areas identified for UN assistance.

Talks on the difficult and intertwined issues of transitional power sharing, the status of the monarchy, and the management of arms and armed personnel progressed rapidly in October. Key problems for the UN were the speed at which the parties obviously expected it to be able to assume its monitoring responsibilities; their insistence that the management of arms and armed personnel be monitored by civilian (ex-military) monitors, a formula that was new to the UN and operationally complicated; and broader political considerations regarding whether a mandate of the General Assembly or the Security Council was more appropriate.

In the Comprehensive Peace Agreement signed on November 21, 2006, the parties committed themselves to finalizing an interim constitution; forming an interim

---

[18] John Tyynela, *Final Report, Conflict Prevention and Peace Forum Nepal Consultancy on Civil Affairs Monitoring*, March 27, 2007, p. 12.

assembly and government, in which the Maoists would take part; and determining the fate of the monarchy in the first meeting of a Constituent Assembly, for which elections were to take place by mid-June 2007. Notably absent from the CPA's provisions were clarity on the critical issue of the fate of Nepal's two armies, commitments to justice and accountability, or provision for a monitoring mechanism for the commitments it did contain. Although the CPA did look forward to a UN role in arms monitoring, this role would only be clarified in the days ahead in tripartite negotiations between Martin and his advisors, the government, and the Maoists. In some respects these talks were the most classically structured and orderly of Nepal's varied negotiations; they were chaired by General Wilhelmsen and concluded in an agreement on November 28 that was signed on December 8, paving the way for the establishment in January 2007 of the United Nations Mission in Nepal (UNMIN).

CONCLUSION

As other chapters in this volume describe, Nepal's comprehensive peace agreement may have marked the end of the armed confrontation, but it also heralded a long and far from completed struggle for sustainable peace. Conflict dynamics that had for much of the decade pitted three contending forces against each other were overtaken by new and more complex demands, rooted in deep-seated issues of identity and exclusion that the peace process had exposed, but by no means fully addressed.

This chapter has concentrated on international peacemaking in Nepal. Assessing its impact is complicated by three distinct factors. First, none of the efforts to promote dialogue before February 2005 resulted in a conventionally structured dialogue, even as the various discussions, sharing of advice, and carrying of messages undoubtedly constituted a sort of informal dialogue of its own. Second, in the post-April 2006 period, although elements of the advice proffered by international actors were picked up and reflected within the ongoing process, much of it was simply not heeded. Third, this chapter does not extend to the period of implementation of the CPA and its complex political processes.

Therefore questions regarding impact both tend toward the counterfactual and defy easy answers. They also should be considered while recalling that one of the central features of the peace process is the extent to which its long and complex trajectory demonstrated the benefits of talking. Across conflict lines, with India and with a wide range of interested outsiders, the parties to Nepal's conflict kept talking – and, in the case of the Maoists in particular, thinking about talking even when the talking itself was not taking place – and thus laid the groundwork for the solution of the conflict by political means.

It is in this area that the benefits of the early efforts by external actors – notably the HD Centre and then the UN – can perhaps be perceived most clearly. The HD Centre's involvement in the early 2000s has been credited with helping initiate "a discourse of dialogue" in Nepal.[19] Public attention to the conflict by the United Nations from 2002 on lifted the discussion of dialogue to a different level: the secretary-general's offer of his good offices and the frequent visits by Tamrat Samuel prompted a healthy public debate on the possibilities of dialogue and a UN role that the HD Centre had neither wanted nor been able to play. This process was continued by the involvement of the Carter Center and others who organized a variety of workshops, study trips, and seminars. A direct correlation between these various efforts and developments in Nepal's peace process is difficult to determine, but their contribution to a landscape in which discussion of dialogue and negotiation became commonplace is undeniable.

The sustained interest in Nepal by the UN secretary-general came no closer than the HD Centre's efforts to initiating a formal and structured dialogue, but it brought with it other benefits. First and foremost, it helped spur interest in Nepal at an international level at a time when the gravity of the situation in Nepal was largely ignored. Second, Samuel's visits managed to ensure that the UN became a regular political interlocutor of all parties in Nepal, as well as of India and other members of the international community. His efforts laid the groundwork for the UN role that gradually developed, initially through the opening of the OHCHR presence; then through the elevation of that office's head, Ian Martin, to a position as a direct representative of the secretary-general; and finally to the establishment of UNMIN in early 2007. Without this progression it is unlikely that a special political mission of the United Nations would have been acceptable either to Nepal or India. Finally, that substantive discussion of issues such as cantonments, weapons lock-up, monitoring, and international supervision of elections had begun well before 2005 undoubtedly helped them find their way into the 12-Point Understanding and the CPA.

There are undoubtedly lessons to be learned from the multiple efforts to pursue peacemaking in Nepal. Nongovernmental actors who were not resident in the country and were simultaneously engaged in activities elsewhere had insufficient capacity to understand the full complexity of the conflict's dynamics and thus the wider context within which their efforts were sited. All the external actors struggled with what to do about India's firmly held suspicion of their involvement. Although the United Nations could at least engage Indian officials from a solid institutional basis, interaction with New Delhi by a country as small as Switzerland, let alone an NGO, was more complex. Tolerance of their interest was the most that could be expected, whether direct engagement was pursued – as in the case of the Carter Center – or, as in the case of the HD Centre, avoided for many years.

A proliferation of international actors was itself confusing for their Nepali counterparts, who accepted the multiple offers of assistance with goodwill, even as they

---

[19] Rajendra Dahal, "Personal View: Nepal's Conflict and the HD Centre," *Centre for Humanitarian Dialogue Annual Report 2006*, p. 7.

found confusing the fragmentation of their partners and their reluctance to collaborate more closely with one another. Padma Ratna Tuladhar saw all the outsiders come and go. He recalled constantly trying to encourage his foreign friends to work together. Yet his efforts were to no avail. "I suppose it is just not in their culture," was his somewhat rueful conclusion.[20]

There are questions to be asked about India's role as well, not least the perception that India's "twin pillar" policy toward Nepal caused it, for too long, to passively accept the country's descent into conflict and institutional decay. The dramatic events of February 2005 and April 2006 precipitated a fundamental change in India's attitude and actions, but it is not too much to have expected a more proactive and less reactive engagement from Delhi at an earlier stage. Similarly, it is important to ask, given the trajectory followed by external actors engaged within Nepal's peace process, whether India's neuralgia toward international involvement was justified.

In the years since the CPA, and in particular since the Maoists emerged as the largest political party in the new Constituent Assembly – confounding India's expectations – questions about the impact of India's strong presence within Nepal have only intensified. A determination to keep the UN within the strict limits of UNMIN's mandate prevented the organization from assuming a prominent role in addressing the differences that continued to arise between Nepal's fractious political actors. The peace process lurched forward, with delays in the CPA's implementation a consequence of denial of some of the fundamental precepts on which it was based (including a need to address future arrangements for the country's two armies). Peacemaking of a kind remained required, but for the most part it has taken the form of intermittent dialogue among national political elites, supplemented by the direct involvement of India at critical moments behind the scenes. Whether this will be sufficient to move toward the stable and democratic Nepal for which hundreds of thousands of Nepalis took to the streets in April 2006 remains to be seen.

---

[20] Interview, March 2008.

7

A Comprehensive Peace? Lessons from Human Rights Monitoring in Nepal

Frederick Rawski and Mandira Sharma

INTRODUCTION

The Maoist insurgency in Nepal took place over a decade during which human rights discourse was growing in influence at the international level. When the conflict began in the mid-1990s, the Office of the United Nations High Commissioner for Human Rights (OHCHR) had only just been created, and Nepal's troubles attracted little international attention. By the end of 2005, Nepal had become host to one of the largest UN human rights field operations in the world, and human rights issues had come to play a central role in national political discourse about the conflict. International monitoring and advocacy helped reduce violence and create space for national actors to push a human rights and pro-democracy agenda culminating in the April 2006 People's Movement.

However, after the signing of the November 2006 Comprehensive Peace Agreement (CPA), human rights seemed to lose their centrality as attention shifted to the complexities of postconflict politics. Little progress was made in addressing the inequality, systemic corruption, and weak rule of law to which the insurgency was largely a response, despite most of the main political actors' public commitments to uphold human rights and end impunity. As human rights advocates and victims' groups adjusted their focus from the prevention of civilian casualties to these root causes, their demands for accountability and change appeared to fall on deaf ears. A range of political actors – including some who supported a robust international presence during the conflict – began to attack international monitoring as a form of interference in sovereign affairs and to make claims that the national human rights agenda was being driven by interests outside Nepal.

This chapter examines the role that human rights advocacy and field monitoring played in Nepal before and after the signing of the peace agreement, with a view toward explaining why human rights figured so prominently during the conflict, and why the human rights community found it difficult to effectively push forward a rights agenda during the post-CPA period. It concludes by drawing lessons from the Nepal experience, focusing on identifying the limitations of international intervention, and offers a few words of caution about the transitional justice approach to postconflict peacebuilding.

HUMAN RIGHTS MONITORING DURING
THE MAOIST CONFLICT IN NEPAL

Impunity, Rights, and the Roots of the Insurgency

The Maoist insurgency must be understood in the context of centuries of ethnic and caste-based discrimination and the exclusion of most of the population from participation in government. For most of its history, government in Nepal has been an authoritarian affair dominated by a small upper caste elite and hereditary kings. Between 1846 and 1950 the monarchy was reduced to a ceremonial role by a series of authoritarian prime ministers drawn from the Rana family, who treated the state as their personal estate and reinforced caste ideology and impunity. A failed attempt at democratic governance in the late 1950s ended with the imposition of monarchic rule in the form of the Panchayat system, which persisted for three decades until it gave way to a constitutional monarchy after the 1990 People's Movement.[1]

A succession of post-1990 governments failed to end these entrenched patterns of patronage and impunity or to shake the overwhelming influence of the king and the army. Political party leaders continued to take direction from the palace, co-opt local government structures, and fill public institutions with their own cadres. Home Minister Sher Bahadur Deuba (and his successors) did the same for the security and criminal justice sectors, resulting in the politicization of both the police and the judiciary. It is not surprising then that, from its founding in 1995, the leaders of the Communist Party of Nepal (Maoist) (CPN-M) characterized the party's objective as completing the unfinished business of the People's Movement abandoned by the other political parties – such as abolishing ethnic and caste-based discrimination and ending the one-sided justice of the Panchayat and its dysfunctional successors.[2]

During the course of the conflict and as international attention intensified, Maoist rhetoric drew increasingly on human rights discourse as a tool to justify the war and to impeach the integrity of the government security forces. Although the term "human rights" does not appear in the Maoists' 1996 40-Point Demand, the

[1] The Panchayat system, established by King Mahendra and enshrined in the 1962 constitution, consisted of a series of party-less political assemblies at the local and national level. Although King Birendra, Mahendra's successor, initiated some democratic reforms to the system in 1980s, the Panchayat system remained a thinly veiled form of direct rule by the monarchy until it was dismantled in 1990.

[2] For more on this, see Deepak Thapa, *A Kingdom under Siege: Nepal's Maoist Insurgency, 1996 to 2004* (2004), pp. 13–50; Ali Riaz and Subho Basu, *Paradise Lost? State Failure in Nepal* (2010), pp. 119–34.

document makes detailed reference to the unfulfilled rights (*adhikar*) of the Nepali people to education, freedom of expression, and freedom from political repression and discrimination based on race, caste, class, gender, geography, and language. As the conflict deepened, both civilian-led governments and the royal government of King Gyanendra characterized the Maoist insurgents as criminals (and later, terrorists) in an attempt to shield the conduct of the war from international scrutiny. Nonetheless, by the time the Royal Nepalese Army (RNA) was deployed in late 2001, the Maoists had developed a sophisticated political and military structure, including parallel government institutions such as rural development bodies and revolutionary tribunals.[3]

Over time, the Maoists adopted tactics incompatible with their own rights-laden rhetoric, much less international human rights standards, including extrajudicial killings, torture, extortion, the targeting of civilians, abductions, and forced labor.[4] Yet as international attention increased, both Maoist rhetoric and behavior continued to evolve. By the time the 2003 ceasefire negotiations began, Maoist references to human rights had become explicit, including demands for the "impartial investigation of the abuse of human rights in the course of the civil war."[5] The clandestine and military leadership soon began to make public commitments that Maoist combatants would abide by international law during combat operations. In January 2004, Maoist leader Pushpa Kamal Dahal, also known as Prachanda, made a statement supporting an international mediation and monitoring role. Maoist leaders later publicly committed to abide by the Geneva Conventions and entered into a ceasefire Code of Conduct, which made reference to the Universal Declaration of Human Rights. In some regions, Maoists selectively invited the International Committee of the Red Cross (ICRC) and other human rights monitors to be present when they released prisoners from their custody to show that they were observing humanitarian law.

These commitments formed part of a larger Maoist strategy to build legitimacy in the eyes of the international community. In turn, international scrutiny – in particular the establishment of the OHCHR in Nepal in 2005 – seemed to have a moderating effect on Maoist abuses. From mid-2005, there was a noticeable drop in

---

3 See *Nepal's Maoists: Their Aims, Structure and Strategy*, International Crisis Group Asia Report No. 104 (October 27, 2005). All ICG reports cited in this chapter are available at http://www.crisisgroup.org.

4 For accounts of Maoist abuses, see *Nepal: A Spiraling Human Rights Crisis*, Amnesty International (April 4, 2002); *Between a Rock and a Hard Place: Civilians Struggle to Survive in Nepal's Civil War*, Human Rights Watch (October 6, 2004); *Nepal: Dealing with a Human Rights Crisis*, International Crisis Group Asia Report No. 94 (March 24, 2005); *Investigations into Violations of International Humanitarian Law in the Context of Attacks and Clashes between the Communist Party of Nepal (Maoist) and Government Security Forces*, Office of the High Commissioner for Human Rights, Nepal (Jan.–March 2006). All OHCHR-Nepal documents cited in this chapter are available at http://nepal.ohchr.org.

5 *Summary of the CPN (Maoist) Proposal Presented for Consideration during 2003 Ceasefire* (April 27, 2003), in D. Thapa, *supra* note 2, at 227.

civilian casualties, torture, and abductions at the hands of their cadres. Nonetheless, a stark contrast remained between Maoist commitments to human rights and their use of violence and intimidation against civilians – a contradiction that continued to dog them well after the conflict formally ended.[6]

Enter the Royal Nepalese Army: International Scrutiny Increases

Although the ICRC had been active in Nepal since 1998, the conflict began to garner the attention of the international community in earnest only after the RNA was deployed in late 2001 to counter increasingly brazen Maoist attacks, primarily against poorly equipped police posts.[7] After a four-month ceasefire broke down in November, the government proclaimed the CPN-M a terrorist organization and declared a state of emergency. It promulgated the Terrorist and Disruptive Activities (Control and Punishment) Ordinance (TADO), which authorized preventive detention and empowered the RNA to take direct control of counterinsurgency operations, including those of the Nepal Police and the newly created Armed Police Force.[8] Allies in the international community, including India, the United Kingdom, and the United States (which added the CPN–M to its Terrorist Exclusion List in 2004),[9] increased their support. Before the state of emergency was lifted in August 2002, more than three thousand lives had been lost, and hundreds of civilians had been disappeared.[10]

RNA tactics developed during the state of emergency carried over into the later stages of the conflict. Conflict-related deaths, both military and civilian, increased dramatically as fighting spread from the mid-western districts to the rest of the country. Typically, the RNA would refrain from engaging with the Maoist People's Liberation Army directly – instead retaliating against individuals and communities suspected of providing them with assistance. Enforced disappearances and extrajudicial executions became common, especially in the immediate aftermath of Maoist

---

[6] For an account of the Maoists' transformation after the CPA, see Chapter 10 by Aditya Adhikari. For more on the evolution of Maoist thinking on the use of violence, see Chapter 3 by Rhoderick Chalmers.

[7] The RNA initially refused to follow the order of the Nepali Congress-led government to engage the Maoists in July 2001. It finally entered the conflict after Maoists attacked a Nepalese Army barracks at Dang that November. For more on these events and why the Army remained on the sidelines for so long, see Chapter 3.

[8] TADO was subsequently adopted by the Parliament as the Terrorist and Disruptive (Control and Punishment) Act (TADA) in 2002. For a legal review of TADO, TADA and other security legislation in Nepal, see *Nepal: National Security Laws and Human Rights Implications*, International Commission of Jurists (August 2009).

[9] Pursuant to Section 411 of the 2001 Patriot Act (8 U.S.C. § 1182), www.state.gov/s/ct/rls/other/des/123086.htm

[10] According to the Informal Sector Service Center (INSEC), 3,525 people were killed during the nine-month state of emergency. INSEC data on conflict violations are available at http://www.inseconline.org.

attacks.[11] These retaliations sometimes included the use of rape; for example, after the Maoist attack on the RNA at Mangalsen, Accham in February 2002. In January 2003, Maoists assassinated Inspector-General Krishna Mohan Shrestha of the Armed Police Force (and his wife) in Kathmandu. Shortly after this act, Maoist leaders called for a ceasefire, but it quickly broke down after the RNA executed 19 unarmed cadres during an August raid of a suspected Maoist meeting in the village of Doramba in Ramechhap District. Military intelligence began to make widespread arrests of suspected Maoist sympathizers, including politicians and journalists in the heart of Kathmandu. Many of those arrested were tortured and disappeared, most notoriously at the Maharajgunj barracks of the RNA's Bhairabnath and Yuddha Bhairab Battalions.[12] The conflict had finally come to the elite in the capital, and the world began to pay closer attention to its human rights consequences.

During this period, rights defenders in Nepal became increasingly united in their public advocacy against both Maoist and army violence. When the army began to detain large numbers of people without producing them before the courts, and to deny or limit access to military detention by the National Human Rights Commission (NHRC) and the ICRC, human rights lawyers filed hundreds of habeas corpus petitions in the Supreme Court – at great personal risk.[13] Documentation of the experiences of detainees released from military custody, including accounts of torture at the hands of RNA personnel, strengthened calls for a suspension of foreign aid to the military. Monitoring by domestic human rights organizations such as the Informal Sector Service Center and Advocacy Forum was also crucial after the breakdown of the ceasefire in 2001 when many international organizations, out of security concerns, either relocated their staff to Kathmandu or left the country entirely.

After King Gyanendra invoked Article 127 of the 1990 constitution to justify the dismissal of then-Prime Minister Sher Bahadur Deuba in October 2002, the alienated leadership of the major political parties began to openly express concerns about human rights violations. The definitive shift occurred after the February 2005 royal coup and the subsequent crackdown on the press and political leaders – many of

---

[11] Members of caste and ethnic groups believed to be sympathetic to the insurgency, such as Tharus in western Nepal, suffered disproportionately from these violations. See *Conflict-Related Disappearances in Bardiya District*, OHCHR-Nepal (December 2008); for the impact on Dalit communities, see *The Missing Piece of the Puzzle: Caste Discrimination and the Conflict in Nepal*, Center for Human Rights and Global Justice (2005), http://www.chrgj.org.

[12] Documented by OHCHR-Nepal in its report *Investigation into Arbitrary Detention, Torture and Disappearances at Maharajgunj RNA Barracks, Kathmandu, in 2003–2004* (May 2006). Accounts by former detainees include Jitman Basnet's *258 Dark Days* (2007).

[13] For instance, the RNA detained and tortured lawyers at the Chisapani Army Barrack in Bardiya for filing habeas petitions on behalf of detainees. For an account of these and other efforts by national human rights organizations, see Mandira Sharma, "Human Rights during the Armed Conflict and Its Aftermath," in Barbara Weyermann (ed.), *Close Encounters: Stories from the Frontline of Human Rights Work in Nepal* (Kathmandu: Himal Books, 2010).

whom were arrested and detained. It was at this point – when the parties themselves became targets – that leaders began to call for international intervention.

The international community outside Nepal then began to voice its concerns more loudly. As early as August 2000, then-UN Special Rapporteur on extrajudicial, summary, or arbitrary executions, Asma Jahangir, had called on the government to investigate the rising number of reported disappearances and extrajudicial killings.[14] Nepali human rights lawyers such as those at the Advocacy Forum and the Nepal Bar Association made frequent submissions to different UN Special Procedures mandates. Major advocacy efforts by international nongovernment organizations (NGOs), such as Human Rights Watch, Amnesty International, and the International Commission of Jurists, and behind-the-scenes work by the Swiss and other governments also helped set the groundwork for a more aggressive and united international stance.[15] After a 2004 visit, the UN Working Group on Enforced or Involuntary Disappearances issued a report making strong recommendations, including that enforced disappearance be criminalized, that TADO (renewed by decree by the King in October 2004) be rescinded, that the NHRC be given access to places of detention, and that the UN Department of Peacekeeping Operations "assess . . . the suitability" of Nepali security forces for participation in peacekeeping operations in view of their poor human rights record.[16] As a result of the campaign by international and national human rights organizations, and despite efforts by the government to keep Nepal off the agenda of the UN Commission on Human Rights (CHR) in Geneva (including by circulating a human rights "commitment" paper to diplomats in March 2004), a Chairperson's Statement was issued at the CHR's 60th session in April 2004 urging the government to agree to the establishment of a human rights monitoring mechanism.[17] Crucially, India did not block this statement.

A Fragile Consensus in Support of International Monitoring

The king's poorly calculated declaration of a state of emergency and dissolution of the government in February 2005 (an announcement made only days after a visit

---

[14] Report of the Special Rapporteur on Extrajudicial, Summary, or Arbitrary Executions, < E/CN.4/2001/9/Add.2 (August 9, 2000).

[15] Joint advocacy by Amnesty, HRW, and the ICJ, in partnership with domestic human rights organizations, started early and proved particularly effective. *Nepal Human Rights Crisis Continues: Member States Must Stand Firm on Nepal at the Commission on Human Rights*, International Commission of Jurists, April 6, 2005.

[16] Report of the Working Group on Enforced or Involuntary Disappearances, E/CN.4/2005/65/Add.1 (January 28, 2005). For a summary of the recommendations and a review of their state of implementation five years later, see *Review of implementation of the recommendations made by the UN Working Group on Enforced or Involuntary Disappearances after its visit to Nepal in December 2004*, Advocacy Forum Occasional Briefing Series Vol. 1 (September 2010).

[17] E/2004/23-E/CN.4/2004/172, para. 716; for more on the March 2004 commitment paper, see ICG, *Dealing with a Human Rights Crisis, supra* note 4.

by UN High Commissioner for Human Rights Louise Arbour), subsequent assault on civil liberties, and arrests of civil society and political leaders helped solidify a growing consensus among human rights defenders and political party leaders in favor of an international monitoring presence. This consensus was supported behind the scenes by sympathetic international actors within certain diplomatic agencies and the UN.[18] This sense of national ownership and the close working relationship that developed between civil society organizations and the UN were crucial to the effectiveness of the OHCHR and set the stage for the Security-Council–mandated political mission, the UN Mission in Nepal (UNMIN).[19]

The case of the establishment of OHCHR-Nepal is instructive. Human rights defenders lobbied intensively for its creation with the UN and diplomatic community in Nepal and abroad. This civil-society–led campaign involved submitting complaints to UN human rights mechanisms, issuing joint public statements, and making multiple trips to Geneva, several European countries, and the European Parliament. It had the support of some members of the NHRC, which had issued a controversial report on the killings at Doramba. The government's targeting of opposition leaders also increased support for an international role among the established political parties, although their house arrest made it difficult for some to engage in international advocacy.

When the issue of Nepal came before the 61st session of the UN Commission on Human Rights in 2005, representatives of 25 Nepali human rights organizations urged it to create a mandate for a Special Rapporteur to look into allegations of human rights violations.[20] Although the motion failed, it created pressure on a reluctant royal government to agree to a technical assistance role for OHCHR. On April 10, 2005, the government entered into an agreement with the High Commissioner for Human Rights setting the framework for the establishment of a field presence. Ten days later, the CHR followed this up with a strong resolution calling on the government to promptly and fully implement the agreement, including the establishment of an OHCHR office "to monitor the situation of human rights and

---

[18] Swiss, Danish, Canadian and British officials and Tamrat Samuel of the UN Department of Political Affairs were among those that played important roles. Human rights advisor to the UNDP John Bevan's work with Sushil Pyakurel of the National Human Rights Commission in lobbying for a human rights accord also helped set the stage for the eventual acceptance of a UN role.

[19] See Chapter 8.

[20] In their appeal, these civil society activists (including one of the authors of this chapter) called for the establishment of a Special Rapporteur under the Commission's Agenda Item 9 (usually employed to censure a country for its poor human rights record). Anticipating strong opposition, they also strategically proposed, as an "alternative," a monitoring mission under Agenda Item 19 (used to authorize various forms of technical assistance). The eventual establishment of such a robust OHCHR field-monitoring presence as part of a technical assistance mandate was unprecedented. *Nepal under Military Rule: The Undermining of Democracy and the Constitution of Nepal*, 5th Public Appeal from the Nepalese Human Rights Community (March 15, 2005), http://www.nepalresearch. com/coup_2005/papers/hr_community_05.pdf.

observance of international humanitarian law, including investigation and verification nationwide."[21]

Importantly, both the United States and the United Kingdom – two of the countries that had bankrolled the RNA for much of the conflict – gave their support to this UN monitoring role. Even India, the RNA's most ardent ally, raised concerns about the direction in which the conflict was heading, having been alienated by the king's overtures to China for support and his forging ahead with the 2005 coup against Indian advice.[22] Concerns about the potential consequences for RNA participation in peacekeeping operations (and the financial benefits that it enjoyed from that participation) were also a factor in the government's ultimate decision to accept a UN presence in Nepal.[23] This set the stage for the establishment of an OHCHR monitoring mission with one of the most robust mandates ever seen for a UN human rights field operation.[24]

OHCHR's presence provided a crucial protection mechanism for human rights defenders and helped expand the political space in which supporters of the democratic movement in general could act. Its public advocacy and visits to individuals in the custody of the military in 2005 and early 2006 almost certainly contributed to a reduction in torture, disappearances, and abductions, and both the army and the Maoists seemed to make genuine efforts to limit civilian casualties. OHCHR issued reports on violations of international humanitarian and human rights law by both the RNA and the Maoists, and Ian Martin, OHCHR's first representative, armed with a mandate that permitted him to engage with nonstate actors (the Maoists) directly, took on a public and behind-the-scenes role in promoting dialogue. Although OHCHR took no official position on the fate of the monarchy, political party and civil society leaders, many of whom OHCHR monitors had visited in detention, subsequently credited the international attention – and OHCHR's monitoring role during the April 2006 street demonstrations in particular – as contributing to the success of the People's Movement.[25]

Once the Comprehensive Peace Agreement was signed, however, the political ground shifted substantially, and the post-CPA period proved hostile to human rights

---

[21] *Agreement between the United Nations High Commissioner for Human Rights and the Government of the Kingdom of Nepal Concerning the Establishment of an Office in Nepal* (April 2005); Human Rights Resolution 2005/78: Technical Cooperation and Advisory Services in Nepal, E/CN.4/RES/2005/78 (25 April 2005).

[22] See Chapter 12.

[23] By early 2006, on the eve of the second People's Movement, the Nepalese Army had 3,485 troops deployed in 17 peacekeeping operations, making it the fifth largest troop contributor worldwide. See "Nepal's Role in the UN Peacekeeping Operations," Ministry of Foreign Affairs, http://www.mofa. gov.np/nepalun/statement7.php.

[24] For example, Article XIV of the Agreement gave OHCHR unprecedented access to prisons and military detention "without prior notice." See OHCHR Agreement, *supra* note 20.

[25] *The April Protests: Democratic Rights and the Excessive Use of Force: Summary of OHCHR-Nepal's Monitoring and Investigations*, OHCHR-Nepal (September 2006).

advocacy, in particular to calls for holding accountable the perpetrators of conflict-related violations. The culture of impunity that predated the conflict and to which the insurgency was in part a response had survived the conflict more or less intact.

THE COMPREHENSIVE PEACE AGREEMENT AND BEYOND: POSTCONFLICT COMPLICATIONS

A sense of euphoria swept Nepal after the massive street demonstrations of April 2006 succeeded in toppling the king's regime, and optimism pervaded Kathmandu. The second half of 2006 saw many changes in Nepal's relationship to the rest of the world. Diplomatic presences began to resume development activities, and discussion got underway for the establishment of UNMIN to oversee the cantonment of the Maoist Army and assist in the holding of Constituent Assembly elections. On November 22, Maoist leader Pushpa Kamal Dahal and Nepali Congress leader Girija Prasad Koirala (on behalf of the interim government) signed the CPA.

The central role that human rights discourse and human rights monitoring played during the conflict is reflected in the agreement that marked its formal ending. From a human rights perspective, the CPA is an extraordinary expression of intent. The text refers to human rights 18 times and makes reference to international law, including the Universal Declaration of Human Rights. It includes provisions on the right to life, civil and political rights, economic and social rights, women and children's rights, and a right to personal liberty. In addition, the agreement both recognizes OHCHR's past monitoring role and gives it an explicit role in monitoring the implementation of the human rights provisions contained therein. The CPA also committed the parties to addressing several of the central demands of the insurgency, such as ending discrimination and land reform.

Only one provision makes reference to impunity (*dandahinta*). Article 7.1.3 includes a "guarantee not to encourage impunity" and a commitment to impartial investigations – although it is not clear that this provision was meant to apply to past conduct. The CPA makes no mention of criminal accountability, but does mandate the creation of a Truth and Reconciliation Commission (5.2.3) and calls on the parties to make known the names and fates of those who were disappeared during the conflict (5.2.5) – a commitment that first appeared in the May 2006 ceasefire Code of Conduct and was later elaborated in the interim constitution.

The many rights-related provisions of the CPA notwithstanding, as the postconflict picture became more complex, human rights disappeared down a long list of other priorities, such as the cantonment of the Maoist army and its integration into the state's security forces, the holding of elections, and the reestablishment of local government. In subsequent years, national and international human rights advocates struggled to keep human rights on the public agenda – in particular, addressing the many violations and abuses that occurred during the conflict. Before long, however, the old patterns of impunity began to reemerge, although in slightly altered forms.

Public Insecurity and the Rise of Ethnic Politics

The post-CPA period saw a reconfiguration of Nepali politics with the entrance of Madhesi and indigenous activists and leaders onto the political scene. These newly empowered actors, many formerly aligned with the Maoists, drew both on Maoist rhetoric and international human and indigenous rights discourse to justify their movements. Their use of threats of violence – modeled on some of the Maoists' own strategies – and the government's inconsistent response (a mixture of inaction by political leaders and excessive use of force by Nepal Police and Armed Police Force personnel) only served to reinforce the underlying culture of impunity at the root of the conflict. The emergence of armed groups with explicitly violent agendas soon followed, creating a public security crisis in Nepal's southern plains, the Terai. Human rights organizations found this to be a difficult environment to navigate. Simultaneous calls for the government to curb rising violence and demands that the security forces be held accountable for abuses carried out in the name of improving public security became muddled and were often interpreted as contradictory by the media and political leaders.

The strength of antigovernment demonstrations in the Terai was met with surprise, and initially indifference, by many members of the human rights and political communities in Kathmandu – both traditionally dominated by high-caste elites from the hills. Yet the street demonstrations of early 2007, known as the *Madhesi Andolan*, profoundly altered Nepali politics, by bringing issues of discrimination and historical marginalization to the forefront of public discourse and preparing the ground for the rise of political parties such as the Madhesi People's Rights Forum (MPRF). During the protests, demonstrators sometimes resorted to violence and threats directed at migrants from the hills (*pahadi*). Migrant communities responded with their own threats of violence, often backed by the largely *pahadi* police force. This period culminated in mob violence in the village of Gaur in March 2007, during which 27 people (nearly all Maoists and including 4 women and a young girl), were killed in clashes with MPRF supporters. In September 2007, another 14 people died in a series of riots and revenge killings in Kapilvastu after the murder of Mohit Khan, a local Muslim landowner, vigilante, and ex-Nepali Congress cadre.[26] Police did not credibly investigate these and many other incidents. Cases against suspects in the Kapilvastu violence were withdrawn, and a local gangster alleged to have instigated the violence in Gaur subsequently ran for election and won a seat in the Constituent Assembly. Human rights monitors, particularly OHCHR, played a role in restraining the police, which, still in conflict mode, threatened to use excessive or lethal force

---

[26] See *Findings of OHCHR-Nepal's Investigations into the 21 March Killings in Gaur and Surrounding Villages* (April 2007), and *Investigation by the Office of the High Commissioner for Human Rights in Nepal into the Violent Incidents in Kapilvastu, Rupandehi and Dang Districts of 16–21 September 2007* (June 2008).

to disperse demonstrations. In the end, however, the Madhesi rights movement reinforced the lessons learned by the Maoists during the conflict – that without the threat of violence, elites in Kathmandu (now including the Maoists themselves) will never listen, and that once you have a seat at the table, little effort will be made to hold you accountable for past sins.

Other groups advocating for various forms of ethnic autonomy followed suit, mixing threats of violence with reference to indigenous rights and filling the law-and-order vacuum left by the withdrawal of the army and a decade of neglect by police. Youth wings of the political parties, in particular the Maoists' Young Communist League, and of indigenous movements, such as the Limbuwan Volunteers in the eastern hills, made efforts to take control over local economies and engaged in acts of extortion. Armed groups reemerged (obscuring their largely criminal activities by asserting mainstream demands for political autonomy), engaged in killings and abductions for ransom, and on occasion attacked vulnerable police posts – a classic Maoist strategy. These groups enjoyed near total impunity for their actions.

For its part, the national political leadership exerted pressure on the judiciary to have criminal cases against well-connected perpetrators withdrawn, a practice that dated at least to the interim government of 1990–1.[27] Almost every agreement struck between post-CPA governments (including under Maoist leadership) and agitating groups included the withdrawal of criminal charges and release of party cadres from police custody. Most recently, the four-point agreement struck between the UCPN-M and the United Democratic Madhesi Front (UDMF) in August 2011, which led to Maoist Baburam Bhattarai becoming Prime Minister, included a provision to withdraw criminal cases against Maoist cadres as well as individuals affiliated with the Madhesi, Janajat, Tharuhat, Dalit and Pichadabarga movements. This led to a strongly negative reaction from national and international human rights organizations.[28]

These movements opened up political space to actors who had never been given an opportunity to benefit from the spoils of participation in government or national politics. Yet the Madhesi and indigenous movements' simultaneous sanction of the use of violence and invocation of rights discourse put human rights advocates in a difficult position. Although the rhetoric of indigenous movement leaders had its roots

[27] The 1990–1 interim government ordered the withdrawal of more than 1,100 cases, and between 1991 and 1997 successive governments ordered the withdrawal of more than 1,400 cases – many of them serious crimes. *Impunity in Nepal: An Exploratory Study* (September 1999), http://www.asiafoundation.org/pdf/nepal_impunity.pdf, at 7–8. More recent withdrawals (which have included a gang rape and the assassination of a candidate in the Constituent Assembly elections) were justified by reference to a provision of the CPA calling on the parties to withdraw "political accusations, claims, complaints and cases;" Article 5 (2) (7).

[28] *Nepal: Cancel Pact for Wartime Amnesty (Joint Letter to Prime Minister Dr. Baburam Bhattarai)*, Advocacy Forum, Amnesty International, Human Rights Watch and the International Commission of Jurists (September 2, 2011); "Int'l rights bodies decry Maoist-UDMF deal," *Republica* (September 2, 2011).

in earlier Maoist demands for the "self-determination of the proletariat," it made more sophisticated reference to international law, including a sometimes deliberate misconstrual of International Labour Organization Convention 169 to support secession and the assumption of local control by indigenous minorities.[29] The *pahadi*-dominated human rights community was slow to respond and was viewed with suspicion by activists in the Terai. The international community, including the OHCHR, was initially regarded as an ally of the indigenous movement and Madhesi parties. However, as ethnicity became increasingly politicized, the messages sent by human rights organizations became less strident in tone and more ambiguous in content as they tried to balance acknowledgment of the movements' concerns with condemnation of violence and the use of strikes. Meanwhile, the Nepal and Indian governments declared off-limits any direct engagement with armed groups, which operated primarily along the border between Nepal and the Indian state of Bihar.[30] As a consequence, human rights reporting about nonstate actors tended to be limited to expressions of concern about the impact of their activities on the general state of lawlessness.[31]

The architects of the CPA had not contemplated the quick emergence and intensity of the Madhesi and indigenous autonomy movements. Similarly, human rights monitors, both international and domestic, failed to anticipate the lack of impact that these movements would have on addressing impunity. It appeared that Nepali political culture and the patterns of impunity and patronage that had characterized it since before the Panchayat era had not been fundamentally altered, even by the combination of the People's Movement, the *Madhesi Andolan*, various indigenous movements, and a looming public security crisis. Whatever effect these events had in prying political space from a small group of high-caste elites, they also reinforced

---

[29] Nepal ratified ILO Convention 169, the Indigenous and Tribal Peoples Convention (1989), in September 2007, and it has since become an important advocacy tool for the indigenous rights movement. It requires states *inter alia* to pursue measures giving indigenous peoples more control over natural resources and to consult in good faith about development projects affecting indigenous communities. Despite public information campaigns and trainings by the ILO, OHCHR, and others, some indigenous leaders and activists have continued to cite ILO 169 to justify activities that the Convention does not protect – such as the imposition of local taxes (for instance, by Limbuwan groups on cardamom in the eastern hills), repossession of land, enforcement of roadblocks, and, in some cases, secession.

[30] Then-UN Resident Coordinator Matthew Kahane's speculation about the role of India in influencing armed groups in Nepal was enough to cause a modest diplomatic firestorm. "UN Plays Down Official Comment on Nepal," *Nepalnews.com* (February 3, 2008), www.nepalnews.com/archive/2008/feb/feb03/news09.phphttp://www.nepalnews.com/archive/2008/feb/feb03/news09.php. When a representative of the UN Office for the Coordination of Humanitarian Affairs met with armed group leaders over the border to elicit guarantees that they would not target humanitarian workers, Indian diplomats also cried foul, accusing the UN of interfering in India's internal matters. "Nepal: UN Mandate under Fire," *International Relations and Security Network* (Dec 4, 2007), http://www.reliefweb.int/rw/rwb.nsf/db900SID/PANA-79KK2D?OpenDocument.

[31] For an overview of the debate about the duties of nonstate actors and its relevance to Nepal, see Frederick Rawski, "Engaging with Armed Groups: A Human Rights Field Perspective from Nepal," 6 *International Organisations Law Review* (2009) n. 2.

the perception that violence is the only – or at least the most expedient – path to power.

INTERNATIONAL CONFLICTS OF INTEREST AND OBSTACLES TO CRIMINAL ACCOUNTABILITY

The extent to which the culture of impunity survived both the conflict and the beginning of the peace process intact is perhaps best illustrated by the successful resistance by both the Nepalese Army and the Maoists to being held accountable for conflict-era human rights violations and abuses. Despite their own public commitments, constant attention from the human rights community, and occasional judicial intervention, both armies stood their ground in refusing to cooperate with investigations of any of their personnel, even at the lowest levels. Over time, this lack of progress began to chip away at the morale and effectiveness of both national and international human rights defenders. Army and Maoist refusals to abide by judicial decisions, including those of the Supreme Court, also came to pose a serious threat to the integrity of Nepal's already weakened judiciary and criminal justice system.

Before the ink began to dry on the CPA, human rights advocates and lawyers had already begun to test the commitments of political leaders to end impunity. Despite serious flaws in the legal framework (for instance, the fact that neither disappearance nor torture constitutes a criminal offense) and an inconsistent record of judicial independence, human rights lawyers and victims' groups engaged aggressively with the courts. Conflict victims and their families, with the support of national and international human rights organizations, attempted to file First Information Reports with the police. When police refused to register them (as was often the case), the victims and families brought petitions before the courts. Civil society efforts were bolstered by several strong reports issued by OHCHR – in particular its reports on enforced disappearances from the RNA's Maharajgunj barrack in Kathmandu, and in the district of Bardiya in the far-western Terai. These various initiatives culminated in a June 2007 decision of the Supreme Court condemning government inaction and calling on the government to initiate criminal prosecutions and establish a commission of inquiry.[32] The Supreme Court eventually ruled in a number of controversial cases involving military or police personnel including the 2004 killing of 15-year-old Maina Sunuwar and the 2005 disappearances of five students in Dhanusha. Yet slow progress in these and other cases caused frustration among victims and human rights defenders, weakening the unity of the human rights community.[33]

---

[32] *Rajendra Dhakal et al. v. Government of Nepal* (writ no. 3575, June 1, 2007).

[33] See *Waiting for Justice: Unpunished Crimes from Nepal's Armed Conflict* (September 2008), and *Still Waiting for Justice: No End to Impunity in Nepal* (October 2009), Advocacy Forum and Human Rights Watch. For an analysis of the systemic weaknesses in the criminal justice system, see Mandira Sharma, "Criminal Justice System in Nepal," in B. Saptoka (ed.), *The Nepali Security Sector: An Almanac* (2009).

Although the army and the Maoists responded in slightly different ways to calls for their personnel to be held accountable, the end result was the same – a refusal to cooperate with investigations and inquiries that had any chance of resulting in criminal liability. The army's approach was primarily one of denial and cover-up. In the Maina Sunuwar case, it refused to honor arrest warrants for serving personnel and court orders to turn over documents. A compromised court-martial disciplined three of the suspects, not for torture and murder, but for failing to follow proper interrogation procedure or to dispose of the body properly. To date, the army continues to maintain that the court-martial verdict was decisive and that the case remains outside of the jurisdiction of the civilian courts, an interpretation of law in conflict with the Supreme Court's ruling.[34] The army responded to OHCHR's report on the Maharajgunj disappearances by issuing a disingenuous and poorly documented set of denials in the form of an internal task force report.[35] Finally, as of mid-2010, the government of Madhav Kumar Nepal, which had become increasingly dependent on the army and its Indian supporters, had not responded to OHCHR's December 2008 report documenting 156 cases of enforced disappearance by the state security forces and 14 abductions by Maoists in Bardiya District between 2001 and 2004.[36]

Maoist rhetoric about human rights remained full of inconsistencies, with leaders making reference both to the universality of rights and to their "class-based" nature – suggesting that different standards apply to acts of violence done in the service of the revolution. The Maoists sometimes acknowledged responsibility for civilian deaths, but justified this violence as an unfortunate necessity – occasionally issuing statements admitting "mistakes" (such as in the aftermath of the June 2005 Madi bus bombing that killed 39 civilians).[37] However, these admissions and acknowledgments did not translate into the acceptance of criminal responsibility, the honoring of commitments to communicate with families of victims, or action against implicated cadres. Like the army, the Maoists flouted the police and courts in cases such as the killings of Arjun Lama, businessman Ram Hari Shrestha (beaten to death at a Maoist cantonment site), and journalist Birendra Sah.[38] Maoist leader Agni Sapkota, a suspect in the killing of Arjun Lama, was even appointed to a ministerial position in the coalition government formed by the Maoists and the Unified Marxist-Leninist

---

[34] For analysis of the legal issues in the case, see *Maina Sunuwar: Separating Fact from Fiction*, Advocacy Forum (2010), www.advocacyforum.org/Maina_english.pdf.

[35] For OHCHR's response to the Army report, see *OHCHR Releases Letter to Prime Minister Calling for Action on Maharajgunj Violations* (20 September 2009).

[36] See OHCHR Bardiya Report, *supra* note 10.

[37] *Attacks against Public Transportation in Chitwan and Kabhrepalanchok Districts*, OHCHR-Nepal Investigative Report (August 18, 2005), par. 38.

[38] For a summary of obstruction and noncooperation in these cases, see *OHCHR Calls for Accountability for Maoist Abuses (Letter to UCPN-M Chairperson Pushpa Kamal Dahal)* (September 25, 2009).

(UML) party in May 2011.[39] This blatant disregard of the authority of the civilian court system shown by the army, Maoists, and other political actors precipitated a crisis of confidence in the entire criminal justice system, even among those human rights lawyers who had engaged that system the most.

International advocacy seemed equally ineffective. A succession of OHCHR press releases, high-level meetings, investigations, and reports to the UN General Assembly and UN human rights bodies fell on deaf ears. The threat of international opprobrium that helped bring the army and the Maoists to moderate their behavior during the conflict had little impact on government intransigence in taking action against perpetrators. The UN found itself sending mixed messages – with OHCHR publicly advocating for accountability on the one hand, and on the other, the department of peacekeeping operations and secretary-general heaping praise on the army for its support for an unprecedented expansion of UN peacekeeping operations.[40] Despite this apparent conflict of interest, OHCHR's ad hoc vetting of army and police officers to be deployed to UN peacekeeping operations offered a meager form of accountability. The withdrawal of the nominations of Generals Dilip Rayamajhi (chief of military intelligence during the time of the disappearances from Maharajgunj) and Toran Bahadur Singh (former commander of the Tenth Brigade) for senior UN posts in 2006 and 2007, as well as the repatriation of Major Niranjan Basnet (one of the suspects in the Maina Sunuwar case) from his deployment with the UN in Chad in December 2009, shook up the army establishment, but did not lead to any change in its entrenched attitude.[41]

Interventions by other UN human rights bodies, such as the office of Manfred Nowak, the Special Rapporteur on Torture (who had visited Nepal in 2005), and the Human Rights Committee of the ICCPR (which issued strong decisions on a disappearance case in November 2008 and a torture case in April 2011), have

[39] The appointment was subsequently challenged, unsuccessfully, in the Supreme Court. "SC refuses interim order against Sapkota's appointment as minister," *Republica* (June 21, 2011); see also *Joint Open Letter to Prime Minister Khanal of Nepal on Persistent Impunity*, Amnesty International, Human Rights Watch and the International Commission of Jurists (May 24, 2011).

[40] In March 2001, Kofi Annan visited Nepal to praise its role in UN peacekeeping. In his first visit after the signing of the CPA, Ban Ki-Moon was similarly effusive in his praise. These visits marked a period during which the number of uniformed UN peacekeepers deployed worldwide doubled (47,778 in November 2001 to 95,419 by August 2009). By the end of the conflict in 2006, Nepal had tripled the number of troops serving with the UN since 2001. See www.un.org/Depts/dpko/dpko/chart.pdf, and www.mofa.gov.np/nepalun/statement7.php.

[41] When Basnet arrived in Nepal from Chad, the army claimed that the UN had violated protocol in the manner in which he was repatriated and that the UN had subsequently "apologized." This claim prompted a press release from the office of Robert Piper, the UN Resident Coordinator in Nepal, stating that the Permanent Representative of Nepal in New York had not complained to the UN and that the UN had not issued an apology. *United Nations Press Statement on Repatriation of Major Niranjan Basnet from the United Nations Mission in the Central African Republic and Chad (MINURCAT)* (January 9, 2010).

also showed little result.[42] For its part, UNMIN's narrow mandate made it difficult to address human rights issues, even those that could feasibly be linked to the integration process (such as the establishment of a mechanism to help ensure that rights abusers among former combatants would not take positions in the national army).[43] Many civil society actors felt that the UN failed to effectively leverage the peacekeeping relationship to pressure the army to improve its human rights record and engage more productively with the peace process.

The diplomatic community also suffered from conflicts of interest when it came to human rights, although at times there was a level of unity among the Western diplomatic corps. Both the United States and the United Kingdom – the army's main Western wartime supporters – struggled with the tensions between their own human rights policies and pressure from their defense ministries to resume military support. Only after the departure of U.S. Ambassador James Moriarty in 2007 and the change in presidential administration in Washington in 2009 did the United States take meaningful steps to enforce the human rights restrictions imposed by Congress on bilateral aid to the military – culminating in a February 2010 announcement that nonhumanitarian assistance to the army would cease until progress was made on human rights. However, despite strong public statements during this period, high-level U.S. military visits and training opportunities for army personnel continued. In contrast, U.S. rhetoric remained strong in regard to the Maoists, with explicit human rights benchmarks announced as prerequisites to removal from the U.S. Terrorist Exclusion List, although there had been a general improvement in U.S.-Maoist relations since the days of outspokenly anti-Maoist Ambassador Moriarty. However, in June 2010, when the U.S. Embassy indicated that it would deny a visa to Constituent Assembly (CA) member Agni Sapkota for his alleged involvement in the murder of Arjun Lama, the Maoists chose to recall its first official mission of Maoist CA members to the United States, rather than remove him from the delegation.[44]

The United Kingdom's record was equally mixed. Nepal's Chief of Army Staff (COAS) General Rookmangud Katawal was given the red carpet treatment on a 2007 visit to London, and Major Ajit Thapa, an alleged perpetrator of torture and disappearances in Bardiya, was awarded a prestigious Chevening scholarship to study in the United Kingdom the same year. Subsequently, the United Kingdom made

---

[42] *Report by the Special Rapporteur on Torture and Other Cruel, Inhuman or Degrading Treatment or Punishment, Manfred Nowak*, UN Doc. E/CN.4/2006/6/Add.5 (January 9, 2006); *Yasoda Sharma v. Nepal*, Communication No. 1469/2006, UN Doc. CCPR/C/94/D/1496/2006 (November 6, 2008); *Yubraj Giri v. Nepal*, Communication No. 1761/2008, UN Doc. CCPR/C/101/D/1761/2008 (April 27, 2011).

[43] In August 2009, OHCHR called for the establishment of such a mechanism. *OHCHR Calls for Comprehensive Human Rights Vetting as Part of Peace Process*, OHCHR-Nepal press release (August 28, 2009).

[44] The Australian Embassy had already denied Sapkota a visa earlier in the year for the same reason. "Maoists Abort US Visit over One Visa Denial," *Republica* (June 25, 2010).

efforts to vet security forces personnel alleged to have been involved in human rights violations for scholarship and training opportunities and to take a stronger public position on human rights accountability. When Major General Toran Singh was promoted to second-in-command of the army, the UK ambassador sent a pointed letter to the government stating that the United Kingdom would not formally deal with him. The stand provoked an act of defiance by the army, which promptly dispatched Singh to greet (and pose for a photo with) the Chief of the General Staff of the British Army at the airport when he visited soon thereafter.

Broader initiatives fared only slightly better. In 2009, a group of 10 embassies issued a joint letter to the government on the International Day of the Disappeared, and nine senior diplomats as well as OHCHR Representative Richard Bennett made a high-profile visit to meet with families of the disappeared in Bardiya. The government's response was muted at best, and in the case of the Bardiya visit, it accused the group of breaching protocol without remarking at all on the substance of the visit.[45]

However, more telling than the shaky Western unity on human rights was the deafening silence of India and China, for which accountability did not seem to register as a topic worth discussing. India gave its overt support to the NA command, with the COAS making high-profile trips to Delhi at key moments (such as on the eve of Toran Singh's promotion). China limited its public statements to condemnations of the activities of Tibetan refugees in Nepal (and criticism of OHCHR, whose staff visited Tibetan demonstrators arrested under conflict-era preventive detention laws). By 2009, this silence was augmented by a resumption of military aid by both India and China. Other Asian diplomatic representatives took a generally negative attitude toward both OHCHR and UNMIN, echoing domestic critiques (in particular by Nepali Congress politicians) that characterized UN personnel as having a pro-Maoist bias.[46]

In the end, fulfilling the promises made in the human rights provisions of the CPA proved easier said than done. Political leaders responded to public demands for accountability with vague promises that transitional justice institutions such as the promised Truth and Reconciliation Commission and Commission of Inquiry on Disappearances would address their concerns. As for the international community, its efforts served largely to illustrate the dearth of influence that the UN and Western countries retained in post-CPA Nepal.

The Consensus Fragments

This frustrating lack of progress took its toll on the national consensus in support of an international monitoring presence that had coalesced during the later years of the

---

45 "Govt: Ambassadors breached protocol," *ekantipur.com* (December 13, 2009)

46 For the reasoning behind this critique, and how Nepali political discourse could accommodate it alongside the Maoist indictment of the UN as pro-imperialist, see Chapter 13 by Prashant Jha.

conflict. However, the army and Maoist leadership were not solely to blame: none of the established political parties placed accountability high on their agendas, and civil society organizations found it increasingly difficult to maintain a united front.

Although the fractured nature of Nepali politics makes it difficult to distinguish official political party positions from the opinions of individual leaders, Nepali Congress and UML politicians consistently opposed calls to hold the army accountable. The government stood equally by COAS Katuwal in his standoff with the Maoist-led government in 2008[47] and his successor General Chhatraman Singh Gurung's promotions of known rights violators and defiance of court orders. Maoist leaders predictably protected alleged perpetrators among their armed forces. Nor did emerging political leaders, including those from the Madhesi parties, take the issue up with any fervor, seemingly content with official recognition of their deceased cadres as "martyrs" and other political concessions. This response is not surprising given that many party leaders were themselves subject to accusations of complicity in human rights violations at one point or another during the conflict. Nepali Congress leaders, including Girija Prasad Koirala, Khum Bahadur Khadka, and Sher Bahadur Deuba, were particularly vulnerable to accusations of responsibility for violations committed by police during anti-Maoist crackdowns; for instance, during Operation Romeo in 1995 and Operation Kilo Sierra in 1998.

Yet what about the human rights community itself? The leaders of many civil society organizations in Nepal have links with political parties, and their advocacy was sometimes influenced by political ideology and party affiliation. The provincial Kathmandu-centered world of Nepali politics meant that many human rights defenders had close ties with politicians (particularly those in the Nepali Congress and UML), government officials, and security forces personnel. During the UML-led coalition government in 2009 and 2010, rights defenders in Kathmandu found themselves under pressure not to criticize the government too vociferously. For instance, it was very difficult to achieve a consensus among human rights organizations on how to respond to Prime Minister Madhav Kumar Nepal's eventual approval of the promotion of General Toran Singh or his unwillingness to confront the army on its noncooperation with police investigations.

Domination of the human rights space by civil society organizations focusing on civil and political rights also generated discontent among organizations representing marginalized groups and focusing on the economic and social consequences of the conflict.[48] Although the extent to which these divisions prevented human rights

---

[47] In May 2009, a confrontation between Maoist leader Pushpa Kamal Dahal (who had assumed the office of prime minister after the Maoists won a plurality in the Constituent Assembly election) and COAS Katuwal led to the resignation of the Maoist-led government. For more on this episode and its consequences, see *Nepal's Future: In Whose Hands?* International Crisis Group Asia Report No. 173 (August 13, 2009).

[48] For one critique, see Tafadzwa Pasipanodya, "A Deeper Justice: Economic and Social Justice as Transitional Justice in Nepal," *International Journal of Transitional Justice*, Vol. 2, 2008.

defenders from taking collective action is often overstated, the different priorities played into the hands of both right-wing and Maoist propagandists, who argued that the human rights community was overpoliticized and therefore untrustworthy. For its part, the NHRC, reborn as a constitutional body after the passage of the 2007 interim constitution, struggled to maintain its credibility after a politicized nomination process resulted in the appointment of commissioners with questionable human rights credentials.[49] Its five commissioners spent much of their time focused on internal squabbles and demonizing OHCHR, which they came to view as a rival for international funding support.

Alliances that had developed during the conflict between the media, human rights defenders, and leaders of the main political parties began to unravel. This began to weaken support for a strong international monitoring presence. Some civil society actors began to criticize OHCHR for softening its position on impunity and shifting its focus to cooperation with the government on economic, social, and cultural rights. Others complained that it focused too narrowly on issues of criminal accountability. Although UNMIN bore the brunt of public criticism for its alleged partiality in favor of the Maoist insurgents on issues of integration, OHCHR was not free from accusations of pro-Maoist bias (and the two organizations were often, sometimes deliberately, confused). Over time, political opposition to OHCHR's broad mandate developed as it focused increasingly on emblematic cases implicating senior military personnel and Maoist leaders, as well as on controversial issues such as caste discrimination.

When OHCHR's mandate came up for renewal in 2007, soon after the police crackdown against protesters in the Terai, the human rights community and representatives of the Madhesi political parties remained broadly supportive. Things were not so easy in 2009 and 2010. In 2009, NHRC commissioners beholden to the political parties for their positions came out strongly opposed to another extension unless OHCHR's mandate was trimmed to a narrowly defined technical assistance role. Misinterpreted remarks by the recently appointed High Commissioner for Human Rights Navanethem Pillay, comparing the situation of victims in Nepal to those in Rwanda, added fuel to the fire; critics construed these comments as a sign of an overly critical UN presence trying to justify its continued existence.[50] Civil society support also weakened, with some human rights defenders expressing the view that OHCHR had softened its advocacy on impunity as part of its mandate-renewal

---

[49] For an assessment of the NHRC, see former commissioner and human rights defender Sushil Pyakurel's account. S. Pyakurel, "National Human Rights Commission," in B. Sapkota (ed.), *The Nepali Security Sector: An Almanac* (2009). For a more critical take, see *The Withdrawal of OHCHR-Nepal: Agreeing an Alibi for Violation?*, Asian Centre for Human Rights, No. 5 (4 March 2010).

[50] Media coverage distorted a remark made by the High Commissioner comparing the experiences of victims that she heard during her time as a judge on the Rwanda tribunal with those that she heard during her visit in Nepal. *UN High Commissioner for Human Rights Statement to the Media* (March 22, 2009).

campaign. In the end, the government granted last-minute three- and nine-month extensions. In 2010, OHCHR's term was extended only after the High Commissioner agreed to "expeditiously" close all field offices in the Terai – a demand widely believed to have been introduced into the negotiations at the last moment at the urging of India, which also opposed the establishment of an OHCHR South Asia regional office in Kathmandu or Delhi. The years of widespread support for UN human rights monitoring had clearly ended.

IMPUNITY, POLITICS, AND THE LIMITS OF INTERNATIONAL INTERVENTION: CONCLUDING OBSERVATIONS

This chapter examined three interrelated factors that contributed to effective international monitoring during the conflict: a gradual evolution in Maoist rhetoric and behavior, scrutiny drawn by the royal coup and violent crackdown on the civilian population, and a widespread – albeit fragile – consensus among civil society and political actors. It then set out to explore some of the difficulties that rights defenders experienced when they shifted their focus from the prevention of civilian casualties to addressing the social, structural, and institutional causes of the conflict. The Madhesi and indigenous movements highlighted the discrimination that much of the population had historically suffered, but did little to challenge the institutionalized impunity that had facilitated discriminatory practices. Once in power after the 2008 elections, the Maoists proved just as resistant to accountability and institutional reform initiatives as had the army and the established political parties. Lack of progress in addressing rights violations in turn contributed to a weakening of support for an international role. As time passed, it became clear that the peace process had not had much effect on the culture of impunity that characterized Nepali politics since well before the start of the war.

This experience suggests that human rights monitoring can play an important role in mitigating violations and opening democratic space at key moments, but that when addressing long-term systemic problems at the heart of institutional and political culture, international interventions (particularly those perceived or misconstrued as being driven by external interests) have serious limitations. The final section of this chapter briefly explores these limitations and attempts to draw some lessons applicable beyond the context of Nepal.

"Logical Conclusions": The More Things Change...

It has become common in the media and in political circles to speak of bringing the peace process to its "logical conclusion" (*tarkik nishkarsha*), but for many that conclusion means a return to the pre-1996 status quo ante (even as the constitution-writing process is underway, prominent politicians advocate a return to the 1990 constitution and deny the need for substantial reform to the political system). What is clear is that the end of the conflict failed to fundamentally alter either the Kathmandu political culture (built on ethnic, class, and caste-based networks of personal patronage) or the way in which those in power view the role of state institutions (not as guarantors of the rule of law, but as tools for strengthening and extending those networks of power).[51]

Politics in Nepal continues to be guided by cultural practices that predate contemporary notions of impunity – a term that some analysts credit the human rights movement itself for bringing into popular usage.[52] Post-CPA Nepal has had a strong tendency to backslide on promises to address impunity, as illustrated by the refusal of any of the major political actors, including those involved in the emerging indigenous rights movement, to subject themselves to the jurisdiction of the courts; the continuing practice of withdrawing criminal cases; a resistance to the reform of corrupt governance and security institutions; the near constant and unanswered threat to enforce strikes and protests with violence; and interference by local and national political actors in the work of the police – all practices characteristic of the political culture that predated the conflict, including the governments established by the 1990 People's Movement.

Control of state institutions – from the ministries in Kathmandu to local development committees – has mainly functioned as a vehicle through which party, ethnic, and caste loyalties are maintained. State responsibilities such as building infrastructure, delivering services, and ensuring the equal application of the law have remained subservient to these interests. In shifting their focus in the postconflict period to the "culture of impunity" and its pervasiveness within the state, human rights organizations increasingly called into question the very basis of the political culture and the integrity of rule of law and governance institutions.

It is not surprising then that, once the dust settled after the April 2006 People's Movement, international scrutiny of the state met with little enthusiasm by those in power. Raising issues such as corruption, impunity, institutional dysfunction, and security sector reform remained taboo, and the international community including both OHCHR and UNMIN frequently came under attack. This critique generally involved accusations of partisanship (in favor of the Maoists) and pushing a pro-Western agenda (manifesting itself in a focus on impunity and human rights).[53] It

---

[51] The ICG's September 2010 report explores this thesis in detail, presenting the clearest analysis of the nature of the "state: in Nepal published to date. *Nepal's Political Rites of Passage*, International Crisis Group Asia Report No. 194 (September 29, 2010). The authors' own thinking on the topic benefited from conversations with Rhoderick Chalmers of the ICG in Kathmandu.

[52] Such as conceptions of *afno manchhe* (one's own people) and *chakari* (obligations formed through gift-giving and receiving). See *Impunity: An Exploratory Study, supra* note 26, at 1 and 7.

[53] More extreme forms of the critique have included accusations of espionage and Christian proselytizing. "Spying under the Pretext of Human Rights," *Drishti Weekly* (May 18, 2010) (accusing OHCHR of spying on behalf of Western countries); "Serving Christians in the Name of Human Rights," *Nepali Patra* (February 19, 2010) (claiming OHCHR and human rights activists were supported by Christian missionaries).

was directed not only at the UN and the Western diplomatic community but also at national human rights defenders and political reformers. International advocacy soon began to see diminishing returns – especially when other regional actors such as Sri Lanka (after the dramatic loss of civilian life during its offensive against the Tamil Tigers in 2009) and Thailand (in its heavy-handed response to the "red shirt" protests in 2010) blatantly ignored their human rights obligations without serious consequence.

Recognizing the Strengths and Limitations of International Monitoring and Advocacy

Although it is dangerous to draw conclusions from events still in progress, there are preliminary lessons to be drawn from the Nepal experience. First, it illustrates that human rights can make a difference if the context is right. Over time, the language of rights came to play a role in the way both parties to the conflict articulated their demands – as reflected in the text of the CPA itself. Even the NA, partly because of its links to UN peacekeeping, found it necessary to justify its actions with reference to international law. There is good reason to believe that the presence of OHCHR, and later UNMIN, had a positive moderating effect during volatile moments. It is also a rare example of international human rights monitoring setting the stage for later international involvement in a peace process. At the very least, the international monitoring presence helped define the boundaries of acceptable behavior and acted as a counterweight to the more extreme tendencies of both Maoist and right-wing political actors. Despite the near constant critique, when push has come to shove, the mandates of both OHCHR and UNMIN had been repeatedly extended (the latter having left in January 2011). Both the UN presence and its critique have apparently remained pertinent.

Second, a broad understanding of the social and political context at the local, national, and regional levels is crucial. Addressing human rights issues such as impunity or discrimination requires taking a long-term view. Linking human rights initiatives so intimately to the CPA and progress in the peace process reinforced the tendency to see events through the eyes of the political elite and their short-term interests. The international community and much of the national intelligentsia misjudged the political climate by viewing developments through a Kathmandu-centered lens. Diplomats and party leaders underestimated the level of support that the Maoists commanded before the Constituent Assembly elections and failed to adequately anticipate the reaction of the Madhesi and indigenous communities.

More recent disappointment in the effectiveness of international human rights advocacy to end impunity may also reflect an insufficient understanding of how politics functions in Nepal. Most of this advocacy has been directed at weak interim and coalition governments – none of which have had the political clout or willingness to make controversial decisions related to conflict-era accountability. International pressure to reform state institutions came up against the entrenched interest of the political elite in maintaining the status quo system, in which government's primary role is not protecting rights or maintaining the rule of law, but serving the political parties and their leaders. Even the incentives that had led the Maoists, army, and political leadership to follow through on certain commitments during the conflict no longer seemed to apply in the post-CPA context. Initiatives to promote accountability thus became hostage to deadlock around the unresolved issue of integrating former Maoist combatants into the national army. Where the UN has tried to play a larger role in good governance and security sector reform, it has been met with resistance.

Nor have the UN and representatives of the Western diplomatic community paid sufficient attention to the influence of India and other regional actors – an influence that has often played a decisive role. This lack of focus further amplified the divide between Asian and Western countries, a division that continues to be exploited wherever possible by political actors seeking to avoid human rights accountability.[54] Closer attention to the nature of politics and the state, the local dynamics underlying the conflict, and political sentiments outside of the capital (including in Delhi) could have increased the ability of internationals and human rights monitors to respond effectively.

Third, international involvement is unlikely to be effective without broad domestic support. OHCHR's entry into the country was the result of intense advocacy from national and international actors working closely together, and its most effective work was accomplished when that partnership was at its strongest. Earlier and broader engagement with leaders outside of government, the Maoist leadership, and mainstream political parties may have helped keep the partnership intact. Likewise, maintaining civil society support requires consistent engagement and a strong public voice. A weak international monitoring presence can be worse than none at all if it displaces national voices with an ambiguous or compromised message.

At its best, the UN helped open up space for these national voices, and it was most effective when it reinforced the advocacy of the national human rights community or took the lead on issues that national actors found difficult to address out of concern for their own security. Perceptions that OHCHR and UNMIN were reluctant to speak out on controversial issues for fear of endangering their mandate extensions weakened civil society support over time. Although the failure of the NHRC to emerge as a credible human rights actor cannot be blamed on the UN (which expended substantial time, resources, and political capital supporting it), many members of civil society were troubled by the extent to which the diminishing public space for human rights became dominated by debates over the presence of OHCHR and the institutional problems of the NHRC.

---

[54] For instance, Foreign Minister Sujata Koirala would meet separately with Western and Asian diplomats on controversial issues – a practice that she reportedly justified on the ground that her sitting room was too small to accommodate everyone.

It is unreasonable to expect that any peace process, and particularly short-term international interventions such as UNMIN and OHCHR, can have an immediate and lasting effect on social and cultural practices. At the same time, efforts that ignore the need to address fundamental root causes are destined to be superficial in their impact. Global peacebuilding experience suggests that the earlier that underlying structural causes of violence can be addressed, the better.[55] It was not until almost three years after the peace agreement was signed that the UN and other international actors began to take initial steps to link development, impunity, and institutional reform; for instance, through projects supported through the UN Peacebuilding Fund and the designation of Nepal as a pilot country for global UN rule of law efforts. Most recently, both international and national actors have placed much emphasis on the role of transitional justice institutions. Such an approach presents both opportunities and risks.

Transitional Justice: Stepping Forward or Standing Still?

Nepal has taken several steps down the path toward the establishment of transitional justice institutions. Together, the CPA and the interim constitution call for the establishment of both a truth commission and commission of inquiry to investigate enforced disappearances and abductions.[56] As of late 2011, legislation setting out the framework for the establishment of both bodies had been drafted but not yet passed by the legislature-parliament. Well-meaning supporters claim that the criminal justice system has too narrow a mandate to address the varied impacts of the conflict and is simply not up to the job. This may be true, but there are dangers with establishing those commissions. The army and the Maoist leadership have used the promise of these commissions as an excuse for their noncooperation with ongoing investigations. The Nepal Police, the Ministry of Home Affairs, and multiple prime ministers have invoked the proposed truth commission to explain their reluctance to push forward politically sensitive investigations or otherwise respond to demands for criminal accountability. High-placed officials of the major parties continue to advocate for a South Africa–style amnesty as part of a transitional justice process (despite the fact that the proposed bills in their current form prohibit amnesties for serious human rights violations) – the possibility of which may have been a motivating factor for including the truth commission provision in the CPA in the first place.[57]

---

[55] For an analysis and comparative study on the relationship between transitional justice and peace-building, see R. Mani, *Beyond Retribution: Seeking Justice in the Shadows of War* (2002), at 12.

[56] For a review of transitional justice provisions in recent peace agreements (in which the CPA figures prominently), see *Inventory of Human Rights and Transitional Justice Aspects of Recent Peace Agreements*, UN Doc. A/HRC/12/18/Add.1 (August 21, 2009).

[57] *Nepal: Peace and Justice*, International Crisis Group Asia Report No. 184 (January 14, 2010), at 20; for a study of the lopsided stature given to the South African commission as a global model, see F. Pizzutelli, *Moving away from the South African Model: Amnesties and Prosecutions in the Practice of*

Unfortunately, both international experience and Nepal's past experience with commissions of inquiry suggest that prospects are dim that transitional justice mechanisms will result in strong accountability measures or have a lasting impact on structural weaknesses, impunity, or social inequities. In Nepal, the creation of commissions with little power and that are open to political influence has been the standard response to all major human rights events. The recommendations of both the Mallik and Rayamajhi Commissions, formed to investigate the suppression of the 1990 and 2006 People's Movements, respectively, have gone unimplemented.[58] The recommendations of a myriad of other smaller *ad hoc* commissions or parliamentary committees established to investigate particular incidents (such as the September 2007 communal violence in Kapilvastu and the killing of civilians by Nepalese Army personnel in Belbari in April 2006) have suffered the same fate. NHRC recommendations are virtually ignored.

The international picture is no rosier. Philip Alston, then-UN Special Rapporteur on extrajudicial, summary, or arbitrary executions, conducted a review of national commissions of inquiry into extrajudicial executions worldwide and concluded that they were "frequently designed to deflect criticism by international actors of the government rather than to address impunity."[59] Closer to home, Sri Lankan commissions of inquiry have thus far been a failure, with the government both obstructing the commissions' work and ignoring their recommendations.[60] Without any real prospect of sanction, there is little reason to think that the army or the Maoists will cooperate any better with transitional justice institutions than they currently do with police investigations. Transitional initiatives may have a role to play, but experience suggests that great care needs to be taken not to draw attention from the need for systemic reform of the criminal justice system.

Since the defeat of the Tamil Tigers, Nepali analysts and politicians have begun to cite the Sri Lankan example to justify increasingly belligerent positions toward human rights.[61] Yet, although Nepal's conflict shares many of its structural and social

---

40 *Truth Commissions*, paper presented at "Taking Stock of Transitional Justice," Oxford University (June 26–8, 2009).

58 Not only unimplemented but also defied – in May 2010, the president awarded a medal of honor to a Deputy Inspector General of the Nepal Police who had been directly implicated by the Rayamajhi Commission (and OHCHR investigations) in the killing of demonstrators during the April 2006 People's Movement. This occurred on the occasion of Republic Day, a holiday celebrating the achievements of that very movement. The award was subsequently revoked. "Cabinet Scraps Republic Day Medals to Two Senior Police Officers," *nepalnew.com* (June 2, 2010), http://www .nepalnews.com/main/index.php/news-archive/1-top-story/6497-cabinet-scraps-republic-day-medals-to-two-senior-police-officers.html.

59 *Report of the Special Rapporteur on Extrajudicial, Summary or Arbitrary Executions*, Philip Alston, UN Doc. A/HRC/8/3 (May 2, 2008).

60 K. Pinto-Jayawardena, *Post-War Justice in Sri Lanka: Rule of Law, The Criminal Justice System and Commissions of Inquiry*, International Commission of Jurists (January 2010).

61 H. Dulal, "Lessons for Nepal," *Republica* (May 25, 2009) (citing Sri Lanka as example for Nepal); B. Peterson, "Nepal: 'Democrats' and the Struggle for Democracy," *Green Left* (May 23, 2009) (claiming

roots with other regional conflicts, Nepal is not Sri Lanka. Successive governments have invited both OHCHR and UNMIN to continue to monitor aspects of the peace agreement. Whatever transitional justice regime emerges from the current process is also likely to be largely donor-funded, and international attention could create some disincentive for abuse. Regional civil society initiatives – especially those involving colleagues in India – aimed at addressing common patterns of impunity and unequal access to justice show particular promise.

The leaders of the 2006 People's Movement, including the Maoists, have fallen short of instituting the radical changes promised in the rhetoric of both the insurgency and the agitating parties – but the story has not ended yet. The post-CPA period – with its messy and volatile political context, unreformed governance institutions, and two unrepentant armies – still offers opportunities. In the end, it may be better to view the peace process not as a discrete transitional period but as part of a much longer political trajectory – one that has already cycled through multiple periods of uniquely Nepali forms of democracy and authoritarianism. As this chapter goes to press, it remains unclear whether the changes ushered in by the Second People's Movement, the *Madhesi Andolan,* and the constitution-writing process will bring an end to this cycle or simply mark the beginning of another of its iterations.

defeat of Tamil Tigers has encouraged Nepali elite). In June 2010, the Sri Lankan Ambassador to Nepal published a lengthy letter in a major English-language daily denying war crimes accusations and offering Sri Lanka as an example to Nepal of a country "able to find home-grown solutions for its people with the assistance from friendly nations." T. Hewage, "Lankan Lessons," *Kathmandu Post* (June 6, 2010).

8

The United Nations and Support to Nepal's Peace Process: The Role of the UN Mission in Nepal

Ian Martin

Nepal's peace process has been exceptional in the extent to which it was a truly national achievement and not one mediated by any international actor. The United Nations Mission in Nepal (UNMIN) too has been unusual among recent UN peace operations, which increasingly have had wide-ranging mandates, in the limited focus of its support, and among UN missions with a military function, in the lightness of its military component. This chapter explains how this mandate and mission configuration – negotiated between the expectations of the parties and the capacities of the UN – came about. It describes the work of UNMIN in monitoring the commitments of the peace agreements regarding the armies and their weapons and in assisting the country on its troubled path toward the election of a Constituent Assembly. It explains how the breakdown of cooperation among the parties after the election success of the Maoists delayed decisions about the future of the combatants and the nature of a federal constitution for the new republic. It concludes by considering the flaws in Nepal's peace process and the strengths and weaknesses of an unusual UN mission in this context, particularly the tensions UNMIN faced between a limited mandate and high expectations, as well as its inability to determine its exit strategy when it depended on decisions that it was largely excluded from assisting.

THE END OF THE WAR

The decision of the political leaders who shaped the peace process to request a significant UN role grew out of a longer period of mostly low-profile political engagement followed by a shorter period of high-profile human rights monitoring.

Ian Martin was Special Representative of the UN Secretary-General in Nepal and head of UNMIN, February 2007–February 2009 and previously served in Nepal as Representative of the UN High Commissioner for Human Rights (May 2005–August 2006) and Personal Representative of the Secretary-General for support to Nepal's peace process (August 2006–February 2007). The views expressed are solely those of the author and do not represent the official views of the UN.

As described elsewhere in this volume,[1] the quiet pursuit of the secretary-general's good offices gradually confirmed the desire of Nepal's Maoist leaders for a UN role in supporting a negotiated end to the armed conflict; increasingly convinced political and civil society leaders in Kathmandu of the potential contribution of such a role; and went some way toward persuading India that this role could serve its interests in a peaceful transition, despite its extreme reluctance to allow the UN to engage politically in its neighborhood. The value of a UN monitoring presence in the field was first tested when the government of King Gyanendra agreed to the establishment in 2005 in Nepal of an Office of the High Commissioner for Human Rights (OHCHR-Nepal). After the king's declaration of a state of emergency had added serious violations of democratic rights to the continuing humanitarian law violations on both sides of the armed conflict, the government faced strong criticism at the 2005 session of the UN Commission on Human Rights. Rather than be subjected to stronger condemnation and the mandating of a special rapporteur, the government opted to accept an OHCHR presence. High Commissioner Louise Arbour negotiated a strong mandate for her office in Nepal, which from May 2005 built up a presence that would grow to more than 120 international and national staff. OHCHR-Nepal immediately set about exercising the right it had been given to make unannounced visits to those detained in army barracks and to speak publicly about major aspects of the human rights situation.[2]

The presence of OHCHR-Nepal and its early monitoring had a significant impact on the conduct of the armed conflict. Its impact was increased by factors that gave it influence with both sides. The Royal Nepalese Army (RNA) was proud of its long-standing role in UN peacekeeping, which not only enhanced its reputation but also benefited financially the institution and its officers. Visiting Nepal in early 2005, the High Commissioner had warned publicly that the RNA's involvement in extrajudicial executions, disappearances, and torture, which had become widespread since it had entered into counterinsurgency operations in late 2001, could threaten its peacekeeping participation. With the arrival of OHCHR-Nepal, disappearances became rare, and eventually all those who had been detained in military barracks were transferred to civilian prisons. The Maoist leadership as well as the beleaguered parliamentary parties had supported the civil society call for a United Nations human rights field operation in Nepal, and it rapidly established a dialogue with them in accordance with its mandate to "engage all relevant actors, including non-state actors, for ensuring the observance of relevant international human rights and humanitarian law." The Maoists were courting both international respectability and an alliance with the parliamentary parties, and they out-maneuvered the king's government by declaring a unilateral ceasefire, which was not reciprocated. Although serious

---

[1] See Chapter 6 by Teresa Whitfield for an account of good offices and mediation efforts.
[2] See Chapter 7 by Frederick Rawski and Mandira Sharma on the role of OHCHR-Nepal.

humanitarian law violations continued, the OHCHR presence and pressures seemed to mitigate the behavior of both armies in the field.[3]

The clearest indication that the UN would be requested to play a role in an eventual peace process came in November 2005 in the 12-Point Understanding signed between the Seven Party Alliance of parties represented in the last parliament (elected in 1999 and dissolved in 2002) and the Communist Party of Nepal (Maoist) (CPN-M). Preceded by extensive negotiations between representatives of the seven parties – in particular Girija Prasad Koirala's Nepali Congress – and the Maoist leadership in Delhi, the 12-Point Understanding set out a partial roadmap for a peace process, when and if its objective of ending the "autocratic monarchy" was achieved. The Seven Party Alliance accepted what had long been the Maoists' objective of establishing a Constituent Assembly to "restructure the state," opening the door to their republican and federal agenda, while the CPN-M committed itself to democratic values and norms. During elections to a Constituent Assembly, the Maoist army and the "royal army" would be kept under the supervision of the UN or a reliable international body. The 12-Point Understanding also stated that international involvement was expected during the process of further talks.

Although King Gyanendra's government refused to reciprocate the Maoists' unilateral ceasefire and attempted to proceed with local elections, the 12-Point Understanding became the basis of a growing movement of demonstrations and civil disobedience, involving civil society and political party activists, with strong Maoist encouragement and participation of its less identifiable cadres. Successive waves of arrests, bans, and curfews proved powerless to prevent this activity from culminating in an extraordinary 19 days of demonstrations across the country – the *Jana Andolan* of April 2006. OHCHR-Nepal's calls for respect for democratic rights, opposition to arbitrary detention, and avoidance of excessive use of force against demonstrators, together with its visits to detainees and monitoring presence at demonstrations, further enhanced the standing of the UN in the eyes of those who would take forward the peace process after Gyanendra was compelled to step aside.[4]

DEFINING THE UN ROLE AND MANDATING UNMIN

The UN role was not modeled on a template from peace operations elsewhere, but was designed during close interaction between UN representatives and the peace process parties, giving birth to an unusual UN mission.

---

[3] See *Report of the United Nations High Commissioner for Human Rights on the situation of human rights and the activities of her Office, including technical cooperation, in Nepal*, E/CN.4/2006/107, February 16, 2006; and United Nations Office of the High Commissioner for Human Rights, Nepal, *Investigations into violations of international humanitarian law in the context of attacks and clashes between the Communist Party of Nepal (Maoist) and Government Security Forces, January-March 2006*.

[4] See United Nations Office of the High Commissioner for Human Rights, Nepal, *The April Protests: Democratic rights and the excessive use of force*, September 2006.

After the success of the *Jana Andolan*, the UN was quick off the mark in opening discussions on its possible future role. By mid-May 2006, UN political, military, and human rights officials had discussed its role in Kathmandu and with Maoist leaders, still as yet in Delhi. More formal discussions required a request from the interim government formed by the Seven Party Alliance. A first letter from the government promptly provoked protest from the Maoists by referring to "decommissioning" their arms, to which they had made no commitment in the 12-Point Understanding or since. However, a UN pre-assessment mission, sent in late July to engage in discussions with the parties, was able to secure identical letters from Prime Minister Girija Prasad Koirala and CPN-M Chairman Prachanda outlining the UN's role, which requested the UN

> to provide its assistance as follows with a view to creating a free and fair atmosphere for the election of a Constituent Assembly and the entire peace process:
>
> 1. Continue its human rights monitoring through the Office of the High Commissioner for Human Rights in Nepal (OHCHR, Nepal).
> 2. Assist the monitoring of the Code of Conduct during the Ceasefire.
> 3. On the basis of the agreement to seek UN assistance in "the management of arms and armed personnel of both the sides," deploy qualified civilian personnel to monitor and verify the confinement of CPN-M combatants and their weapons within designated cantonment areas . . .
> 4. Monitor the Nepal Army to ensure that it remains in its barracks and its weapons are not used for or against any side . . .
> 5. Provide election observation for the election of the Constituent Assembly in consultation with the parties.[5]

The most contentious issue was the modality for monitoring the Maoists' weapons, and the letters left this to be worked out at a later stage. The pre-assessment mission recommended that a senior resident UN political interlocutor be immediately designated to maintain continuous engagement with all sides in Nepal and the region, and in late August 2006 Secretary-General Kofi Annan appointed me as his Personal Representative in Nepal for support to the peace process, to be joined by a very small team of political, military, electoral, and ceasefire monitoring advisors. The presence of the Office of the Personal Representative in Kathmandu enabled the UN to explain further to the parties what the UN could and could not do, obtain clarity in the formulation of a mandate, and get planning underway.[6]

The Office of the Personal Representative engaged closely with the parties during their negotiations, which culminated in the signing of a Comprehensive Peace

---

[5] The letters are reproduced in *Letter dated 22 November 2006 from the Secretary-General to the President of the Security Council*, S/2006/920, November 27, 2006.

[6] On the value of mission planning being led from the field, see Teresa Whitfield, *Focused Mission: Not So Limited Duration – Identifying Lessons from the United Nations Mission in Nepal (UNMIN)*, Center on International Cooperation, New York University, February 2010.

Agreement (CPA) on November 22, 2006. Although the Maoists in particular wanted a third-party presence in the negotiations and had initially preferred it to be the UN, any such international presence was successfully resisted by India, which argued that independent Nepalis could play that role. A team of five prominent civil society observers was appointed by the two sides, but played only a very limited role. There was thus no formal facilitation of the overall negotiations, although the UN, a Swiss conflict advisor, a South African consultant contracted through USAID, and the Indian Embassy engaged continuously with members of both the government and Maoist negotiating teams.[7]

The management of arms and armed personnel continued to be a central issue in the overall negotiations, and the last to be agreed. Although the 12-Point Understanding had included the commitment to international supervision of the two armies during elections, there was no commitment to decommissioning Maoist arms. The government side, strongly supported by India and the United States, insisted on "weapons separation" before the Maoists could join an interim parliament and government. The Maoists agreed to storage of their weapons, but resisted the government proposal of a dual-key arrangement with the UN. Eventually, agreement was reached on a single-key arrangement with the Maoists retaining control, but with UN monitoring including a "device" with a siren, recording facility, and camera monitoring. The same number and type of weapons of the Nepalese Army would be similarly stored and monitored – equal treatment that was only symbolic, because the arms covered constituted merely a fraction of the state's weaponry.

Both sides were clear that they did not want a peacekeeping mission, with armed troops, to monitor their military commitments: they instead asked for "qualified civilian personnel." The pride that the Royal Nepalese Army and establishment took in Nepal's long-standing participation in UN peacekeeping was reflected in its reluctance to become a recipient of blue helmets. The Maoist leadership had developed some confidence in UN impartiality, but suspicion of military interventions was rife in its ranks. India had only reluctantly come to accept the need for any UN role and initially hoped that Nepal could be kept away from the Security Council: it certainly did not want to see a UN peacekeeping force in a neighboring country with which it has an open border.

This request for civilian personnel caused considerable unease at UN headquarters, which would have strongly preferred to deploy serving military personnel, both in principle and also because the UN lacked an established process for recruiting and deploying former officers. Eventually the parties were persuaded to agree to accept a mix of active and former officers, on the understanding that all would be unarmed and in civilian attire.

---

[7] See Teresa Whitfield, *Masala Peacemaking: Nepal's Peace Process and the Contribution of Outsiders*, Conflict Prevention and Peace Forum, October 2008, and Chapter 6.

When the parties agreed on the arrangements for weapons storage on November 8, 2006, they further agreed that the Maoist army combatants would be assembled in cantonments and their arms stored under UN monitoring by November 21 – despite the obvious inability to meet this timeline (cantonment sites had not yet been identified, let alone preparations made) and despite the fact that modalities for UN monitoring had yet to be negotiated. The UN had given clear notice as to the steps that would be necessary for it to monitor the agreement and submitted to the parties an agenda for negotiations and a draft agreement on the management of arms and armies that would meet requirements for effective monitoring. After intensive negotiations chaired by the UN's Military Advisor, who brought with him the experience of having headed the Nuba Mountains Joint Military Commission in Sudan,[8] government and Maoist representatives signed the Agreement on Monitoring the Management of Arms and Armed Personnel (AMMAA) on December 8, 2006, with the UN as witness.

Other aspects of the request also required clarification and discussion. The signing of a Ceasefire Code of Conduct in late May had given rise to considerable discussion as to how it was to be monitored. Some in Nepal suggested that OHCHR-Nepal could take on broader monitoring requirements, both because of its established presence and credibility and to avoid a further UN mandate, especially one that would engage the Security Council. However, the UN made clear that OHCHR could not operate beyond a strictly human rights mandate. Others insisted that only national monitoring was required. In the end, the government and the CPN-M appointed a National Monitoring Committee to monitor implementation of the Ceasefire Code of Conduct and the 12-Point Understanding, and requested UN support. In addition, the government side particularly wanted a strong international observation presence for the forthcoming Constituent Assembly elections. The parliamentary parties hoped that this presence would require the Maoists to allow activists of other parties to return and campaign in areas from which they had been driven out during the armed conflict, and – as the expected losers – to accept an internationally certified outcome. The UN explained that it does not itself undertake large-scale electoral observation, but could offer its assistance to the electoral process.

The UN did not wait for the signing of the CPA before moving with unusual speed toward the establishment of a mission to carry out the tasks requested by the parties. The secretary-general wrote to the Security Council on November 22, stating his intention to deploy advance teams of up to 35 arms monitors and up to 25 electoral personnel, even in advance of a technical assessment mission.[9] By

---

[8] Brigadier-General Jan Erik Wilhelmsen of Norway, who subsequently became Chief Arms Monitor.
[9] *Letter dated 22 November 2006 from the Secretary-General to the President of the Security Council.* The response of the Security Council is in *Statement by the President of the Security Council,* S/PRST/2006/49, December 1, 2006. My briefing of the Security Council on November 29, 2006, and all my subsequent briefings, can be found in Ian Martin (ed.), *Nepal's Peace Process at the United Nations,* Himal Books, 2010.

mid-December, a technical assessment mission had begun its work in Nepal, and its proposals for a political mission were presented in a report of January 9, 2007,[10] to the Security Council, which adopted its resolution mandating the UN Mission in Nepal (UNMIN) on January 23.[11]

UNMIN was to have three major substantive components, corresponding to the requests for monitoring arms and armies, supporting the Constituent Assembly election, and assisting with more general monitoring of the peace process at the local level. Its monitoring responsibilities under the AMMAA would be carried out by up to 186 active and former military officers, unarmed and in civilian attire, headed by a brigadier-general as Chief Arms Monitor. The electoral component would include advisors providing assistance to the Election Commission of Nepal at headquarters, regional, and district levels, and a small police advisory team would advise on the planning and execution of election security. A civil affairs component, including staff deployed to the regions, would complement the mission's monitoring of arms and armies and electoral assistance, as well as OHCHR's human rights monitoring, by providing support to the work both of a national independent monitoring mechanism and to local structures and mechanisms to be established within the framework of the peace process.

Several issues arose regarding the congruence between the design of the mission and the parties' request and wishes. As noted, the first emphasis of the parties' request in the electoral context had been for UN observation. Instead the UN had offered technical assistance, and the Chief Election Commissioner persuaded the political parties of the Election Commission's need for this assistance. Although the UN had indicated that international observers had to come from elsewhere (and would later actively encourage appropriate organizations to deploy as many as possible), it responded to this desire for a UN election monitoring role by proposing to deploy a small team of five expert monitors to review all technical aspects of the electoral process. To avoid any conflict of interest with UNMIN's electoral assistance role, this Electoral Expert Monitoring Team would be appointed by, and report to, the secretary-general. At the same time, the presence of electoral advisors, civil affairs officers, and OHCHR human rights officers in the regions – and in the case of electoral advisors, in each of the 75 districts – would together constitute a significant UN presence beyond Kathmandu, responding to the desire for a substantial confidence-building role in the countryside.

The UN noted that ensuring adequate political space and a level playing field for all parties in the rural areas, where there had been a prolonged absence of an effective state, would be crucial for the credibility of the election. If the Nepal government failed to restore local government, the secretary-general's report warned,

[10] *Report of the Secretary-General on the request of Nepal for United Nations assistance in support of its peace process*, S/2007/7, January 9, 2007.
[11] S/RES/1740 (2007).

there would be a clear lack of democratic space for the political parties in advance of the election. The civil affairs officers were to seek to promote the functioning of local government and the freedom of all political parties to operate normally throughout the country, working closely with local government and civil society to develop and promote conflict mitigation and dispute resolution strategies at the local level.[12] However, the intended national counterparts to the civil affairs component never materialized. Despite repeated commitments by the parties and consistent urging by UNMIN and other international actors, no national monitoring mechanism was ever established to succeed the one that had functioned under the Ceasefire Code of Conduct (terminated with the signing of the CPA). In addition, the parties failed to agree on a formula to reestablish local government bodies, and plans to establish local peace committees were poorly conceived, implemented belatedly and only partly, and quickly politicized. As a result, UNMIN was left without either a mandate to report directly on all aspects of the peace process or a national mechanism into which to feed its knowledge of what was unfolding on the ground, thereby exposing it to criticism either for exceeding its mandate or for failing to share its information.

In a context where police posts were only being gradually reestablished in large parts of the country from which the Maoists had driven them out, the UN also believed that security during voter registration, campaigning, and polling would be crucial and that a UN police advisory presence could be valuable. UNMIN's small team of eight police advisors was politely received, but the Nepal Police kept the door firmly shut against UN advice, regarding its own role in UN peace operations elsewhere as placing it beyond any such need and reluctant to expose itself to professional scrutiny.

Although the Security Council's resolution mandating UNMIN narrowly specified the roles requested, the UN saw these roles as key elements in its overall support to the peace process, to which it would continue to contribute good offices through the Special Representative of the Secretary-General as the head of the mission, supported by a small team of political officers. The UN was also conscious that it was assuming the responsibility of monitoring temporary arrangements for the two armies with only a vague definition in the peace agreements of a process to move forward the "integration and rehabilitation" of Maoist combatants and the "democratization" of the Nepalese Army. The UN would have wanted to offer technical assistance in resolving these security sector issues in the mandate and was told that eventually such UN assistance would be required. Yet, Nepal's deference to Indian wishes precluded any reference to this future need in the original or subsequent mandates.

From the outset, the UN recognized this and other difficulties that lay ahead. Perhaps the most prophetic warning in the secretary-general's first report of January 9, 2007, was that "the debate over the country's political future could...swiftly

---

[12] *Report of the Secretary-General*, January 9, 2007, paras. 18, 46.

exacerbate ethnic, regional, linguistic and other tensions. If Nepal fails to meaningfully include traditionally marginalized groups in the peace process and in the
election, the country will . . . leave some of the key underlying causes of the conflict
unaddressed."[13]

CANTONMENTS, ARMS, AND ARMIES

The most urgent challenges for the new mission were to put in place the arrangements for monitoring arms and armies and to enable political power sharing and the
Constituent Assembly election to proceed. Carrying out the complex and sometimes
novel tasks involved would inevitably be attended by political controversy.

The speed with which the parties wanted to proceed regarding the cantonment
of the Maoist army and storage of its weapons was a consequence of the political
bargain they had struck. The Seven Party Alliance would agree to the Maoists' entry
into an interim legislature only after the weapons storage process had begun and
into a new interim government only after the process was complete. The timetable
they had agreed on November 8 was wildly unrealistic from their own perspective,
let alone that of the UN: the CPA was to be signed on November 16, the Maoist
combatants cantoned and their weapons stored and verified by the UN by November
21, the interim constitution promulgated and the new interim legislature formed by
November 26, the new interim council of ministers constituted by December 1, and
the Constituent Assembly election held by mid-June 2007.

The Maoists in particular were impatient with the UN's forecasts of when it could
have its arms monitors at the cantonments, even though the tiny UN team was
working intensively with the parties to reach agreement on 7 main and 21 satellite
cantonment sites, have weapons storage containers in readiness, establish minimal
requirements for the first arms monitors to camp at the cantonments, and develop
plans for registration of weapons and personnel.[14] To mount an around-the-clock
presence at weapons storage sites even before sufficient UN monitors could be
deployed, the Maoists and the government proposed the recruitment of an Interim
Task Force (ITF) of Nepali ex-servicemen from the Indian Army. This unorthodox
arrangement gave rise to more nervousness at UN headquarters, and UNMIN took
no formal responsibility for the ITF. However, its 111 members, selected by consensus
between the two sides, became invaluable to the overall monitoring presence at the
cantonments, even after the full deployment of UNMIN's arms monitors.

The oversight of the monitoring arrangements rested with the Joint Monitoring
Coordination Committee (JMCC), chaired by UNMIN's Chief Arms Monitor, with
senior officers from the Nepalese Army (NA) and the Maoist army as vice chairmen.

---

[13] Ibid., para. 20.
[14] The containers were provided by India, Norway supported the first basic UN sites at the cantonments,
and UNDP brought in registration experience from Afghanistan, all with exemplary speed.

The hostility between the armies that had needed to be contained by the political leaders during the negotiation of the AMMAA soon developed into wary cooperation, although UNMIN's wish to use tripartite joint monitoring teams was constrained by the NA chief's refusal to have Maoist army representatives share in monitoring NA barracks. Joint monitoring teams were eventually trained and deployed, and they proved the ability of members of the two armies to work together well under UN auspices; however, these teams could only be used for confidence building and investigations of alleged violations of the AMMAA away from the barracks and cantonments.

By mid-January 2007, the advance team of arms monitors was in Nepal, and the registration of Maoist weapons and personnel was ready to begin. Thus on January 15 the interim constitution was promulgated, and the old parliament dissolved and replaced by the new interim legislature-parliament with Maoist representation. The parties had committed themselves to hold the Constituent Assembly election by June 2007, and although other factors would eventually lead to postponements of the election date, the pressure remained on UNMIN to complete registration quickly, as the precondition to the Maoists' entry into a new government.

UNMIN's responsibility for registering and verifying Maoist combatants was greatly complicated by the fact that the number of persons who were now in the cantonments was hugely in excess of any reasonable estimates of the real strength of the Maoists' Peoples Liberation Army (PLA), which placed it toward 10,000 by mid-2005.[15] It was well known that, in addition, the CPN-M had tens of thousands of locally based militia, some of whom had been mobilized to support the PLA in major attacks. In October 2005, the CPN(M) expanded the PLA from three to seven divisions, bringing in some of the militia and political cadres. These soldiers then became eligible for registration at the cantonments and eventual integration or rehabilitation when May 25, 2006 (the date of signing the Ceasefire Code of Conduct, which prohibited further recruitment by either army) became the cut-off date for eligibility to be regarded as a Maoist combatant. As the cantonments were being established in late 2006, it was widely reported that the Maoists, in violation of the agreements, were increasing their numbers by bringing in more young people, attracted by promises of salary payments and future recruitment into the security forces. Finally, more than 31,000 people presented themselves for registration at the cantonments. Many of them appeared to be minors, although it had been agreed that their age would be determined only at the second stage of the process.

At the same time, the Maoists announced the reestablishment of its Young Communist League (YCL). It became clear that the Maoists, once again in violation of the peace agreements, had kept some key PLA commanders out of the cantonments to provide leadership to the YCL, which was the new home for many former

---

[15] See International Crisis Group, *Nepal's Future: In Whose Hands?*, Asia Report No. 173, August 13, 2009, p. 10.

militia and other younger cadres. Only the PLA, and not the Maoist militia, had been addressed in the negotiations, although the different components of the Maoist movement had in fact been fluid. Privately, Maoist leaders justified this by the need to maintain discipline over cadres who would otherwise cause problems, although this was undoubtedly only part of the motivation, as would become clearer from the strong-arm role of the YCL, especially during the Constituent Assembly election.[16]

However, the immediate focus was on completing weapons storage. Here too there was inevitable controversy. It was known that the Maoist army had fought the war with weapons greatly limited in numbers and sophistication – most captured from the security forces and others homemade. An attempt by the Nepalese Army to argue that only a Maoist combatant who produced a weapon should be eligible for registration bore no relation to this reality. The Maoists presented to UNMIN a total of 3,475 weapons, and when this figure was made public, it was widely asserted that it was far short of the likely total, especially when contrasted with 31,000 claimed combatants. The Nepalese Army had provided UNMIN with a list, by type, of 3,430 weapons "looted" by the Maoists from the NA, Armed Police Force, and Nepal Police, 781 of which were not identified among those registered. Whatever the suspicions, with the completion of the storage of Maoist weapons, the parties moved on to the formation on April 1, 2007, of a new interim government, still under Prime Minister Koirala, but now with CPN-M ministers holding 5 of 22 cabinet positions. The Nepali Congress retained for itself the Defense, Home, and Finance Ministries, as well as a newly created Ministry of Peace and Reconstruction with key responsibilities for peace process implementation.

UNMIN was now ready to proceed to the second stage of the registration and verification process, during which each claimed combatant would be interviewed to assess whether he or she had been a member of the PLA before May 25, 2006, and was over 18 years of age on that date; the agreements stipulated that those who were minors should be immediately discharged. Several irritants between the Maoists and the other political parties stalled the process from moving forward. The Maoist leadership would not allow the verification process to start until cantonment conditions were improved, the government provided salaries as promised to those registered there, and a special committee was formed, as required by the CPA and interim constitution, to supervise and consider the future of the Maoist combatants.

Living conditions in the cantonments – accommodation, water and electricity supply, and medical provision – were indeed abysmal, especially once the monsoon season began. The lack of planning and execution by the interim government at national and local levels, as well as the Maoist insistence on having 28 sites, made the poor condition of the cantonments a shared responsibility. Non-Maoist ministers were reluctant to act, as they resented being expected to fund the living costs and pay salaries for numbers of Maoist personnel they knew to be grossly inflated, and

[16] See Chapter 10 by Aditya Adhikari on the nature of the Young Communist League.

to do so by handing over lump sums that they knew would be used for wider party purposes, including sustaining the YCL.

The UN had never been asked or agreed to assume any responsibility for cantonment conditions, but UNMIN testified to its arms monitors' knowledge of the acute need for improvement, and the UN Development Programme (UNDP) and others in the international community offered assistance. However, the Maoists were reluctant to accept international support to improve conditions, insisting that it was a responsibility of the government, whereas ministers of other parties argued that donors should not prioritize the needs of Maoist combatants over those of victims of the Maoists. At last, the government committed funds to construct better shelter for 15,000 combatants in the cantonments, and a first tranche of salary payments was disbursed. The Maoist leadership finally allowed UNMIN to proceed with verification in mid-June.

Verification of the Maoist combatants was a novel exercise, preceded by careful preparation and negotiation. PLA identity cards, as well as birth and education certificates, would be scrutinized, but could not be relied on. Individual interviews with claimed combatants were essential and were carried out by teams composed of UNMIN arms monitors, UNDP registration experts, and UNICEF child protection officers. Although the nature of the questions to be asked was discussed and agreed with the Maoist army and NA representatives in the JMCC, UNMIN denied the Maoists' wish to have their commanders present in the interviews.

The Maoist army divisions would be verified sequentially, so that the UN personnel and logistical support required could move on from one main cantonment site to the next. The results for the first division in which verification was carried out shocked the Maoists: UNMIN disqualified about 40% of those who had been registered, finding most of them to have been minors and others recruited after the cut-off date of May 25, 2006. The Maoists mounted heavy pressure on UNMIN, publicly attacking the way the verification teams had allegedly carried out their questioning. Recognizing that this had been a first application of a novel process, UNMIN undertook further training of its teams and agreed to review a small number of cases for which the Maoist commanders were most insistent that mistakes had been made. However, UNMIN stood firm on the integrity of the process.

Although the Maoists eventually agreed to cooperate in the resumption of verification, they appeared to have tried to limit further embarrassment by sending away from the cantonments many of those most likely to be disqualified by UNMIN. As the verification proceeded, one division at a time, the proportion of those originally registered who were verified remained fairly consistent, but the proportion of those who failed to present themselves increased greatly from the first division. When verification was finally completed in December 2007, 19,602 Maoist army combatants had been verified, 8,640 had left the cantonments without going through the process, and 4,008 remained to be discharged, of whom 2,973 were assessed as having been under age 18 in May 2006. A long struggle to agree arrangements for their discharge then began.

Because the final total of verified combatants became known at a time when the parties' priority was to head toward the Constituent Assembly election, it was accepted as a basis for going forward – but not without skepticism, because it still exceeded most estimates of the strength of the PLA, some of whose longer term personnel were now in the YCL. It would become the subject of major controversy in May 2009, when a video was released of a January 2008 address by Prachanda to members of the PLA, in which he appeared to boast that the Maoists had hoodwinked UNMIN into verifying a vastly inflated number of combatants, when the true strength of the PLA had been between 7,000 and 8,000. The widespread assumption in Kathmandu's media that this declared strength was to be set against the 19,602 verified by UNMIN took no account, however, of the expansion of the PLA between mid-2005 and the ceasefire.[17]

The focus of public attention on UNMIN's registration and verification at the cantonments, together with very few breaches of the AMMAA by either army, tended to obscure the importance and the success of the Joint Monitoring and Coordination Committee (JMCC) in preventing or resolving issues that could have threatened the peace process. Those issues that received the most public attention involved Maoist combatants being, or alleged to be, outside the cantonments with weapons. No weapons were ever found to have been removed from the storage containers. Yet the parties had agreed in the AMMAA that 30 registered weapons would be kept out of storage at each main cantonment site and 15 at each satellite site, strictly for perimeter security. Moreover, in a separate protracted negotiation without UN facilitation, they had agreed that a small detachment of registered personnel with weapons would remain outside the cantonments to provide security to senior Maoist leaders. On occasion, Maoist personnel were found with these categories of registered weapons in unauthorized contexts or with small arms acquired outside the cantonments. The most obvious breaches of the AMMAA occurred on the few occasions when armed and uniformed PLA came out of cantonments on brief (and disciplined) demonstrations at moments of political protest or to supplement security for Maoist leaders. All such known violations were promptly brought before the JMCC and protested by UNMIN.

The biggest blow to the credibility of UNMIN's monitoring of the cantonments, albeit based on a misunderstanding or misrepresentation of UNMIN's role, came in April 2008, when it was discovered that a businessman in dispute with a Maoist commander had been taken to a cantonment site and beaten to death. Both UNMIN and OHCHR promptly and strongly condemned the violation, and they pressed

---

[17] For a careful contextualization and analysis of the video, see *Nepal's Future: In Whose Hands?*, pp. 9–11.

publicly and privately for the Maoist commander to submit himself to justice. However, it was widely asserted that the fact that this violation could occur without the knowledge of arms monitors at the cantonment revealed a weakness or complacency in UNMIN's monitoring, despite explanations that they were intended to maintain around-the-clock surveillance only of the weapons containers, and not of the tens of thousands of personnel in 28 open cantonment sites.

The greatest threat of actual hostilities, and of derailing the Constituent Assembly election at the last moment, received the least public attention. In the last stages of the election campaign, Maoist cadres, after a series of clashes in one locality, abducted supporters of the Unified Marxist-Leninist Party (UML), among whom were two Nepalese Army soldiers on leave in their home district. The Nepalese Army Chief of Army Staff (COAS) ordered preparation of a rescue mission and special forces to stand ready to surround the CPN-M headquarters in Kathmandu. Because of the relationships forged within the JMCC, UNMIN was able to intervene at the political level where this rash intention was not yet known: the two soldiers were released and the preparations for the operations were aborted.

The breach of peace agreements that would eventually have the most serious political consequences was the Nepalese Army's determination to undertake new recruitment to fill vacancies and maintain its authorized strength, which had more than doubled after it had entered the armed conflict and stood at nearly 96,000. The CPA envisaged the need to "determine the appropriate number" of the NA (i.e., to downsize it to peacetime requirements and affordability), as well as to develop its "national and inclusive character" – a reference to the need to recruit from underrepresented groups. It also provided for the "integration and rehabilitation" of the Maoist army combatants – integration being understood by the negotiators on both sides, notwithstanding later interpretations, to mean integration into the security forces, including the Nepalese Army. The Ceasefire Code of Conduct unambiguously committed both parties "not to recruit new people," a provision that was later reconfirmed when the AMMAA prohibited "recruiting additional armed forces" unless mutually agreed by the parties. As already noted, the Maoists were the first to breach this provision by bringing thousands of new recruits, many of them minors, into their cantonments.

In mid-2007, the Maoists complained to the JMCC that the Nepalese Army was undertaking recruitment. When challenged, the NA argued that recruitment to fill vacancies was not a breach of any agreement, although the fact that the JMCC had not been notified called into question its good faith. UNMIN formally advised the prime minister and the COAS that this was indeed a breach of the AMMAA, which gave the representative of the secretary-general final authority for reporting on compliance with the agreement. However, at a time when negotiations to resume momentum toward the Constituent Assembly election were the main preoccupation for all parties involved, the Maoist leadership – despite great resentment in the Maoist cantonments – did not pursue the issue any further. The recruitment issue would, however, return as a major element in the political crisis of April–May 2009.

Cantonment of the Maoist combatants and corresponding restrictions on the Nepalese Army were initially envisaged as arrangements for a short period, while an early Constituent Assembly election was held and the future of both armies decided by an interim government that would include the Maoists. For the UN, such decisions were crucial to its own exit strategy: the electoral aspects of UNMIN's mandate would have been discharged once the election was held, but the monitoring of arms and armies required decisions on the future of the combatants, which for the Maoists – and according to the CPA – were to be taken in parallel with decisions about the Nepalese Army. The CPA had only papered over fundamental disagreements between the Maoists, on the one hand, and other political parties, the Nepalese Army, and India, on the other. With no mandate even to advise in this area, the best UNMIN could do was to press the parties to begin the processes they themselves had agreed: the formation of a special committee to supervise, integrate, and rehabilitate the combatants of the Maoist army and the formulation of an action plan for the democratization of the Nepalese Army. The Council of Ministers established the special committee in mid-2007, but it was stillborn. It met once, with offers of technical assistance from the UN and the United Kingdom, but never met again until long after the election.

At times the Maoists seemed to want to press ahead with the special committee, especially in response to the frustration of those in the cantonments about the uncertainty of their future. Yet ultimately their leaders preferred that hard decisions be left until after the election: the continued existence of their army strengthened their hand while the election was being held and beyond, whereas settling its future was bound to be a difficult issue inside the party and the PLA. The other parties assumed that their position would be strengthened and that of the Maoists weakened after the election, and then the issue of the armies would be easier to solve on their chosen terms. This view seems to have been shared by India, but it was to prove a fundamental miscalculation.

TOWARD THE CONSTITUENT ASSEMBLY ELECTION

The holding of the Constituent Assembly election required not only technical preparations that were in significant respects unprecedented for Nepal but also addressing demands for inclusion from hitherto marginalized groups and achieving a climate of adequate security.

Nepal's Election Commission itself faced a major challenge, which it began to tackle when new commissioners acceptable to all parties were appointed. The Chief Election Commissioner was a former Home Secretary, whose integrity and independence had prevented his earlier appointment to the position by the king.[18] The commission rapidly began to update the registration of voters and to plan for the logistical challenges of a June election throughout Nepal's far-flung districts, some inaccessible by road. Once the UN's electoral advisors understood that their role was to be supportive of a commission that possessed the independence and much of the competence to manage a credible process, and staff as well as members of the commission came to recognize the advisors' value, they worked together well. Yet the commission could not set full preparations in motion until the necessary legislation was enacted. Its work also required some reasonable expectation that adequate security could be assured by the time of the poll.

These requirements had been made much more difficult by the discontent of groups that had long been marginalized within the public life of Nepal and that, despite their participation in the *Jana Andolan*, had little influence over the peace process negotiations. They were now determined to ensure adequate representation in the Constituent Assembly and the restructured state. Groups representing Madhesis – the people of the Terai plains along Nepal's southern border who are not of hill origin – engaged in widening protests from January to March 2007. Some demonstrations turned violent and were met with excessive use of force by police, resulting in deaths and injuries among demonstrators. Tensions were high between Madhesi groups, including emerging armed groups, and the Maoists, who believed that the Madhesi movement was being encouraged by royalists and by India to weaken its own base in the region. Groups representing the Janajatis, indigenous peoples of Nepal, asserted parallel demands for inclusion. The demands from traditionally marginalized groups threatened to overtake the government–Maoist peace process.

The Seven Party Alliance and the Maoists eventually recognized the legitimacy of the claims for inclusion. They agreed to allocate 49% of the Constituent Assembly seats to the Terai region, proportional to its population according to Nepal's last census, and to amend the interim constitution to incorporate a commitment to a future federal state. Negotiating teams were established to consider other demands. However, the security situation remained turbulent. On March 21, at least 27 people, all or almost all linked to the CPN-M, were killed in a Terai town after violence broke out at simultaneous rallies of the Madhesi People's Rights Forum (MPRF) and the Maoists – this was the greatest loss of life in any single incident outside the armed conflict. Elsewhere in the country, the Maoists continued to engage in a persistent pattern of intimidation, threats, and extortion, and their YCL carried out abductions and quasi-policing activities.

With the legislation determining the electoral system still to be adopted, it was increasingly apparent that a June election was not feasible and that time was needed to address the security situation. However, none of the parties wanted to acknowledge

---

[18] See Chief Election Commissioner Bhojraj Pokharel's own account of how he approached his responsibility in Chapter 9.1.

this reality. Thus it fell to the Election Commission to announce that an election by mid-June had become impossible and to specify the minimum period necessary after legislation was enacted, requiring a postponement until after the June–September monsoon season. An unhappy period followed, marked by accusations and counter-accusations within the eight-party governing coalition regarding the responsibility for the failure to hold the election within the agreed period, an extremely volatile security situation featuring clashes and killings in the Terai, intense criticism of the activities of the YCL, and lack of progress across the board on implementation of peace process commitments. Finally, at the very end of May, constructive dialogue among the eight parties and with Madhesi and Janajati groups resumed; the parties set a new deadline of mid-December for the election, and in mid-June the legislature passed the key electoral law.

Throughout this period, UNMIN struggled to get the process of verification of Maoist combatants underway, supported the Election Commission as it grappled with the implications of changing timetables and potential electoral arrangements, pressed the Maoists to bring their cadres within the law, and generally encouraged the political parties to maintain their peace process consensus and reach out to marginalized groups. Public calls by Madhesi groups for UN participation in their talks with the government embroiled UNMIN in some controversy. A first-ever meeting between the UN and a cross-party group of Madhesi representatives at the end of 2007, with the modest objective of understanding Madhesi grievances, brought an Indian rebuke that UNMIN allegedly exceeded its mandate. A cross-border meeting of UN humanitarian representatives with a Madhesi armed group based in India, seeking to ensure the safety of non-Madhesi staff delivering relief supplies after severe flooding in the Terai, was widely misrepresented as an UNMIN political initiative. In fact, the UN had told Madhesis who sought its involvement that it could only involve itself in facilitation if requested by the government, which made clear it had no such desire. However, UNMIN civil affairs officers, working in conjunction with OHCHR staff, could and did try to mitigate local conflicts, which were sometimes becoming communal in character. Both UNMIN and OHCHR felt it right for the UN to be a voice for inclusion, both as a matter of principle and because its recognition was crucial to the success of the Constituent Assembly election that UNMIN was mandated to support. The mission also repeatedly drew attention to the almost total exclusion of women from participation in public life and from the peace process, insisting that this issue should receive no less attention simply because women were less likely to press their legitimate claims through violence or disruption.

The electoral system that was enacted in June would be critical to ensuring inclusion in the Constituent Assembly, although it would be further amended. It was to be a mixed system, with half of the 480 elected seats filled by first-past-the-post races in single-member constituencies and half from a proportional representation list. A complex quota system prescribed the extent to which each party needed to include members of marginalized groups and women among its nominees and winning candidates.[19]

The election was to be the cornerstone of the peace process, but during the second half of 2007, the peace process itself was in deep trouble, requiring new rounds of intense discussion and negotiations between the two sides and with the new actors.

Jeopardizing the path toward the election now were the Maoists. Discontent had been rising within the CPN-M, including within the cantonments, at the compromises made by its leadership, and the future of the cadres remained uncertain. This dissatisfaction had to be addressed in a plenum[20] of the party in early August. The party leadership was worried that it would be going into the election weakened in particular by the Madhesi movement in the Terai. It also expressed concern that those who, in its view, wanted to save the monarchy and block the Maoist agenda of a federal republic would continue their efforts to undermine the party. The CPN-M emerged from the meeting having agreed to take a tougher line in relation to its coalition partners and to make an effort to rebuild alliances with traditionally marginalized groups, which had been a major part of its support base. Thus the Maoists, in contradiction to existing agreements, called for a fully proportional electoral system, as demanded by the marginalized groups, and the declaration of a republic by the interim legislature before the election of the Constituent Assembly.

The Maoist leaders explained the major adjustments they were demanding as a consequence of changed political circumstances following the postponement of the ballot, pointing to the alleged resurgence of "regressive" monarchist forces bent on undermining the peace process and preventing the election. Others accused them of simply being unwilling to face electoral defeat. When their demands were not met, the Maoists withdrew their ministers from the government. Other parties, too, were barely ready for a November election: it was only in late September that the Nepali Congress sealed protracted negotiations for reunification with the breakaway Nepali Congress (Democratic) and adopted a federal republican platform, both essential for its own electoral prospects. In spite of the Election Commission's repeated extension of deadlines for nominations to allow more time for parties to resolve their differences, party leaders, in early October, had to agree to postpone the election a second time.

The prospects for the election to take place at all now looked bleak. Despite an agreement between the government and the MPRF, political and criminal violence had escalated in parts of the Terai, including a serious outbreak of communal violence in one central region district. UNMIN's view was that, beyond the claimed

---

[19] See Chapter 9 by Catinca Slavu for a more detailed explanation of the electoral system.
[20] A substantially expanded central committee meeting.

and proximate causes, the crisis had occurred first and foremost because of the lack of implementation of a wide range of agreements. The reluctance of the CPN-M to ensure that the YCL ceased using violence and intimidation had eroded confidence in the Maoists' democratic commitment, whereas the lack of progress within the coalition government in discussing the future of the Maoist combatants and security sector reform had contributed to Maoist concerns that the other parties lacked sincerity in their commitments. There needed to be a renewed effort to reestablish the common purpose of the 12-Point Understanding and develop a shared roadmap for moving forward the peace process and creating the conditions for the Constituent Assembly election.

Cooperation between UNMIN and India over the practicalities of cantonment and election preparations had been good, but now positions began to diverge. Although India immediately sent an envoy to press the parties for the earliest possible rescheduling of the election, the UN believed that a more fundamental recommitment by the parties was needed. The Secretariat told the Security Council that

> the peace process will not come to a successful conclusion, absent political agreements that could potentially be nurtured, as well, with the assistance of the United Nations. Unfortunately we are limited in that regard. Although we have a sizeable presence and capacity to assist in the political management of the peace process – a role that the United Nations has played successfully in other peace processes around the world – we are constrained in the case of Nepal by the limited focus of UNMIN's mandate.[21]

On the ground, UNMIN began discreetly bringing together key leaders of the Maoist and non-Maoist parties. Its suggestions, in New York and Kathmandu, as to how it could do more to assist the process were modest: providing support to the implementation of the peace process and agreements reached; assisting a discussion on the future of the country's security sector, including a managed transition from the temporary cantonments and arms monitoring to long-term solutions; and providing greater advisory support to the police on promoting public security.

Whatever the value of the encouragement by the UN or other international organizations may or may not have been, it was once again the Nepalis' capacity for dialogue with each other that produced a fresh agreement. On December 23, the parties signed a 23-Point Agreement that struck new compromises closer to the Maoist position. The interim constitution was amended to state that Nepal should be a "federal democratic republic" and that the republic would be implemented at the first meeting of the Constituent Assembly. The role of the king was further downgraded by stipulating that until an elected government was in place the prime minister would conduct all duties of head of state. The mixed electoral system was

---

[21] Briefing by Assistant Secretary-General for Political Affairs Angela Kane, Security Council Informal Consultations, October 9, 2007.

amended, most significantly by increasing the number of seats distributed under proportional representation, which expanded the size of the future assembly from 497 to a gargantuan 601 members. The 23-Point Agreement set new ambitious timelines for the implementation of yet to be fulfilled commitments stemming from the peace agreements, and the Maoists rejoined the interim government on December 30. The parties resolved that the election would be held by April 10, 2008.

However, one major hurdle to the election still had to be overcome. The electoral formula contained in the 23-Point Agreement had again been decided by the governing alliance without consultation with the Madhesi and Janajati groups, which, already incensed that agreements signed with them in August 2007 had yet to be implemented, complained that it fell short of full proportional representation. A broadened Madhesi Front launched a protest movement, seeking to prevent the election unless their demands were met. Deaths at demonstrations and blockades of essential supplies to the Kathmandu Valley soon followed. Armed groups continued to engage in killings, abductions, and extortion, taking advantage of the open border with India, and the proportion of rural areas in the Terai without public officials increased further after targeted assassinations.

With time slipping away before the election date of April 10, it took strong Indian intervention in the government's negotiations with the Madhesi Front to broker an agreement sufficient to pave the way for the participation of the Madhesi parties; a similar agreement was quickly signed with Janajati representatives.[22] Most armed groups rejected the agreement and attempted to persist with protests, including violence, but with limited effect, as Madhesis overwhelmingly showed their wish to assert themselves through the ballot box and India tightened border security. The fact that the 23-Point Agreement had gone the way of other agreements, with few of its commitments implemented by the stipulated deadlines, did not trouble the political parties as they at last applied their energies to their election campaigns.

THE CONSTITUENT ASSEMBLY ELECTION

The election on April 10, 2008, was a major technical accomplishment, but it was much more: it was a historic event, bringing into being an assembly of unprecedented representation. Yet its imperfections and shock result would bring new hurdles to completion of the peace process.

As attested by the UN's Electoral Expert Monitoring Team[23] and other international observers, Nepal's Election Commission successfully overcame all the considerable technical and logistical challenges it faced.[24] Not the least of these

---

[22] See Chapter 13 by Prashant Jha on the Madhesi movement and the role of India.

[23] Executive summaries of the five reports of the Electoral Expert Monitoring Team can be found at http://www.unmin.org.np/?d=activities&p=electoral.

[24] See Chapter 9 for more details on elections challenges.

challenges were the printing and distribution of giant ballot papers for the two races once all nominations had been submitted, within a period of time that had been shortened to allow for the final negotiations, as well as efforts to inform voters of the complex process, in a country where partial proportional representation was being used for the first time. Throughout the frustrations of postponements and missed deadlines, the Chief Election Commissioner wisely took the view that the election was to serve the peace process and should not be derailed by inflexibility on the part of the commission.[25] UNMIN had its own frustrations with the postponements, because it had twice mobilized and stood down the UN volunteers who were to deploy as district election advisors for June and then for November 2007. The mission also had to overcome security concerns regarding the volunteers' deployment: an international presence was most needed in the districts where the situation was most troubled. However, finally all the district staff were in place for the April election.

Even more daunting than the technical preparations was promoting a level playing field for all parties. The UN coordinated the deployment of UNMIN's civil affairs officers and OHCHR's human rights officers to prioritize the districts and constituencies where voting was likely to be most problematic. From New York and Kathmandu, the UN had pressed to maximize the overall international observation effort: on polling day, nearly 800 international observers were in Nepal, but many of these came only for Election Day itself. Three organizations – the Carter Center, the European Union, and the Asian Network for Free Elections (ANFREL) – provided longer term observation and greater outreach into rural areas. Donors invested substantially in national observer groups, which could be expected to reach more remote areas, but later complaints of intimidation and malpractice suggest that a claimed 60,000 national observers did not have the impact that might be expected of such numbers.

Campaigning was peaceful in many constituencies, but there was persistent obstruction of the activities of other political parties, involving intimidation and violent clashes by the YCL and other Maoist cadres, particularly in the hill districts that had been their strongholds. There was also election violence in Terai constituencies, mostly between parties other than the Maoists. Although Maoist cadres were most widely involved in election-related violence, they also suffered the largest number of fatalities in the weeks preceding the election. UNMIN issued three reports, based on UNMIN and OHCHR monitoring, describing the violence and other breaches of the Code of Conduct,[26] and publicly and privately, at the national and local level, it pressed the Maoist and other party leaders to control their supporters.

---

[25] See Chapter 9.1 for the Chief Election Commissioner's own explanation of his approach.
[26] UNMIN, *Report on conditions for the 10 April Constituent Assembly election*, March 22, March 30, and April 6, 2008, http://www.unmin.org.np/?d=media&p=press&mode=&offset=30.

A particular UNMIN responsibility was to do its utmost to ensure that the two armies stayed out of the election – the starting point in the 12-Point Understanding for the UN role. The AMMAA's provision allowing up to 12% of personnel from any cantonment or barracks to be on leave at any point in time was a potential loophole in this respect, and UNMIN urged both armies to suspend all leaves. Both did so, although not before there were reports, some of which were confirmed and protested by UNMIN, of Maoist combatants from the cantonments engaging in election activity. UNMIN stretched its arms monitoring capacity to its limits at the cantonments, for the first time fielding a simultaneous presence at all satellites as well as the main sites and conducting head counts. On Election Day, Maoist army and NA personnel who were registered to vote in the proportional representation race (but not in the constituencies where they were stationed) cast their ballots in an orderly fashion at polling centers outside their cantonments and barracks.

On polling day there were four deaths, including that of one candidate, and reports of "booth-capturing" by various parties – a long-established malpractice in Nepal. However, the immediate statements of interested governments and reports of observers were highly positive – including those of the national observer organizations, whose political ties were mostly to the UML and Nepali Congress. Some of the enthusiasm in Kathmandu turned to dismay as the results began to come in, with the CPN-M winning exactly half the first-past the-post contests and just under 30% of the proportional vote, giving them a total of 38% of the elected seats in the Constituent Assembly. The main disappointed parties, the Nepali Congress and the UML, each polled just more than 20% of the vote, whereas the Madhesi parties were strongly represented with 81 members. The quota system, together with the greater diversity of Maoist constituency candidates, produced an assembly with unprecedented representation of most social groups in the country and nearly one-third women – far in excess of the global average of around 18% of women representatives in elected bodies.

The inquest among the disappointed parties was in part self-critical, but also attributed the Maoist victory to obstruction and violence inhibiting the campaigning of their rivals, intimidation of voters, and polling-day abuses. The criticism that this obstruction had been understated by international observers (who did not reach the more remote areas of the country) was not without some justification, although the national observers had been equally positive about the election and the criticism did not properly apply to the UN, whose reports had been among the frankest. There were also clear indications that some voters had voted for the Maoists for fear that armed conflict might resume if they were heavily defeated, a fear played on by Maoist campaign rhetoric. Yet the Maoist victory was no less in constituencies under the eye of observers in the Kathmandu valley, and peaceful by-elections one year later would show little change in the relative support of the parties. There could be no doubt that the vote was one for change and a rebuff to the old parties, but receiving less than one-third of the vote was hardly an unqualified endorsement of the ideology of the CPN-M.

MAKING AND BREAKING GOVERNMENTS

The people of Nepal could thus be said to have mandated the parties to work together to complete the peace process and draft a new constitution, as indeed the major parties had all committed themselves to do. Indeed, the parties did honor their first, historic commitment: that the opening session of the Constituent Assembly would implement the republic. It was convened on May 28, 2008, and the vote to end the 239-year-old monarchy overwhelmingly passed by a margin of 560 to 4. Within an allotted 15 days, former king Gyanendra Shah left the palace, without incident, to remain peacefully in Nepal.

However, behind the scenes, divisions and hard bargaining had already begun. It soon became clear that the election had caused a breakdown in cooperation among the parties and an inability to agree on terms to work together in successive governments, impeding any resolution of the future of the combatants or sufficient consensus on a new constitution within the two-year deadline of the interim constitution.

The interim constitution required the government to conduct itself "consistently with the aspirations of the united people's movement, political consensus and culture of mutual cooperation," and the pre-election assumption was that a new interim government to steer Nepal through the process of drafting the new constitution would comprise all major parties in accordance with their respective strength at the ballot box. Despite the allegations about their methods, there was grudging recognition that the Maoists had won the right to head the government. Prime Minister Koirala, however, appeared in no hurry to step down, while the former alliance parties engaged in protracted negotiations over the basis for proceeding to a new government.

The interim constitution provided for a prime minister to be selected by political consensus or, failing that, by a two-thirds majority and similarly to be subject to removal by a two-thirds majority vote. Because the CPN-M had a blocking minority of well over one-third of the seats in the Constituent Assembly, a Maoist prime minister, once installed, would not be able to be removed even by a combination of all other parties. Therefore, the other major parties would not let the assembly proceed until the Maoists had agreed to an amendment of the interim constitution allowing for the prime minister to be elected or ousted by a simple – rather than two-thirds – majority and to the introduction of a nonexecutive presidency.

Both the Nepali Congress and the UML laid claim to the new presidency, with the former stating that it would not otherwise participate in a Maoist-led government: its candidate would be Girija Prasad Koirala. With Prachanda as prime minister, a Koirala presidency would have kept in play the partnership that had been the main pillar of the peace process. However, the Maoists feared that the presidency would create a strong alternative power center to their prime minister. During lengthy maneuvering, the Maoists alienated not only the Nepali Congress but also the UML by appearing to promise and then renege on support for the presidency to Madhav Kumar Nepal, who had resigned as UML general secretary after losing in both of the two constituencies he contested. Eventually, the Maoists sought to elect a sympathetic president, nominating a Madhesi who was not from any of the major parties. However, this effort backfired, and almost all parties united against the Maoists to elect as president Ram Baran Yadav, a Madhesi parliamentarian of the Nepali Congress.

Relations among the parties were now irrevocably soured. The UML was reluctant to join a Maoist-led government without the Nepali Congress. As conditions for joining an all-party government, the Nepali Congress demanded implementation of Maoist commitments to return all property seized during the People's War and to end the "paramilitary functioning" of the YCL, and it insisted that it must hold the Defense Ministry. The mood in the Nepali Congress was against joining the government, and when negotiations for a consensus government eventually failed, it alone opposed the election of Prachanda as prime minister in the Constituent Assembly, leaving the CPN-M and UML to combine with the MPRF and some smaller left and Madhesi parties to form the new interim government.

The coalition government led by the world's first democratically elected Maoist prime minister lasted for less than nine months. Its failure was due to the Maoists' inexperience, their internal divisions over strategy and tactics, and the CPN-M's incomplete transformation into a democratic party (yet rapid assimilation to some of the bad habits of previous parties in power), in the face of considerable obstruction by the Nepali Congress and others. UNMIN's responsibility remained to try to keep the peace process on track and to accomplish its own exit strategy through the resolution of the issues regarding the former combatants.

First and foremost, this task required the establishment of the special committee to supervise, integrate, and rehabilitate the Maoist combatants. Against a fractious background, it was only in late October 2008 – not coincidentally, on the eve of a visit to Nepal by UN Secretary-General Ban Ki-moon – that the government announced the reestablishment of the special committee; it was only in January 2009 that inter-party differences regarding its composition and terms of reference had been resolved and the special committee held its first meeting. During the long period in which no serious negotiation or technical analysis of options had taken place, public statements by political and military voices demonstrated the clash of divergent opinions. The Nepalese Army, led by COAS General Rookmangud Katawal, was politically active in resisting both integration of Maoist combatants into its ranks and any need for its own "democratization" or major steps toward more inclusive recruitment.

The crisis that led to the downfall of the Maoist-led government began in November 2008 when the Nepalese Army, without authorization from the Maoist-held Ministry of Defense, began a new round of recruitment to fill vacancies. At a time when no progress was being made regarding the future of Maoist army personnel, this was the subject of strong exception within the cantonments. The Maoist army declared that it too would recruit "to fill vacancies." UNMIN stated its consistent position that any new recruitment by either army constituted a breach of the AMMAA. After a cabinet discussion, the Ministry of Defense wrote to instruct the Nepalese Army to suspend its recruitment; the army replied that suspension would be inappropriate because the process was almost complete, and it proceeded with its later stages.

This defiance, along with two further cases of perceived insubordination, was cited by the Maoist leadership in resolving to dismiss General Katawal. Strong Indian pressure, as well as Katawal's politicking and the mood among the Kathmandu elite, ensured that the Maoists lacked the support of any other parties when the cabinet proceeded to dismiss him. Eighteen political parties, including the Nepali Congress and the UML, urged President Ram Baran Yadav to intervene, and he wrote to Katawal instructing him to remain in his post. With the withdrawal of UML support guaranteeing the loss of the government's Constituent Assembly majority, Prachanda resigned as prime minister, denouncing the president's action as unconstitutional and asserting the need for civilian supremacy over the army.[27]

After the episode, some contended that the Maoists' true intention in replacing COAS General Katawal was a complete capture of the state – a view supported by the strategically timed release of a January 2008 video of Prachanda speaking to Maoist combatants of preparations for revolt. Others asserted that the army was on the verge of a coup, to be fronted by the president.[28] Those close to the president maintained that he had withstood pressures to take more radical action.

Whatever risks may have been averted, the change of government came about peacefully. With the active encouragement of India, almost all other parties united behind Madhav Kumar Nepal of the UML as the new prime minister, to head a government with a jumbo cabinet to accommodate them. The most significant group to stay outside the new government, apart from the Maoists, was the MPRF faction led by the outgoing foreign minister Upendra Yadav, whose party split over whether to join the new coalition.

There was little prospect that the Maoists would allow a government that excluded them to preside over the integration and rehabilitation of their combatants and the promulgation of a new constitution. They only briefly permitted the functioning of the legislature and waged a campaign of demonstrations and non-cooperation outside, demanding recognition of the impropriety of the president's action and

---

[27] See Chapter 13 in this volume for further details.
[28] For a detailed analysis, see *Nepal's Future: In Whose Hands?*, p. 16.

clarification of his limited powers, as well as civilian supremacy over the army. All parties paid lip service to the need for cooperation among the major political forces and indeed for a national unity government to include the Maoists. However, the Maoists insisted on their right to return to head it, and majority factions within each of the main parties, strongly encouraged by India, resisted this push.

The death of Girija Prasad Koirala on March 20, 2010, removed from the scene the person with the strongest vision of the peace process, although despite his stature he had ceased being able to impose this vision on his own or other parties. As all pretense that a constitution would be drafted by the deadline of May 28, 2010, had to be abandoned, the issue became whether and on what terms the Maoists would vote to extend the life of the Constituent Assembly and avert a constitutional crisis. A last-minute vote to extend it for another year was based on a commitment that Prime Minister Nepal would resign, and ill-tempered negotiations began on the terms for formation of the third postelection government.

NO EXIT FOR UNMIN

The secretary-general had told the Security Council at the outset that UNMIN was expected to be "a focused mission of limited duration" – initially 12 months. The Constituent Assembly election was intended to be held by June 2007, and the future of the former combatants was also supposed to be addressed by the first interim government. The successive postponements of the election, followed by the failure of successive governments to resolve the future of the combatants, made repeated extensions of the mission's duration inevitable, but the scope of its mandate was more controversial.

As already noted, the UN regarded the political crisis around the second post-ponement as a serious crisis in the peace process and believed that it could assist by providing broader support to implementation. It also had a greater sense of urgency than the parties regarding the future of the armies, not only because of its own exit strategy but also because, as the secretary-general would remind the Security Council, "experience in various countries has demonstrated the dangers of failing to address successfully the issue of former combatants and the risks that this can pose to durable stability."[29]

Many of the leading Nepali actors privately welcomed a broader UN role, but were not prepared to defy Indian pressures by making this support explicit. India expected and obtained close consultation by the government of Nepal over the terms of each successive request to the UN. Thus when the first formal request for extension of UNMIN's presence was made in December 2007, Nepal asked for no expansion of the mandate.

---

[29] *Report of the Secretary-General on the request of Nepal for United Nations assistance in support of its peace process*, S/2008/670, October 24, 2008, para. 62.

The successful holding of the election in April 2008 raised larger questions when UNMIN's mandate approached its next expiration in July of that year. Kathmandu media repeatedly presented mandate renewal as something desired by the UN, which might be graciously granted by Nepal. They failed to understand that the ultimate decision was to be made by the Security Council, for which Nepal was not a high priority, where financial considerations weighed heavily, and which – although impressed with what had been accomplished – was becomingly increasingly impatient with repeated disregard for deadlines. In his first postelection report, the secretary-general said that he did not anticipate a further extension of the mandate beyond July, although the UN would discuss with the new government any assistance it might request for the completion and consolidation of the peace process and for the long-term development of Nepal.

However, the termination of UNMIN by July 2008 could only have proved realistic if the parties had proceeded, in a mood of postelection cooperation, to early resolution of the future of the combatants. What happened was the opposite. With the long delay in forming the new government, let alone the special committee, UNMIN remained trapped in its role of monitoring the cantonments. All leading political actors made clear privately that they would expect UN assistance in resolving this issue, but when the formal request for another extension came – once again, at the last minute – it related only to monitoring the management of arms and army personnel. The terms of the request were so narrow that the secretary-general stated that it lacked the clarity for him to recommend to the Security Council a continuing special political mission, and he sought clarification from the government that indeed it desired a mission headed by a Special Representative with political staffing, and thus a good offices role. The government provided such clarification, to the displeasure of India, which – having succeeded in ensuring the limited nature of the Nepali request in the first place – complained publicly to the Security Council that the UN was engaging in "a consistent effort to expand the definition of what Nepal seeks in terms of support to include a role in the Nepali peace process, irrespective of the desire of Nepali interlocutors."[30]

Immediately after the election, UNMIN had begun downsizing through the withdrawal of electoral personnel, and in July 2008 it closed its five regional offices and withdrew its civil affairs officers – not without regret, because their presence and the frequent visits they had made to the districts had had a significant mitigating effect on local conflicts, which had yet to be addressed by effective local governance or peace committees. The arms monitors remained at approximately half their original strength, and UNMIN suggested that when the special committee was reconstituted, it could reduce the number of cantonments and the requirement for around-the-clock surveillance at eight weapons storage areas. No such progress was made, but

---

[30] Statement by H. E. Mr, Nirupam Sen, Permanent Representative of India, at the Security Council, July 18, 2008.

when the Security Council had no option but to extend UNMIN beyond January 2009, the mission was further downsized: at its pre-election peak, it had had just over one thousand international and national staff, and during 2009 this number fell to around 250.

UNMIN's main focus was now to maintain its arms monitoring, while encouraging progress regarding the future of the combatants through providing assistance to the technical committee that the special committee had appointed to advise it. In early 2010, it achieved at last the long overdue discharge of those still in the cantonments, who had been disqualified in UNMIN's verification as minors or late recruits. Its monitoring of the Maoist army was periodically criticized as weak and inadequate – by the very politicians who had insisted on a minimal presence in the first place and who were responsible for the lack of progress, under governments led in turn by the Nepali Congress, the CPN-M, and the UML, in fulfilling the CPA commitments regarding the future of the armies. Both armies were restive: the Maoist combatants at the uncertainty about their future and the failure to make any positive use of them in the meantime; the Nepalese Army at the continuing constraints that the CPA and AMMAA placed on its desire to return to business as usual. What is remarkable is not that there were occasional violations of the AMMAA, but the extent to which discipline prevailed, especially on the part of a rebel army. In July 2009, January 2010, and May 2010, the government of Nepal submitted last-minute requests for further extensions of UNMIN's mandate, and an increasingly frustrated Security Council saw no option but to accede, despite the futility of its attempts to insist on deadlines for the completion of the mission's tasks. Finally in September 2010, after a government reduced to caretaker status ill advisedly sought to abandon the CPA by having UNMIN remain to monitor the Maoist army only, the Security Council decided that UNMIN would withdraw at the end of a final extension in January 2011.

CONCLUSION

The achievements of Nepal's peace process are extraordinary. In mid-2005, the armed conflict was heading into its tenth year, with grave violations of international humanitarian law being committed by the Maoists and by the state security forces, and the government then headed by a king curtailing democratic rights, as it apparently sought to take Nepal back to a period preceding its first democracy movement of 1990. Three years later, Nepal had seen an end to the armed conflict, the election of a first genuinely inclusive assembly to shape a new constitution, and a peaceful transition to a republic. All this had been achieved not by international intervention or mediation, but by Nepal's own political and civil society leaders, driven by the demand for peace and change that was so powerfully expressed by the people of Nepal in the *Jana Andolan* and again at the ballot box.

Yet four years after the peace agreement, the two armies that fought the war remained in separate existence, the deadline for agreement on a new constitution had passed, the Madhesis and other groups remained marginalized despite their representation in the Constituent Assembly, and the political parties seemed unable to overcome the divisions among and within themselves to cooperate to complete the peace process. One must ask: What have been the weaknesses of the peace process and of the UN's support of it?[31]

The most dangerous flaw in the peace agreements was the failure to negotiate more fully the future of the armies and of the Maoist militia; instead they merely set out processes toward vaguely formulated objectives: the "integration and rehabilitation" of Maoist combatants and the "democratization" of the Nepalese Army. An internationally mediated process would probably have insisted on greater clarity, even at the price of a longer and more difficult negotiation. Yet perhaps an insistence on clarity would have prevented any agreement, while the passage of time has at least made a return to war increasingly unthinkable.

The UN could be criticized for accepting the responsibility to monitor the management of arms and armies, with no ability to ensure its exit strategy. Should it have insisted on a more robust military presence and on a mandate to advise on reform of the security sector? Neither would have been realistic. India would have ensured that Nepal made no such request, whereas other members of the Security Council would have opposed any mandate not requested by Nepal itself.

Some in the non-Maoist parties now argue that it was a mistake to proceed to the Constituent Assembly election while the Maoist army was still in existence. This argument too lacks realism: the state had proved unable to defeat the Maoist army, and the terms on which the CPN-M agreed, in the 12-Point Understanding, to end the war were that their army would remain in existence, under international supervision, until after the election. An interim government and legislature based on no democratic mandate, as regards the inclusion of the Maoists, or on one that had expired, in the case of the parliamentarians, lacked legitimacy. Only an election could produce an assembly reflecting the new realities of Nepal – as it did.

Madhesis, Janajatis, Dalits, and other marginalized groups were nonetheless excluded from almost all stages of peace process negotiations, and the separate agreements struck with them came as afterthoughts when they had forced their way onto the agenda, sometimes by violence and disruption. Peace negotiations remained a matter for a small group of political leaders, mostly from higher castes – and all men.

---

[31] I offered a fuller analysis in a November 2009 lecture at the New School, "The Peace Process in Nepal: Is It Failing?" published as the afterword in Ian Martin (ed.), *Nepal's Peace Process at the United Nations*, and online at http://www.newschool.edu/uploadedFiles/ici/News_and_Events/ IM_NewSchool_6Nov09_final.pdf.

Beyond whatever flaws there were in the agreements themselves, there was – throughout the different governments – a persistent weakness of implementation. This exacerbated recriminations among the political parties and failed the victims of the conflict. Repeated agreements to establish commissions or committees to steer or monitor the process as a whole remained unfulfilled. Four years after the first commitment to make known the fate of disappeared persons, an investigation commission had yet to be established; civil society and OHCHR-Nepal have been unable to keep human rights issues high on the agenda of the peace process, where all parties have colluded in perpetuating impunity. After many months of promises and complaints, a parliamentary committee was charged with monitoring the return of property seized by the Maoists, but this did not amount to a practical approach to bringing about its return. Much could have been achieved if the UN had been allowed to work more closely with a less partisan Peace Ministry on issues of implementation. Ideally, the tripartite formula of the JMCC – the only implementation body that met regularly, convened and minuted by the UN – could have been applied to nonmilitary peace process implementation. The haphazard and personalized manner in which the peace process was conducted by the political leaders was a major weakness. UNMIN's urging of a more structured and systematic approach was not heeded, and offers of assistance were all too easily represented as "mandate creep."

The limitations of UNMIN's mandate contrasted sharply with the high expectations of its role, leaving it in an often uncomfortable position. Although a mission of around one thousand personnel in a country of 27 million constituted in UN terms a light footprint, it was the most visible foreign presence Nepal had seen. This visibility was in part desired to have an impact on the pre-election context, just as OHCHR-Nepal's arrival in 2005 had a psychological reach beyond its actual resources. Yet it also exposed UNMIN to resentment at the inevitable white vehicles, and to appearing toothless when unable to enforce compliance with agreements, even when they were outside its mandate. UNMIN found itself simultaneously criticized for not preventing failings in the peace process and for exceeding or seeking to expand its mandate.

The very politicians who had wanted only a light military monitoring role became critics of the inability of UNMIN to control the personnel and weapons of the Maoist army and to prevent rather than investigate and protest breaches of the AMMAA. UNMIN's arms monitoring component was not planned for a long-term role and was downsized after the election, when the Security Council expected the parties to move swiftly to solutions allowing UNMIN's exit. If it had been anticipated that monitoring would be prolonged into a fourth year, in a climate of increasing political tension, perhaps the monitoring could and should have been planned as a more robust operation. Alternatively, given the limitations of mandate and capacity which the Nepali actors had requested, more could have been done to explain these publicly. Yet there was merit in leaving the responsibility clearly with the parties, and in terms of any international comparison, it is remarkable that there have been so few serious breaches of agreements and that none provoked fresh clashes between the armies and threatened breakdown of the ceasefire.

There are positive lessons from the UN role in Nepal that may have relevance in other settings.[32] UN human rights activism is sometimes assumed to complicate UN peacemaking, but in Nepal a human rights monitoring presence, following and then accompanying low-key but proactive good offices, helped create a more positive climate for the peace process and paved the way to broader UN support to it. A light military monitoring presence proved sufficient to help sustain a ceasefire that became a lasting peace. Even without a mandate to mediate or facilitate, a UN political presence was able to provide encouragement to political actors, notwithstanding their divisions, to maintain a focus on the peace process, and many felt it to be a deterrent to greater confrontation and a return to conflict. It also helped sustain the hope of the people of Nepal that their political leaders would rise to their demand for peace and change – a hope that is yet to be fulfilled.

---

[32] The conclusions of a workshop identifying lessons from the experience of UNMIN are set out in Teresa Whitfield, *Focused Mission: Not So Limited Duration*, p. 7. See also Astri Suhrke, "Virtues of a Narrow Mission: The UN Peace Operation in Nepal," *Global Governance*, Vol. 17, January 2011. My views regarding broader lessons for the UN system are in Ian Martin, "All Peace Operations Are Political: A Case for Designer Missions and the Next UN Reform," *Review of Political Missions*, Center on International Cooperation, New York University, September 2010.

9

The 2008 Constituent Assembly Election:
Social Inclusion for Peace

Catinca Slavu

A BALANCING ACT

Electoral processes are not serving their main purpose, that of consolidating or deepening democracy, unless they are fostering a political system representative of the society and advancing human rights. The election for Nepal's long-pursued Constituent Assembly was meant to ensure such a democratic transformation and, with it, the deliverance from a decade-long conflict. In the context in which large-scale social exclusion had been the root cause of the conflict in Nepal, this chapter focuses on the opportunities and limitations for peace and state-building through electoral processes from the perspective of inclusive representation.

Two circular paradigms framed the Constituent Assembly electoral process. Holding an early election would sustain the necessary momentum for the peace process by maintaining the trust between the main parties to it, the Seven Party Alliance[1] and the Communist Party of Nepal (Maoist) (CPN-M). At the same time, holding the election *before* granting the traditionally marginalized communities the freedom to elect their own representatives was prone to opening a new dimension for the conflict.

After faltering commitments, growing mistrust among all parties, a pervasive climate of fear and insecurity, a radicalization of ethnic demands, and two postponements of the polls, the election was successfully held in April 2008 with high voter turnout. Thanks to a new electoral system that introduced proportional representation with inclusion quotas alongside the traditional first-past-the-post system and, as importantly, the CPN-M's selection of minority group candidates for the first-past-the-post race, the Constituent Assembly became the most inclusive state institution in Nepal's history.

---

[1] A coalition established against the royal takeover of February 1, 2005, by seven main political parties that held approximately 90% of the seats in the 1999 House of Representatives.

Yet, the success of the election failed to provide a boost to the peace process and state-building efforts. The unexpected Maoist victory united conservative status quo forces in an opposition front, leading to political deadlock. In addition, the formidable representation of ethnic and religious minorities cemented identity politics, largely as the result of a mismanaged peace and political process in the run-up to the election. Given that the postelection period has seen a return to exclusionary politics and power struggles among the parties, this legacy is likely to continue to haunt Nepal in times ahead. Until and unless partisan agendas make room for a genuine state-building process, peace will keep faltering, ultimately jeopardizing the momentous accomplishments of the election.

LESSONS FROM THE PAST

The demand for a constituent assembly elected by the people had long been at the core of Nepal's political transformation agenda. Underlying this demand was the decades-long quest for multiparty democracy and the hope it would deliver Nepal from its most fundamental democracy deficit: the large-scale social exclusion and the conflict that had metastasized around it.

A first opportunity to achieve these ideals presented itself in 1950–1 when an armed revolt toppled a century-long autocratic dynasty of hereditary Rana prime ministers. The 1951 interim constitution was meant to pave the way for a Constituent Assembly to be elected within two years. However, several amendments to this constitution resulted rather in the consolidation of the king's powers and the shelving of any plans to establish a Constituent Assembly. Not until February 1959 could an election finally be held, but for a parliament instead. The undisputed success of that election as a herald of change was reversed in December 1960 by King Mahendra's royal coup, which established a new autocratic regime of Panchayat rule that would last for three decades.[2] It was only in February 1990, in the wake of a popular uprising (the first People's Movement), that democratic inroads would be made again.

The new 1990 constitution laid the foundation for democratic governance built on regular, party-based elections. Legislative elections were held in 1991, 1994, and 1999 and local elections in 1992 and 1997. In the political transition context of the 1990s, these elections should be evaluated in terms of their contribution to democratization and state-building rather than as isolated, technical events.

There is no doubt that the significance of the elections in the 1990s lies in their successful restoration of multiparty governance[3] and the alternation of power they

---

[2] A party-less system of governance imposed to ensure autocratic control.

[3] In 1980 a referendum was organized by the royal rule on the Panchayat system versus the restoration of multiparty democracy, with 54.7% of the voters officially, albeit subject to claims of electoral fraud, reported to favor preserving the Panchayat system. Legislative elections were then organized in 1981 and 1986 and local elections in 1987. Candidates' party affiliation was banned, so they had to stand as independents. As a result, the 1981 election was formally boycotted by the then-reformist parties,

delivered – between the main parties of the day, the Nepali Congress (NC) and the Communist Party of Nepal (Unified Marxist-Leninist) (UML). Despite significant challenges – prominently among them low levels of literacy[4] requiring extensive voter education and logistical challenges brought about by Nepal's terrain – the elections were largely deemed *free* and *fair*[5] and were marked by a fairly high voter turnout,[6] as well as a relatively effective performance of the Election Commission, which enjoyed broad confidence from the parties.[7]

At the same time, these elections failed to deliver on social inclusion as both the vehicle and measure of democratic change, foiling the aspirations that had been created by the democratic transition. The 1991 legislative election achieved incipient, albeit minor, progress in terms of social emancipation, sending to parliament a small number of women and ethnic and religious communities as well as a new regional party.[8] In a period marked by an increasingly acute struggle for social inclusion, the legislative elections in 1994 and 1999, however, failed to build on this progress and delivered little more than an alternation of power. Minority representation even declined,[9] reinforcing the continuation of exclusionary politics and feeding the growing agitation of the radical left. Unsurprisingly, the 1997 local and 1999 legislative electoral processes saw increasing violence and intimidation,[10] and in 1999 a phased election ended up being justified in the name of security.[11]

---

including the NC. Although the boycott continued for the second Panchayat election of 1986, these parties decided to participate in the 1987 local elections.

[4] According to Dr. Sushan Acharya (*Democracy, Gender Equality and Women's Literacy: Experience from Nepal*, UNESCO Kathmandu Series of Monographs and Working Papers No. 1, September 2004), in 1991 literacy rates for men reached 38% and for women, 13%. By 2001, these rates rose to 62.2% for men and 34.6% for women (all rates are given for the age category 15 years and above). Both men and women also showed lower caste and ethnic disparities.

[5] Andrea Matles Savada (ed.), *Nepal – A Country Study*, published by the Federal Research Division of the Library of Congress under the Country Studies, Area Handbook Series, September 1991, with an introduction of March 3, 1993.

[6] The percentages were 65.15% for 1991, 61.86% for 1994, and 65.79% for 1999 (http://www.election.gov .np/EN/prevelection.html).

[7] Savada, *Nepal – A Country Study*.

[8] 1991: seven women, one Dalit, and five Muslims were elected. Central Bureau of Statistics 2002 and Election Commission of Nepal as quoted in Krishna Khanal, *The Future of Democracy*, April 2005. The figures for Janajatis and Madhesis are not available segregated as such.

[9] 1994: seven women, four Muslims, no Dalits, 12.2% Janajatis, and 20.0% Madhesis. 1999: 12 women, 2 Muslims, no Dalits (four Dalits were appointed in the Upper House). Central Bureau of Statistics 2002 and Election Commission of Nepal as quoted in Khanal, *The Future of Democracy*.

[10] Democracy and Election Alliance Nepal (DEAN), *Election and Political Violence in Nepal, Final Report* (26 November 2007 – 30 April 2008), June 26, 2008, reports 10 deaths for the 1991 elections and an increase in electoral violence for the subsequent elections.

[11] The phasing of the 1999 legislative election was justified by the Election Commission, as supported by the NC, because of security threats and insufficient protection measures. However, both the UML and the parties outside government were highly concerned that the phasing would increase the scope for malpractice. Both local elections had been conducted in two phases, for ease of administration.

The failure to make progress on social inclusion was to a large extent a consequence of insufficiently progressive changes in the 1990 constitution. Although it laid the foundation for parliamentary democracy, it maintained key exclusionary features – imposing Nepali as the only official language, reaffirming Nepal as a Hindu state, and maintaining highly centralized state structures, thereby allowing the political parties to resist internal democratization.[12]

The constitutional introduction of the first-past-the-post electoral system was another factor reinforcing social exclusion. This system uses single-member constituencies in which the candidate receiving the highest number of votes (a plurality) is elected. In the elections during the Panchayat regime, Nepal's 75 administrative districts served as single- or dual-member constituencies from which a total of 112 seats were returned. Because population density varies significantly across Nepal's districts, the 1990 constitution expanded the number of constituencies from 75 to 205[13] to achieve a more equitable geographic representation. Together with later adjustments in the number of constituencies allocated per district to account for population shifts,[14] this expansion constituted a significant step forward and an important legacy for the future since the most populous districts were in the Terai, the southern lowlands along the Indian border and home to the historically marginalized Madhesis.[15] However, given the constitutional provisions for each administrative district to be individually represented, the disparity of vote weight between constituencies remained high,[16] likely as a result of the intention of the new political elite – now including the political parties – to control their access to power.

One of the main advantages of the first-past-the-post system is that it links elected representatives to their constituencies, fostering accountability. It is also credited with generating stable parliamentary majorities through the development of bipolar party-political systems, a feature that may be either advantageous or detrimental in different political and social contexts because it sidelines smaller parties representing

[12] Among other internal democracy problems, candidacy was determined centrally instead of by the local committees. See Karl-Heinz Kraemer, *Elections in Nepal: 1999 and Before*, in Informal Sector Service Centre (INSEC) (ed.), *Human Rights Yearbook 2000*.

[13] Parliament comprised the 205-member House of Representatives, which was directly elected and the 60-member National Council, of whom 35 were elected (through proportional representation, including a reservation for three women) by the House of Representatives, 10 were elected as representatives of the Regional Development Areas, and 10 were appointed by the king.

[14] For the 1994 and 1999 elections the number of seats was redistributed among districts, with some districts seeing a reduction in the number of seats, whereas others saw an increase. See details in Ramjee P. Parajulee, *The Democratic Transition in Nepal*, 2000.

[15] According to John Bevan and Bhaskar Gautam, *Political Economy Analysis: The Madhes/Tarai*, draft report of August 15, 2008. Madhesi is a term describing the non-hill-origin people in the Madhes, which includes the inner and outer Terai, and who share cultural ties with people living in the bordering Indian states of Bihar and Uttar Pradesh. The Madhesis comprise approximately a third of Nepal's population.

[16] The sparsely populated district of Manang received a seat for a mere 6,249 voters, whereas the average was 50,000 voters per constituency and the largest constituency (in Kathmandu) was 102,632 voters. *Spotlight*, May 10, 1991, as quoted in Parajulee, *The Democratic Transition in Nepal*, p. 14.

minority interests. Although a sense of accountability of elected representatives failed to take root in Nepal, the system certainly helped Nepal's two major parties, the NC and the UML, gain dominant positions (in 1999, the two parties won 182 of 205 seats in the House of Representatives). However, unlike proportional electoral systems, this system does not easily accommodate affirmative action. When coupled, as in Nepal, with low levels of internal democracy within the parties and with discriminatory registration of voters, the first-past-the-post system can be fatal to social inclusion. Seeing social inclusion as a threat to the elite ruling them, the main parties successfully opposed proposals in the 1990s to replace the first-past-the-post system with a proportional one.[17]

The Election Commission, too, was not beyond reproach. In the course of the 1990s, it became increasingly politicized, with the NC gaining increasing influence over the appointments of commissioners through its de facto control of the Constitutional Council, which recommended candidates to the king. In this light, the Election Commission's widely reported failure to establish an accurate and inclusive voter register and educate voters should be read more as additional means of maintaining an elite system – promoted by an increasingly elitist NC – and not merely as administrative weaknesses.

In fact, inequities in voter registration reinforced the exclusionary nature of the electoral system. The requirement to prove permanent residence in a given constituency discriminated against internal migrants and the landless, who were typically Dalits,[18] Madhesis, and the poorer segments of the population. Additional inequities came with the fact that voter lists in areas affected by the People's War were often not kept up to date. Moreover, entrusting the registration of voters to the village development committees (VDCs)[19] instead of the electoral officials was meant to reinforce the bias toward the Pahadis, the group originating from the hills, and the higher castes in general because the VDCs were composed almost entirely of higher castes and Pahadis. These problems were compounded by patterns of discrimination on Election Day, such as the systematic failure by election officials to stamp and validate ballots of uneducated voters from minority groups, a practice made possible by the Election Commission's limited efforts to educate voters.[20]

In the same vein, the Election Commission refused to register parties representing minority groups or regions. Although it found lenience for the Hindu-based Madhesis' Nepal Sadbhavana Party and the Rastrya Jana Mukti Morcha (a confederation

---

[17] Ibid. (quoting John Whelpton's *The General Elections of May 1991*, in Michael Hutt [ed.], *Nepal in the Nineties: Versions of the Past, Visions of the Future*, 1994). The major political parties rejected the idea because, among others, "they believed that the traditional system of voting would benefit them."

[18] Group of outcastes from the Hindu caste system, considered untouchable by this system.

[19] The lowest state structure with a combination of administrative and development responsibilities, reporting to the Ministry of Local Development.

[20] Various electoral assessment reports, such as Ian Smith and Dr. Julia Buxton, *Electoral Process Strengthening in Nepal*, July 2005.

of Janajatis[21]), it denied registration for all other parties representing non-Hindu groups.[22]

Therefore, it can be concluded that throughout the 1990s internal agendas of the traditional parties replaced the broad democratization agenda that had underpinned the 1990 People's Movement and that incipient electoral progress was overshadowed by the systemic failure to ensure genuine social inclusion. Against a creeping return to autocracy culminating in the royal coup of February 2005, the compromised local elections of 2006 would deal a final blow to Nepal's emerging electoral culture.

In the middle of the Maoist insurgency and a context increasingly aggravated by human rights abuses, in February 2006, King Gyanendra organized municipal elections, against all advice,[23] in an attempt to legitimize his 2005 coup. In the absence of conditions for credibility,[24] the main political parties, with the notable exception of the royalist Rastryia Prajatantra Party, refused to participate in the elections (the boycotting parties were later to coalesce as the Seven Party Alliance [SPA]). Large numbers of voters joined the election boycott, resulting in a symbolically low turnout of 20%.[25] The reputation of the already discredited Election Commission[26] and the electoral officials' morale sank to new lows.[27] Nationwide clashes between police and protesters marred the elections, reflecting widespread discontent with the establishment and foreshadowing greater upheavals to come. Organized *against* democracy, the 2006 local elections thus not only failed to consolidate the king's

---

[21] Nepal's indigenous ethnic groups as a whole.

[22] Parajulee, *The Democratic Transition in Nepal*. For the 1994 elections this number grew to six. Kraemer, *Elections in Nepal: 1999 and Before*). The 1990 constitution prevented the registration of parties formed based on religion, community, caste, tribe, or region. It has been assessed that these two parties were able to register because their names did not indicate any communal identity.

[23] A few written examples on the risks and consequences of organizing these elections could be found in Danida's *An Assessment of Nepal's Electoral Environment*; May 2004 Smith and Buxton, *Electoral Process Strengthening in Nepal*; and International Crisis Group (ICG), *Electing Chaos*, Asia Report no. 111, January 2006.

[24] ICG, *Electing Chaos*. The lack of credible conditions also prompted the European Union to label the elections "another step backward for democracy" before they even took place.

[25] See South Asia Analysis Group, *Nepal: Municipal Elections 2006: No Winners but Losers*, Update 83 by Dr. S. Chandrasekharan, February 13, 2006. Other sources indicate turnout between lower than 20 and 25 percent. Of the voters who had participated in the polls, not many were reported to have done so voluntarily.

[26] As reflected in Smith and Buxton, *Electoral Process Strengthening in Nepal*, the governments of Denmark, Norway, Switzerland, and the United Kingdom, having provided electoral assistance to Nepal, had by July 2005 "decided to withhold support to the [Election Commission] and municipal elections until the human rights and security situation improve[d]." Moreover, according to the ICG report *Electing Chaos*, the Election Commission was not only "palace-leaning" but also the Chief Election Commissioner appointed by the king had been found by the judicial commission (the Malik Commission) – established to investigate abuses committed by the Panchayat government in suppressing protests – to have ordered the police to fire on civilians in his then-capacity as Chief District Officer.

[27] It is not surprising that the website of the Election Commission reestablished in October 2006 does not carry any reference to the 2006 municipal elections.

regime but also provided additional momentum for a second People's Movement. The election results as well as all the previous local government appointments would be annulled by the SPA government in May 2006.

A Misguided Start

Even before the failed 2006 municipal elections, the SPA and the Maoists, in an effort to reinstall democracy, had initiated peace negotiations, reaching a formal agreement in November 2005 and laying the ground for a new People's Movement in April 2006. This movement consolidated the ongoing peace negotiations and provided a firm base for the election of a constituent assembly as the vehicle to an "inclusive, democratic and progressive" state.[28]

While the explicit goal of the election was to enable the formation of a democratic constitution-making platform, this was accompanied by a number of implicit goals. In light of the widespread mistrust in the political parties' ability to ensure that the new constitution would reflect the people's interests, the election was also to guarantee that the constitution-making process was genuinely representative of the diversity of interests of Nepal's social composition. For the Maoists and their growing constituency, Nepal's transformation into a republic became another goal of the election. Last but not least, the election was to replace bullets with ballots and firmly anchor the Maoists into the peace process. With such goals, the election became the very embodiment of the peace process, placing a premium on enabling conditions to ensure its credibility.

Yet, partisan agendas prevailed once again, and the mainstream parties, with the NC in the lead, concerned about allowing the Maoists enough time to consolidate their constituency, pressed for an early election in which they believed they themselves would thrive. The NC also took it for granted that the Maoists would fare badly in the elections, after which it would be able to dictate the terms of the peace process – and the earlier that happened, the better. An early election was likewise favored by the Maoists, who believed it would confirm their legitimacy as a political – as opposed to military – force and enable them to take advantage of the peace process. As such, a 2007 spring election was discussed during the peace negotiations in the summer and fall of 2006. In November, the election was

---

[28] This goal was defined already in the Comprehensive Peace Agreement through which the parties agreed "(3.5.) To carry out an inclusive, democratic and progressive restructuring of the state by ending the current centralized and unitary form of the state in order to address the problems related to women, Dalit, indigenous people, Janajatis, Madheshi, oppressed, neglected and minority communities and backward regions by ending discrimination based on class, caste, language, gender, culture, religion, and region."

formally scheduled to take place by mid-June 2007, allowing just seven months for its preparation.²⁹

The ambitious timeline exacerbated the inherent challenges of holding elections in a postconflict environment, all the more so as the parties had not even agreed on a clear roadmap. Indeed, at the time the election date was set, a number of conditions essential for ensuring credible elections were remarkable by their absence: a solid political settlement, a safe and secure environment, agreement on the electoral legislation, including the electoral system, a voter list, and sufficient voter awareness. Moreover, the Election Commission was weak and discredited, and the ability of its fledgling Secretariat, already burdened by inexperienced staff, to begin any electoral planning was complicated by a prolonged legal and policy vacuum. The state of affairs was not better in the districts, where approximately 40% of the district election offices had become inoperative as a result of the People's War.³⁰

After a decade of conflict, the state was slow to reestablish its presence and authority in much of the country.³¹ Where present, police and law enforcement were weak, corrupt, and demoralized.³² A well-organized Maoist machine continued to retain de facto control over many districts, often resorting to violence and intimidation. Human rights violations were widespread and impunity prevailed. Internally displaced persons were still prevented by fear or intimidation from returning. The media were attacked and threatened on an almost daily basis.³³ At another level, the coexistence of two armies – the Maoist People's Liberation Army (PLA) and the Nepalese Army (NA) – and the unwillingness of their political masters to reach an agreement over their future fueled insecurity and deepened distrust between the parties.

The early election date also hindered the establishment of a level playing field for the political parties because it restricted the time necessary for new parties

---

²⁹ The date was established in the preliminary peace agreement (the Six-Point Agreement) signed between the SPA and the CPN-M on November 8, 2006, and reiterated in the Comprehensive Peace Agreement concluded on November 21, 2006.

³⁰ Information received from the Election Commission Secretariat in October 2007.

³¹ According to the UN's Nepal Situation Overview (http://www.un.org.np/sites/default/files/situation_ updates/tid_188/20060811062501.pdf) of July 2006 (published on August 11, 2006), in July 2006, 68% of the VDC secretaries – the only administration representatives at the subdistrict level in the absence of elected officials – were displaced from their posting. This assessment uses the presence of the VDC secretaries as a proxy indicator for the reach of the state.

³² Three hundred of the approximately 1,300 pre-conflict stations and posts (*Report of the UN Secretary-General on the request of Nepal for United Nations assistance in support of its peace process*, 9 January 2007). See also Dan Huntington, *District and VDC level changes in politics and state functioning, in particular since the elections, with special reference to conflict dynamics*, August 2008 (political economy report prepared for DFID Nepal).

³³ Nepal Human Rights Commission (NHRC) Summary Report on the *Status of Human Rights under the Comprehensive Peace Accord* (covering the period between February 26 and July 16, 2007), November 7, 2007.

to form and organize a campaign. This rushed situation was aggravated by the constitutional requirements for the Election Commission to register only political parties, thereby excluding civil society organizations from contesting the election, and for new parties to submit as many as 10,000 support signatures to be registered for the election.[34] Needless to say, the most affected groups were those that did not wish to associate themselves with the traditional parties and the obsolete political climate these represented. As is analyzed later, another highly problematic consequence of a rushed election was that it would not allow sufficient time to redraw the inequitable boundaries of the single-member constituencies inherited from the 1990s for the first-past-the-post race and the parties used the short timeframe they themselves imposed to justify the retention of these boundaries.

Thus, the risks of holding an election *before* conditions were in place to ensure broad participation and inclusion were not properly weighed by the parties. Thus, parties did not properly weigh the risks of holding an election *before* conditions were in place to ensure broad participation and inclusion. Instead, a concern prevailed that a late or delayed election would stall the peace process and give the parties time to entrench themselves into hard-line positions. The damaging consequences a rushed and therefore failed election could have for the peace process were never seriously taken into consideration by the key national or international actors, either.[35] Instead, once the election date was announced, postponing it was seen even more strongly as a major challenge to the country's transition out of fragility.[36] In the end, having become hostage to an incomplete political settlement, the election took place on April 10, 2008, after two postponements and – more gravely – increased ethnic violence, proving that the initial timeline had been dangerously unrealistic.

It was in this context of a hasty election without sufficient credibility premises that, on October 30, 2006, a Chief Election Commissioner was appointed, shortly followed by two additional commissioners, of whom one was a woman. Because the initial appointments included only members put forward by the NC and the UML, two more commissioners were appointed in January 2007 on CPN-M's insistence, this time expanding the membership to a Janajati and a Madhesi. Not least because of their high professional standing, the commissioners' appointments were widely accepted, reflecting a first commitment to a credible election by the parties.

---

[34] Signature requirements are a normal feature in contexts where political party registration can at times be undertaken solely for the reason of obtaining financial support, office space, or even a phone line from the state budget. Ten thousand signatures can be seen as a quite high requirement, thus potentially limiting the access of small parties to the process.

[35] India, for example, pressed for early elections because of interests serving internal agendas (see details at the end of this chapter in *Assistance and Influence*).

[36] See ICG Asia Report No. 126, *Nepal's Peace Agreement: Making it Work*, December 15, 2006. Even NHRC considered setting the election date for June 2007 one of the very few "positive improvements in the human rights sector" (NHRC Summary Report).

Because of the tight timeline, the degraded state of its infrastructure, and the low level of expertise of its Secretariat and district election offices, the newly appointed Election Commission was faced with a daunting challenge. Complex logistical preparations had to be initiated at the same time as undertaking the registration of voters, all in the absence of any legal framework to regulate even the status and activity of the Election Commission or the conduct of voter registration. Priority had to be accorded to drafting all the necessary laws and regulations and to elaborating and implementing a plan for ensuring the operation of the election offices in the districts. Yet the commission's task that was most critical for the peace process was the elaboration of the framework for translating the principles of representation agreed on by the parties into the electoral system.

Lessons Unlearned

Most remarkably, the mainstream parties, led by the NC, continued their elitist business-as-usual approach to politics, while the CPN-M focused increasingly on consolidating power and influence. The peace negotiations, led chiefly by the NC and the CPN-M, concentrated on ensuring the best platform for political gains rather than addressing the conflict's very root cause: social exclusion.

Engrossed in negotiating an urgently needed agreement on arms monitoring,[37] the parties delayed the formation of the new government and legislature. Crucially for the election, the parties also delayed the promulgation of the interim constitution until January 15, 2007, and, with it, the establishment of the electoral system: it was to be a "mixed electoral system" for the election of 409 representatives to the Constituent Assembly. This system retained the 205 single-member constituencies from 1999 under which representatives would be elected in the first-past-the-post race through a relative majority, and it introduced a "proportional" system for 204 additional seats, which used Nepal as a single constituency. Sixteen more representatives were to be appointed by the Interim Council of Ministers from among prominent national figures on the basis of consensus.

The choice of the mixed electoral system reflected a rushed compromise between the NC and other mainstream parties, which wanted to retain a pure first-past-the-post system, and the CPN-M, which preferred a list proportional system for the entire assembly. Although each camp was convinced (mistakenly, as it would turn out) that it would fare better under the electoral system it promoted, the CPN-M could assume the moral high ground, championing the list proportional system in the

---

37 Although an agreement limited to the monitoring of the management of arms and armies (by UNMIN) was reached on December 8, 2006, the main and thorny issue of security sector reform was deferred, both parties believing they would control it better after the election. However, "addressing longer-term army restructuring and merging of Maoist fighters into the national army [was necessary . . .] as soon as the interim government [was] formed" (ICG, *Nepal's Peace Agreement: Making It Work*).

name of inclusiveness.[38] However, in the end, CPN-M decided not to pursue large-scale proportional and therefore inclusive representation, preferring to prioritize the integration of their combatants into a unified army on the upcoming negotiation agenda.

Mixed electoral systems can take the form of either a parallel system or a mixed-member proportional one. Under the first version,[39] the two races would not have any connection with each other. Their results would be considered separately and have no impact on each other, being therefore only partially proportional; namely, to the votes received by the parties contesting the election in the proportional representation part of the vote. Under the mixed-member proportional model,[40] the advantages of the list proportional system would be combined with those of the single-member constituencies to produce a fully proportional result for the combined races. Proportional representation of the parties on the basis of votes received by each party would be guaranteed by supplementing the seats gained in the first-past-the-post race with a number of seats gained in the proportional one.[41]

However, the interim constitution did not specify whether the mixed electoral system should be a parallel or a mixed-member proportional one, allowing the two main parties to negotiate the method of representation in backroom deals. In another victory for the NC, in February 2007 the parties opted for the parallel system, which was to retain a first-past-the-post component that would be unaffected by the result in the proportional vote. The NC's position prevailed mainly because of its superior technical expertise on the issue.

In pursuing their narrow power political interests in the negotiations of the electoral system, the two parties were oblivious to the unique representation requirements of the Constituent Assembly, operating instead on the assumption that the electoral system adopted this time would serve as precedent for future elections.[42] However, the responsibility for undertaking substantial electoral reform should have belonged to the Constituent Assembly itself – and to an electoral reform commission – through consultative and transparent debates. It thus became clear that the election's goal of a political settlement prevailed over that of ensuring the assembly's social representation as a premise for sociopolitical transformation and state-building.

---

[38] The list proportional system facilitates the representation of smaller regional and ethnic parties and allows for the application of affirmative action quotas.

[39] This system is used, for instance, in Japan, Mexico, and Thailand.

[40] This system is used, for instance, in Germany and New Zealand.

[41] Under this system, the list proportional race determines the parties' seat ratio in the elected body. The allocation of seats won on the basis of the party list is determined in conjunction with the outcome of the plurality (or majority) election so that any lack of proportionality resulted in that race is compensated for. This is done by allocating to each party only those seats necessary to reach the ratio they are entitled to as a result of the list proportional outcome.

[42] Although the Constituent Assembly was also to have legislative responsibilities, it is clear that its main objective was to formulate a new constitution and that this constitution was to reflect the aspirations for social inclusion.

The adoption of the electoral system took place in the absence of any meaningful consultation with civil society or electoral experts. Unsurprisingly, the historically marginalized communities, in particular the Madhesis, whose interests were represented neither by the mainstream parties nor the CPN-M, felt that their once-in-a-lifetime opportunity to correct historical injustices was sacrificed again. This perception, more than any other aspect of the transition, contributed to the Madhesi uprising in January 2007, which left 30 people dead and introduced a highly volatile dimension into the peace process.

Reluctant and piecemeal expansions of the inclusion measures through the electoral system and the reluctance of the NC and the CPN-M to ensure genuine consultation on social emancipation were key factors delaying the election until April 2008. These factors also aggravated the mounting conflict between Madhesis, on the one hand, and the Maoists and Pahadis, on the other, culminating in outbursts of extreme ethnic violence in the Terai in March and September 2007.[43]

In the meantime, the lack of clarity in the formulation of the electoral system in the interim constitution further complicated matters. The constitution's general provisions guaranteed representation of women and the country's marginalized communities in the state structures *based on the principles of proportional inclusion*,[44] in which "proportional" referred to population ratios and not to a type of electoral system. "Proportional" thus became a term to define social instead of political representation. In some ways, this definition gave impetus to the argument in favor of the parallel system, because it did not justify any need for the Constituent Assembly to reflect an ideological proportionality.

In any event, setting the premises for enhanced inclusion through the introduction of the list proportional system – whether in parallel or in addition to the first-past-the-post race – for less than 50% of the seats was only going to go some way toward achieving broad social representation. Because it is not feasible to impose quotas on the first-past-the-post election without compromising democratic principles,[45] representation could not be guaranteed in the single-member constituencies. This task was reserved for the proportional contest and its 204 seats. This meant that to

---

[43] Twenty-seven Maoists were brutally killed in the Gaur ambush by the Madhesi People's Rights Forum (MPRF) (or Madhesi Janadhikar Forum [MJF]) in March 2007, and 14 persons were killed in the Terai in the Kapilvastu incident in September 2007 (NHRC Summary Report).

[44] Art. 21 states that "[w]omen, Dalits, indigenous ethnic groups, Madhesi communities, oppressed group, the poor farmers and labourers, who are economically, socially or educationally backward, shall have the right to participate in state structures on the basis of principles of proportional inclusion." Moreover, art. 63 (4) states, "The principle of inclusiveness shall be taken into consideration by the parties while selecting candidates [for the first-past-the-post race] and, while making the list of candidates [for the list proportional race], the political parties shall ensure the proportional representation of women, Dalits, oppressed communities/indigenous groups, backward regions, Madhesis and other groups, in accordance with the law."

[45] Imposing affirmative action quotas in the first-past-the-post race would have deprived voters of the freedom to select their preferred representatives in a given constituency.

guarantee, for instance, the 33% constitutional requirement for the representation of women in the Constituent Assembly (which was the only defined representation bar), up to 66% of the 204 seats would have to be reserved for women. The same principle would apply for all other communities for which quotas would be instituted, provided that these communities could be sufficiently clearly defined.[46] However, the interim constitution was silent on the modalities through which representation was to be achieved or even on the extent to which marginalized communities needed to be represented, implying the need to facilitate inclusiveness through internal political party procedures. Given the democracy deficit within the mainstream parties, representation of women, Dalits, Janajatis, or Madhesis was bound to be difficult to achieve without imposing a particular list order or clear quotas on the results.

Arguably one of the main achievements of the Election Commission, albeit delayed until June 2007 because of a generalized paralysis of the peace negotiations, was the conceptualization of the quota system introduced to implement and consequently guarantee the principles of representation in the interim constitution.[47] As formalized in the electoral law, parties fielding candidates for the proportional race were obliged to put forward candidates on closed lists in accordance with their share of the population as per the 2001 census: 37.8% Janajatis, 32.1% Madhesis, 13% Dalits, and 4% "backward regions."[48] A separate category called "other" with a quota of 30.2% was also introduced by the legislators to cover overlapping social categories. In an impressive departure from past practices and one that owed much to the active lobbying from women's rights advocates, women were to constitute 50% of all candidate lists for the proportional race and a minimum of 33% of the candidates for both races.

Reflecting the elite-driven nature of Nepali politics, the category called "other" was subsequently expanded by the interim parliament to include high-caste groups, thereby defying the very purpose of the quota provisions.[49] Moreover, the electoral law allowed the Election Commission to grant the parties a 10% dispensation from compliance with the set quotas, enabling a further skewing of the quota system. Likewise, because the quotas were not based on accurate and updated population data but on the incomplete and outdated census from 2001, it was disputed whether they reflected the respective communities' real share of the population. In this respect, independent analysts claim that the most significant discrimination was

---

[46] Many of these categorizations actually overlap.

[47] This was one of the main areas of electoral assistance received through the UN (see the later section, *Assistance and Influence*).

[48] The eight least developed western and far-western districts are Accham, Bajhang, Bajura, Dolpa, Humla, Jumla, Kalikot, and Mugu.

[49] Because these categories overlap, the sum of their percentages exceeds 100 (it is 116.2), and candidates were allowed to define themselves as belonging to one or another category.

legalized against the Dalits, because they were undercounted in the 2001 census and therefore were not accorded their appropriate share in the quota system.[50]

Another significant drawback of the representation system was the power granted by the electoral law to the parties to select candidates from their registered closed lists *after* the certification of the election results, undermining transparency and potentially widening the gap between the party representative and the constituency. This practice had previously only been used in two other countries, where electoral experts widely criticized it for the same reasons.[51] Smaller parties who fielded candidates for only 20% of the seats allocated to the proportional race were also granted a dispensation from the affirmative action system of quotas, albeit not from the women quota. Last-minute political concessions granted to the Madhesis in 2008 would turn this initial flexibility into a somewhat discriminatory aspect of the electoral process.

Last but not least, retaining the constituency delimitation of 1999 for the first-past-the post segment of the election was another deviation from best practice. The inherited disparity in vote weight between the hills and the Terai put the Madhesis in a considerably discriminatory position. At its extreme, this disparity was illustrated by the fact that the 117,209 voters registered in the fifth constituency of Jhapa, in the Terai, had over 17 times less influence in electing their representative than the 6,812 voters registered in the single constituency of Manang, in the hills.[52] In spite of this disparity, the interim constitution preempted the possibility of redrawing constituency boundaries. However, in the aftermath of the Madhesi movement in January 2007, the interim government agreed to review the existing boundaries and established an Electoral Constituency Delimitation Commission. Nevertheless, this Commission's report, released in April 2007 and drawn up in the absence of any public consultations, turned out to favor the hills, leaving the Madhesis dismayed and triggering violence against Pahadis in the Terai.

Inequities in vote weight between the hills and the Terai were compounded by a flawed voter registration process. An effort to update the voter lists in early 2007 failed to register large numbers of internal migrants and a large number of Madhesis and members of other marginalized groups, who were formally recognized as Nepali citizens by the state[53] only after the voter lists were updated by the

---

[50] According to Human Rights Watch, some nongovernmental organizations estimate the Dalit population at 21% (quoted in *Nepal – The Constituent Assembly Election 2008*, Report of the International Election Observation Mission by the Asian Network for Free Elections [ANFREL], July 2008). However, the Election Commission claims that the Dalit representatives were in fact in agreement with the set 14% of the population, but then demanded a further 50% to compensate for past injustices (in which case the percentage would have reached 21).

[51] Guyana and Serbia, *Nepal's Election and Beyond*, ICG Asia Report No. 149, April 2, 2008.

[52] These are preregistration figures. It is estimated that after the 2007 voter registration process, the disparity did not decrease. For more information on vote weight, see http://www.aceproject.org.

[53] Citizenship – which is a requirement for voter registration – is certified by the authorities through citizenship certificates. Nepal does not use identity cards.

Election Commission.[54] Moreover, voter lists were not updated after the election was postponed by a year, thereby disenfranchising a large number of young voters who came of voting age after the initial cut-off date of December 15, 2006. Of particular concern for the Madhesis, this situation was aggravated by the fact that the festering conflict in the Terai complicated the Election Commission's access to some areas during the voter registration process.

Many of these flaws were arguably by design rather than oversight. Indeed, it was certainly in the interest of both the SPA and the CPN-M to discriminate against certain categories of voters: disenfranchising the young voters who were more likely to favor the CPN-M was balanced by disenfranchising the internal migrants who were more likely to favor the NC and the mainstream parties in general. Disenfranchising the Madhesis presented an advantage to both the mainstream parties and the CPN-M.[55] Although subsequent changes to the electoral system succeeded in keeping the fragile peace process on track, the disenfranchisement through voter registration remained the weakest point of the electoral process as a whole.

By April 2007, in the absence of an electoral law, postponing the June election became inevitable. However, the parties failed to assume the responsibility of declaring the postponement themselves, fearing that they would be blamed for derailing the peace process. Instead they left it to the Election Commission to announce the postponement on April 12, 2007. Accepting this responsibility had dual consequences for the electoral process. On the one hand, it allowed the commission to present itself as an independent institution, which refused to go ahead with a flawed process, thus enhancing its professional credibility. On the other hand, it raised its profile as a peace process actor in its own right, placing a crucial responsibility in its hands and further raising the peacebuilding stakes of the election.

Shortly after the postponement of the election, the interim parliament adopted a second amendment to the interim constitution, increasing the number of single-member constituencies from 204 to 240 and, in this context, requesting the Electoral Constituency Delimitation Commission to review its April report. This amendment

---

[54] Observer reports, such as those by the European Union Election Observation Mission (EU EOM) and ANFREL, as well as the ICG report *Nepal's Election and Beyond*. According to Dr. Hari Bansh Jha in *Nepal: Citizenship Laws and Stateless Citizens*, South Asia Analysis Group, February 14, 2010, up to 2.4 million Nepalis might still have been deprived of their right to citizenship. The limited voter list update carried out by the Election Commission after the Madhesis were granted citizenship certificates did not reach more than some ten thousand voters. Despite these weaknesses and the inability to remove duplicate registrants or records belonging to the deceased from the lists, the registration of voters was assessed remarkably positively by both the parties and the majority of observers. As noted by the EU EOM, this assessment was positive mostly because the voter register had expanded by 15% compared to 2006.

[55] This could be corroborated with the election results: together the CPN-M, the NC, and the UML won approximately two-thirds of the seats in the Terai (Mick Moore, *Nepal in 2008: Conflict, Drivers of Change, and the Political Economy of Economic Growth*, Synthesis Report for DFID, October 6, 2006).

enabled the finalization of the electoral law and its adoption on June 22, 2007. With the framework finally in place, the Election Commission could undertake all preparations for an election to be held in November 2007, as agreed by the parties in May. However, once again, the existence of a framework alone would prove inadequate. Continuing to suffer from insufficiently inclusive features, in particular in relation to the vote weight between the hills and the Terai, the measures taken would prove nominal.

Representation at Last

By August 2007, the election again became a political bargaining chip for the CPN-M. By that point, the Maoist leadership had come under increasing pressure from hard-liners in their own party for having failed to extract greater concessions in the peace process. In light of the Madhesi uprising, the Maoist strategists were also concerned that the party had lost critical support among the Madhesis. In an effort to appease its base and shore up support among marginalized groups, the CPN-M presented to the negotiation table a set of "necessary preconditions" for holding the election. Chief among them were demands for Nepal to be declared a republic and for the election to be held under a fully proportional representation system. Although these demands resonated with a large constituency, including marginalized groups, they were in contradiction with the initial peace agreement and were thus considered by the mainstream parties and the majority of the international actors a major blow to the peace process. When their demands were not met, the Maoists pulled out of the government,[56] triggering another postponement of the election and casting a new shadow over the peace process.

In December 2007, after considerable negotiations and international advocacy and diplomacy, the parties reached another interim agreement, pulling the peace process back from the brink. The election-related provisions of this agreement included a further expansion of the number of seats to be elected through the proportional representation system from 240 to 335 and an increase in the number of appointed members from 17 to 26, with a special provision for Janajati representation. The agreement was subsequently enshrined in a third amendment to the interim constitution,[57] and a new election date was set for mid-April 2008.

However, in reaching this agreement the parties had once again failed to consult the marginalized groups, including the Madhesis. Unrest in the Terai intensified, and the newly established Madhesi parties allied to form a common front. With tensions in the Terai reaching a boiling point and strikes and roadblocks paralyzing the country's economy, the mainstream parties finally relented, signing special

[56] October 5, 2007.
[57] December 15, 2007.

agreements with representatives of the Madhesis and Janajatis in late February and early March 2008, respectively, and paving the way to the election.[58]

One of the concessions made to the Madhesis that further distorted the imperfect equity of the quota system was to expand the quota exemption granted to small parties. Increasing the exemption for parties fielding candidates from 20% of the proportional seats to 30% practically enabled the Madhesi parties, which were to field candidates for more than 20% and less than 30%, to circumvent the quota system altogether and discriminate against lower castes, particularly Dalits, within their own ranks.

Nevertheless, the hard-fought agreements concluded between December 2007 and March 2008 indicated that inclusiveness could no longer be ignored. Following suit, the Election Commission extended the deadline for the registration of candidates and enabled a smooth operation of the polls. Its voter education efforts, however, failed to reach the areas where they were most needed.[59]

The commitment to a peaceful and credible election manifested itself in an unexpectedly calm Election Day[60] with encouragingly high voter turnout (more than 60%[61]). This success was all the more remarkable as the pre-election period had been marred by political tension and violence, resulting in as many as 50 deaths,[62] because the government, through the police and armed police forces, had been unable to maintain the security of voters and candidates. A number of incidents of electoral violence or other electoral complaints were brought to the attention of the Election Commission, which had both the mandate and the power to enforce the electoral legislation.[63] However, it chose not to take action in response to these claims, reinforcing the general impunity with which parties had been violating the electoral Code of Conduct during the campaign period.[64] The

---

[58] These agreements guaranteed specific community representation in state and government bodies and the implementation of previous agreements, including federalism. The last agreement was signed with the Limbuwans, an indigenous hill ethnic group, on March 19, barely three weeks before the election.

[59] ANFREL electoral observation report.

[60] ICG, *Nepal's Election and Beyond*, reports the occurrence of four deaths. According to the same report, quoting the Election Commission, re-polling was necessary because of electoral security incidents in 106 stations across 21 constituencies and 12 districts (constituting 0.5% of the total polling locations) and was accomplished successfully by April 19, 2008.

[61] The Election Commission reported 63.3% turnout in the proportional system race and 61.7% turnout in the first-past-the-post one.

[62] Recorded – alongside 1,286 injuries – by DEAN between November 26, 2007, and April 30, 2008. During this period DEAN recorded 485 incidents of violence, including 116 kidnappings (*Election and Political Violence in Nepal*). DEAN's monitoring covered 61 of Nepal's 75 districts.

[63] In accordance with the electoral law, art. 73, the Election Commission officials have the power to seek assistance from the government in relation to security matters and could have asked the police to act in response to specific incidents brought to their attention.

[64] Both ANFREL (electoral observation report) and ICG (*Nepal's Election and Beyond*) suggest that the Election Commission's inaction was based on a concern not to upset the peace process. The

commission's tolerance of such infringements illustrated once again its high profile as a peace process actor while chipping away its profile as guardian of electoral due process.

Another commitment to peace came from the voters, along with a strong message of change both in the political and in the social representation realms. The election results brought the Maoists to power and paved the way for unprecedented representation of women and marginalized communities in the Constituent Assembly. The inherent message of change was both substantial and wide-ranging.

The Madhesis made particularly dramatic gains, securing 35.5% (or 204) of the total seats, despite the insecurity in the Terai during the pre-election period. Madhesi parties collectively earned 83 seats in their own right, which was a significant achievement considering that they competed in less than half of the constituencies. Janajatis and Dalits, too, fared relatively well, gaining 33.2% and 8.7% (or 191 and 50) of the seats, respectively.[65] The need to form ethnic-based parties and to advance ethnic rights through own ethnic lines, however, opened the door to large-scale ethnic political polarization.

The increase in women's representation was one of the most powerful messages from the voters: women obtained more than 33% (191 seats) of the Assembly seats, not only marking a clear departure from Nepal's past but also catapulting Nepal to the 14th position in the global ranking of female representation in national legislatures. This electoral gain was mainly owed to the CPN-M, which had, unlike the other parties, put forward a high number of female candidates along with candidates from ethnic and religious minorities. Their returning 24 of a total of 30 women who won seats in the first-past-the-post contest was a major value-added to the results of the proportional race (which were bound to include 50% women by law) and ensured that women members exceeded 33% in the Constituent Assembly. By contrast, only seven other women gained representation in the first-past-the-post race on the tickets of other parties, demonstrating the centrality of the proportional race in ensuring social inclusion.

What constituted nothing short of a political landslide was the resounding Maoist victory. Widely expected to trail in third place after the NC and the UML, the CPN-M won 120 of the 240 seats in the first-past-the-post race and 30% in the proportional one. With 38% (221) of total seats, they fell considerably short of an absolute majority but turned out to be by far the largest party in the Constituent Assembly, holding exactly twice as many seats as the second-ranking NC, which won overall less than 20% of seats, closely followed by the UML with around 18%. Remarkably, royalist parties failed to carry a single constituency, but received a combined 4.5% of the proportional vote, which gave them 15 seats in the Constituent

304 formal complaints received by the Election Commission were neither investigated nor acted on (ANFREL electoral observation report).
[65] ICG, *Nepal's Election and Beyond.*

Assembly. As significantly, parties that could not win any seats in the first-past-the-post election were able to be represented through the proportional one. Overall, 25 parties gained representation.[66]

In addition to the parties' eventual commitment to inclusion and to a credible election altogether, the overall impartial and effective performance of the Election Commission played an important role in this achievement. The UN's assistance to the Election Commission as well as various civic empowerment projects helped deliver the message and kept the peace process on track. A plethora of national and international observers sealed the success through overwhelmingly positive reports.[67]

Whether a more representative Constituent Assembly is sufficient to advance the democratic transformation agenda and the peacebuilding process remains to be seen. Not long after the election, the mainstream parties and their civil society affiliates began a bitter recrimination campaign, despite the initially promising messages of cooperation. Not unexpectedly, given the wrong assumptions of electoral victory especially within the NC's ranks, the mistrust between the mainstream parties and the CPN-M has widened, leaving unresolved many of the issues that had posed legitimate threats to the electoral process.

The Constituent Assembly abolished the monarchy in its first session, but has achieved little since then and has already failed to meet the interim constitution's deadline of finalizing a new constitution within the prescribed two years. The culture of impunity, coupled with the state's inaction on the protection and promotion of human rights, has been strengthened by the CPN-M's inability to rid itself of its violent arm, the Young Communist League (YCL), and an increase in the use of violence by outlets linked to the NC or the UML. Above all, the lack of progress in the area of security sector reform and the unremitting insecurity in the Terai continue to undermine the peace process. In the absence of a solid roadmap for peace and for building a genuinely democratic state, the positive outcome of the election is contingent on all parties' ability to transform and serve their only democratic purpose of representing the aspirations of their constituencies.

---

[66] For comprehensive results see the Election Commission's website, http://www.election.gov.np/reports/CAResults/reportBody.php.

[67] In addition to a small electoral monitoring mission deployed by the UN secretary-general, EU EOM, ANFREL and the Carter Center, as well as numerous domestic umbrella organizations with observers throughout the country, all issued positive statements in the aftermath of the polls. These ranged from "*landmark elections*" (ANFREL) to "*a crucial step for the restoration of representative democracy in Nepal*" (EU EOM). The three main domestic observer groups – DEAN, the National Election Monitoring Alliance (NEMA), and the National Election Observation Committee (NEOC) – issued similar statements, respectively: "[the Constituent Assembly election] was *a crucial step towards creating an inclusive democracy and a peaceful new Nepal*"; "*The Constituent Assembly election is a major achievement of the Nepalese people* [. . .]. *Although acts of violence occurred during the pre-election period, the elections themselves were markedly peaceful and well-carried out*"; and "*historically successful election.*"

ASSISTANCE AND INFLUENCE

To a remarkable degree, Nepal's peace process has been domestically driven. However, already during the early stages of the peace negotiations, in 2005, it was clear to the SPA and the CPN-M that the UN would have to play a role in monitoring both armed forces during the electoral process for it to succeed.

As the peace process started taking a clearer shape, both the SPA and the CPN-M understood also that a guarantee of legitimization could be obtained through a UN monitoring of the election, and they sent formal requests to the UN to that effect.[68] Once established and after a thorough assessment of the context, the Office of the Personal Representative of the UN Secretary-General (OPRSG) determined that an electoral assistance mandate would best serve Nepal's interest; a UN pre-assessment mission conducted in August 2006, before the establishment of the OPRSG, had been of a similar view. However, as negotiations regarding the UN mandate progressed, to retain overall domestic control over the peace process, the SPA strongly rejected that option, maintaining their request for monitoring alone.[69] Realizing the overwhelming challenges posed by the initial timeline, the newly appointed Chief Election Commissioner appealed to the SPA and the CPN-M, as well as the Personal Representative of the UN Secretary-General, for the mandate to include electoral assistance. The SPA finally agreed to a compromise – sealed by the Security Council in the form of the mandate for the UN Mission in Nepal (UNMIN) – in which electoral assistance was added to that of the electoral monitoring mandate. To minimize the conflict of interest thus arising, the monitoring component became symbolic and was realized in the deployment of a small electoral expert monitoring team.[70]

---

[68] On August 9, 2006, the SPA and the CPN-M sent separate letters requesting the UN to "observe" the election. The future agreements of November 8 and 21, 2006, envisaged a "monitoring" and "supervisory" role, respectively (although the difference in terminology may be the result of translation from Nepali). Largely through the UN's mere presence on the ground, monitoring was likely seen by the SPA as a palliative for rubber-stamping the election, whereas the CPN-M arguably perceived the UN as a neutral defender of its interests in the face of SPA manipulation and fraud.

[69] The parties ignored the fact that the UN does not engage in observing elections – in special circumstances the UN agrees to play limited monitoring roles, as had hitherto been the case in the Solomon Islands in 2002 and in Timor Leste in 2006. Following negotiations by the Chief Election Commissioner with the government, this appeal was formalized in a request for electoral assistance in addition to electoral monitoring. The Government of Nepal formally submitted the request to the UN on November 16, 2006.

[70] The UN Mission in Nepal (UNMIN) was established and mandated through the UN Security Council Resolution (UNSCR) 1740/2007. Despite the UN not engaging in electoral observation, a decision was made in the case of UNMIN to include an electoral monitoring component, because such was the initial request of the parties. As replacing this initial remit with one of assistance was not politically palatable for Nepal's government, a dual mandate was negotiated to include electoral assistance while preserving a small monitoring component (see ftn. 69 and UNSCR 1740/2007 para. 1. (d): *To provide technical support for the planning, preparation and conduct of the election of a Constituent Assembly in*

The UN's electoral assistance activities, agreed on by the Election Commission and the OPRSG, entailed the facilitation of technical advice at headquarter, regional, and district levels, as well as the coordination of international support to the process. The district-level deployment was envisaged to provide both confidence in the process through the presence of UN field staff on the ground and the necessary support for election organization at the lowest administration level possible. A major contribution to the electoral process was the assistance provided by international expertise made available by Norway and facilitated by the UN in the development of the formula for translating the minority quotas into numbers of seats.

In conjunction with the other components of its mandate,[71] the UN's dual role of providing technical assistance and confidence-building for the election added legitimacy to the electoral process.[72] The deployment and positive reports of the small electoral expert monitoring mission consolidated this legitimacy.[73]

In the withering negotiating environment and the intensified violence preceding the election, confidence-building became a UN imperative. Rallying behind the Election Commission, the UN appealed to the international community for increased support for international and domestic observation, because observation was rightly seen as a deterrent to violence, intimidation, and malpractice. Thus, alongside approximately 850 international observers, more than 60,000 domestic observers were financed – the vast majority of them with donor support – to cover the approximately 21,000 polling locations. However, the deployment and reporting of the domestic observers did not come without the taint of their notorious political affiliation. Although not compromising their confidence-building role, the evident political bias of the majority of these organizations[74] left a tainted watermark on

---

a free and fair atmosphere, in consultation with the parties; and (e) *To provide a small team of electoral monitors to review all technical aspects of the electoral process, and report on the conduct of the election).*

[71] Ibid.: *"to monitor the management of arms and armed personnel of both sides; to assist the parties in implementing their agreement on the management of arms and armed personnel of both sides; and to assist in the monitoring of the cease-fire arrangements."* UNMIN's mandate to coordinate international support to the electoral process materialized in the provision of technical assistance for donor coordination to the Election Commission as well as in the establishment of – as agreed jointly with the Government of Nepal – an electoral component for the UN Peace Fund for Nepal. The technical assistance enabled the Election Commission to harmonize in-kind and financial donor contributions to elections, the latter provided through the Government of Nepal's Peace Trust Fund. The UN Peace Fund for Nepal, which operates under the same governance structures as the government's Trust Fund, provided financing for several electoral support projects undertaken by UNDP.

[72] Acknowledged in the presentation made by the Chief Commissioner to the UN Secretariat on November 7, 2008, and in ICG, *Nepal's Election: A Peaceful Revolution?*, Asia Report No. 155, July 3, 2008 (citing commentaries of district election officers).

[73] This mission was deployed under the auspices of the secretary-general and did not report to UNMIN in order to alleviate the conflict of interest with UNMIN's electoral assistance mandate.

[74] Of the three main domestic networks (DEAN, NEMA, and NEOC), DEAN appears the most professional and impartial, whereas NEOC, known to be associated with the UML, is at the opposite end of the spectrum.

their future role as impartial supporters of peace and state-building. Nevertheless, despite all weaknesses,[75] the observers' contribution to the electoral process and the momentum they helped build, particularly through their positive statements, were highly relevant.

As important a contribution to the electoral process came from a myriad of civil society organizations in their long-term capacity as advocates and defenders of human rights, social inclusion, and political and economic empowerment. For years, their extensive efforts, supported by most Western donors, raised the necessary awareness that enabled the People's Movements and supplied the base for the political parties' fight against the king's autocracy. However, alongside these efforts also developed a strong sense of identity as each group focused on delivering its own people from marginalization.[76] Surprisingly, the one group most difficult to define,[77] and least supported, has been that closest to India both geographically and ethnically: the Madhesis.

Despite broad international support for the peace process, self-serving interests and miscalculations of who would win the election made the U.S. electoral support highly conspicuous, because it came with the formal condition of excluding the Maoists or Maoist-affiliated organizations from receiving any U.S. assistance. However, the United States changed its position in the aftermath of the polls when it acknowledged the success of the election, and it eventually established a relationship with the Maoists.

Less conspicuously but as problematically, India's role extended beyond supporting some civic education efforts. India was one of the most influential driving forces behind an early election – appearing thus to support what was believed to maintain the peace process on track. At the same time, it provided support to certain armed movements in the Terai, which represented a contradictory position only at face value. In fact, fueling the armed conflict in the Terai went hand in hand with Delhi's constant drive for an election before and therefore *against* a solid political settlement and guarantees for the political inclusion of its own kin, the Madhesis. This approach to Nepal's peace process was inward oriented and based on an erroneous prediction of the election results. India saw an early election in Nepal as providing a political example to India's own Maoist fighters (the Naxalites) while consolidating a power hold that would not include the CPN-M – for Nepal to provide a useful

---

75 International observers are not spared criticism either. Key areas of concern were the failure to deploy to remote areas or even to conduct activities before Election Day. Even the mission of the Carter Center, one of the three long-term international NGOs together with ANFREL and the EU EOM, was perceived to be at least hasty with its preliminary conclusion (see ICG's *Nepal Election: A Peaceful Revolution?*) as well as presenting a conflict of interest between its role as observer and that of "peacefully resolve[ing] electoral or political disputes" at the same time.

76 The National Coalition against Racial Discrimination (NCARD) is the only major national organization fighting against discrimination based on gender, ethnicity, caste, and religion.

77 Bevan and Gautam, *Political Economy Analysis: The Madhes/Tarai.*

example to India's own backyard, the Maoists were supposed to participate in the political process and give up their arms but not take over power.

However, Delhi's calculations that the CPN-M would trail behind the NC and the UML in the polls and its foreign affairs position established on that basis are likely to prove destabilizing for the future of Nepal. Before the election, India decided to back armed movements in the Terai as a precautionary alternative to the Maoists' return to arms in the aftermath of their expected electoral defeat. Delhi's duplicitous approach to the peace process continued after the election: the fear that the CPN-M's electoral victory could enable the integration of Nepal's Maoists into the Nepalese Army, with mirroring consequences at home, caused India to support the NC in stalling any progress in reform of the security sector.

Although India's approach to an early election at the expense of the Madhesis had its own political roots, it is quite intriguing that the vast majority of national and international actors and observers of the peace process took the same position.[78]

---

[78] See Chapter 8 by Ian Martin for an overview of the opportunities and limitations associated with the UN's role.

9.1

Elections: A Nepali Perspective

Bhojraj Pokharel

A DAUNTING TIMELINE

When I was appointed the Chief Election Commissioner on October 30, 2006, I could sense the urgency among the major political party leaders to conduct the elections as soon as possible. The octogenarian Prime Minister Girija Prasad Koirala had expressed concerns about his weakening health and insisted on early elections "so that I can see them happen before I die." Concerns about the prime minister's health were echoed by other party leaders who saw the political veteran and five-time prime minister as the only leader who could stand up to potential peace spoilers. There were several other factors that tipped the scales in favor of early elections: the widespread hope that they would institutionalize the peace process and consolidate it by bringing the Maoist insurgents into the democratic fold; the understanding that only a Constituent Assembly (CA) could implement the Maoists' core demand of the transformation of Nepal into an inclusive, democratic republic; the expectation of the Nepali people that early elections would restore peace and stability in the country; the fear among the political parties that a delay in elections would allow regressive forces to regroup and disrupt them; and the desire of the international community to see a legitimate and representative government reestablished in Nepal as soon as possible. The three main political parties (the Nepali Congress, UML, and CPN-M) had a strong interest in early elections, because each expected to secure a majority. This explains why political parties scheduled elections for the earliest possible date, in June 2007, without considering the necessary political and technical implications and making my role as Chief Election Commissioner extremely challenging.

The Election Commission (EC) started its work in the context of a strong commitment for elections from the government and major political parties, but a weak electoral infrastructure. Because the interim constitution had yet to be finalized, the commission lacked clarity on fundamental questions, such as the model of the

electoral system, eligibility requirements for voters, the size of the CA, the number
of constituencies, or the amount of resources required. When I began my work as
the Chief Election Commissioner, I soon realized that, on these and other vital
components, we had to start from scratch.

The challenge of the assignment appeared all the more daunting once I mapped
out the following key tasks that had to be carried out by the relevant actors – the
government, parliament, and the Election Commission – within the remaining
seven and half months until the elections.

Promulgation of the interim constitution
Formation of an interim parliament that would include the Maoists
Agreement on the electoral system
Drafting and ratification of the electoral legislation (six new laws were necessary)
Drafting of bylaws, directives, and guidelines based on the electoral legislation
    (45 such documents had to be finalized)
Acquisition and managing of necessary human, financial, and material resources
Delineation of electoral constituencies according to constitutional provisions
Voter registration, voter education, and the registration of political parties
Logistical preparations, such as procurement, printing, and transport of ballot
    papers and other electoral material
Training for and mobilizing of around 275,000 poll workers

THE LEGACY OF THE CONFLICT

Implementing this agenda was complicated by the challenges inherent in Nepal's
postconflict environment. Unsurprisingly, after 10 years of armed conflict a sense of
fear and insecurity prevailed among the people, with government officials, voters,
and political workers feeling particularly under threat. The political parties seemed
somewhat impervious to people's fears and made little efforts to address them. The
peace agreements explicitly forbade mobilization of the Nepalese Army, which had
provided the backbone of electoral security during past elections. The police force
was highly demoralized and had limited reach. The police posts that had been
destroyed during the Maoist insurgency were slow to be reestablished, and even
those posts that had reopened were often dysfunctional, their work disrupted by local
Maoist cadres. The political parties' decisions to avoid dealing with the integration
of the Maoist combatants into the state's security apparatus and their rehabilitation
in the community until after the elections added a potentially destabilizing element.
Indeed, the electoral process was marked by competition between unequal players:
the CPN-M with an army (although cantoned in UN-monitored camps) and the
other political parties without armed forces.

Conducting elections was further challenged by an administrative vacuum in
large parts of the country. Because of the armed conflict the last local-level elections

were held in 1997, and since 2001 there were no local governing bodies in districts. The presence of the state was limited to urban centers and district headquarters. Similarly, most Village Development Committees were either closed down or not functioning. Because most government officials were based in the capital, offices at the local level were vacant. Only half of the positions in the district election offices were filled.

Our work was also complicated by the aforementioned lack of a legislative framework. Despite their commitment to holding the elections in June, the political parties delayed finalization of the interim constitution by failing to agree on essential issues, such as the nature of the electoral system, the modalities of representation, and the size of the Constituent Assembly. As a result, the Election Commission was unable to prepare drafts of any major election-related legislation.

REBUILDING THE ELECTION COMMISSION'S CREDIBILITY

In Nepal's politically fragile situation, the trust and confidence of stakeholders in the Election Commission were vital. The most critical challenge for the commission was thus to rebuild its institutional credibility. This credibility had been severely damaged by its role in overseeing the municipal election sham in February 2006, which the king had called to shore up his democratic credentials in the aftermath of the royal coup.

I understood that, to rebuild its credibility, the commission had to go beyond its traditionally limited and purely technical function and play a more proactive role. For instance, in the face of the political parties' failure to finalize the interim constitution, I repeatedly and publicly pressured them to finalize it and take other necessary steps to allow elections to take place in June. The commission was also trying to influence the political parties' decision making on electoral affairs. Initially, they were reluctant to consult the commission on any issues pertaining to the elections, even on technical ones.[1] However, by using the commission's convening power and helping bring the political forces together on key electoral issues, I created opportunities to shape decision making on the design of the electoral system, ensuring that certain provisions would find entry into the interim constitution. At times, this required confronting the political parties whose decisions tended to be guided more by partisan interests than technical feasibility. For instance, the commission successfully pushed for proportional representation to be made mandatory for the candidate selection process rather than only in the nomination process as had been the parties' strong preference.

---

[1] This may be because of Nepal's political culture where the political parties do not have a consultative approach and top leaders make major decisions in most cases even without broader inter-party discussions.

Throughout the process, the Election Commission was careful to engage in participatory and consultative outreach to gain the confidence of key stakeholders. In addition to the political parties, the EC organized a series of regular consultative meetings with civil society, academia, ethnic groups, the private sector, and the international community. We also successfully used the media to communicate our activities to the people. This outreach ensured that the views and concerns of these various constituencies were reflected in the electoral legislation and decision making. It also provided us with important feedback on what the public expected from the commission, such as playing an assertive role in implementing the proportional representation system.

My proactive approach was not universally applauded. For instance, a full-page article entitled "*An Over Smart CEC*" appeared in *Janamanch*, a Nepali weekly, arguing that it was the job of the politicians and the government rather than the EC to push for the elections.[2] Yet, I felt that an active role was necessary to keep the political parties on track, because they were otherwise distracted by their own partisan agendas. For these players, party unification (for the NC), strengthening local organizations (for the UML), and cultivating constituencies in the urban areas and penetration into professional organizations (for the Maoists) prevailed over holding the elections within the scheduled timeframe.

REPEATED POSTPONEMENTS

In spite of the Election Commission's best efforts, the government failed to pass critical election laws in time, forcing the EC to declare that June elections were not feasible. Along with this declaration, the Election Commission also put in place a condition that it would need a minimum of 110 days for technical preparations of rescheduled elections after all election-related legislation was in place. Although the cancellation of the June elections was disappointing in many ways, they had never been a realistic proposition in the first place, given the unresolved issues, first and foremost electoral legislation. The political parties should thus be blamed not so much for the postponement but for their irresponsibility in setting an election schedule that was almost impossible to meet.

A constitutional amendment later rescheduled elections for November 2007, and the Parliament started working on a Constituent Assembly Members Election Bill, adoption of which was the minimum requirement for beginning any election-related preparations. The EC played a leading role in its formulation.

One of the EC's major contributions to this bill was designing the quotas within the proportional representation (PR) system. Although the political parties had decided to adopt a mixed system with both the first-past-the-post (FPTP) and PR, they had not specified how to implement the PR system. Because the mixed system was

---

[2] *Janmanch Weekly*, November 4, 2006, Kathmandu, Nepal.

new to Nepal, the commission invited national and international assistance and sought the UN's technical support. Initially, the usefulness of the UN's technical assistance efforts was undermined by difficulties in understanding both the local context and our needs. Subsequently, however, both the UN and the Norwegian government offered invaluable insights on various alternative international practices of implementing a quota system. Kare Vollan, an election expert, worked with the Election Commission and local experts to devise a formula for the quota allocation for marginalized ethnic groups and castes, as well as for women and people from the so-called backward regions. The bill was drafted after extensive consultations with all stakeholders including political parties, women leaders, and ethnic groups. Finally, the legislature-parliament passed the much-awaited Constituent Assembly Members Election Act on June 14, 2007, providing the main legal framework for the Constituent Assembly elections and spelling out the procedural guidelines for implementing the election system. The legislation stipulated a mixed system with both proportional and majoritarian components. With the main legislation in hand, the Election Commission went ahead with the necessary preparations for the November elections, ensuring that they stayed well on track from a technical perspective.

According to initial legislation, a total of 425 legislators would make up the CA body, with 205 members elected through the PR system and another 204 through the FPTP. The Council of Ministers would nominate the remaining 16 members. Subsequently, the act was twice amended to incorporate changes made to the interim constitution, increasing to 497 and finally to 601 the total number of legislators. However, once again, political developments derailed the process. In August 2007, the Maoist leaders, confronted with a groundswell of discontent among their cadres who felt that too many compromises were made for too little in return, released a list of 22 demands and threatened to leave the government if they were not met. The demands included the immediate declaration of Nepal as a republic and the transformation of the CA electoral system to a fully proportional system. Faced with the other governing parties' unwillingness to seriously negotiate these demands, the Maoists followed through on their threat and left the government on September 18, pledging, among other things, to disrupt all electoral preparations – thereby rejecting the commission's Election Code of Conduct.

Thus, even though the Election Commission had showed utmost flexibility in providing parties with enough time to reach a political compromise, the elections were canceled yet again, marking the second time the long-awaited vote was delayed. For me, one of the most disheartening moments during the election process was when I received the news about the cancellation of the elections during a meeting on election preparations with the visiting State Minister of Finland. Earlier, a few high-level political leaders had informally suggested to go ahead with elections without Maoist participation. However, the Election Commission had immediately dismissed this proposal, because it would have run counter to the goal of the entire peace process, which was to bring the Maoists into the democratic process. With-out their participation, the election would be meaningless. The cancellation of the November elections proved that a stable political environment was at least as important to ensuring successful elections as adequate technical preparations.

Although the political parties and the Maoists subsequently settled their differences and, in December 2007, signed a 23-Point Agreement allowing the setting of a new date for the elections in April 2008, the immediate implications of the cancellation of the November elections were enormous. The delay generated deep doubts among the voters, stakeholders, and even the commission's staff whether CA elections would ever take place.

THE NEED FOR FLEXIBILITY

Two key lessons I learned during my time as Chief Election Commissioner were the primacy of politics and the need for an Election Commission operating in a postconflict environment to be prepared to be highly accommodating and show utmost flexibility in the face of a highly fluid political situation. Two examples illustrate these lessons.

First, in January 2008, as the preparations for April elections were well under-way, the Terai-based Madhesi parties embarked on a protest program against the government for ignoring their demand for greater representation in the Constituent Assembly and state institutions. Activists from other parties and electoral staff were constantly threatened and harassed. Madhesi leaders refused to field candidates and submit nomination lists until an agreement was reached, forcing the Election Commission to extend the deadline twice for candidate nominations for the Madhesi parties. As a result, the government and the Madhesi leaders reached an understanding that entailed changes in a few election system clauses just shortly before the elections. Extending the nomination datelines repeatedly and incorporating these last-minute changes in the electoral system and legislation was highly inconvenient for the commission, but such flexibility was essential in the context of the peace process; as a result all the Madhesi political parties participated in the elections.

Second, on nomination day, the government issued an ordinance to amend the electoral laws to allow any candidate from a political party to be nominated even if their names were not on the voters' list, which had been a mandatory requirement. This amendment had the purpose of giving those Maoist leaders who had not already registered their names an opportunity to file their nomination.[3] Although such a scenario would be highly unlikely in a normal election environment, the EC had to accommodate changes of this kind in the interest of the peace process.

---

[3] The Maoists insisted on this amendment because they realized that on nomination day some of their key candidates were not registered on the voters' list, jeopardizing the Maoists' ability to stand for elections.

THE CHALLENGE OF INSECURITY

Widespread violence in the campaign period was another major challenge for the commission. The fact that the Maoists still maintained a standing army created a climate of fear among voters, party workers, election officials, and government agencies, which the highly demoralized police force was unable to mitigate. Unfortunately, there was little the Election Commission could do. I had hoped that the UN could assist Nepal in improving public security and discussed various options with the head of the UN Mission in Nepal (UNMIN), Ian Martin, who shared our concerns. UNMIN repeatedly offered to make available to Nepali authorities the expertise of UN Police Advisors to improve election security. In what I consider to be a mistake, this offer was rejected by the Home Ministry and the Nepal Police, which were averse to outside interference.

At the same time, ignoring repeated pleas and complaints by the parties, the law enforcement authorities primarily the Nepal Police did not take any action against the (primarily Maoist) political party workers who repeatedly resorted to violence during the campaign period. The passivity of the police in the face of Maoist abuses can partly be explained by their fear of retaliation. Partly, however, it was also a reflection of the Home Ministry's concern not to provide the Maoists with any excuse to pull out of the election process. Indeed, most observers were speculating at the time that the Maoists would emerge as a distant third or possibly worse in the elections, creating fears that they might decide at the last moment to boycott the election rather than face defeat. However, the inaction by the government and security agencies led to impunity and a deterioration of the security situation. The threat of the Maoists abandoning the election process also compelled the EC to remain silent, even in the face of serious violations of the Code of Conduct. Although the Election Commission's inaction further contributed to the environment of impunity, we felt it was a compromise worth making in the interest of the peace process. The major dilemma I faced as the Chief Commissioner throughout the election was where to draw the line in making compromises between the election norms and the peace process.

On April 10, 2008, the Constituent Assembly elections were finally held. They suffered from some minor technical shortcomings in the areas of voter identification, voter registration, political party registration, voter education, counting, complaints adjudication, and the sanctions process. However, such technical flaws have been a steady feature of Nepali polls since the early 1990s and are a natural reflection of the country's relative inexperience in holding free and fair elections. The Election Commission's ability to prevent these shortcomings was undermined by time constraints, lack of capacities, the remoteness of many polling stations, poor transport and communication infrastructure, culture of electoral violence among the political parties, and a low literacy rate. Logistical hurdles such as daily power cuts (up to 10 hours a day, even in Kathmandu), fuel shortages, and frequent strikes or *bandhs* added to the challenge. However, despite these difficulties, the elections were held more peacefully than expected, and the results were widely accepted. The election further anchored the Maoists in the democratic process, established a democratically elected government for the first time in nine years, and created an inclusive body to lay the constitutional foundation for the country. For the first time, significant affirmative action was exercised to ensure representation of previously excluded groups in the constitution-making process. Most remarkably, representation of women increased from less than 6% in the last legislature to 33% in the Constituent Assembly.

THE ROLE OF INTERNATIONAL ASSISTANCE

The international community played an important role throughout the electoral process, supporting the Election Commission at every step. The UN's involvement from the very beginning of the peace process was crucial in creating a politically conducive environment for credible elections and subsequently helped legitimize their results.

Initially, Nepal had requested the UN to deploy an election observation mission before my appointment. As the Chief Commissioner I instead sought the UN's technical election assistance, because its involvement would help provide the elections with international legitimacy. UNMIN's mere presence contributed to a favorable political environment for the elections, and its head, Ian Martin, with whom I consulted regularly, was helpful in assisting to create an enabling political environment inside the country and in mobilizing resources by encouraging both donors and international observers to step up to the plate. UNMIN's involvement also helped attract global attention to the elections. International electoral experts provided their invaluable expert opinion in various technical areas to improve the electoral processes.

UNMIN's role in providing electoral assistance, however, received mixed reactions, and its delivery fell short of expectations. The Election Commission is partly to blame because we did not properly assess and communicate our needs or the role we expected UNMIN to play. We assumed UNMIN's short-term involvement with us would magically solve all our problems. My own expectation was that, once we had international experts working with us, we could create a strong institutional capacity for future elections. In my experience, UNMIN's role was most effective and visible in the areas where the commission did not have prior experience. For instance, the commission adopted a media code of conduct, which set out certain rules for fair reporting on the election and the parties' campaign activities, and on UNMIN's advice, the EC established a unit to monitor its implementation with violations subject to sanctions by the commission. However, in the areas where the commission was confident, UNMIN's role was understandably limited.

UNMIN's presence at the central, regional, and district levels was helpful in building the public's confidence and encouraging participation in the election process. However, its effectiveness was undermined by several factors, first and foremost the language barrier. With most of UNMIN's electoral staff coming from outside Nepal, some of their interaction with local, district, and central authorities got lost in translation. UNMIN's radio campaigns were not always well received by the people or the Nepali authorities because they tended to give the impression that UNMIN rather than the Nepali authorities was leading the election process. Lastly, UNMIN, because of its restrictive security regulations, was initially slow to deploy its staff to where they were most needed (i.e., to particularly volatile areas). This issue, however, was eventually resolved. Additionally, the UN Electoral Expert Monitoring Team (EEMT) played a positive role in sharing their international experience and assisting the Election Commission during critical times. The EEMT – a five-member team independent of UNMIN that reported directly to the UN secretary-general – was responsible for reviewing and monitoring all technical aspects of the electoral process. Citing examples of elections in other postconflict countries, the EEMT, particularly its Chairman Prof. Rafael Pintor, provided me with the valuable advice that the Election Commission would need to remain flexible in the political process.

The support from UN headquarters especially by Craig Jenness, Director of the UN's Electoral Assistance Division and his team was extremely helpful in providing expert opinion as well as to field the experts at extremely short notice. He was always available to listen to us to meet our needs and priorities.

In addition to the UN, other bilateral and multilateral external partners including Australia, China, Denmark (including DANIDA), the European Commission, Finland, Germany, India, Japan (including JICA), Korea (including KOICA), Norway, the United Kingdom (including DFID), and the United States (including USAID) offered valuable support to the election process, not least by footing its significant bill. However, international assistance was marred by some inefficiencies and inequities. For instance, although there was often a duplication of voter and civic education programs in more easily accessible areas, very little support was provided to conduct such programs in remote districts.

Donors also invested significantly in domestic election observation. However, the selection of Nepali observer organizations for such investment suffered from a lack of transparency and an absence of clear criteria. On the advice of UNMIN and international observer groups, the EC developed a more liberal policy to increase the number of domestic election observers. The lax selection guidelines helped attract a large number of domestic observers (around 60,000), with varying levels of professionalism. Indeed, there were complaints that some of the internationally funded domestic observer organizations did not maintain political neutrality and acted unprofessionally, and in a few cases the commission had to withdraw the permission of these individual observers. The Election Commission also had to spend considerable energy in resolving conflicts between organizations that received donor funds and those that did not.

International observers did play a significant role in the electoral process. Nepal's need for robust country-wide coverage, including in remote and conflict affected areas, was of course difficult to meet. However, deployment of long-term and short-term observers – in particular by the Carter Center, Asian Network for Free Elections (ANFREL), and the European Union – despite repeated postponements and uncertainty about the elections added significant legitimacy to the electoral process, as did several visits of former president Jimmy Carter and other distinguished members of international observation teams.

CONCLUSION

The support of the international community notwithstanding, the Nepali people played the most crucial role in the success of the elections by their enthusiastic participation in the voting and their continuous commitment to the elections. Similarly, civil society organizations and the media were sources of energy and motivation to the Election Commission. They played an invaluable role in building people's confidence in the election process and in pressuring the government and political actors to meet their commitments. Most importantly, the elections would not have been possible without the willingness of the political leaders who ultimately came together to make the elections happen.

Although it is too early to predict whether the success of the Constituent Assembly elections will lead to the consolidation of democracy and a return to complete peace, there is no denying that the alternatives to the elections were worse. For now, I think the elections should be viewed at as a step toward restoring democracy and moving the peace process forward. The CA elections have also created an opportunity to break from Nepal's past problems. It is now up to the political actors to determine what these changes will mean for the future of Nepal.

10

Revolution by Other Means: The Transformation of Nepal's Maoists in a Time of Peace

Aditya Adhikari

This chapter traces the transformation of the Maoist party since the end of the People's War. The Maoists saw the peace process as a bargain through which they would enter peaceful multiparty competition; abandon crucial sources of power, in particular the People's Liberation Army and parallel government structures; and renounce all use of force in return for the abolition of the monarchy and the socioeconomic transformation of the Nepali state and society.

Yet, as the peace process progressed, the Maoist party found other means of expanding its power base. From its inception, the Maoists shored up their popular support through their far-reaching transformation agenda, which contrasted sharply with the other parties' general lack of programmatic vision. The Maoists also exploited a weak state to expand their reach into society through illiberal methods.

This chapter focuses primarily on the strategies the Maoists pursued to emerge as the dominant political force in Nepal. The first section analyzes the differing approaches of the two most important international players in the peace process – the United Nations Mission in Nepal (UNMIN) and India – to facilitate the democratization of the Maoist party. The following three sections detail how the Maoists expanded their influence over society, how they maintained strict discipline and unity within their party in the face of attempted manipulation by other political forces, and what they sought to achieve during their time in government between August 2008 and May 2009. The subsequent section analyzes how the Maoists were able to exploit the weakness of the state to increase their power at the expense of others and explains how the older parliamentary parties and India attempted to stop this process. The conclusion sums up the Maoists' achievements so far and the challenges they continue to face in accomplishing their goals. The first draft was written in late 2009, and while it was updated to include later developments, still deals chiefly with the initial three years of the peace process. Many important developments have taken place since then, and this chapter is thus best read as an account of the difficulties and struggles involved in the early years of the Maoist rebels' transition into a mainstream political force.

TWO ACTORS, TWO METHODS

UNMIN and India shared the important but somewhat intangible function of providing international legitimacy to the peace process enshrined in the various agreements signed in 2005 and 2006. Their presence and commitment to the peace process also helped prevent further military action by the Maoists, the state, and the monarchists who resented the palace's marginalized position after the 2006 People's Movement (*Jana Andolan*). Both India and UNMIN created the necessary space for the development of the relationship between the traditional parliamentary parties and the Maoists.

As the peace process progressed, however, significant differences in approach and objectives emerged between the two actors. The UN Security Council provided UNMIN a "special political mission," in UN parlance, with the rather limited and technical mandate to assist in the implementation of specific elements of the Comprehensive Peace Agreement (CPA), such as supporting elections to a Constituent Assembly and monitoring the management of arms and armies. However, both the public and political actors understood UNMIN's role to be broader, and the mission, particularly during the tenure of Special Representative of the Secretary-General (SRSG) Ian Martin (January 2007–January 2009), exerted an influence that was informal but greater than its limited mandate would suggest. In particular, although the impression that UNMIN was the arbiter of the peace process would be overstating its role, Nepali political actors took seriously its views on broader politics and, on occasion, even sought its advice.

Indeed UNMIN did have a broader vision of the steps that were necessary for the process to succeed. SRSG Ian Martin and other UNMIN officials repeatedly stated – correctly, it appears in hindsight – that the major weakness of the peace process was the failure to implement commitments made in the CPA and other agreements. The mistrust among parties led them to engage in various power games to weaken each other, rather than focusing on implementing the peace process agreements.

Recognizing the peace agreement implementation deficit, SRSG Ian Martin, in November 2007, asked the Nepal government for an expansion of UNMIN's responsibilities; for instance, by setting up a UN-assisted mechanism to support the "impartial monitoring and implementation of the return of property." He further suggested that UN police advisors be provided who would support the Nepal Police during the elections and offer assistance in security sector reform, including integration of the Maoist People's Liberation Army (PLA).[1]

---

[1] For instance, Martin, 2007.

Because of sovereignty concerns expressed by some members of Nepal's political class and by India, UNMIN was not granted such an extension of responsibility. Lacking any enforcement capacity, all UNMIN could do was to draw attention to unfulfilled commitments and breaches of the peace agreements and exhort the political parties to take steps to fulfill them. It was aware that to focus on the outcomes of particular negotiations was to open itself to criticisms of being biased toward one party or the other. Therefore, it limited itself to providing advice on the necessity of setting up structures and mechanisms that would, it was hoped, help move the peace process forward,[2] such as a committee that would decide the future of Maoist combatants or a High-Level Government Coordination Committee that could move forward crucial aspects of the peace process in the face of increasing political polarization.

Along with the focus on implementation and process, a related aspect of UNMIN's role was to facilitate the entry of the Maoists into the political mainstream. Experience from other UN missions demonstrated that, after peace agreements were signed, the state parties, seeing themselves as the only legitimate actors, often tried to marginalize the – in their view, illegitimate – rebel parties, leading to the rise of hard-liners on both sides and undermining of the peace process. UNMIN thus insisted on its "effective involvement with both sides" of the peace process,[3] constantly reminding the political actors of the CPA's commitments to integration of Maoist combatants and democratization of the Nepalese Army. UN officials felt that lack of progress on these issues would radicalize the cantoned Maoist combatants and the indoctrinated Maoist base, thereby limiting the party leadership's ability to make compromises in the peace process.[4]

UNMIN's stance nurtured suspicions among the parliamentary parties and the Indian establishment that the mission was biased in favor of the Maoists. In fact, India's approach to the peace process was diametrically opposed to that of UNMIN. New Delhi, keen to return to the status quo ante bellum, rejected the Maoists' state transformation agenda and worked to weaken the Maoists.

The Indian establishment was familiar with and deeply enmeshed in the political culture of Kathmandu, where a small number of actors played a perpetual game of shifting alliances and soliciting support from powerful interest groups. Immersion in this system had through the 1990s and the early 2000s gradually weakened the ties of the party leaders to their constituencies outside of Kathmandu. It was only during general elections – held only three times between 1990 and 2006 – that public opinion played any role in who gained power. Yet, in between elections, governments changed frequently through recourse to three major sources of power: first, other parties in parliament, with whom alliances could be formed, majorities created, and

[2] For instance, Martin, 2009a.
[3] Martin, 2009b.
[4] Interviews with UNMIN officials, August 2008.

positions in government gained; second, the institution of the monarchy, which –
until 2005 when all parliamentary parties turned against it – served as the ultimate
arbiter, at times supporting particular parliamentary groups and undermining others;
and third, India, which cultivated indebtedness through financial and other support
to various political leaders and exploited divisions within and between parties. India
was comfortable with this political system and its key actors who had barely changed
since the early 1990s, repeated government alternations notwithstanding. Indian
embassy officials were deeply familiar with these leaders' susceptibility to external
influence and skilled in exploiting their personal ambitions.

The entry of the Maoists into the political mainstream in 2006 was marked by
great optimism. It was felt that an unprecedented shift in Nepal's political history had
occurred that heralded the beginning of far-reaching changes in Nepal's political
culture. Yet at the time (and, to a large degree, to this day), all the envisioned changes
existed only on paper. The political culture of the post-1990 democratic experiment
had survived the People's War and the peace process largely unscathed, as did many
of its key players – both institutions and individuals – with the notable exception of
the monarchy. In fact, the major objective of the mainstream political parties – the
Nepali Congress, in particular – was to entrap the Maoists into this political process,
the rules of which the former rebels were thought to be unfamiliar with.

Although since 2005 sections of the Indian establishment had actively cultivated
a relationship with the Maoist leadership, this relationship could not grow as close
as the one Delhi maintained with the older political parties. For one, the Maoists
had not been part of the power games of the post-1990 era (except for a brief
period in the early 1990s), and their leaders had thus not been exposed to the
perks and punishments that the Indian establishment could provide. Moreover, the
Maoist organization, suspicious of outsiders and consisting of a militant and tightly
disciplined cadre indoctrinated in anti-parliamentarian and anti-Indian beliefs, was
less easily co-opted than the other parties.

The Maoists had good reason to be cautious. After all, India's goal was to see them
transform into a party like the others: demilitarized and socialized into the political
culture of Kathmandu, responsive to the same incentives. The Maoist state reform
agenda was considered secondary. Some – both in New Delhi and among the older
parties – even thought that their agenda would prevent their transformation into a
mainstream political party in the existing system. For instance, measures such as the
"democratization" of the Nepalese Army would enable Maoists to consolidate their
control over the state to an undesirable extent and thus reinforce their authoritarian
tendencies. On such matters the interests of the older parliamentary parties and the
Indian establishment converged.

In contrast to UNMIN, India had little interest in the implementation of most of
the CPA's provisions (such as the establishment of commissions for Truth and Reconciliation, disappearances, and land reform). It was also staunchly opposed to the
implementation of those provisions that would shake up the political structure and

expand Maoist power, in particular any steps that would increase Maoist influence in and over the Nepalese Army (NA). In that vein, Indian officials were willing to consider integration of, at most, a few thousand Maoist combatants into the lowest ranks of the NA. However, Delhi was opposed both to the Maoist vision of "merging" the two armies on equal terms and to more substantive security sector reform, including the CPA provisions mandating "right-sizing" and "democratization" of the NA. India saw the NA as the ultimate bulwark against an attempted Maoist military takeover and thought that no action that could undermine that institution's cohesion and morale should be taken.

The one provision of the peace agreements that India was adamant should be implemented was holding elections to the Constituent Assembly (CA), because they believed that elections were the only means to confer legitimacy on the parties and the political transition. Elections would further entangle the Maoists in the multiparty political system and make it more difficult for them to return to a state of conflict. Perhaps most importantly, India thought that the Maoists would perform poorly in the elections. Right up to the day of the CA elections, the conventional wisdom in Kathmandu and Delhi was that the Maoists would emerge a "distant third" in the elections after the Nepali Congress and the Communist Party of Nepal – United Marxist-Leninist (CPN-UML). After all, it was believed that the Maoists had not acquired the skills of electoral competition and that the population was aggrieved with them for thrusting the country into a decade of violence. The expected electoral defeat would diminish the Maoists' credibility while enhancing the role of the older political parties, making it possible to negotiate with the rebels from a position of strength on issues such as the future of the Maoist army and democratization of the NA.

THE PENETRATION OF SOCIETY

The parliamentary parties and India were of course shocked when the Maoists emerged as the largest party in the Constituent Assembly, winning an astonishing 220 of 575 elected seats (the Nepali Congress, which emerged second, won only 110). As the scale of the Maoist victory became clear, leaders from the Nepali Congress and the CPN-UML complained bitterly that they done so poorly only because of Maoist violence and intimidation during the campaign period and massive vote rigging on Election Day.

It was true that Maoists and the Maoist-affiliated Young Communist League had engaged in a series of abuses, beating up and temporarily abducting members of rival political parties, disrupting their campaigns, and intimidating voters. Yet violence alone does not explain why the Maoists performed so well in the elections. Their victory occurred because, since the peace process took off, the Maoists had successfully penetrated and politicized areas of society that had previously only a superficial immersion in politics. In parallel with cantoning their army and

dissolving parallel government structures, the Maoists methodically used other elements of their party organization – the student union, the trade union, and, most
importantly, their militia – to consolidate and establish new power bases throughout the country. They also reorganized their party and campaign machinery in the
run-up to the elections, allowing them to reach remote villages where other parties
did not campaign at all or only made sporadic appearances. Maoist cadres educated
the populace about the electoral system and how to fill out ballots in places that
not even the Election Commission's voter education volunteers visited. In addition,
they made serious efforts to field candidates from a broad range of caste and ethnic
groups who were native to their constituencies. When other political parties finally
began campaigning outside district headquarters, they had difficulties competing
with the established local Maoist presence.

The most important of the party's affiliate organizations was the Young Communist League (YCL), which was formed (or reestablished) in December 2006, a
month after the CPA was signed. According to the YCL in-charge Kul Prasad K.C.
"Sonam,"[5] "the main force of the PLA was put in the cantonments, but the secondary force, the village and local defense teams, became the YCL."[6] Recognizing
that the YCL held greater potential than the PLA in increasing the party's strength
and propagating its ideology, the party's leadership transferred a number of PLA
commanders and commissars to the YCL. For instance, the YCL's president in the
years after 2006, Ganesh Man Pun, had served as a PLA division commander at the
end of the conflict.

Although not mentioned in the peace agreements, the YCL began to receive
much attention soon after it was formed. YCL leaders liked to claim that their chief
purpose was to serve the people, and in the months after the organization was formed,
YCL cadres were frequently seen on the streets of Kathmandu, in red bandanas and
with flags, drawing attention to themselves by ostentatiously collecting garbage,
demolishing illegal makeshift shelters built by the poor on public land, and even
building roads. However, most of these activities were abandoned almost as soon as
they began, and it was clear that they were mostly for show, aimed at improving the
YCL's image among the wider population.

Its public relations campaign notwithstanding, the YCL's core business remained
intimidation and coercion. Taking advantage of the state's weak capacities to enforce
the rule of law, the YCL established itself as a parallel law enforcement mechanism.
YCL cadres regularly abducted or abused individuals accused of corrupt or criminal
activities and often handed them over to the police. The YCL thus made itself an
alternative judicial recourse mechanism, and many who felt they had been victims

---

[5] Most Maoist leaders and cadre possess a party name in addition to their real one. The party name has
    been appended in quotation marks to their real ones in this chapter.
[6] World People's Resistance Movement (Britain), 2009.

of a crime or injustice, but had been unable to gain redress from the state's legal system, sought its help to punish their tormentors – as did various people who simply wanted action taken against their adversaries.[7]

Much of the actions of the YCL were directed toward creating space for the Maoist party during the elections, and there was a significant drop in YCL abuses after the CA elections took place. In response to pressure from other political parties and the international community – all of which insisted that a paramilitary organization such as the YCL had no place in a democracy – the Maoist chairman made repeated promises to use the YCL only for peaceful purposes, and it was renamed the Young Communist Democratic League (YCDL) in January 2008.

The YCL did indeed become less violent, partially as a result of external pressure, but for other reasons as well. For one, the mere threat of violence was sufficient to ensure compliance with Maoist demands, reducing the need to engage in actual violence. In addition, in the absence of effective state-controlled public security, the YCL gradually gained acceptance, if not as a legitimate institution of force, then at least as an acknowledged one. Rather than antagonizing the YCL, it was thought better to collude with it. In a number of districts, the police force used the help of the YCL to apprehend criminals.

The conclusion of the CA elections also meant that the YCL could shift its attention from ensuring a Maoist electoral victory to the pursuit of financial gain. For instance, the Carter Center reported that the YCL was "brokering real estate deals and taking percentage cuts of the profits in Kaski [district]," as well as "using intimidation to obtain development contracts for beneficiaries, and taking a cut of the deal for 'mediation services.'"[8]

Other Maoist sister organizations similarly expanded their influence in their respective spheres. Maoist trade unions penetrated industries and businesses, causing disruption sufficient for the owners to relent and work in collusion with the Maoists rather than to oppose them. For instance, all of Kathmandu's casinos pay major Maoist trade unions significant cuts of their profits in return for protection.[9]

In essence, the Maoists penetrated all areas where there were breaches of the contract between the state and its citizens. They stepped in where the state could not provide security and charged fees for the services provided, took advantage of the corrupt practices through which the government granted contracts, and installed themselves as dominant players. They exploited the lack of law enforcement and a demoralized police force to undermine the state and other political parties and provide quasi-governmental services, thereby both raising revenue for the party and strengthening their grip over large sections of the populace.

---

[7] See UNOHCHR, Nepal, 2009 .
[8] Carter Center-Nepal, 2009.
[9] Pokhrel, 2009.

THE DEMANDS OF LOYALTY

In several ways, the transformation of the Maoists from a rebel group into a mass party mirrored the transformations of the Nepali Congress and the CPN-UML in the early 1990s. Since the early 1990s, these parties had successfully expanded their networks far beyond their initial power base – creating alliances, forming relationships of mutual dependence, and seeking the support of powerful interest groups. For instance, soon after the 1990 People's Movement, the Nepali Congress welcomed into its ranks former officials of the Panchayat regime it had helped oust. Norms of both the state and the parties were subverted to provide patronage to sections of society that would contribute to the power of the individual leader. On occasion, a leader would use his support base to undermine the position of a rival within the same party, gradually weakening the cohesion of the parliamentary parties in the 1990s. Leaders of these parties expected that the Maoists would respond to the same inducements and be similarly transformed into parties just like theirs.

The Maoist party, after entering multiparty competition, expanded their networks and brought large numbers of people hitherto ambivalent or antagonistic to the Maoist cause into the party fold, diluting their militant ideology along the way. Various party leaders formed profitable relationships with powerful business interests in Kathmandu. Yet for the first few years of the peace process, the party leadership maintained remarkable cohesion and did not allow the party to become beholden to powerful external interests. The expectation that the Maoists could easily be co-opted and fractured proved to be wishful thinking.

This is not to say that the Maoist leadership was consistently united regarding the tactical and strategic direction it should follow in the peace process. At key intervals, the Standing Committee, the party's top decision-making body, faced serious internal divisions, which trickled down through the party's hierarchy. Indeed, the momentous decisions of the Maoist leadership in 2005 to form an alliance with the other political parties against the monarchy and, after the royal regime was toppled, to enter multiparty politics remain controversial within Maoist ranks to this very day.

The chief architect of this strategy was the party's second-ranking leader Baburam Bhattarai. Hard-liners within the party accused him of betraying the revolution. He countered that Maoist cooperation with the traditional political parties against the monarchy constituted an alliance with the bourgeois democratic forces against feudalism. Keeping with classic Marxist doctrine of historical materialism, he pronounced, in 2005, the "Federal Democratic Line," arguing that Nepal was still a semi-feudal country and therefore had to first go through a transition period of capitalist democracy before it could complete the revolution that would usher in the establishment of a socialist state. Large sections of the party leadership, schooled in revolutionary Maoist doctrine, did not find this analysis satisfactory, but reluctantly accepted it out of tactical considerations: the party had realized that it had reached a military stalemate and would not be able to capture the state through the use of force. With King Gyanendra having concentrated all executive power in his hands and bent on a military onslaught against the Maoists, the best option at that time was to work together with the parliamentary parties, which were also chafing under what they called the "royal regression," to organize a mass movement against Gyanendra's regime.

However, once the 2006 *Jana Andolan* had toppled the monarchical regime and the focus had shifted to negotiations with the other political parties over the terms of the peace process, it was natural that the Maoists perceived the traditional parliamentary parties as much as antagonists as allies. Particularly at times when the Maoists felt that the NC and the CPN-UML were reneging on their commitments and on assimilating a Maoist party that had lost its military force and militant discipline into the old political system, hard-liners within the party would raise their voices and urge their leaders to adopt a more aggressive posture against the other political parties.

The ideological leader of the faction commonly known as the "hard-liners" is Mohan Baidya "Kiran." This elderly Maoist leader, who during the 1970s and 1980s was mentor to numerous communist activists who are now top-ranking Maoists, argued consistently that, with the removal of the monarchy from Nepal's political scene, the utility of the alliance with the other parties had come to an end. The abolition of the monarchy meant that a decisive blow had been struck against feudalism. It was now time to strike against Indian expansionism and its domestic representatives – the Nepali Congress, in particular, but also the CPN-UML. The objective was to stage a decisive "people's revolt" that would enable the Maoists to seize state power and establish a "People's Democracy" along the lines advocated by Mao Zedong.

The traditional parties and India hoped that the divisions between the supporters of Bhattarai's and Kiran's line would become so severe as to lead to a split in and weakening of the Maoist party. There were a few occasions – notably in the run-up to the gathering of the party's top 1,100 members at the November 2008 Kharipati Convention held at a time when Maoist Chairman Prachanda was prime minister – when the debates between the opposing groups led by Kiran and Bhattarai/Prachanda were so acrimonious that a party split did indeed seem imminent. However, in this and other instances of intra-party strain, whether in the Standing Committee, the Politburo, or the Central Committee, the party leadership emerged with a unanimous stance on its political direction, at least until 2010 when party differences became increasingly unmanageable.

One of the ways in which the hard-liners were placated is through the incorporation of their ideological line in political documents that the Maoist party frequently puts out after its strategic meetings. At the Kharipati Convention, for example, Prachanda agreed to include in the outcome document the thesis that, with the demise of the monarchy, the Nepali Congress had emerged as the representative of all the feudal and reactionary elements and would therefore have to be considered the Maoists' principal adversary. It also stated that greater attention had to be paid to the issue of "national sovereignty," accusing the traditional parliamentary parties of acting as proxies of "expansionist" India.

On other occasions when Kiran demanded an immediate "people's revolt," he was assured that, although this was of course the party's long-term goal, the current balance of power in Nepali politics did not allow its immediate implementation. The course of the peace process should therefore be continued and the Maoist agenda pursued on the streets and in parliament with a view toward creating conditions in which the Maoists could take complete control of the state.

However, the grievances of Kiran's supporters within the party went beyond the ideological. The party's mode of functioning since its entry into the peace process caused a sense of unease among this group. First, there was the issue of the change in lifestyle of party leaders. At almost every major meeting of the Central Committee or other senior officials, the leadership was criticized for becoming too enamored with the luxuries and trappings of power. Then, there was anxiety that Prachanda and those leaders who were involved in negotiations with other political parties had expanded their connections with powerful groups in society and were in the process of being co-opted at the expense of the interests of the party.

Indeed, while in government, Maoist leaders had started to cultivate influential people from outside the party, with a view toward bringing them into the party fold and benefiting from their experiences in governance. For instance, Prachanda appointed a former royalist – Hira Bahadur Thapa – as his foreign policy advisor. Actions such as these made much of the party's cadre feel betrayed. After spending years committed to the Maoist cause, they felt they had been sidelined when it came to senior appointments in the party hierarchy.

In addition to ideological matters, Kiran picked up these themes in his criticism, expressed during the 2008 Kharipati Convention, of the entire direction taken by the party; he pressured the leadership to remain committed to the party's revolutionary ideals and agenda and to set themselves apart from other political forces. The Kharipati document describes, for instance, how "suddenly [the party leadership's] lifestyles, food habits and family haughtiness have begun to look like that of the upper class" while "the standard of living for the thousands of revolutionary warriors is generally poor and miserable." As a result, "serious concerns and rage have surfaced within the party." Therefore, "the party centre needs to form a high-level committee, and determine an objective system by which to find an appropriate solution to this sensitive problem."[10]

Similarly, the document claimed that in the course of the peace process "reactionary gangs and murderers of the past encircle[d] the leaders or cadres, and increase[d] the gap [between party members] by instigating one against the other."

[10] CPN(Maoist), 2008.

The entire party was strongly urged to rectify this shortcoming for, "no matter how nice they try to be, reactionaries are reactionaries and revolutionaries are revolutionaries, no matter how harshly anyone talks about them."

What the Kharipati Convention accomplished was a kind of equilibrium between those in the party keen to ensure continued participation in the peace process and those dismayed with the ideological and organizational compromises the party had to make as a result. Prachanda was able to elicit the party's continued commitment to participation in multiparty politics, but limits were placed on his freedom of action in the broader political sphere: the section of the party that was in government was to be made subordinate to those with organizational control over the party, and engagement with nonparty political forces was to be restricted.

Of course, one cannot expect that important matters such as these can be resolved at a single convention. The debate over the political direction and the behavior of party leaders resurfaced at regular intervals. Maoist leaders and cadres alike were reminded that they owe their power to the party organization and that their political future will be at risk if they start cultivating other sources of power at the expense of the party.

The Maoists thus have held onto a modus operandi that had prevailed during the course of the conflict when open dispute was permitted and even encouraged as a way to vent grievances and to consolidate party unity. The Maoists had been trained during their long years as a rebel group to be receptive and accommodating to rival viewpoints from within the party. This style had justification in the Maoist conception of the "two-line struggle," in which debates were seen as primarily based on differing ideological analyses rather than on personal grievances. The Maoists were thus able in the initial years of the peace process to avoid the harm that had befallen other political parties in which disputes had degenerated into factionalism, caused personal enmity, and on occasion led to party splits. Over time, however, as the Maoists became immersed in mainstream politics and the relations between the "moderates" and "hardliners" became increasingly acrimonious, these methods became less effective.

THE INFILTRATION OF THE STATE

The Maoists' first tenure in government, which began in August 2008, lasted for six months after the Kharipati Convention. During that time, disillusionment with and fear of their actions grew among the other political parties. Nepali Congress leaders took to brandishing and quoting from leaked Maoist documents at public events to demonstrate that the Maoists were still bent on capturing the state through violent means. They also pointed to alleged Maoist abuses of government power to show that their priority was to penetrate and dominate all state institutions.

Indeed, once in government, the Maoists attempted to shake up the civil service to a degree unprecedented in the post-1990 period. As civil servants were transferred from ministry to ministry, there was a widespread perception that those sympathetic toward the Maoist party were being accorded positions of privilege. The party also managed to alienate much of the bureaucracy by declaring that civil servants over the age of 50 or with more than 20 years of service would be retired, that no civil servant would be allowed to moonlight to supplement his or her income (a common practice, given the dismal government salaries), and that civil servants' children would have to be educated in government-owned schools (considered to be vastly inferior to the country's private schools).[11]

Similarly, the Maoist government alienated the judiciary when it attempted to force a member of the Judicial Council to resign.[12] It also turned the entire private school industry against it by announcing that all educational institutions would in due course be nationalized, but that in the meantime private schools would have to pay heavy taxes to subsidize the government-run education system. And they alienated the Nepalese Army, first when they refused to renew the tenure of eight prominent generals up for retirement and then when they attempted to fire Chief of Army Staff (COAS) Rookmangud Katawal on charges of insubordination. Already deeply resentful of the Maoist demand for integration into the national army, the NA perceived these moves as part of a Maoist attempt to weaken its organizational cohesion and thus establish control over it. At the end, it was the Maoist attempt to fire the COAS that united all political forces and India in an effort to engineer the collapse of the Maoist-led government and its replacement by the CPN-UML in May 2009.

Claims that the Maoists were intent on capturing the state by taking control and demolishing the capabilities of the Nepalese Army, seen as the sole institution that could prevent a Maoist takeover, were no doubt exaggerated. One motivation behind the Maoists' actions was to genuinely reform corrupt and dysfunctional institutions of the state. Yet there was truth to the claim that the Maoists were keen to expand their influence over the entire state machinery in ways that would benefit the party. In fact, this was what all successive governments during the post-1990 democratic experiment had attempted, and so the older political parties understood only too well what the Maoists were doing. Impunity and weak rule of law had been a constant feature of the Nepali state. Those in power had always used patronage to ensure influence in state institutions, undermining them in the process – the efforts by the

---

[11] Rawal, 2009.

[12] In December 2008, the Maoist Minister of Law and Justice Dev Gurung demanded the resignation of Judicial Council member Moti Kaji Sthapit on the grounds that he was a political appointee of the previous Nepali Congress government and thus needed to be replaced with someone more favorable to the Maoists. Sthapit maintained that the interim constitution stated that the term of his appointment was for four years and that the government could not seek his resignation. The media and other political parties severely criticized the Maoists for this move, interpreting it as an attempt by the executive to infringe on the independence of the judiciary.

Nepali Congress to penetrate the police force and make it loyal to the party are an oft-cited example.

However, the Maoists' actions differed from those of previous governments in the haste and degree to which they attempted to consolidate control over state organs and enlist them in the pursuit of the Maoist agenda. As has been observed by a number of commentators, the mistake the party made while in power was to intervene on too many fronts too soon, thereby threatening the interests of a wide variety of the traditional institutions of power and causing widespread fear and disillusionment.

The other main cause of concern was the Maoists' strong and disciplined party organization. Even during the 1990s when the Nepali Congress and, for a much shorter period, the CPN-UML were in power, their organizational strength nowhere matched that of the Maoists.

Much of the patronage the Maoists were now able to distribute directly benefited the party. The health minister in the Maoist-led government, Giriraj Mani Pokharel, gave a grant of Rs 10 million (approximately US$140,000) to the Maoist-owned Janamaitri Hospital,[13] in violation of the rule that grants could not be provided to private health care institutions. In accordance with the Kharipati directive that the party's organizational machinery would implement government policy on the ground, Finance Minister Baburam Bhattarai prepared to form bodies, consisting mainly of Maoist cadres, that would help in the collection of taxes and investigate tax evaders, potentially giving control over government revenues to the Maoists. In addition, leaders of the Nepali Congress and other traditional parliamentary parties claimed that funds allocated to the Finance Ministry's self-employment program flowed primarily into the hands of YCL and other Maoist cadres.[14] Considering how quickly the Maoists had adopted the system of patronage, this claim would quite possibly have become a reality if the Maoist-led government had remained in office for a longer period of time.

India already held an anti-Maoist disposition, and these factors further contributed to its antagonism toward the party. In addition, India became increasingly alienated from the Maoists because of the latter's efforts to cultivate China while distancing Nepal from India.[15] This outreach to China, combined with worries that the Maoists were intent on decisively marginalizing the other parties, convinced India that it had to support the political forces that opposed the Maoists' decision to sack the army chief and to coerce the unwilling into withdrawing support from the Maoist government.

[13] Rawal, 2009.
[14] Ibid.
[15] See Chapter 13 by Prashant Jha and Chapter 11 by Rajeev Chaturvedy and David Malone for more details.

THE PRACTICE OF DEMOCRACY

The practice of democracy in the post-1990 period took place in a context of a weak state with a highly limited implementation capacity. Even the most conscientious politicians who entered the halls of power in the 1990s were quickly disabused of any notion they may have had of gaining stature and legitimacy through the implementation of service-oriented projects that would benefit the people at large. They soon realized that it was far easier to expand one's support base – although perhaps not one's stature and legitimacy – through the dispensation of patronage to particular individuals or groups. Of course, this effort would not lead to any tangible output, but it would enable them to cultivate a pool of cadres and voters.

Meanwhile, the bureaucracy and other state institutions such as the police showed that they were eminently susceptible to the lures that their political bosses offered them. Patronage could make government officials loyal to a particular politician or party. For politicians, then, one of the purposes of entering government became the co-optation of the bureaucracy, which they could use toward partisan ends in events such as elections. While out of government, they were wracked with paranoia that their political rivals would expand their influence at their expense.

However, the structure of Nepal's political system and its culture helped mitigate these fears. Except for brief periods in the late 1950s and early 1990s, no single party received an absolute majority in national elections. Therefore, parties that wished to form a government had to first cobble together a coalition, often of vastly diverging interests. This enabled the smaller parties to keep in check the larger parties' unrestrained control over government organs and patronage networks. In addition, before this process went too far and before the party leading the government became too powerful, the government tended to collapse. Disinclined to countenance the head of government's power expansion, his coalition partners or, on occasion, rivals within his own party would engineer his downfall. The maintenance of a relative equilibrium of power among parties through such restrictions imposed on their tenure and actions in government became an informal but important value of this political system.

It was into this political dynamic that the Maoists were reintroduced in 2006 (they briefly participated in parliament in the early 1990s, having won nine seats in the 1991 elections). However, the implementation of the CPA and other agreements between the parliamentary parties and the Maoists required a very different functioning of the system. It required political institutions that were more developed and independent from direct political control, in particular a bureaucracy capable of mediating conflict between various groups and influencing the behavior of political parties, rather than being manipulated by them. A bureaucracy capable of independently following up on and completing directives given to it by the political class, for example, would have been of great help in ensuring that provisions in the CPA were put into force. It would also have limited politicians' attempts to selectively implement commitments according to calculations based on what would increase and what would undermine their own power.

The recognition that the state's institutions faced difficulties in executing the kind of activities required by the peace process was implicit when UNMIN offered to take responsibility for monitoring the implementation of agreements in November 2007. The proper implementation of the peace agreements would mean that the Maoists' brute force would be neutralized but their agenda of socioeconomic transformation adopted.

In effect, what UNMIN had offered to do was to carry out some governance functions on behalf of a state that lacked the capacity to perform them itself. Although we will never know whether UNMIN would have been able to properly execute the proposed tasks, it is certain that it would have faced a major challenge had the government taken it up on its offer. The development of mechanisms for the implementation of agreements would have required the rapid creation of good faith by the political parties, both in each other and in the UN mission. The provision of police advisors to help improve public security was based on the assumptions that an effective and noncorrupt police force could be formed in a short period of time and that the political parties, particularly the Maoists, would either develop enough faith in the security forces to end their parallel enforcement activities or that groups like the YCL could be effectively neutralized by the state.

In other words, UNMIN's offer was directed toward at least a partial transformation of the nation's political culture, a strengthening of its institutions, and a change in the mindset of its politicians toward both the state and each other. Although the mechanisms that UNMIN would have set up could no doubt have been of some utility, other strong institutions would have been required to complement them – and these could not have been supplied by the UN.

UNMIN's repeated urging to make progress in implementation of the peace agreements ran up against the absence of institutions able to mediate between political forces to make possible the translation of these commitments into action. The peace process became a raw struggle for power between the old parliamentary parties and the Maoists, in which most Nepali political institutions – whether the bureaucracy or trade unions or student unions – were instrumentalized and abused for parochial interests.

The traditional parliamentary parties, fearful of the Maoists' actions while in government, thus came together to replace the Maoist-led government with one consisting of 22 other parties including the CPN-UML and the Nepali Congress. Through manipulation and coercion India helped ensure that all parties in the Maoist-led coalition withdrew their support and that most of the parties in parliament came together to support the CPN-UML–led government.

New Delhi hoped that being forced out of power would lead the Maoists to undergo a "course correction." They thought that depriving the party of access to state resources would diminish its patronage power, thereby increasing restiveness among the Maoist rank and file and discontent with the party leadership. In addition, in May 2009, the Indian government, in alliance with the mainstream parliamentary parties, noticeably hardened its stance on key Maoist demands, most importantly on the integration of Maoist combatants into the NA. It was thought that these actions would expose to Maoist combatants their leadership's inability to deliver what it had promised, thereby undermining its authority.

India further hoped that fostering dissatisfaction among the Maoists' rank and file would cause cracks within the party, forcing its leadership to appear before New Delhi in a "walk to Canossa" to renegotiate the terms and conditions under which they would be allowed to return to power. If these negotiations succeeded, a suitably chastened and compliant Maoist party could once again enjoy the perks of power. If not, tensions within the Maoists would keep increasing, individual leaders would seek support from other power centers, the party would gradually open up to penetration and influence from Delhi, and it would thus lose its strength. These methods were entirely in accord with the political culture of the 1990s, as well as with the strategies India had adopted, sometimes successfully, in dealing with insurgent groups in Northeast India.

In a number of limited ways, this approach seemed to work with Nepal's Maoists as well. Confusion over policy and strategy arose within the party as a result of being forced to stay in opposition. Without access to state power, the Maoists found it difficult to push forward their agenda and thus demonstrate to the public that they were the only agents of radical change in Nepal. In addition, being deprived of state resources, they found it difficult to maintain and expand networks of patronage they had cultivated during their time in power. The party thus decided to focus most of its energies on protests meant to oust the CPN-UML–led government. Most parties in the Constituent Assembly and India stood firmly behind the government, however, and the Maoists found it difficult to regain their place at the helm of the state.

This situation gave rise to major tensions within the party. The rivalry between the top two Maoist leaders – Prachanda and Baburam Bhattarai – became increasingly bitter. Their disagreements had much to do with strategy: Prachanda advocated a confrontational posture against India and the other parties, whereas Bhattarai preferred a more conciliatory approach. Yet clearly personal ambition played a major role in their disagreements as well. The party's rank and file increasingly felt neglected and began resenting the leadership for engaging in power games in Kathmandu. Afflicted by a sense of a major loss of power and unable to return to war or to participate in any activity that would channel their energies and give them a sense of direction, the Maoist party body began to feel demoralized.

However, a year after the Maoists quit the government, India had made little progress in exploiting tensions within the party, gaining influence with its leaders, or cultivating them as sources of information. The party's chain of command remained intact and largely impenetrable to external interests. Instead, the Maoists staged nationwide protests against "Indian interference" in Nepal and the "puppet-government" it supported, further angering the Indians.

New Delhi continued to believe that the Maoists pose a major threat to its interests and that it was possible to neutralize them by keeping them out of power. Meanwhile the governing coalition that replaced the Maoists was unwieldy, suffering from a lack of legitimacy and unable to exercise effective political authority. Because of the prevailing antagonism between the Maoists and the government there was no progress in settling issues regarding the integration and rehabilitation of Maoist combatants and the drafting of the new constitution. Stagnation and polarization thus continued to afflict the country's politics, as did the process of slow erosion of state authority.

The continuing battles between the older parliamentary parties and the Maoists finally led to two changes in government: the first in February 2011 when the UML's Jhalanath Khanal became prime minister with the Maoists' backing, the second in August 2011 when Baburam Bhattarai was elected prime minister. As Bhattarai and Prachanda increasingly felt that the stalemate was damaging to the wider political process, they attempted to repair relations with Delhi and reached an agreement with the other political parties on the integration and rehabilitation of Maoist combatants in October 2011 that marked a significant compromise on their original position. This led to an improvement in relations between parties and to optimism that the completion of the peace and constitution drafting processes was now imminent. The hardliners led by Kiran, however, vehemently protested against this agreement and other compromises that they felt Prachanda and Bhattarai had made. The old methods of maintaining party unity became increasingly ineffective and many now believe that it is only a matter of time before the party splits.

CONCLUSION

The Maoists have always maintained that, rather than having entered the political mainstream, they are in the process of creating a new one. They understand this process to mean pursuing two objectives: first, the deepening of participation in Nepal's political sphere to include the voices of classes and ethnic/caste groups that have historically been marginalized, and, second, the creation of an effective and sovereign state that is able to reduce the excessive influence of traditionally powerful interest groups and external powers.

During the course of the war, the Maoists thought that these objectives could be achieved through the total capture of state power and the establishment of a "dictatorship of the proletariat." After their acceptance of the multiparty system, the Maoists have sought to accomplish these objectives through peace-process–driven state restructuring, advocating a federal system that would grant various ethnic and caste groups special rights in their ancestral regions. They have also been pushing to replace the current parliamentary system with a presidential one in which a powerful, directly elected president would act as head both of state and government, making it difficult to bring down governments before their term is up and thus avoiding the instability of the 1990s when shifting parliamentary coalitions led to rapid government turnover.

The Maoists have pursued the objectives of greater social inclusion and the concentration of power within the party. They have formed sister organizations representing key constituencies (such as Dalits, peasants, and students) and have reached out to form alliances with leaders of ethnic groups. Their expansion of control over society through the YCL and other groups also reflects their ambition of establishing party dominance over all sections of society. Meanwhile, power is still heavily concentrated in the party leadership.

In the broader political sphere, however, the Maoists are still far from accomplishing their goals. Although the Maoist movement has encouraged the assertion of marginalized ethnic and social groups, the party has not succeeded in establishing firm leadership over them. Many groups representing various ethnicities and castes feel, not without reason, that the Maoist leadership – still dominated by the upper castes – is not wholly committed to their empowerment. Thus much to the annoyance of the Maoists, independent parties representing specific ethnicities/castes and led by those who once were part of the Maoist movement have emerged over the years of the peace process. A number of these parties – representing Madhesis, Limbus, and Tharus, for instance – have achieved significant influence over the communities they seek to represent. These assertions, while contributing to the deeper democratization of Nepali society, have fragmented the political field further, making it increasingly difficult for the Maoists to achieve their goal of a strong state under their leadership.

Growing Maoist influence on state and society elicited adamant opposition from the older parliamentary parties. The fear with which the parliamentary parties view the Maoists was reflected in the broad anti-Maoist alliance that replaced the Maoist government in May 2009, leading to a deep polarization of Nepali politics (and society) and opening the door for India to further expand its influence in Nepal. Already weakened by the Maoists' decade-long armed assault against it and by more recent assertions of previously marginalized groups, the state became paralyzed by the conflicts between the Maoists and the traditional parties.

Against this background, the Maoists continued to be ambivalent toward the peace process. Some voices insisted that the only way to change the Nepali state and society was through a total capture of state power. However, it gradually became clear that it would be difficult for the Maoists to achieve total hegemony over Nepal's political space. They have no option but to pursue their goals in the forums of multiparty politics, which will necessary entail even more difficult negotiations and uncomfortable compromises.

REFERENCES

Basnet, Madhav. 2008. "Farak matka fasad" (The Alternative Direction Dilemma). *Nepal Weekly Magazine*, November 30.
Carter Center, Nepal. 2009. "First Interim Report," August 26, at http://www.cartercenter.org/resources/pdfs/news/pr/Nepal-first-interim-report-082609-eng.pdf; accessed October 14, 2009.
Communist Party of Nepal (Maoist). 2006. "Ekkaisau shatabdima janabadko bikasbare prastav" (The Development of Democracy in the 21st Century). In *Nepal Communist Party (Maobadi) ka aitihasik dastavejharu* (Historical Documents of the Nepal Communist Party (Maoist)), pp. 228–42. Kathmandu: Prasavi Publications.
Communist Party of Nepal (Maoist). 2008. *Kharipati Document*. November.
"Kiran," Mohan Vaidya. 2008. "Bartaman sandarvama party ra krantiko karyabhar" (The line of the Party and Revolution in the Present Context), *Dishabodh*, November 16–30.
Martin, Ian. 2007. "Press Conference: Transcript of Question & Answer Session – Reporters' Club," November 16, 2007, at http://www.unmin.org.np/downloads/pressreleases/2007–11–16-UNMIN.SRSG.Reporters.Club.QnA.Transcript.ENG.pdf; accessed on October 14, 2009.
Martin, Ian. 2009a. "Briefing by SRSG at Meeting of the Security Council," January 17, at http://www.unmin.org.np/downloads/keydocs/2009–01–17-UNMIN.SRSG.Briefing.Security.Council.ENG. pdf; accessed on October 14, 2009.
Martin, Ian. 2009b. *Interview with the Kathmandu Post*. February 2, at http://www.ekantipur.com/the-kathmandu-post/2009/02/02/interview/i-regret-that-the-offer-for-un-assistance-wasnt-taken-up/178268/.
Pokhrel, Upendra. 2009. "Udhyog-Byavasaya rananiti" (Industry-Business Strategy), *Nepal Weekly Magazine*, May 10.
Rawal, Ram Bahadur. 2009. "Misan Maobadi" (Mission Maoist), *Nepal*, May 10.
United Nations Office of the High Commissioner for Human Rights (OHCHR), Nepal. 2007. "Allegations of Human Rights Abuses by the Young Communist League (YCL)," June.
World People's Resistance Movement (Britain). 2009. "Interview with Comrade Sonam, 13 September 2009," at http://www.wprmbritain.org/?p=767; accessed on October 14, 2009.

Regional Dynamics

11

A Yam between Two Boulders: Nepal's Foreign Policy Caught between India and China

Rajeev Ranjan Chaturvedy and David M. Malone

INTRODUCTION

Since the emergence of modern Nepal, its foreign relations, conditioned by its geography, have been remarkably limited. This chapter discusses the international significance of Nepal and seeks to shed light on the forces driving Nepal's foreign policy in recent decades. Like many countries with a powerful neighbor and significant economic interdependence across a long border, Nepal's ties with India, which dwarf all others, breed both familiarity and resentment. In this chapter, we discuss why this is likely to remain the case, even at a time when Nepal's links to China through Tibet are growing. Nepal is a hotbed of conspiracy theories that blame all internal problems on its southern neighbor, an unhappy disposition if it is to forge a more mutually beneficial relationship with New Delhi, which Nepal's current harsh economic and other realities cry out for.

This chapter starts by highlighting the importance of geography as a major determinant of Nepal's foreign relations and then provides a brief historical overview of Nepal's foreign relations over the past two centuries. It then examines the interests, concerns, and perceptions of Nepal and India with respect to each other, focusing on cooperation over water sharing that could considerably benefit both countries were more trust to develop between them. It subsequently examines China's increasing profile in Nepal and how it affects India–Nepal relations. The chapter concludes that Nepal has limited options to maneuver in its foreign relations and needs to focus on making the best of its geographical constraints through positive engagement, including with India.

This chapter is best read in conjunction with Chapter 13 by Prashant Jha, which explores whether Indian actions in Kathmandu by a plethora of players (the embassy,

We are deeply grateful to Robert Templer, director of the International Crisis Group's Asia Program, for his extensive input. We are also grateful to Archana Pandya for her research and insights into Nepal's history and its wider foreign policy.

including its sometimes seemingly self-directed intelligence elements, and the many political, business, and religious visitors, some of them empowered to speak for India, and many more not) are guided by a central design blessed from on high in Delhi. Whereas Indian meddling in Kathmandu is a constant reality, the extent to which it is coordinated and thought through in Delhi remains murky. Indeed, within Nepal too much may often be read into reported and actual statements and initiatives by Indian officials in Kathmandu relative to the weight that might be given them in Delhi. Nepal is rarely among the top three concerns in Delhi, whereas India is almost constantly a top concern in Kathmandu, where conspiracy theories abound. Despite this atmosphere in Kathmandu of near-systematic suspicion of Delhi's motives, criticism of much Indian maneuvering in Nepal as gauche and all too frequently counterproductive is often on the mark. Chapter 12 by S. D. Muni analyzes much more intricately than we ever could the complexities of the recent and current relationship between India and Nepal, so we confine ourselves to its broad outlines and structures.

GEOGRAPHY

Prithvi Narayan Shah of the House of Gorkha, who, through, his conquest of the Kathmandu valley and regions beyond forged modern Nepal in the late 18th century, assessed Nepal's geographic position this way: "This Kingdom is like a traul (yam) between two boulders. Great friendship should be maintained with the Chinese Empire. Friendship should also be maintained with the emperor beyond the southern seas," a reference to Great Britain, then increasingly exercising power over India. Shah's assessment was thus interpreted to favor "equal friendship" with China and India.[1] Nepal's relations with its neighbors did not always live up to these lofty ideals.

This is partly a function of Nepal's geography, the single most important determinant of its foreign relations. Although it shares long borders with both India and China, the fact that Nepal is insulated from China by the Himalayan chain while sharing an open border with India across lowlands that extend well into the North Indian heartland states of Bihar and Uttar Pradesh means that, politically and economically, it is heavily southward-oriented.[2] In addition, its foreign trade is largely dependent on access to and through India, not China.[3]

---

[1] See Pradyumna P. Karan and Hiroshi Ishii, *Nepal: A Himalayan Kingdom in Transition* (New Delhi: Bookwell, 1997), p. 1, and Leo E. Rose and Margret W. Fisher, *The Politics of Nepal: Persistence and Change in an Asian Monarchy* (Ithaca: Cornell University Press, 1970), p. 144.

[2] See Ram Sharan Mahat, *In Defence of Democracy: Dynamics and Fault lines of Nepal's Political Economy* (New Delhi: Adroit Publishers, 2005), p. 225. Also see John Whelpton, *A History of Nepal* (Cambridge: Cambridge University Press, 2005).

[3] Pradyumna P. Karan and Hiroshi Ishii, *Nepal: A Himalayan Kingdom in Transition* (New Delhi: Bookwell, 1997), p. 6.

Before unification, its many principalities and fiefdoms related to each other and to neighboring polities and economies such as those of Tibet, Sikkim, Bhutan, and of the North Indian region through trade and other forms of largely localized exchange. Only when mountaineering and the lure of the world's highest peaks attracted foreigners keen to brave them did Nepal commend itself to the world's fleeting attention, notably through the conquest of Everest by Edmund Hillary and his Sherpa Tenzing Norgay in 1953.

Geography also endowed Nepal with a degree of strategic importance to India. Despite the country's limited size, resources, and military capability, Nepal controls a number of important strategic passes such as Kuti-Kodari, Mustang, Hatia, and Kerong that connect the Indian subcontinent with China through Tibet.[4] Difficult though they are to cross, they provided one gateway for invaders from the north to penetrate into the Indian subcontinent. Nepalis tend to cultivate a self-image of a "bridge" between different subregions and "tend to view their homeland as an intermediate zone between South and Central Asia, belonging to both regions but not exclusively affiliated with either. This has been a critical factor in the formulation of Nepal's contemporary foreign policy and its attitude towards relations with neighboring states."[5]

Nepal's potential natural resource wealth is not yet established, having been too little explored, but its considerable hydroelectric potential should be contributing more than it does to meet the needs of its fledgling industries and even to provide export earnings. However, successive Nepali governments have failed to encourage economic growth or to provide the infrastructure that would have made it a more readily achievable goal; instead they have often blamed their failure on the unequal terms they and other Nepalis believe India has offered the country for its assistance in developing the critical hydroelectric sector.

India has been a magnet for many unemployed and often unskilled Nepalis. An open border and close economic and cultural ties with India have facilitated the continuous movement of people across the India–Nepal border in both directions, although Nepali migration into India in recent decades has vastly exceeded movement in the opposite direction.[6] Maya Chadda draws attention to the pressure for

---

[4] S. K. Jha, *Uneasy Partners: India and Nepal in the Post-Colonial Era* (New Delhi: Manas, 1975), p. 3. Also see Susan M. Walcott, "Bordering the Eastern Himalaya: Boundaries, Passes, Power Contestations," *Geopolitics*, Volume 15, Issue 1 (2010), pp. 62–81.

[5] Leo E. Rose, "Regional Developments in South Asia," in S. P. Varma and K. P. Misra (eds.), *Foreign Policies in South Asia* (New Delhi: Orient Longmans, 1969), p. 357.

[6] Migration figures between India and Nepal are not authoritatively documented. Officially, about 589,000 Nepalis work in India; they constitute 77% of all documented Nepali migrants. By contrast, Nepali immigrant associations estimate that there are up to 3 million Nepalis in India. See, Susan Thieme, *Social Networks and Migration: Far West Nepalese Migrants in Delhi* (Münster: LIT Publishing House, 2006), p. 1. According to a British Broadcasting Corporation article, approximately five million citizens of Nepal work and own property in India. See Sunil Raman, "Nepal Maoists Seek New Order with India," at http://news.bbc.co.uk/2/hi/7616316.stm. There are no reliable statistics on

an autonomous "Ghorkaland" in India's Darjeeling Hills that extensive migration into the area from Nepal has helped produce. As of this writing, calls for autonomy continue to create a volatile political situation in this sensitive district of the state of West Bengal, with negative economic consequences for the local economy.[7] High population pressure on the land has encouraged Nepalis to seek employment in the Gulf and in Southeast Asia as far afield as Singapore.[8] Brutal conditions and often exploitative environments await unskilled Nepalis in most directions. Like several of its South Asian neighbors, Nepal does not have the means to provide even basic support to its growing migrant population abroad, who feed the remittance economy that both keeps Nepal afloat and largely enables an unproductive domestic economic model to remain in place, given the absence of a coherent government economic plan.

A BRIEF HISTORY

After Gurkha conquests resulted in a unified Nepal in 1769, further expansion moved the country's borders as far west as Kumaon and to Sikkim in the east.[9] Fueled by long-standing difficulties in trade and economic relations between Nepal and Tibet, the Gurkhas invaded and defeated Tibet in 1788–9. Even after its victory, Nepal pursued an aggressive policy toward Tibet, triggering a successful Chinese military intervention on behalf of Tibet that forced the Gurkhas to surrender on the terms of Chinese suzerainty over the kingdom in 1792 (although this suzerainty largely remained a paper agreement, given the large distance between the two countries and the growing power of the British to the south).[10] While China kept Nepal's northward expansion in check, Gurkha expansion southward in the Terai lands and the ensuing rivalry between Nepal and the British East India Company eventually led to the Anglo-Nepali War of 1814–16. After initial difficulties, the British defeated Nepal and forced the signing of the Sugauli Treaty ceding one-third of Nepal's

---

Indian migrants in Nepal. "Government departments keep silence in connection with the number of Indian migrants working in Nepal. Two decades ago, the Ministry of Foreign [sic] Affairs of India had mentioned . . . that there were 3.8 million Indian migrants in Nepal. But at the same time, another . . . source . . . mentioned the number to be only 150,000. Along with these contradictory facts, the population census of Nepal 1971 gives the data to be 137,583." See Bishnu Rimal, "GEFONT and Migrant Workers," at http://www.gefont.org/.../GEFONT%20and%20Migrant%20Workers.doc.

[7] See Maya Chadda, "Rebellion and State Formation in Nepal: Implications for South Asian Security," in T. V. Gill (ed.), *South Asia's Weak States: Understanding the Regional Insecurity Predicament* (Palo Alto, CA: Stanford University Press, 2010), p. 281.

[8] See Michael Kollmair et al., "New Figures for Old Stories: Migration and Remittances in Nepal," *Migration Letters*, Vol. 3, No. 2 (October 2006), pp. 151–60.

[9] S. D. Muni, *Foreign Policy of Nepal* (New Delhi: National Publishing House, 1973), p. 2; Whelpton, *A History of Nepal*, p. 35; see also Leo E. Rose & John T. Scholz, *Nepal: Profile of a Himalayan Kingdom* (Boulder, CO: Westview Press, 1980), pp. 34–9.

[10] Leo E. Rose, *Nepal: Strategy for Survival* (Berkeley: University of California Press, 1971), pp. 35–49.

territory in Sikkim, Kumaon, and Garhwal (the latter two now part of the Indian state of Uttarkhand), as well as portions of land in eastern and western Terai.[11]

Despite the expansionist aspirations of the Gurkhas, Nepal pursued a policy of physical isolation from and exclusion of foreigners to keep the country as free from contact with British India as possible. Moreover, to avoid being absorbed into China or British India, Nepal sought occasionally to play off its southern and northern neighbors against each other.[12] For instance, Kathmandu unsuccessfully appealed to the British for help during the 1791–2 war with China, whereas in the 1814–16 war with the British, political and material assistance was sought from Beijing.[13]

Significant change followed the rise of the hereditary Rana regime of strong prime ministers nominally serving the monarchy (1846–1951), which ushered in a new era of understanding and cooperation between Nepal and the British.[14] In 1856, when Nepal launched an attack on Tibet (*inter alia*, because Nepali traders were facing difficulties in Lhasa),[15] the British permitted the transport of Nepali troops through their territory and the purchase of arms by Nepal through private sources in India.[16] Moreover, under the reign of Jung Bahadur, Nepali troops helped the British against Indian "mutineers" in 1857, which resulted in the return of some annexed Terai land to Nepal.[17] To reduce the likelihood of further Anglo-Nepali conflict, the British not only recruited Gurkha troops for their army but also encouraged economic and cultural exchanges between the two governments.[18] Indeed, Gurkha troops famously fought under the British and with its allies during both world wars (and still form part of the Indian and British armies).[19]

Overall, however, the Ranas followed a policy of isolation, largely focused on appeasing the East India Company. Nepal's external affairs were therefore mostly limited to its immediate neighbors until the fall of the Ranas in 1951. Yet although the Nepali public's response to the intrusion of Indian influence in the immediate post-Rana period was often vocally hostile, this tenor was seldom reflected in government policy. For instance, there was no autonomous Nepali foreign policy as such between 1951–5, as New Delhi defined both the principles and the

---

[11] Kanchanmoy Mojumdar, *Anglo-Nepalese Relations in the Nineteenth Century* (Calcutta: Firma K. L. Mukhopadhyay, 1973), p. 5; S. D. Muni, *Foreign Policy of Nepal*, p. 5.

[12] Rishikesh Shaha, *Nepali Politics: Retrospect and Prospect* (Delhi: Oxford University Press, 1978), p. 107.

[13] Rose & Scholz, *Nepal: Profile of a Himalayan Kingdom*, p. 119.

[14] Rose, *Nepal: Strategy for Survival*, p. 107.

[15] Ibid., pp. 109–10.

[16] Muni, *Foreign Policy of Nepal*, p. 8.

[17] Whelpton, *A History of Nepal*, pp. 46–7; see also Mojumdar, *Anglo-Nepalese Relations in the Nineteenth Century*, pp. 70–84.

[18] Muni, *Foreign Policy of Nepal*, p. 38.

[19] Whelpton, *A History of Nepal*, pp. 64, 67.

conditions under which Nepal participated in international affairs.[20] Rose and Dial note,

> Independent India was a far greater challenge to Nepal's national integrity than the British rulers of India. The latter had posed a political problem, which had been threatening only on rare occasions and had been handled by relatively simple political responses. India, in contrast, cannot be treated as an alien power because Indian influence at all levels – political, economic, cultural, and religious – is so pervasive that Nepalis have to struggle continually against absorption into the "mother culture." Nepalis were bound to be strongly agitated by the Indian threat to their political integrity, no matter how "benevolent" and "altruistic" the Indian authorities may have been in their attitude towards Nepal.[21]

Nevertheless, Nepal established diplomatic relations with other countries, gradually at first, providing a hedge against its dependence on India. The United States offered ambassadorial-level representation in August 1951, and Ambassador Chester Bowles journeyed over the coolie path from India to Kathmandu in February 1952. The French ambassador in Delhi followed suit one month later. After succeeding to power in March 1955, King Mahendra accelerated the diversification of Nepal's foreign affairs, moving away from the policy of "special relations" with India and establishing a degree of equidistance to its neighbors.[22] He sought to lessen Nepal's dependence on India by very slowly establishing relations with other countries, including China and the Soviet Union.[23] In 1955 Nepal was admitted into the United Nations.[24] "In one decade Nepal was transformed from . . . one of the world's most closed societies to . . . one of the more accessible of the small states in the Third World."[25] By the 1990s, it enjoyed diplomatic relations with approximately 100 countries.[26]

Nepal also developed strong bilateral relations with major providers of economic aid.[27] India, China, and the United States were key donors during the 1960s and

---

[20] Leo E. Rose and Roger Dial, "Can a Ministate Find True Happiness in a World Dominated by Protagonist Powers?: The Nepal Case," *Annals of the American Academy of Political and Social Science*, Vol. 386 (1969), p. 92.

[21] Ibid., p. 91.

[22] MacAlister Brown, "The Diplomatic Development of Nepal," *Asian Survey*, Vol. 11, No.7 (July 1971), pp. 664–5. See also Werner Levi, "Nepal in World Politics," *Pacific Affairs*, Vol. 30, No. 3 (September 1957), pp. 236–48.

[23] Rishikesh Shaha, *Nepali Politics: Retrospect and Prospect* (Delhi: Oxford University Press, 1978), p. 143.

[24] Enayetur Rahim, "Nepal: Government and Politics," in Andrea Matles Savada (ed.), *Nepal and Bhutan: Country Studies* (Washington, DC: Federal Research Division, Library of Congress, 1993), p. 191.

[25] Rose & Scholz, *Nepal: Profile of a Himalayan Kingdom*, p. 123.

[26] Rahim, "Nepal: Government and Politics," p. 179.

[27] Library of Congress – Federal Research Division, "Country Profile: Nepal," November 2005, at http://lcweb2.loc.gov/frd/cs/profiles/Nepal.pdf; see also Vishwa S. Shukla, "Nepal: The Economy," in

1970s.[28] Thereafter, aid from other countries, notably Japan and Germany, grew strongly, with Japan eventually taking the lead among bilateral donors and the Asian Development Bank among multilateral actors.[29] Other multilateral institutions, notably the International Monetary Fund, the World Bank, and the South Asian Association for Regional Cooperation (whose secretariat is headquartered in Kathmandu), are also active in Nepal.[30] Chapter 4.1. by Jörg Frieden and Chapter 4 by Devendra Raj Panday analyze the benefits and also potential drawbacks of Nepal's ties with its foreign donors.

Worth noting are Nepal's strained relations with Bhutan over the latter's expulsion in 1990 of tens of thousands of ethnic Nepalis long resident in Bhutan who viewed themselves as Bhutanese. Transiting through a narrow patch of India, which did nothing to oppose this forced population movement, these displaced people found themselves confined to seven camps in eastern Nepal monitored by the UN High Commissioner for Refugees (UNHCR); they subsequently served as pawns in a bitter feud between the two mountain kingdoms (as they were both then known).[31] With Bhutan displaying not the slightest intention of accepting the return of any members of this community, whose families grew considerably in the camps to exceed 100,000, a solution only took shape around 2006 when the United States led several other large-scale immigration countries (notably Canada and Australia), working with UNHCR, to resettle the bulk of the refugees. Successive governments of Nepal had previously opposed resettlement as rewarding Bhutan, but international pressure and the offer by new host countries eventually wore down Kathmandu's resistance. By 2009, significant numbers were on their way to distant new homes.[32]

THE CENTRALITY OF INDIA FOR NEPAL

The absence of any physical barrier against its southern neighbor makes Nepal an integral geographical component of the vast Indian peninsula. Relations between India and Nepal, long controlled by Raj interests, have, since 1947, experienced the tensions and interdependencies that small neighbors typically have with large ones.

Andrea Matles Savada (Ed.) *Nepal and Bhutan: Country Studies* (Washington, DC: Federal Research Division, Library of Congress, 1993), pp. 119–21.

[28] Shaha, *Nepali Politics: Retrospect and Prospect*, p. 159.

[29] Whelpton, *A History of Nepal*, p. 134.

[30] Library of Congress – Federal Research Division, p. 21.

[31] John Quigly, "Bhutanese Refugees in Nepal: What Role Now for the European Union and the United Nations High Commission for Refugees?" *Contemporary South Asia*, Vol. 13, No. 2 (June 2004), p. 187. India's apparent complicity with Bhutan over this mass expulsion, or at very best its passivity, has led successive Nepali governments to view the episode as an international rather than a bilateral one.

[32] See Integrated Regional Information Networks (IRIN), "Nepal: Bhutanese Refugees Find New Life beyond the Camps," November 10, 2008, at http://www.unhcr.org/refworld/docid/491946b81e.html. See also Rajesh S. Kharat, "Bhutanese Refugees in Nepal: Survival and Prospects," *Economic and Political Weekly*, Vol. 38, No. 4 (Jan. 25–31, 2003), pp. 285–9.

Historical, geographical, economic, political, religious, and sociocultural links, as well as constant flows of population across borders, conspire to create deep associations and attachments but also deep resentments.[33] The open border, "national treatment" granted to the nationals of the other country (even though there is asymmetry in how the two countries implement the facility), and long-standing familial links at various levels underline the exceptionally close interactions between these two neighbors. However, they have also contributed to frequent friction, leading to an economic blockade imposed by an exasperated India against Nepal in 1989 ostensibly due to unpaid Nepali bills, but in fact provoked mainly by Nepali weapons purchases from China, further discussed later. The blockade created widespread inconvenience in Nepal without achieving much for India, except a consolidation of its reputation in some quarters as a neighborhood bully.

The Treaty of Peace and Friendship concluded between India and Nepal on July 31, 1950, forms the basis of Indian policy toward Nepal.[34] From an Indian perspective, the 1950 treaty was driven by security considerations. Prime Minister Nehru made clear to the Parliament in Delhi the significance of the treaty:

> Apart from our sympathetic interest in Nepal, we are also interested in the security of our own country. From time immemorial, the Himalayas have provided us with a magnificent frontier. Of course, they are no longer as impassable as they used to be, but they are still fairly effective. We cannot allow that barrier to be penetrated because it is also the principal barrier to India.[35]

The 1950 treaty obligated the governments of Nepal and India to consult with each other and cooperate should either country face any security threat. It stipulated that they would inform each other of any serious friction or misunderstanding with any neighboring country likely to adversely affect their own friendly ties.[36] It also provided that the government of Nepal "shall be free to import, from or through the territory of India, arms, ammunition or war like material and equipment necessary for the security of Nepal."[37]

Fifteen years later, in the wake of the Sino-Indian border war of 1962, India and Nepal concluded a "secret" Arms Assistance Agreement, in which India undertook

---

[33] Sita Kaushik, "Indo-Nepal Relations: Some Political and Security Issues," in V. T. Patil and Nalini Kant Jha (eds.), *India in a Turbulent World: Perspectives on Foreign and Security Policies* (New Delhi: South Asian Publishers Pvt. Ltd., 2003), p. 74.

[34] Raj Kumar Jha, *The Himalayan Kingdoms in Indian Foreign Policy* (Ranchi: Maitryee Publications, 1986), pp. 347–50.

[35] Jawaharlal Nehru, *India's Foreign Policy: Selected Speeches, September 1946–April 1961* (New Delhi: Publication Division, 1971), p. 436.

[36] For the text of the treaty, see Treaty of Peace and Friendship between the Government of India and the Government of Nepal signed at Kathmandu, on July 31, 1950, *United Nations Treaty Series No 1302*, 1951, at http://untreaty.un.org/unts/1_60000/3/9/00004432.pdf.

[37] Article 5 of the 1950 treaty. Delhi clearly believed and may still believe that this provision is an exclusive one, barring Nepal from acquiring weaponry from other sources without its consent; witness the 1989 blockade of Nepal by India.

to "supply arms, ammunitions and equipment for the entire Nepalese Army," and to "replace the existing Nepalese stock by modern weapons as soon as available and also to provide maintenance of and replacement for the equipment to be supplied by them."[38]

Further, under the terms of the 1950 treaty, each government was to treat citizens of the other country as their own nationals, allowing them to participate in the development of the country, by granting them, on a reciprocal basis, rights to property ownership and participation in trade and commerce, free movement, and other privileges of a similar nature, although this provision has often been ignored by Nepal's political elite.[39] Thus, India adopted a variety of measures (including economic ones), to induce Nepal to remain within the broader Indian security sphere.[40]

Views on the treaties differ. Indians tend to think that they have proved of greater advantage to Nepal, whereas the Nepalis think otherwise. In all likelihood benefits have accrued to both sides. The security and many other aspects of the 1950 treaty have gradually, to a degree, become irrelevant, but India remains highly sensitive to China's impressive military presence in Tibet. The only aspect of the treaty that still remains fully operational relates to national treatment, on which Nepal is clearly the main beneficiary.

Indo-Nepali direct and transit trade has been governed by a series of treaties successively signed in 1950, 1960, 1971, and 1978. The last expired in March 1988 amidst serious negotiating difficulties and political tensions.[41] New Delhi then adopted a tough tone and played its "geographic trump card" – its open border with Nepal on which Kathmandu was so reliant.[42] In March 1989, Delhi closed all but 2 of the 21 bilateral trade routes between the two countries and 13 of the 15 transit routes agreed under the 1978 treaty. The disruption to the Nepali economy was significant, not least because of the interruption of fuel supplies. In June 1990, the new Nepali prime minister agreed to revert to past practice in matters of trade and transit, and each country consented to respect fully the other's security interests.[43]

India thus succeeded in securing some concessions from the hard-pressed Nepali government, including the removal of the work permit arrangements for Indian

---

[38] Surya P. Subedi, "India-Nepal Security Relations and the 1950 Treaty: Time for New Perspectives," *Asian Survey*, Vol. 34, No. 3 (Mar. 1994), p. 276.

[39] Articles 6 and 7 of the treaty.

[40] Surya P. Subedi, "Indo-Nepal Relations: The Causes of Conflict and Their Resolution," in S. K. Mitra and D. Rothermund (eds.), *Legitimacy and Conflict in South-Asia* (New Delhi: South Asia Institute, Manohar, 1997), p. 220.

[41] John W. Garver, "China-India Rivalry in Nepal: The Clash over Chinese Arms Sales," *Asian Survey*, Vol. 31, No. 10 (Oct. 1991), pp. 956–75. The most sensitive issue for Delhi was the import by Nepal of Chinese weapons in June 1988.

[42] Garver, *Protracted Contest*, p. 144.

[43] See Garver, "China-India Rivalry in Nepal," pp. 958–9. See also Padmaja Murthy, "India and Nepal: Security and Economic Dimensions," *Strategic Analysis*, Vol. 23, No. 9 (1999), pp. 1531–47.

nationals working in Nepal, trade preferences, the introduction of a concept of common rivers applying to water resources of rivers passing the border – such as the Mahakali – and the accommodation of India's security concerns, particularly with respect to Chinese arms imports by Nepal.[44] A new transit treaty of 1991 endorsed the provisions of the 1978 treaty, which diluted Nepal's right of access to and from the sea on the principle of reciprocity.[45]

Nepali resentment of Indian domination has impinged directly on India's effort to uphold its special security relations with Nepal. Indian economic, political, and cultural influence on Nepal has been and remains pervasive, producing at best ambiguous sentiments in Nepal. For Nepal's government, India is the ultimate guarantor of law and order (through close links between the armed forces of the two countries, which became controversial in 2009 when India appeared to stand by the Nepalese Army's chief of staff who had refused to step down at the request of Nepal's Maoist prime minister, leading to the latter's resignation). Culturally, India's universities, religious and artistic institutions, media, and scientific-technological institutions also exercise a strong influence on Nepal, such that to the Nepalis, India is an inescapable presence in their lives.[46]

NEPALI INTERESTS AND CONCERNS

The key objectives of both Nepal's domestic and foreign policy – (1) to achieve internal stability, peace, and economic development; (2) to pursue an independent domestic and foreign policy; and (3) to play a growing role in both regional and international relations – have to be understood in the context of India's pervasive influence. The difficulty is that none of these goals can realistically be pursued without a degree of Indian acquiescence and, in some matters including economic ones, active support. Although faster economic development would help ease the constraints posed by Nepal's geopolitical situation, the goal of economic development itself rests on how effectively Nepal manages its ties with India in the meanwhile.[47]

Nepali resentment of dependence on India is not helped by an often patronizing Indian attitude. India considers Nepal mainly as a source of cheap, and not always welcome, labor. Further, India seems not to have decided whether to treat Nepal as one of its neglected northeastern states or as a sovereign country. Indeed, in a recent

---

[44] Subedi, "Indo-Nepal Relations," pp. 230–2; also see Surya P. Subedi, "The United Nations and the Trade Transit Problems of Land-Locked States," in M. I. Glassener (ed.), *The United Nations at Work* (Westport, CT: Praeger, 1998), pp. 134–60.

[45] Surya P. Subedi, "Transit Arrangement between Nepal and India: A Study in International Law," in D. Hodder, S. J. Lloyd, and K. McLachlan (eds.), *Geopolitics and International Boundaries* (London: Frank Cass, 1997), p. 190.

[46] Garver, *Protracted Contest*, pp. 139–43.

[47] Narayan Khadka, "Geopolitics and Development: A Nepalese Perspective," *Asian Affairs*, Vol. 19, No. 3 (Fall 1992), p. 143.

book on Indian foreign policy, former Indian diplomat Rajiv Sikri wrote, "Indians have taken Nepal too much for granted. India's approach towards Nepal has been dismissive and neglectful. The Indian government and public have never shown adequate sensitivity to Nepali pride and uniqueness."[48]

There is both appreciation and anxiety in Nepal over the depth of religious and cultural affinities with India, which breeds fear of assimilation. Such apprehensions are accentuated when Indians speak publicly of unique or extraordinary relationships. Religious affinity was played up during the monarchy when Nepal was officially a Hindu kingdom. At the same time, occasional anti-Indian propaganda by the palace in Kathmandu from the 1960s onward, seemingly at times to deflect attention from the deficiencies of its own policies, helped foster a widely held belief in Nepal that the various treaties and agreements between the two countries are "unequal" and not in Nepal's interests, particularly regarding cooperation over shared water resources.

Further, the very large Indian share in Nepal's trade, tourism, and investment has also been manipulated politically to foster resentment and apprehensions about India. In addition, the employment opportunities available in India are taken for granted and discounted, although many Nepalis are acutely aware of India's growing economic success and their own stagnation. This is not least because of the accelerated economic growth (in the 11% range in 2009–10) achieved by the erstwhile laggard state of Bihar, one of India's five states that border Nepal, largely due to much improved governance under Chief Minister Nitish Kumar since 2005. Recent progress in Bihar provides a pointed hint to the political community in Kathmandu on what economic growth might be possible in Nepal with a sharper focus on government performance there.

Familial connections also foster shared interests across the border: these connections involve both the Madhesis and the hill elite. The daily reality of relations between India and Nepal, away from the formulations of think tanks and security experts, is one of a deep and wide engagement in everything from religion to crime, culture to violence, and trade to tourism. Around 10 million Indians describe themselves as ethnic Nepali, whereas many Nepalis have close cultural ties across the border. Criminals operate not just across the border in Bihar and Uttar Pradesh but also in extensive networks across the subcontinent. The Indian Army employs approximately 35,000 Gurkha soldiers and maintains extensive welfare programs for them when they retire.[49]

The Maoists above all complain of the "unequal" nature of the treaties signed with India, particularly the 1950 treaty. However, in 2008 when India agreed in principle to renegotiate the treaty, the Maoists, as others in the excitable Nepali political

---

[48] Rajiv Sikri, *Challenge and Strategy: Rethinking India's Foreign Policy* (New Delhi: Sage Publications India Pvt Ltd, 2009), pp. 83–4.

[49] See RSN Singh, "Indian Hypocrisy and Security," *Indian Defence Review*, Vol. 23, No. 1, at http://www.indiandefencereview.com/2008/05/indian-energy-security.html.

world, had few specifics to propose.[50] (Doubtless, they would like to establish more firmly the independence from Indian influence of the Nepali armed forces, but this is not so much treaty-based as rooted in tradition and reinforced by training in and provision of equipment from India.) India's overall approach to the treaty renegotiation process has been phlegmatic and somewhat aloof. A more proactive approach, including a set of specific proposals (at least to be held in reserve), might serve its interests better.

INDIA'S INTERESTS AND CONCERNS

India has challenging and often unsettled relationships with all its neighbors except Bhutan and the Maldives. Its size, sometimes inept and coercive diplomacy in past decades, security obsessions, and introspection as a massive, diverse country focused on domestic issues all contribute to an environment in which its neighbors feel a mix of dependence, victimization, solicitude, awe, and resentment. Nepali elites spend much time worrying about what New Delhi is thinking and doing (when quite often the major centers of power in Delhi are not thinking much about Nepal, although local activities of Indian intelligence and other agencies sometimes create an impression that Nepali matters are preoccupying Delhi more than they actually do); Indian elites mostly regard Nepal as very low on their list of priorities. This is as true geostrategically as economically. The Indian Ministry of External Affairs retains significant knowledge of Nepal, and among senior officials, the foreign secretary personally takes charge of the most important issues as with other neighbors, but India's political class is loathe to be disturbed by Nepali anxieties or activities. Despite being neighbors, India and Nepal endure rather than enjoy a slow-moving relationship marked by lengthy periods of occasional mutual contempt and neglect followed by intense interactions that leave neither side satisfied. In brief, as seen from Delhi, the relationship could be summed up as a joyless psychodrama.

Since the low-water mark in bilateral relations in the late 1980s, India has gradually shifted to a more sympathetic approach to Nepal, as it has done with most of its neighbors. Indeed, in part because of helpful interventions of the Indian Communist Party (Marxist), notably under Sitaram Yechury's influence on its foreign policy thinking, India shifted from a position of unbridled hostility vis-à-vis Nepal's Maoists toward a willingness to accommodate their participation in talks on Nepal's governance in India from 2006 onward.[51] India's communists and other Indian political actors argued strongly that the Maoists needed to renounce their armed insurgency

---

[50] See "Joint Press Statement on Official Visit of Rt. Hon'ble Pushpa Kamal Dahal 'Prachanda,' Prime Minister of Nepal to India (14–18 September 2008)" on September 17, 2008, at http://meaindia.nic.in/.

[51] After 2004 informal talks had been arranged at several places in India between Nepali Maoist leaders and Indians with strong connections to the government, sometimes through contacts established while those Nepalese were attending university in India some decades earlier. S. D. Muni was reported to be an important go-between early on, as was Yechury.

and join the political process; to the surprise of many in both India and Nepal, the Maoists agreed to the latter demand in stages in 2005 and 2006.

In a parallel process, India, which had generally been hostile to the United Nations' involvement in its neighborhood since the world organization failed to uphold Indian claims over Kashmir in 1948, unsuccessfully resisted a country-wide resident mission of the Office of the UN High Commissioner for Human Rights in 2005. However, it accepted more willingly, if not enthusiastically, a meaningful role for the United Nations in monitoring agreements entered into by political parties in Nepal in 2006. As documented by Prashant Jha in Chapter 13, India supported the electoral process that brought the Maoists to power in early 2008, but tensions thereafter developed between the Maoists and India (fueled in part by the enhanced relationship that the Nepali Maoists seemed keen to build with Beijing). In the run-up to and after the 2009 political crisis over the Maoist demand that the Chief of Army Staff, General Katawal, be sacked, India's multiple interventions in Nepal's political processes have reversed an earlier more hands-off approach. Although some Nepalis are reassured to know that India continues to oppose unfettered Maoist domination of politics in Kathmandu, the manner of its local actions and statements will have made it few local friends.[52]

For India, the foremost issue with respect to Nepal is China and its evolving relationship with Kathmandu. Obviously other factors are at play as well, including Indian worries over neglect and mismanagement of the constitution-writing process and a view held even within Indian's Communist Party that the Maoists, when in power and since, "lost the plot" with respect to the main mandate of the Constituent Assembly elected in 2008. Indeed, Sitaram Yechury, member of both India's Upper House of Parliament and the key Communist Party of India (Marxist) and an advo-cate of an assertive, positive role for India in resolving Nepal's crisis during the years 2004–6, notes,

> In Nepal there has been a misreading of what a Constituent Assembly can and should do. People voted for an inclusive process with a strong Maoist presence. Prachanda misinterpreted the vote. A Constituent Assembly can not lend itself to government by an interim Cabinet over an extended period of time. Its business is to debate and adopt a constitution, after which elections should be held for a parliament that can underpin government on the basis of that constitution. The Maoists and others lost track of this basic fact during 2009, and much time was wasted and goodwill dispelled.[53]

India is increasingly concerned by Beijing's growing engagement in South Asian countries, including Nepal. China has made inroads in Nepal by concluding treaties, offering grants of economic aid, promoting exchange of delegations, and providing

[52] See Siddharth Varadarajan's extended essay, "The Danger in India's Nepal Policy," *The Hindu*, August 16, 2010.

[53] Interview, Delhi, and then correspondence with Sitaram Yechury dated February 19, 2010.

facilities for Nepali students in China.[54] China's policy of engagement with Nepal on infrastructure projects is part of a wider program of extending its commercial (and perhaps, Indian think tanks worry, strategic) reach into countries on India's periphery. Although China is pursuing its interests in a largely nonthreatening way, Delhi is unconvinced by the velvet glove Beijing wears in Nepal and betrays concern over even minor Chinese initiatives in the country.

The fear of Chinese influence is also the first factor Indian officials and analysts cite when asked to comment on the problems of the Maoist-led government in 2008 and 2009. At that time, and quite deliberately, the Maoists pursued better relations with Beijing in an attempt to develop leverage vis-à-vis New Delhi, crossing a major Indian "red line."[55] Indeed, after becoming prime minister, Prachanda chose China instead of India as the destination of his first foreign visit, ruffling Indian feathers, even though the visit was linked to the Beijing Olympics and coincided with trips there by dozens of heads of state. Talk of a proposed new bilateral cooperation treaty between China and Nepal raised further concern.[56] In this context, some analysts in Kathmandu suggested that India might have pushed the Maoists toward a crisis over the army chief precisely to thwart conclusion of such a treaty; Prachanda himself has hinted at such a possibility.[57]

In contrast, a rash of stories in the Indian press a few days after the fall of the Maoist government in 2009 suggested, on the basis of unidentified sources, that China had encouraged Prachanda to seek a confrontation with the Nepalese Army that eventually led to the Maoist government's downfall.[58] However, there is no evidence of China's purported advice, and Beijing is likely too prudent to imagine that it could displace or trump India's influence in Nepal in the short or even

---

[54] On December 26, 2009 during the Nepali prime minister's visit to China three agreements were signed, notably increasing Chinese economic and technical cooperation and providing for financial support for construction of Nepal's Consulate in Lhasa. See "Political, Economic and Social Development in Nepal in the Year 2009," at http://www.fesnepal.org/reports/2009/annual_report/report_2009.htm.

[55] As one more sympathetic retired Indian official put it, "The way the Maoists cozied up to China makes it simply impossible to defend them [in Delhi]. However unfairly Delhi may have treated them, they just went too far." Confidential interview, New Delhi, June 2009.

[56] Pranab Dhal Samanta, "Process in Pieces," *Indian Express*, May 5, 2009. See also Aditi Phadnis, "Once a Revolutionary . . . ," *Business Standard*, May 8, 2009.

[57] For example, one (anti-Indian but also anti-Maoist) weekly suggested that Indian intelligence operatives instigated the crisis to derail the visit. "RAW Mission Successful?," *People's Review*, May 7, 2009. Prachanda used an interview with the Indian press to say that the Indian withdrawal of support to the Maoist-led government could have been "a planned strategy or a coincidence," adding "[t]here are forces that did not want the (Beijing) visit to take place." While acknowledging the desire to conclude a friendship treaty with China, he insisted that it would have had "no negative impact on our friendship with India" and noted the "imaginary fear in Indian political circles that Maoists [might] play the China card against India." See "We'll Not Bow to Foreign Pressure: Prachanda," *The Times of India*, May 9, 2009.

[58] "China Pushed Prachanda into Sacking Army Chief: Sources," *The Times of India*, May 9, 2009.

medium term. There are also few signs to support the theory that either the Maoists or China were then considering a dramatic strategic realignment.

Yet, the rapprochement between Beijing and the Maoists may explain to some degree why India's supportive attitude vis-à-vis the Maoists and their integration into Nepali mainstream politics as part of the peace process has given way to barely veiled hostility toward the Maoist party.[59] A former Indian intelligence officer and prolific regional analyst wrote in 2009,

> China would try its best to see that the Maoists stay in power. Their continuance in power in Kathmandu is important for stability in Tibet. In the past, we supported the Maoists thinking that Prachanda would take a neutral line between India and China. These hopes were elusive. Should we facilitate the Chinese designs in Nepal by bringing about a political compromise which would enable the Maoists to continue in power or has the time come to work for a non-Maoist alternative? This requires serious examination in our policy-making circles.[60]

One former Indian foreign minister observed that such fears were well founded: "We are pouring a thousand crores [ten billion rupees][61] into Nepal. Yet China is more active in Nepal than we are. Prachanda feels quite comfortable with that."[62] In New Delhi's views of China, perceptions matter as much as reality, if not more, and fears over Chinese influence in Nepal form part of a larger picture: "It's not just about Nepal," cautioned one Indian diplomat. "It's how [Chinese influence there] fits into a broader pattern of worrying behaviour."[63]

At the same time, theories about Chinese machinations in Nepal conveniently overshadowed unflattering headlines about Indian policy miscalculations – it notably failed to anticipate the Maoist win in the 2008 elections, having asserted its confidence that the Maoists would run third or, at worst, second. Delhi's concern in constraining Maoist influence over the Nepalese Army doubtless had as much to do

---

59 See Pranab Dhal Samanta, "Facing Maoist Protests, Nepal Premier Gets India's Support," *The Indian Express*, May 2, 2010; "Nepal: Himalayan Precipice," *The Economist*, May 6, 2010; and Prashant Jha, "Nepal: Rumblings of Anarchy," *South Asia Intelligence Review Weekly Assessments & Briefings*, Vol. 8, No. 44 (May 10, 2010), at http://www.satp.org/satporgtp/sair/Archives/sair8/8_44.htm#assessment1.

60 B. Raman, "China Wants Prachanda to Stay in Nepal," rediff.com, May 4, 2009. In an earlier paper, the same analyst had cautioned, "China has a Look South policy to counter our Look East policy. As we try to move Eastwards to cultivate the countries of South-East Asia, it is trying to move southwards to outflank us. China is not a South Asian power, but it already has a growing South Asian strategic presence – in Pakistan, Sri Lanka and Bangladesh. It is hoping to acquire a similar presence in Nepal with the co-operation of a Maoist-dominated Government.... India will find itself in Nepal in a situation not dissimilar to the situation in Myanmar – all the time having to compete with China for political influence and economic benefits." B. Raman, "Rise of Maoists in Nepal: Implications for India," paper presented at a seminar organized by the Asia Centre, Bangalore, August 9, 2008, at http://www.southasiaanalysis.org/papers29/paper2802.html.

61 Roughly the equivalent of $220 million dollars at the time of this writing.

62 K. Natwar Singh, "Neighborhood in Turmoil," *Indian Express*, May 5, 2009.

63 Confidential interview, Indian diplomat, July 2009.

with constraining unbridled Maoist power than it did with a larger strategic conflict with China. Indeed, one senior Indian diplomat underlined that China's line differed little from India's: "I don't think Prachanda heard anything from [the Chinese ambassador] that he didn't hear from us: I understand that he counselled caution and urged the prime minister to build consensus for any such step."[64]

After China, it is Pakistan that holds the pride of second place in the list of New Delhi's major security concerns with respect to Nepal. Indians fear that Pakistan has over the past 15 years or more been making covert use of the open border to promote subversive activities against India.[65] Even the major political parties in Nepal have sometimes failed to appreciate the depth and rational nature of India's concerns in the matter, preferring to ignore risks potentially arising from Pakistani activities, which has worried other partners of Nepal as well. Although Pakistan denies the validity of such concerns, in the past groups operating from within Pakistan have targeted India murderously through Nepal. Notably, in December 1999 Indian Airlines Flight IC 814 from Kathmandu to Delhi was hijacked by five members of the Pakistani terrorist group, Harkat-ul-Mujahideen. The hijackers killed one of the Indian passengers and injured several others during an odyssey that culminated in Kandahar where the passengers were released in exchange for Islamic militants jailed in India, who were handed over in the presence of Indian Foreign Minister Jaswant Singh. This incident was widely viewed in India, which had vowed not to negotiate with terrorists, as a humiliation.[66] India is believed to closely watch the activities of Pakistani-affiliated individuals and groups in Nepal, but it is difficult to chart their relationships with madrasas and individuals there, as well as the cross-border activities. Thus considerable Indian anxiety attends Pakistan's relationship with Nepal, the legitimate, formal dimensions of which remain slight, if only for lack of physical contiguity.

India has also been concerned with the possibility (and past reality) of Maoist interaction with some of the plethora of insurgencies within India. In recent years Indian Prime Minister Singh has noted several times that India's own Naxalite (Maoist) insurgencies, affecting roughly a quarter of India's districts, represent the

---

[64] Confidential interview, Kathmandu, May 2009.

[65] A report titled "Pakistan's Anti-India Activities in Nepal" detailed various aspects of Pakistan's "undeclared war" and its modus operandi, including support to NGOs promoting ill will against India among the Nepali Muslim community by circulating propaganda material received from Pakistan and elsewhere, support to radicalization in an increasing number of mosques along the border, and the use of such mosques and religious centers to facilitate the movement of terrorist cadres and material across the border. See Farzand Ahmed, "Nepal: Wake-Up Call" at http://www.india-today .com/itoday/20000619/neighbors.html. See also Harinder Baweja, "Terrorism: The Kathmandu Nexus," at http://www.india-today.com/itoday/20000612/nation2.html.

[66] A detailed account of the painful episode is available in Jaswant Singh's book, *A Call to Honour: In Service of Emergent India* (New Delhi: Rupa & Co., 2006), pp. 229–47. Also see Ranbir Vohra, *The Making of India: A Historical Survey* (New York: M. E. Sharpe, 2000), p. 318.

greatest security threat to the country. Any outside official or officially organized covert support of these insurgencies (and none is apparent today from within either Nepal or China) would be a cause for great concern in India. In addition, the gradual transformation of Nepal's Maoist movement could be held up by Indians as a positive example to the Naxalites. The Maoist-led government in Nepal in 2008–9 was careful never to give any hint of the slightest sympathy for the Naxalites.[67] Thus, it remains unlikely that Nepali support (as opposed to the inevitable commercially and criminally driven gun-running across most of India's borders including Nepal's) for the Naxalite insurgencies will be forthcoming, even under left-wing coalitions or a Maoist government in Nepal.

The open border is a matter of concern and also perhaps of opportunity. Given its importance to both sides, any restrictions in cross-border connectivity would come at significant cost to both countries. Indeed, "connectivity" has become a significant concept in India's neighborhood policy.[68] Curtailing illegal trade and other illicit activities including drug trafficking, money laundering, and counterfeit currency smuggling would require a degree of regulation and much better monitoring across the India–Nepal border. Yet the number of Nepali nationals working in India, some seasonally, could not be meaningfully reduced without a major upheaval and massive human distress.

COOPERATION ON WATER: A SADLY NEGLECTED OPPORTUNITY
FOR NEPAL AND INDIA

Water is the source of much tension between India and Nepal, but could potentially be the greatest asset to their relationship if a more confident, respectful, and cooperative approach could be engineered by the two governments. India's ever-increasing energy requirement speaks to its potentially most important economic interest in Nepal – the largely untapped hydropower potential. A major part of the downstream discharge of the Ganga (Ganges) is contributed by flows either originating in Nepal or transiting Nepal from sources in Tibet, most notably the Kosi, Gandak, and Karnali systems. Because of the terrain, Nepal provides the best, if not the only, option for downstream flood control and dry season augmentation. A change in course of the Kosi in 2008 produced massive flooding in Bihar as well

---

[67] In an interesting interview with Nepali Maoist leader Prachanda, Siddharth Varadarajan elicited the view from him that the political triumph of the Maoists in Nepal should be interpreted by Indian Maoists as a signal that electoral strategies, as opposed to violent insurgency, can best deliver positive outcomes. See Siddharth Varadarajan, "We want new unity on a new basis with India: without taking cooperation with India forward, we cannot do anything for Nepal, says Parachanda," *The Hindu*, April 28, 2008.

[68] For example, see "Does India Have a Neighborhood Policy?"– Talk by Foreign Secretary at ICWA, September 9, 2006, at http://www.meaindia.nic.in/speech/2006/09/09ss02.htm.

as in Nepal, displacing millions and occasioning much loss of life. Well-managed Indo-Nepali cooperation on water could benefit both countries.[69]

The first recorded water resource negotiations between Nepal and India occurred between 1910 and 1920 when British India needed to harness the Sarda (Mahakali) river, which formed the western boundary between Nepal and British India, to develop irrigation in the United Province (now Uttar Pradesh). Nepal, then lacking understanding of the value of water resource development, agreed to the 1920 Sarda Treaty, which involved an exchange of territory, but not an advantageous one for Nepal. However, since then, the Nepalis have learned the value of their consent to India's plans pertaining to water.[70]

Indian insistence on management control and its refusal to allow independent assessment of downstream benefits have created suspicions in Nepal, resulting in stalling tactics.[71] The relationship between the two countries on water resources has been unsettled at best and inconclusive.[72] India enjoys most benefits of the Kosi and Gandak treaties (of 1954 and 1959), mainly covering irrigation and flood control, because they led to the construction of dams that primarily irrigate and protect Indian lands. Many in Nepal viewed the outcome of these treaties as a "sellout" of their natural resources (although it was resistance in Nepal that prevented construction of larger dams that would have accrued more benefits to it).[73] These tensions are part of a wider pattern with regard to agreements on rivers, now further underlined by the earlier mentioned disastrous 2008 Kosi breach.[74]

In this climate of mutual distrust, despite discussions between the two nations on several multipurpose projects (Karnali, Pancheswar, Saptkosi, etc.) over three decades, little progress has been made. As in India, environmental concerns, worries about the displacement of people, and misgivings about large projects in the seismically active Himalayan region have militated against large-scale centralized generation of hydroelectric power (in Nepal's case, largely for export).

There is an increasingly popular view in Nepal that rejects large-scale water development, advocating instead for decentralized, relatively small, environmentally benign projects (whether for irrigation or for hydroelectric power) primarily for

---

[69] B. C. Upreti, *Politics of Himalayan River Waters* (New Delhi: Nirala Publications, 1993), pp. 84–8.

[70] Dipak Gyawali, "Nepal-India Water Resource Relations," in I. William Zartman and Jeffrey Z. Rubin (eds.), *Power & Negotiations* (Ann Arbor: University of Michigan Press, 2002), p. 137.

[71] Ibid., pp. 137–8.

[72] Dwarika Nath Dhungel, "Historical Eye View," in D. N. Dhungel and S. B. Pun (eds.), *The Nepal–India Water Relationship: Challenges* (Kathmandu: Springer and Institute for Integrated Development Studies, 2009), p. 12.

[73] B. G. Verghese and R. R. Iyer (eds.), *Harnessing the Eastern Himalayan Rivers: Regional Co-Operation in South Asia* (New Delhi: Konark Publishers., 1993), pp. 200–3; see also B. C. Upreti, *The Politics of Himalayan River Water* (New Delhi: Nirala Publications, 1993), pp. 98–118.

[74] The Kosi was breached in Kusaha in Nepal on August 18, 2008, not for the first time but this time upstream of the Kosi Barrage. On this and earlier floods, see Dinesh Kumar Mishra, "The Kosi and the Embankment Story," *Economic and Political Weekly*, November 15, 2008, pp. 47–52.

Nepal's own needs rather than for meeting the needs of other countries. This view does not rule out the export of electricity, but large generation primarily for export to a single large buyer (India) under intergovernmental arrangements is not considered desirable. This alternative approach of national capacity-building, local government participation, and use of cheap and reliable electricity to give national industries a competitive edge could help resolve some of the challenges Nepal faces. This approach (as opposed to that of only inviting external contractors and consultants) would enhance local resilience that would contribute to demonstrable societal well-being.[75]

Nepal does not have much of a manufacturing base, but its hydroelectric potential alone is more than sufficient to transform the economy in a dramatic manner. Nepal's apprehensions regarding the inadequacy of its arable land and therefore the difficulty and potential political unpopularity of creating large water reservoirs are understandable, as are worries over the challenge of people displaced by hydroelectric development. However, Nepal's inability to take constructive action where it could generate income is unfortunate and, alas, typical. Until serious improvements are made in this area, Nepal will remain a net importer of electricity from India despite its achievable hydropower potential of nearly 42,000 megawatts.[76] This is a tragic state of affairs, not least considering the highly profitable business that nearby Bhutan has been able to generate through Indian-designed hydroelectric projects on its soil. (Bhutan is today inclined also to open tenders for additional such hydroelectric projects to other international bidders, while India will benefit as the main client for the electricity produced.)

CHINA'S INTERESTS AND CONCERNS

Beijing has focused its policies vis-à-vis Nepal on encouraging the Himalayan state's neutrality by trying to reduce its dependence on India in the political, economic, and security arena.[77] Indeed, in recent decades, the main aim of China's policy in Nepal was to complicate India's relationship with Kathmandu so as to limit New Delhi's ability to take effective action beyond the South Asian region.[78]

China's occupation of Tibet in 1950 heightened both Chinese interests in and influence over Nepal. On the one hand, Beijing feared that Nepal, bordering Tibet, would be used by its Cold War rivals for anti-China activities, a problem that was

[75] See Dipak Gyawali and Ajaya Dixit, "Mahakali Impasse and Indo-Nepal Water Conflict," *Economic and Political Weekly*, February 27, 1999, pp. 553–64.

[76] R. B. Shah, "Ganges-Brahmaputra: The Outlook for the Twenty-First Century," in A. K. Biswas and J. I. Uitto (eds.), *Sustainable Development of the Ganges-Brahmaputra-Meghna Basins* (Tokyo: United Nations University Press, 2001), p. 23.

[77] Manish Dabhade and Harsh V. Pant, "Coping with Challenges to Sovereignty: Sino-Indian Rivalry and Nepal's Foreign Policy," *Contemporary South Asia*, Vol. 13, No. 2 (June 2004), p. 160.

[78] Leo E. Rose, "King Mahendra's China Policy," in S. D. Muni (ed.), *Nepal: An Assertive Monarch* (New Delhi: Chetna Publications, 1977), p. 234.

further compounded over the years by the growing presence of Tibetan refugees in Nepal.[79] On the other hand, the occupation of Tibet extended Beijing's reach into Nepal. China reportedly regarded Tibet as the palm and Nepal, Bhutan, Sikkim, Ladakh, and the region today covered by much of the Indian state of Arunachal Pradesh as the five fingers of Tibet.

In the decade after the Tibetan invasion, Beijing was careful not to raise Indian concerns about Chinese expansionism. In 1955 China yielded to Indian wishes and refrained from establishing a resident embassy in Kathmandu, and in 1956 it obtained India's approval before signing a treaty with Tibet.

However, by 1959 Beijing began to encourage forms of anti-Indianism in Nepal, seeking opportunities to exploit friction between Kathmandu and Delhi while entering into direct confrontation with India in the Himalayas, culminating in the 1962 China–India border war. However, its attempts to sow seeds of discord between India and Nepal during B. P. Koirala's premiership (1959–60) largely failed.[80]

Around that time, Beijing also started to flex its muscle vis-à-vis Kathmandu. In 1960, China unexpectedly staked a claim to Mount Everest, setting off a nationalistic frenzy in Nepal, which culminated in an unprecedentedly large anti-Chinese demonstration in Kathmandu on April 21, 1960, to affirm Nepal's sovereignty over the world's highest mountain (and Nepal's most visible asset globally). In another incident on June 28, 1960, Chinese troops intruded into the Mustang region of northwest Nepal, killing one and capturing several other Nepali border guards. Nepal protested this action energetically the following day. Chinese Prime Minister Chou En-lai expressed deep regret over the incident, returned the prisoners, and paid compensation for the killing of the Nepali guard.[81]

After this episode, China was careful to allay Nepali fears about possible China's expansionist designs in order to maintain the goodwill of Nepal while it consolidated its position in Tibet. In 1961, King Mahendra paid a state visit to China on the latter's invitation, during which an agreement was reached on construction of the Kathmandu-Kodari road,[82] popularly known as the Kathmandu-Lhasa road, which Beijing agreed to finance.

Today, Beijing's policy toward Nepal appears to be driven by the twin objectives of expanding influence in Nepal and suppressing anti-China activities of the Tibetan community residing there.[83] China's interest and involvement in Nepal are perhaps greater than Beijing claims, but also significantly more modest than India fears. One

---

[79] Narayan Khadka, "Chinese Foreign Policy towards Nepal in Cold War Period: An Assessment," *China Report*, Vol. 35, No. 1 (1999), pp. 62–5.

[80] Shashi Bhushan Prasad, *The China Factor in Indo-Nepalese Relations 1955–72* (New Delhi: Commonwealth Publishers, 1989), pp. 70, 73–5.

[81] Ibid., pp. 75–6.

[82] An agreement to construct an all-weather highway linking Kathmandu with Tibet was signed in October 1961 – at a time when neither Kathmandu nor Beijing had cordial relations with New Delhi. The Kathmandu-Kodari road opened in May 1967.

[83] See Thierry Mathou, "Tibet and Its Neighbors: Moving toward a New Chinese Strategy in the Himalayan Region," *Asian Survey*, Vol. 45, No. 4 (Jul.–Aug. 2005), pp. 517–18.

issue – Tibet – continues to override all others. China makes friends with any Nepali government that keeps a lid on political activity by the estimated 20,000 Tibetans in the country.[84] Whether monarchist, Maoist, or led by the traditional parties – the nature of the government has made little difference to Beijing, which has moved effortlessly from supporting one to the next. China's top priority is to stifle any protests among the Tibetans in Nepal and to stop other "anti-Chinese" activities. On this topic, Chinese diplomats and Beijing are vocal and insistent.[85] Nepali governments of any political color have little choice but to bow to their powerful neighbor's primary (indeed only important) concern. Indeed, Beijing's concerns are not entirely irrational: external encouragement of the Khampa rebellion in the 1960s was pronounced from Nepal. Yet China's efforts to cut off access for Tibetans to Nepal runs counter to the preferences of Western powers, such as the United States, and may also (quietly) distress India.

Chinese apprehension is at its most intense in times when its occupation of Tibet is potentially the most controversial, as in the run-up to the 2008 Olympic Games in Beijing. Most recently it has expanded security and police posts along Nepal's border with Tibet, significantly reducing the number of people crossing the border to seek refuge in Nepal and beyond.[86] China has spent little to win friends in Nepal. It invests next to nothing in the relationship compared to India, but it tends to be more successful at making sure its very limited interests are protected. Thus, its construction of new road access from Tibet into Nepal is accompanied by sharp messaging on the need to curtail access to India through Nepal by Tibetans seeking contact with the Dalai Lama and other Buddhist religious figures; China went as far as pressing the Kathmandu government in 2010 to cease honoring the so-called Gentleman's Agreement providing safe transit for Tibetans to India through Nepal.[87]

Initially, Beijing had demonstrated little interest in or worry about the Maoist insurgency. Indeed, it seemed embarrassed to witness the Maoist brand usurped by a movement of which it knew little and whose principal ties were with India. As mentioned earlier, Beijing's attitude toward the Maoists warmed considerably as the peace process progressed. The increasing number of visits back and forth by Chinese and Nepali governmental and nongovernmental delegations after the Maoists took over the government in 2008 was closely followed in India.

Yet, even during Maoist-led rule, Beijing remained equally comfortable with other political actors, inviting senior delegations of various Nepali parties to

---

[84] Nishchal N. Pandey, "Bhutanese and Tibetan Refugees in Nepal: Implications for Regional Security," *ISAS Insights*, No. 17 (December 19, 2006), p. 2.

[85] See "Nepal's Future: In Whose Hands?", International Crisis Group, Asia Report No. 173, August 13, 2009, at http://www.crisisgroup.org/~/media/Files/asia/southasia/nepal/173_nepals_future_ _in_whose_hands.ashx.

[86] Jim Yardley, "China Intensifies Tug of War with Indian on Nepal," *New York Times*, February 18, 2010.

[87] Confidential interviews, Kathmandu, April 2010.

Beijing.[88] Chinese diplomats, who entertained cordial relations with the royal family, today consort happily with Foreign Minister Sujata Koirala, daughter of the former Nepali Congress leader.

Since 2006, China has stepped up aid, opened new cultural centers, expanded visits, and offered Nepal nonlethal military aid and training by the Chinese People's Liberation Army (PLA).[89] Yet, China did not lavish money on the Maoist party or the government it led, just as its relations with the royal family led to only negligible practical assistance, be it financial or military, after the royal coup. (If nothing else, this rate of return on cautious investments looks shrewd. In contrast, New Delhi finds the support of the very parties, politicians, and local communities that it so generously showers with financial inducements often elusive.)

Assurances of nonintervention from neighboring countries can always be taken with a grain of salt. Nevertheless, the evidence that China is interfering in Nepal or pursuing hidden agendas is most notable for its absence. It certainly views Nepal as lying on an important strategic boundary at the juncture of its and India's spheres of influence but, except for boosting commercial ties and establishing a number of China study centers, including in the Terai, it shows absolutely no signs of wishing to push that boundary further south.

However, China's long-term intentions toward Nepal are not inherently benign: they depend entirely on China's perceptions of its self-interest, which could demand less friendly approaches. However, for now, its mantra of noninterference in internal affairs looks close to the truth.[90] "What China is doing in Nepal is to help the country achieve development and stability," explained a Chinese diplomat. "This is in line with China's international role and the aspirations of the international community. We are not stopping any other country from doing the same for Nepal."[91]

Indeed, China's growing preoccupation with Nepal appears to be commercial and economic, as it seeks outlets for the manufacturing that drives its own phenomenal growth. Trade between China and Nepal is growing significantly. In addition to the older Kathmandu-Kodari Highway, which is widely used for transit of Chinese goods to other parts of the region,[92] the other seven important transit points between China

[88] A Nepali Congress delegation, headed by Vice President Prakash Man Singh, visited China before an official postelection party trip to India had taken place ("After Prachanda, Koirala's Party Heads for China," thaindian.com, August 29, 2008). Several other visits from rival parties followed.

[89] "China Agrees to Provide Non-Lethal Military Support," The Rising Nepal, December 9, 2008; RSN Singh, "The China Factor in Nepal," *India Defence Review*, Vol. 25, No. 2 (April–June 2010), at http://www.indiandefencereview.com/2010/05/the-china-factor-in-nepal.html.

[90] The difference with India is most striking in New York where China, a permanent member of the UN Security Council, is almost silent on Nepal, whereas India, not a Council Member between 1993 and 2011 and vocally committed to Nepal's independence, is tireless at the UN in its advocacy of Nepal's "sovereign" views.

[91] Interview comment by a Chinese diplomat in Beijing in July 2009, relayed by the International Crisis Group.

[92] Mahendra P. Lama, "India-China Border Trade Connectivity: Economic and Strategic Implications and India's Response" in *Connectivity Issues in India's Neighborhood* (New Delhi: Asian Institute of Transport Development, 2008), pp. 101–2.

and Nepal are being strengthened. Total trade jumped from INR 2.2 billion[93] in 1998–9 to INR 5.4 billion[94] in 2000–1. Since then it has very steadily increased to INR 6.8 billion.[95,96] In March 2006, Nepal and China signed an agreement promising further economic and trade cooperation that could benefit Nepal.[97]

Transit of Chinese goods through Nepal to India could prove an important means to increase what is already India's foremost trade relationship as of 2009. It is interesting to note that Nepal's trade deficit with China has shot up from INR 953 million[98] in 1991–2 to more than INR 11 billion[99] in 2005–6, with many of the Chinese goods heading toward Nepal finding their way into the Indian market via Dhulabari, Pashupatinagar Kakarbhitta, Raxaul, Gorakhpur, Nepalganj, Sunaoli, Tanakpur, and Birgunj. Thus, although potentially threatening, China's rising profile in Nepal can also be seen in India as a harbinger of further trade and hence of prosperity and peace in the region.

CONCLUSION

Nepal displays the sensitivities of many smaller countries contending with large neighbors. However, most countries understand the advantages of boosting economic ties with these large neighbors and manage their resentments to achieve this wider end. The Nepali leadership would seem to have much to gain from promoting a national consensus on its economic relations with adjacent states, notably building on the provisions of India's "Gujral Doctrine," which although implemented only fitfully by Delhi, much to the disappointment of the late former Indian Prime Minister Inder K. Gujral, remains a touchstone in Indian foreign policy doctrine.[100] This doctrine advocates good neighborly relations and seeks no reciprocal concessions from poor bordering countries.[101]

---

93 Roughly the equivalent of $52 million dollars in 1998–9.
94 Roughly the equivalent of $117 million dollars in 2000–1.
95 Roughly the equivalent of $148 million dollars at the time of writing. Ibid.
96 Lama, "India-China Border Trade Connectivity," pp. 101–2.
97 Ibid., p. 102.
98 Roughly the equivalent of $44 million dollars in 1991–2.
99 Roughly the equivalent of $247 million dollars in 2005–6.
100 I. K. Gujral's willingness to go the extra mile in resolving problems with neighbors and his refusal to insist on reciprocity came to be widely termed as the "Gujral Doctrine." It was articulated by Gujral in a speech in London in September 1996, outlining five points: "First, with its neighbors like Bangladesh, Bhutan, Maldives, Nepal and Sri Lanka, India does not ask for reciprocity, but gives and accommodates what it can in good faith and trust. Second, we believe that no South Asian country should allow its territory to be used against the interests of another country of the region. Third, that none should interfere in the internal affairs of another. Fourth, all South Asian countries must respect each other's territorial integrity and sovereignty. And finally, they should settle all their disputes through peaceful bilateral negotiations." See I. K. Gujral, *A Foreign Policy for India* (New Delhi: Ministry of External Affairs, 1998), pp. 69–81. Also see I. K. Gujral, *Continuity and Change: India's Foreign Policy* (New Delhi: Macmillan, 2003), pp. 107–74.
101 P. D. Kaushik, "Indo-Nepal Relations and Gujral Doctrine – Bouquets and Brickbats," in M. D. Dharmdasani (ed.), *India and Nepal: Big Power-Small Power Relations in South Asia* (New Delhi:

Although India can be and frequently is criticized for its "heavy hand" in Nepal, its current stance and behavior represent a quantum leap from its earlier outright domination of the country through a dependent Nepali royal family and other allies. It has demonstrated a willingness to accommodate Nepali political actors it would have rejected outright only a few years ago. And, although India's nervousness about China's intent in Nepal is palpable, so is its considered judgment that China will play its cards prudently in that country. This is perhaps only because in China's wider calculus relating to control over Tibet, it knows that India holds some key cards.

Of course, India also needs a positive agenda in Nepal. It might be more proactive and supportive of economic renewal in Nepal and of strengthening democracy and civil society. Concessions offered to Nepal under various Indo-Nepal trade treaties do not seem to have contributed much to long-term growth of the Nepali economy.[102] The whole sphere of economic relations between the two countries definitely needs more attention in both capitals, particularly in Kathmandu, with Nepal having potentially the most to gain.

India's approach too often appears reactive to events on the ground, suggesting a lack of actual strategy vis-à-vis this important and troubled neighbor. This sense of drift is summed up tartly by Mohan Guruswamy: "The confusion in [Delhi] over Nepal is not because that choice is difficult owing to a number of alternatives. We suffer no *embarras de richesses* in terms of options, but a poverty of clarity and hence muddle takes the place of policy."[103] This confusion is all the more significant in a period marked by the Maoists' abandonment of power in Kathmandu in early 2009.[104]

A virtual standoff between Delhi (through its local proxies and allies) and the Maoists cannot continue indefinitely.[105] S. D. Muni, in correspondence with us in 2010,[106] suggests,

The standoff between India and Nepal resulted from a number of factors, principal among them was the Maoists' deviations from assurances sought by India and given

South Asian Pub., 2001), pp. 55–62; also see B. C. Upreti, *Uneasy Friends: Readings on Indo-Nepal Relations* (New Delhi: Kalinga Pub., 2001), p. 186.

[102] Nisha Taneja, Subhanil Chowdhury, "Role of Treaties in Facilitating Nepal's Trade with India," *Economic and Political Weekly*, Vol. XLV, No. 7 (February 13, 2010), pp. 27–9.

[103] Mohan Guruswamy, *India's World: Essays on Foreign Policy and Security Issues* (Gurgaon: Hope India Publications, 2006), pp. 208–9.

[104] Sudeshna Sarkar, "India Asks Nepal Not to Meddle with Army," April 26, 2009, at http://www.thaindian.com/newsportal/politics/india-asks-nepal-not-to-meddle-with-army_100184871.html; also see Kanchan Chandra and Yubaraj Ghimire, "Why Nepal Will Stay Democratic," *The Indian Express*, May 12, 2009; and S. D. Muni, "The Civil-Military Crisis in Nepal," *The Hindu*, May 6, 2009.

[105] This is based on one of the authors' discussion with Nepali scholars including Uddhab P. Pyakurael on November 11, 2009. Uddhab recently published a book, *Maoist Movement in Nepal: A Sociological Perspective*. See also S. D. Muni, "Manmohan Singh-II: The Foreign Policy Challenges," *ISAS Insights*, No. 9, May 26, 2009, at http://www.isasnus.org/events/insights/70.pdf.

[106] Correspondence, November 11, 2009.

by them on a number of bilateral issues; their propensity to use the China card beyond the "red lines" drawn by India; and their unwillingness or incapacity to give up strong-arm methods in dealing with their political opponents. Relevant as well was the abrasive diplomatic behaviour of Kathmandu-based Indian diplomacy; India's fears that the Maoists were inclined to and capable of changing Nepal's domestic power equations; and finally Delhi's fears that a Constitution drafted under assertive Maoist leadership may not be compatible with the democratic profile of Nepal.[107]

However, he added,

Both India and the Maoists seem to be uncomfortable with the standoff and may want to end it. While the Maoists would want their recognition by New Delhi as the most powerful political force in Nepal, New Delhi may want the Maoists to respect its sensitivities inherent in the issues identified above. India can accept a gradual social transformation in Nepal, but the Maoist agenda of radical change may not be compatible with its own view of stability and order in the sensitive Himalayan state.

The tensions inherent in the relationship between India's government and the Maoists in Nepal point to the wider challenges that India faces in analyzing and influencing developments in neighboring countries. Senior Maoist leader and former finance minister Baburam Bhattarai adopted the convenient view that India mishandled the crisis over the Army Chief General Katawal in 2009 because Indian politicians were too busy with elections and left it to blundering bureaucrats.[108] It is true that Indian political leaders, including ministers, have taken remarkably little responsibility for a Nepal policy. Indian diplomats have doubtless done little more than implement on the ground guidance crafted by senior officials in Delhi with ministerial approval. However, it is all too easy to demonize Indian diplomats assigned to Kathmandu. The real challenges lie beyond (and often closer to home).

As for China, it will doubtless continue to develop its commercial and other ties to Nepal as circumstances allow. Kathmandu does not appear to be a major focus of its attention or activity. Rather, the inevitable expansion of Chinese influence across Asia will continue to be felt in Nepal, just as India's growing influence in East and Southeast Asia is accommodated by China.

Nonregional powers such as the United States, heavily weighed down in Afghanistan and recently in Iraq, will continue to be engaged with Nepal, but not as major geostrategic players. Donor countries looking for worthy recipients will be attracted to Nepal by its people and its poverty, but may increasingly be repelled by the incompetence of its successive governments, the rapaciousness of local elites, the blatant nature of corruption in Nepal, and by the sense that Nepal's future is

---

[107] Muni also notes the extent to which political actors in Kathmandu connect regularly with counterparts in Delhi, amplifying concerns on both sides about quiet lobbying.
[108] "India Blundered, Lost the Respect It Once Had," interview, *Outlook*, May 18, 2009.

ultimately tied up in more sensible relations between it and its key regional partners than in distant and increasingly cash-strapped Western and Asian nations such as Germany and Japan. The Asian Development Bank will likely remain the best friend and quiet critic of Nepal, providing support but also advice that Nepali governments should heed.

Thus, recent developments, despite their sounds and fury between 2006 and today, have brought about no fundamental change in Nepal's foreign policy options. It remains "caught between two yams" and must learn to make the best of this situation, which could be considerably better than the current dispensation.

12

Bringing the Maoists down from the Hills: India's Role

S. D. Muni

The transition of Nepal's Maoist insurgency into a peaceful democratic process in 2006 has been one of the most remarkable developments in the history of efforts to resolve communist rebellions. Peaceful resolutions of insurgencies are not entirely new in South Asia. The Tamil, Punjabi, and Assam separatist movements in India and the Sindhi agitation for identity assertion in Pakistan are other examples. However, the case of a left extremist insurgency joining hands with bourgeoisie parties to resolve a 10-year-old violent conflict has rarely been seen. Yet, the Maoists of Nepal transformed their violent People's War and agreed to confront the monarchist state through peaceful civil agitation in alliance with the established mainstream political parties. The People's Movement, or *Jana Andolan II*, launched by the mainstream parties and the Maoists against the monarchy, was ultimately the product of various forces coming together in reaction to the royal coup of February 2005. The alliance between the Maoists and the mainstream parties was also greatly facilitated and influenced by the international community, especially India. In this role, India gradually changed its position from that of supporting the monarchy against the Maoist insurgency to favoring an alliance between the Maoists and the political parties to marginalize the monarchy. In doing so, India acted indirectly but in concert with other members of the international community and, through the Nepali players, nudging them to forge alliances, mobilize people, and carry the People's Movement to its conclusion. This chapter critically examines the shift in India's position in response to rapidly unfolding developments in Nepal, particularly after 2005.

THE MAIN PLAYERS

There were four main players in Nepal's political transition: the Maoists, the mainstream political parties, the king, and the international community within which India was the dominant actor. The Maoists were obviously the principal "game changers." They set the agenda of transition – a People's Republic through an elected Constituent Assembly – through their decade-long armed struggle, the People's War. The Maoists had sought to forge an alliance with the other parties with the objective of eliminating the monarchy even before the palace massacre of June 2001, at a time when they still enjoyed support and some patronage from the palace.[1] Indeed, King Birendra had encouraged covert links with the Maoists through his younger brother Dhirendra Shah and other trusted interlocutors. The unstated political objective behind these outreach efforts was to resolve the Maoist insurgency and marginalize the "unscrupulous" and "power hungry" leaders of the mainstream parties. Within the Maoist party, there existed a nationalist wing that was not averse to cutting a deal with the king in order to come to power. What ultimately prevented an alliance between the palace and the Maoists was the strong Maoist position advocating a republican Nepal. King Birendra was of course unwilling to consider his own abdication, even though the Maoists were willing to offer him the post of first president of a republican Nepal. Prachanda, the Maoist supremo, disclosing this fact recently, said, "Birendra's youngest brother Dhirendra was in touch with us and we were to start direct talks with him within a month with the request to abdicate his throne and become the country's first president. He was killed in this backdrop."[2]

Soon after the palace massacre, on August 16, 2001, the Maoists convened a meeting of the parties in Siliguri (in West Bengal, India) in which all the prominent left parties of Nepal participated, including the Communist Party of Nepal – United Marxist-Leninist (CPN-UML).[3] The Maoist proposal of a broad leftist alliance based on a republican platform was widely rejected, except by one group led by Bamdev Gautam (CPN-Marxist-Leninist). However, the Maoists did not give up and pursued their contacts subsequently with other political leaders, including Girija Prasad Koirala of the Nepali Congress. The Maoists also sought contacts with the international community and Indian establishment to mobilize support for their cause and counter their image as a terrorist group.

That the Maoists pursued contacts with the mainstream political parties and the international community and engaged in periodic dialogue with the palace while they were still waging their People's War required some ideological justification. This justification was provided by adapting to Nepal the classic Maoist concept of the "two-line struggle" (2LS), which accepts the relevance of working through other

---

[1] The Maoist leader Dr. Baburam Bhattarai acknowledged this patronage and support in his article written days after the palace massacre. Baburam Bhattarai, *"Naya Kot Parva Lai Manyata Dinu Hundeina"* (The New Palace Massacre Can Not Be Legitimized), *Kantipur*, June 6, 2001 (Kathmandu). The Maoist leader Prachanda again echoed this pro-palace line by blaming India for being behind the palace massacre because King Birendra was moving Nepal's foreign policy toward greater independence from India. *The Telegraph* (Kathmandu), January 22, 2010.
[2] *The Hindustan Times* (New Delhi), January 10, 2010.
[3] Those who attended the meeting were Bamdev Gautam (CPN-UML), Madhav Kumar Nepal (CPN-ML), Narayn Man Bijukchhe (Nepal Peasants and Workers Party), Mohan Bikram Singh (CPN-Mashal), Prakash (Nepal Unity center), and Lila Mani Pokherel (United People's Front).

systems for achieving "revolutionary" goals. Its roots can be traced to the broader Marxist-Leninist concept of the "united front": to isolate the principal enemy (or contradiction). Its ideological and conceptual definition was recast by the Nepal Maoists as the *"Prachanda Path"* to rationalize the "zigzag" movement of their struggle for establishing a "new democratic revolution" or "new democracy." In this struggle, the Maoists first engaged with the Nepali monarchy because, during the early stages of the People's War, the Maoists had to concentrate on confronting the various governments led by the mainstream political parties, first and foremost the Nepali Congress. It was only after two rounds of negotiations when the united front with the monarchy did not work out that the Maoists allied with the political parties. This alliance led to the 2005 12-Point Understanding with the Seven Party Alliance (SPA) and the *Jana Andolan II* and eventually culminated in the establishment of Nepal as a democratic republic in 2008.

The Maoists' failure to engineer the transition from "democratic republic" to "new democracy" under their leadership was precipitated by the breakdown of their alliance with the SPA and their exit from power in May 2009. To prevent the party from splitting, the Maoists again debated the 2LS in that context: "right opportunism" and "reformism" while carrying forward the "correct ideological line" to lead the Nepali people to "a victorious conclusion of a new democratic revolution." Underneath the ideological jargon, the Maoists have since been caught in an internal conflict between the two approaches: one, led by Mohan Vaidya, pleads for a revolutionary struggle to achieve the ultimate ideological goal of a "new democracy" without any compromise or accommodation. The other approach, led by Dr. Baburam Bhattarai, argues for a gradual movement toward the ultimate goal by working through the "federal democratic transition" because both the national and international strategic context of Nepal and the reality of its socioeconomic level of development, which calls for pragmatism, cannot be ignored.[4] These two ideological positions also reflect a strong personality clash between their respective proponents. Prachanda, the chief of the party, has been cleverly playing on them to preserve his leadership in the party. Some critics of the Maoists have labeled this "pragmatism" and the 2LS strategy "opportunism."[5]

In the Seven Party Alliance, the Nepali Congress and its leader Girija Prasad Koirala had played the leading role in broadening Nepal's antimonarchy struggle. Ironically, it was G. P. Koirala whose government had advocated using the maximum force against the Maoists in the early years of their People's War. However,

---

4 For the two strong arguments on the "two-line struggle," see the statements by the Central Committee member Basanta (http://southasiarev.wordpress.com/2009/09/12/2-line-struggle-at-paris-height-report-from-k . . .) and Hisila Yami (http://www.kantipuronline.com/columns.php?&nid=208193), August 6, 2009; both accessed on February 1, 2010.

5 Mohan Bikram Singh, "The Royal Palace Massacre and the Maoists' Pro-King Political Line," in Arjun Karki and David Seddon (eds.), *The Peoples War in Nepal: Left Perspectives* (New Delhi: Adroit Publishers, 2003), pp. 315–74.

the palace thwarted his move to use the Royal Nepalese Army (RNA) against the Maoists, compelling him to resign as prime minister in July 2001 and encouraging the split of the Nepali Congress, with a breakaway faction led by Sher Bahadur Deuba establishing the Nepali-Congress (Democratic). This episode prompted Koirala to look toward the Maoists, with whom he found convergence in their shared desire to break the palace's control over the RNA. Maoist leaders Prachanda and Bhattarai met Koirala for the first time in 2002 in India. Koirala's domestic political stature and broader international acceptability enabled him to bring other political parties, particularly the CPN-UML, together in building the People's Movement with the Maoists. Koirala's commitment to mobilize an antimonarchy struggle was strengthened after King Gyanendra's dissolution of parliament on May 22, 2002, and the *Jana Andolan II* was formally announced in 2003 under his leadership. However, its momentum fizzled when the king succeeded in splitting the parties and in July 2004 formed a government under Sher Bahadur Deuba, who led the breakaway group of the Nepali Congress mentioned earlier.

Yet another irony of the Nepali transition was that no one did more to mobilize the antimonarchy people's movement than King Gyanendra himself. His penchant for overplaying his hand and usurping all constitutional powers led to his undoing. His undemocratic moves in 2002, which were exceeded by his direct takeover of power in 2005, gradually drove political parties away from him. He even managed to alienate India, the United States, and the European Union, which had been inclined to protect the monarchy as a pillar of stability and an anticommunist bulwark. They also had preferred the king because strategically it was easier to deal with a center of power dominated by one person than with a host of political forces represented by various parties. The king failed to realize the depth to which the monarchy's credibility had fallen among the common Nepalis after the palace massacre of June 2001 and his assumption of the crown. As the main beneficiaries, he and his son were widely suspected to be part of a conspiracy orchestrating the massacre.[6]

The international community that eventually played a decisive role in the massive political change in Nepal was dominated by four key players or groups of players: India, the West (that is, the United States, United Kingdom, and the European Union), the United Nations, and China. All these players changed their respective policies to keep pace with the evolving Nepali situation. India and the West reversed their support for the monarchy, and China moved from a position of being indifferent to active support of the monarchy. The United Nations began its work quietly following the secretary-general's offer of "good offices" in 2002, but subsequently with the establishment of the Office of the UN High Commissioner for Human

---

[6] Pointers to this effect are found in a political novel by Krishna Aviral, *Raktakund* (Pond of Blood), (Kathmandu: Pairavi Book House, 2006); also see Manjushree Thapa, *Forget Kathmandu: An Elegy for Democracy* (New Delhi: Penguin, 2005).

Rights in 2005 and a full fledged UN Mission in Nepal (UNMIN) in 2007, it emerged as a major player in the peace process.

One would be amiss to exclude the people of Nepal from the list of those who played a decisive role in the success of the People's Movement. Civil society leaders[7] played a major role in mobilizing the general population for the cause of democracy even when the mainstream political parties were in disarray. To different degrees, all these leaders endorsed the Maoist agenda. They joined the Maoists in bringing people on the streets even at the last moment in April 2006 when party leaders were still not sure whether the protests would be effective.[8]

INDIA'S ROLE

India's Nepal policy has not always been the outcome of rational choices. Although ensuring Nepal's political stability and economic well-being through the development of its hydropower potential and a smooth flow of trade has been India's stated priority, its approach to Nepal has largely been determined by its own security interests. These security interests have been defined in the context of evolving India–Nepal relations and regional concerns and, more broadly, in terms of preserving and consolidating India's strategic space in Nepal. India has been very sensitive to the strategic presence in Nepal of extraregional powers like the United States and of its known adversaries like China and Pakistan. Nepali nationals as well as ill-intended foreigners have been known to use India's open borders with Nepal to weaken India's security.

The precise thrust of India's interests and approach at any given point in time is shaped by the balance of forces among multiple stakeholders in India's Nepal policy. These stakeholders are diverse and varied and their positions often mutually incompatible. Some are even beyond the reach of India's Ministry of External Affairs. Prominent among these actors are the recognized political/administrative establishments (the Home, Finance, and Commerce Ministries; intelligence and national security organizations; and the Prime Minister's Office); the Indian army, which has traditional fraternal relations with the RNA and has maintained seven Gurkha regiments since independence; the business community; the members of the former princely ruling class who have close matrimonial and family relations with Nepal's feudal rulers (both the Shahs and the Ranas); Indian political parties and their leaders who maintain close institutional and personal relations with their

---

[7] Such as Dr. Devendra Raj Panday, Padma Ratna Tuladhar, Mathura Shrestha, Daman Dhungana, academics, journalists, and others.

[8] This was reflected in the shaky confidence of the representatives of the three main parties as the date for launching the movement (April 6, 2006) approached quickly. I met with these representatives on March 29 when they wanted to be assured that the Maoists would be able to bring around 100,000 demonstrators on the streets of Kathmandu on April 6. The party leaders were not sure if their people, even those living in Kathmandu, would come in full strength.

Nepali counterparts; the Hindu religious interest groups;[9] and, finally, the Indian states bordering Nepal. There is also a large Nepali diaspora in India (an estimated population of 10 million), which has extensive social and matrimonial ties with the Indians. Most of these stakeholders harbor strong anti-Maoist feelings, not only because of their radical ideology and violent tactics but also because of the Maoists' anti-Indian stance, which regularly denounces Nepal's neighbor as "expansionist" and "exploitative." In addition, because the Maoists had also linked themselves to the Maoists of India (the Naxalites), as well as other Maoist groups in South Asia and elsewhere (under the Revolutionary International Movement [RIM]), many in the Indian security establishment perceived them as a direct security challenge to the stability of India and the whole South Asian region. The intelligence establishment in India, particularly the Intelligence Bureau (IB), has been ideologically structured to face the challenge of communists in general and leftist extremists in particular ever since the British days.

By the time Nepal entered its momentous transition phase, India's Nepal policy had long been based on two pillars: the constitutional monarchy and multiparty democracy. Yet this premise could not be sustained in the face of rapidly growing tensions between these two pillars, resulting from the king's attack on democratic institutions and processes. For analytical convenience, India's policy toward Nepal's People's Movement and its approach toward the Maoists, can be looked at in three phases: (1) pre-palace massacre, (2) post-palace massacre (2001–5), and (3) the period from the February 2005 royal coup to the People's Movement (2005–6). During the momentous developments of the third phase and even earlier, all the major players in Nepal's People's Movement were in contact at different levels with the Indian government and political leadership.

Pre-Palace Massacre

Immediately before the royal massacre, Indian policy makers were busy mopping up the dust and din created in bilateral relations by the hijacking of Flight IC 814 from Kathmandu to Delhi by Pakistani terrorists in December 1999 and protests over alleged remarks (derogatory to Nepali nationalism) by Indian Bollywood hero Hritik Roshan (which he never made) in December 2000.[10] India was unhappy with the way the Nepali government and the palace were handling these sensitive issues, behind both of which Delhi suspected a covert Pakistani hand. The Nepali government and

---

9 Such as the *Shankaracharyas, Vishwa Hindu Parishad*, and *the Rastriya Swayam Sevak Sangh.*

10 In December 1999, Indian Airlines flight IC 814 from Kathmandu to New Delhi was hijacked by Pakistani terrorists and was taken to Kandahar in Afghanistan. India had to release three Pakistani terrorists to save nearly 160 passengers on the plane.

In the other incident, an Indian Bollywood hero, Hritik Roshan, was attacked and anti-India emotions were whipped up in Kathmandu over allegations that he had denigrated Nepal and the Nepalese. No anti-Nepal statement was ever made by Hritik Roshan.

the palace had long resisted India's proposed special security arrangements to deal with such incidents.

New Delhi rarely paid much attention to the Maoist insurgency and links between the Nepali Maoists and the Indian Naxalites. Instead, it treated the possible security spillover of the Maoist insurgency as a routine law-and-order problem to be handled by the bordering Indian states.[11]

Post-Palace Massacre

The Maoist insurgency did not figure prominently in India–Nepal discussions during the visit of Indian Foreign Minister Jaswant Singh to Nepal in August 2001, shortly after the palace massacre.[12] This was despite the fact that the Maoists had accused India's intelligence agency, the Research & Analysis Wing (RAW), of having been involved in the palace massacre along with the U.S. Central Intelligence Agency. Perhaps the reason for Delhi's lack of interest was that the Maoists had not yet attacked the RNA and their People's War was still confined to Nepal's hills. Nepal's new government under Prime Minister Deuba was preparing to talk with the Maoists, which India quietly encouraged, hoping for a peaceful negotiated resolution of the insurgency.

When the Maoists first attacked the RNA in November 2001, the 9/11 terrorist attacks had just taken place, bringing the question of terrorism upfront on the global agenda. India had responded to the 9/11 attacks with a swift change in its approach to terrorism. By joining hands with the United States in the "Global War on Terror," Delhi hoped it would be able to pressure Pakistan on cross-border terrorism and also receive international support in fighting terrorism at the regional level. Analysts in India and Nepal started linking Nepal's Maoists with the Naxalite insurgency in India and with global terrorism networks. India branded the Nepal Maoists as terrorists even while the Nepali government was talking to them under a mutually agreed temporary truce. These talks collapsed on November 21, 2001, over the Maoist insistence on a Constituent Assembly.

Complications for India's policy on the Maoist issue were created by subsequent developments. The Maoists launched successful attacks on the RNA, capturing large amounts of its arms. On October 4, 2002, the king dismissed Deuba's government, dissolved parliament, and took the administration into his own hands, appointing a royalist, Lokendra Bahadur Chand, as prime minister on October 11, 2002. This

---

[11] This is based on the then-Foreign Minister Jaswant Singh's comments to me in an informal discussion at India International Center, New Delhi, December 2000.

[12] For an analysis of Jaswant Singh's visit to Nepal by a former foreign secretary of India who rose to become the national security advisor under the UPA government, which came to power in May 2004, see J. N. Dixit, "Jaswant Singh's visit to Nepal," September 10, 2001, *India News Online*, http://news.indiamart.com/news-analysis/jaswant-singh-s-visit-5161.html; accessed on September 30, 2009.

royal administration stepped up moves to mobilize military support from various countries including India, the United States, the United Kingdom, China, and Pakistan. Driven by its "Global War on Terror" the United States, followed by the United Kingdom, expanded military cooperation with Nepal and stationed advisors with the RNA in the areas of live conflict with the Maoists. The growing interest of Nepal's government in diversifying sources of military support was prompted by the palace's suspicion that India was sympathetic to the Maoists. The fact that the Maoists were able to convene the earlier mentioned meeting with other leftist parties in Siliguri was seen as evidence of the Indian intelligence agencies' connivance with the Maoists. The regime encouraged the pliant Nepali media to highlight such "connivance." All this made New Delhi uneasy and angry.

India was in close contact with the United States and United Kingdom on the overall strategy of fighting terrorism in South Asia, and they discussed the Maoist question. However, the growing U.S. military presence in Nepal, its deepening military relationship, and increasing provision of supplies to the RNA raised many eyebrows in New Delhi, because India has always been sensitive toward other powers' involvement in Nepal's security sector. It feared that a growing U.S. presence in Nepal could prompt China to do the same, which was not acceptable to India. This concern also sowed the seeds of distrust between the Indian government and King Gyanendra, who was seen as seeking defence assistance from countries other than India under the pretext of fighting Maoist terrorism.

Sensing the undercurrent of unease between the United States and India and also realizing that increasing international support for the RNA was gradually creating difficulties in the conduct of their People's War, the Maoists reached out to India by sending Maoist leader Baburam Bhattarai to New Delhi in early 2002 to quietly establish political contacts.[13] However, no meaningful Indian political leader was willing to see him, not even Dr. Bhattarai's erstwhile Jawaharlal Nehru University (JNU) colleagues like Sitaram Yechury of the Communist Party of India – Marxist, D. P. Tripathi of the Nationalist Congress Party, and Digvijay Singh of the Janata Dal. Much has been made of these actors' support for the Maoists, but that came only in 2005. The former prime minister I. K. Gujral also declined a meeting with Maoist leaders, as did several junior Congress and Socialist leaders. The terrorist tag on the Maoists and their loudly proclaimed anti-Indian position made them untouchable for the Indian political class.

However, when the Maoists' request for an opportunity to make their case in Delhi was taken to the Indian Prime Minister's Office in June 2002, there was a hesitant but cautiously encouraging response. The Maoists were asked to put their point of view

---

[13] It seems that with the launching of direct attacks on the RNA, the Maoists' top leadership moved to India quietly and guided most of their military campaign from safe places in the north Indian states of Uttar Pradesh, Bihar, and Himachal Pradesh and also Mumbai and Delhi. The Maoist leader Prachanda confessed subsequently that during the insurgency period, he was hiding mostly in India.

in writing, which they reluctantly did.[14] Packaged in radical rhetoric, the letter written by the Maoist duo, Prachanda and Baburam Bhattarai, assured the Indian leaders that they wanted the best of relations with India and would not do anything to harm its critical interests. The response to this letter came after a couple of months: the intelligence surveillance and restrictions on the Maoists' movements in India were relaxed, and an IB team held discussions with the Maoist representatives. The Maoists reiterated their position again in writing to the IB sleuths. This was followed by more contacts and meetings between the Maoists and the RAW. Maoists could now move with greater ease and could also contact other Nepali political leaders in India.

The Maoist message to Koirala and other mainstream political leaders in Nepal was that they were prepared to join the democratic process, in return for support for a republican Nepal. Koirala and other political parties were not yet ready to consider the complete abolition of the monarchy, but were prepared to work to liberate the Nepali state from the stranglehold of the palace. Prachanda also wrote to many other international leaders and the UN secretary-general emphasizing the Maoists' commitment to "universal democratic values and principles."

The partial thaw between the Maoists and the Indian security agencies was marred by the arrest of Maoist leaders C. P. Gajurel in Chennai in August 2003 and Mohan Vaidya "Kiran" in Siliguri in March 2004. The arrests can be attributed to various factors. One was an ongoing turf war between the IB and the RAW, in which the former carried out the arrests to upstage the latter. The IB also seemed increasingly concerned by the frequent media reports of growing contacts between the Nepal Maoists and the Naxalites. In some reports, the Nepali Maoist leader Prachanda was even credited with facilitating the merger of India's People's War Group (PWG) and the Maoist Coordination Committee (MCC) in September 2004.[15] There were also reports that the Nepali and Indian Maoists were collaborating to create a Compact Revolutionary Zone (CRZ) stretching from central and eastern India to Nepal. However, when India's Foreign Ministry specifically asked the IB and the RAW about the exact nature of the Nepal Maoists' support to the Indian Naxalites, no hard evidence was forthcoming. At the most there could have been local level and ideological links, but there were no organized or structured efforts between the two Maoist groups across the Indo-Nepal borders.[16]

---

[14] The PMO was initially furious with the Maoists' demand to abolish the monarchy. However, after a discussion that centered on the complete failure of the monarchy to ensure India's security and developmental interests in Nepal, the PMO softened its stance a bit and agreed to look into the Maoist position on issues affecting India if they were put in writing by their top leadership. The letter addressed by the Maoists tried to reassure India that they were a genuine political movement and not a bunch of terrorists and that they recognized the need to sustain the close ties between India and Nepal as necessary for Nepal to advance.

[15] These were Indian left-extremist groups fighting for a communist revolution. They were based in Andhra Pradesh with links and branches in other Indian provinces. They were also members of the Revolutionary Internationalist Movement, where they had come into contact with the Nepal Maoists.

[16] This was disclosed by a highly placed foreign ministry officer to me in an interview in New Delhi.

There was also pressure on New Delhi to counter allegations from Kathmandu that it was clandestinely supporting the Maoists. Arresting Maoist leaders in India was one way to prove these allegations wrong. Some of the arrested members of the Nepal Maoist Central Committee, such as Suresh Ale Magar, Matrika Yadav, and Bamdev Chettri, were handed over to the king's government. Interestingly, except for Chettri, most of these leaders belonged to the hard-line group of the Maoists that was trying to marginalize the moderate group around Baburam Bhattarai. Whether intended or not, these arrests also served to send a message to the Maoist hard-liners not to harm the moderates and not to deviate from the mainstream line of seeking an alliance with the Nepali parliamentary parties. Yet, in retrospect, the arrests contributed to the deep and persistent Maoist suspicions of India and made India a factor in the ongoing power struggles between the different wings within the Maoist Party.

Royal Coup and Jana Andolan II

The situation in Nepal took a sharp turn with King Gyanendra's power grab on February 1, 2005. He dismissed his own appointee, Prime Minister Deuba, and constituted a government under his direct leadership. He declared a state of emergency, detained all the major political party leaders, and gave the RNA free rein to crush the Maoists and any other political opposition. India and the international community came to realize that there was no military solution to Nepal's insurgency. Since 2002 India had been repeatedly cautioning the king against an assault on democratic institutions, but to little effect. The king's drastic action came as a shock to New Delhi, which reacted strongly. Reminiscent of India's reaction to King Mahendra's similar coup in December 1960, it described Gyanendra's move as a "serious setback to the cause of democracy" in Nepal and a "matter of grave concern to India." It is worth quoting from the Ministry of External Affairs' statement issued after the meeting of the Cabinet Committee on Security on the day of the king's coup:

India has consistently supported multiparty democracy and constitutional monarchy enshrined in Nepal's constitution as the two pillars of political stability in Nepal. This principle has now been violated with the King forming the government under his Chairmanship.

We have always considered that in Nepal, it is imperative to *evolve a broad national consensus*, particularly between the monarchy and political parties, to deal with the political and economic challenges facing the country.

The latest developments in Nepal bring the monarchy and the mainstream political parties in direct confrontation with each other. This can only benefit the *forces that not only wish to undermine democracy but the institution of monarchy as well* (italics added).

The statement was interesting for its implicit references to the Maoists. First, it talked of "broad national consensus," which could also include the Maoists, although the emphasis was on "mainstream parties." Second, it cautioned the king that his move would strengthen the Maoists, because only they wished to "undermine . . . the institution of monarchy."

As it evolved in response to the changing situation in Nepal, India's policy had three major objectives: (1) to pressure the king to reverse his February 2005 move and build consensus with the political parties, (2) to rally the international community around New Delhi's approach, and (3) to bring mainstream political parties together in their opposition to the king's move and facilitate their alliance with the Maoists to increase pressure on the monarch.

To pressure the king to reverse the coup, India stopped its arms supplies to the RNA. A number of processes led to this decision. In one, Minister of External Affairs Natwar Singh held consultations with experts outside the government, in which proponents of halting arms supplies prevailed.[17] India refused to attend the South-Asian Association for Regional Cooperation (SAARC) summit scheduled to take place in Dhaka in February 2005, under the pretext of poor security arrangements. However, the king was given adequate hints that the real reason was that the Indian prime minister did not want to share the dais with him. On February 3, 2005, then Army Chief J. J. Singh turned down an invitation to visit Nepal on the advice of the government. A few days later, on February 9, 2005, an already scheduled India–Nepal Joint Security Group meeting, expected to work out the details of arms supplies to Nepal, was canceled. The Indian prime minister also personally spoke to the king on two occasions – in April 2005 in Jakarta and in November 2005 in Dhaka – urging him to reverse his actions and engage the political parties. India's attempts to pressure the king proved in vain. In response, all that the king did was to lift the emergency rule after three months and give some freedom of movement to the Nepali leaders. His dictum reflecting on India's efforts was "they must say what they must say and we must do what we must do."[18] He also flagrantly played the China card, telling India that he had other options and could not care less for India's sensitivities.

To counter the Indian pressures, the king tried to cultivate U.S. support, but when this effort failed, he secured military support from China and Pakistan. This action

---

[17] Within a couple of days of the king's coup, the External Affairs Minister K. Natwar Singh called a small group of India's Nepal hands (academics and former ambassadors) to take stock of the situation. In that discussion, opinion was divided on whether arms supplies to the RNA should be halted immediately as that would strengthen and embolden the Maoists. However, the proponents of a tough line vis-à-vis the monarchy who favored the stoppage of arms prevailed, and supplies were stopped immediately, including even those arms that were already in the pipeline. However, a formal announcement was only made weeks later, on February 22, 2005. I was present in those discussions.

The question of resuming arms supplies came up again in April 2005, when a king's emissary, Ramesh Nath Pandey, managed to secure at least a one-time resumption in view of the deteriorating security situation in Nepal. However, the lethal components of the deal were not allowed to go through due to a last-minute technical hitch raised by then-Foreign Secretary Shyam Saran.

[18] *South Asian Tribune*, February 27, 2005.

further alienated India as well as the rest of the international community. Nepal's purchase of US$ 1.2 million worth of ammunition from China in August 2005 was the proverbial last straw on the camel's back that changed India's approach to the king. During his arms purchase negotiations in China, the Nepali foreign minister promised to push for China's participation in the upcoming SAARC summit. He also expressed reservations about India's bid for a permanent seat in the UN Security Council (UNSC).[19]

Earlier, when Indian Minister of State for External Affairs Rao Indrajit Singh visited Kathmandu in July 2005 to request the king's support for India's UNSC bid, King Gyanendra's response was that such support would be conditional on resumed arms sales and withdrawal of then-Indian Ambassador Shiv Shanker Mukherjee, who had offended the king by his public support for the democratic forces. The king informally dispatched a series of personal envoys to India and tried to mobilize lobbies sympathetic to him to weigh in on his behalf with the India government. His message to Delhi was that, in return for political support, he was willing to accept all of Delhi's economic and diplomatic demands.[20] India reiterated its expectation that the king make up with the political parties, restore democratic institutions, and desist from involving external interests in dealing with the Maoists. It was the persistent refusal of King Gyanendra to heed this advice that drove New Delhi away. After July-August 2005, India was inching toward a position in favor of jettisoning King Gyanendra, if the circumstances so warranted, while protecting the institution of the monarchy. I return to this point later.

While pressuring the king, India was keen to have the international community on its side. A strategic shift to closer relations had been gradually occurring in Indo-U.S. relations since the 1999 Kargil conflict between India and Pakistan[21] and President Clinton's visit to India in March 2000. As noted, there was a convergence of India and the United States on the issue of counterterrorism in the aftermath of 9/11. However, views in India and the United States continued to differ on how to approach Nepal. The media speculated about the possibility of Maoists developing links with Al Qaeda and Muslim extremists, given the marked growth in Islamic religious schools (madrasas) in the Terai, the southern flatlands bordering India. In addition, Pakistan's intelligence agencies were already active in Nepal. Therefore the United States suddenly became more active in Nepal's security sector, with Secretary

---

[19] See the text of Ramesh Nath Pandey's speech on August 16 in Beijing. Nepali Ministry of Foreign Affairs website, http://www.mofa.gov.np/uploads/news/20060310112705.pdf; accessed on October 10, 2009.

[20] One such message was also conveyed by Foreign Minister Ramesh Nath Pandey to his Indian counterpart Natwar Singh through me.

[21] The conflict between India and Pakistan took place in 1999, starting in the Kargil district of Kashmir. The United States took a serious exception to Pakistan for launching this conflict and called Pakistan's Prime Minister Nawaz Sharif to Washington in July 1999 to ensure that the Line of Control between India and Pakistan in Kashmir was not violated. This was seen in Delhi as a positive change in the U.S. position on India–Pakistan issues.

of State Colin Powell and his Assistant Secretary for South Asia, Christina Rocca, visiting Nepal in January and December 2002. These visits brought in substantial military support in terms of arms and even the placement of U.S. security personnel in Nepal for exercises and training.[22] British military assistance also started increasing in Nepal. Britain even appointed a Special Envoy, Jeffrey James, in 2003 to help coordinate Britain's counterinsurgency assistance and reduce differences between the king and the political parties. Although India was also providing significant military support to Nepal, it was not very comfortable with the growing military presence of the West in its backyard.

Throughout 2005, India kept the lid on its arms supplies to Nepal, fearing that any relaxation on this count would encourage other countries to resume their support to Nepal's security forces. India was worried about the escalation of conflict within Nepal and its possible spillover into India. Its preference was for the king to come to terms with the political parties and seek a peaceful resolution of the Maoist insurgency. Whereas the United States looked sympathetically to the increasing role of the United Nations and various international NGOs in the Nepali conflict for mediation and conflict resolution, India was not comfortable with this development.

Gradually, through continuous discussions at the highest levels, India's differences with the United States and the other Western powers on Nepal narrowed. The king's refusal to accommodate the political parties and a growing realization on the part of India, the United States, and the United Kingdom that the king's war against the Maoists was militarily unwinnable led to a strategic convergence with respect to Nepal. The parallel movement toward an Indo-U.S. strategic partnership during the first term of President George W. Bush also facilitated this convergence. The United States and the other Western actors generally agreed to follow India's lead in relation to Nepal, keeping intact their respective nuances on finer points. Most of these nuances related to the assessment of the Maoists, the military presence of the West, and the role of international organizations in Nepal. Differences on these issues remained even after the victory of the *Jana Andolan II*, and when the U.S. Secretary of State for South and Central Asian Affairs Richard Boucher visited Kathmandu in November 2006, he acknowledged "slightly different approaches."[23] Nevertheless, this was the first time since 1947 that India and the West's respective approaches toward Nepal were broadly in harmony.

India was also not very happy with the increasing role of the United Nations and various NGOs like the Swiss-based Centre for Humanitarian Dialogue and the U.S.-based Carter Center.[24] The question of expanding the role of the UN to handle the disarmament of Maoist cadres assumed a critical dimension in the post–*Jana*

[22] For some details on this aspect, see Sumanta Banerjee, "Nepal: A Flashpoint?," *Economic and Political Weekly*, Vol. 37, No. 36 (September 3–7, 2002), pp. 3715–16; Rita Manchanda, "Nepal's Challenges," *Frontline*, Vol. 20, Issue 12, June 7–20, 2003.

[23] For the text of Mr. Boucher's statement, see http://nepal.usembassy.gov/sp11-16-2006.html.

[24] See Chapter 6 by Teresa Whitfield for more details on the role of NGOs in Nepal's peace process.

Andolan II peace process. India wanted Nepali security forces to undertake this task. In addition to the fact that this proposal was a nonstarter for the Maoists, the RNA was not well equipped to take on this responsibility. India's opposition to the UN role was softened only when the Interim Prime Minister G. P. Koirala, during his first post–*Jana Andolan* state visit to India in June 2006, told Delhi that if it was not willing to let the UN manage the Maoist disarmament, India should take on this role itself, something that Delhi was not prepared to do.[25]

The task of bringing the mainstream political parties together was greatly facilitated by the king's coup. Before his coup, he had succeeded in dividing the political parties, as was evident in the coalition put together under Deuba's second term in July 2004. The leftist CPN-UML, the royalists, and the Terai-based Sadbhawana party joined the coalition led by the Nepali Congress-Democratic (NC-D), but the Nepali Congress refused to do so. However, the dismissal of Deuba's government in February 2005 set all the political parties in opposition to the king. Therefore, Delhi's diplomacy was directed toward forging a united front of the Nepali mainstream parties in support of the restoration of democracy. Toward this end, pressure was also put on the king to release political leaders and enable them to move freely.

The Seven Party Alliance (SPA) emerged out of these efforts as a major front for democracy in Nepal. In effect, the SPA was a combination of three major political formations: the Nepali Congress led by Koirala, the CPN-UML, and the NC-D led by Deuba. The Terai- and Kathmandu-based smaller parties also came into the SPA fold, but the three royalist parties of Surya Bahadur Thapa, Pashupati Shumsher Rana, and Kamal Thapa refused to join the antimonarchy platform. The SPA was to lead the *Jana Andolan II* and, after its success, Nepal's peace process.

In India, a number of political activists from the main Indian parties had formed the Nepal Democracy Solidarity Group in the aftermath of the king's takeover. This group included former Jawaharlal Nehru University students like D. P. Tripathi of the Indian National Congress Party (NCP) and Sita Ram Yechury of the Communist Party of India-Marxist (CPM). Both their parties were the key constituents of the ruling United Progressive Alliance (UPA), and these leaders had easy access to the prime minister. One of the Congress Party's General Secretaries, Digvijay Singh, was also involved in the group. Some of this group's members were in a position to facilitate three-way communications among the SPA, the Maoists, and the Indian government. India's support of the SPA was directly correlated to the degree of defiance shown by King Gyanendra. For instance, as soon as the king secured arms from China in August 2005, India encouraged the Nepali Congress to adopt a resolution in support of democracy, which, for the first time, did not include a reference to the constitutional monarchy. This resolution was the Nepali Congress's first concrete move toward the Maoist agenda of a republican Nepal.

---

[25] Teresa Whitfield (Chapter 6) and Ian Martin (Chapter 8) cover the role of the UN in Nepal's peace process.

While bringing the Nepali mainstream parties together on the democracy agenda, India further encouraged the rapprochement between the Maoists and the SPA. However, Delhi avoided direct contacts with the Maoists because of their "terrorist" tag and because doing so would have complicated India's stance in relation to the king and the United States/international community. There was also the domestic political imperative not to be seen associating with the Nepal Maoists in view of the Naxalite challenge. Nevertheless, the Maoists managed to make further headway in their high-level political contacts in India with Baburam Bhattarai's meeting in May 2005 with Prakash Karat, Secretary General of the CPM.[26] Karat's meeting with Baburam opened the door to frequent contacts between the Maoists and members of the Nepal Democratic Solidarity Group. Prominent among those members figured Sita Ram Yechury, who gradually emerged as the primary channel between the Maoists and the Indian top political establishment, including Prime Minister Man Mohan Singh and Foreign Ministers Natwar Singh and Pranab Mukherjee.

A good personal connection between new RAW Chief Hermis Tharakan and Baburam Bhattarai[27] facilitated better understanding between the Maoists and the RAW, which kept in regular contact with the Maoist leadership. Tharakan was politically progressive and viewed Nepal's Maoists as leading a genuine struggle for Nepal's socioeconomic transformation. By contrast, he had a rather low opinion of the integrity of other Nepali mainstream party leaders. However, the Maoists' attempts to establish direct contacts with senior foreign ministry officials succeeded only in July 2005.[28]

The Indian policy establishment clearly held two views of the Maoists. Those who knew Nepal well were in favor of testing the Maoists on their promise of democratic mainstreaming, not least because of the hope that it would facilitate solutions to the Naxalites and counter the consolidation of leftist extremist groups in the larger South Asian region. Bringing the Maoists into the democratic fold would also force King Gyanendra back on the path of constitutionalism. This view was held by the Ministry of External Affairs and RAW, and its active proponents were the RAW Chief Tharakan and the Foreign Secretary Shyam Saran. It has been noted earlier that the Ministry of External Affairs had ascertained that there were no operational links between the Nepal Maoists and Indian Naxalite insurgents. Political activists, such as the members of the Nepal Democratic Solidarity Group, and individuals in

---

[26] Contrary to reports at the time that the meeting was organized by intelligence agencies, it was, in fact, brought about by me, as Prakash Karat, Bhattarai, and I knew each other from our time at JNU. Prakash Karat was a student in my center, and Bhattarai used to visit me frequently when he was pursuing research work for his Ph.D. in the Center of Regional Development Studies in the School of Social Sciences.

[27] Baburam Bhattarai spent time studying in Kerala, Hermis Tharakan's home state, while Tharakan spent time working in Nepal.

[28] I also enabled this contact. It was during my third meeting with Foreign Secretary Mr. Shyam Saran on this subject that he finally agreed to meet the Maoist leaders. Later, the logistics of this meeting were perhaps worked out by RAW.

the media and academic circles also wanted to see the Maoists join the democratic mainstream.

The other view was hostile to the Maoists; it was strongly influenced by the members of the princely order and the defense and internal security establishments. The national security advisor to the prime minister, M.K. Narayanan, was a strong proponent of this line. The intelligence agencies, especially the IB, which had a deeply rooted anticommunist outlook, remained suspicious of the Maoists' long-term intentions. India's armed forces, particularly the army, which had a longstanding relationship with the RNA, detested the Maoists. Because of their continuing matrimonial relations with the royal family, the members of India's old princely households felt sympathetic and committed to the Nepali monarchy. All these components of the Indian establishment were also sensitive to the position of the West, which did not approve of Maoist ideology and their violent methods.

In an effort to bridge these differing views, it was decided to nudge the Maoists into the political mainstream but under the dominance of the SPA, as part of an overall strategy of building pressure on the king. There were strong reservations against formally according political legitimacy to the Maoists. Those who were skeptical of paving the Maoists' way into multiparty democracy were mollified by intelligence assessments concluding that they enjoyed little popular support in Nepal because of their oppressive acts against the Nepalis in rural areas. It was thought – falsely as it later turned out – that, once the Maoists competed in democratic elections, they would be marginalized. Moreover, India had not yet committed itself to a republican Nepal and looked forward to the institution of the monarchy, without King Gyanendra if necessary, playing an important role even in a new and democratic Nepal.

The continuing reservations in India and among SPA members about both the Maoists and their republican agenda became clear in the negotiations for the November 2005 12-Point Understanding. Allegations, propagated at the time by the palace, that Delhi presented the SPA and the Maoists with a final draft of the Understanding and made them sign on the dotted lines are false. Rather, the document emerged from the continuous parlays between the SPA and the Maoists, along the way informally consulting trusted interlocutors and officials in India.[29] However, Delhi, using informal channels, managed to influence the 12-Point Understanding on three critical aspects. One was that the document was not called an "agreement" but only an "understanding," implying that there was no binding commitment on either side. Second, even as an "understanding," it was not jointly signed or announced at one place by the SPA and Maoist leaders. As such, the Maoists were still treated as an "outsider" group and were denied the political legitimacy and limelight they were frantically seeking. The only concession made to them was the simultaneous

---

[29] The 12-point draft was shown to me on several occasions by members of the negotiating teams of the SPA and the Maoists.

announcement of the 12-Point Understanding by the Maoists and the SPA from their separate headquarters on November 25, 2005.[30] Third, the word "republic" was completely avoided in the document. The Maoists had to be satisfied with phrases like "end of the autocratic monarchy" and ensuring "full democracy." The thrust was on taming the monarchy, not abolishing it. The Maoists and the SPA agreed on an elected Constituent Assembly, but differed on how to bring it about. Whereas the SPA wanted to simply see a restoration of the 2002 parliament, the Maoists wanted the Constituent Assembly to be established through a "national political conference" of all the "agitating democratic forces." India sided with the SPA in providing full support to the *Jana Andolan II*.

However, Delhi's continued support for the monarchy even in the face of a popular antimonarchy uprising became evident when it sent Dr. Karan Singh, a scion of the Indian feudal order, to Nepal as a special envoy to bring an end to the *Jana Andolan II*. Dr. Singh, a member of the Indian Princely Order of Kashmir and a relative of Nepal's royal family, met all key political leaders except the Maoists in an effort to persuade the king to cede his authority. It is widely believed that Dr. Singh assured King Gyanendra that, in return, India would not allow the king to be disgraced or the institution of the monarchy to be abolished. A crucial element in Delhi's efforts to get the king to yield power was the lengthy talk between then-Foreign Secretary Shyam Saran, who had accompanied Singh, and the RNA Chief General Pyar Jung Thapa. In a tense and explosive situation, General Thapa had orders to shoot at protesters if they breached the special security zone. After 90-minute discussion, General Thapa was persuaded to plead with the king that there was no military solution to either the *Jana Andolan II* or the Maoist insurgency. This left the king with no other option but to give in.

On April 21, 2006, the king yielded to Delhi's demands and issued a proclamation announcing his intention to install a prime minister from the mainstream parties. However, both the Maoists and the SPA were unimpressed and continued their agitation; they rebuffed high-level efforts by India to accept the king's proclamation.[31] By supporting the king's proclamation, India's credibility as a champion of democracy in Nepal suffered a serious dent.[32] In an effort to limit the damage to India's reputation, India's Foreign Secretary Shyam Saran summoned a press conference on April 22, 2006, in which he presented Delhi as the leading force in the restoration of democracy in Nepal.

India then leaned heavily on the king to issue a second proclamation on April 24, which was virtually dictated by G. P. Koirala in consultation with other SPA

---

[30] Having failed to persuade G. P. Koirala to sign the 12-Point Understanding together with the Maoist leader Prachanda, this was proposed as the best way out.

[31] With the prime minister on a European visit, it was then-Defense Minister Pranab Mukherjee who pleaded via telephone with key political actors of the SPA to accept the king's proclamation.

[32] There were rumors afloat in Kathmandu that some Pakistani-inspired text messages were going round to provoke Nepali agitators against an India-brokered deal.

members and the Indian Embassy. This proclamation reinstated the Nepali parliament's House of Representatives, which had been dissolved on May 22, 2002 so
as to "resolve the ongoing violent conflict... according to the road map of Seven
Party Alliance." The proclamation also referred to the "sovereignty inherent in the
people of Nepal" and expressed "condolences to all those who lost their lives in the
peoples' movement." The Maoists accepted the second proclamation, although with
reservations. Thus the *Jana Andolan II* came to an end. Given that the proclamation
was born out of the culmination of a vague consensus whose various key players
still maintained their differences, the road ahead was full of challenges that started
unfolding as soon as G. P. Koirala took charge as interim prime minister.

SUMMING UP

The Maoists came "down from the hills" to join the democratic mainstream because,
in their own assessment, they were unable to take over the Nepali state militarily
and hold it under the prevailing national, regional, and international conditions.
However, the Maoists have not given up their socioeconomic agenda of trans-
forming Nepal from a feudal to a modern, inclusive, and egalitarian society. It
is still being debated whether they have fully committed themselves to peaceful
and democratic politics; a section of the Maoist leadership still believes that their
goals could be achieved through the use of force. However, many of their internal
discourses and public pronouncements at the highest levels of leadership reiterate the futility of such methods again and again, although through radical Marxist
jargon.

The mainstream political parties of Nepal and the international community, particularly India, joined the Maoists in the *Jana Andolan II* in pursuit of their respective
objectives in response to King Gyanendra's autocratic moves. They supported the
Maoist agenda only half-heartedly and tactically, if at all, and only to force themselves back into the power structure. It is doubtful whether the mainstream political
parties realize the depth to which the Maoist agenda of Nepal's socioeconomic transformation has penetrated the psyche of ordinary Nepali people. India, which played
a key role in bringing the Maoists and the mainstream parties together during the
Jana Andolan II, became disenchanted with the Maoists during their nine months
in power from August 2008 to May 2009 on issues of India–Nepal bilateral relations
and the Maoists' political conduct. Since then there has been a concerted effort
by the mainstream parties and sections of the international community, especially
India, to keep the Maoists politically marginalized in order to weaken them in the
long run. The worst casualty of this development has been Nepal's peace process
and its task of establishing a new democratic constitution.

The responsibility of mainstreaming the Maoists into a democratic process does
not exclusively lie with the Maoists. The mainstream political parties and the

international community have to do their share to help them in this process. The Maoists can be neither kept out of power nor can the thrust of their agenda be ignored. As long as that effort continues, the vision of a new Nepal unleashed by the *Jana Andolan II* will remain a mirage, and the domestic peace and stability in Nepal will continue to hang in a precarious balance.

13

A Nepali Perspective on International Involvement in Nepal

Prashant Jha

Since the inception of the peace process in Nepal, the involvement of international actors has had both enormously constructive and fairly destructive political conse-quences. At key moments, the role of "outsiders" has enabled political consensus, aided the peace process, and pushed Nepal toward the process of creating a stable, democratic, and just state. Yet there have been other moments when international involvement – either intentionally or unintentionally, directly or indirectly – has led to greater political polarization and contributed to an unstable impasse.

This chapter recognizes that the international community in Nepal constitutes a heterogeneous category. Although the United Kingdom and other European donors have paid many of the bills to make the peace process viable, this chapter confines itself to assessing the political role and actions of India (the key regional actor), the United Nations Mission in Nepal (the lead international organization), China (the other neighbor), and the United States (the most powerful player globally). The chapter thereby broadly covers the period between the 12-Point Understanding signed by the Maoists and parties in November 2005 to May 2010 when the tenure of the Constituent Assembly was extended by a year.

In discussing the roles of these actors, the chapter primarily focuses on the role of India at key moments since 2005. Direct and subtle shifts in Indian policy have had deep implications for the political transition in Nepal, and Delhi's support is widely seen as indispensable for any political party to survive in the formal power structure. India also provokes the most respect, awe, fear, criticism, and anger among key politicians.

The United Nations Mission in Nepal (UNMIN) has had a legitimate but limited mandate with regard to the peace process and its share of controversies. China's engagement in Nepal has increased since 2007, sparking Indian concerns. The U.S. stance has evolved from a rabidly anti-Maoist posture and deep skepticism about the peace process to a more restrained and supportive attitude.

A unified Nepali perspective on the role of international actors is obviously a fiction. Ultranationalist and monarchist forces in Nepal, who lost out after the change in 2006, have been critical of the peace process and its international supporters. The political parties often take an instrumentalist view, seeing international actors as helpful or unhelpful depending on circumstances and their partisan interests. Describing and analyzing the role of the international actors, this chapter alludes to these multiple domestic positions, while locating itself in a perspective that views the peace process as a remarkable, although fragile, achievement.

INDIA'S CENTRALITY

If there is one point on which most domestic politicians agree, it is the centrality of India to developments in Nepal.

One has to sample some of the rhetoric to get a sense of how India is held responsible for all that happens in Nepali politics. Monarchists, sections of the military, and established parliamentary parties claim that Delhi provided the Maoists with a safe haven during the war, got them to Kathmandu, destroyed the monarchy, and effected regime change. Others praise India for helping end the war. Meanwhile, in numerous formal party documents the Maoists have referred to India as an "expansionist force" that backs local "reactionaries, feudals, and comprador bourgeoisie." Maoist Chairman Pushpa Kamal Dahal "Prachanda," when resigning from office in May 2009, claimed he did not accept the diktats of "foreign forces," hinting at New Delhi's hand behind the political developments. During the peak of the Madhesi crisis, Former Prime Minister Girija Prasad Koirala said, "If India wants, the Terai problem can be solved immediately." For their part, the Madhesi leaders have criticized India for "only using [the] Madhes as a pawn" to serve its larger objectives in Kathmandu politics.

Is there such a shocking lack of agency among domestic actors? Or is this merely political sloganeering using India as a convenient scapegoat to stoke "nationalism" and enhance their own legitimacy? Or are there many Indias when it comes to Nepal and these seemingly contradictory acts have different backers within the broad establishment?

Maoists and the Peace Process

This section briefly examines India's role in five processes: (1) bringing the Maoists down from the hills and "facilitating" the 12-Point Understanding, (2) its response to the April 2006 movement, (3) its support for Constituent Assembly elections and its attitude and actions after the surprising election results, (4) India's growing estrangement from the Maoists during their stint in power, and (5) the crisis over the army chief's dismissal in 2009 and India's subsequent strong support to the Madhav

Nepal government given to force the Maoists to undergo a "course correction." On that basis, this section highlights some patterns in India's motivations and strategy vis-à-vis Nepali national politics, as well as the perception of diverse Nepali actors.

12-Point Understanding

For years, India had maintained a "twin pillar" policy toward Nepal, supporting both the constitutional monarchy and multiparty democracy. However, its dual policy suffered a jolt with the royal takeover on February 1, 2005, when then-King Gyanendra assumed absolute power against India's wishes, pitting the two pillars against each other. New Delhi – in particular, then-Foreign Secretary Shyam Saran; Chief of the External Intelligence Agency, Research and Analysis Wing (RAW) P. K. Hermis Tharakan; and Indian envoy to Nepal, Shiv Shanker Mukherjee – instinctively recognized that the monarch's move was not sustainable. It was also a time when Saran had begun articulating India's vision of a "peaceful periphery" and how a stable neighborhood was essential for India to emerge as a global power.[1] Saran could see that the king's action would only push Nepal further into conflict and instability. Even though communication lines in Nepal were shut off, it was clear that the entire spectrum of democratic opinion in the country was against the move.

Delhi's reaction to the royal coup was swift, calling it a "setback"[2] and postponing the South-Asian Association for Regional Cooperation (SAARC) summit scheduled for February 6–7 in Dhaka to send a signal to the king that he would not be awarded international legitimacy. India also suspended arms supplies to the Nepalese Army (NA). In addition, several Indian political parties, led by the left, came together to form the Nepal Democracy Solidarity Committee.

At the same time, India continued its efforts to convince the king of the need for a course correction, trying to foster a partnership between the monarchy and the political parties. However, the disjunction between the king's private assurances to India that he would restore political freedoms, while he continued to repress political parties back home, strengthened those in Delhi who felt that Gyanendra was unreliable. Against this background, India placed increasing emphasis on encouraging the warring parliamentary parties to resolve their differences and form an alliance. As an official put it, "We told them the royal takeover was the consequence of their infighting and if they continued with the same politics, they would lose their relevance."[3] In addition to providing political support, multiple sources confirm that India also

---

[1] See Saran, "India and Its Neighbours," speech at IIC, Delhi, http://www.indianembassy.org/Speeches/ 1.htm.

[2] Government of India, "Statement on Developments in Nepal," February 1 2005, http://meaindia.nic. in/pressrelease/2005/02/01pro1.htm, and Media Briefing by Foreign Secretary Saran on February 2, 2005.

[3] Interview, senior Indian official, New Delhi, March 2009.

extended financial support to these parties' leaders for organizational purposes and to prepare for a movement.

According to Indian intelligence officials, India's engagement with the Maoists had deepened back in 2002–3 and then intensified after the king's move. In the middle of 2005, Maoist leaders Dr Baburam Bhattarai and Krishna Bahadur Mahara met with most mainstream Nepali politicians in Delhi who were either staying in or visiting there. Prachanda himself met Nepali Congress President Girija Prasad Koirala in May 2005 in Delhi.[4] Bhattarai also met Indian politicians to assure them that the Maoists were committed to a democratic path and were not against India.

Even at that point, in the summer of 2005, it was not a certainty that India would back a rapprochement between the parties and Maoists. Several powerful constituencies in Delhi – the Indian Army, the old princely rulers, the Hindu right, and sections of the security establishment – supported the royal takeover.[5] However, as the monarch's domestic base eroded, and as his opponents started to rally together, the Indian political establishment recognized that the status quo was not a workable option. Many see the Dhaka SAARC summit in November 2005 as a breaking point; there Gyanendra backed China's inclusion as an observer and was seen as trying to block Afghanistan's entry into the grouping, conveying to India that he could not be relied on to support its broader strategic interests.[6]

This set of factors paved the way for the 12-Point Understanding, in which the Maoists and political parties pledged to establish "absolute democracy by ending autocratic monarchy" and "permanent peace in the country through constituent assembly elections." The Maoists in turn agreed to abide by "democratic norms." The document was signed in New Delhi by top political leaders, and Indian officials are understood to have seen the draft of the text.[7] Nepali actors saw India as a guarantor of the agreement. India's presence gave the parties the confidence that they had an ally against Maoist adventurism and gave the Maoists much needed international recognition as a legitimate stakeholder in the polity.[8]

The most authoritative interpretation and acceptance of India's involvement came later, in January 2009. Pranab Mukherjee, who served as India's external affairs minister until May 2009, told an interviewer, "We persuaded . . . the Maoists in Nepal, that they give up violence and participate in mainstream national polit-ical activities. They agreed, listened to our advice, and now in collaboration

---

4 For details, see Whitfield, "Masala Peacemaking in Nepal," http://www.cic.nyu.edu/staff/Staff%20Docs/Teresa%20Whitfield,%20Masala%20peacemaking%20in%20Nepal,%2010_%202008.pdf.
5 See Dixit, 'Flip-flop,' *Nepali Times*, http://www.nepalitimes.com.np/issue/2005/05/20/Fromthe NepaliPress/317.
6 Interview, senior Indian officials, New Delhi, March 2009.
7 For details of the Indian role in the 12-Point Understanding, see Chapter 12 by S. D. Muni.
8 For details, see ICG report, "Nepal's New Alliance: The Mainstream Parties and the Maoists," November 28, 2005; and Whitfield, "Masala Peacemaking."

with other democratic parties they formed the government, they are leading the government."[9]

Within Nepal, the reaction to the 12-Point Understanding was largely euphoric, but coupled with caution and opposition from other quarters. Political party activists, media, and civil society – who had all opposed the royal regime – largely welcomed the pact and saw it as a sign that the political conflict would finally end. Most saw India's role as constructive, as being on the side of democracy and peace.[10] In contrast, royal ministers and others sympathetic to the monarchy pounced on it as a grand Indian plot to weaken the Nepali state and to destroy the symbol of nationalism that, in defying Delhi's policy advice, had stood up against the powerful southern neighbor.[11]

From People's Movement to the Peace Process
April 2006 marked a decisive turn in Nepal's political evolution. Delhi's response to the People's Movement was symptomatic of how the Indian establishment has cautious instincts, hesitates to change course, and then tries to catch up with events – in the process losing plenty of hard-earned goodwill.

In the Indian assessment, the king's intransigence, fused with an increasingly radical, violent, and out-of-control mass of protestors ready to storm the palace, could lead to a bloody outcome – the consequences of which would be difficult to manage politically and would perhaps allow the Maoists to claim an absolute victory. Delhi and by extension the Indian embassy in Kathmandu wished to avoid this scenario at all costs, although local diplomats recognized the on-the-ground sentiment that it might be too late for a compromise that included the king.[12]

Delhi continued to pressure the palace to revoke its royal coup. It sent senior Congress leader and a distant relative of Gyanendra, Karan Singh, as a special envoy to persuade the monarch. The move was seen with suspicion within Nepal as a ploy to save the monarchy, although Indian officials insisted they chose Singh because they felt that "Gyanendra would listen only to someone who was of royal blood like him."[13] This sounded like empty rhetoric when the king's first announcement

---

[9] For details, see "Interview: Pranab Mukherjee," *Al Jazeera*, http://english.aljazeera.net/news/asia/2009/01/20091271817658725.html.

[10] See "On the Move," *Nepali Times*, http://www.nepalitimes.com.np/issue/2005/12/02/Headline/9236; C. K. Lal, "Precursors to Peace," http://www.nepalitimes.com.np/issue/2005/12/02/StateOfTheState/9238; "12 Point Understanding Installs New Hope: Dr Panday," http://www.nepalnews.com.np/archive/2005/nov/nov26/news02.php; "Rights Groups Welcome Parties-Maoist Understanding," http://www.nepalnews.com.np/archive/2005/nov/nov25/news14.php; "Thousands Take Part in UML Rally," http://www.nepalnews.com.np/archive/2005/nov/nov25/news17.php; and ICG, "Nepal's New Alliance."

[11] See "Foreigners behind Party-Maoist Understanding: Dhakal," *Nepal News*, http://www.nepalnews.com.np/archive/2005/nov/nov23/news14.php.

[12] Interviews, Indian officials, New Delhi and Kathmandu, March 2009.

[13] Interviews, Indian officials, New Delhi and Kathmandu, March, 2009.

on April 21 – asking the Seven Party Alliance to nominate a prime minister – was welcomed by India, even though it fell far short of the demands of the parties, Maoists, and protestors. The Nepali political forces were quick to dismiss the announcement, and suddenly India was in danger of squandering all the goodwill it had earned with Nepali democratic forces and of being on the wrong side of history.

In response Delhi went into damage-control mode. Key decision makers spoke to Nepali leaders and realized that nothing less than the reinstatement of parliament would satisfy popular sentiment. On April 22, Shyam Saran briefed the press, clarifying that India's welcome of the king's first proclamation did not indicate its support for monarchy and that the final decision rested with the Nepali people.[14]

Over the next two days, multiple levels of private negotiations between Indian and Nepali actors took place. India asked the Royal Nepalese Army (RNA) to restrain the king, and the chief of army staff reportedly told the palace that the armed forces might not be able to control the crowd.[15] The palace was also talking to NC leader Girija Prasad Koirala and UML leader Madhav Kumar Nepal about the draft of a new proclamation, while the parties kept an open dialogue with the Maoists. On April 24, the king officially recognized that sovereignty lay with the people and accepted the roadmap of the parties.

In the last stages of the movement, Indian diplomacy came across as confused and incoherent. The actions of Special Envoy Karan Singh became a metaphor for Delhi's lack of grasp of the reality on the ground. Yet to be fair, Delhi's recovery was swift, and Saran's briefing marked India's first public departure from its twin pillar policy, moving toward acceptance of a possibly republican Nepal. In addition, after parliament was reinstated and Maoists emerged above ground, India continued to support the peace process and pushed for speedy elections.

Elections, Before and After

The period after the People's Movement was characterized by complex negotiations over the peace accord; the drafting of the interim constitution; the formation of the interim parliament, interim government, and the electoral system; and the development of terms under which polls to the Constituent Assembly would take place.

India was involved in important aspects of these negotiations. It was keen to detach the Maoist army from the party structure and keep the forces in cantonments. However, it only reluctantly agreed to the idea that there could be "possible integration" of these combatants into the state's security forces, especially the RNA. At most, the Indian position argued for token integration of a few thousand Maoist fighters into the army at low levels.

---

[14] See "Press Briefing by Shyam Saran on Nepal," April 22, 2006, http://www.meaindia.nic.in.
[15] See Varadarajan, "Nepal Army Chief Helped Convince Gyanendra," *The Hindu*, April 27, 2006, http://svaradarajan.blogspot.com/2006/04/nepal-army-chief-helped-convince.html.

However, India's core concern through 2007–8 was to push for elections, and it grew increasingly nervous when polls were postponed twice in the process. The initial June 2007 date for the elections was missed because of a lack of technical preparations. Elections could not be held in November 2007 either, after the Maoists walked out of the interim government and demanded the declaration of a republic and a full proportional representation system as preconditions for their return.

India felt that elections were the best way to "lock" the Maoists into mainstream democratic politics. Some other international actors, especially UNMIN, empha-sized the need to make progress on other aspects of the peace process – especially the fate of the Maoist fighters – before holding the elections. These concerns were brushed aside. Delhi and a large section of the non-Maoist Nepali political class felt that elections would alter the balance of power, assuming that the Maoists would rank a distant third. India's National Security Advisor M. K. Narayanan even went on record before the polls to state his preference for the Nepali Congress. After the NC would win the elections, the calculation was that the future of the Maoist army and the constitution could be written on terms favorable to the "democratic forces."

Of course, the election results in April 2008 altered everything. The Maoists emerged as the single largest party in the Constituent Assembly by a huge margin, winning more seats than the NC and the UML combined. However, after the results trickled in, India engaged in some deft diplomacy. They immediately reached out to the Maoists, dismissing suggestions that Delhi would try to subvert the results and cobble together an anti-Maoist alliance. India also insisted that it had no preferred electoral outcome and made it clear privately that the electoral mandate dictated a Maoist-led government.[16] Those in Delhi directly responsible for facilitating the Maoist entry into mainstream politics publicly argued that this was the best outcome India could have hoped for – defending themselves against critics who accused them of "losing Nepal."[17]

An immediate consequent of the elections was the controversy over who would be the republic's first president. This episode is of particular interest because it revealed India's changed calculations in the new context, how India ended up enmeshed in all key crucial Nepali processes, how this role largely remained opaque and gave rise to multiple and conflicting perceptions, and how Delhi does not necessarily have its way all the time.

In bestowing on the Maoists the status of legitimate political actors, Girija Prasad Koirala expected that they would support him for his role, and thus he demanded the presidential post for himself. Some Nepali Congress leaders suggested that this was in fact agreed on before the elections, although the Maoists denied the existence of

[16] At the end of April, India invited senior Maoist leader C. P. Gajurel and Minister Hisila Yami to a prescheduled Nepal–India conference in Patna after the results became public. In his opening remarks at the conference, Saran stated that India had no preferred outcome.

[17] See Tharakan, "Best of All Certainties," *Indian Express*, April 22, 2008, http://www.indianexpress.com/news/best-of-all-uncertainties/299851/o.

any such deal. When the issue of who would be president emerged, Indian officials told Nepali observers that they would not be taking sides. As a diplomat put it in July 2008, "If we back [Koirala], the Maoists will be angry with us. And we don't want to add to the mistrust so soon after their election victory – we know we have to do business with them. If we oppose [Koirala], he will be angry with us and feel that we have dumped him. So we are staying out of this."[18] However, by not backing Koirala explicitly, the perception that India did not want Koirala as president gained ground.

Yet India's position appeared to have changed in the immediate run-up to the election of the president by the Constituent Assembly in July 2008. Sections of the Indian establishment took the view that having Koirala as president was the only way to take the peace process forward smoothly – both as its guarantor of the peace process and to balance Maoist power, not least as it was widely understood that the president, as the king's successor as head of state, would be the supreme commander of the armed forces.[19] However, by then, Maoists had taken a firm decision not to back Koirala or even a UML candidate, and a contest had become inevitable between the Maoist candidate Ram Raja Prasad Singh and the last minute NC-UML candidate,[20] Dr. Ram Baran Yadav. Dr. Yadav won the elections, becoming the country's first president, but the politics of consensus that had marked the first two years of the peace process had collapsed.

After the presidential elections, key Nepali actors were left harboring a sense of resentment against India. Koirala felt that India's intervention on his behalf was too little, too late, whereas the Maoists characterized Delhi's last-minute support for Koirala as a stab in the back. Although India's precise role during those polarizing days remains murky, in the battle of perceptions, India was once again seen to be trying to shape political outcomes.

Steady Estrangement

After Prachanda was sworn in as prime minister in August 2008, his first act in office was a visit to Beijing to witness the closing ceremony of the Olympics, breaking a tradition under which the Nepali prime minister would pay the first bilateral visit to New Delhi. Although Prachanda insisted that the Beijing visit was merely a result of

---

[18] Interview, Indian diplomat, Kathmandu, May 2008. Senior NC leaders, who were involved in lobbying for Koirala's election as president, confirmed this fact. Their visits to New Delhi had little success. Interview, senior NC leader, Kathmandu, July 2008.

[19] When Maoists were later asked about their contacts with Indian officials on the presidential question, Prachanda went on record to say that India wanted the Maoists to back Koirala. See "We Have Lost the Moral Ground to Stake a Claim to Form a New Government: Prachanda," *Spotlight, Nepal News*, http://www.nepalnews.com.np/contents/2008/englishweekly/spotlight/jul/jul25/interview.php; and Chandrashekharan, "Nepal: Presidential Elections, More Confusion," South Asia Analysis Group, http://www.southasiaanalysis.org/%5Cnotes5%5Cnote460.html.

[20] Later also backed by the Madhesi Janadhikar Forum (MJF).

special circumstances and that his first political visit would be to India,[21] this episode strengthened the hard-liners within the Indian establishment who had been warning that a Maoist-led government would diminish India's strategic space in Nepal and strengthen China's influence.

A warm reception for Prachanda in India the following month – by political leaders across the spectrum as well as the bureaucratic establishment, which termed him a statesman in private briefings – gave rise to the impression that New Delhi and the Maoists had put aside any differences. However, the China factor, as is elaborated in a later section, was going to continue to disturb the relationship.

If the Maoist attempt at refashioning its relationship with China was one reason for Indian suspicions, domestic policies and actions of the Maoists inside Nepal were another. The Maoists attempted to break an age-old tradition of having priests from south India serve at the Pashupati temple in Kathmandu, and they appointed Nepali priests instead. This led to a political backlash from religious conservatives both in India and Nepal. In addition, the Maoist decision to raise taxes, including an education tax imposed on private schools, alienated an influential class in Kathmandu. Sporadic attacks on the media strengthened the anti-Maoist undertone that characterized the urban media's projection of the former rebels and sowed further doubts about their democratic credentials. In addition, the rising tensions between the Maoists and the Nepalese Army was seen by many politically powerful constituencies not as an issue of military defiance of civilian authority, but as a Maoist attempt to cripple the last institution capable of standing up to them.[22]

This constituency – businessmen, media owners, religious leadership, leaders from other political parties, senior generals, and others – had begun lobbying with the Indian establishment about the dangers of the Maoist government and the need to think of an alternative.

May 2009 Crisis and After

The breaking point in India–Maoist relations was the Maoist government's attempt to dismiss the then-army chief, General Rookmangud Katawal, in May 2009.

After the Maoists assumed control of the government, the tension between them and the Nepalese Army (NA) steadily increased. The Maoist leadership argued that Katawal had repeatedly been making political statements and that he was a stumbling block in advancing the process of integrating Maoist fighters into the NA. The defense minister, an influential Maoist leader, shared an extremely uneasy relationship with the army chief, and there were instances of the government and NA adopting different positions. For example, the NA began recruiting soldiers to its

---

[21] See "My First Political Visit Will Be to India: Prachanda," http://www.expressindia.com/latest-news/My-first-political-visit-will-be-to-India-says-Prachanda/354060/.

[22] For a Maoist record in government and tensions with powerful constituencies, see ICG report, "Nepal's Future: In Whose Hands," August 13, 2009.

ranks, defying the government's stance that this was a violation of the peace accord. In turn, the government did not extend the tenure of eight brigadier generals, ignoring the NA's recommendation. Both these cases went to the Supreme Court. The army chief had also presented a paper to the Constituent Assembly that included proposals at odds with the general political consensus on issues like secularism. Against this backdrop, the government asked Katawal for a clarification of his repeated "defiance of civilian authority" as precursor to his dismissal.

A large section of the non-Maoist political class, as well as India, saw the Maoist move to sack Katawal as an attempt to take over the state. They alleged that the Maoist game plan was to appoint a pliant army chief who would support bulk integration of their combatants, in the process changing the character and structure of the NA and thereby neutralizing it.

Indian officials insist that, during Prachanda's visit to India, one of the clear red-lines conveyed to him was not to touch the Nepalese Army. India had assured the NA – with which its own army shared fraternal links – that its structure, interests, and privileges would be safeguarded. This was widely understood to be the quid pro quo for the NA's support to the peace process. Seeing the Nepalese Army as the final bulwark against the Maoists, Delhi decided the risks of allowing the Maoists to take over the NA were too high and that it had to invest its political and diplomatic capital to prevent such a scenario.[23]

In the most public of its interventions since the peace process began, the Indian establishment went into overdrive. In meeting after meeting, Indian Ambassador Rakesh Sood warned Prachanda of the consequences of going ahead with the general's dismissal. Indian diplomats lobbied the entire non-Maoist political class – most of whom were suspicious of Maoist intentions in any case – to join forces in defiance of Prachanda's impending move.

Given the wider geopolitical context and the rising opposition from Nepali allies, it became clear that Katawal's dismissal would come at too high a cost to the peace process. Why did the Maoists take what even at the time was evident to be a reckless risk? The most convincing explanation is that by that time Prachanda had come under pressure from the party's hard-liners, who had been increasingly disillusioned with the party's performance and yearned for reconfirmation of their "revolutionary" credentials by confronting the army chief and defying India. Prachanda appeared to have felt that to go through with the dismissal was the best way to preserve his position within the party and maintain its united framework.

When the Maoist-led government – despite a walkout by the UML and notes of dissent by other parties – decided to sack the army chief on the morning of May 3, the Indian establishment acted immediately to block the implementation of the decision. They did so by encouraging the UML to withdraw support from the government and by passing on a message to the president – whom Ambassador

23 Interview, Indian officials, Delhi and Kathmandu, April–July 2009.

Sood had met a few days earlier – that he should ask the army chief to stay in office. Prachanda resigned the next day, indirectly blaming India for the collapse of the government. The extent of India's involvement became even more apparent in the formation of a successor government when India used its influence among various parties to back UML leader Madhav Kumar Nepal as prime minister.[24]

Throughout 2009–10, India played a crucial role in keeping the Madhav Nepal government intact. This was no mean achievement given the inherent fragility of the ruling alliance, led by a prime minister who had lost in two constituencies in the 2008 elections. Similarly, most ministers in the government were not members of the parliament and belonged to the discredited old guard of the 1990s. Lastly, there were enormous contradictions between and within the 22 parties constituting the anti-Maoist grouping that was holding Madhav Nepal's alliance afloat. India's leverage with domestic actors and its warnings that giving in to the Maoists would result in an authoritarian communist regime did much to keep the government together.

Delhi insisted that the Maoists could not be allowed to return to power unless they reformed. This meant that the Maoists would have to give up control over their army, with a token integration of some fighters into the security forces while the rest would be rehabilitated, and renounce violence. They would also have to disband their militant youth wing, the Young Communist League. The Maoists would further be expected to behave like a responsible opposition and not obstruct parliament, stop all forms of "anti-India" rhetoric that they frequently used, and end any attempts to change the "geo-political balance" of South Asia.[25] These demands have been echoed by other Nepali parties since then. Both India and non-Maoist parties maintain that only if the Maoists realize that fundamental reforms are a necessary precondition for returning to power will they have an incentive to develop into a "reliable" and "democratic" party of the political mainstream.

The reaction to India's involvement within Nepal has been varied. The Maoists have publicly blamed India's intransigence for the domestic political impasse. Maoist leaders privately say that what India means when it issues calls for them to reform is to become like the other parties, pliant to Delhi. Toward the end of 2009, Prachanda launched a campaign for "national independence," insisting that the unequal bilateral relationship between the two countries,[26] the trade deficit, border disputes, and India's engagement in Nepali politics had to be adapted to the "new realities." As part of the campaign Maoists organized visits to disputed border areas and blocked Indian

---

[24] India's role in this period has been reconstructed through detailed interviews with leaders of different political parties and Indian officials both in New Delhi and Kathmandu.
[25] Interview with an Indian official, June 2009.
[26] Reflected in the 1950 Indo-Nepal Treaty of Peace and Friendship, which allows for free movement of people and goods between the two nations and creates a close collaboration on matters of defense and foreign affairs. Critics charge, however, that Nepal cedes much of its sovereignty under the treaty.

hydropower companies from operating smoothly, and Prachanda visited China to seek support. All this only served to further harden positions in Delhi.

Meanwhile, leaders of non-Maoist political parties rejected accusations that they were acting on India's orders. They said that it was not any external pressure, but the widespread distrust of the Maoists within Nepal, that held the 22 ideologically diverse parties together. After all, they argued that India, throughout the peace process, had repeatedly extended support to the Maoists, who tended to selectively (and hypocritically) complain about Indian intervention only when it ran counter to their interests.

Broad Patterns

Delhi's engagement with the Maoists and its perception of the peace process, recounted here through specific incidents, reveal certain distinct patterns.

For one, India does not act in a vacuum. As we have seen during the April 2006 People's Movement, when the Nepali people and parties speak with one voice or when there is a political consensus within Nepal, there is very little space for India to act in ways that runs counter to this consensus. By contrast, when politics within the country is fragmented, Indian involvement can be decisive in tilting the domestic balance of power. No developments in Nepal, however, are solely externally driven, as some Nepali actors both on the far right and far left of the political spectrum tend to suggest.

Two, in a fragmented political environment, there will always be some sector of the political landscape criticizing India, no matter what it does or does not do. The big question for Indian policy makers always is whether an issue is important enough to invest political capital in, at the cost of generating resentment.

Three, India has had two objectives during Nepal's political transition, which have often clashed with each other. It wanted the Maoists to enter mainstream politics, and it supported various facets of the peace process to make this happen – from opening up to a role for the UN, pressing for and assisting elections, jettisoning the monarchy, and providing logistical and financial support for specific aspects of the process. At the same time, it has wanted to strengthen the middle ground of Nepali politics, supporting the non-Maoist parties and preventing the center from turning too far to the left. In this quest, India initially favored a monarchy–party pact in April 2006, supported Madhesi groups (to be explained later), endorsed the Nepali Congress before the elections, and supported the NA and president in the Katawal crisis. These often conflicting objectives have contributed to a lack of clarity in Delhi's Nepal policy, with key policy makers getting cold feet about the peace process they had helped initiate. The process has had the (from the Indian perspective, unintended) consequence of further legitimizing the Maoists and helping them emerge as the strongest political force in Nepal.

The Indian-supported peace process has also set in motion developments that may fundamentally alter both the political landscape (dominated by Maoists) and the Nepali state (heading toward an institutionalized democracy with a federal struc-ture). In this scenario, established parties will be increasingly challenged by newer ethnic and regional forces that will be less inclined to seek as close relationships with Indian political elites as the established parties did in the past. India has to make a difficult choice – whether it is willing to live with what may be a Maoist-dominated government and a different kind of Nepali state or whether the risks of that scenario are too high and it would rather try to block these changes, even at the cost of instability and conflict.

For now India has adopted a strategy toward the Maoists that it has used with some success toward its own militant groups in Kashmir and the Northeast; namely, to engage, coerce, co-opt, and try to divide the leadership without making any concessions, while working toward frustrating, weakening, and isolating the cadres. At no point has Delhi stopped engaging with the Maoists since the peace process began, even when their relations hit ever new lows. At the same time, India has been steadfast in its determination not to allow Maoists back into government until certain conditions are met. India has carefully tried to stoke the already existing divisions between the top political leaders, and the Maoists have been pushed to a corner where they can neither go back to war nor come back to power. In the broader context, this means that Nepal remains stuck in a political stalemate, but as long as this situation does not cross the threshold of controlled instability, India is not too worried.

IN THE TERAI

In November 2006, Prime Minister Koirala and Prachanda signed a Comprehen-sive Peace Agreement (CPA) formally ending the People's War. A month later, in accordance with the CPA, the government drafted an interim constitution, which was widely seen as a remarkable achievement. However, particularly in the Terai, concerns were voiced that the constitution did not adequately reflect the concerns of ethnic groups. The Sadbhavana Party, which was then the only established Madhesi party, raised objections to the inequitable electoral system and the statute's silence on federalism.[27] Protests in the Terai condemning the state's continuing exclusion-ary practices gained strength, even leading to violence and riots in the western town of Nepalgunj.[28]

---

[27] For an analysis of the 2007 Madhesi movement, description of political actors, and its evolu-tion, see ICG report, "Nepal's Troubled Terai Region," July 2007; *Nepali Times Madhes Special* at http://nepalitimes.com/special/madesh.php; and ACHR briefing "Madhes: The Challenges and Opportunities for a Stable Nepal," September 2009.

[28] For description of the Nepalgunj riots, see Dhital, "A Comparison of Two Communal Riots in Nepalgunj," *European Bulletin of Himalayan Research*, 33–4.

Despite the agitation in the Terai, the interim legislature promulgated the interim constitution in mid-January without taking into account any of the Madhesis' concerns. The Madhesi Janaadhikar Forum (MJF) – then an ethnic platform that had membership across party lines – burnt the copy of the draft constitution the next day, on January 16, in Kathmandu. Its top leaders were then arrested, but activists in the Terai kept up the protests. The January 19 shooting of an MJF activist by a Maoist cadre in the southeastern town of Lahan provided the trigger for a mass movement across the plains. The movement, which was widely seen as a struggle for dignity, rights, and representation against the background of historical discrimination, acquired a sharp anti-Kathmandu and anti-Maoist tinge. Its core demands included a change in the electoral system, a firm commitment to federalism, and proportionate inclusion in state structures on the basis of population. After 21 days of protests, Prime Minister G. P. Koirala addressed the nation and promised to fulfill all the demands of the Madhesi groups.

As the movement broke out, the Maoists adopted a defensive posture. During the People's War, they had heavily mobilized Madhesis against the state, seeking their support by fighting for a federalist state structure to counter the "internal colonialism" of the Terai by the centralized state. However, as the agitation picked up, the Maoists were painted as the villains in the popular narrative – as the force that had used the Madhesis tactically, only to betray them once they had entered the halls of power.

The Maoists reacted by repeatedly blaming royalists, Hindu fundamentalists, and foreign powers for instigating the protests, further alienating the Madhesis. Over time, Maoist accusations that the Indian establishment, sections of cross-border politicians in the Indian states of Bihar and Uttar Pradesh, and elements of the Indian Hindu right were behind the Madhesi unrest gained traction among the wider population.

The Movement

However, India had not engineered the Madhesi movement. Over the years, as they did with other Nepali politicians, sections of the Indian establishment patronized small Madhesi groups, but these outfits lacked an organizational base and were never encouraged to create a mass stir. After 2003, India increased its development aid to the Terai. India also cultivated relationships with the two most influential Madhesi political players. The Sadbhavana Party led by Gajendra Narayan Singh was seen as close to India and ever since the 1990s was known to seek guidance from Delhi. Toward the end of the People's War, an official Madhesi Janaadhikar Forum (MJF) delegation visited Delhi in November–December 2005 to meet a range of political actors and officials. Although India's outreach may have had the objective of creating a reliable constituency of support within Nepal, it was not geared toward promoting a radical ethnic or separatist agenda. In fact, one of the most common complaints of Madhesi leaders has been that India "used them as pawns" but never pressured Kathmandu to give Madhesis the rights they demanded.[29]

Indian officials seemed to have been taken aback by the intensity of the agitation in January 2007 and were concerned that the problems in the Terai would upset the peace process. At the same time, after the movement picked up, Delhi recognized its potential in weakening the Maoists in the plains, right across the Indian border.

The movement also found active support among the Indian Hindu right, which, worried about the Hindu monarchy in Kathmandu being under siege, saw the unrest in the Terai as an opportunity to regain influence in Nepali politics. Prominent Hindu fanatical leaders met Madhesi leaders in the run-up to and during the movement,[30] and directly across the border from Nepal, local chapters of major ultra-Hindu nationalist groups also backed the protests politically and materially.[31]

Armed Groups

There is also a widely held perception among Nepalis, particularly in Kathmandu, that the armed groups in the Terai have been created and supported by India.

It is true that some local groups and regional political parties in Bihar and Uttar Pradesh have provided limited support to the armed Madhesi militants, and key Madhesi underground leaders[32] continue to be based in bordering areas. The local Indian administration is usually aware of their whereabouts, but as long as the militants do not carry weapons and engage in illegal activities on the Indian side, they are free to pursue their activities from Indian soil. It is difficult to ascertain the levels of interaction with Indian intelligence agencies, but both officials and armed group activists admit that they have been in contact.[33]

Indian officials, however, deny any involvement in stirring up unrest in the Terai, blaming Nepali authorities for a weak law-and-order machinery and for not sharing actionable intelligence. They also point to the dismal governance in its states bordering Nepal and the proliferation of criminal gangs to show that this lawlessness occurred not because of the Indian state, but despite it.[34]

Yet, it is also clear that India has leverage over Nepali political groups, which it uses only when it wants to. This was visible in April 2008 when India's pressure on armed groups based in India not to disrupt the Constituent Assembly election, combined

---

[29] Interviews, Madhesi leaders, Kathmandu and Terai, between 2007–9.

[30] See "Nepal Should Be a Hindu Rashtra Again," *Nepali Times*, September 7, 2009, http://www.nepalitimes.com.np/issue/365/Interview/13940.

[31] Interview, Seema Jagaran Manch leaders, Raxaul, Bihar, June 2007.

[32] Such as Jai Krishna Goit, Nagendra Paswan (aka Jwala Singh), and others.

[33] See ACHR briefing, "Madhes: The Challenges and Opportunities."

[34] Interviews, local police officials, Sitamarhi and Raxaul, Bihar.

with strict instructions to local authorities to tighten the border, limited the militants' operational abilities and helped prevent any large-scale election violence.

Party Politics

From 2007–10, Indian involvement in Madhesi mainstream politics – from determining its shape, influencing intra-party dynamics, backing certain actors and discouraging others, and shaping agendas – increased sharply.

India encouraged several Madhesi leaders of established national parties to come together to form the Terai Madhesi Democratic Party (TMDP) in December 2007. Delhi's pressure played an important part in breaking the impasse in negotiations between the government and Madhesi groups on two occasions – it facilitated an agreement between the government and MJF in August 2007 and then visibly mediated an Eight-Point Agreement between the government and the United Democratic Madhesi Front (UDMF) in February 2008.[35] Among the points were an autonomous Madhesi province, group entry of Madhesis into the Nepalese Army, and revisions in electoral law to satisfy Madhesi demands.

In the postelection context, the most significant Indian role in Madhesi politics came during the Maoist government's attempt to dismiss the army chief, which was recounted earlier. The MJF, which had emerged as the biggest Madhesi party in the elections and had since become an important Maoist ally, was divided on the question. Once the Maoist government fell, there were indications that MJF party chairman and foreign minister Upendra Yadav might ally with the Maoists and make a prime ministerial bid himself. However, India's preference was for an UML-led government. Although the entire MJF party voted for Madhav Nepal on the floor of the house, the government's decision to appoint another senior MJF leader, Bijay Gachhedar, as the deputy prime minister led to a split within the party – with Upendra Yadav's faction withdrawing support from the government. India's fairly open support to the Gachhedar faction was instrumental in influencing the choices of many parliamentarians.

Broad Patterns

This cursory glance at key events in Madhesi politics during the last few years reveals three crucial features of India's role.

One, Delhi has clearly sought to build a reliable constituency of support that can be instrumentally used in Kathmandu politics. Furthermore, because of Madhesi

---

[35] The 23-Point Agreement eventually failed to calm the unrests in the Terai, because its demands were not properly implemented and led to a split within MJF. The treaty was succeeded by the February 2008 Eight-Point Agreement.

politicians' tendency to lobby and seek support from India on a range of issues, Delhi has an almost legitimate space to intervene in Madhesi affairs.

Two, Delhi has also tried to play a mediatory role between Kathmandu and Madhesi forces, because neither an unmanageable separatist struggle in the Terai nor a completely hill-elite–dominated Kathmandu system is in its interest. Characterizing India as one-sidedly backing Kathmandu against the Terai, or the Terai against Kathmandu, is far too simplistic. India's motives depend on specific circumstances and the overriding Indian policy aim at that particular moment. Quite often, its objectives on the national stage – for instance, ousting the Maoist government or preserving the Madhav Nepal government – have trumped protecting what may be called Madhesi interests by splitting powerful Madhesi parties or asking Madhesi protestors to tone down their strident rhetoric.

Three, although much of Nepali perceptions about India's role in the Terai may emanate from the old hill-centric nationalist hysteria, there is also a valid basis to be suspicious of Indian intentions. Some of Delhi's actions have added to the mistrust, so that Nepali actors are not quite confident of what India wants and suspect Delhi of relishing the instability in the Terai, even if that may not be India's real intent.

THE NEW ENTRANT: UNMIN

The United Nations Mission in Nepal (UNMIN) formally set up operations in Nepal in January 2007. It was mandated, initially for one year, to monitor the management of arms and armed personnel of both sides to the conflict, assist in the monitoring of ceasefire arrangements, and provide technical support for the planning, preparation, and conduct of the election of a Constituent Assembly.[36] By the time the mission drew down in January 2011, the initial one-year mandate had been extended seven times for a period of six months each at the request of the parties to the conflict.

UNMIN's arrival was greeted with much celebration across the political spectrum, media, and civil society, which saw the mission's mere presence as a sign that the war had ended and that Nepal might finally be on its way to peace and political stability. However, as domestic polarization within Nepal grew, UNMIN came to spark different, and often conflicting, reactions. There are those who viewed the mission as a nonpartisan force that acted as a deterrent to a resumption of violence and those who accused it of incompetence and political prejudice. This section examines how UNMIN has been viewed both in Kathmandu and in the Terai, particularly among Madhesi actors.

Peace Process

As part of its mandate, UNMIN successfully registered and stored the weapons of the People's Liberation Army's (PLA; and an equivalent number of the NA's weapons)

---

[36] "Security Council Establishes UN Political Mission in Nepal," United Nations, http://www.un.org/News/Press/docs/2007/sc8942.doc.htm.

and cantoned Maoist fighters at various sites across the country (and barracked a limited number of NA personnel). It was generally assumed that UNMIN would continue its monitoring activities until the political parties and Maoists reached a final agreement on the future of the former PLA combatants, including integration of at least part of the Maoist force into Nepal's security forces. Due to a misunderstanding of its mandate or sometimes due to a mischievous interpretation of the same for partisan purposes, the arms monitoring part of UNMIN's engagement has drawn the most criticism from Nepali actors.[37]

The first criticism against UNMIN, which continues to be raised to this day by Nepali Congress leaders and sections of the Indian establishment, was that it allowed the Maoists to get away with not registering all the weapons in the cantonments. There was indeed a significant discrepancy between the number of Maoist combatants and of registered and stored weapons. However, most military experts agree that the Maoists possessed far fewer weapons than they had combatants. In addition, UNMIN was not mandated to evaluate whether Maoists had indeed deposited all their weapons in the containers. Nevertheless, the widespread public suspicion remains that UNMIN has negligently allowed the former insurgents to keep hidden arms caches.

Second, UNMIN has been widely criticized for verifying thousands of combatants who had never been part of the PLA, thus making them potentially eligible for integration into the state's security forces. Although there is some evidence – including a leaked tape of the Maoist chairman speaking to his cadres about "fooling UNMIN" – that the Maoists succeeded in inflating their numbers in the verification process, UNMIN argues that it was the political parties themselves who had determined the verification criteria and that the verification results were subsequently accepted by the Nepalese Army.[38] Critics counter that the UN should have used its long international experience to help Nepali actors design a more rigorous peace deal.[39]

The third criticism accused UNMIN of failing in its task of supervising the cantonments, pointing to the killing of a Kathmandu businessman in a PLA cantonment site in the middle of 2008 and instances of groups of verified combatants leaving the cantonments with weapons.[40] Yet, UNMIN was never given the mandate or resources to exert any kind of supervision that could have prevented such

---

[37] For details on some of the major criticisms and UNMIN's response, see Ian Martin's interview on Kantipur Television, December 2008, http://www.unmin.org.np/downloads/interview/2008–12–01-UNMIN.SRSG.Interview.KantipurTV.Fireside.ENG.pdf.

[38] The verification criteria were limited to the age of the combatants (under-aged fighters were not accepted) and recruitment date (those who joined the PLA after the ceasefire of May 25, 2006, were disqualified). UNMIN did not have to judge whether a particular combatant had fought a battle or if other fighters had not registered with the PLA or had joined another wing of the party.

[39] "UNMIN and Accountability," *Republica*, May 9, 2009, http://www.myrepublica.com/portal/index.php?action=news_details&news_id=4815.

[40] "PLA out of Cantonments," *Republica*, August 26, 2009, http://www.myrepublica.com/portal/index.php?action=news_details&news_id=9041.

transgressions. UNMIN only had a very limited number of arms monitors because the NC and India had insisted on a mission with a light footprint. In addition, UNMIN also had no supervision, let alone enforcement, authority and could only monitor and report acts of noncompliance of the two armies. Yet, although UNMIN may not have had enforcement authority, it was a referee with a whistle, and not whistling more loudly at times dented its credibility.

As a result of these various criticisms, some domestic forces viewed the mission as a pro-Maoist institution, with an NC leader going as far as to label former UNMIN chief, Ian Martin, as a communist. This is ironic given that Maoist dogmatists, in their propaganda, have often depicted the UN as a tool of imperialists.

What the critics missed was that UNMIN was in Nepal to assist in the peace process, in which the Maoists happen to be a 50% stakeholder. UNMIN's mandate and work thus required very close collaboration with the Maoists at multiple levels – the party and the PLA, at the center and in the districts. There might have been UNMIN officials who privately sympathized with the Maoists and the challenge they pose to the older parties that are perceived to be upholding the status quo and exclusionary state structures. There is little evidence, however, to suggest that these personal beliefs had an impact on UNMIN's larger procedural role.

Still, despite efforts to reach out to multiple constituencies, the fact remains that UNMIN lost the propaganda war. However, perhaps the utility of the presence of a neutral outside body was that domestic actors could use it as a scapegoat for their own failures.

In the Terai

UNMIN was the first international institution that seriously tried to understand the grievances of the Madhesi community. Recognizing that the inclusion of the marginalized communities was a part of all peace agreements and, aware that if left unaddressed, it could potentially derail the peace process, UNMIN officials engaged closely with these groups.[41]

As the negotiations over the exact mandate of UNMIN personnel were taking place between the government and the Maoists, political unrest in the Terai was growing, with the emergence of armed groups, violence, and assertive voices in favor of federalism and ethnic autonomy by smaller Madhesi parties. Even before the mission's formal launch, toward the end of 2006, then-Personal Representative of the Secretary-General, Ian Martin, met Madhesi leaders across party lines. When UNMIN established its offices in January 2007, the Madhesi movement broke out in full force, forcing the mission to keep track closely of developments in the plains.[42]

UNMIN's fairly intensive engagement with the Madhesi issue provoked both support and opposition. The support came largely from the Madhesi political leadership

---

[41] Ian Martin press conference, October 10, 2007, http://www.unmin.org.np.
[42] Interviews, UNMIN officials, Kathmandu, Biratnagar, Janakpur, Pokhara, Nepalgunj, 2007–8.

and, more importantly, civil society, which for the first time saw any international attention devoted to their complaints. They also saw UNMIN's involvement as a great opportunity for the Madhesi movement to gain international legitimacy.[43] However, this involvement also created expectations, which soon turned into disappointment for many of UNMIN's political and civil society interlocutors in the Terai. These interlocutors commonly complained that UNMIN staff would "arrive in their big cars, talk to us, and then go back and nothing changes. Instead of doing anything for us, they write reports to headquarters. They are like journalists."[44] Eventually, the limited understanding of UNMIN's mandate, the failure of the UN machinery to explain its role, and the absence of a national monitoring committee with which UNMIN could share local-level information and push for action turned the Madhesis' initial enthusiasm about UNMIN into a degree of indifference.

In contrast, UNMIN's inability to influence dynamics on the ground in the Terai was welcomed by several other groups who opposed a UN role. This opposition came from three different constituencies, which sometimes overlapped.

The first group was the hill-centric establishment that consisted of castes and classes who were reluctant to accept the history of discrimination and to share power. This group was already feeling besieged by the Maoist agenda and saw UNMIN as partial to the Maoists. It also thought that UNMIN's efforts in the Terai would further undermine the state's integrity by contributing to radical ethnic/regional/separatist agendas.

The second source of opposition came from both pragmatic and nationalist quarters. These groups pointed out that UNMIN had no mandate for this level of engagement in the Terai. Although UNMIN repeatedly made a pitch for a mandate extension that would allow it to play a good offices role in the Terai, no such extension was ever granted. Even among those who understood that Madhesi assertions had to be accommodated, there was a widespread feeling that involvement of any international actors would only complicate this process because they would be unable to deal effectively with Nepal's complex social fabric and the heterogeneity of social groups and political outfits – including violent ones - within the Madhesis.[45]

The third source of opposition was India, which shares open borders with the Terai. India has been extremely sensitive about international meddling on what it considers to be its home turf. A reluctant convert to the idea of a UN presence in Nepal, India was concerned that the UN would "use the Madhesi card" to steadily expand its mandate and term to stay on and treat Nepal as its protectorate.[46]

[43] Interviews, Madhesi leaders, Kathmandu and Terai, 2007–8.
[44] Interviews, journalists and civil society activists, Terai, 2007–8.
[45] Professor Chaitanya Mishra, cited in Suhrke, "Nepal as the Exceptional Case," CMI working paper, 2009.
[46] Interviews, Indian officials, Kathmandu and Delhi, June 2007.

THE CHINA CARD

Despite a historically close political and economic relationship and a long shared border, the contemporary Nepal–China relationship is notable for the absence of any dense networks of interdependence. This is especially true when compared to the complex, multilayered ties that bind Nepal and India.

For most of its modern history, Nepal's road connectivity with China has remained poor, and social relationships have been limited except in areas bordering the high Himalayas. In addition, the Nepali state has not relied on China for essential imports such as fuel. Generally the Nepal–India economic networks far outweigh the influence of the few Chinese businesses that operate in Nepal. Lastly, China's penetration into Nepali party politics has been limited, while seeking good relations with whoever ran the government of the day. In combination, these facts demonstrate limited Chinese interests and leverage in Nepal.

However, China has influenced Nepal's geostrategic thinking and internal politics. When King Mahendra took power in 1960, and India encouraged political groups, including the Nepali Congress, to nurture an opposition from the safety of its territory, the king played what has now come to be called the "China card." Exploiting the deteriorating Sino-India relationship, which culminated in a war in 1962, to his political benefit, the king threatened Delhi with the prospect of a closer relationship between Kathmandu and Beijing. The loss of Nepal as a neutral buffer state would have left India vulnerable on another front and diminished the value of the Himalayas as a natural security frontier. The king's "politics of balance" succeeded.[47] Delhi realized that the geostrategic costs of antagonizing the Nepali rulers could be high and developed a working relationship with the monarch.

As far as China was concerned, its core concern in Nepal is simple – Tibet. Nepal firmly backed the One China Policy,[48] and when Tibetan protestors in Nepal tried to stir up unrest in the mid-1970s, Kathmandu acted fast to curtail their activities. As long as the state was sensitive to its core security concern, China did not worry about Nepali political dynamics. Focused on its internal consolidation, navigating a complex Cold War dynamic after its fallout with the USSR, and aware of the far more intimate relationship between India and Nepal at the people-to-people level, the Chinese regime recognized that it could not be a substitute for India in Nepal. Chinese leaders, including Chairman Mao, are understood to have told visiting Nepali leaders repeatedly to keep good relations with India while protecting the country's sovereignty.[49]

Indian Prime Minister Rajiv Gandhi's visit to Beijing in 1988, during which China is understood to have informally agreed that Nepal and Bhutan were in the

---

[47] Leo Rose, *Nepal: Strategy for Survival*, University of California Press, 1971.
[48] By accepting the One China Policy, Nepal recognizes Tibet as part of China.
[49] Interviews, Nepali officials, Kathmandu, 2008–9.

Indian sphere of influence, marked the beginning of Sino-Indian rapprochement. The Nepali monarchy did not understand the significant geopolitical shift that this new relationship represented. When King Birendra's government tried to acquire arms from China around the same time, India asserted itself and blocked most entry points into Nepal – crippling its economy and depriving it of essential supplies. When China did little to rescue the Nepali regime, the limits of the "China card" became all too clear. Without means to sustain itself, the autocratic monarchical system was overthrown by popular demonstrations in 1990.

This broader historical context is crucial to understanding China's role in the recent Nepali political transition.

Contrary to misconceptions that may emanate from the name of Nepal's rebel force, China did not support the Maoists during the war. In fact, China even refused to call them Maoists, referring to them instead as "anti-state forces." When King Gyanendra took over power in 2005, the Chinese government was one of the few in the world that backed the royal regime and refused to condemn its actions, which it categorized as part of Nepal's "internal affairs." This was a source of much comfort and confidence for Gyanendra, on which he intended to build when, at the SAARC summit in Dhaka in 2005, he proposed to add China as an observing member to the regional organization – a move with which India was distinctly uncomfortable. Unlike in 1960, this time, the king's hopes of neutralizing India's opposition to his regime or scaring Delhi into supporting him were disappointed.

Gyanendra was misguided if he had thought that China would invest its political capital, risk its relations with the rest of the Nepali political class, and antagonize India to help the besieged king. Although initially China backed him, thinking he was their best bet to ensure a stable central government, they subtly changed track once they realized his rule was unsustainable. In fact, India and China had been talking to each other about Nepal. In January 2006, China noted "changes in Nepal's political situation" and called on "all parties" to narrow their differences through dialogue. In March 2006, a Chinese official met mainstream political leaders on a visit to Kathmandu, in a clear signal to the palace.

After the king yielded his authority in the wake of the People's Movement, China officially recognized the government led by Girija Prasad Koirala. Beijing began engaging with all political parties, including the Maoists, more proactively than ever before. With the lame-duck monarchy on the verge of being abolished, China, like everyone else, was not quite sure which political force would emerge strongest and be a reliable future ally sensitive to its security concerns.

The turning point in China's approach to Nepal came in March 2008 in the run-up to the Beijing Olympics when "free Tibet" protests rocked Tibet as well as Kathmandu. Protests continued for almost a month, and the international media, which had no or little access to Tibet itself, descended onto Kathmandu to report on the extent of discontent. China was furious with the Nepali government, led by the Nepali Congress, for not swiftly reining in the protests.[50] For Beijing, it was proof that Western influence in Nepal had grown and that the increasingly strong India–U.S. strategic partnership meant that Delhi was no longer a reliable partner when it came to keeping international actors out of the region. China felt that the open border between India and Nepal was a major problem, because Tibetans could use it not only to flee to exile but also to return to foment protests in Nepal and Tibet. China had also been concerned about developments in the Terai, especially the Madhesi movement, seeing it both as an Indian ploy to expand influence over Nepali territory and a threat to Nepali sovereignty.

Beijing's disappointment with the Nepali government coincided with the victory of the Maoists in the elections, heralding a strategic shift in Beijing's approach to Nepal. After Prachanda took office in August 2008, China was quick to invite him to attend the closing ceremony of the Olympics – an invitation that the Maoist leader accepted even though he knew it would not win him friends in New Delhi. Subsequently, there were successive high-level visits of political and military delegations from China and Tibet's Autonomous Region (TAR) to Nepal, and Nepali political party representatives from across the spectrum traveled to China. Beijing also expanded its outreach to all parties, including the ones based in the Terai, with a Chinese Communist Party (CCP) representative even attending MJF's party convention as a guest in early 2009. Chinese businesses too increased investment in various sectors across Nepal, especially in infrastructure, construction, and the hotel industry. A number of Chinese study centers were set up. Lastly, the two countries enhanced their military ties, with China promising more aid and support to the Nepalese Army. Even as the Maoists were talking about renegotiating the 1950 Treaty of Peace and Friendship with India, the Chinese reportedly offered to sign a similar treaty with Nepal.

The Maoist government read these signs to mean that this was the right moment to balance Nepal's relations with India and implement its policy of keeping equidistance with both countries. The subtext was building a closer party-to-party relationship with the CCP. After they formed the government, the defense minister, Ram Bahadur Thapa "Badal," Krishna Bahadur Mahara and another Maoist leader secretly went across the border accompanied by a Chinese military attaché from the embassy and reportedly met Chinese officials. The "secret" nature of the visit led to suspicions in Kathmandu about its real motivation. There were reports that China had offered to train the PLA commander, Nand Kishore Pun "Pasang" – if true, this was a direct sign of support for the integration of the former Maoist combatants in the Nepalese Army because Pasang was a natural claimant to a senior rank in the NA structure.

---

[50] For the broader Sino-India dynamic and role in Nepal, see Kunda Dixit, "A New Himalayan Game," *Fletcher Forum of World Affairs*, Winter 2010, Vol. 34:1.

The Maoist–China ties only strengthened those hard-liners in Delhi who had warned against trusting the Maoists. However, as it turned out, Beijing's relationship with Kathmandu was not built on a solid foundation. When India stepped in to build an anti-Maoist alliance in 2009, China did little to rescue the Maoists. After Prachanda resigned from government, Chinese diplomats in Kathmandu were uncharacteristically vocal about the need for a national unity government and power sharing, which would include the Maoists. Yet beyond that, China did not invest any political capital to try to alter domestic political outcomes. Instead, Beijing quickly adapted to the political change and began working with Madhav Nepal's new government, urging it to reiterate Nepal's commitment to the One China Policy and to deploy more security forces on the northern border.

This glance at China's role during the Nepali transition suggests that, at a broad level, China and India share a common aim in Nepal – a degree of political stability with a government that is sensitive to their respective security interests. However, India remains far more central in shaping Nepali politics. China's engagement is steadily growing, and it may use it to influence internal political dynamics and intervene at some point – but has not shown that inclination yet. What is certain is that it will be increasingly challenging for successive Nepali governments to navigate the India–China relationship, as the two countries grow and compete for influence in South Asia.

THE GRADUAL SHIFT: THE U.S. ROLE

During Nepal's conflict, the United States was one of the strongest backers of anti-Maoist forces. In the aftermath of the 9/11 attacks, Washington designated the Maoists a terrorist organization. It provided generous aid, equipment, and training to the Royal Nepalese Army and defended the monarchy in international forums against criticism for human rights violations. The United States also encouraged the "constitutional forces," meaning the monarchy and the political parties, to unite to fight the Maoist threat.

The king's 2005 takeover complicated the United States' stance on Nepal. Although it promptly condemned the monarch's move and emphasized that it would like to see democracy and freedom restored, Washington continued to see the Maoists as a part of the problem and not the solution to the conflict.

However, with the rapprochement between Maoists and political parties in 2005 and the emerging peace process, combined with India's growing disenchantment with the monarchy in the aftermath of the royal coup, the United States risked getting stranded on the wrong side of history. Still, U.S. Ambassador James Moriarty did what he could until the very end to block any rapprochement between the Maoists and the political parties. Framing it as a battle for freedom in line with the U.S. president's policy of democracy promotion around the world, Moriarty told a Kathmandu audience in August 2005, "Every day the Maoists assail democracy itself through attacks on political party workers, local government offices, journalists, human rights workers, and other innocent civilians who want nothing more than peace. The Maoists have done nothing to indicate that they are prepared to change, and they do not abide by democracy. Their actions speak louder than their words." Asking the king and parties to reach out to each other, he added, "The way to achieve peace is with a democratic government united against the Maoist assault on Nepal."[51]

As talks between parties and Maoists picked up, the United States noted "with alarm recent reports in the Nepali media on the emerging potential for an 'alliance' between one or more of the major political parties and the Maoist rebels."[52] Moriarty followed top Nepali political leaders to Delhi in mid-November 2005 to lobby against what subsequently became the 12-Point Understanding. However, once the deal was signed, the United States "cautiously welcomed the new political understanding,"[53] while emphasizing that parties should not formally work with the Maoists until the latter gave up violence, put down their weapons, and formally committed to the democratic process. Despite the changing political winds, the United States also continued to call the palace a legitimate political actor.[54]

The United States' cautious welcome may have had something to do with the increasingly good relations between Delhi and Washington, whose initial negotiations over the U.S.–Indian nuclear deal reflected their new strategic partnership. On regional issues, with the exception of those related to Pakistan, the U.S. administration was content to give India the lead. Nepali politicians who visited Washington to lobby against the king recount that they were told that the United States would not block or obstruct an Indian initiative – even though the White House did not think talking to "terrorists" was a good idea. Indian officials in Kathmandu, Delhi, and Washington were careful to keep the United States in the loop. To some extent, it helped India that the United States kept up its tough rhetoric toward the rebels. Even if its stance was not coordinated, it allowed India and the United States to play, in the words of an Indian diplomat, "good cop–bad cop"[55] with the Maoists, signaling that no blank checks were given to the rebels and that their actions would be under constant scrutiny. This dual approach continued until well after the Maoists joined open politics.

As the popular movement against the monarchy picked up in April 2006, the United States became increasingly critical of the king and his refusal to reach out to the parties. Washington remained suspicious of the Maoists' intentions, but the

[51] Speech to the Nepal Council of World Affairs, August 9, 2005.
[52] US Embassy in Nepal Press Release, November 4, 2005, as quoted in IGC report, "Nepal's New Alliance: The Mainstream Parties and the Maoists," November 2005, p. 22.
[53] "US, India Welcome New Political Development," *The Kathmandu Post*, November 24, 2005, as quoted in IGC report, "Nepal's New Alliance," p. 23.
[54] Ibid.
[55] Interview, senior official, Kathmandu, June 2007.

palace was not conceding an inch, and the popular mood was firmly antimonarchy, making it impossible for Ambassador Moriarty to continue to push the parties to engage with the palace. When King Gyanendra made his first proclamation, the United States, in a final attempt to back the monarchy, followed India's lead in welcoming the announcement and asking the parties to respond positively. Eventually though, when the king was forced to retract his statement and announced that sovereignty lay with the people, the United States expressed its eagerness to work with the new government.[56] However, after the Maoists emerged above ground and began engaging closely with other political parties, civil society, media, and sections of the international community, the United States maintained its distance, refusing to treat the Maoists (who to date remain on one of three U.S. terrorist designation lists) as a political party.

Moriarty repeatedly warned mainstream parties and the NC-led government not to give concessions or space in the interim legislature and government to the Maoists until they reformed and gave up violence and guns. In a farewell speech in June 2007, Moriarty said that the first obstacle to democracy and prosperity in Nepal was the "Maoist failure to bring their conduct in line with the standards of mainstream political parties in multiparty democracies." He added that Maoist behavior had not changed in line with their commitments and argued, "No mainstream political party anywhere in a multi-party democratic system is allowed to maintain its own armed groups. . . . Nor should a political party be permitted to carry out, with impunity, crimes of extortion, abduction, and intimidation."[57]

Throughout this period, U.S. policy was widely criticized not only by the Maoists but also by many in civil society who found Washington's approach unhelpful at a time of a complex transition. However, the general sense among most Nepali political actors was that the United States had "outsourced" its Nepal policy to New Delhi and would not go beyond a certain threshold.

The arrival of a new U.S. ambassador, Nancy Powell, may not have changed Washington's policy in substance, but her sober style and restrained public statements were seen by most Nepali politicians as a welcome departure from Moriarty's undiplomatic conduct. Powell maintained that the Maoists had to implement peace process commitments and renounce violence, but was more supportive of the broader roadmap to peace, including the CA elections. Like everyone else, the United States was also taken aback by the Maoist election success, but used the moment to begin a long overdue process of formal engagement with the former rebels. Shortly after the elections, the ambassador met Maoist leaders, and around the same time a senior administration official met with Prachanda. The United States officially stated that its main policy priorities included "consolidation of gains

56 See ICG reports, "Nepal's Crisis; Mobilizing International Influence," April 2006 and "Nepal: From People Power to Peace?" May 2006.
57 Speech at the Community Information Centre, Pokhara, June 2007.

in the peace process, promotion of security sector reform and strengthening demo-cratic institutions." After Prachanda took office as prime minister, the United States engaged with him as the head of the Nepali government.

The most visible proof of change in the U.S. tone, from the days of James Moriarty to now, came during the February 2010 Senate confirmation hearing of the newly appointed U.S. ambassador, Scott Delisi. He noted that the United States was engaging with the Maoists, who had made great strides in signing the peace agreement, participating in elections and the constitution-drafting process, discharging disqualified combatants from cantonments, and allowing parliament to function. Yet, recounting that the Maoists had not yet renounced violence as a political instrument and that its youth wing continued with violent and criminal activities, he concluded that "we've [the United States] got a mixed bag with the Maoists. Yes, we have to engage them; we have to talk to them both as a key political actor and as part of the peace process. We hope that they will take some of the steps that will allow us to look at removing them from the terrorist exclusion list."[58]

CONCLUSION

Even a brief narrative of the Nepali political transition – which has not covered all events or all international actors operating in Nepal – reveals how external actors, their relations with each other, and their approach toward domestic politics have influenced developments in the country. Encouragement by the international com-munity created space for warring sides to look for a political solution to a military conflict, and the presence of international actors has assisted the country in imple-menting key aspects of the peace deal. At the same time, political polarization also tended to sharpen because of the insecurities of other countries. Political develop-ments then became hostage to the national interest of neighbors and the agenda of other internationals, and problems became more difficult to solve because of different approaches and conflicting prescriptions.

The lessons from the Nepali peace process are both complex and simple. As long as the key principal domestic actors see an incentive in working together and maintain a consensus, the involvement of international actors can be channeled constructively. When that consensus unravels and politics begins to fragment, those international actors with major interests in the country end up contributing to the instability deliberately or inadvertently.

---

[58] "Maoist Need to Renounce Violence as a Political Instrument," February 24, 2010, http://www.indianexpress.com/news/maoist-need-to-renounce-violence-as-a-political-instrument/575462/o.

Conclusions

14

Conclusions

Sebastian von Einsiedel, David M. Malone, and Suman Pradhan

Nepal is struggling with multiple interlocking transitions: from war to peace, from autocracy to democracy, and from an exclusionary and centralized state to a more inclusive and federal one. As elsewhere, in Nepal this postconflict transition, which is embedded in broader state transformation, has not been linear, has suffered setbacks, is likely to see future reversals, and is unlikely any time soon to be "completed." To be sustainable, these multiple transitions will need to be underpinned by another transformation: from economic laggard to an economy offering both inclusion and growth, as well as economic governance reform.

All these transitions have been and should be largely domestically driven. Yet, at times outsiders have played a significant, often useful, but sometimes unhelpful role – as this volume has highlighted. This concluding chapter first assesses achievements so far and then examines key outstanding challenges facing major actors, both inside and outside Nepal.

SIGNIFICANT ACHIEVEMENTS

In the two years from 2006 to 2008, Nepal's peace process registered significant achievements in a remarkably short period of time. In the context of the People's Movement in the spring of 2006, the king was stripped of all executive powers and parliament was restored. In its first session, the restored parliament declared Nepal a secular state. Both parties to the conflict, the Maoists and the state's security forces, by and large refrained from the use of lethal force. The Maoist Army has remained in cantonments while awaiting resolution of its future, and the Nepalese Army has largely remained in its barracks. Some of the key transitional arrangements laid

The views expressed in this chapter are solely those of the authors and do not represent the official views of the United Nations or the International Development Research Centre.

down by the Comprehensive Peace Agreement have been implemented. Within a few months an interim constitution was adopted, which included provisions defining as fundamental rights both nondiscrimination and the right not to be subjected to "untouchability." Shortly thereafter, an interim legislature-parliament and interim government were set up, both with significant Maoist participation. Despite all of the day-to-day ups and downs, with hindsight of several years, these developments are tremendously encouraging.

In the crowning achievement of Nepal's transition so far, Nepalis in April 2008 elected a 601-member Constituent Assembly (also serving as Parliament) after two postponements generating a delay of ten months. The Maoists, who only two years earlier had been engaged in active insurgency, emerged to the surprise of many, not least the Indian government, as the largest party in the Constituent Assembly, holding one-third of all seats. The election yielded the most inclusive legislature in Nepal's history, with most marginalized groups represented in rough proportion to their share of the population.[1] Shortly thereafter, Nepal was proclaimed a federal democratic republican state by the Constituent Assembly, ending the 239-year-old monarchy. Although this proclamation was symbolically important, Nepalis have yet to decide what model of federalism and what type of democracy to espouse. Most important of all, the contours and substantive responsibilities of a transformed Nepali state remain elusive.

Perhaps because so much was yet to be settled, the declaration of the republic seemed strangely anticlimactic, arousing little emotional response among the public. Since then, the political world of Nepal has been caught up in permanent crisis. Five years into the peace process, none of the remaining key players in Nepal, the royal family having lost out decisively early on, were prepared to offer compromise or even creative negotiating strategies until late 2011 when a slew of agreements renewed hopes of positive progress. The circumscribed role of the UN Mission in Nepal (UNMIN), although offering some reassurance to the population at large, did not allow it, after 2008, to nudge the key political actors toward more productive engagement with each other. The other international actors, several with much greater weight than the UN, either could not or would not assume that role either.

Thus, Nepal's transition to peace, democracy, and an inclusive state with better economic prospects remains at risk, and the country seems stuck with interim arrangements never designed for the long haul and that could fray dangerously in the years ahead.

---

[1] Madhesi, Hill Muslim, Inner Tarai Janajati, Hill Dalit, Tarai Janajati, and Hill Janajati populations were almost proportionally represented, with the only significantly underrepresented group being those who had always suffered double discrimination as a result of their caste and geographic provenance: Madhesi Dalits, which made up 2.4% of the CA members as compared to their 4.7% share of the population. See inclusiveness analysis prepared by UN Mission in Nepal (UNMIN), internal document, May 2008.

TRANSITION FROM WAR TO PEACE

In many respects, the situation today in Nepal continues to resemble more that of an extended ceasefire than a dynamic peace process, mainly because of the continued existence of two standing, formerly opposed, and still potentially contending armies. In spite of provisions in the 2006 peace accords foreseeing the integration of the People's Liberation Army (PLA) into Nepal's security forces, close to 20,000 Maoist soldiers remain cantoned in 28 sites across the country as of late 2011, with ready access to more than 3,000 guns (albeit poor-quality ones) and in the context of unresolved political differences. A breakthrough "Seven-Point Agreement" of November 1, 2011 foresees integration of 6,500 of its cantoned former combatants into the government's security forces. While implementation of the deal will pose a challenge and may see delays, it is the first time that the parties could agree on specific numbers.

Meanwhile, the Nepalese Army (NA), while having remained largely confined to its barracks, has successfully blocked the aspects of the peace accords relating to its downsizing and "democratization." Having doubled in size during the conflict, the NA remains more than 90,000 strong and has displayed no intention of shrinking its numbers to prewar levels. Meanwhile, successive postconflict governments in Kathmandu have done little to develop the institutional capacity to exert meaningful civilian and democratic oversight of the NA. In September 2006, the restored parliament adopted the Army Act, providing a legal framework for civilian oversight, accountability, and political neutrality of the army. However, with the Defense Ministry being nothing more than a shell, the law is merely notional or at best symbolic for now.

The lack of meaningful progress on integration of the Maoist combatants and security sector reform since the outset of the peace process is rooted in continuing deep mutual suspicion among the parties formerly engaged in conflict. With neither of the two armies defeated on the battlefield, both remained to a large extent unwilling to make the sacrifices necessary for implementation of the security-sector–related aspects of the peace accords. Even the November 2011 agreement has not fully resolved that doubt. The very concept of "demobilization and disarmament" is anathema to the Maoists, who view a newly integrated national army as the crown jewel of a restructured state and an important symbol of the new Nepal. As Rhoderick Chalmers argues in this volume, this notion renders any political settlement that leaves the NA unchanged irrelevant and unacceptable for the Maoists, who believe that failing to restructure the army would also inhibit radical social political change on other fronts. The NA, unlike the Maoist Army, is a largely autonomous actor unresponsive to political direction that rejects meaningful oversight from democratically elected authorities, as well as any reform that it sees as undermining its self-assigned role as the last line of defense against a Maoist power grab. A case in point is the "Katawal episode," referred to in several chapters of this volume, during which the Army Chief of Staff orchestrated opposition to his dismissal by Prime Minister Prachanda in 2009, leading to the resignation of the Maoist government.

The political parties – first and foremost the Nepali Congress (NC) and the Communist Party of Nepal – Unified Marxist-Leninist (UML), which is quite bourgeois and traditionalist in outlook, contrary to what its name might suggest – although themselves wary of an autonomous army that only a few years ago assisted the king in reintroducing absolute monarchy, quietly prefer a powerful military (even a military unresponsive to democratic control) over one that is neutered through significant integration of Maoist combatants. However, the decisive support for the NA's intransigent position comes from India, which, even before the end of the monarchy, had replaced the king as the ultimate authority to which the army responds.

Even if the Seven-Point Agreement of November 1, 2011 on the integration of Maoist ex-combatants will be eventually implemented, the absence of any meaningful reform of the Nepalese Army constitutes a continuing challenge to the peace process. As long as the question of the future of PLA personnel and the reform of the Nepalese Army remain unresolved, both parties will be ultimately prepared for a return to conflict. International efforts to facilitate movement in this area have been stymied by India, which rejects third-party involvement on security issues in its backyard. Faced with reservations from Delhi, donors remain reluctant to step up their engagement on security-sector–reform programming. India also militated against efforts by UNMIN to obtain a mandate from the Security Council to provide assistance in this area.

That said, the UN has one potential lever over the Nepalese Army that it has so far chosen not to use: the fact that Nepal has been for many decades a proud participant in UN peacekeeping operations and as of late 2010 ranks as its seventh largest troop contributor overall. In addition to the reputational benefit the NA derives from its peacekeeping role (and the cushy jobs it provides for senior officers), it remains highly dependent on UN peacekeeping as a source of financing for its Army Welfare Fund. Yet, faced with a chronic shortfall in the supply of peacekeepers from a limited pool of contributors and wary of setting a precedent, the UN has so far hoped that the Nepalese Army would reform on its own – particularly with respect to a more cooperative attitude on the integration of Maoist personnel and on accountability for human rights violations committed during the conflict – rather than through the imposition of any conditionality.

A lack of trust between political actors and, even more so, between military ones formerly in conflict in the framework of a civil war, is hardly exceptional. Indeed, the contrary would be surprising. For example in Central America and in African civil wars such as that of Mozambique, outside actors (neighboring countries, regional powers, the permanent five members of the UN Security Council, and other influential states) supplied considerable suasion and confidence-building measures to induce compromise, accommodation, and a degree of ideological sacrifice.[2] This

---

[2] For a comprehensive account of efforts to wind down a number of murderous civil wars, see Stephen John Stedman, Donald Rothchild, and Elizabeth M. Cousens (Eds.), *Ending Civil Wars: The Implementation of Peace Agreements*, Boulder, CO: Lynne Rienner, 2002.

influence has been largely absent in Nepal, and therefore the deadlock among political actors and between the Nepalese Army and the Maoists should come as no surprise. We do not exclude the possibility that some combination of external actors could come together in months or years ahead to play this role. Conceivably, with significant political will, discipline, dexterity, and flexibility, India, particularly if it were careful not to alienate the Maoists, could do so on its own. However, Nepal never seems quite important enough relative to other priorities in New Delhi for the disparate Indian actors who would need to be involved in such delicate maneuvers to come together. In addition, the Indian security establishment, deeply suspicious of the Maoists, seems to prefer a degree of instability to a Maoist-controlled government in Kathmandu.

The seeming inability of Nepali actors to resolve their disputes has frustrated well-meaning outside actors, particularly in years since the Constituent Assembly election. As a result, they are increasingly looking elsewhere to the many other crises making claims on their attention. This is disturbing because research and scholarship demonstrate that a key precursor and predictor of civil wars is an earlier such conflict within a country.[3] Although it is hard to imagine the Maoists lightly taking up arms again, other forces may be impelled by the country's frustration with the status quo in Kathmandu to challenge the Maoists as well as the rest of the political establishment in the future, especially if the economy continues to stagnate.[4] Enduring horizontal inequalities, from which Nepal suffers considerably, are well known to encourage conflict and were a significant factor in the People's War. Little of concrete value is being done to address them today.[5]

BUILDING A FEDERAL AND INCLUSIVE STATE

With both the future of the Maoist army and the democratization of the Nepalese Army still in limbo, the process of state transformation is similarly languishing. The election of a highly representative Constituent Assembly was an important achievement, but as long as it does not deliver what it was created for – a new constitution - this milestone remains largely symbolic. The original deadline for

---

3 See, for example, Fen Osler Hampson and David M. Malone (Eds.), *From Reaction to Conflict Prevention: Opportunities for the UN System*, Boulder, CO: Lynne Rienner, 2002, particularly pp. 14–40 by Anne-Marie Gardner.
4 For the saliency of economic factors in civil wars, see Paul Collier and Nicholas Sambanis, *Understanding Civil War: Evidence and Analysis*, Vol. 1: Africa and Vol. 2: Europe, Central Asia, and Other Regions, Washington, DC: World Bank, 2005. For contending speculations on what matters most in causality of civil wars, see Mats Berdal and David M. Malone (Eds.), *Greed and Grievance: Economic Agendas in Civil Wars*, Boulder, CO: Lynne Rienner, 2000. For important dimensions on what international institutional frameworks and processes can contribute to the resolution of civil wars, see Michael W. Doyle and Nicholas Sambanis, *Making War and Building Peace: United Nations Peace Operations*, Princeton, NJ: Princeton University Press, 2006.
5 See, for example, Frances Stewart, *Horizontal Inequalities and Conflict: Understanding Group Conflict in Multiethnic Societies*, Basingstoke, UK: Palgrave Macmillan, 2008.

agreement on a constitution, set for May 2010, passed without the assembly having started a serious drafting process. Several further deadlines that were half-heartedly advanced have come and gone as well, with none in the body politic apparently much indisposed. Stasis prevails in the Constituent Assembly, which appears to have lost sight of this, its only important role (as opposed to that of a regular parliament, from which more wide-ranging legislation is expected). The lack of progress reflects the deep divide over the nature of the future federal republic.

At the time of this writing, the most difficult challenge facing the drafters of the constitution is still the design of a federal system appropriate to Nepal. This is not surprising given the complexities of the country, which have been discussed throughout the volume, and of federalism, which has needed to take very different forms in different countries (as students of the federal systems of Germany and Switzerland, or Canada and the United States, to cite only two sets of countries living in close proximity geographically, ideologically, and culturally, would readily recognize).

On federalism and other constitutional questions, a great deal of international advice – from the International Institute for Democracy and Electoral Assistance to the International Commission of Jurists, the Forum of Federations, and the UN Development Programme – has been on offer to help members of the assembly assess options and weigh strategies. Although this expertise has found an attentive audience among some within the Constituent Assembly, there is little evidence that it is being taken into consideration during the negotiations. Indeed, the convergence of flights from all over carrying much international constitutional expertise to Kathmandu occasionally takes on an unreal air, given the disjuncture between plentiful supply of international advice and limited demand for it within the assembly, particularly relative to experience from far-flung places with little resemblance to Nepal's current circumstances.

When they talk about federalism, most Nepalis discuss it in terms of ethnicity – either for or against ethnic-based federalism – a fact missed by many international experts. Yet, creating ethnically homogeneous regions out of such an intricate ethnic mosaic as Nepal's is bound to create minorities in any new administrative or governance unit, no matter how the pie is sliced. Meanwhile, the promise of federal solutions, which seemed quite exciting to some of the major political actors and the public three or four years ago, has now invited a backlash from traditional elite groups. As a 2010 report of the International Crisis Group puts it succinctly, "Powerful elites are not keen on dismantling the unitary state and are even less happy to relinquish their privileged access to jobs, money and political power."[6] In any event, federalism per se could address only a few of Nepal's entrenched economic

---

[6] International Crisis Group, *Nepal's Political Rites de Passage*, Asia Report no. 194, September 29, 2010, p. i.

and social problems and would not necessarily reduce its deeply ingrained discrimination along lines of caste. In some areas, it might merely facilitate the capture of political power by ethnic-based local elites.

Beyond election of the Constituent Assembly, there has been little practical progress toward more inclusive state structures and bodies. *Attentisme* (a wait-and-see attitude) prevails, or as cynical Haitians sometimes say of their political establishment (which has quite a bit in common with that of Nepal), *le dilatoire* (the art of postponement dressed up in rhetoric) triumphs. Progress, if any, exists mostly on paper. An August 2007 Civil Service Bill, requiring that 45% of posts be reserved for women and marginalized groups, and an October 2007 decision by the government to hire 45% of new recruits to the Nepal Police and Armed Police Force from traditionally marginalized groups are largely unimplemented and are likely to remain so until forward momentum on state reform resumes – which can only happen seriously once a constitution has been agreed.7 As Mahendra Lawoti shows in this volume, although formal and legally enshrined discrimination may have ended, informal discrimination continues to be prevalent in Nepal. In addition, no progress has been made on the land reform mandated by the Comprehensive Peace Agreement.8 This is all the more worrisome because the distribution of land ownership and the exploitative relationships that have developed around it contributed mightily to the conflict in Nepal.

Ultimately, the major challenge to state transformation is that traditional elites have very little intention of abandoning their privileged position and of sharing (or worse, ceding) control over patronage networks and access to state assets. Indeed, many of these elites consider their privileged position as God-given and a natural state of affairs. A poll taken in 2007, which showed that only 5.2% of Brahmins and Chettris feel they have more power than they should, illustrates both the need for and the likely significant obstacles to that aspect of state transformation (notwithstanding the fact that a large proportion of high-caste Nepalis are among the poor and downtrodden). Indeed, traditional elites and powerbrokers have been required to give up very little in the peace process to date – and when they saw their power challenged by new actors, such as the Maoists in power or new voices in the Terai, they sought to enlist India's help in countering them.

Thus, the root causes of the Maoist insurgency remain mostly unaddressed. Dangerously, attempts to address the underlying factors in a haphazard way risk igniting a much more violent conflict than before because of the infusion of grievance-based identity politics into an already volatile mix.

---

7 International Crisis Group, *Nepal's Fitful Peace Process*, Crisis Group Asia Briefing no. 120, April 7, 2011, p. 16.
8 The issue is unhelpfully linked with land confiscated by Maoists during the conflict. As of late 2007, Maoists still occupy confiscated land in 132 of 401 VDCs surveyed. 2007 OCHA/WFP sample data.

TRANSITION FROM AUTOCRACY TO DEMOCRACY

Nepal's transition to democracy is similarly stuck and still has a long way to go. One successful election does not a democracy make, and Nepal has yet to fulfill the minimum criterion for democracy established by Samuel Huntington – that of two consecutive changes of government brought about by free and fair elections. Indeed, Freedom House's 2010 list of the world's 115 electoral democracies does not include Nepal.[9] The country is still far from qualifying as a liberal democracy in which the procedural aspect of elections is complemented by respect of individual liberty, the rule of law, and the respect of basic rights, all of which are secured by checks on the power of each branch of government, equality under the law, impartial courts and tribunals, and separation of religion and state. Noticing a growing trend around the world toward the phenomenon of illiberal democracies since the end of the Cold War, Fareed Zakaria has observed that, although in the Western European experience constitutional liberalism has led to democracy, "democracy does not seem to bring constitutional liberalism."[10] Even if future elections in Nepal generate peaceful transitions of power, Nepalis may still not be able to enjoy the full benefits of democracy.

The political and socioeconomic environment in Nepal is arguably not particularly conducive to deep democratization, because several of the key facilitating conditions such as higher levels of per capita GDP; an active, well-organized civil society; and mass democratic attitudes and values have not been met. The endemic weakness of the state and its institutions, partly a result of the decade-long civil war, poses additional hurdles to democratization. As democracy scholar Larry Diamond points out, "Before a country can have a democratic state, it must first have a state – a set of political institutions that exercise authority over a territory, make and execute policies, extract and distribute revenue, produce public goods, and maintain order by wielding an effective monopoly over the means of violence."[11] None of these factors are fully present in Nepal, and except for the success of the Nepali people in getting rid of the authoritarian king, the country still has a long way to go to regenerate and nurture legitimate power. This task is complicated by widespread corruption and the predatory, self-seeking behavior of government officials, which have a corrosive effect on the public's confidence in both the state and on the promise of democracy.

Attitudes of the key political actors are not encouraging either. The leaders of mainstream political parties prefer to strengthen their position through patronage and close links to Delhi over building popular constituencies at home. Internally, party structures remain highly centralized and undemocratic. Meanwhile, the new

---

9　See http://www.freedomhouse.org/template.cfm?page=548&year=2010.

10　Fareed Zakaria, "The Rise of Illiberal Democracy," *Foreign Affairs*, Vol. 76, no. 6 (1997), pp. 23–44.

11　Larry Diamond, "Promoting Democracy in Post-Conflict and Failed States: Lessons and Challenges," presentation prepared for the National Policy Forum on Terrorism, Security, and America's Purpose, Washington, DC, September 6–7, 2005.

kids on the block – the Maoists – although paying lip service to democracy and displaying a degree of pragmatism while in government – hold an understanding of democracy that gives rise to widespread suspicion, with leading party members continuing to subscribe to the goal of establishing a "dictatorship of the proletariat." Their opposition to the term "pluralism" in the draft constitution has ignited further concerns. Meanwhile, the Madhesis, the other potential game-changers in this process, also have failed to advance beyond an agenda of ethnically based federalism.

Instilling democratic values, attitudes, and practices in the body politic is of course a long-term endeavor. A more immediate opportunity to place democracy in Nepal on a sound footing presents itself in the constitution-making process, in which Nepalis face the challenge of designing institutions with a high degree of democratic resilience. The experience of democratic transitions in other countries suggests that constitutional arrangements featuring elements of power sharing increase the probability of democratic governance's succeeding. Among the key power-sharing features associated with higher democratic performance in divided or multiethnic societies are proportional representation (PR) electoral systems.[12] These systems provide a potent impetus toward consensus democracy, in particular when used in combination with a parliamentary system of government. Oft-repeated fears that such systems will lead to weak and unstable cabinets have little support in empirical evidence.[13] In multiethnic societies such as Nepal, PR systems facilitate minority representation in parliament, whereas majoritarian systems, such as the "winner-takes-all" first-past-the-post system employed in Nepali elections throughout the 1990s, actively excludes them. Catinca Slavu, in her chapter, points out that "these elections failed to deliver on social inclusion . . . foiling the aspirations that had been created by the democratic transition." By contrast, it was the strong proportional representation features of the mixed system adopted for the Constituent Assembly election combined with the imposition of quotas that ensured its highly representative composition. The inter-party struggles described by Slavu that led to the agreement on the mixed system remind us that the design of electoral systems is not a technical exercise but rather a highly political and contentious exercise.

PUBLIC SECURITY AND IMPUNITY

As in many other postconflict countries, Nepal has seen high levels of nonpolitically motivated violence in some parts of the country, and public security is poor, especially along the country's southern strip bordering on India. A number of armed groups, dressing up largely criminal agendas behind political slogans often centered

[12] Pippa Norris, *Driving Democracy: Do Power-Sharing Institutions Work?*, Cambridge: Cambridge University Press, 2008, pp. 103–31, 211–12, and 214.
[13] Arend Lijphart, *Patterns of Democracy: Government Forms and Performance in Thirty-Six Countries*, New Haven: Yale University Press, 1999, pp. 258–75.

on the demand for Madhesi autonomy, have turned kidnapping and extortion into a cottage industry in the central and eastern Terai. In some areas, this activity has contributed to a general sense of exasperation with lawlessness and also led to ethnic polarization. Armed groups often collude with local officials and political parties. Indeed, much of the violence in the Terai revolves around a struggle for control over patronage networks.

Police forces across Nepal remain woefully unprepared, in terms of doctrine, training, and equipment, to ensure public security and to safeguard basic human rights, particularly in the Terai. Instead of receiving strategic guidance from responsible civilian leaders, they are subjected to constant self-interested political interference, reinforcing festering corruption within their own ranks. Police often responded with brute force to protests and other actions during the Madhesi *Andolan* (movement) in 2007 and 2008. Security forces were directly involved in at least nine politically related killings during the Constituent Assembly election campaign. Meanwhile, according to Advocacy Forum, a leading Nepali human rights NGO, more than three years after the end of the People's War, almost one in five detainees endures torture at the hands of state agents.[14] Torture is still not criminalized by law.

The public security vacuum is aggravated by the difficulty the state faces in reestablishing its presence and authority in many rural areas after having been chased out by the Maoists during the People's War. In fact, the void is often filled by Maoist cadres, who have continued openly to fulfill state functions (as during the war), on occasion receiving explicit recognition from the police or the local administration. In some areas, such as the Eastern Hills, people are increasingly seeking redress from their own ethnic networks and structures rather than from the state, potentially storing up significant interethnic problems for the future.

Nepal's judiciary faces equally serious problems. The vast majority of accused persons in Nepal do not have access to counsel. Quasi-judicial bodies and agencies, including Chief District Officers (CDOs), district forest officers, park wardens, and border officers, are given vast jurisdiction to try criminal cases, even though most of them have no judicial training. Yet, despite the generally poor state of Nepal's justice system and the Maoists' efforts to intimidate the judiciary, Nepal's courts have remained remarkably independent. That said, Frederick Rawski and Mandira Sharma explain in their chapter that the judiciary faces continuous pressure from the political leadership of post–peace-agreement governments, including those under Maoist leadership, to have cases against well-connected perpetrators withdrawn, thereby reinforcing the state of impunity.

Against this backdrop of weak state control and delivery of services, impunity continues to reign. According to the International Committee of the Red Cross, as of December 2009, more than 1,300 families (some Nepali NGOs provide much higher figures) were still seeking information on relatives who had gone missing

---

[14] Advocacy Forum, Submission to the UN Special Rapporteur on Torture, August 28, 2009.

during the People's War.[15] Although the large majority of the "disappeared" are believed to be victims of the Nepalese Army, the PLA, too, has failed to make public the fate of those who disappeared in its custody.[16] Most disappointingly, as of December 2011, not a single person responsible for grave human rights violations during or after the conflict has been convicted in a civilian court.

Approaches to reconciliation have varied from country to country in the wake of civil wars, and formulas that work well in one have often failed in others. Yet reconciliation has required active engineering (short of wide-scale prosecutions, which poor countries cannot afford or generally pull off very credibly) in most former theaters of conflict.[17] And although the parties in November 2011 agreed to set up the Truth and Reconciliation Commission foreseen by the Comprehensive Peace Agreement within "one month," it is unlikely to see the light of day for some time. Even if it does, it is unlikely to quell significant concerns about its mandate, structure, and operations. For the moment, both camps of former combatants share an interest in suppressing accountability for past crimes, concrete evidence of which is still mostly missing, and there is no widespread domestic political or international pressure on them to shift their stance.

TRANSFORMATION OF THE MAOISTS

As S. D. Muni puts it in this volume, the Maoists are the main game-changers in Nepal. Although their central role in Nepali politics is the result of the military threat they posed to the state, their transformative power does not rely solely on their coercive potential. Undeniably, the Maoists incarnate at the political level the popular will, and indeed the demand for change. Those who wanted change and who voted for them in the Constituent Assembly elections were not mistaken insofar as the Maoists were the only leading political formation that advanced a recognizable agenda for state transformation.

The Maoist 2008 electoral platform conveyed their historic sense of mission, advancing the objective of "creating a new history" bringing "[t]he dark era of feudalism and monarchism . . . to an end." In line with the classic Marxist doctrine of historical materialism, the Maoists saw the establishment of industrial capitalism as a necessary intermediary step in the country's path from feudalism to socialism. Beyond the demand for "revolutionary land reform . . . on the basis of the principle of 'land to tillers,'" the Maoists' stated economic policy was moderate, by any standard, identifying as priorities the development of tourism, national industrialization, water resources, hydropower, as well as physical infrastructure. That said,

---

15 ICRC 2009 Annual Report, p. 212.
16 105 according to the Informal Service Sector Center (INSEC), a national human rights organization.
17 For an interesting discussion of Truth Commissions and their relevance to reconciliation, see Priscilla B. Hayner, *Unspeakable Truths: Transitional Justice and the Challenge of Truth Commissions* (2nd ed.), Abingdon, UK: Routledge, 2010.

the Maoist tenure in government in 2008 and 2009 revealed that its leaders had only a rudimentary notion of how to translate headline goals into economic policy, let alone how to implement their ideas. At the same time, the Maoists were prepared to be pragmatic (at the expense of disappointing some of their supporters by failing to be transformative). Meanwhile, the traditional political parties, particularly the NC and UML, missed no opportunity to demonstrate that they have no specific policies or wider solutions to offer that might improve the abject performance of Nepal's economy, and their rhetoric about social inclusion is widely understood to be just that.

The outcome of the Constituent Assembly elections initially looked pregnant with possibility (as well as risk). The Maoists achieved significant credibility by coming in first by winning one-third of the seats, providing them with a blocking minority, meaning that nothing could be achieved without their active concurrence. In negotiations over the formation of an interim government, they won over sufficient support to form a cabinet.

Yet they then decisively failed to generate buy-in from their partners in government to achieve anything much. Rather than power sharing, paralysis ensued. The Maoists lacked both experience in and the mindset for democratic governance, and the traditional parties were deeply versed in frustrating change while talking about it a great deal. The Maoists' brief spell at the helm of the interim government in 2008–9 proved a failed opportunity for them and for the country, especially as Prachanda seemed gratuitously to alienate an India that needed little provocation to imagine the worst at play in Kathmandu.[18]

In addition, Maoist actions show that they have not entirely forsworn the use of violence. Maoists continue to rely on rule-by-fear in a significant portion of the country. During the April 2008 Constituent Assembly election campaign, aggressive use of the Young Communist League (YCL), with former members of the PLA in command positions, aimed to achieve widespread intimidation, and it did resonate loudly among those who had reason to fear the Maoists. Throughout the peace process, Maoist-affiliated groups, in particular the YCL, continued to carry out abductions. The YCL and other Maoist-affiliated groups have repeatedly attacked local government offices and public bodies, threatening and on occasion attacking civil servants. Continuing reports, four years after the signing of the peace accords, of YCL "law enforcement" activities, including sentencing of people to forced labor, are worrying. Periodic intimidation of and pressure on the media by Maoist-affiliated groups, although not particularly effective, have also been disturbing. Perhaps most pervasive, extortion of financial support from businesses in Kathmandu and outside the capital (sometimes in league with several trade unions) suggests contempt for the

---

[18] Maoist Prime Minister Baburam Bhattarai's visit to India in October 2011 proved a much defter performance than the self-aggrandizing Prachanda had achieved on his earlier pilgrimage to Delhi, even though few concrete outcomes were immediately apparent.

basic rule of law and a lack of understanding of the investment climate Nepal will need to develop in order to emerge sustainably from its economic doldrums. That the Maoists continue to run "parallel structures" in some parts of the country, with police in some areas requiring approval from the Maoists even for basic operations, is hardly surprising, given the absence of a state capacity to fill the vacuum left by years of civil war. Nevertheless, it is hardly reassuring.

That said, although the Maoists have retained their capacity for the use of violence and make sure that everyone knows it, Aditya Adhikari's chapter suggests that they have taken the risk of restructuring their operations for participation in politics, and away from an organizational mode that would favor a return to war. Political life has not come cost-free for them: it has encouraged and triggered occasionally sharp, surprisingly public divisions within the party's leadership, with Prachanda, although still in control, not always emerging strengthened in the eyes of either fellow party cadres or compatriots at large. In particular, tension over how to deal with India remains significant within the Maoist leadership.

THOUGHTS ON THE POLITICAL PARTIES

A number of authors in this volume place a fair share of blame for Nepal's stasis on political parties. It should come as no surprise that, as argued earlier, the traditional political parties have not driven change in Nepal in recent years. Although they objected to the episodic and ultimately catastrophic absolutism of the royal family, their leadership (to a large degree unchanged since the 1990s) is recruited from the country's long-standing elite, which ostensibly has the most to lose from meaningful state transformation (although, arguably, if Nepal's economy were stimulated to perform at the level of others in its neighborhood, there could be many winners, including the elite families). Perhaps hardest to change is the attachment of these politicians and their political parties to deeply entrenched patronage networks that have helped them win elections. As Devendra Panday explains in his chapter, initially idealistically inclined politicians mostly find it difficult to challenge this system and often ultimately succumb to promotion of their personal, family, and network interests. As Sujeev Shakya shows in his chapter, the Maoists, while in power in 2008–9, were similarly susceptible to the temptations of patronage.

Frustration among the population of Nepal with the political and economic situation of their country runs deep. So far, no party has produced a platform for change sufficiently compelling as to command anything close to a consensus or even a mandate for rule undiluted by coalition politics. In that sense, there has been no progress on meaningful reforms since the breakthrough of 2005. Thus, although the large majority of Nepalis, in particular those from marginalized groups of society, have high expectations for the role of the state and the politicians running it, the ambitions of the existing parties other than the Maoists rarely seem to address these aspirations.

The life of politicians has been made easier by the fact that civil society, after having led, alongside the political parties, the People's Movement that swept away monarchic rule in the spring of 2006, has subsided into inertia ever since and, although patently disappointed and frustrated, has failed to play more than a passive watchdog role. Civil society in Nepal comprises many organizations, some focused on self-help, local improvement, and certain forms of economic and social activity, generally of a useful sort, and others heavily politicized – with many nongovern- mental organizations (NGOs) being largely an extension of their political "mother parties" or creations of foreign donors. These latter NGOs are unlikely to call into a question a corrupt system they are inherently a part of, whereas the former ones will tend to stick to their local knitting. The monitoring activities of international NGOs and even the activities of the Office of the UN High Commissioner for Human Rights, although useful in exposing and documenting the worst excesses of the combatants and the body politic, have brought about little major change.

THE ROLE OF INDIA

S. D. Muni's authoritative contribution to this volume demonstrates that India can make and has made positive contributions to breaking political deadlocks in Nepal. Indeed, the peace negotiations of 2004–6 would never have been possible without active Indian support, first from the Communist Party of India (Marxist), then a member of the governing alliance in New Delhi providing support in parliament to the narrower governing coalition. Later, at first passively and tentatively, then more actively, the government as a whole encouraged negotiation of the Comprehensive Peace Agreement. A skeptical opposition did not seek to undermine the government's positive role on this issue. S. D. Muni's account shows that New Delhi's policy will inevitably and likely always be rooted in India's self-interest – a notion further reinforced in the chapter by Rajeev Chaturvedy and David Malone. However, all three authors believe that India's and Nepal's interests need not be in conflict. On the contrary, Chaturvedy and Malone make a strong argument for joint action by India and Nepal to develop resources and cooperative policies that can do much to enrich both countries.

Malone, a long-time resident of the Middle East, recognizes in Nepal something of the syndrome he used to observe in Lebanon. Encircled by two powerful neighbors (Israel and Syria) that have often interfered in its internal affairs, Lebanon displays a disposition to interpret and proclaim anything bad that happens as originating with or directly caused by one or more outside powers, thus ignoring the role of domestic actors (in league with foreign powers or as free agents) and relieving them of responsibility for any untoward developments. Nepal's relationship with India is pathological from this perspective and not unlike that characterizing many others between a small, vulnerable country alongside a powerful, often heedless neighbor. This type of dynamic gives rise to reflexive anti-Indianism, which, as Prashant Jha points out in this volume, is reinforced by the increasingly polarized atmosphere in Kathmandu: "in a fragmented landscape, India will get criticized by some section of Nepali political opinion for whatever it does or does not do."

India, no doubt, is adept at exploiting divisions among Nepali political actors to increase its influence, playing in the words of Devendra Panday "a game of divide and rule with multiple power centers competing for Indian support." Yet, Panday also notes that "India's strategy is facilitated by the subservient behavior of the self-serving Nepali leadership," which throws the door wide open for India to manipulate the political process. As Jha has persuasively argued, leeway for Indian interference shrinks dramatically in situations in which Nepali political actors are united.

These observations do not exonerate India, nor do they constitute an argument for the wisdom of its policies on Nepal. Quite clearly, the extent and depth of animus against India in Nepal arise from a degree of Indian insensitivity to Nepal's sense of sovereignty and independence, as well as a number of mistakes of judgment it has made over the years, sometimes aggravated by an arrogance of manner and tone. The fact that India, in the past, has shown no hesitation to use its control of land routes to its landlocked neighbor as leverage to secure political and economic concessions has significantly contributed to the development of the Nepali mindset. India may well have been trying in recent years to be a kinder, gentler regional hegemon and less interfering with neighbors, as Malone argues elsewhere.[19] Yet, India's policy in support of the Nepalese Army and traditional conservative elements within mainstream parties since 2008 has elicited fury in sizable segments of Nepal's intelligentsia and easily excitable media.

Meanwhile, that frustrations with India run deep in all political camps in Nepal may be a function of Delhi's pursuit, throughout the peace process, of objectives that are difficult to reconcile: on the one hand facilitating Maoist entry into "mainstream politics," while, on the other, seeking to strengthen the "middle ground" of Nepali politics by often siding with the non-Maoist parties in their arguments with the Maoists. Jha concludes in this volume that "India has to make a difficult choice – whether it is willing to live with what may be a Maoist-dominated power structure and a different kind of Nepali state, or whether the risks of that scenario are too high and it would rather try to block these changes, even at the cost of instability and conflict."

India may end up choosing the latter option, despite its new-found affinity to work with the Maoist-led government of Prime Minister Baburam Bhattarai. Nepal rarely features among India's foreign policy priorities, and there is a tendency in Delhi to look at the country through a national security lens in the context of concerns about China's growing influence in the region. As a result, Delhi's Nepal policy tends to be dominated by its security organs, which are among the most conservative elements

---

[19] See David M. Malone, *Does the Elephant Dance: Contemporary Indian Foreign Policy*, Oxford: Oxford University Press, 2011, pp. 101–28.

within the Indian policy establishment and which view the Maoists with considerable suspicion. Meanwhile, key outside powers are loath to openly contravene Indian interests in the region. Thus, as of early 2011, although some key outside players showed signs of aligning their objectives to achieve progress in Nepal, they did so largely by quietly backing India's positions, for example on the closure of UNMIN. China, meanwhile, dances to a different tune. Its engagement with Nepal is driven almost exclusively by its preoccupation with ensuring that the activities of the Tibetan exile community remain in check, and any government in Kathmandu that delivers on this front will be met with benevolence in Beijing.

Yet India might expect political actors in Nepal, including the Maoists, to take into account the sensitivity of its parliament and media to what many Indians believe is a deliberate and systematic Chinese policy of penetration of India's sphere of influence, including in Nepal. However, the Nepalis see this policy as New Delhi's problem, not their own, and some see China's growing interest in and cooperation with their country as a geostrategic opportunity for Nepal. Indeed Nepal should profit from a maturing economic and wider relationship with China as best it can. Yet to provoke New Delhi without much purpose or strategy (as the Maoists have done from time to time since 2008) is bound to exact a price.

THE UNITED NATIONS

After India, the United Nations has been the most visible outside actor in Nepal's peace process. The United Nations was an important player in Nepal's transition phase even before the peace process got underway and had been present as a development actor for several decades. In 2005, in the aftermath of the king's coup and in the context of gross human rights abuses of its government, a broad coalition of international donors and Nepali civil society used the UN Commission on Human Rights as a forum to exert pressure on the regime in Kathmandu, leading to its acceptance of a deployment of the human rights mission in 2005. As Frederick Rawski and Mandira Sharma remind us, OHCHR's monitoring presence helped reduce the level of violence by both conflict parties, provided a degree of protection to key leaders on both sides of the conflict, and helped to change the dynamics on the street. This mission, by gaining the trust of both sides of the conflict, also opened up space and paved the way for the deployment of the UN Mission in Nepal in 2006, which gave the UN a (limited) political role, reluctantly conceded by India.

UNMIN's presence yielded qualified results. Authors in this volume agree that the mission was important as a confidence-building measure. Its credibility among the conflict parties (built first through quiet "good offices" diplomacy pursued by UN headquarters in New York since 2003 and later through the good work of the human rights mission) allowed the Maoists to accede to cantonment arrangements they otherwise would have eschewed in all likelihood. The leadership and staff of the mission were widely (if not always or universally) praised. Inevitably, UNMIN became the subject of many local conspiracy theories. By UN standards, it was a small mission and always intended as a supportive rather than a decisive actor. Continuing, indeed increasing, Indian ambivalence over its role, constrained its freedom of maneuver and influence after 2008. Ironically, it was above all the Maoists who argued most forcefully for the repeated extension of UNMIN's mandate, with the traditional political parties, closer to India, displaying increasing discomfort over the mission's presence.

Aspects of the mission were technically successful and potentially precedential for other such international operations.[20] In particular, its arms monitoring regime was very innovative, providing helpful lessons for future such UN missions. It was the first UN operation with an arms monitoring mandate, and although this function was largely a symbolic one, UNMIN discharged the mandate credibly. It hired local civilian staff extensively, including in analytical and policy roles, significantly contributing to its thorough understanding of Nepali political dynamics. The establishment of an UN-chaired joint body made up of representatives of the Nepalese Army and its Maoist counterparts played a useful role in confidence-building. Even though the mission, with its 186 unarmed observers, had neither the mandate nor the strength to prevent the former conflict parties from returning to war, its presence served as a security guarantee, as a "tripwire" as one scholar put it, that was linked to the Security Council.[21] And the involvement of the Security Council, although it was distant and not unduly preoccupied with Nepal compared to several other much more pressing crises, was useful in reminding the parties that a sword of Damocles potentially remained suspended over them were they to behave very disruptively. However, the UN was unable to generate real momentum to see through the peace accords, particularly after the 2008 elections, in part because of the levels and drivers of political inertia in Nepal and in part because of India's anxieties and reservations. At heart, these actors did not accept the results of the elections and blamed the UN for that as well.

When evaluated in relation to its formal mandate, UNMIN will be considered by most experts as a success for its arms monitoring role and the conditions it helped create for credible elections to a Constituent Assembly. We particularly want to pay tribute to one of the authors in this volume, Ian Martin, for his successful and in many ways highly innovative leadership of UNMIN, which was in keeping with his earlier work for the UN in many other, even more difficult situations around the globe over two decades. His successor, Karin Landgren, came on the scene as the

---

[20] For a summary of the Nepal Mission alongside narratives and statistical data on other UN political missions, see *Review of Political Missions*, 2010, New York: Centre on International Cooperation, New York University, pp. 89–94, available at http://www.cic.nyu.edu/politicalmissions/index.html. For an executive summary, see http://www.cic.nyu.edu/politicalmissions/docs_missions/strategicsummary.pdf.

[21] Astri Suhrke, *UN Support for Peacebuilding: Nepal as the Exceptional Case*, Chr. Michelsen Institute, Working Paper No 2009:7, Bergen 2009, S. 45, http://www.cmi.no/publications/file/?3468=un-support-for-peacebuilding.

UN's role became a less promising one. Throughout, she performed admirably and expertly, all the more so for having to paint on a shrinking canvas.

Criticism of UNMIN inside and outside of Nepal was often based on (sometimes deliberate) misunderstanding of its mandate and capacities. Indeed, criticisms that UNMIN showed a pro-Maoist bias in the registration and verification process of Maoist weapons and combatants and in monitoring cantonment sites came mostly from champions of the status quo, who rejected key premises on which the peace process was built.

Sometimes, however, even successful microsurgery fails to heal a patient. Ultimately, UNMIN's limited mandate tied its hands and precluded it from addressing, effectively or otherwise, the big challenges of the peace process: (1) the integration of the Maoist army as the first step of broader security sector reform and (2) mitigation of the potentially destabilizing impact of the fears and hopes fueling the federalism debate, including the attendant unrest in the Terai. Although the UN and other international donors, many of which have had a presence in Nepal for decades, can assume a modest share of the blame for Nepal's poor economic performance, no short-term UN political mission could meaningfully address the root causes of a conflict such as Nepal's, which centred on poverty and social exclusion. As an illustration of the constraints, discreet efforts by UNMIN to assist Nepal on challenges relating to the security sector were met with resistance from India and the Nepalese Army, whereas comments by UNMIN's leadership relating to marginalized groups in the Terai and elsewhere were rejected by the government and some others as unacceptable interference into Nepal's sovereign affairs.

These considerations raise the question of whether the UN could or should have sought a wider mandate at the outset of the mission. In his chapter, Ian Martin insists that, in January 2007, India would certainly have prevented an ambitious, wide-ranging UNMIN mandate. Key UN Member States (and the UN Secretariat) were unwilling to confront India on an issue that was not among their highest priorities.

After yielding ever diminishing returns post-2008, the mission's mandate expired in January 2011, with the future of the PLA still uncertain. The UN faced a "catch-22" dilemma by then: had it stayed, it would have been criticized for being increasingly ineffective and would have had to share responsibility for future political upheavals in the country without being able to mitigate them. In departing, it opened itself to criticism that it displayed too short an attention span and that it failed to complete a complex and inevitably lengthy job. In one respect, UNMIN's departure may have pressured the body politic to move beyond the deadlock on power sharing to establish a functioning government that would address more contentious issues of Maoist army integration and rehabilitation and drafting of the constitution. Indeed, by August 2011, the parties – and India – agreed to allow the Maoists back into power, but only under the leadership of Bhattarai (not Prachanda) and only after the Maoists pledged significant concessions in areas of integration of former combatants and issues related to drafting of the constitution. By November of that year, a new round of agreement seemed to have revived the optimism in the peace process. However, the international safety net created by UNMIN's presence is now missing, should serious bumps in the road to sustainable democracy develop.

In any case, UNMIN's mandate, design, and small footprint make it an interesting case study of a smaller UN peace operation, with an essentially political character, in contrast to more ambitious classical peacekeeping operations (PKOs); the military deployments of such PKOs quite often extend well beyond 10,000 and, increasingly after 1990, also have involved a large number of civilian components, which often also feature ambitious mandates. With the UN stretched very thin, and its capacity to manage effectively the more than 100,000 troops under its control internationally as of late 2010 in some doubt, smaller political field missions may offer a useful model of what can be achieved at much lesser cost and with considerably less risk than massive peacekeeping operations – provided that the security situation is permissive and protection of civilians is not part of the mandate.

DEVELOPMENT PARTNERS

With UNMIN gone, the international community's presence will increasingly shift its focus to Nepal's longer term development challenge, the unfinished peace process notwithstanding. In their efforts to ensure that development interventions bolster the ongoing transition, bilateral and multilateral donors as well as UN agencies will want to learn from past mistakes.

Devendra Panday is highly critical of the donors' role over past decades, lamenting their practice of imposing the international development doctrine of the day on Nepal without assessing how it could address local needs and challenges. Not only did they fail to indentify the exclusionary nature of the state as a root cause of failed development and conflict, but also their programming and funding practices ended up strengthening traditional elites and fueling patronage networks. At the same time, they shied away from promoting the type of (admittedly hugely challenging) reforms that could have sustainably addressed deeply entrenched social injustice, such as land reform. Jörg Frieden, in his chapter, focuses his criticism of donors on their belated adjustment to the realities of the violent conflict in Nepal, arguing that years into the conflict they still refused to accept its political nature, allowed the lion's share of development resources to be captured by a small elite, and failed to defend the development space against the pretensions of the insurgents and the interference of the security forces.

Yet, both Panday and Frieden acknowledge that donors, in the wake of King Gyanendra's 2005 coup, embarked on a steep learning curve, distancing themselves from an increasingly illegitimate king, ensuring that the poorest segments of the population and in particular the marginalized groups would benefit from external interventions, embedding development activities into specific context analysis (starting with attempts to identify the agents and beneficiaries of development programs and their links to the conflict parties), engaging constructively with the conflict parties, proactively promoting human rights, and helping push for a UN role in the peace process in the face of Indian resistance. Yet, once the peace process got stuck, donors too found it difficult to translate the considerable development aid they extended to Nepal into political leverage to prod the actors into more cooperative behavior.

Panday argues that donors should fundamentally revisit their engagement with Nepal and design development strategies that are tailored to address the specific challenges of the country. He advocates an approach under which national actors take the lead in defining priorities, programs, and implementation, while making them more accountable for their performance both vis-à-vis donors (who should stand ready to respond to nonperformance with targeted or comprehensive assistance interruption) as well as their domestic constituencies. He concludes that "[f]or the immediate future, it would be preferable to see governance framed as a conditionality rather than a program that finances all kinds of largely unproductive expenditures on behalf of nonperforming political leaders and their cohorts in civil society."

Although reformed donor practices may indeed improve the effectiveness of development aid, it is worth noting that donors cannot be and should not be the main drivers of development anywhere. Indeed, in the economic boom of China, India, and Brazil, outside aid has been largely irrelevant. The earlier rise of the other Asian Tigers was equally domestically led. At the same time, China, India, Brazil, and the Asian Tigers benefited from investment flows and trading opportunities that will not be available to Nepal, a marginal player in the world economy, which offers little in terms of comparative advantage. It will doubtless need to rely on investment from immediate neighbours and multilateral institutions.

Sujeev Shakya points to the sectors that harbor economic potential and that, if harnessed, could drive domestically led growth: hydropower, agriculture (with special focus on the commercial potential of Nepal's biodiversity), and tourism. Yet, to ensure that investments in these areas are productive, they need to be complemented by reforms that strengthen Nepal's institutions (in particular its hopelessly ineffective bureaucracy), promote democratic governance, and reduce corruption; there need to be investments in the education and health sectors as well. At the same time, new and serious efforts will need to be deployed to ensure that the benefits of economic growth reach all regions and classes of society.

ENVOI

Whether Nepal's polity is able to meet these considerable challenges in the foreseeable future will depend to a large degree on whether the current process of bargaining among key political players in Kathmandu within the framework of the peace process will allow state transformation to proceed and ultimately deliver a new social contract on which a new polity can be built.

We wish we could be more optimistic than we are today that the necessary conditions will be met and these widely desired outcomes achieved. However, some of the domestic political developments in Nepal in late 2011 provide a ray of hope.

Index

383

Made in the USA
Lexington, KY
16 December 2013